drive $45 $90 90
shop: $45 $45 90
Suit: $120 $90 45
$205 $225 ~~85~~
$315

INTRODUCTION TO ECONOMICS

INTRODUCTION TO ECONOMICS

Social Issues and Economic Thinking

Wendy A. Stock
Montana State University

WILEY

VP & EXECUTIVE PUBLISHER George Hoffman
EXECUTIVE EDITOR Joel Hollenbeck
CONTENT EDITOR Jennifer Manias
EDITORIAL ASSISTANT Erica Horowitz
MARKETING MANAGER Jesse Cruz
PRODUCTION MANAGER Janis Soo
ASSISTANT PRODUCTION EDITOR Elaine S. Chew
PHOTO EDITOR Sheena Goldstein
PRODUCT DESIGNER Greg Chaput
MEDIA SPECIALIST Elena Santa Maria
COVER DESIGNER Wendy Lai
COVER PHOTO © Gustaf Brundin/iStockphoto

This book was set in 10 pt MinionPro by MPS Limited, Chennai and printed and bound by Courier Kendallville, Inc. The cover was printed by Courier Kendallville, Inc.

This book is printed on acid free paper. ♾

Founded in 1807, John Wiley & Sons, Inc. has been a valued source of knowledge and understanding for more than 200 years, helping people around the world meet their needs and fulfill their aspirations. Our company is built on a foundation of principles that include responsibility to the communities we serve and where we live and work. In 2008, we launched a Corporate Citizenship Initiative, a global effort to address the environmental, social, economic, and ethical challenges we face in our business. Among the issues we are addressing are carbon impact, paper specifications and procurement, ethical conduct within our business and among our vendors, and community and charitable support. For more information, please visit our website: www.wiley.com/go/citizenship.

Copyright © 2013 John Wiley & Sons, Inc. All rights reserved. No part of this publication may be reproduced, stored in a retrieval system or transmitted in any form or by any means, electronic, mechanical, photocopying, recording, scanning or otherwise, except as permitted under Sections 107 or 108 of the 1976 United States Copyright Act, without either the prior written permission of the Publisher, or authorization through payment of the appropriate per-copy fee to the Copyright Clearance Center, Inc. 222 Rosewood Drive, Danvers, MA 01923, website www.copyright.com. Requests to the Publisher for permission should be addressed to the Permissions Department, John Wiley & Sons, Inc., 111 River Street, Hoboken, NJ 07030-5774, (201)748-6011, fax (201)748-6008, website http://www.wiley.com/go/permissions.

Evaluation copies are provided to qualified academics and professionals for review purposes only, for use in their courses during the next academic year. These copies are licensed and may not be sold or transferred to a third party. Upon completion of the review period, please return the evaluation copy to Wiley. Return instructions and a free of charge return mailing label are available at www.wiley.com/go/returnlabel. If you have chosen to adopt this textbook for use in your course, please accept this book as your complimentary desk copy. Outside of the United States, please contact your local sales representative

Library of Congress Cataloging-in-Publication Data

Stock, Wendy A.
Introduction to economics : social issues and economic thinking / Wendy A. Stock, Montana State University.
pages cm
Includes bibliographical references and index.
ISBN 978-0-470-57478-2 (pbk. : alk. paper) 1. Economics. I. Title.
HB171.5.S8946 2013
330—dc23

2012032700

Printed in the United States of America
10 9 8 7 6 5 4 3 2 1

Brief Contents

Contents

About the Author

Dr. Wendy Stock is a Professor of Economics and Department Head of the Department of Agricultural Economics and Economics at Montana State University in Bozeman, Montana. She holds Ph.D. and M.A. degrees in economics from Michigan State University and a B.A. in economics from Weber State University. Dr. Stock has taught economics at the introductory through graduate levels for more than two decades. She served on the American Economic Association Committee on Economic Education from 2005 to 2011, coordinated the group's annual poster session on active learning techniques in economics from 2007 to 2011, and has directed the American Economic Association Graduate Studies in Economics website since 2006. She was awarded the Montana State University James and Mary Ross Provost's Award for Excellence in 2010 in recognition of teaching and scholarship excellence. She was named Professor of the Month by the Montana State University Mortar Board in 2009, earned an Award for Excellence from Montana State in 2006 and again in 2009, was the winner of the Montana State University Betty Coffey Award in 2005 in recognition of her contributions on behalf of women, and was awarded the William L. Stamey Undergraduate Teaching Award at Kansas State University in 1998. She currently teaches ECON 101 *The Economic Way of Thinking* to several hundred Montana State University students each semester. She also teaches Peer Leadership, Labor and Human Resource Economics, and graduate and undergraduate Econometrics at Montana State.

Dr. Stock has published numerous research articles and has presented her work at locations across the United States. Her most recent research includes examining the relationship between education and health among Native Americans, assessing trends in female labor force participation, and investigating the labor market effects of disability discrimination laws, race and sex discrimination laws, and age discrimination laws. She also conducts research on graduate and undergraduate education in economics, where her work has been funded by the Ford Foundation, the Spencer Foundation, and the Calvin K. Kazanjian Economics Foundation.

Dr. Stock lives in Bozeman with her husband, Ken, her two children, and the family's assortment of pets, including dogs, cats, gerbils, and fish. All give her great utility.

Preface

Many students reading this text will be enrolled in their *first* class in economics. For many (indeed, perhaps for most), it will also be their *last* class in economics. Why? Not everyone wants to be an economist, business owner, banker, or any of the myriad careers for which the study of economics is essential. So what can a course in economics do besides provide a few credits for those on their way toward degrees in engineering, environmental resources, nursing, graphic design, education, or other disciplines? Frankly, for those willing to put forth the effort to understand the basics of the economic way of thinking, even one course in economics can do a lot. My goal in writing *Introduction to Economics: Social Issues and Economic Thinking* is to foster an understanding of the basic tools and core reasoning that underly decision making and problem solving, and to teach students to apply this way of thinking to an array of social and personal issues. Although specific occupations may require particular skills, these particular skill sets necessarily change and evolve over time. The need for people who can think, learn, and solve problems does not change. In *Introduction to Economics*, I emphasize these critical-thinking and problem-solving skills.

Introductory courses in economics are generally taught using either a principles of economics approach or an issues in economics approach. Based on my own teaching experiences using each pedagogical approach for several years, students tend to be more involved and enthusiastic about the material when taught using the issues-based approach. The issues approach is also more fun for the professor and has drawn more students into the economics major at my institution. In their investigations of the issues pedagogy, Grimes and Nelson (1998)[1] conducted controlled experiments to examine learning outcomes in issues-based versus traditional principles of economics courses. They found no significant difference in learning outcomes between the two pedagogical approaches but higher rates of course completion for students in the issues-based course.

My intent is that *Introduction to Economics* will bring to the issues market a better integration of the issues-based pedagogy with the conceptual framework of social welfare economics. The toolkit chapters are essential to doing this, in particular the chapters Consumer Surplus, Producer Surplus, and Economic Efficiency (Chapter 3) and the Power and Limits of Markets (Chapter 8). These chapters are often overlooked (or completely excluded) as a means to provide an accessible conceptual framework for students to judge the tradeoffs associated with market interventions and other social policies. By fully illustrating the concepts of efficiency and social welfare and by highlighting that economic systems face tradeoffs between efficiency and equity and between security and liberty, these chapters provide students with a method for evaluating social problems and policy

1 Grimes, Paul and Nelson, P., 1988, "The Social Issues Pedagogy vs. the Traditional Principles of Economics: An Empirical Examination," *The American Economist* 41(1): 56–64.

responses and the inherent tradeoffs they pose. Students should finish the text with an appreciation of the great power of markets to organize societies and with an appreciation for the times in which markets alone cannot yield optimal outcomes. I hope the text will be a "myth buster" for students, who often hold very naïve black-and-white ideas about be-all and end-all policy responses on both the laissez-faire and government intervention ends of the spectrum.

INTENDED AUDIENCES

This book is aimed at a dual audience: students beginning majors in economics and students simply fulfilling general education requirements. The book is somewhat less rigorous than a traditional principles text, but it trades coverage of topics including minimum average variable cost and the shutdown rule, indifference curves, and marginal propensities to consume for application-based coverage of issues. As noted by Bill Becker in his 2000 critique of teaching methods in economics, "... more headline-grabbing material ... needs to be in prominent places (in economics courses)."[2] My experience on the American Economic Association (AEA) Committee on Economic Education (CEE) and as coordinator of the CEE-sponsored poster session on active learning techniques at the AEA meetings for several years is that applied, issues-based teaching generates more interest and motivation among students than having their first exposure to economics in the traditional principles classes, where coverage of applications and social issues is necessarily lighter due to time constraints. For the student for whom this text is part of their first and last course in economics, exposure to the breadth of issues that economics can address and most importantly the marginal benefit/marginal cost lens through which economists view these issues is much more valuable and lasting than exposure to the more technical treatment provided in principles courses and texts.

FEATURES

Several features of *Introduction to Economics* enhance student learning of the material and appreciation for the field of economics.

- Flexibility. The first eight chapters constitute "the economics toolkit." The remaining chapters apply the concepts from the toolkit to examine an array of social and economic issues. Instructors can select from the chapters based on their interests and the goals of their particular course.
- Chapters begin with learning objectives and vignettes to help draw students into each chapter.
- Each chapter includes several "Think for Yourself" self-quiz problems, with answers at the end of the book.
- Student-friendly writing style, extensive use of examples, figures, and tables.
- Global perspective incorporated throughout the text.
- Each chapter includes at least one profile of an influential economic thinker; Smith, Ricardo, Marx, Galbraith, Marshall, Mill, and many others are highlighted throughout the text.
- End-of-chapter materials include discussion questions, problems, and multiple choice questions. Answers are available to instructors.

---

2 Becker, William, 2000, "Teaching Economics in the 21st Century," *Journal of Economic Perspectives*, 14(4): Winter 2000, 109–119.

INSTRUCTOR AND STUDENT RESOURCES

Several resources are made available for instructors and students on the book companion site: www.wiley.com/college/stock.

Instructors can access an Instructor's Manual, Test Bank, and Outline PowerPoint Presentations.

Students can access Practice Quizzes, which provide instant feedback.

Acknowledgments

This book has benefited from input from friends, mentors, and colleagues around the country, and I am deeply indebted to them. Richard Alston, emeritus professor from Weber State University, provided expert guidance on textbook writing in general and gave substantial feedback on the early chapter drafts. Colleagues at Montana State University commented on several chapters and corrected some of my misconceptions regarding the economics of agricultural programs. I am grateful for their input. Students in several of my Economics 101 courses at Montana State suffered through using early drafts of the text, and I appreciate their feedback and willingness to help me root out the many typographical errors that crop up in the early stages of writing.

I am also grateful to the many reviewers who reviewed the text and provided constructive criticism and insight. The book is much improved because of their help.

Olugbenga Ajilore, University of Toledo
Ademar Bechtold, Notre Dame of Maryland University
John Blair, Wright State University
Natalia Boliari, Manhattan College
John Conant, Indiana State University
Diana Denison, Red Rocks Community College
Abbas P. Grammy, California State University, Bakersfield
Adam Grossberg, Trinity College
Randi Hawkins, Bloomfield College
Tom Larson, California State University, Los Angeles
Cheryl A. McGaughey, Angelo State University
Inge O'Connor, Syracuse University
Zuohong Pan, Western Connecticut State University
Chris Phillips, Somerset Community College
Terry Riddle, Central Virginia Community College
Mary Ann Rittenhouse, University of Nebraska at Kearney
Fred J. Ruppel, Eastern Kentucky University
Michael Ryan, Western Michigan University
Sue Lynn Sasser, University of Central Oklahoma
David Schutte, Mountain View College
Robert Schuttler, Marian University
Arun Kumar Srinivasan, Indiana University Southeast
Tara Thornberry, Kentucky Community and Technical College
Darlene Voeltz, Rochester Community and Technical College
Russel Neil Walter, Dixie State College of Utah
Bassam Yousif, Indiana State University
Ernest Zampelli, Catholic University of America

I also want to give a special thank you to my family and friends. They have been very supportive of my writing the text, from reading sample chapters and providing feedback, to prodding me to finish, to supporting the intrusion on family time that was necessary to get the work done. Thanks, guys.

SECTION

The Economics Toolkit

© Shuan Lowe/iStockphoto

An Introduction to the Economic Way of Thinking

After studying this chapter, you should be able to:

- Define economics
- Explain how scarce resources influence choices
- Describe the influence of benefits and costs on deciding among alternatives
- Identify the decision rules individuals and firms use to make choices
- Explain why decisions are made "at the margin"
- Assess the general conditions that generate maximum utility or profits

Economics is a subject that students tend to learn best by using examples, so we'll start our study of economics with an example. At many colleges and universities, a substantial number of students drive to campus. If you attend one of these colleges, you have probably engaged in "trolling" for a parking spot. You might have been hovering and circling your car around the parking lots on campus while waiting for other students finishing classes to drive off and open up a parking space for you. Trolling for parking spaces is a common practice on college campuses (and at grocery stores and shopping malls). Trolling on campus is particularly popular during the morning hours, at the beginning of the school year, on campuses in colder climates, or where public transportation is either unavailable or inconvenient.

Perhaps as you circled your car around and around and around, you thought to yourself, "Why don't they build more parking spaces?" or "Why didn't I ride my bike today?" or "Why didn't

I spring for that expensive reserved parking space?" Believe it or not, trolling is an interesting illustration of economic behavior. Deciding how many parking spots to produce, whether to drive to and park on campus, or whether to spend money on an expensive parking space are all choices. Choices are what **economics** is all about.

Economics is the study of choices.

This is the basic definition of economics. "Wait," you might protest, "I thought economics was about the economy, the stock market, interest rates, inflation, and money." Well, it is certainly about all of those things. But economics is also about much more. More than just a subject of study and memorization, economics is a tool or way of looking at the world.

The tools of economics help us to understand all kinds of choices, ranging from how to preserve the environment, to deciding how much workers are paid, to understanding why some activities, like public education, are socially provided, while others, like the sale of recreational marijuana, are prohibited. Economics helps us understand why societies choose to allow pollution, unemployment, or poverty to persist. Although we'll examine these and many more choices throughout the text, in this chapter we focus on some of the fundamental concepts that underlie economic choices.

Microeconomics and Macroeconomics

Macroeconomics deals with choices that societies make.

Microeconomics deals with the choices individuals, households, and businesses make.

Economics is divided into two branches that differ according to the kinds of choices people make. **Macroeconomics** deals with the choices we make as a society, such as how much tax to pay and how many programs the government should sponsor. **Microeconomics** deals with the choices individuals, households, or businesses make, such as a high school graduate's decision to attend college, the decision for both spouses in a family to have paid employment, and the decisions firms make when hiring workers.

We will learn about macroeconomic and microeconomic choices in many chapters of this book, but first let's focus on *your* choice to study economics.

Why Study Economics?

Although you may not plan to become a professional economist, studying economics can help you in many ways.

- Studying economics can improve your decision-making skills. The focus on analyzing choices can help you make better decisions.
- Studying economics can improve your critical thinking skills. The economic way of thinking encourages skepticism and critical analysis. Rather than relying on assertions or opinions, economics uses a logical, evidence-based approach to evaluating problems.
- Studying economics will help you develop analytical and quantitative skills. Approaching complex problems in a logical, organized way helps you to identify the crux of issues and problems.
- Using the tools and principles of economics, you will understand many current issues, whether they are local, national, or global problems.
- Approach controversial issues with objectivity and clarity. People airing their views about such issues as immigration, international trade, illegal drugs, or politics often cite subjective opinions rather than fact. Economics provides a tool for viewing controversial issues objectively.

- Studying economics can help you prepare for graduate school in many fields. In fact, studies have found that economics majors score among the highest of those taking the Law School Admissions Test (LSAT).[1]

Employers want workers who are able to think critically and carefully and who are able to learn new things and solve problems. Studying economics can advance your critical thinking skills, improve your prospects as a job candidate, and make you more valuable on almost any job.

SCARCITY AND BASIC ECONOMIC RESOURCES

It might seem as if much of what you do has little to do with making choices. You *must* wake up at 6:00 a.m. to get to class, you *must* go to work, and you *must* pass your exams to graduate. Most economists would disagree and instead would propose that even in these situations (and all others) you are making choices. Choices arise from **scarcity**. Something is scarce if the amount of it is limited and there is more than one alternative use for it. In the cases of waking up at 6:00 a.m., going to work, and studying for exams, your time is scarce. Your time is limited, and you have many other uses for your time. You could sleep in, hang out with friends, or watch TV instead of going to class, working, or studying.

Scarcity occurs when we have fewer resources than we have uses for those resources.

In these instances, we consider time use as labor. *Labor* is one of the three **basic economic resources** available to individuals or societies: laborers combine time and energy to produce goods or services. The other two basic economic resources are *land* and *capital*. Economists categorize natural resources, water, and clean air as *land*; long-lasting tools or skills used in producing goods and services are categorized as *capital*.

The basic economic resources are land, labor, and capital.

All of these resources are scarce. We have less time, fewer natural resources, and less capital than we have uses for them. In fact, once you think about it, it appears that practically *everything* is scarce.

Notice the difference between the economic definition of scarcity—alternative uses and limited resources—and a more familiar definition of scarcity—something is scarce if there isn't very much of it. It is easy to understand that diamonds or rare coins or someone's time is scarce, since quantities of these things are very limited. But it is also true that air and water are scarce, even though there is much air and water in the environment. Air and water are scarce because we can think of alternative uses for them. We can breathe, bottle, or emit smoke into air. We can swim in, drink, and set up fisheries in water, or we may use it as a garbage dump.

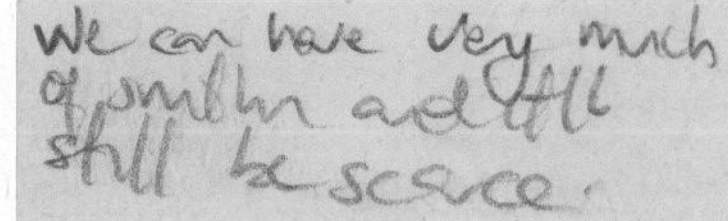

Scarcity forces us to allocate our scarce resources among the many uses for them, and we have to make choices or tradeoffs between these various uses. Economic tools help us to understand and analyze choices and their implications.

HOW DO DECISION MAKERS MAKE CHOICES?

In order to study choices, we must make a few general assumptions regarding how people make choices. Economists assume that decision makers compare the costs benefits of alternative choices and that decision makers choose options that make them as well off as they can be. This section presents the basic assumptions that economists use to describe how decision makers make choices.

---

1 Nieswiadomy, Michael, "LSAT Scores of Economics Majors," *Journal of Economic Education* (Fall 1998): 377–379.

Decision Makers Compare Benefits and Costs

*The **cost** of a choice is what you give up to make the choice.*

*The **benefit** of a choice is what you gain when you make the choice.*

***Utility** is a synonym for satisfaction or happiness and describes the benefit individuals get from their choices.*

***Profit** is the difference between the earnings that a firm receives from selling its good or service and the costs incurred to produce the good or service. Profit is the benefit that firms get from their choices.*

*The **opportunity cost** of a choice is the value of the next-best alternative foregone.*

Economists assume that all choices have a cost and a benefit. The **cost** of a choice is what you give up when the choice is made. If you decide to buy a college t-shirt, the cost is the price of the t-shirt and the time and effort it takes to choose and buy the shirt. The **benefit** of a choice is what is gained when a choice is made. The warmth and coverage of the t-shirt or the school pride gained when wearing it are examples of benefits.

In the case of individuals and households, economists use the concept of **utility** to describe the benefits obtained when making choices. Utility is a synonym for satisfaction or happiness. For an individual, increases in utility mean that the individual is becoming happier or more satisfied.

In the case of business firms, economists use the concept of **profit** to describe the benefits obtained when making choices. Profit is the difference between the earnings that a firm receives from selling its good or service and the costs incurred to produce the good or service.

In economics, the concept of cost is not based on prices, dollars, or cents but rather on opportunities foregone or values of choices not made. Economists use the term **opportunity cost** to denote that the cost of a choice includes the value of what is given up to make that choice. That is, when we make a choice, we give up an alternative opportunity that was available instead. Opportunity cost is a valuation of the next-best alternative opportunity not chosen.

What is the opportunity cost of going to college? According to The College Board, the average cost of a year's tuition and fees at a private four-year college was over $27,000 in 2011. Attending a public four-year college cost an average of $7,600.[2] Books can easily run $1,000 per year. But the cost of tuition and books alone fails to capture the full opportunity cost of attending college. High school graduates who choose not to attend college can get jobs that earn an average of about $26,000 per year. A reasonable estimate of the opportunity cost of going to a public college for a year would include the cost of tuition and books ($8,600) plus the earnings from the job a student would have gotten instead ($26,000). Thus, the opportunity cost of a year of college is about $34,600.

THINK FOR YOURSELF

What are the opportunity costs of each of these choices? (1)You chose to take this class; (2) You chose to put your money in a savings account; (3) You choose to have a mutually exclusive relationship with your boyfriend or girlfriend.

Decision Makers Maximize

Economists make a basic assumption about the way people make choices: *decision makers weigh the costs and benefits associated with any choice in order to maximize the value of some objective.* In the case of individuals, economists assume that they maximize their utility, or satisfaction, when making choices. In the case of business

2 Source: The College Board, "Trends in College Pricing," http://trends.collegeboard.org/.

firms, economists assume that they maximize their profits when making choices. As the benefits of making a particular choice increase, you are more likely to make the choice. As the costs of making the choice increase, you are less likely to make the choice. We can summarize this behavior by saying that "incentives matter." When the incentives to do an activity or make a choice change, people tend to change their actions or choices. When people respond to incentives and consider costs and benefits of their possible choices in order to maximize their utility or profit, they engage in the economic way of thinking.

Hulton Archive/Getty Images, Inc.

Adam Smith and the Economic Way of Thinking

Adam Smith (1723–1790) was a philosopher who is widely cited as the father of modern economics. His book *An Inquiry into the Nature and Causes of the Wealth of Nations* is one of the most influential books ever published and is the foundation of modern economics. In referring to the power of incentives to drive choices, Smith said, "It is not from the benevolence of the butcher, the brewer, or the baker, that we expect our dinner, but from their regard to their own interest. We address ourselves, not to their humanity but to their self-love, and never talk to them of our own necessities but of their advantages." In other words, Smith believed that people's self-interested responses to incentives would benefit society as a whole.

To illustrate the economic way of thinking, let's go back to our example of the parking spaces. Did you buy a parking permit for your campus this year? If you did, economists would argue that you expected the benefits of buying the permit would be higher than the costs of buying the permit. The benefits of buying the permit include easier parking, closer parking, and the comfort of driving instead of walking or biking to school. The costs of buying the permit include money plus the time and effort involved in buying the permit. If you did not buy a parking permit, economists would argue that you perceived the costs of buying the permit to be greater than the benefits you expected from owning the permit. The costs could exceed the benefits because you carpool, live on campus, are not allowed to park on campus, or prefer to walk or bike to school.

Now think about how your choice might have changed if the incentives to buy the parking permit were different. Imagine two different scenarios. First, suppose the price of a parking permit is cut by half. Some students will change their decision about buying the permit. If the cost of a permit falls, more people will buy one. Second, suppose the parking authority announces that it will sell five times as many permits as in the past but will leave the number of parking spaces unchanged. Some students will change their decision about buying a permit since the expected benefits fall when it is less likely that they will be able to find a parking space (which will happen if there are more drivers trolling out there). If the benefit of having a permit falls, fewer people will buy one.

The parking example highlights two other important concepts in economics, the concept of *ceteris paribus* and the fact that decisions are made by comparing *marginal costs* and *marginal benefits.*

Ceteris Paribus

Ceteris paribus is a Latin term that means "all other things remaining constant" or "all else equal." Whether we are studying people's choices in economics, chemical

Ceteris paribus means all other things remaining constant or all else equal.

reactions in chemistry, or the impact of fertilizer on plant growth in agronomy, we are often studying cause and effect relationships. If the price of a parking permit is increased, fewer people will choose to buy parking permits. If you add yellow dye to a beaker of blue water, the resulting fluid will be green. If a fertilizer is effective, plant growth will increase. To isolate the effect of some causal event (the price change, the yellow dye, the fertilizer application) on an outcome (the decline in permits purchased, the green fluid, and the increased plant growth), other factors that might also affect the outcome cannot be allowed to change. Without the ceteris paribus assumption, it would be difficult to isolate cause and effect when studying various economic or scientific outcomes.

For example, if there is a drastic drop in the price of gasoline at the same time that the price of parking permits increases, the number of permits purchased could increase. The increase in the number of permits purchased does not mean that an increase in price causes more people to buy permits but is instead a reflection of ceteris paribus not being true. If you add yellow dye to a beaker of blue water but your lab partner also adds black dye, the resulting fluid may not be green, not because yellow and blue do not make green but rather because other factors were not held constant. If the correct amount of fertilizer is added to a crop and at the same time there is a heat wave and drought, the crop yield may actually fall. Again, this reflects that ceteris paribus was violated rather than that the fertilizer is not effective. When other factors are changing, it is impossible to predict how changes in benefits and costs will impact people's choices because you cannot isolate whether the choices are caused by a change in other factors.

Economists, just like other scientists, use the concept of ceteris paribus to isolate important relationships. Note, however, that just because other factors (the price of gasoline, the black dye, the drought) are initially held constant with the ceteris paribus assumption, they do not need to be held constant forever. Analysis of economic choices often involves relaxing the ceteris paribus assumption in a series of steps. Much like a chemist adds one chemical at a time to a mixture to determine the resulting reaction, an economist relaxes one ceteris paribus assumption at a time to observe the results.

Decisions Are Made Incrementally or "At the Margin"

For many students, the change in the price or number of parking permits might not have changed their behavior at all. Does this mean that for them, an increase in the cost of something does not influence their choice behavior? No. Instead, it is likely that those who do not change their behavior as a result of a change in incentives are not "at the margin" of choice. To be at the margin of choice means that you are just on the edge of changing your choice, so that a small change in either the costs or benefits of the choice is enough to change your behavior. If Sue, for example, is doggedly determined to avoid driving to campus, the change in the price of the parking permit might not be relevant to her. Alternatively, if Jane is just on the edge and cannot quite decide whether or not to drive to campus, the price change might be enough to change her behavior.

*The **marginal cost** of a choice is the additional or incremental cost associated with the choice.*

...inal benefit of a choice is ... or incremental benefit ... hoice.

Economic decisions are made by comparing the **marginal costs** and **marginal benefits** of various choices. In this context, "marginal" means "incremental." Making a choice involves comparing the additional or incremental costs associated with the choice, the marginal costs, against the additional or incremental benefits associated with the choice, the marginal benefits.

Another example of choices being made at the margin comes from examining the impact of the minimum wage (the lowest wage that can be paid to workers by law) on high school enrollment. Economic research suggests that increasing the minimum wage is associated with an increase in high school dropout rates.[3] To some students, this may not seem logical because graduating high school is highly valuable and important to them: the marginal benefits of dropping out are smaller than the marginal costs of dropping out. For other students, however, the costs of attending school seem high (lots of studying, missing out on activities such as work in order to attend classes), and a change in the minimum wage raises those costs because they can now earn more in their time outside class. For students who are not on the margin of dropping out of high school, a change in the minimum wage does not change their dropout choice. For students who are on the margin of dropping out, however, an increase in the minimum wage can be just enough to make dropping out the more attractive choice.

Law of Diminishing Marginal Benefits

Decisions tend to be made incrementally or at the margin by comparing the marginal benefits and marginal costs of different activities. The marginal benefits of most activities share a common characteristic: they are subject to the **law of diminishing marginal benefits**. At the beginning of the activity, the marginal benefits tend to be relatively high. As the activity is continued, however, the marginal benefits start to diminish.

The law of diminishing marginal benefits: Ceteris paribus, as more and more of an activity is done, the marginal benefits derived from the activity tend to diminish.

Imagine, for example, that you are sitting down one evening to enjoy some ice cream. Its creaminess and yummy taste bring you lots of utility. We can get a rough measure of the dollar value of the ice cream to you by asking how much you are willing to pay for the ice cream. Suppose you are willing to pay \$5.00 for the first bowl of ice cream. This \$5.00 is a dollar-value representation of the amount of benefit you received from consuming the first bowl of ice cream. Now suppose that after you finish the first bowl, you decide you'd like another one, and then another, and another. By the fourth bowl of ice cream, however, you decide that its creaminess and yummy taste have lost some of their charm for you. Indeed, while you were willing to pay \$5.00 for the first bowl, you are only willing to pay \$2.00 for the fourth bowl. This situation arises because of the law of diminishing marginal benefits. After some point, each successive bowl of ice cream that you consume that evening brings you less and less additional utility, which is reflected in a lower willingness to pay for each successive bowl of ice cream.

Table 1.1 illustrates your hypothetical marginal and total benefit values for ice cream. Since you were willing to pay \$5.00 for the first bowl of ice cream, its marginal

Table 1.1 Marginal and Total Benefit from Ice Cream

Bowl of Ice Cream	Marginal Benefit	Number of Bowls of Ice Cream (per evening)	Total Benefit
1st	\$5.00	1	\$5.00
2nd	\$4.00	2	\$9.00
3rd	\$3.00	3	\$12.00
4th	\$2.00	4	\$14.00
5th	\$1.00	5	\$15.00

3 Neumark, David and William Wascher, 1996, "The Effects of Minimum Wages on Teenage Employment and Enrollment: Estimates from Matched CPS Data," *Research in Labor Economics*, pp. 25–64.

benefit to you is $5.00, as illustrated in the Marginal Benefit column of the table. Since you were willing to pay $4.00 for the second bowl of ice cream, its marginal benefit is $4.00. The marginal benefit of the third bowl of ice cream is $3.00, and so on through the fifth bowl of ice cream, for which you are willing to pay only $1.00. If you were to eat more and more bowls of ice cream, the marginal benefit you get from each successive bowl declines, as illustrated by the marginal benefit numbers getting smaller and smaller.

The Total Benefit column of Table 1.1 illustrates the total benefit you get from eating ice cream. When you eat one bowl, the total benefit is $5.00. The second bowl provides you with $4.00 in marginal benefit, so that if you eat two bowls, your total benefit is $9.00 ($5.00 from the first bowl plus $4.00 from the second bowl). Notice that the total benefit you get from eating ice cream grows as you eat each bowl, since each bowl provides you with positive benefits. However, the total benefit grows by smaller and smaller increments with each bowl of ice cream you eat, which reflects the law of diminishing marginal benefits.

The marginal benefit from eating ice cream is illustrated graphically in Figure 1.1. The marginal benefit of eating ice cream is measured on the vertical axis, and the quantity of ice cream is measured on the horizontal axis. When the quantity of ice cream you eat is low, the marginal benefit of eating ice cream is high. As you eat a second, third, and fourth bowl of ice cream, the marginal benefit gained from each bowl of ice cream diminishes. This generates the downward-sloping marginal benefit line in Figure 1.1.

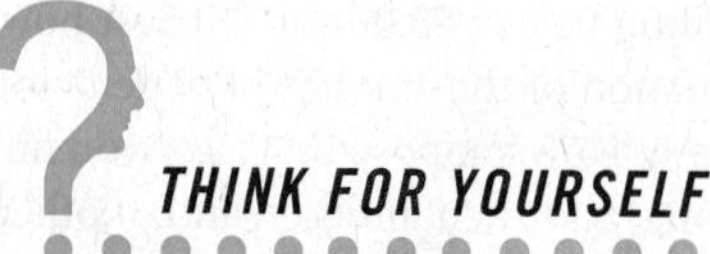

THINK FOR YOURSELF

In 2009, news organizations reported that Suresh Joachim broke his own Guinness World Record by watching TV for 72 hours straight. Joachim reportedly drank between 25 and 30 cups of coffee while watching three seasons of Kiefer Sutherland's *24* without pause. Use the concept of diminishing marginal utility to explain why nonstop TV watching is uncommon.

Figure 1.1 **Marginal Benefits of Ice Cream**

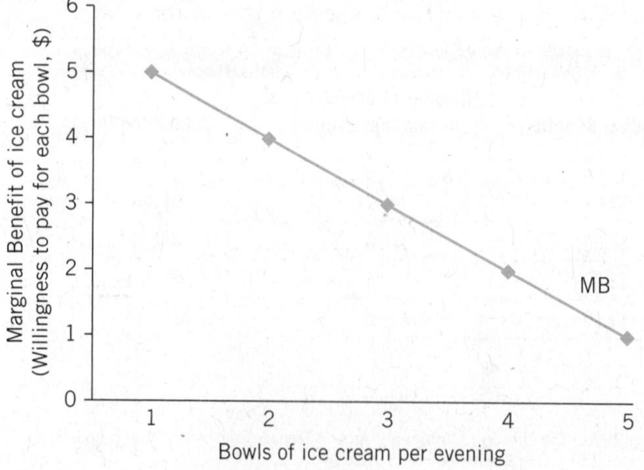

The marginal benefit you obtain from eating ice cream is refelected by your willingness to pay for each bowl, as measured on the vertial axis. As you eat more and more ice cream, the marginal benefit of each successive bowl of ice cream falls, as illustrated by the downward sloping MB curve.

Law of Increasing Marginal Costs

As is the case with marginal benefits, the marginal costs of most activities share a common characteristic: **the law of increasing marginal costs**. At the beginning of the activity, the marginal costs tend to be relatively low. As the activity is continued, however, the marginal costs start to increase.

The law of increasing marginal costs: Ceteris paribus, as more and more of an activity is done, the marginal costs of the activity tend to increase.

Imagine, for example, that Jan is training to run a 10K road race. In the past, she has run a fairly decent time of 60 minutes, which averages to just over 10 minutes per mile. This season, however, she wants to improve her time by 5 minutes. To accomplish that, it will take 30 minutes more per week of fast running than she currently performs, meaning that improving her 10K time from 60 to 55 minutes will "cost" Jan 30 extra minutes of training per week. Now suppose that she wants to improve her time by another 5 minutes, so that she finishes the 10K race in 50 minutes. Improving her time by another 5 minutes will likely take more than an additional 30 minutes of training per week, and will be accompanied by an increased probability of injury. The marginal cost of the second 5-minute improvement in Jan's 10K time is higher than the marginal cost of her first 5-minute improvement. If Jan tries to cut her overall time by 10, 15, or 20 minutes, the marginal cost of each 5-minute improvement in race time will increase because she will have to devote more time to training and because she faces increased probability of injury when she trains more.

Table 1.2 illustrates the concept of increasing marginal cost using our ice cream example. Let's suppose that the price of each bowl of ice cream is $2.00. Because eating ice cream can affect our health, we need to consider the health costs associated with consuming each bowl of ice cream. For the first bowl of ice cream, the marginal cost is the $2.00 you paid for the ice cream. The health costs are probably zero because eating one bowl of ice cream probably won't have negative health consequences. As you move on to eating the second bowl of ice cream, the marginal cost rises relative to the first bowl because the second bowl will probably have negative health consequences by spiking your sugar level. The second bowl is also more likely than the first to put you in a calorie surplus because you're consuming more calories than you burn. Including the price of the ice cream, suppose the marginal cost is $3.00. For the third bowl, the marginal cost is $4.00. By the fourth bowl, the marginal cost is $5.00 and includes even more negative health consequences as well as discomfort from eating so much.

The Total Cost column of Table 1.2 shows the total costs associated with eating ice cream. For the first bowl, the total cost includes only the price of the ice cream. If you eat two bowls, the total cost is $5.00, which is made up of $2.00 from the first bowl of ice cream plus $3.00 from the second bowl. The total cost of three bowls is $9.00, and so on.

Table 1.2 Marginal and Total Cost from Ice Cream

Bowl of Ice Cream	Marginal Cost	Number of Bowls of Ice Cream (per evening)	Total Cost
1st	$2.00	1	$2.00
2nd	$3.00	2	$5.00
3rd	$4.00	3	$9.00
4th	$5.00	4	$14.00
5th	$6.00	5	$20.00

Figure 1.2 shows the marginal costs of ice cream graphically. The first bowl of ice cream has marginal cost of $2.00. The second bowl has higher marginal cost, $3.00. As you eat more and more ice cream, the marginal cost rises. The increasing marginal cost of eating ice cream generates the upward-sloping marginal cost curve shown in the figure.

Figure 1.2 **Marginal Costs of Ice Cream**

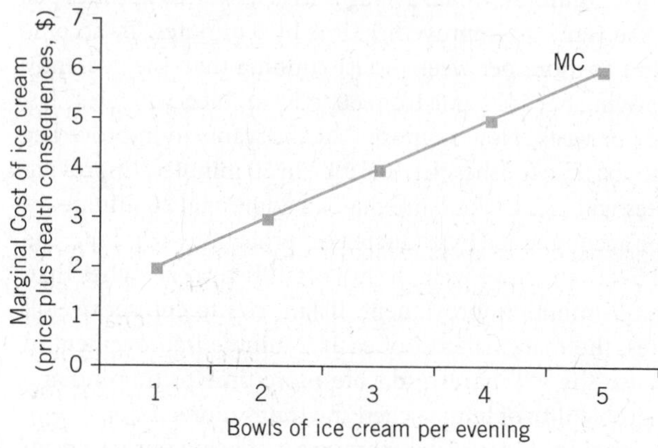

The marginal cost of ice cream includes its price plus the health consequences of eating ice cream and is reflected on the vertical axis. As you eat more and more bowls of ice cream, the marginal costs increase, as illustrated by the upward-sloping MC curve.

The Marginal Decision Rule

We can use marginal benefits and marginal costs to illustrate a general rule for making decisions: when the marginal benefit of an activity is greater than its marginal cost, we can increase our utility or profits by engaging in more of the activity. If the marginal cost is greater than the marginal benefit, engaging in more of the activity will make us worse off by decreasing our utility or our profits.

The net benefit of an activity is equal to its total benefit minus its total cost.

Table 1.3 illustrates the marginal decision rule using our ice cream example. The columns of the table report the marginal costs and benefits and total costs and benefits from eating ice cream. The last column reports the **net benefit** of eating ice cream. The net benefit from eating ice cream is the total benefit minus the total cost of eating ice cream.

When you eat three bowls of ice cream, the total benefit you receive is $12.00. The total cost you incur is $9.00. The net benefit is $3.00, which is the difference between the total benefit and total cost associated with consuming three bowls of ice cream.

When you consume one bowl of ice cream, the marginal cost is $2.00 and the marginal benefit is $5.00, so you increase your net benefit by consuming the first bowl of ice cream. For the second bowl of ice cream, the marginal cost is $3.00 and the marginal benefit is $4.00, so your net benefit rises by $1.00 when you consume

Table 1.3 **Benefits and Costs from Ice Cream**

Bowl of Ice Cream	Marginal Cost	Marginal Benefit	Total Cost (per evening)	Total Benefit (per evening)	Net Benefit (per evening)
1st	$2.00	$5.00	$2.00	$5.00	$3.00
2nd	$3.00	$4.00	$5.00	$9.00	$4.00
3rd	$4.00	$3.00	$9.00	$12.00	$3.00
4th	$5.00	$2.00	$14.00	$14.00	$0.00
5th	$6.00	$1.00	$20.00	$15.00	−$5.00

the second bowl of ice cream. If you consume a third bowl of ice cream, the marginal cost is $4.00, but the marginal benefit is only $3.00. Consuming the third bowl of ice cream will thus lower your net benefit by $1.00 relative to consuming two bowls of ice cream. If you consumed a fourth bowl of ice cream, your net benefits would fall again because the marginal cost of the fourth bowl of ice cream is more than the marginal benefit of the fourth bowl of ice cream. If you wanted to maximize your utility from eating ice cream, the optimal number of bowls for you to eat is somewhere between two and three. The second bowl of ice cream gives you marginal benefit that exceeds marginal cost, but the third bowl of ice cream gives marginal cost greater than marginal benefit. If you were restricted to eating only whole bowls of ice cream, you would maximize your utility by consuming two bowls. If you could eat partial bowls, you might maximize your utility by consuming, say, two and a half bowls.

Figure 1.3 graphically illustrates the marginal benefits and costs of eating ice cream. When you aren't eating very much ice cream, the marginal benefit of an additional bowl is high and the marginal cost of an additional bowl is low. As you eat more ice cream, however, the marginal benefit falls and the marginal cost rises. Beyond about two and a half bowls of ice cream, the marginal cost of eating additional bowls of ice cream is higher than the marginal benefit, which means that eating more bowls actually makes you worse off. Thus, the optimal number of bowls of ice cream for you is two and a half, which is where the MC and MB curves intersect in Figure 1.3. This example shows the **marginal decision rule** in action. You can maximize the net benefit you receive from an activity when you engage in that activity until the marginal benefits are just equal to the marginal costs.

*The **marginal decision rule** states that you can maximize the net benefit you receive from an activity when you engage in that activity until the marginal benefits are equal to the marginal costs.*

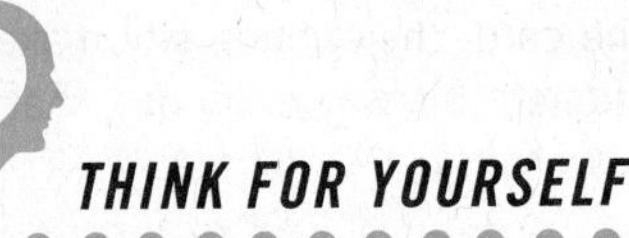

THINK FOR YOURSELF

Suppose that the price of a bowl of ice cream is $3.00 instead of $2.00 but all the other costs and benefits are the same as in Table 1.3. What would be the total cost of consuming four bowls of ice cream? What would be the optimal number of bowls of ice cream to eat per evening?

Figure 1.3 **Marginal Benefits and Marginal Costs of Ice Cream**

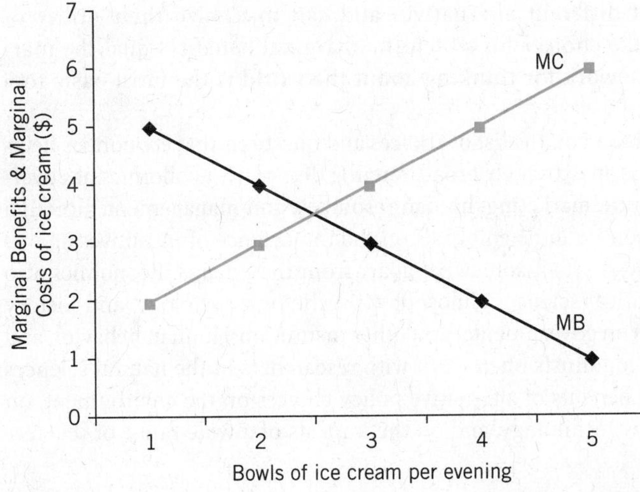

When you eat one or two bowls of ice cream, the marginal benefit of more ice cream is higher than the marginal cost of more ice cream. So eating more ice cream will make you better off. When you eat three or more bowls of ice cream, the marginal cost is higher than the marginal benefit, so eating more ice cream makes you worse off. The optimal amount of ice cream to eat is where MB = MC.

A sunk cost is a cost that, once incurred, cannot be recovered. Sunk costs are irrelevant when making decisions at the margin.

Sunk costs

In making sound decisions, it is important to evaluate costs correctly. If people include **sunk costs**, their decisions will not be correct. Sunk costs are costs that, once incurred, cannot be recovered. For example, suppose that you recently purchased a car for $25,000, but your job now requires you to relocate to another country and you are considering selling your car. The best price you have been offered for the car is $15,000. Should you sell it? The answer depends on whether you will derive more benefit from selling it than from not selling it, *not* based on the price you paid for it, since the $25,000 you paid is a sunk cost.

Sunk Costs and Penny Auctions

People make poor choices when they allow sunk costs to affect their decisions. Indeed, online auction sites like QuiBids, Skoreit, and beezid survive in part because their customers consider sunk costs in their decision making. Each time a user bids on an item, he or she must pay an average of $0.60. In addition, each bid made extends the length of the auction by a few seconds. As an item's price rises, some customers think to themselves, "I don't want give up on bidding on this item, since I've already spent $10 (or $20 or $50 . . .) bidding on it." Because of this reasoning, users continue to bid on items because they don't want to "lose" their sunk costs (which, in fact, are already lost and once placed have no influence on whether or not the user will win the auction). It is typical for items on penny auction sites to sell for 90 percent less than their retail price. How do the sites make money? As an example, when a $25 gift card sells for $2 after 100 bids are placed for the card, the auction site makes $60 on the bid charges, for a net profit of $37. Since thousands of items are auctioned this way every day, that's a lot of sunk cost!

SUMMARY

Economics is the study of choices. Choices arise because resources are scarce—we have less of them than we have uses for them. Decision makers weigh the costs and benefits of different alternatives and can maximize their utility or profits when they make choices for which the marginal benefits equal the marginal costs. This framework for thinking about the world is the most basic tool of economics.

As you can guess based on the list of choices and questions that economics helps to address, economics is an extremely broad-ranging discipline. Economics has overlap with business, finance, marketing, human resources, and management, although the grounding of economics in its emphasis on the importance of incentives and its use of theoretical analysis sets it somewhat apart from these fields. Economics also overlaps with law, political science, philosophy, psychology, sociology, and history because of its emphasis on governmental and other institutions, human behavior, and human interactions. Economists often work with researchers in the natural sciences to assess the costs and benefits of alternative policy choices on the environment, on the introduction of new technology, and on the impacts of a wide range of science-related outcomes.

KEY CONCEPTS

- Economics
- Macroeconomics
- Microeconomics
- Basic economic resources
- Scarcity
- Cost
- Benefit
- Utility
- Profit
- Opportunity cost
- Ceteris paribus
- Marginal cost
- Marginal benefit
- Law of diminishing marginal benefits
- Law of increasing marginal costs
- Net benefit
- Marginal decision rule
- Sunk cost

DISCUSSION QUESTIONS AND PROBLEMS

1. Suppose you are a fly-fishing guide. Your bookings of late have been low, and you are thinking of lowering the price of your guide service. If you lower your price, you'd expect more clients, ceteris paribus. But if other events occur at the same time as you decrease your prices, the expected increase in clients might not happen. Discuss possible outcomes in the following situations:
   a. You lower your price, and at the same time, many of the local rivers are closed to fishing due to a drought or forest fires.
   b. You lower your price, and at the same time, a new movie about fly-fishing is released and draws record attendance at the theaters.
2. Discuss the costs and benefits of each of the following activities; include at least one nonmonetary cost and benefit in your discussion of each:
   a. Studying for an exam
   b. Going skiing on a class day
   c. Taking a job
   d. Watching television
3. Suppose that a friend of yours recently opened her own business. She is happy because it generated $25,000 in earnings last year. How can you tell whether this was a good investment?
4. Economists are fond of saying that "there is no such thing as a free lunch." Use opportunity cost to explain the meaning of this saying.
5. In his book *The Wealth of Nations*, Adam Smith noted the contradiction that, "Nothing is more useful than water: but it will purchase scarce anything; scarce anything can be had in exchange for it. A diamond, on the contrary, has scarce any value in use; but a very great quantity of other goods may frequently be had in exchange for it."[4] This is situation is known as the diamond-water paradox. How does thinking at the margin help to explain the paradox?
6. It is common for people trying to lose weight to notice that the first 10 pounds are much easier to lose than the last 10 pounds. Use the concept of increasing marginal cost of explain why this is the case.
7. Suppose that you have 6 hours per day to devote to studying economics and accounting. You estimate your benefits of studying for each subject as follows:

Hours Studying Economics Per Day	Expected Score on Economics Exam	Marginal Benefit of Studying Economics (increase in economics score)	Hours Studying Accounting Per Day	Expected Score on Accounting Exam	Marginal Benefit of Studying Accounting (increase in accounting score)
0	44	-	0	70	-
1	62	18	1	80	10
2	76	14	2	88	8
3	86	10	3	94	6
4	94	8	4	96	2
5	100	6	5	96	0
6	100	0	6	96	0

What is the best way for you to divide up your study time in order to maximize your grades in both classes? (Hint: What is the marginal cost of studying economics? What is the marginal cost of studying accounting?)

4 Smith, Adam. *The Wealth of Nations*. Bantam Classic Edition, March 2003, New York: Bantam Dell (p. 41).

MULTIPLE CHOICE QUESTIONS

Quantity	Marginal Benefit ($)
1	45
2	35
3	30
4	27
5	25

1. Ross is a passionate vinyl record collector. He is interested in obtaining one or more rare vinyl records for his collection. His marginal willingness to pay (i.e., his marginal benefit) for these records is detailed in the table shown. How much is Ross willing to pay for the third record?
   a. $45
   b. $30
   c. $110
   d. $5
   e. Not enough information, since the price of a record is not given

2. Using the table, what is Ross's total willingness to pay for three records?
   a. $45
   b. $30
   c. $110
   d. $5
   e. Not enough information, since the price of a record is not given

3. Using the table, if the local record store has their records on sale for $28 each, how many will Ross want to purchase?
   a. 1
   b. 2
   c. 3
   d. 4
   e. 5

4. The branch of economics that is concerned with broad choices and the overall performance of the economy is
   a. resource economics.
   b. contemporary economics.
   c. macroeconomics.
   d. microeconomics.

5. Assuming that rational people are motivated by incentives, what would occur if the average salary of education majors falls by 30 percent and the average salary of economics majors rises by 10 percent, ceteris paribus?
   a. Some students will shift majors from economics to education.
   b. Some students will shift majors from education to economics.
   c. Some students will stop majoring in both economics and education.
   d. Some students will drop out of college.

Number of Sushi Rolls	Total Benefit	Sushi Roll	Marginal Benefit
1	$8.00	1st	$8.00
2	$14.50	2nd	?
3	$19.25	3rd	?
4	$22.00	4th	?
5	$23.50	5th	$1.50

6. Dave loves sushi. There are always sushi rolls that Dave is willing to try (or eat for a second or third time!). The left side of the table above shows Dave's total benefits (or total willingness to pay) associated with eating sushi during a night. The column on the right shows Dave's marginal benefit. Suppose that sushi rolls are priced at $5.00. How many rolls will Dave choose to buy in a night?
   a. 1
   b. 2
   c. 3
   d. 4
   e. 5

7. Using the table above, suppose that sushi rolls are on sale for $2.50. How many rolls will Dave choose to buy in a night?
   a. 1
   b. 2
   c. 3
   d. 4
   e. 5

Total number of Wands	Total Benefit ($)	Total Cost ($)
1	1,800	500
2	3,300	1,000
3	4,500	1,500
4	5,400	2,000

Total number of Wands	Total Benefit ($)	Total Cost ($)
5	6,000	2,500
6	6,400	3,000
7	6,600	3,500

8. Tom Riddle is planning to use rare magic wands to attack wizards in London. He needs to buy many wands because their powers work differently on certain wizards. The table above reflects Tom's total benefits and total costs associated with buying magic wands. Based on this information, Tom's ***net*** benefit of buying three wands would be___.
   a. $9,600
   b. $4,500
   c. $3,000
   d. $6,000
   e. $6,600

9. Based on the table above, the marginal cost of the fourth wand for Tom is:
   a. $5,000
   b. $3,500
   c. $3,400
   d. $2,000
   e. $500

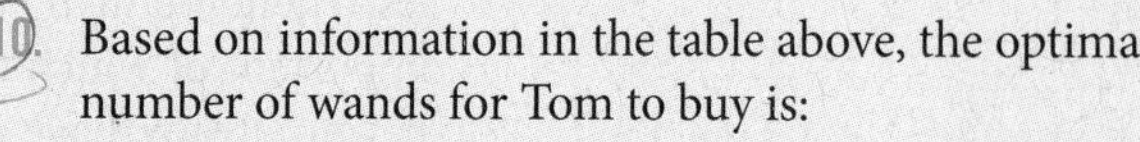

10. Based on information in the table above, the optimal number of wands for Tom to buy is:
   a. 1
   b. 2
   c. 4
   d. 5
   e. More than 7

ADDITIONAL READINGS AND WEB RESOURCES

Heilbroner, Robert. (1999) *The Worldly Philosophers: The Lives, Times And Ideas of the Great Economic Thinkers*, 7th ed. Touchstone Publishers.

Smith, Adam. (2011) *An Inquiry into the Nature and Causes of the Wealth of Nations*, Simon & Brown Publishers.

Wheelan, Charles. (2010) *Naked Economics: Undressing the Dismal Science* (Fully Revised and Updated), W. W. Norton & Company.

http://marketplace.publicradio.org/ This website accompanies the Marketplace radio show. It includes coverage of current economic events, the economics of current issues, financial advice, and current policy debates.

http://www.thebigmoney.com/ The Big Money website. Economic and current events, news, and commentary without technical jargon.

http://econ161.berkeley.edu/ The blog site of Berkeley economist Brad DeLong. Focuses on current economic debates, and explains basic economics concepts.

http://www.freakonomics.com/ The Freakonomics website is a spinoff of the best-selling book *Freakonomics: A Rogue Economist Explores the Hidden Side of Everything.* The website includes blog posts and links to the Freakonomics radio, RSS feed, Twitter, and Facebook sites.

http://gregmankiw.blogspot.com/ Blog by Harvard economist Greg Mankiw. Presents discussions of economic issues, useful links, and "random observations for students of economics."

Chapter 1 Appendix Working with Graphs

Understanding how to read and construct graphs will be crucial to learning economics. There are many reasons why economists use graphs to present ideas, the most important of which matches the old saying, "a picture is worth a thousand words." If you already have experience with graphs, you probably don't need to read this Appendix. If you don't have experience with graphs, fear not! This Appendix will introduce the fundamentals of constructing and interpreting graphs.

CONSTRUCTING GRAPHS

Graphs are visual representations of relationships between two or more variables. Although graphs can take many forms, most are constructed in the same way. This section describes how graphs are constructed.

Obtain Data

The first step in constructing a graph is obtaining the data you want to show in the graph. Economic data can come from government agencies, from surveys, and from business records. Suppose that we are interested in graphing the number of students enrolled in college across time. We can obtain data on this relationship from the U.S. Department of Education's National Center for Education Statistics. Table A1.1 shows enrollment in U.S. colleges and universities for each year between 2000 and 2009.

Table A1.1 U.S. College and University Enrollment over Time

Year	2000	2001	2002	2003	2004	2005	2006	2007	2008	2009
Total (in 000s)	15,312	15,928	16,612	16,911	17,272	17,487	17,759	18,248	19,103	20,428

Source: U.S. Department of Education National Center for Education Statistics. www.nces.ed.gov

Draw and Label Axes

The second step in constructing a graph is drawing and labeling the axes of the graph. For many graphs, data is shown on the Cartesian coordinate system, named after René Descartes, the French philosopher and mathematician who invented this graphing system. The Cartesian coordinate system graphs data using a set of two axes to represent values of two variables. The axes are drawn perpendicular to each other, and the point where they intersect is called the origin of the graph. The horizontal axis is called the x-axis, and the vertical axis is called the y-axis.The variable that is measured on the y-axis is the y-variable. The variable that is measured on the x-axis is the x-variable. Rightward movements along the x-axis correspond to increases in the value of the x-variable. Similarly, upward movements along the y-axis correspond to increases in the value of the y-variable. Figure A1.1 shows the axes for a graph that will depict college enrollment over time. The years are labeled on the x-axis, and the enrollment numbers are labeled on the y-axis.

Figure A1.1 **Draw and Label Axes**

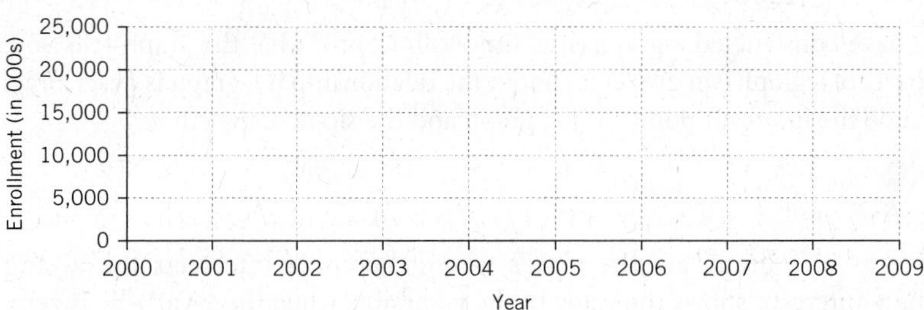

The first step in constructing a graph is to draw and label the graph's axes. The horizontal axis is called the *x*-axis. The vertical axis is called the *y*-axis. Rightward movements along the horizontal axis and upward movements along the vertical axis represent increases in the values of the *x*-and *y*-variables, respectively. Vertical and horizontal gridlines can be drawn at each of the values on the *x*- and *y*-axis.

Plot Points

The next step in constructing a graph is to plot the corresponding data points on the graph. Corresponding data points are the data values that go together. We can see from Table A1.1 that college enrollment in year 2000 was 15,312,000 students. So the year value of 2000 and the enrollment value of 15,312 correspond to one another. Point A in Figure A1.2 shows this corresponding data point. Similarly, enrollment in year 2002 was 16,612,000 students, which is shown by point B in Figure A1.2. Plotting all of the corresponding data points for each of the years in Table A1.1 generates points shown in Figure A1.2.

Figure A1.2 **Plot the Corresponding Data Points**

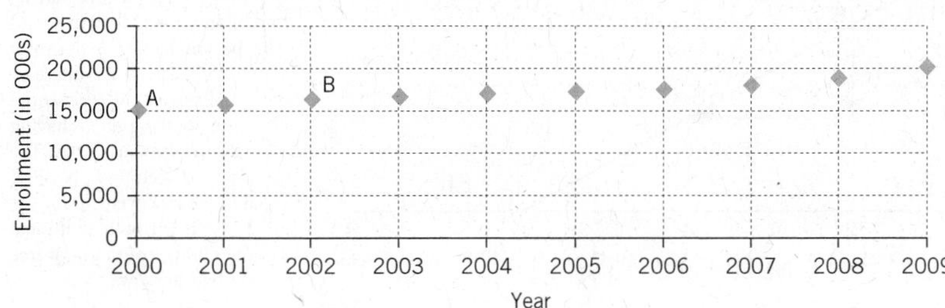

The second step in constructing a graph is to plot the corresponding data points onto the graph. In year 2000, college enrollment was 15,312 thousand students, so point A plots the value 15,312 to correspond to the year 2000. College enrollment was 16,612 thousand students in 2002, so we plot the value 16,612 to correspond with year 2002 (point B).

Draw the Curve

The third step in constructing a graph is to connect the data points and label the resulting curve or line. By convention, the term "curve" is used to describe the connected data points, regardless of whether the curve is a straight line or not. The curve showing enrollment over time is labeled Enrollment in Figure A1.3.

Figure A1.3 **Draw the Curve**

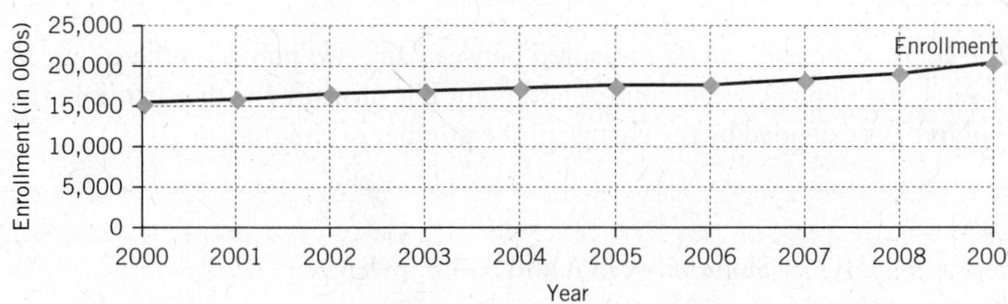

The third step in constructing a graph is to connect the data points and label the resulting curve.

INTERPRETING AND MODIFYING GRAPHS

Once you have constructed a graph, it is time to interpret what the graph tells you. Two key parts of a graph can give clues about the relationship the graph is describing. These include the intercept points of the graph and the slope of the curve.

Intercepts

The intercepts of a graph are the places where the curve intersects the *y*- and *x*-axes. The *y*-intercept shows the value of the *y*-variable when the *x*-variable is zero. The *x*-intercept shows the value of the *x*-variable when the *y*-variable is zero. Curve FT in Figure A1.4 graphs hypothetical data showing the relationship between the number of children and the amount of free time that a parent has. The *y*-intercept of Figure A1.4 tells us that people with 0 children have 6 hours of free time each day. The *x*-intercept tells us that people with 6 children have 0 hours of free time each day. In graphs like Figure A1.3, that depict changes in variables over time, the *y*-intercept usually corresponds to the first time period in our data.

Figure A1.4 **Intercepts and Slope**

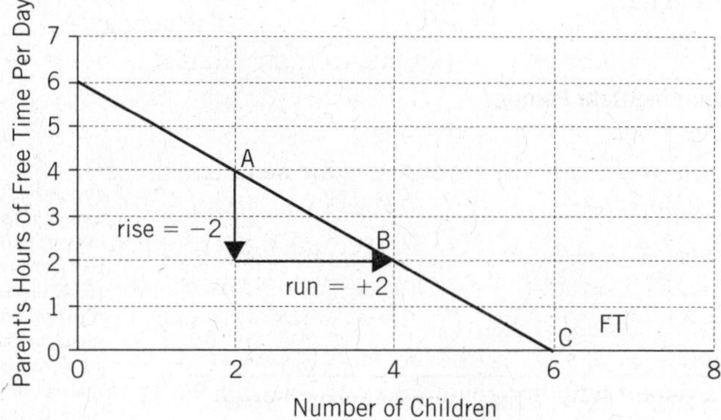

Curve FT shows the relationship between a parent's free time and the number of children he or she has. The *y*-intercept tells us that having zero children would correspond to the person having 6 hours of free time each day. The *x*-intercept shows that having 6 children would correspond to the parent having 0 hours of free time each day. The slope of FT between point A and B is equal to the rise over the run, or $-2/+2 = -1$. For each additional child, the number of hours of free time falls by 1 per day.

Slope

Another important key to understanding the relationships described by graphs is the slope of the curve shown in a graph. The slope of a curve tells us how much one variable changes when another variable changes. Just like the slope of the roof of a house, the slope of a curve is equal to the "rise over the run," or the change in the value of the *y*-variable over the change in the value of the *x*-variable between two data points.

$$\text{Slope} = \frac{\text{rise}}{\text{run}} = \frac{\text{change in the } y\text{-variable}}{\text{change in the } x\text{-variable}}$$

The slope of a curve can be measured between any two points on the curve. In Figure A1.4, the slope between point A and point B is measured as the change in the hours of free time divided by the change in the number of children, or

$$\text{Slope between A and B} = \frac{-2}{+2} = -1.$$

We can interpret this slope value of −1 as indicating that an increase in the number of children in a family by 1 is associated in a reduction in the parent's amount of free time by 1 hour per day. In Figure A1.4, the slope of the curve FT would be −1 regardless of whether we measured the slope between points A and B, between points A and C, between points B and C, or between any other two points on the graph. In other words, curve FT has a constant slope. All straight lines have a constant slope. In Figure A1.3, however, the slope of the Enrollment curve changes between different points on the graph.

The negative value of the slope of the FT curve in Figure A1.4 implies that the number of children and hours of free time have an inverse or negative relationship with one another. When variables are inversely or negatively related, an increase in the x-variable is associated with a decrease in the y-variable and vice versa. Alternatively, the slope of the Enrollment curve in Figure A1.3 is positive, indicating that there is a direct or positive relationship between college enrollment and time. In other words, as time passes, college enrollment has risen.

Moving Along a Curve versus Shifting a Curve

As you progress through the text, it will be important to distinguish between *moving along* a curve and *shifting* a curve. In Figure A1.5, curve FT shows the tradeoff between a parent's free time and the number of children he or she has, just as in Figure A1.4. At point A, the parent has 2 children and 4 hours of free time per day. All else equal, when the number of children increases from 2 to 4, the number of hours of free time the parent has falls from 4 hours per day to 2 hours per day, as shown by the movement along the curve FT from Point A to Point B.

Now suppose that the parent changes the amount of time he or she works outside the home, perhaps moving from a full-time job to a part-time job. Changing the hours that the parent works will change the amount of free time the parent has, even if the number of children the parent has stays the same. For example, a parent with 2 children may be able to have 6 hours of free time instead of only 4 hours of free time, as shown by the movement from point A on curve FT to point D on curve FT′. Alternatively, on curve FT, a parent who has 2 children was able to have 4 hours of free time, but a parent working fewer hours could have 4 hours of free time even if they have 4 children, as shown by the movement from point A on curve FT to point C on curve FT′. The change in the amount of time a parent works outside the home causes a shift from curve FT to curve FT′.

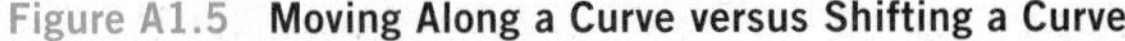
Figure A1.5 Moving Along a Curve versus Shifting a Curve

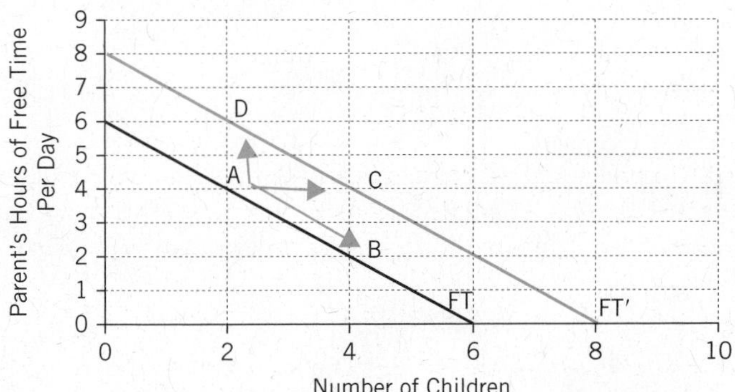

Curve FT shows the relationship between a parent's free time and the number of children he or she has, ceteris paribus. When the number of children changes, ceteris paribus, there is a movement along the curve FT from point A to point B. If the parent changes the amount of time he or she works outside the home, the relationship between free time and the number of children changes, as shown by the curve FT′. Ceteris paribus, changes in variables measured on the axes cause movements along the FT curve. Changes in variables that are not measured on the axes cause a shift in the curve from FT to FT′.

More generally, a movement along a curve happens when one of the variables measured on the axes changes, ceteris paribus. A shift in a curve occurs when a variable that is not measured on the axes changes. In Figure A1.5, the movement from A to B occurs because the number of children changes. The shift from curve FT to FT' occurs because of the change in the amount of time the parent works outside the home.

You will gain experience with graphs throughout your class in economics. As you are studying each of the chapters in the book, you can deepen your understanding if you take the time to draw each of the graphs in the book on your own and use your own words to describe what the graph is telling you.

Pedro Portal/©AP/Wide World Photos

Production Possibilities

After studying this chapter, you should be able to:

- Explain the importance of models in economics
- Describe the production possibilities model
- Illustrate the use of the production possibilities model
- Calculate opportunity costs of production
- Define the concept of comparative advantage
- Apply the concept of comparative advantage to demonstrate the benefits of specialization and trade
- Discuss the difference between positive and normative economics

Each spring, high school and college graduates hear commencement addresses as part of their graduation ceremonies. Typically, graduation speakers such as U.S. President Barak Obama, who spoke to Miami-Dade College graduates in 2011, encourage graduates to "reach their potential." But what is your potential? What are the possibilities available for you? Do you have the skills to become a physician or veterinarian? Would your writing and language abilities prepare you for a career as a language teacher or author? If you are interested in mathematics and logic, could you go on to become an engineer or scientist? Your possible potential depends on the skills and resources available to you and the choices you make about how to use those resources.

Like individuals, economies also have a "potential." The available resources and the choices citizens make about how to use those resources determine a society's economic potential.

This potential includes the amount of goods and services that can be produced in order to satisfy the needs of the people living in the economy. But an economy's potential is much more than nuts and bolts and TVs and cars. The choices we make about how to use our economy's resources determine our society's level of well-being, social and financial stability, and future growth. In this chapter, we introduce a model of an economy's potential, the production possibilities model.

MODELS IN ECONOMICS

To understand an economy's production possibilities, we will use a model that simplifies the many economic opportunities available. Models are used in economics and most other sciences to represent reality. You have probably encountered models before. Maps are examples of models. The map shown here is of the Norris Geyser Basin in Yellowstone National Park. The picture is of Steamboat Geyser, located in the Norris Geyser Basin. As a model of Norris Geyser Basin, the map is a representation of the important features of the area (such as the location of roads, campgrounds, and trails), but it abstracts from many of the details (the colors, terrain, and geyser eruptions shown in the picture). A model is a simplification that captures the most important features of something but does not include each and every detail.

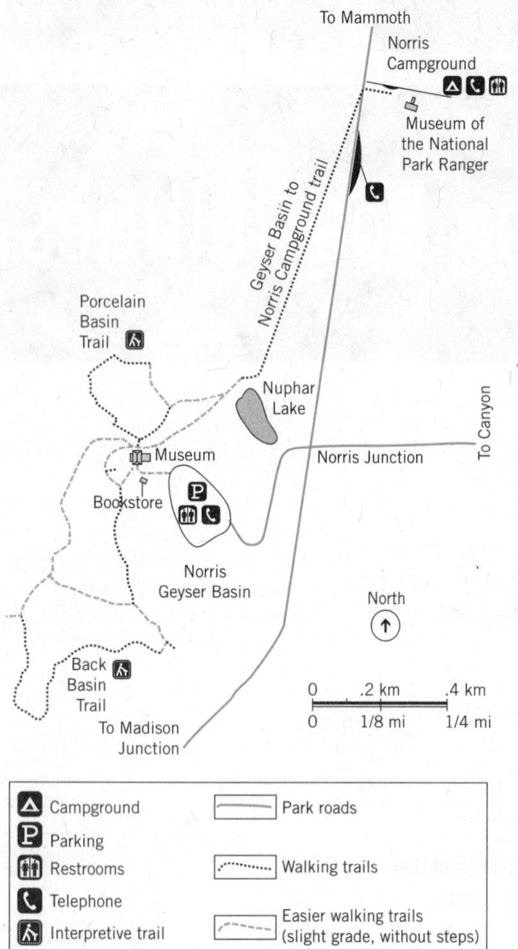

Most sciences use models. Before a NASA engineer builds a Mars-bound rocket, she first builds a small-scale model of the rocket to test her ideas. Before a chemist conducts an experiment to test the reactions between two molecules, he builds a model of the molecules to capture their relevant features and possible interactions. Economists build models to help make predictions about economic outcomes. When building economic models, we first account for the most important features in an economic relationship, and we assume that other factors are either irrelevant or are held constant (using the ceteris paribus concept described in Chapter 1). We can later add details to our economic models by relaxing the ceteris paribus assumption in a systematic way and drawing conclusions about how outcomes change as a result.

The production possibilities model, which we discuss next, is one of the most basic and useful models in economics. It describes an economy's potential, it can be used to illustrate how scarcity leads to choices, and it helps us understand that some choices provide more efficient uses of our resources than others.

PRODUCTION POSSIBILITIES MODEL

*A **production possibilities model** tells us combinations of goods or services that can be produced by an individual, a group, or an entire economy given the resources available and the state of technology.*

The **production possibilities model** identifies the choices available to an individual, a group, or an entire economy given the resources available. Most often, we use the model to determine the potential goods and services that an economy can produce.

Let's first use the production possibilities model to evaluate the choices that face an individual. We will then extend this simple model to one that predicts the choices for an entire economy. To build the model, you must start with your resources. Suppose that they consist of four hours of time per day, this textbook, and a finance textbook. Although you might be able to do all sorts of activities with this set of resources, let's focus on just two: earning points on economics homework and earning points on finance homework.

Table 2.1 presents hypothetical production levels you could generate with your resources. If you choose to devote all your resources to studying finance, you could earn 10 points on your finance homework. This is combination A in Table 2.1. If you choose to split your time evenly between studying economics and studying finance, you could produce combination B, and if you choose to study economics but not finance, you could produce combination C.

Table 2.1 Production Possibilities for Economics and Finance Points

Combination	Number of Points Earned in Economics Per Day	Number of Points Earned in Finance Per Day
A	0	10
B	5	5
C	10	0

Your production possibilities can also be shown graphically, as in Figure 2.1. The axes of Figure 2.1 show the number of points you could earn in economics and finance per day. There is no independent or dependent variable in the production possibilities model, so we could measure either economics or finance points on the y-axis or x-axis. In Figure 2.1, we measure economics points earned per day on the x-axis and finance points earned per day on the y-axis. Combinations A, B, and C from Table 2.1 are plotted in Figure 2.1. The line that connects points A, B, and C shows all of the infinite number of possible combinations of economics and finance points that you could produce with your resources. This line is called your **production possibilities frontier** (PPF) for economics and finance points, given the set of resources available to you. It illustrates the maximum amount of economics and finance points that you could produce with your resources, ceteris paribus.

A production possibilities frontier (PPF) illustrates the maximum amount of output that can be produced with a given set of resources and technology, ceteris paribus.

Figure 2.1 Production Possibilities for Economics and Finance Points

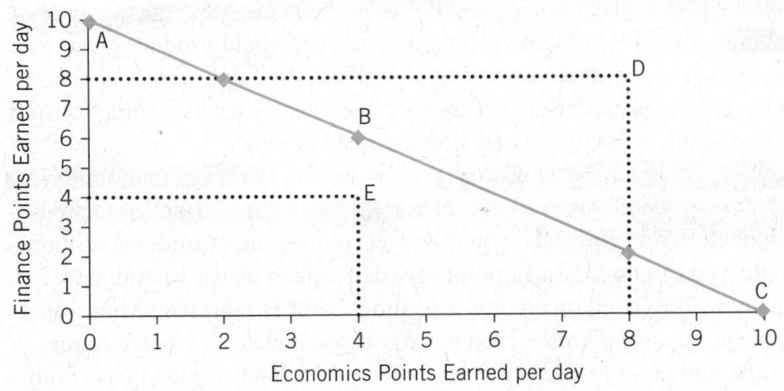

Line ABC shows the maximum combination of finance and economics points that could be earned per day given the resources available. Point D represents an unattainable choice given the available resources. Point E represents an attainable, but inefficient choice.

Although it's simple, the production possibilities model in Figure 2.1 shows some important relationships that are typical of any production possibilities model, even one that represents the choices facing an entire economy.

Scarcity and Tradeoffs

Something is scarce when there is a limited amount of it available but more than one alternative use for it. In our simple model, the scarce resources are time and the textbooks. They are scarce because they have more than one possible use because you can use them for either studying finance or studying economics. If you decide to change your time use to include more economics studying, that time is no longer available for studying finance. If you made such a choice, you would move, for example, from point A to point C on the PPF, where you have traded points in finance for points in economics.

Attainable and Unattainable Choices

Points on or inside the PPF are attainable choices, ceteris paribus.

Points outside the PPF are unattainable choices, ceteris paribus.

In Figure 2.1, points A, B, C, and any other point on or inside the PPF are all **attainable choices**, given the resource set available to you. They are combinations of economics and finance points that you could achieve given your resources. Notice that point D, which represents the combination of 8 points per day in economics and 8 points per day in finance, lies outside the PPF. That combination, and any other combination outside the PPF, is an **unattainable choice**, given your resource set.

Efficiency and Inefficiency

Combinations of output that lie on the PPF represent efficient choices.

Combinations of output that lie inside the PPF represent inefficient choices.

Points that lie on the production possibilities frontier, such as A, B, and C, are **efficient choices** of how to use your resources because they represent the maximum output that can be produced using the resources available. Point E, which lies inside the PPF in Figure 2.1, represents 4 points in economics and 4 points in finance earned per day. Because you had dedicated enough resources to earn more points than this, point E represents an **inefficient choice** about how to use your resources. It is inefficient because at point E you have the potential to produce more points in economics, more points in finance, or more of both with the same set of resources, but you don't meet that potential.

Ceteris Paribus

Each PPF represents the production possibilities while holding the particular level of resources fixed. The PPF in Figure 2.1 shows what you could produce given four hours of time and your two textbooks, ceteris paribus. Why does it matter that we hold the level of resources fixed? Suppose we relax the ceteris paribus assumption and allow the time available to increase to six hours instead of four.

The change in the resource set means that you have a new set of economics and finance production possibilities available, so the PPF in Figure 2.1 no longer represents your production possibilities. If you spend all your resources studying economics, for example, you can now earn 12 points per day instead of just 10. In Figure 2.2, we draw your new PPF based on six hours of time. Point H represents your potential economics and finance points earned per day if you devote all your resources to studying finance, and point J represents your potential economics and finance points

Figure 2.2 **Production Possibilities after an Increase in Resources**

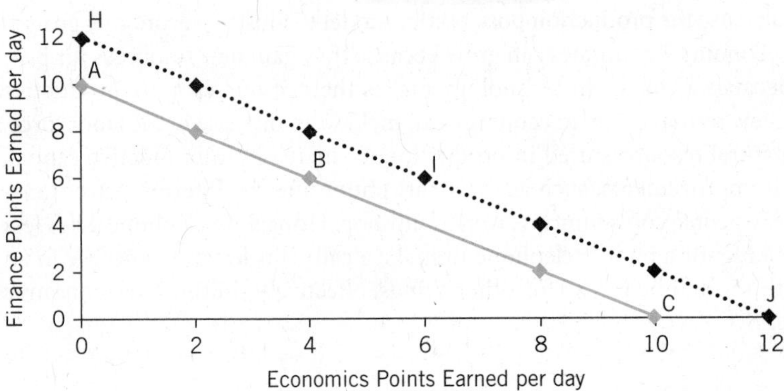

The PPF ABC represents production possiblities when you have 4 hours to study per day. The PPF HIJ represents the production possibilities available when your resources increase from 4 to 6 hours of study time per day. When more resources are available, the PPF shifts outward.

earned per day if you devote all your resources to studying economics. When we draw a given PPF, we must hold other factors constant because changes in other factors such as technology or the amount of resources available will generate a different PPF.

Economic Growth

When the PPF shifts to the right, as it does in Figure 2.2, you have the ability to produce more than you did before. In the graph, the outward shift of the curve represents economic growth, which is an increase in the amount of output that you can produce. This economic growth resulted from an increase in the resources available to you. Your PPF could also move outward because of a change in technology. Technology that generates overall improvements in production possibilities would shift the PPF outward, as in Figure 2.2. If technology increases production possibilities in some goods but not others, the PPF will move differently than in Figure 2.2.

Imagine that you find an economics podcast that helps you to understand economics (but not finance) better. How would such a technological change affect your PPF? Figure 2.3 illustrates the impact on your PPF of a technological change that allows you to produce more of one good but not more of another. If you devote all of your time to studying economics, you can now earn 20 points per day rather than 10 points per day. Because the technology does not improve your understanding of finance, you can still earn only 10 points per day if you devote all of your resources to studying finance.

Figure 2.3 **Production Possibilities After Technological Innovation that Improves Economics Understanding**

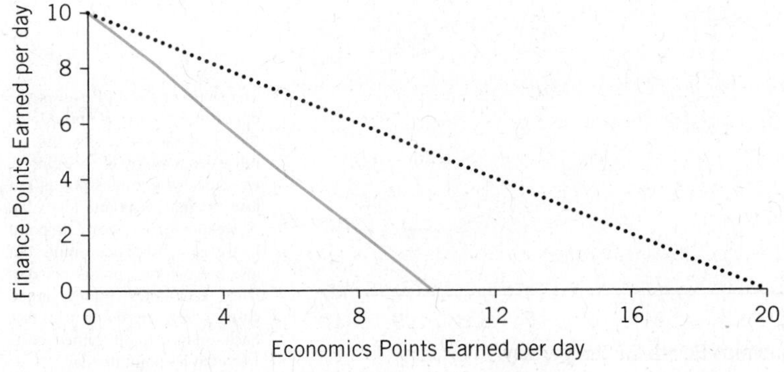

The solid PPF represents original production possibilities. The dotted PPF represents production possibilities after a technological innovation that improves your economics understanding but not your finance understanding. When a technological innovation increases the production of one good but not another, the PPF rotates outward.

Thus, a technological change that improves your ability to produce one output but not another generates an outward rotation in your PPF.

We can also use the production possibilities model to illustrate economic growth for an entire economy. Economies can grow because they gain new resources for production or because a change in technology makes their resources more productive than before. New resources for an economy can include an increase in the labor force, the land or natural resources used in production, or increases in productive capital. Technological improvements, such as the smart phone and the Internet, have transformed the way people communicate, work, and shop. Using a smart phone takes less time than looking for a public telephone to make a call. This leaves the people in an economy with more time to use for other things, effectively shifting the economy's PPF outward.

Opportunity Cost

We can also use the production possibilities model to determine the tradeoffs associated with different choices. As you move from one point to another on a PPF, you gain more of one good but must give up some of another good. For example, if you move from point A to point B in Figure 2.1, you gain 4 points per day in economics, but you give up 4 points per day in finance. In other words, your opportunity cost of 4 points in economics is 4 points in finance. If instead you moved from point C to point B, you would gain 6 points in finance at an opportunity cost of 6 points in economics.

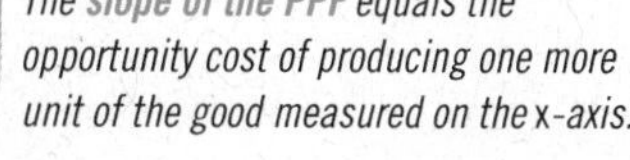

The ***slope of the PPF*** *equals the opportunity cost of producing one more unit of the good measured on the x-axis.*

Opportunity cost can be illustrated using the slope of the PPF. The slope between any two points on a line or a curve is equal to the rise over the run between those points. That is, it equals the change in the value on the *y*-axis that occurs as we move from one point to the other divided by the change in the value on the *x*-axis between the same points. In our production possibilities model, the **slope of the PPF** shows the amount of the good measured on the *y*-axis that must be given up in order to gain one more unit of the good measured on the *x*-axis. This is the opportunity cost of one more unit of the good measured on the *x*-axis.

Figure 2.4 shows your PPF again for economics and finance points when you have four hours available. Suppose you are initially at point K, where you earn 8 points in finance per day and 2 points in economics per day. If you move to point B,

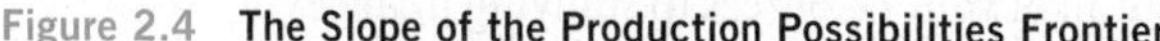

Figure 2.4 **The Slope of the Production Possibilities Frontier**

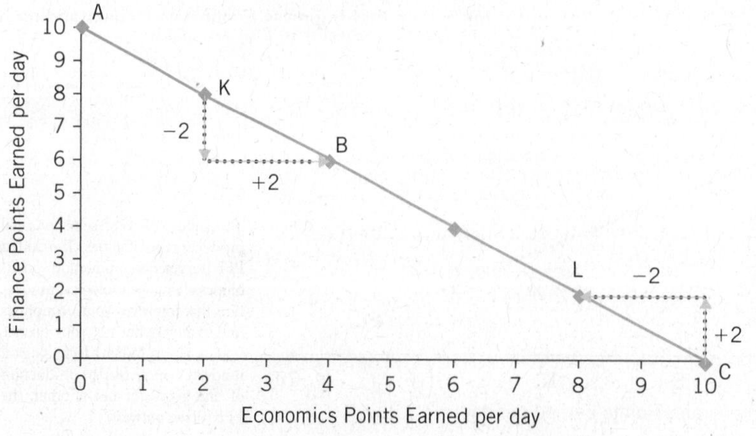

The slope of the PPF shows the opportunity cost of producing the good on the *x*-axis. As we move from point K to point B, we gain 2 economics points but lose 2 finance points per day. As we move from point C to point L, we gain 2 finance points but lose 2 economics points per day. Each economics point gained costs 1 finance point per day. Each finance point gained costs 1 economics point per day.

the change in the amount of points you earn in finance (the good measured on the y-axis) is minus 2 points and the change in the amount of points you earn in economics (the good measured on the x-axis) is plus 2 points. The slope of the PPF between point K and point B is

$$-2/+2 = -1$$

In order to gain 2 points in economics you must give up 2 points in finance.

Suppose instead that you are initially at point C, earning 10 points per day in economics and 0 points in finance. If you move to point L, you gain 2 points in finance but give up 2 points in economics. The slope of the PPF between point C and point L is

$$+2/-2 = -1$$

Because the PPF in Figure 2.4 is a straight line, its slope is the same between any points on the PPF. This implies that each point gained in finance costs a constant amount of points in economics given up, and vice versa, regardless of whether you are moving from 2 points per day in economics to 4 points per day in economics or moving from 8 points per day in economics to 10 points per day in economics.

THINK FOR YOURSELF

How many points in finance could you attain if you also earned 6 points in economics per day? What if instead you earned 1 point in economics per day? What is the opportunity cost of each point you earn in economics? What is the opportunity cost of each point you earn in finance?

Increasing Costs and Specialized Resources

In Figures 2.1 through 2.4, we used a production possibilities model with a constant slope. Each additional point that you earned in finance meant 1 less point that you could earn in economics. This tradeoff was the same regardless of whether you spent 15 minutes, 30 minutes, or 3 hours studying economics. The opportunity cost of an additional point in finance was *constant*.

In most situations, costs are not constant. Instead, they tend to increase as you engage in more of an activity. This idea was introduced in Chapter 1, when discussing the law of increasing marginal costs. The production possibilities model can help us understand why increasing costs are so prevalent.

Figure 2.5 shows a model of the production possibilities frontier for two typical goods produced in an economy: housing and food. Suppose that this economy is initially at point A, where all the resources are used to produce housing and none are used to produce food. Given the resources available, if the citizens in the economy want to obtain food, they must reduce their housing production. The movement from point A to point B is one possibility that represents more food and less housing production per year. As the economy moves from point A to point B, citizens gain 1 unit of food. At the same time, there is a change in housing production from 20 units per year to 18 units per year. The cost of the first unit of food gained is the 2 units of housing foregone. Table 2.2 also shows the cost of increasing food

Figure 2.5 **Production Possibilities for Housing and Food**

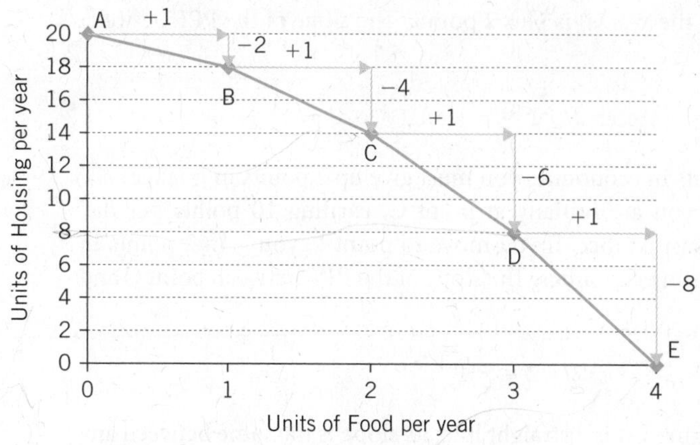

The opportunity cost of producing food increases as more food is produced. This is reflected by the increasing slope of the PPF as we move along the *x*-axis. The bowed-out shape of the PPF also reflects increasing opportunity cost of production.

Table 2.2 Opportunity Cost of Food

Move (in Figure 2.4)	Gain (food units per year)	Cost (housing units per year)
A→B	1	2
B→C	1	4
C→D	1	6
D→E	1	8

production in the economy. The first row of the table shows that when the economy moves from point A to point B, its citizens gain 1 unit of food per year at a cost of 2 units of housing per year.

Suppose that citizens want still more food, so they choose to move from producing 1 unit of food at point B to producing 2 units of food at point C. Although they again gain 1 unit of food, they must now give up 4 units of housing to get it. Thus, the opportunity cost of the second unit of food gained is 4 units of housing. The second row of Table 2.2 also illustrates this tradeoff. One unit of food is gained as the economy moves from point B to point C, and 4 units of housing are given up. If the economy moves from point C to point D, citizens gain 1 more unit of food, but its cost is 6 units of housing. Finally, if the economy moves from point D to point E, citizens gain a fourth unit of food, at a cost of 8 units of housing.

Notice how the opportunity cost of food increased each time the economy gained an additional unit of food. As citizens obtained more and more food, the amount of housing they had to give up increased. Why do opportunity costs increase? Think about the resources that are used to produce housing and food. Land that is used to grow food may vary in its fertility and slope. When the economy first moves resources into food production, it uses the most fertile and flattest land first. Because that land is well suited to food production, we won't need much land to obtain 1 unit of food. Because we don't need much land, we don't have to give up much housing. However, as food production is expanded to less productive land, it will take more and more acres to get 1 unit of food output. This implies that we have to give up more housing than we did for the first unit of food we produced. It is often the case that resources are better suited for producing some goods than they are for producing other goods, which implies that moving production from one good or service to another increases opportunity costs.

In any PPF, the slope tells us the opportunity cost of producing another unit of the good measured on the *x*-axis. Unlike Figures 2.1 through 2.4, where the linear PPFs had constant slopes and constant opportunity costs, the slope of the curve in Figure 2.5 is not constant. The slope of the PPF changes and becomes steeper as we move from A to B to C and so on. Between points A and B, the slope is -2, which illustrates that when we gain the first unit of food, we give up 2 units of housing. Between points D and E, the slope is -8, which illustrates that when we gain the fourth unit of food, we give up 8 units of housing. The increasing steepness of the slope corresponds to the increasing opportunity cost of production. The bowed-out shape of the PPF is also an indication of increasing costs of production.

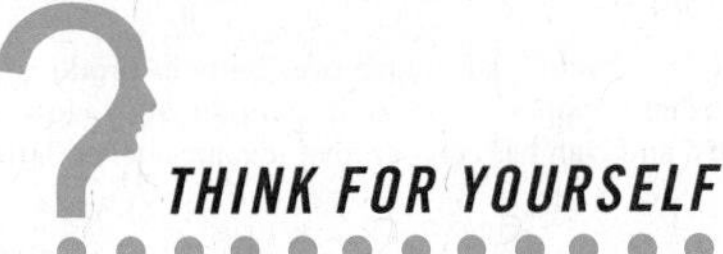

THINK FOR YOURSELF

Table 2.2 and Figure 2.5 show that the opportunity cost of food production increases as we produce more of it. Suppose that we start at point E and move to point D (and then points C, B, and A). How much housing do we gain, and how much food must we give up as we move in that direction along the PPF? Does the opportunity cost of each unit of housing produced increase as more housing is produced?

THE PPF, OPPORTUNITY COSTS, AND THE THEORY OF COMPARATIVE ADVANTAGE

When a person or business is better at producing a good or service than you are, you can benefit from buying that good rather than producing it yourself. Most people don't keep their own dairy cows or bake their own bagels. Instead, you typically buy food items such as bread, bagels, milk, cheese, yogurt, and ice cream from producers who have the skills and technology to produce these products more cheaply than you can. By buying goods and services from people who can produce them more cheaply than you, you gain time to specialize in producing the things you can produce more effectively than others. By trading goods or services that you produce at lower cost for goods and services that others have lower costs of producing, you can make yourself better off than if you tried to produce everything yourself. To demonstrate how this kind of specialization can make people better off, let's use the simple example shown in Figure 2.6.

The graphs in Figure 2.6 show hypothetical daily production possibilities frontiers for Dan and Betty for their production of bagels and yogurt. For simplicity, we've assumed constant opportunity costs of production for both individuals.

If Dan devotes all his resources to bagel production, the maximum number of bagels that he could produce in a given day is 300. If all his resources are instead devoted to yogurt production, he could produce 60 pints per day. Similarly, if Betty devotes all her resources to bagel production, she can make 120 bagels per day. If she devotes all her resources to yogurt production, she could produce 40 pints per day.

Absolute advantage is the ability to produce something with fewer resources or to produce more with the same resources as another producer.

Notice that Dan is able to produce higher levels of output of both bagels and yogurt. Dan has an **absolute advantage** in producing bagels and yogurt relative to

Figure 2.6 **Production Possibilities for Dan and Betty**

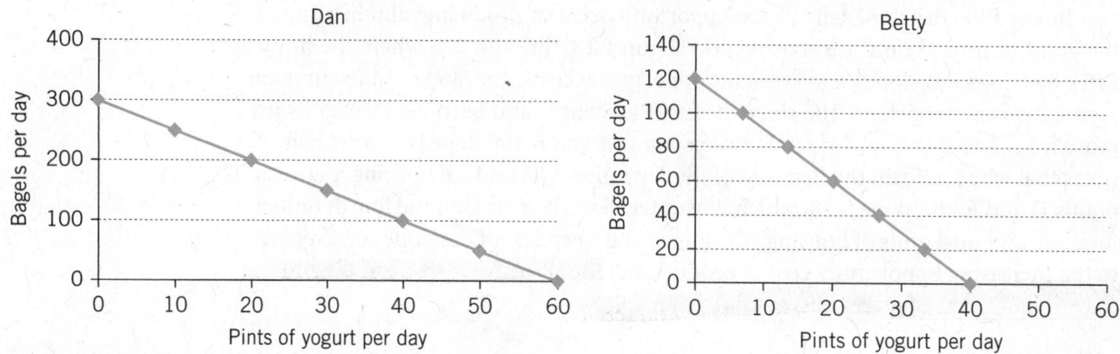

Dan's PPF shows that he can produce more yogurt and more bagels than Betty, which means that he has absolute advantage over Betty in producing bagels and yogurt. The slope of Dan's PPF (-5) is larger than the slope of Betty's PPF (-3). This means that the opportunity cost of producing yogurt is higher for Dan than it is for Betty. Thus, Betty has comparative advantage over Dan in producing yogurt, and Dan has comparative advantage over Betty in producing bagels.

Betty because he can produce more of them. Absolute advantage is the ability to produce more output than another producer of the product.

Comparative advantage is the ability to produce a good or service at a lower opportunity cost than another producer.

Even though Dan has absolute advantage in producing bagels and yogurt compared to Betty, they can both gain from trading with each other. The benefits from trading arise because the two individuals have different opportunity costs of production for bagels and yogurt. This means that they have **comparative advantage** relative to one another in the production of these two goods. Having comparative advantage in the production of a good or service means being able to produce the good or service at a lower opportunity cost than another producer.

If Dan and Betty specialize in producing the goods for which they have a comparative advantage, the total output produced by the two of them can be increased. In addition, both of them have potential to benefit from this specialization if they trade their output with one another. To determine the comparative advantage of each person, we need to know his or her opportunity costs of production. Dan's PPF shows all the combinations of bagels and yogurt that he could produce with his given set of resources, ceteris paribus. If Dan produces only yogurt (Y), he can produce 60 pints per day. If Dan produces only bagels (B), he can produce 300 bagels per day. Because these two combinations use all of Dan's available resources for producing bagels and yogurt, we can express these outcomes mathematically as

$$60\text{Y} = \text{all Dan's available resources} = 300\text{B}$$

so

$$60\text{Y} = 300\text{B}$$

Because 300 bagels or 60 pints of yogurt each reflect the production that can be obtained by using the same amount of Dan's resources, they are equivalent. Producing 300 pints of yogurt per day uses the same amount of resources for Dan as producing 60 bagels per day. We can use this equivalency to show that the slope of Dan's PPF is -300/60 or -5. The slope of the PPF tells us the opportunity cost of the good on the *x*-axis of the PPF, so the opportunity cost of producing 1 pint of yogurt per day for Dan is 5 bagels per day. With the resources used to produce each pint of yogurt per day, Dan could have instead produced 5 bagels per day. We can show Dan's opportunity cost of yogurt as

$$1Y = 5B$$

If we divide both sides of the equation by 5 we can also see that the cost of producing 1 bagel for Dan is 1/5 pint of yogurt.

$$1B = 1/5Y = 0.2Y$$

For Betty, the opportunity cost of 1 pint of yogurt per day is 120/40 = 3 bagels. For each pint of yogurt Betty produces per day, she gives up the production of 3 bagels. Alternatively, for each bagel she produces per day, she gives up 0.33 pints of yogurt. For Betty,

$$1Y = 3B$$

and

$$1B = 1/3Y = 0.33Y$$

The opportunity cost of producing yogurt is lower for Betty than it is for Dan, since the cost of producing 1 pint of yogurt for Dan is 5 bagels, and the cost of producing 1 pint of yogurt for Betty is 3 bagels. Because Betty can produce yogurt at a lower opportunity cost than Dan, she has comparative advantage relative to him in producing yogurt. Because Dan's cost of producing 1 bagel (0.2Y) is lower than Betty's (0.33Y), Dan has comparative advantage relative to Betty in producing bagels.

When people, firms, and even countries trade according to their comparative advantage, both trading parties are better off. If Dan and Betty do not trade with one another, their consumption is limited to what they can produce. Their production possibilities frontiers also represent their consumption possibilities frontiers.

Now suppose that Dan and Betty decide to specialize in the production of the good for which they each have comparative advantage, and then trade with one another. Dan will specialize in producing bagels, and Betty will specialize in producing yogurt. Their PPFs indicate that Dan will produce 300 bagels and no yogurt. Betty will produce 40 pints of yogurt and no bagels.

How do the two decide how much of each good to trade? It will depend on their bargaining power and preferences for yogurt and bagels. The trade arrangement they reach will generate a "price" or rate of exchange of the number of pints of yogurt to be traded for each bagel or the number of bagels to be traded for each pint of yogurt. There are an infinite number of possible prices that will generate mutual gains for Dan and Betty. What these possible prices all have in common is that they lie between the two individuals' opportunity costs of producing the good.

In our example, Betty will produce yogurt and exchange it for bagels. In order to be better off by trading her yogurt for bagels, she will need to obtain more bagels for her yogurt than she could if she just produced the bagels herself. Because her opportunity cost of producing 1 pint of yogurt is 3 bagels, she will need to obtain more than 3 bagels for each pint of yogurt she trades to Dan. For Dan to be better off buying yogurt from Betty than he would be producing yogurt himself, he needs to obtain each pint of yogurt for less than 5 bagels, which is his opportunity cost of producing yogurt. Betty and Dan's opportunity costs imply that the price of 1 pint of yogurt needs to be greater than 3 bagels but less than

5 bagels in order to make them both better off by trading Betty's yogurt for Dan's bagels. Mathematically,

$$3B < 1Y < 5B$$[1]

The price of 1Y for 4B fits the criteria. If, for example, Dan trades 100 bagels to Betty at this price, he will receive 25 pints of yogurt in return.

$$1Y = 4B$$

so

$$25Y = 100B$$

Figure 2.7 illustrates how this trade impacts Dan and Betty. When Dan specializes in producing bagels, he can produce 300 bagels per day. If Dan trades away 100 of his bagels, he will be left with 200 bagels he can consume. He will also be able to consume the 25 pints of yogurt he obtained from Betty. This level of consumption of yogurt and bagels is illustrated by point A in Figure 2.7, which lies outside Dan's production possibilities frontier. Indeed, any trades at this price will generate consumption for Dan that lies beyond his PPF. Figure 2.7 illustrates the new consumption possibilities frontier for Dan if he and Betty trade at the price of 1Y = 4B. When Betty trades 25 units of yogurt to Dan for 100 bagels, she will also move to a point outside her PPF. At point A on Betty's consumption possibilities frontier, she can consume 100 bagels and 15 units of yogurt.

THINK FOR YOURSELF

Draw consumption possibilities frontiers for Dan and Betty if they exchange at a rate of 1Y = 4.5B.

Figure 2.7 **Production and Consumption Possibilities Frontiers**

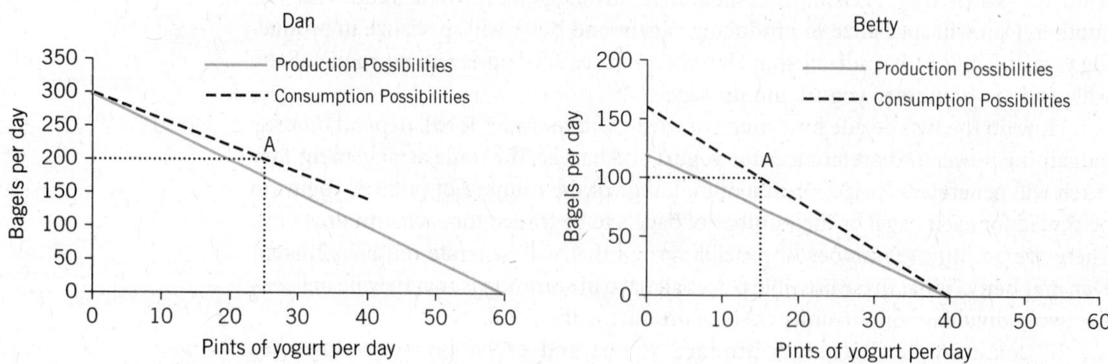

If Dan and Betty specialize according to their comparative advantage, Dan will produce only bagels and Betty will produce only yogurt. If they trade at a price of 1 pint of yogurt for 4 bagels, they will be able to consume at levels outside their production possibilities frontiers. Point A represents one possible point of consumption for Dan and Betty.

---

1 We could also illustrate the trade in terms of the price per bagel instead of the price per pint of yogurt. Since Betty's opportunity cost of bagels is 0.33Y, she will need to be able to obtain bagels at a price lower than 0.33Y in order to be better off. Since Dan is producing bagels at an opportunity cost of 0.2Y, he will need to sell bagels at price higher than 0.2Y in order to be better off. Betty and Dan's opportunity costs imply that the price of bagels needs to be between 0.2Y and 0.33Y in order to make them both better off by trading Betty's yogurt for Dan's bagels. This implies that $0.2Y < 1B < 0.33Y$.

Notice that Dan gains from trade with Betty even though he has an absolute advantage in producing both goods. Although this example is simple, it shows that trading according to comparative advantage can make both parties better off. The same conclusion applies to more complex situations, such as countries trading with one another.

Comparative advantage helps explain the choices made in economies. As a consumer, you buy milk from a dairy firm because it has comparative advantage in producing milk. Similarly, you buy bagels from the bakery because it has a comparative advantage in producing bagels. You might sell your services as a physician, author, or engineer because you have comparative advantage relative to others in producing medical, writing, or engineering services.

Hulton Archive/Getty Images, Inc.

David Ricardo and the Theory of Comparative Advantage

The theory of comparative advantage is usually ascribed to David Ricardo (1772–1823). In his book *Principles of Political Economy* (1817), Ricardo presented his theory of comparative advantage to advocate against policies in place at that time in Britain that limited international trade. His theory forms the foundation of the economics of international trade.

WHERE TO PRODUCE ON THE PPF

What is the best combination of outputs on a PPF? There is no right answer to that question because it depends on the values of the trading partners or the economies engaged in international trade. It also depends on how trading partners or economies decide to allocate their resources.

In deciding the "best" combination of outputs on a PPF, like that in Figure 2.5, some might say that food is better or more important than housing, so we should produce more food. Others might say that more housing should be produced. Still others might opt for somewhere in the middle. Deciding which combination is best involves a value judgment. Value judgments and decisions regarding *how things should be* fall under the realm of **normative economics**. Objective descriptions regarding *how things are* fall under the realm of **positive economics**. Economists tend to agree on positive economic issues. For example, virtually all economists would agree with the positive statement that both point B and point C on the PPF in Figure 2.4 represent efficient uses of resources. They would disagree with the normative statement that producing at point B is better than at point C.

Normative economics deals with value judgments and decisions regarding how things should be.

Positive economics is more objective and provides descriptions of how things are.

When individuals or entire economies decide where to produce on the PPF, they are choosing how to allocate scarce resources. In essence, they are answering three **basic economic questions**: What to produce? How to produce it? For whom to produce? The answers to these basic economic questions determine the allocation of goods and services in the society.

The three basic economic questions regarding resource allocation are: What to produce? How to produce it? For whom to produce?

How a society answers the basic economic questions depends on their economic system. In the United States, we rely primarily on markets to determine where to produce on our PPF. In Chapter 3, we'll learn the details of how markets serve to allocate society's resources and thus generate outcomes along the PPF.

SUMMARY

Economists use models to describe important features of economic relationships and to make predictions about economic outcomes. The production possibilities model shows the combinations of goods or services that can be produced with a given set of scarce resources and illustrates the opportunity cost involved when we choose one combination of outputs instead of another. Points inside a PPF are considered inefficient choices because they represent combinations of output that are below an economy's potential. Points outside a PPF represent combinations of output that are unattainable, given a society's resources and technology. The slope of a PPF is equal to the opportunity cost of producing one more unit of the good measured on the x-axis. Linear PPFs demonstrate constant opportunity costs, whereas PPFs that are bowed-out demonstrate increasing opportunity costs. The PPF model also illustrates how specialization and trade according to comparative advantage can generate increased consumption possibilities for both trading partners. Decisions about where to produce on a society's PPF involve answering the basic economic questions of what, how, and for whom to produce.

KEY CONCEPTS

- Production possibilities model
- Production possibilities frontier
- Attainable choices
- Unattainable choices
- Efficient choices
- Inefficient choices
- Slope of the PPF
- Absolute advantage
- Comparative advantage
- Normative economics
- Positive economics
- Basic economic questions

DISCUSSION QUESTIONS AND PROBLEMS

1. Use a graph to demonstrate how a country's PPF will shift if additional resources become available to the country.
2. Use a graph to demonstrate how an improvement in technology used for the production of one good but not the other will affect the PPF.
3. Compare positive and normative economics. Find examples from the newspaper or an Internet news site of positive and normative statements by political and community leaders.
4. Draw two production possibilities frontier graphs. In one, illustrate the situation of unemployed resources in an economy. In the other, illustrate the impact of a reduction in available resources. Your two graphs should be different. Why?

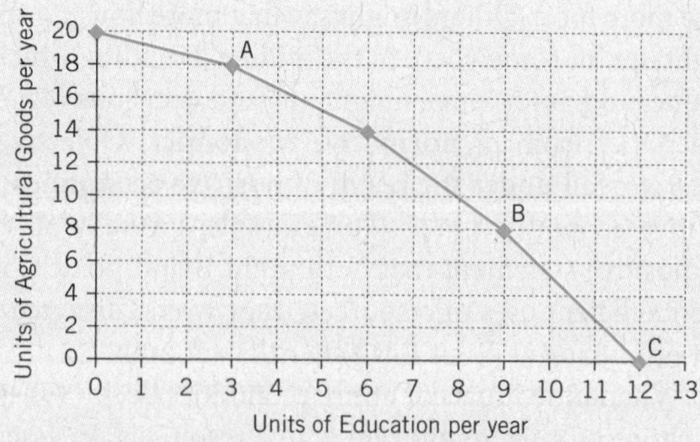

5. The accompanying PPF shows possible alternative combinations of agricultural goods and education that can be produced in a given economy in a given year.
   a. If the economy is operating efficiently and producing 14 units of agricultural production, how much education can it also produce?

b. If the economy is operating at point A, what is the cost of 3 additional units of education per year? What is the cost if the economy is operating at point B?
c. If the economy is operating at point A, what is the approximate cost of 1 additional unit of education per year? What is the approximate cost if the economy is operating at point B? Does this PPF illustrate increasing costs of production of education?
d. If the economy is operating at point C, what is the approximate cost of 1 additional unit of agricultural production per year? What is the approximate cost if the economy is operating at point B? What is the approximate cost if the economy is operating at point A? Does this PPF illustrate increasing costs of production of agricultural goods?

6. Suppose Ted the track team trainer can produce two outputs, fast runners (R) and strong shot putters (S). If Ted works 40 hours per week, Ted's production possibilities frontier (PPF) per season for these two outputs is given by the equation:

$$S = -(1/3)R + 5$$

or

$$R = -3S + 15$$

Number of Trained Runners Per Season	Number of Trained Shot Putters Per Season
15	
12	
9	
6	
3	
0	

a. Complete the accompanying table by using the PPF equation to determine the number of shot putters trained per season.
b. Graph Ted's PPF for runners and shot putters.
c. Suppose Ted is currently producing 0 shot putters. What is Ted's opportunity cost of increasing his production of shot putters from 0 to 2?
d. Suppose Ted is currently producing 2 shot putters. What is Ted's opportunity cost of increasing production of shot putters from 2 to 4?
e. Does Ted's PPF exhibit increasing, decreasing, or constant opportunity costs? Explain. Does this seem realistic? Explain.
f. What is Ted's opportunity cost for each shot putter produced? What is Ted's opportunity cost for each runner produced?
g. What would you say about Ted's production if 3 shot putters and 2 runners were produced in a given season? Would he be operating on his PPF?
h. Suppose that Ted's computer crashes. His computer contains the only copy of his program for optimal nutrition and training requirements for athletes, making it harder to train the runners and shot putters as well as before. Sketch a new PPF for Ted that illustrates what this will do to his production possibilities. Briefly explain what has happened to Ted's PPF and why.
i. Starting from Ted's original PPF, suppose that the athletic department hires an assistant for Ted, allowing him to further refine his training techniques. Sketch a new PPF for Ted that illustrates what this will do to his production possibilities. Explain what has happened to Ted's PPF and why.

7. In one year, two producers, Bjorn and Xian, can produce boats and cars according to the production possibilities given in the following table:

Individual	Production Possibilities Per Year
Bjorn	15 boats or 10 cars
Xian	20 boats or 40 cars

a. Graph the production possibilities curves for the two producers, assuming constant opportunity costs.
b. Which good does Bjorn have comparative advantage in producing? Why?
c. Which good does Xian have comparative advantage in producing? Why?
d. If the two individuals specialize in production who should specialize in producing boats and who should specialize in producing cars? Why?
e. Suggest a trade that would make both individuals better off than if they produced and consumed independently of one another. In your graphs, show that their new point of consumption possibilities based on your trade terms moves each individual beyond their PPF.

MULTIPLE CHOICE QUESTIONS

1. Which of the following is true of production possibility frontiers (PPFs)?
   a. The slope of the PPF reflects the opportunity costs of producing different combinations of two goods.
   b. Combinations of goods can be produced inside or outside the PPF, ceteris paribus.
   c. Points inside the PPF boundary are attainable and efficient.
   d. Only points along the frontier line are attainable and efficient.
   e. Both A and C
   f. Both A and D

2. The first hour you study on Thursday night for your Friday morning Economics 101 final exam will improve your grade on the final exam from a score of 50 percent to a score of 70 percent. The next hour you study improves your exam grade to a score of 85 percent. The third hour of studying moves your grade up to a score of 90 percent. This is an example of what?
   a. The marginal costs of studying
   b. The marginal benefits of studying
   c. The opportunity costs of studying
   d. The sunk costs of studying

3. John can produce 6 tents or 12 sleeping bags per month. Jane can produce 4 tents or 12 sleeping bags per month. If John and Jane specialize and trade according to comparative advantage, which of the potential trades below would make them both better off?
   a. John will trade away sleeping bags for tents.
   b. Jane will trade away tents for sleeping bags.
   c. Jane will trade away sleeping bags for tents.
   d. John will trade away tents for sleeping bags.
   e. Both A and B
   f. Both C and D
   g. None of the above because John can produce more tents and the same amount of sleeping bags as Jane.

4. The first hour you study on Thursday night for your Friday morning Economics 101 final exam will improve your grade on the final exam from a score of 50 percent to a score of 70 percent. The next hour you study improves your exam grade to a score of 85 percent. The third hour of studying moves your grade up to a score of 90 percent. This illustrates which of the following?
   a. Constant marginal costs
   b. Decreasing marginal costs
   c. Increasing marginal benefits
   d. Decreasing marginal benefits
   e. Constant marginal benefits

5. John can produce 6 tents or 12 sleeping bags per month. Jane can produce 4 tents or 12 sleeping bags per month. Under which of the following scenarios would both parties be willing to trade?
   a. Jane trades away 2 tents for 5 sleeping bags.
   b. John trades away 1 tent for 1 sleeping bag.
   c. John trades away 2 tents for 3 sleeping bags.
   d. John trades away 1 tent for 2 sleeping bags.
   e. John trades away 2 tents for 5 sleeping bags.

Country	Production per Month
Colombia	900 million units of natural gas or 300 million units of soybeans
Bolivia	400 million units of natural gas or 200 million units of soybeans

6. The accompanying table shows the production possibilities for two countries, Columbia and Bolivia, which produce natural gas and soybeans. Based on this information and assuming constant opportunity costs for simplicity, the opportunity cost of producing 1 unit of soybeans in Bolivia is
   a. 2 units of natural gas.
   b. 1 unit of natural gas.
   c. 1/2 unit of natural gas.
   d. 2 units of soybeans.

7. The table shows the production possibilities for two countries, Colombia and Bolivia, which produce natural gas and soybeans. Ceteris paribus, based on this information and assuming constant opportunity costs for simplicity, ______ has a comparative advantage in producing natural gas and ______ has a comparative advantage in producing soybeans.
   a. Colombia; Bolivia
   b. Bolivia; Bolivia
   c. Colombia; Colombia
   d. Bolivia; Colombia

8. The table shows the production possibilities for two countries, Colombia and Bolivia, which produce natural gas and soybeans. Ceteris paribus, based on this information and assuming constant opportunity costs for simplicity, which of the following trades would be possible and would make both countries better off?
   a. Colombia trades away 100 units of soybeans for 250 units of natural gas from Bolivia.

b. Bolivia trades away 300 units of soybeans for 200 units of natural gas from Colombia.
c. Bolivia trades away 100 units of soybeans for 250 units of natural gas from Colombia.
d. Bolivia trades away 100 units of soybeans for 100 units of natural gas from Colombia.

9. In one day, John Smith, a professional assassin, can blow up two buildings or kill five bad guys. His partner Jane can blow up four buildings or kill six bad guys in one day. John and Jane can gain from specialization and trade if Jane ______ and John ______.
   a. kills bad guys; blows up buildings
   b. kills bad guys; kills bad guys
   c. blows up buildings; kills bad guys
   d. blows up buildings; blows up buildings
   e. None of the above, Jane should do everything since she is better at being an assassin than John is.

10. Last year Martha could grow 20 bushels of basil or 25 bushels of cilantro on each acre of land that she farmed. This spring, she discovered a free organic fertilizer that allows her to double the amount of cilantro that she can grow on each acre, ceteris paribus. How has Martha's opportunity cost changed with this discovery?
    a. The opportunity cost of cilantro stays the same because the discovery will allow Martha to produce more of both goods.
    b. The opportunity cost of cilantro stays the same because the discovery does not change the amount of basil that Martha can produce.
    c. The opportunity cost of cilantro has increased.
    d. The opportunity cost of cilantro has decreased.

© Sean Locke/iStockphoto

3 Demand and Supply

After studying this chapter, you should be able to:

- Describe the relationship between price and quantity demanded
- Describe the relationship between price and quantity supplied
- Diagram demand and supply relationships and identify market equilibrium
- Describe factors that shift demand and supply
- Illustrate how changes in demand or supply affect market equilibrium

The three basic economic questions that a society must answer regarding how to allocate its scare resources are: What to produce? How to produce it? For whom to produce? In many countries, including the United States, markets are a primary means of answering these questions. A market exists anywhere there are buyers willing to buy a good and sellers willing to sell it. Markets are pervasive institutions of trade. A market can be a physical location, like a grocery store, gas station, or bakery. Markets also exist in cyberspace at sites like eBay, Amazon, Monster.com, or iTunes. Markets can be very formal, involving legal contracts specifying the terms and conditions of a trade, or they can be informal, where deals are sealed with no more than a handshake. Markets are used to trade everything from cars and books to labor services and music. Despite their many forms, all markets have a similar basic structure. Economists use a model called demand and supply, which is introduced in this chapter, to explain the interactions of buyers and sellers in markets and to make predictions about the prices of quantities of goods bought and sold.

DEMAND

If you've ever bought anything, you've experienced the "demand" in the demand and supply model. In the demand and supply model, **demand** represents the buyers' side of the market and describes the relationship between the price of a good and the quantity of the good that buyers are willing and able to buy at that price.

Demand: *The relationship between the price of a good and the quantity of the good that buyers are willing and able to buy at that price, ceteris paribus.*

The quantity of a good that buyers are willing and able to buy at a given price is called the **quantity demanded** of the good. The quantity demanded of a good changes as the price of the good changes, ceteris paribus. We can observe the demand for a good by tracking changes in the price of a good and the resulting changes in quantity demanded.

Quantity demanded: *The amount of a good that buyers are willing and able to buy at a given price, ceteris paribus.*

Demand Table

We can illustrate the concepts of demand and quantity demanded using a table or a graph. Let's start with a table. The data in Table 3.1 show the hypothetical demand for loaves of bread per day at a local bakery. The column labeled P shows the price of each loaf of bread. The column labeled Q^D shows the quantity of bread demanded at each price. It tells how many loaves consumers will be willing and able to buy per day at each possible price and holding all other things constant.

Table 3.1 Demand for Bread

P ($/loaf)	Q^D (loaves/day)
0	10
1	9
2	8
3	7
4	6
5	5
6	4
7	3
8	2
9	1
10	0

When the price of bread is $3 per loaf, for example, the bakery's customers are willing and able to buy 7 loaves per day. In shorthand, when P = $3 per loaf, Q^D = 7 loaves per day. When the price is $1 per loaf, the quantity demanded is 9 loaves per day, and when the price is $5 per loaf, the quantity demanded is 5 loaves per day. When the price hits $10 per loaf, no one buys bread from the bakery. If the bakery's bread were free, people would "buy" 10 loaves per day.

Demand Graph

Figure 3.1 shows a demand relationship visually in a graph. By convention, price is measured on the *y*-axis and quantity is measured on the *x*-axis of the graph. The line connecting the points Q^D = 5, P = $5; Q^D = 7, P = $3, and so on, is called a

Figure 3.1 **The Demand for Bread**

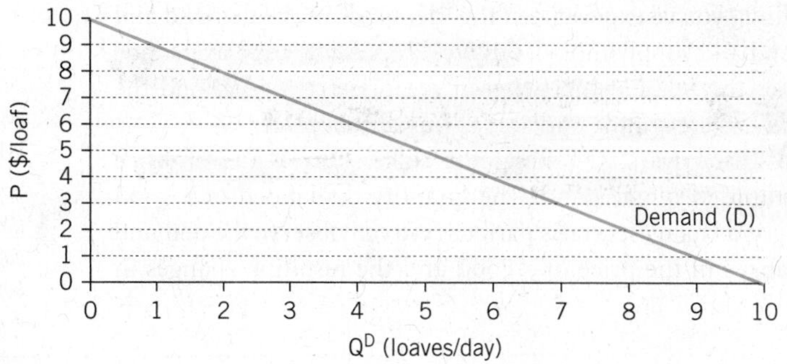

The demand curve D shows the price of bread on the *y*-axis and the corresponding quantity of bread demanded at each price on the *x*-axis.

demand curve and is labeled D. Demand relationships can be linear, as in Figure 3.1, or curved. Regardless of the shape, the graphs are called demand curves.

Demand versus Quantity Demanded

There is an important difference between demand and quantity demanded. *Quantity demanded* is the amount of a good or service that consumers are willing and able to buy at a given price and holding all other things equal. Each quantity demanded is one point in the demand table or one point on the demand curve. *Demand* shows us all the prices and all the quantities demanded in entire table or graph.

The Law of Demand

The relationship between the price and quantity demanded is an inverse or negative relationship. For the demand curve, the inverse relationship means that as the price of bread rises, ceteris paribus, the quantity of bread demanded falls. Similarly, as the price of bread falls, the quantity of bread demanded rises. The inverse relationship between the price of a good and its quantity demanded is so common that it is called the **law of demand**. It is difficult to find examples of goods or services for which the law of demand does not hold. The *income effect*, the *substitution effect*, and the *law of diminishing marginal utility*, all described next, contribute to the inverse relationship between price and quantity demanded.

The law of demand: There is an inverse relationship between price and quantity demanded.

The Income Effect

Suppose you are headed to the bakery to buy bread. You want to buy seven loaves of bread at $3 per loaf, so you carry $21 in your wallet. When you get to the bakery, you see that the price has risen to $5 per loaf. You can no longer afford to buy the seven loaves you wanted. This is the **income effect** of the increase in price. When the price of a good rises, ceteris paribus, a given level of income is no longer enough to purchase the same quantity of the good as before. In other words, the purchasing power of your income declines when the price of a good rises. The income effect also works in reverse—if the price of bread were $1 instead of $3 per loaf, your $21 would be able to buy more bread than before. The income effect causes increases in quantity demanded when the price of a good falls and causes decreases in Q^D when P rises.

The income effect implies that changes in the price of a good affect the amount of it that you can afford, which results in a change in quantity demanded, ceteris paribus. can be an increase or decrease

The Consumer Substitution Effect

The law of demand also arises from the substitution effect, which describes how you respond to changes in *relative prices*. A relative price is a good's price in comparison to the prices of other goods you could buy. Because the increase in the price of bread makes bagels seem relatively cheaper, you may respond to the higher price of bread by increasing the amount of bagels you buy, ceteris paribus. This is the **consumer substitution effect** of the increase in price. The substitution effect tells us that you will respond to a higher price of a good, ceteris paribus, by decreasing your quantity demanded of that good and substituting instead into goods whose prices have not changed. For example, a price change for one good changes its price relative to other goods. As the price of pears rises, we decrease our quantity demanded for pears and instead substitute into buying apples since they are now relatively cheaper in comparison to pears.

The consumer substitution effect implies that consumers will respond to a higher price of a good, ceteris paribus, by decreasing their quantity demanded of that good and substituting instead into goods whose prices have not changed.

The Law of Diminishing Marginal Utility

The law of diminishing marginal utility also contributes to the law of demand. According to the **law of diminishing marginal utility**, people obtain less satisfaction from each successive unit of a good consumed; consequently there is a decrease in their willingness to pay for additional units of the good.

The law of diminishing marginal utility implies that the extra utility you get from consuming a good gets smaller as more of the good is consumed. As a result, your willingness to pay for another unit of a good decreases as more of the good is consumed.

As an example of the law of diminishing marginal utility, imagine that you walk into the bakery to buy a bagel for your lunch. Because you are hungry and you expect that a bagel will satisfy your hunger, you are willing to pay a lot for the bagel. After you finish that first bagel, you have the choice of purchasing a second bagel. How will your willingness to pay for the second bagel compare to what you were willing to pay for the first bagel? Chances are you won't expect as much satisfaction from the second bagel as you did from the first, primarily because some of your hunger has been satisfied. In other words, you expect that your marginal utility will be smaller for the second bagel than it was for the first bagel. As a result, you would not be willing to pay as much for the second bagel as you did for the first bagel. Similarly, as you consume a third and fourth bagel, your willingness to pay for additional bagels will fall incrementally. The price you are willing to pay for a bagel falls with the more bagels you consume.

The law of diminishing marginal utility explains why "all you can eat" businesses can remain profitable. When hungry Harry goes to the buffet, he pays an up-front price, say $15.00, for access to the buffet. After that up-front cost, the price of obtaining more of any dish is zero. Why doesn't Harry continue to eat more and more if the price is zero? Because eventually his marginal utility of eating the food falls to a point where even though the food is free, he gets more satisfaction from other activities than from eating. If the law of diminishing marginal utility did not hold, Harry would be at the buffet forever.

Mark Lennihan/©AP/Wide World Photos

Diminishing Marginal Utility: How often are you using your Wii Fit?

Wii Fit is video game for the Nintendo Wii entertainment system in which players move their entire body in various workout scenarios. The game was released in late 2007 and became a popular alternative to traditional video games. Players can use the "balance board" to measure center of gravity, weight, and various fitness statistics. New users tend to use the system often, but the novelty or newness of the game wears off over time. Economists use the law of diminishing marginal benefits to explain this behavior.

The law of diminishing marginal utility is an alternative way to explain the demand for goods and services, as represented by the demand curve. We can view demand as describing how much of a good consumers are willing and able to buy at a given price. Think of this as a "horizontal" interpretation in the sense that demand shows the quantity demanded, measured on the horizontal axis, for a given price. Another way to think about demand is that it is the maximum amount that consumers are willing and able to pay to obtain each unit of a good. This is a "vertical" interpretation of demand in the sense that it shows the dollar amount, measured on the vertical axis, of consumers' willingness to pay for each unit of the good consumed. Later in the text, we'll interchange the "price and quantity demanded" and "willingness to pay" interpretations when we apply the demand curve to different situations.

Changes in Demand

When we draw a demand curve, we rely heavily on the ceteris paribus assumption. We plot the price and quantities demanded at a point in time and hold constant any other factor that might influence demand. When we relax this assumption, we can allow demand to respond to changes in factors such as a consumer's income or the prices of other goods and services. Before we relax ceteris paribus, we must be careful to distinguish between changes in the quantity demanded of a good and changes in the demand for the good.

A change in quantity demanded results from a change in the price of the good, ceteris paribus. It is represented by a movement along the demand curve.

When the price of a good changes, ceteris paribus, there is a **change in quantity demanded**, but not a change in demand, for the good. To demonstrate this difference, suppose the price of bread changes in our bakery example. When bread costs \$4 per loaf, the quantity demanded is 6 loaves per day. Point A in Figure 3.2 shows this price and quantity. If the price increases to \$7 per loaf, quantity demanded falls to 3 loaves per day. In the graph, this change in price is shown by a movement along the demand curve from point A to point B.

An increase in demand means that quantity demanded increases at each price. As a result, the demand curve shifts outward to the right.

In contrast, a change in demand means that the whole relationship between price and quantity demanded changes. An **increase in demand** means that, at each price, quantity demanded is more than before. The increase in demand is illustrated in column $Q^{D'}$ in Table 3.2. At each of the prices in Table 3.2, quantity demanded is 2 loaves higher per day than before. Originally, when P is \$7 per loaf, Q^D is 3 loaves per day. After the increase in demand, $Q^{D'}$ is 5 loaves per day when P is \$7 per loaf.

The increase in demand is also depicted in Figure 3.3. At each price, the new demand curve, D′, lies to the right of the old demand curve, illustrating an increase in the quantity demanded at each price. Because the quantity demanded increased, the points on the new demand curve D′ are to the right of those on the original demand curve D. Thus, an increase in demand generates an outward shift in the demand curve.

Figure 3.2 **A Change in the Quantity Demanded of Bread**

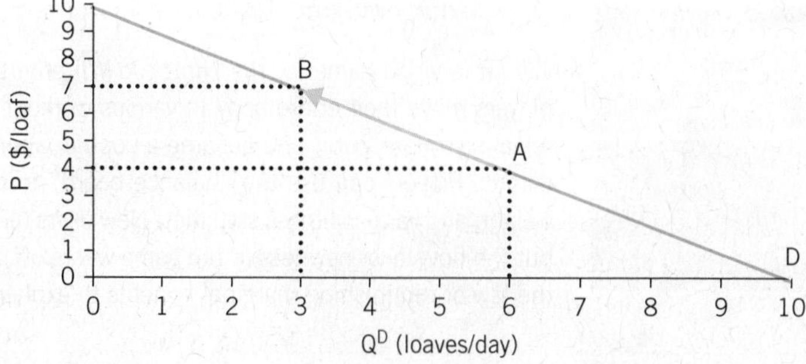

When the price of bread increases, we move along the demand curve for bread. The *quantity demanded* of bread changes, but the *demand* for bread does not change.

Table 3.2 An Increase in the Demand for Bread

P ($/loaf)	Q^D (loaves/day)	$Q^{D'}$ (loaves/day)
0	10	12
1	9	11
2	8	10
3	7	9
4	6	8
5	5	7
6	4	6
7	3	5
8	2	4
9	1	3
10	0	2

Figure 3.3 An Increase in Demand for Bread

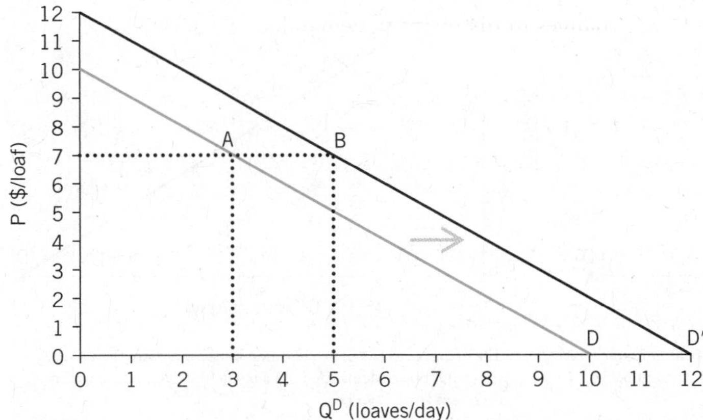

When there is an increase in the demand for bread, the demand curve shifts outward. At each of the prices, the quantity of bread demanded is more than it was before. Point A represents Q^D when P = $7 on the original demand curve (D). Point B represents $Q^{D'}$, the quantity demanded when P = $7 on the new demand curve (D′).

A **decrease in demand** means that at each price, quantity demanded is less than before. If the demand for bread decreases, then at each price in the demand table, the quantity demanded of bread will be less than before. We could illustrate a decrease in demand by moving from $Q^{D'}$ to Q^D in Table 3.2 or by moving from D′ to D in Figure 3.3.

A decrease in demand means that quantity demanded decreases at each price. As a result, the demand curve shifts inward to the left.

Factors That Shift Demand

What factors cause the demand curve to shift? In this section, we will look at changes in consumers' income, the prices of related goods, consumers' expectations, consumers' tastes and preferences, and the number of consumers in the market, to see the impact each factor has on demand.

Income

The effect of a change in income on demand depends on whether the good is a **normal good** or an **inferior good**. For normal goods, increases in income cause demand to increase. Most goods tend to fit into this category. For inferior goods, increases in income cause demand to decrease. Individual preferences determine whether goods are normal or inferior for a particular person. For some consumers, potatoes, canned soup, and ramen noodles are inferior goods, and a decrease in their incomes will increase in their

For normal goods, an increase in income generates an increase in demand.

For inferior goods, an increase in income generates a decrease in demand.

demand for potatoes and ramen noodles. For most consumers, new clothing is a normal good, so that when incomes rise, people tend to increase their demand for new clothing.

Prices of Related Goods

Increases or decreases in the prices of related goods can cause the demand for a good to change. Bagels and peanut butter are goods related to bread. How the prices of these goods affect the demand for bread depends on whether the goods are **complements** or **substitutes**.

Complements are goods that tend to be used together.

Complement goods are goods that tend to be used together. Examples of complement goods include iPods and iTunes downloads, ski equipment and ski passes, and bread and peanut butter. When the price of peanut butter, a complement to bread, falls, the quantity demanded of peanut butter rises and in turn the demand for bread rises. Figure 3.4 illustrates this relationship.

Figure 3.4 **The Relationship between the Price of a Complement Good and Demand**

A Decrease in the Price of Peanut Butter

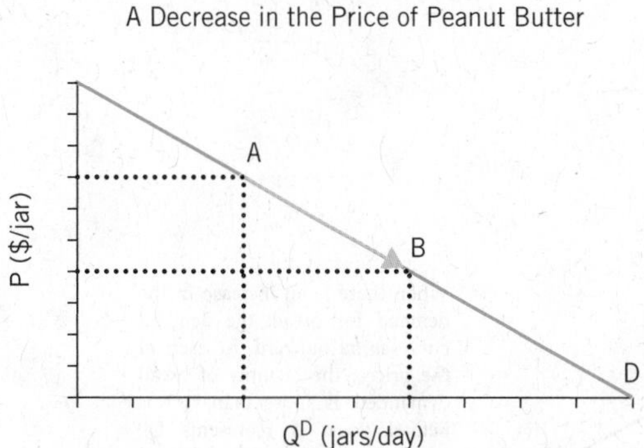

As the price of peanut butter falls, the quantity of peanut butter demanded rises, as in the movement from point A to point B.

An Increase in Demand for Bread

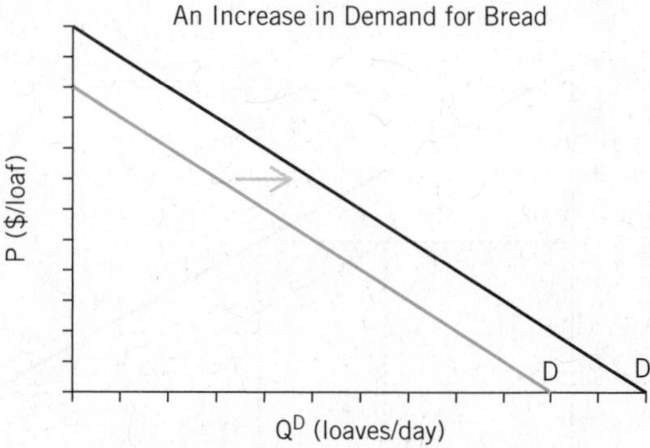

The decrease in the price of peanut butter increases the quantity of peanut butter demanded. As a result, the demand for bread increases from D to D′.

The demand for peanut butter is shown in the graph on the left. If the price of peanut butter falls, the quantity of peanut butter demanded rises, as shown by the movement from point A to point B. Now that people are using more peanut butter than before, they increase their demand for bread since peanut butter and bread are used together. The increase in the demand for bread is illustrated in the graph on the right. The demand for bread rises from D to D′ when the price of peanut butter falls.

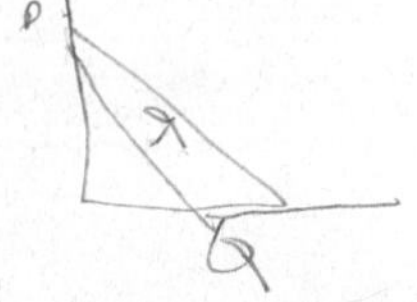

THINK FOR YOURSELF

iPods and iTunes downloads are complements. Draw a graph that shows the change in demand for iTunes downloads resulting from a decrease in the price of iPods.

Substitutes are goods that tend to be used in place of one another.

Substitute goods are goods that tend to be consumed in place of one another. Examples of substitute goods include bread and bagels, butter and margarine, DVD

Figure 3.5 **The Relationship between the Price of a Substitute Good and Demand**

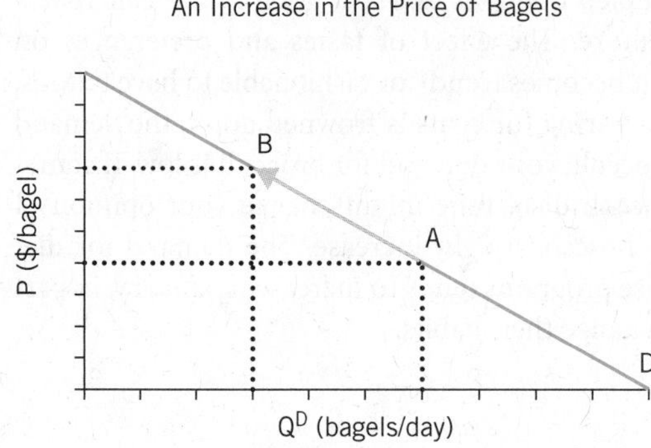

As the price of bagels rises, the quantity of bagels demanded falls, as in the movement from point A to point B.

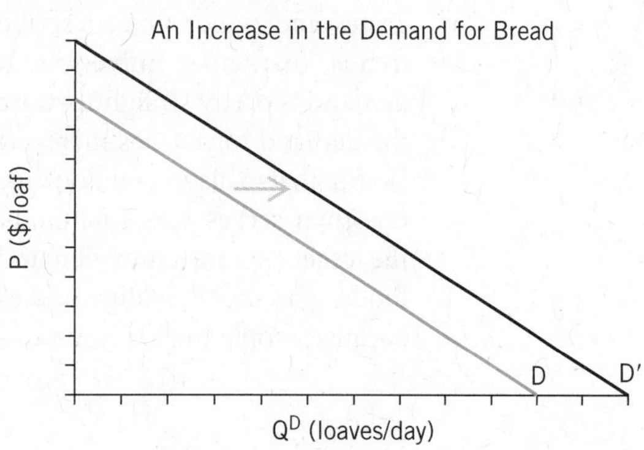

The increase in the price of bagels decreases the quantity of bagels demanded. As a result, the demand for bread increases from D to D′.

purchases and DVD rentals, Wii gaming systems and X-box gaming systems, and Coke and Pepsi. When the price of bagels rises, the quantity demanded of bagels falls and in turn the demand for bread rises. Figure 3.5 illustrates this relationship.

When the price of bagels rises, the quantity of bagels demanded falls, as shown by the movement from point A to point B in the graph on the left. Because people have reduced the quantity of bagels they demand, they instead decide to purchase bread. This increases the demand for bread, as shown by the movement from D to D′ in the graph on the right.

Be careful when thinking about substitutes and complements and their effects on demand for the original good. Changes in the price of bread generate changes in its quantity demanded, not changes in its demand. Changes in the price of peanut butter or bagels generate changes in the demand for bread.

Netflix Busts Blockbuster

At the end of the 1990s, movie rental giant Blockbuster accounted for nearly half of Hollywood studios' rental income from new movies, a very profitable business. By 2002, however, the company was losing approximately $1 billion per year. What accounted for this change in the company's fortunes? A primary factor was the emergence of a competitor providing consumers with a substitute. Founded in 1997, Netflix is an online retailer that offers home delivery or streaming of DVDs in exchange for a set monthly fee. Its emergence introduced a low-price substitute into the DVD rental market. Not surprisingly, the demand for DVD rentals from traditional brick-and-mortar outlets such as Blockbuster has declined dramatically. Indeed, Blockbuster closed 290 stores in 2006 and 282 in 2007. Blockbuster has spent the years since then changing its store-based business model to better compete with online streaming. In the meantime, Netflix continues to grow rapidly, with over 23 million subscribers in 2011.[1]

Jin Lee/Bloomberg/GettyImages, Inc.

1 Sources: "Hollywood New Zombie: The last days of Blockbuster," Edward Jay Epstein. 1/9/2006 http://www.slate.com/id/2133995/ "Blockbuster to shutter 282 U.S. stores this year," Carolyn Pritchard. MarketWatch 6/28/2007 and Netflix financial statements from the investor relations link at www.netflix.com

Tastes and Preferences

Tastes and preferences describe people's opinions about a good. They can reflect trends, marketing influences, or culture. The effect of tastes and preferences on demand is pretty straightforward. If it becomes trendy or fashionable to have tattoos, the demand for tattoos increases. If wearing fur coats is frowned upon, the demand for fur coats falls. If you don't like broccoli, your demand for broccoli is low. If someone then serves you a fabulous broccoli dish, they might change your opinion of the vegetable and your demand for broccoli might increase. The demand for diet foods, gym memberships, and exercise programs tends to increase in January, in part because people make resolutions to change their habits.

Expectations

Expectations describe our notions about what we think will happen in the future. Expectations for the future affect our choices today. For example, imagine that you are living the pauper's life of a college student during the spring semester of college just before your graduation. You get offered and accept a high-paying job that will start in July, a month after graduation. You may go out and buy a new wardrobe or car to get ready for your new job. Your increase in demand for these goods isn't a reflection of a change in your income, since that hasn't happened yet. Instead, the change in demand is due to your *expectation* of increased income.

The effect of expectations can happen in reverse as well. If a firm starts to lay off its workers, employees who aren't laid off are likely to change their spending habits to cut back on nonessential items. Even though their jobs and incomes are secure at the moment, they are worried that they could lose their jobs in the future. To prepare for this possibility, they decrease their demand for many goods and services. A similar shift in demand happens when we have expectations about the future price of a good. Even though a good's price has not yet changed, if we expect that the good's price will rise, we might increase our demand today to buy the good before the price increase.

Expectations are an important factor in shifting demand because they are often self-fulfilling. For example, when an autoworker is worried about a layoff, he may cut his spending on clothing, restaurant meals, appliances, and other discretionary spending items. Other workers will tend to do the same. As a result, producers of clothing, restaurant meals, and appliances will see a decrease in the demand for their products. This may cause them to lay off workers or cut back on their employees' hours. These employees then see a reduction in their incomes and decrease their demand for normal goods like cars, clothing, and restaurant meals, resulting in a round of layoffs in the auto, textiles, and services industries.

Number of Consumers in the Market

When we build a demand curve, we can describe the behavior of an individual or the behavior of all of the consumers in a market, meaning, we can describe your demand for bread or the demand for bread by all of the consumers in your city. If the number of consumers in your city increases, the overall demand for bread will also increase. Since 1980, for example, tortilla sales in the United States have increased fivefold, from $300 million to over $1.5 billion per year. Although tortillas are traditionally made by hand, many small firms have had to automate to keep up with the increasing demand. The increase in demand has been fueled in large part by increased immigration from Mexico.

Our discussion of demand summarizes behavior on the buyers' side of the market. We see that price and quantity demanded move inversely to one another, and also that changes in factors other than price will shift the demand relationship. Now let's look at the suppliers' side of the market. Even though they represent opposite sides of the market, there are many parallels between demand and supply, as you'll see in the next section.

SUPPLY

In the demand and supply model, supply represents the seller's side of the market. The fundamental relationship on the supply side is between the price of the good and the quantity that sellers are willing and able to sell at that price. This quantity is called the **quantity supplied**, and it changes as the price of the good changes. As with demand, letting the price of the good change and then observing the resulting changes in quantity supplied yields an overall relationship between price and quantity supplied, called the **supply** of the good.

Quantity supplied: The amount of a good that sellers are willing and able to sell at a given price and time, ceteris paribus.

Supply: The relationship between the price of a good and its quantity supplied, ceteris paribus.

Supply Table

As with demand, we can represent a supply relationship using a table or a graph. Using our bread example, Table 3.3 shows a hypothetical supply of bread at a local bakery. The column labeled P shows the price of each loaf of bread, and the column labeled Q^S shows the quantity of bread supplied at each price. Column Q^S shows how many loaves the bakery is willing and able to sell per day at each of the possible prices.

At prices below $3 per loaf, the price is too low to cover the costs of production, so the bakery will not try to sell any loaves of bread at those prices. When bread is $3 per loaf, the bakery is willing and able to sell 1 loaf per day. Using our shorthand, when P = $3 per loaf, Q^S = 1 loaf per day. When the price is $5 per loaf, the quantity supplied is 3 loaves per day, and when the price is $8 per loaf, the quantity supplied is 6 loaves per day.

Table 3.3 Supply of Bread

P ($/loaf)	Q^S (loaves/day)
0	0
1	0
2	0
3	1
4	2
5	3
6	4
7	5
8	6
9	7
10	8

Supply Graph

Figure 3.6 is a graph of the data in Table 3.3. As in the demand graph, price is measured on the *y*-axis and quantity is measured on the *x*-axis. The line connecting each of the price and quantity supplied combinations is called a supply curve and is labeled S.

Figure 3.6 **The Supply of Bread**

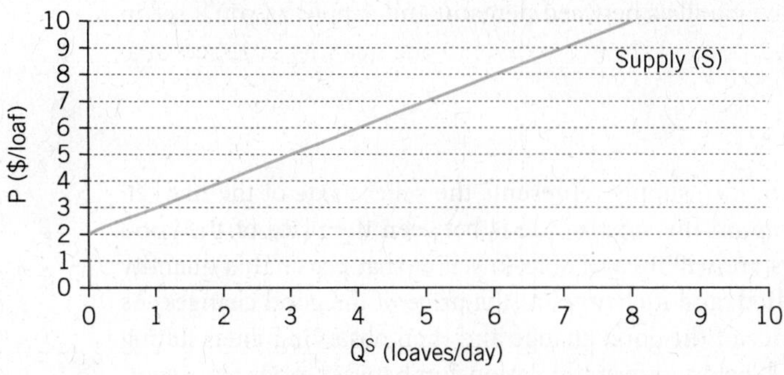

The supply curve S shows the price of bread on the *y*-axis and the corresponding quantity of bread supplied at each price on the *x*-axis.

As with the demand case, supply relationships can be linear, as in Figure 3.6, or curved. Regardless of the shape, the graphs are called supply curves.

Supply versus Quantity Supplied

It is important to understand the difference between quantity supplied and supply. *Quantity supplied* is the amount of a good or service that sellers are willing and able to sell at a given price. Each quantity supplied is one point in the supply table or one point on the supply curve. *Supply* shows us all the prices and all the quantities supplied in the entire table or graph.

The Law of Supply

The law of supply: There is a positive relationship between price and quantity supplied.

The relationship between the price and quantity supplied is a direct or positive relationship. As the price of bread rises, ceteris paribus, the quantity of bread supplied also rises. Similarly, as the price of bread falls, the quantity of bread supplied falls. The positive relationship between the price of a good and its quantity supplied is called the **law of supply**. It is difficult to find examples of goods or services for which the law of supply does not hold.

There are several factors that contribute to the positive relationship between price and quantity supplied: the *scale effect*, the *substitution effect*, and the *law of increasing marginal costs*.

The Scale Effect

The scale effect of a price increase generates increased incentives for producers to expand their scale of production, thus increasing the quantity supplied.

Imagine that you are a baker. When bread prices are low, the scale or level of your bread production is likely to be low because you will not be able to cover the costs of hiring lots of employees and renting a large building. When prices rise, you may be able to expand the scale of your production and bake more bread by hiring additional labor, paying your workers overtime to work longer hours, and expanding to a larger facility. The **scale effect** implies that when the price of a good rises, producers increase their quantity supplied because they can afford to increase their scale of production. When the price of a good falls, producers decrease their quantity supplied because they cannot afford to keep up their current scale of production.

The Producer Substitution Effect

If a good's price changes relative to other goods, producers might choose to supply more of it. In response to a higher price for bread, you may respond by moving some of your oven space and labor efforts out of production of pies or cookies and into bread production. When the relative price of bread rises, you substitute some of your production resources, such as labor and machines, into bread production. This is the **producer substitution effect**, and it causes increases in the quantity supplied of a good when the good's price rises.

The producer substitution effect of a price increase occurs when changes in the relative price of a good cause producers to move their production into the now relatively higher priced goods.

The Law of Increasing Marginal Costs

A third factor generating the positive relationship between prices and quantities supplied is the law of increasing marginal costs. The law of increasing marginal costs asserts that, ceteris paribus, the costs of production tend to rise as successive units of a good are produced. These increasing costs are then reflected in increases in the minimum prices that producers are willing to accept for the good as quantities of the good increase. You encountered the concept of increasing marginal costs in the discussion of the production possibilities curve in Chapter 2. Increasing marginal cost arises because resources are specialized—they are not equally productive at producing all goods and services.

In the case of bread baking, the costs of bread production increase as we produce more bread for several reasons. First, we will likely use our best baker to produce the first batch of bread. He is highly efficient and can make his way around the kitchen quickly. To produce the second batch of bread, our next best baker is used. She is not quite as skilled as our first baker, so it takes her longer to produce the bread. Because it takes her longer, it costs us more in time and wages to make the second batch of bread. By the time we move on to our third baker, the kitchen is getting crowded, it is harder to make the bread as quickly, and so it takes even longer to produce the third loaf.

The explanation of the law of increasing marginal cost is an alternative way of thinking about a supply curve. On the one hand, we can view supply as describing how much of a good producers are willing and able to sell at a given price. As with the demand curve, this is a "horizontal" reflection in the sense that supply shows the quantity supplied, measured on the horizontal axis, for a given price. Another way to think about supply is that it reflects the minimum amount that producers are willing and able to accept in order to sell a given amount of a good. This is a "vertical" interpretation of supply in the sense that it shows the minimum dollar amount, measured on the vertical axis, that producers will accept in payment for a given quantity of the good. We'll use the price and quantity supplied and willingness to accept or marginal cost interpretations when we apply the supply curve to different situations later in the text.

Changes in Supply

When we draw a supply curve, we rely heavily on the ceteris paribus assumption. We draw the price and quantity supplied relationship at a point in time and holding other things constant. When we relax this assumption, we can allow supply to respond to changes in other factors such as technology and the prices of inputs.

As with the demand curve, it is important to distinguish between a **change in quantity supplied** of a good and a change in the supply of the good. When the price of a good changes, ceteris paribus, only the quantity supplied, but not the overall supply, of the good changes. To distinguish between the two cases, let's change the price of bread.

A change in quantity supplied results from a change in the price of the good, ceteris paribus. It is represented by a movement along the supply curve.

Suppose the price of bread is initially $4 per loaf, so that quantity supplied is 2 loaves per day. The P = $4 and Q^S = 2 pair of values corresponds to point A on

Figure 3.7 A Change in the Quantity Supplied of Bread

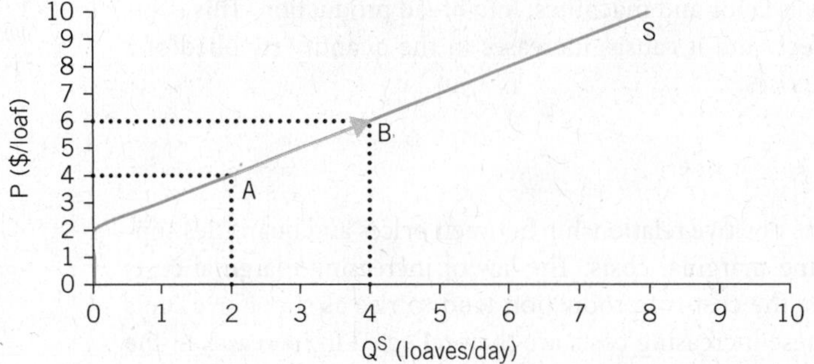

When the price of bread increases, we move along the supply curve for bread from point A to point B. The *quantity supplied* of bread changes, but the *supply* of bread does not change.

the supply curve in Figure 3.7. If the price rises to $6 per loaf, the quantity supplied increases to 4 loaves per day, shown by point B. When the price of bread changes, ceteris paribus, the quantity supplied changes, and there is a movement along the supply curve for bread.

When supply changes, we no longer move within the existing supply table or along the original supply curve. Instead, there is an entirely new relationship between price and quantity supplied. As with demand, an increase in supply means that at each price, quantity supplied is larger than it was before. A decrease in supply means that at each price, quantity supplied is less than it was before.

An increase in supply is illustrated in Table 3.4 and Figure 3.8. In column $Q^{S'}$ of Table 3.4, when the price of bread is $6 per loaf, quantity supplied is now 6 loaves per day rather than 4 loaves per day. When the price is $3 per loaf, quantity supplied is 3 loaves per day instead of 1 loaf per day.

Because the quantity supplied increased at each price, the points on the new supply curve S′ are to the right of those on the original supply curve S, as shown in Figure 3.8. An **increase in supply** generates an outward shift in the supply curve.

An increase in supply means that quantity supplied increases at each price. As a result, the supply curve shifts outward.

A change in supply, then, implies a fundamental change in the overall supply relationship—a new column of the supply table is needed, as in Table 3.4, and the supply curve shifts, as in Figure 3.8. In comparison, a change in quantity supplied which comes only from a change in the price of the good, ceteris paribus, does not imply a

Table 3.4 An Increase in the Supply of Bread

P ($/loaf)	Q^S (loaves/day)	$Q^{S'}$ (loaves/day)
0	0	0
1	0	1
2	0	2
3	1	3
4	2	4
5	3	5
6	4	6
7	5	7
8	6	8
9	7	9
10	8	10

Figure 3.8 **An Increase in the Supply of Bread**

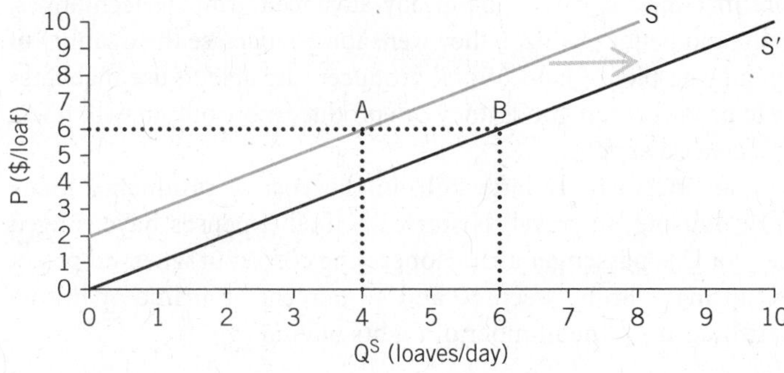

When there is an increase in the supply of bread, the supply curve shifts outward. At each of the prices, the quantity of bread supplied is more than it was before. Point A represents Q^S when P = \$6 on the original supply curve (S). Point B represents $Q^{S'}$, the quantity supplied when P = \$6 on the new supply curve.

change in the overall relationship but rather a movement within the relationship, as was shown in Figure 3.7.

A **decrease in supply** is reflected in movements in the opposite direction. If supply decreases, quantity supplied at each price is less than before. This is illustrated by moving from $Q^{S'}$ to Q^S in Table 3.4. It could also be illustrated by moving from curve S′ to curve S in Figure 3.8.

A decrease in supply means that quantity supplied decreases at each price. As a result, the supply curve shifts inward.

Notice that increases or decreases in supply and demand move the curves in similar directions along the *x*-axis. When supply or demand increase, the respective curve moves outward along the *x*-axis. When supply or demand decrease, the respective curve moves inward along the *x*-axis. Do not view an increase in supply as an upward movement in the supply curve and a decrease in supply as a downward movement in the supply curve. An upward movement in the supply curve would actually imply less quantity supplied at each price. Think instead of the movements as leftward and rightward shifts rather than as upward or downward shifts.

Draw two graphs, one that depicts a decrease in supply and another that depicts a decrease in demand.

Factors That Shift Supply

What factors can generate shifts in supply? The primary factors are the costs of production, the prices of alternative goods that could be produced, seller expectations, and the number of suppliers in the market.

Costs of Production

The expenses involved in production include the costs of inputs, the costs to get goods or services to market, and the technology used to produce the goods and services. When the costs of production of a good or service increase, ceteris paribus, the supply of the good or service will decrease. For example, poor weather pushed the cost of wheat to record highs in 2011. As a result, bakeries had to adjust by cutting their use of wheat in other goods or by baking fewer loaves of bread per day. Increases in technology generally decrease the costs of production, as occurred in U.S. agricultural production in the last half of the 20th century. As farmers changed their production to use more machines and technologically-advanced growing techniques, disease resistant seeds, and better fertilizer, they were able to increase the quantity of food produced from a given plot of land. When producers are able to use machines or other technology to produce their goods, they can produce more output with fewer resources, allowing increased supply.

Fuel prices play an increasingly large role in the cost of producing many goods, from food, to housing, to travel. Historically, fuel expenses have ranged from 10 to 15 percent of U.S. passenger airline operating costs, but when oil prices rise, fuel expenses can make up between 30 and 40 percent of airline operating costs. In response, airlines drop the number of flights offered.

Prices of Alternative Goods That Could Be Produced

The supply of a good can change when the price of alternative goods that use similar resources changes. For example, if the price of cookies rises, ceteris paribus, you face an incentive to use your bakery to produce more cookies and less bread.

THINK FOR YOURSELF

Assume that barley and wheat are alternative goods that could be produced on a given plot of land. In one graph, show how a decrease in the price of barley will change the quantity of barley supplied. In the other graph, illustrate how the supply of wheat will change.

Producer Expectations

As with demand, supply can change in response to changes in producers' expectations about the future. When producers expect sales to increase in the future, they may increase their production today in order to have adequate inventories. For example, if you expect people to buy more bread for a long weekend or a holiday, you may increase your production a few days ahead of time. Alternatively, if producers expect that future sales are going to be lower, they may decrease their supply today in order to avoid having inventories grow.

Number of Sellers in the Market

As the number of sellers in the market rises, the market supply of a good rises. Consider the change in the quantity of coffee available each time Starbucks opens another store.

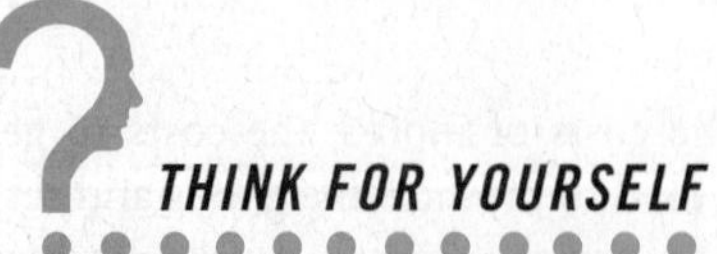

THINK FOR YOURSELF

Draw a graphical depiction of the change in supply that will occur due to an increase in the number of sellers in the market.

MARKET EQUILIBRIUM

We can now combine what we know about the behavior of buyers and sellers in markets to describe how markets set the prices and quantities of goods that are traded. The interactions between consumers or demanders and sellers or suppliers in a market determine the eventual price and amount of the good sold.

When buyers can obtain all of the good that they are willing and able to buy at a given price and sellers can sell all of the good that they are willing and able to sell at a given price, the market is in equilibrium. Table 3.5 combines the prices and quantities for both buyers and sellers in the market for bread. There is one point where the quantity demanded equals the quantity supplied. At that point price is \$6 per loaf, the quantity demanded is 4 loaves per day, and the quantity supplied is 4 loaves per day.

Table 3.5 Demand and Supply of Bread

Q^D (loaves/day)	P (\$/loaf)	Q^S (loaves/day)
10	0	0
9	1	0
8	2	0
7	3	1
6	4	2
5	5	3
4	6	4
3	7	5
2	8	6
1	9	7
0	10	8

Market equilibrium occurs at the price where quantity demanded is equal to quantity supplied.

Figure 3.9 shows the same information graphically. At point E, the demand and supply curves intersect; this point represents the equilibrium in the bread market. Here P = \$6 per loaf, and the quantity demanded and quantity supplied are both 4 loaves per day.

A market in equilibrium is analogous to a slackliner or tightrope walker. When she is in equilibrium, she is well balanced on the line and is stable. When a market is in equilibrium, the price and quantity combination in the market gives buyers and sellers no incentive to change or rebalance their behavior. When a slackliner is tilting to one side or another, she automatically wants to correct this imbalance and get back to equilibrium. Similarly, when a market is not in equilibrium, buyers and sellers notice incentives or "market forces" that act as signals to change their behavior. These market forces take the form of market shortages and surpluses, which we turn to next.

© Sean Locke/iStockphoto

Figure 3.9 **Equilibrium in the Market for Bread**

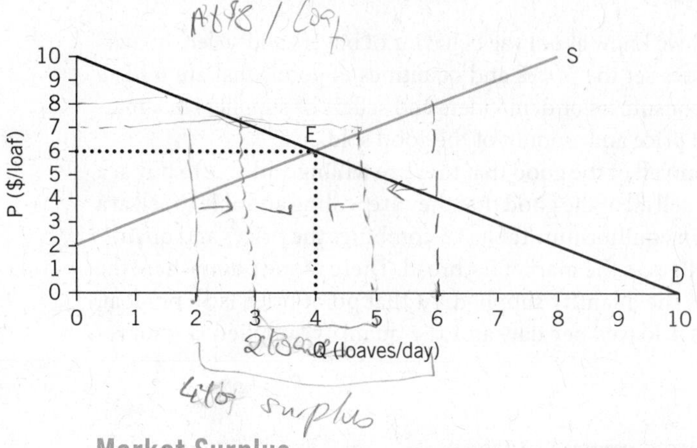

When the market is in equilibrium, the quantity demanded and the quantity supplied are equal to one another at a given price. At point E, the price is $6 per loaf and Q^S and Q^D are both 4 loaves per day.

Market Surplus

Market surplus occurs when the price of a good is above its equilibrium price. In a market surplus, Q^S is greater than Q^D at a given price.

How does a market react when the price of a good is above its equilibrium level? Suppose the price of bread is $8 per loaf. At that price, $Q^S = 6$ loaves per day, which corresponds to point A in Figure 3.10. At the price of $8 per loaf, $Q^D = 2$ loaves per day, shown as point B in Figure 3.10. When the price is $8 per loaf, sellers are willing and able to sell 6 loaves per day, but buyers are willing and able to buy only 2 loaves per day. There will be 4 more loaves of bread offered for sale than will be bought per day.

How does the market adjust when there is a surplus? The market surplus is a signal to sellers to lower their price. If they don't, they will be stuck with excess bread day after day. As the price of bread falls, the quantity of bread supplied per day will fall, shown by the arrow that begins at point A in Figure 3.10. At lower prices, fewer bakers will find it worthwhile to bake as intensely, for example. The lower price will also increase the quantity demanded per day, shown by the arrow that begins at point B. More consumers will be able to buy bread at a lower price, and others will decide to substitute away from other foods, such as bagels, and into purchases of bread.

Market Shortage

Market shortage occurs when the price of a good is below its equilibrium price. In a market shortage, Q^D is greater than Q^S at a given price.

How does the market react when the price of a good or service is below its equilibrium price? Suppose the price of bread is $3 per loaf. At that price, Q^S is 1 loaf per day,

Figure 3.10 **Market Surplus and Adjustment to Equilibrium**

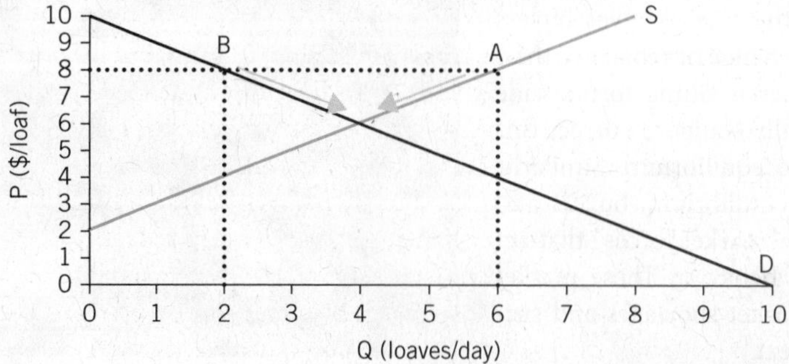

When the price is above equilibrium, Q^S is more than Q^D and there is a market surplus. The amount of the market surplus is the difference between Q^S and Q^D at points A and B. The market surplus gives suppliers an incentive to lower their prices. As prices fall, Q^D increases and Q^S falls, moving the market to equilibrium.

Figure 3.11 **Market Shortage and Adjustment to Equilibrium**

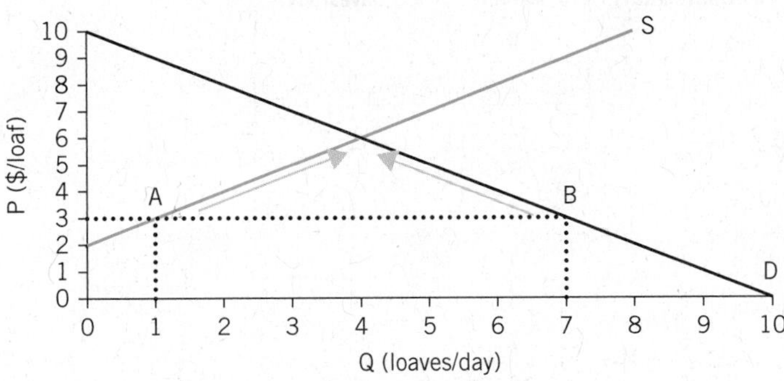

When the price is below equilibrium, Q^S is less than Q^D and there is a market shortage. The amount of the market shortage is the difference between Q^D and Q^S at points A and B. The market shortage gives suppliers an incentive to raise their prices. As prices rise, Q^D falls and Q^S rises, moving the market to equilibrium.

which is point A in Figure 3.11. When P = \$3 per loaf, Q^D is 7 loaves per day, shown by point B. At a price of \$3 per loaf, consumers are willing to buy 6 more loaves per day than producers are willing to sell. When there are market shortages, stores have empty sales bins or lines of customers waiting to buy goods. Market shortages send a signal to suppliers to increase prices. As producers raise their prices, some customers will decide to buy less, so quantity demanded will decrease, as shown by the arrow that begins at point B. At the same time, the higher price makes it easier for sellers to cover the cost of producing more, so that the quantity supplied rises, as shown by the arrow that starts at point A in Figure 3.11.

MARKET ADJUSTMENTS TO CHANGES IN DEMAND AND SUPPLY

It is rare to find a slackliner who can stand in one place on the line for a long period of time. The wind may push her or friends might distract her, disturbing her equilibrium and requiring an adjustment to get back in balance. In like manner, the factors that shift the demand and supply curves are also always in motion. New technological innovations might increase supply or lower production costs, consumers move to new markets, consumers and producers may alter their expectations—all these shifts in demand and supply affect price and quantity and move the market away from equilibrium. We now turn to a discussion of events that disrupt the market and the adjustments that restore equilibrium. In each case, we begin with a market that is in equilibrium. We then observe the effect of the shift on market price and quantity and the process that allows the market to reach a new equilibrium.

Market Adjustment to an Increase in Demand

First let's consider how a market responds to an increase in demand. The original demand and supply values are shown in the first and last columns of Table 3.6 and plotted in Figure 3.12. Figure 3.12 shows the original demand (D) and supply (S) curves, as well as the original equilibrium price and quantity of bread per day (point B).

Now suppose that the demand for bread increases. This increase in demand is shown in column $Q^{D'}$ in Table 3.6. Notice that at each price, the quantity demanded values in column $Q^{D'}$ are more than those in column Q^D. This increase in demand could occur for any of several reasons. The incomes of consumers could have risen (assuming bread is a normal good), the price of a substitute good (such as bagels)

Table 3.6 **An Increase in the Demand for Bread**

Q^D (loaves/day)	$Q^{D'}$ (loaves/day)	P ($/loaf)	Q^S (loaves/day)
10	12	0	0
9	11	1	0
8	10	2	0
7	9	3	1
6	8	4	2
5	7	5	3
4	6	6	4
3	5	7	5
2	4	8	6
1	3	9	7
0	2	10	8

could have risen, the price of a complement good (such as peanut butter) could have fallen, tastes and preferences could have shifted toward increased bread consumption, consumers' expectations may have changed, or more consumers could have entered this market.

If the price of bread remains at $6 per loaf after demand increases, there will be a shortage in the market for bread. Because the demand has increased, the $Q^{D'}$ column rather than the Q^D column represents the amounts that consumers are willing and able to buy at each price. The shortage would occur at the old equilibrium price because when $P = \$6$, $Q^S = 4$ loaves per day and $Q^{D'} = 6$ loaves per day.

Figure 3.12 shows the new demand curve in the market, D′. When demand increases, the market moves to a new equilibrium at point E. The market moves to the new price and quantity as it responds to the market shortage that is created at the old equilibrium price ($P = \$6$) and the new level of demand (D′). With the new demand curve, at the original equilibrium price of $P = \$6$ per loaf, $Q^{D'}$ is 6 loaves per day (point A), but Q^S is only 4 loaves per day (point B). If nothing changes in response to the increase in demand, the bakery will see its bread bins empty but still have customers willing and able to buy bread. This shortage acts as an incentive for producers to raise the price of bread. As they do, they can cover the cost of increased bread

Figure 3.12 **Market Adjustment to an Increase in Demand**

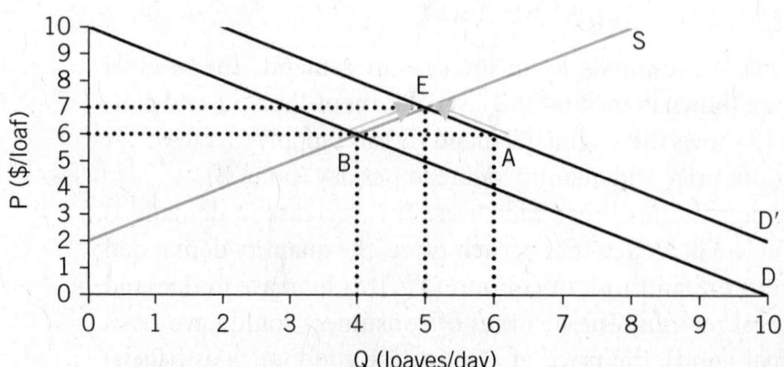

When demand increases, there is a market shortage of the good at the original equilibrium price, shown by points A and B. The market shortage gives suppliers an incentive to raise their prices. As prices rise, $Q^{D'}$ (on the new demand curve) falls and Q^S rises, moving the market to a new equilibrium. At the new equilibrium, price and quantity are both higher than in the original equilibrium.

production. At the same time, the higher price induces some consumers to decrease their quantity demanded, moving along the demand curve D′ from point A to point E. This adjustment is indicated by the arrows in Figure 3.12. The new equilibrium price is $7 per loaf, and the new equilibrium quantity traded is 5 loaves per day (point E).

From this analysis, we can see that an increase in demand for a good or service, ceteris paribus, generates new equilibrium price and quantity values that are higher than the original values.

Market Adjustment to a Decrease in Demand

Suppose that the demand for bread decreases. A decrease in demand is shown in column $Q^{D''}$ in Table 3.7. At each price, the quantity demanded in column $Q^{D''}$ is less than in column Q^D. Demand for bread might decrease if incomes of consumers have fallen (assuming bread is a normal good), the price of a substitute good (such as bagels) drops, the price of a complement good (such as peanut butter) rises, tastes and preferences have changed, consumers' expectations have changed, or consumers could have left this market.

If the price of bread remains at $6 per loaf after demand decreases, there will be a surplus in the market for bread. Because demand has decreased, the $Q^{D''}$ column rather than the Q^D column represents the amounts that consumers are willing and able to buy at each price. The surplus would occur at the old equilibrium price because when P = $6, Q^S = 4 loaves per day and $Q^{D''}$ = 2 loaves per day.

The data in Table 3.7 are plotted in Figure 3.13, which shows the new demand curve, D″. When demand decreases, the market moves to a new equilibrium (E). The market moves to the new price and quantity as it responds to the market surplus that is created at the old equilibrium price (P = $6) and the new level of demand (D″). With the new demand curve, but original equilibrium price, $Q^{D''}$ is 2 loaves per day, but Q^S is 4 loaves per day. If nothing changes in response to the increase in demand, the bakery will see that its bread bins always have 2 extra loaves at the end of each day. The surplus causes producers to lower the price of bread. As they do, they will also want to decrease their bread production, since they cannot cover the costs of the old level of output at the new, lower price. The change in Q^S is illustrated by the arrow from B to E in Figure 3.13. At the same time, the lower price induces some consumers to move along the new demand curve to increase their quantity demanded. The

Table 3.7 A Decrease in the Demand for Bread

Q^D (loaves/day)	$Q^{D''}$ (loaves/day)	P ($/loaf)	Q^S (loaves/day)
10	8	0	0
9	7	1	0
8	6	2	0
7	5	3	1
6	4	4	2
5	3	5	3
4	2	6	4
3	1	7	5
2	0	8	6
1	0	9	7
0	0	10	8

Figure 3.13 **Market Adjustment to a Decrease in Demand**

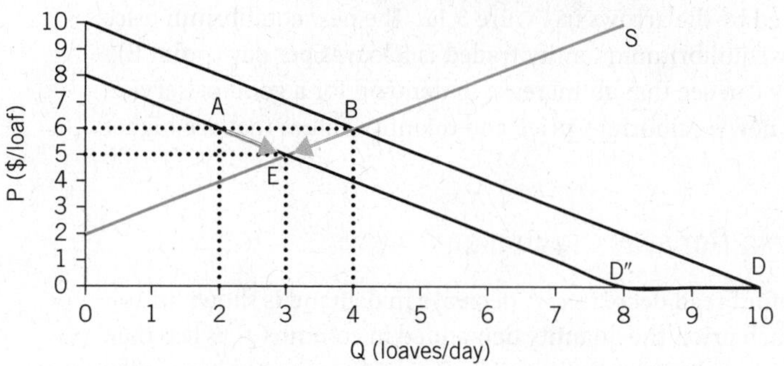

When demand decreases, there is a market surplus of the good at the original equilibrium price, shown by points A and B. The market surplus gives suppliers an incentive to lower their prices. As prices fall, $Q^{D''}$ (on the new demand curve) rises and Q^S falls, moving the market to a new equilibrium (E). At the new equilibrium, price and quantity are both lower than in the original equilibrium.

arrow from A to E shows this adjustment. The new equilibrium price is $5 per loaf, and the new equilibrium quantity traded is 3 loaves per day. A decrease in demand for a good or service, ceteris paribus, generates new equilibrium price and quantity values that are lower than the original values.

The Granger Collection, New York

Alfred Marshall and the Demand and Supply Model

Widely considered one of the most influential economists of all time, Alfred Marshall (1842–1924) helped to move economics from a discipline that focused primarily on the workings of markets and into a discipline focused on the study of human behavior. His work on formalizing the demand and supply model as a tool for understanding how prices are determined and on describing the relationship between marginal utility and prices helped set the stage for modern economics.

Market Adjustment to an Increase in Supply

An increase in supply is shown in column $Q^{S'}$ in Table 3.8. At each of the prices, the quantity supplied in column $Q^{S'}$ is more than in column Q^S. This increase could have occured for any of several reasons: the costs of production could have fallen, there could be new technology to speed up production, there could be a drop in the price of a substitute production good (such as cinnamon rolls) inducing producers to produce bread instead of cinnamon rolls, producers' expectations may have changed, or more producers could have entered this market.

If the price of bread remains at $6 per loaf after supply increases, there will be a surplus in the market for bread. Because supply has increased, the $Q^{S'}$ column rather than the Q^S column represents the amounts that producers are willing to sell at each price. The surplus would occur at the old equilibrium price because when P = $6, $Q^{S'}$ = 6 loaves per day and Q^D = 4 loaves per day.

Figure 3.14 illustrates the new supply curve in the market, S′. When supply increases, the market moves to a new equilibrium (E). The market moves to the new price and quantity as it responds to the market surplus that is created at the old equilibrium price (P = $6) and the new level of supply (S′). With the new supply curve, but original equilibrium price, Q^D is 4 loaves per day (point A), but $Q^{S'}$ is 6 loaves per day (point B).

Table 3.8 **An Increase in the Supply of Bread**

Q^D (loaves/day)	P ($/loaf)	Q^S (loaves/day)	$Q^{S'}$ (loaves/day)
10	0	0	0
9	1	0	1
8	2	0	2
7	3	1	3
6	4	2	4
5	5	3	5
4	6	4	6
3	7	5	7
2	8	6	8
1	9	7	9
0	10	8	10

Figure 3.14 **Market Adjustment to an Increase in Supply**

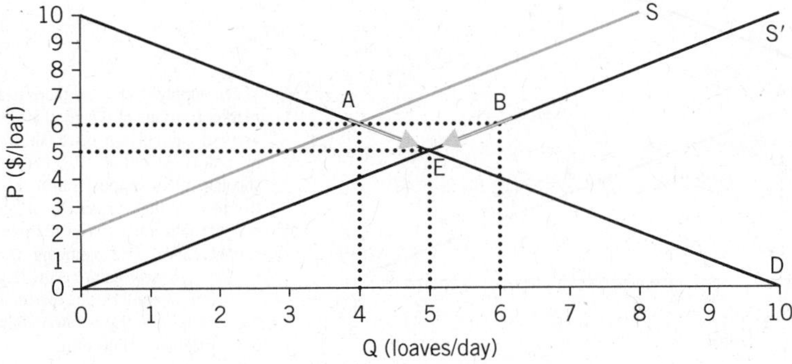

When supply increases, there is a market surplus of the good at the original equilibrium price, shown by points A and B. The market surplus gives suppliers an incentive to lower their prices. As prices fall, Q^D rises and $Q^{S'}$ (on the new supply curve) falls, moving the market to a new equilibrium. At the new equilibrium, price is lower and quantity is higher than in the original equilibrium.

If nothing changes in response to the increase in supply, the bakery will find that its bread bins always have 2 extra loaves at the end of each day. The surplus causes producers to lower the price of bread. As they do, they will also want to decrease their bread production, since they cannot cover the costs of the old level of output at the new, lower price. The change in $Q^{S'}$ is illustrated by the arrow from B to E in Figure 3.14. At the same time, the lower price induces some consumers to move along the demand curve to increase their quantity demanded. The arrow from A to E shows this adjustment. The new equilibrium price is $5 per loaf, and the new equilibrium quantity traded is 5 loaves per day. An increase in the supply of a good or service, ceteris paribus, generates new equilibrium price that is lower and a new equilibrium quantity that is higher than the original equilibrium values.

Market Adjustment to a Decrease in Supply

Now suppose that the supply of bread decreases. A decrease in supply is shown in column $Q^{S''}$ in Table 3.9. At each of the prices, the quantity supplied in column $Q^{S''}$ is less than in column Q^S. This could have occured for any of several reasons. For example, the costs of production could have risen, the price of a substitute production good (such as cinnamon rolls) could have risen (inducing the producers to make cinnamon rolls instead of bread), producers' expectations may have changed, or producers could have moved away from this market.

Table 3.9 A Decrease in the Supply of Bread

Q^D (loaves/day)	P ($/loaf)	Q^S (loaves/day)	$Q^{S''}$ (loaves/day)
10	0	0	0
9	1	0	0
8	2	0	0
7	3	1	0
6	4	2	0
5	5	3	1
4	6	4	2
3	7	5	3
2	8	6	4
1	9	7	5
0	10	8	6

Figure 3.15 Market Adjustment to a Decrease in Supply

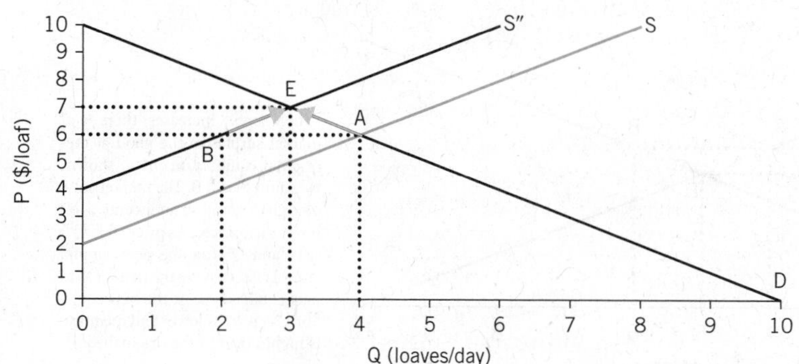

When supply decreases, there is a market shortage of the good at the original equilibrium price, shown by points A and B. The market shortage gives suppliers an incentive to raise their prices. As prices rise, Q^D falls and $Q^{S''}$ (on the new supply curve) rises, moving the market to a new equilibrium (E). At the new equilibrium, price is higher and quantity is lower than in the original equilibrium.

Figure 3.15 illustrates the new supply curve in the market, S″. The market moves to the new price and quantity as it responds to the market shortage that is created at the old equilibrium price (P = \$6) and the new level of supply (S″). With the new supply curve, but original equilibrium price, Q^D is 4 loaves per day (point A), but $Q^{S''}$ is 2 loaves per day (point B). If nothing changes in response to the decrease in supply, the bakery will see its bread bins empty but still have customers willing and able to buy bread. This shortage acts as an incentive for producers to raise the price of bread. As they do, they can cover the cost of increased bread production. The increase in quantity supplied is shown by the arrow from B to E. At the same time, the higher price induces some consumers to decrease their quantity demanded, moving along the demand curve as shown by the arrow from point A to point E. The new equilibrium price is \$7 per loaf, and the new equilibrium quantity traded is 3 loaves per day. A decrease in the supply of a good or service, ceteris paribus, generates a new equilibrium price that is higher and a new equilibrium quantity that is lower than the original equilibrium values.

Market Adjustments to Simultaneous Shifts in Demand and Supply

So far we have analyzed how markets adjust to independent changes in demand or supply. Oftentimes, however, demand and supply both change at the same time. For example, it could be the case that the price of flour used to make bread increases, and at the same time consumers change their preferences away from eating bread and other carbohydrates and toward eating more fruits and vegetables. When demand

Figure 3.16 **Market Adjustment to Change in Demand and Supply**

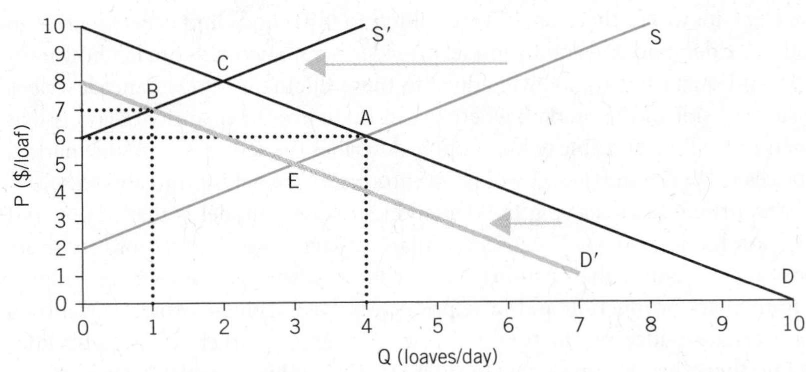

When supply and demand change at the same time, the net impact on equilibrium price and quantity depends on the relative sizes of the supply and demand shifts. Ceteris paribus, the decrease in supply from S to S′ would cause equilibrium price to rise and equilibrium quantity to fall (point C). Ceteris paribus, the decrease in demand from D to D′ would cause both equilibrium price and quantity to fall (point E). The decrease in demand and the decrease in supply cause the equilibrium quantity to fall. The increase in price in equilibrium (point B) occurs because the supply shift is larger than the demand shift.

and supply shift at the same time, we can still make predictions about the changes in equilibrium price and quantity, as long as we know the relative sizes of the demand and supply changes.

Figure 3.16 shows how the market could respond to a simultaneous decrease in supply and decrease in demand. The market is initially in equilibrium at point A (P = $6 and Q = 4 loaves per day). An increase in the price of flour will cause the supply of bread to decrease to S′. At the same time, the change in consumer tastes and preferences causes the demand for bread to decrease to D′. To determine how the equilibrium price and quantity of bread will respond to these changes, we first examine the impacts of the changes in demand and supply separately. Then we assess whether the changes cause similar or opposing impacts on equilibrium price and quantity. In the situation shown in Figure 3.16, if we ignore the change in demand and focus only on the decrease in supply from S to S′ we can predict that the equilibrium would move from point A to point C. As a result of the supply shift, the equilibrium price of bread would rise and the equilibrium quantity of bread would fall. If we ignore the shift in supply and focus only on the shift in demand from D to D′, the equilibrium would move from point A to point E. As a result of the demand shift, the equilibrium price of bread would fall and the equilibrium quantity of bread would fall. Putting both of these shifts together, the equilibrium moves from point A to point B (P = $7 and Q = 1 loaf per day). The equilibrium quantity of bread falls, which is caused by both the decrease in supply and the decrease in demand. The increase in the equilibrium price of bread occurs because the decrease in supply (which pushes equilibrium price up) is larger than the decrease in demand (which pushes equilibrium price down). If the decrease in demand were larger than the decrease in supply, the equilibrium price of bread would have fallen instead of risen. When the demand and supply curves shift simultaneously, the impact on equilibrium price and quantity depends on the relative sizes and directions of the demand and supply shifts.

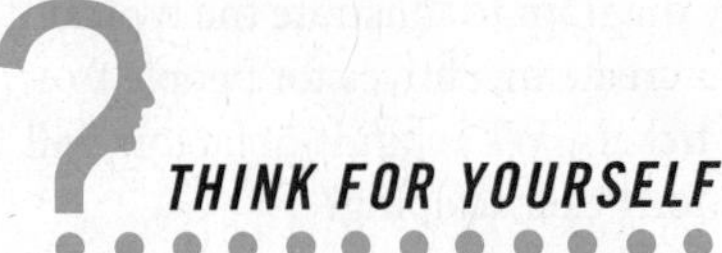

Predict what will happen to equilibrium price and quantity when (1) a large increase in supply occurs simultaneously with a smaller decrease in demand; (2) a small decrease in supply occurs simultaneously with a larger increase in demand; (3) a small decrease in supply occurs simultaneously with a larger decrease in demand; and (4) a small decrease in supply occurs simultaneously with a small increase in demand.

SUMMARY

Markets exist anywhere there are buyers willing to buy goods and sellers willing to sell goods. The demand and supply model provides a framework to predict how market prices and quantities traded will adjust to these fluctuations. Demand describes the consumers' side of the market, where prices influence the quantity of goods that consumers are willing and able to buy. Supply describes the sellers' side of the market, where prices influence the quantity of goods producers are willing and able to sell.

A basic principle underlying the demand and supply model is that buyers and sellers respond to incentives. The prices in markets serve as incentives for producers and consumers to adjust their actions. Market shortages provide incentives for producers to increase production and raise prices. Market surpluses provide incentives for producers to reduce production and prices. When a market is in equilibrium, there are no incentives for producers to change prices and no incentives for consumers to adjust the amount of goods they buy. However, there are many factors that cause demand or supply to shift, and these factors are always in motion. Any change in demand or supply will result in market shortages or surpluses that signal producers to change their prices. In response to changing prices, quantity demanded and quantity supplied adjust to move the market to a new equilibrium price and quantity.

KEY CONCEPTS

- Demand
- Quantity demanded
- Law of demand
- Income effect
- Consumer substitution effect
- Law of diminishing marginal utility
- Change in quantity demanded
- Increase in demand
- Decrease in demand
- Normal goods
- Inferior goods
- Complements
- Substitutes
- Quantity supplied
- Supply
- Law of supply
- Scale effect
- Producer substitution effect
- Change in quantity supplied
- Increase in supply
- Decrease in supply
- Market equilibrium
- Market surplus
- Market shortage

DISCUSSION QUESTIONS AND PROBLEMS

1. A perennial problem at grocery stores and shopping malls is that they tend to have too few parking spaces. Offer solutions to the problem that focus on (1) price changes; (2) a shift in demand; (3) a shift in supply. Which of your proposed solutions do you think is the best? Why?
2. In some places it is common to see ticket scalpers, people who resell or "scalp," tickets for admission, at events such as concerts and football games. Draw a demand and supply diagram to illustrate the typical situation that would create incentives for people to scalp their football tickets. What kinds of factors will increase incentives for ticket scalping?
3. What is a normal good for you? How will your demand for this good change when your income rises? How will your demand for the good change when your income falls? How do your answers change if the good is an inferior good?

4. Suppose the demand and supply for sweatshirts are given by:

Price ($/sweatshirt)	Q^D (#/year)	Q^S (#/year)
10	4000	400
20	3200	800
30	2400	1200
40	1600	1600
50	800	2000
60	0	2400

a. Graph these demand and supply curves. Be sure to correctly label the axes. At what price does equilibrium occur? What quantity is traded at that price?

b. Suppose the price of cotton, a production input for sweatshirts, falls such that at each price, quantity supplied changes by 1200 units. Add the new supply curve to your graph from part a. Label it S′. What is the new equilibrium price? What is the new equilibrium quantity?

c. Draw another graph of the original demand and supply figures. Now suppose that the price of sweatpants, a compliment consumption good to sweatshirts, rises, ceteris paribus. As a result, the quantity of sweatshirts demanded changes by 1200 at each price. Add the new demand curve to your graph. Label it D′. What is the new equilibrium price? What is the new equilibrium quantity?

MULTIPLE CHOICE QUESTIONS

1. Ceteris paribus, an increase in the price of Coke could be caused by
   a. a decrease in the demand for Coke.
   b. an increase in the supply of Coke.
   c. an increase in the demand for Coke.
   d. a decrease in consumer incomes, assuming that Coke is a normal good.
   e. a decrease in consumer tastes and preferences for Coke.

2. Tarantino's pizza and Mackenzie River pizza are substitute goods in Pizzatown. Ceteris paribus, if the price of Mackenzie River pizza rises, what can we expect to happen in the Pizzatown pizza market?
   a. The demand for Tarantino's pizza will decrease.
   b. The demand for Mackenzie River pizza will decrease.
   c. The demand for Tarantino's pizza will increase.
   d. The supply of Mackenzie River pizza will decrease.
   e. Both b and c.

3. Suppose there is a shortage in the market for Hula-Hoops. Ceteris paribus, we would expect to observe ___ as the market moved to equilibrium.
   a. the price of Hula-Hoops rising
   b. the price of Hula-Hoops falling
   c. the demand for Hula-Hoops falling
   d. the quantity of Hula-Hoops demanded rising
   e. Both a and d

4. Netflix subscriptions and Hulu Plus subscriptions are substitutes. Ceteris paribus, if the price of Hulu Plus subscriptions falls,
   a. the demand for Hulu Plus subscriptions increases.
   b. the demand for Netflix subscriptions increases.
   c. the demand for Netflix subscriptions decreases.
   d. the demand for Hulu Plus subscriptions decreases.
   e. both a and c.

Quantity Demanded Per Month	Price Per Pizza	Quantity Supplied Per Month
700	8	100
600	10	300
500	12	500
400	14	700
300	16	900

5. The accompanying table shows the demand and supply of pizzas at Tarantino's, a local pizza joint. At what price would this market be in equilibrium?
   a. P = $8
   b. P = $10
   c. P = $12
   d. P = $14
   e. P = $16

6. The table shows the demand and supply of pizzas at Tarantino's, a local pizza joint. If the price of a pizza is $10, there is a

   a. shortage of pizzas and the price will rise as the market moves to equilibrium
   b. surplus of pizzas and the price will rise as the market moves to equilibrium
   c. shortage of pizzas and the price will fall as the market moves to equilibrium
   d. surplus of pizzas and the price will fall as the market moves to equilibrium

7. The table shows the demand and supply of pizzas at Tarantino's, a local pizza joint. If the price of cheese, and input to pizzas, rises, a possible new equilibrium would be

   a. P = $10; Q = 600
   b. P = $10; Q = 300
   c. P = $16; Q = 900
   d. P = $16; Q = 300

8. Computer printers and printer ink cartridges are complements. If the price of printers decreases, the

   a. demand for ink cartridges will increase
   b. supply of ink cartridges will decrease
   c. quantity supplied of printers will increase
   d. quantity demanded of printers will decrease

9. Which of the following would shift the supply curve for cigarettes?

   a. A change in household incomes
   b. A change in the price of cigars, a substitute good in consumption but not production
   c. A change in the number of smokers
   d. Higher costs of tobacco production
   e. Both b and d

Price (per bowl of soup)	Quantity of Soup Demanded (bowls per month)	Price (per salad)
1	20	1
1	40	2
2	10	1
2	30	2

10. Imagine that you own a restaurant. The accompanying table shows different prices of soup and the corresponding number of bowls of soup that were purchased at your restaurant last month. At different times, you also charged different prices for salads. According to these data, soup and salad are (hint: sketch the graph)

    a. complement goods.
    b. substitute goods.
    c. inferior goods.
    d. normal goods.
    e. unrelated goods.

©Krystian Kaczmarski/iStockphoto

4

Consumer Surplus, Producer Surplus, and Economic Efficiency

After studying this chapter, you should be able to:

- Describe consumer surplus, producer surplus, economic surplus, and deadweight loss
- Illustrate and compute consumer surplus, producer surplus, and deadweight loss
- Describe how economic surplus can represent social welfare and economic efficiency
- Assess the impact of market interventions on economic surplus and social welfare
- Identify groups who benefit and are hurt by market interventions

Suppose that Sam is shopping for a used car. He has had his eye on a particular used car for the past week and is willing to pay $15,000 for it. Fred is selling the used car. He bought the car for $8,000, drove it for a year, spent $2,000 in maintenance and detailing work to get it ready for sale, and is now willing to sell it for $10,000. After a bit of negotiation, Sam and Fred settle on a price of $12,500 for the car. Sam and Fred are both better off after making this trade. Sam was able to buy the car for less than he was willing to pay for it, and Fred was able to sell the car for more than he was willing to accept for it. This chapter focuses on the benefits that buyers and sellers obtain when they trade with one another. Using the demand and supply model, we can assess how changes in market prices impact the benefits from trade. Because economists use these benefits as a measure of social welfare and economic efficiency, we can also determine how various government policies influence social welfare and economic efficiency.

CONSUMER SURPLUS

Consumer surplus is the difference between what someone is willing and able to pay for a good or service and the price of the good or service. It is the net benefit buyers get from buying a good or service.

Consumer surplus is the difference between what you are willing and able to pay for a good and the price that you actually pay for the good. Consumer surplus can also be viewed as the net benefit you receive from obtaining a good or service, since it is the difference between the benefit you receive from a good, measured as your willingness to pay for the good, and the price you pay for the good.

In the example in the chapter introduction, Sam derived $2,500 in consumer surplus from buying the used car because he was willing to pay $15,000 for it but its price was only $12,500. If the price of the car had been $10,000, Sam would have derived $5,000 in consumer surplus from buying the car. Imagine instead that the car's price was $15,000, as Sam had originally expected. Would he still buy it? Yes, since he had already determined that he was willing to pay $15,000 for it. Would he still have derived consumer surplus from the purchase? No, since the price he paid would be exactly what he was willing to pay for the car.

We can use the demand curve to illustrate consumer surplus. In Chapter 3 you learned that the "horizontal" interpretation of a demand relationship describes how much of a good consumers are willing and able to buy at a given price. The "vertical" interpretation of a demand relationship describes the maximum amount that consumers are willing and able to pay to obtain a given amount of a good. Using the vertical interpretation of the demand relationship, the demand curve illustrates the marginal utility consumers get from each additional unit of a good consumed.

Consider the demand curve in Figure 4.1, which illustrates your hypothetical demand for tutoring services. Point A on the demand curve, where Q = 1 and P = $40, illustrates that you are willing to pay $40 for 1 hour of tutoring. Suppose that the price of tutoring is $30 per hour, illustrated as point B. If you buy the first hour of tutoring, you will have consumer surplus of $10. This difference between what you are willing to pay for the first hour of tutoring and the price of the tutoring is illustrated by the vertical difference between points A and B. Your willingness to pay for a second hour of tutoring is $35, shown at point C. If the price of the second hour of tutoring is $30, you would gain consumer surplus of $5, the distance between points C and F. For the third hour, your willingness to pay is $30 (point G). If the price of tutoring is $30, you would still buy the third hour of tutoring, but you would not get consumer surplus from the third hour since the price is exactly equal to what you are willing to pay for it.

The sum of the vertical distances AB and CF ignores much of the lightly shaded triangle HGJ under the demand curve in Figure 4.1. The triangle illustrates the distance between the demand curve and the price for all potential quantities of tutoring up to

Figure 4.1 **The Demand for Tutoring**

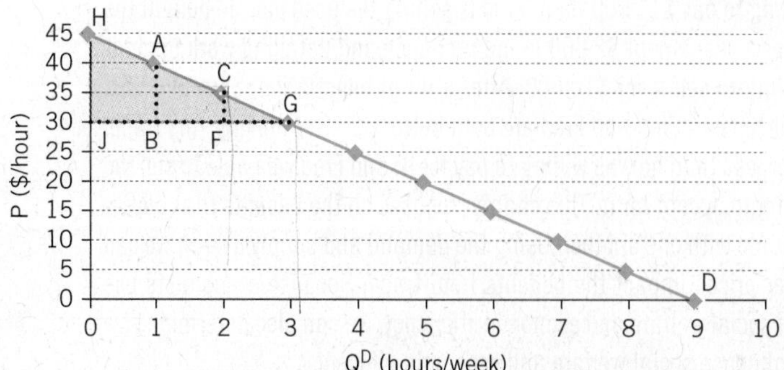

Your willingness to pay for the first hour of tutoring per week is $40, shown at point A. If the price of tutoring is $30 per hour, you obtain $10 in consumer surplus from buying that hour of tutoring (the vertical distance AB). Your total consumer surplus for 3 hours of tutoring when the price is $30 per hour is the area of the triangle HGJ.

Q = 3. Tutoring services are divisible, so you could buy one-half hour of tutoring, one-quarter of an hour, or even one-tenth of an hour. Since the demand curve shows the amount you are willing to pay for each marginal unit of tutoring, you can measure your total consumer surplus as the difference between the demand curve and the price at each of these smaller quantities. Consumer surplus at price = $30 per hour is the area below the demand curve but above the price, which is the area of triangle HGJ.

For linear demand curves like the one in Figure 4.1, we can calculate the dollar value of consumer surplus using the area for a triangle:

$$\text{Area of a triangle} = ½ * \text{base} * \text{height}$$

For the demand for tutoring in Figure 4.1, if the price per hour is $30, you would buy 3 hours of tutoring per week and your consumer surplus would be

$$½ * 3 * (\$45 - \$30) = ½ * 3 * \$15 = \$22.50 \text{ per week}$$

What happens to your consumer surplus if the price of the good changes? Changes in the price of the good will change the consumer surplus derived from the good. If the price of tutoring was $20 per hour, you would buy 5 hours of tutoring per week and your consumer surplus would be

$$½ * 5 * (\$45 - \$20) = ½ * 5 * \$25 = \$37.50 \text{ per week}$$

THINK FOR YOURSELF

What would consumer surplus be if the price of tutoring was $25 per hour? $10 per hour?

PRODUCER SURPLUS

Producer surplus is the difference between the price at which a seller is willing and able to sell a good and the price that he or she actually receives for the good. Like consumer surplus, producer surplus can be viewed as the net benefit sellers earn from selling a good or service, since it is the difference between the benefit they receive (the revenue they earn from the sale) and the cost of producing and selling the good.

Producer surplus is the difference between the price at which a seller is willing and able to sell a given good and the actual price received for the good. It is the net benefit sellers get from selling a good or service.

In the chapter introduction example, Fred derived $2,500 in producer surplus from selling the used car because he was willing to sell it for $10,000, but the sale price was $12,500. If the sale price was $14,000, Fred's producer surplus would have been $4,000 instead of $2,500.

We can illustrate the concept of producer surplus using a supply curve. In Chapter 3 we learned that the vertical interpretation of a supply relationship describes the minimum amount a producer is willing to accept to sell a good or service. This minimum amount reflects the seller's cost to produce additional unit of a good, which is the marginal cost of producing the good.

Figure 4.2 shows the supply curve for tutoring services. Point A illustrates the marginal cost of producing the first hour of tutoring, $20. If the price of tutoring is

Figure 4.2 **Supply of Tutoring**

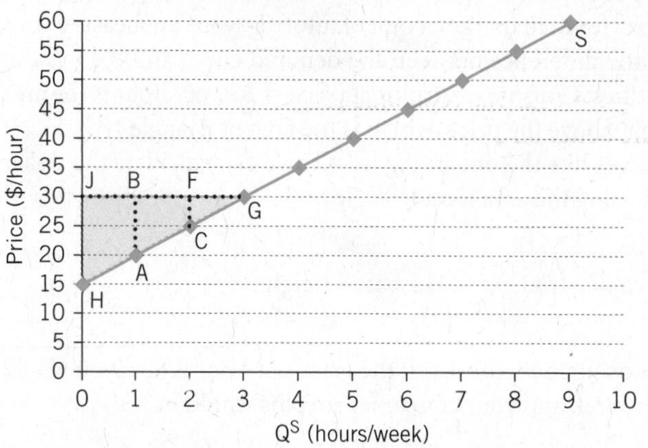

The marginal cost to produce the first hour of tutoring per week is $20, shown at point A. If the price of tutoring is $30 per hour, tutors obtain $10 in producer surplus from selling that hour of tutoring (the vertical distance AB). Total producer surplus for 3 hours of tutoring when the price is $30 per hour is the area of the triangle HGJ.

$30, the tutor earns $10 in producer surplus per week for that hour of tutoring services. This is shown as the vertical distance between points A and B. The marginal cost of the second hour of tutoring produced per week is $25, shown at point C. For that hour of tutoring, the tutor would earn $5 in producer surplus per week, the vertical distance between points C and F. Since the marginal cost of the third hour of tutoring per week is $30 (point G), if the price of tutoring is $30 per hour, the tutor would not earn producer surplus on the third hour of tutoring per week.

As with consumer surplus, we can compute producer surplus as the area of the triangle that lies above the supply curve and below the price. The triangle HJG illustrates the distance between the supply curve and the price for all potential quantities of tutoring up to Q = 3. So producer surplus when Q = 3 is:

$$\frac{1}{2} * 3 * (\$30 - \$15) = \frac{1}{2} * 3 * \$15 = \$22.50 \text{ per week}$$

If the price of tutoring services changes, the producer surplus will also change. For example, if the price of tutoring is $50, then 7 hours of tutoring services would be supplied per week and producer surplus would be

$$\frac{1}{2} * 7 * (\$50 - \$15) = \frac{1}{2} * 7 * \$35 = \$122.50 \text{ per week}$$

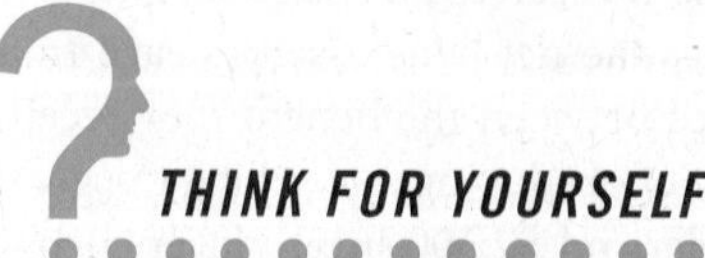

THINK FOR YOURSELF

What would producer surplus be if the price of tutoring was $20 per hour? $40 per hour?

ECONOMIC SURPLUS AND ECONOMIC EFFICIENCY

Economic surplus is the sum of consumer surplus plus producer surplus.

When trades occur, as in our used car and tutoring examples, sellers and buyers can both gain from the trade. The sum of the consumer surplus obtained by the buyers and the producer surplus obtained by the sellers is the **economic surplus** obtained from the transaction.

Figure 4.3 shows the market for tutoring services. The equilibrium price is $30 per hour and the equilibrium quantity is 3 hours per week, shown at point E. At equilibrium, consumer surplus is the triangle ABE ($22.50 per week), and producer surplus is the triangle CBE ($22.50 per week). The economic surplus is the triangle ACE, equal to $45 per week. The economic surplus tells us that the buyers and sellers in this market are better off by $45 than they would have been if the trade had not taken place.

Figure 4.3 **Economic Surplus in the Market for Tutoring**

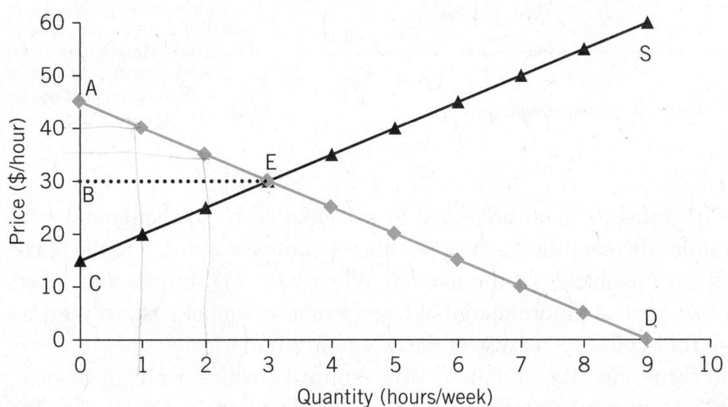

The equilibrium quantity of tutoring services is 3 hours per week at a price of $30 per hour (point E). At equilibrium, producer surplus is the triangle CBE and consumer surplus is the triangle ABE.

We can use the concept of economic surplus to assess how policy changes, demand and supply changes, or other factors affect social welfare or social well-being. Why? We learned in Chapter 1 that we can maximize the net benefit we receive from an activity when we engage in that activity until the marginal benefits are just equal to the marginal costs. In Chapter 2, we learned that choices on the production possibilities frontier are efficient choices regarding how to use resources because they represent the maximum output that can be produced using the resources available. Finally, in Chapter 3, we learned that the demand curve represents the marginal benefits of an activity, and the supply curve represents the marginal costs of an activity. If we combine all of these ideas, we learn that (1) efficient outcomes are those for which we get the maximum net benefit or net output from our resources; (2) we can arrive at efficient outcomes by choosing opportunities where the marginal benefits are greater than the marginal costs; and (3) because the market equilibrium equates the marginal benefit obtained from a good or service with its marginal cost of production, market equilibriums represent efficient uses of our resources.

Figure 4.4 illustrates an inefficient outcome in the market for tutoring. If the price of tutoring services was fixed at $35 per hour, 2 hours of tutoring services would be traded each week. The marginal cost of producing a third hour of tutoring services per week is shown between points BE on the supply curve. The amount that consumers are willing to pay to obtain a third hour of tutoring services per week is shown by AE. The marginal benefit to consumers of moving from two to three hours of tutoring services per week is higher than the marginal cost of moving from two to three hours of tutoring services per week. If the third hour of tutoring services is not traded, the economic surplus is reduced by triangle ABE, or $15 per week. This is the amount by which producers and consumers are made worse off by the disequilibrium price.

Figure 4.4 **Disequilibrium and Inefficiency**

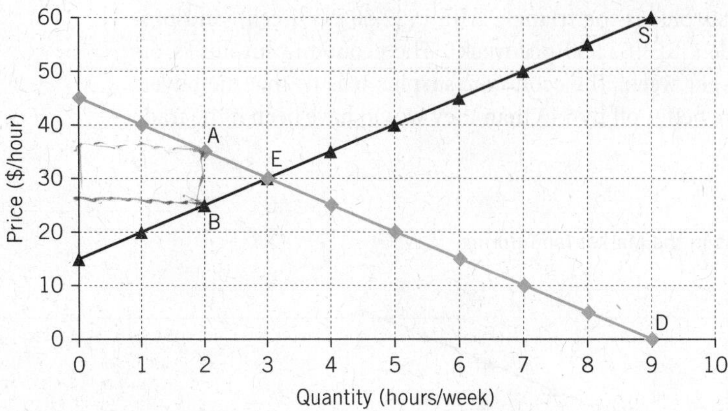

If the price of tutoring services is $35 per hour, 2 hours of tutoring services will be traded. Because the marginal cost of increasing production of tutoring services from 2 to 3 hours per week (shown by BE) is less than the marginal benefit of increasing production of tutoring services (AE), there is a loss of ABE in economic surplus per week.

At equilibrium, marginal benefits are equal to marginal costs, so that equilibrium generates economic efficiency, the highest possible economic surplus, and the maximum social welfare possible from the market. When P = $35, buyers and sellers forego choices that generate more marginal benefit than marginal cost, so they are less well off than they could be because of the disequilibrium price.

Deadweight loss is the loss in economic surplus that results from disequilibrium market outcomes.

Market interventions, like quotas or price controls, which we turn to next, can generate disequilibrium outcomes like the one depicted in Figure 4.4. The reduction in economic surplus that results from disequilibrium outcomes is called **deadweight loss**. Deadweight loss represents the decrease in economic welfare or economic surplus that results from disequilibrium market outcomes. In Figure 4.4, the triangle ABE is the deadweight loss that results from the above-equilibrium price of tutoring.

Economists frequently use the concept of deadweight loss to measure the social costs of economic policies. We will later discuss policies that generate deadweight loss: quotas and price controls, which include price ceilings and price floors. We will see more examples of price controls and quotas in later chapters.

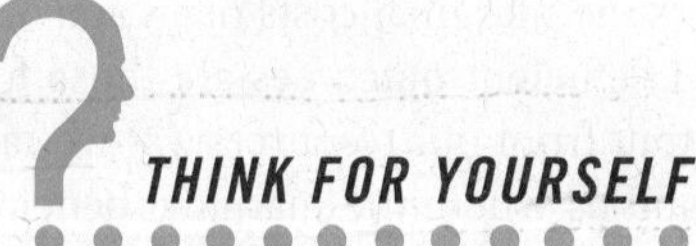

THINK FOR YOURSELF

What would economic surplus be if the price of tutoring was $35 per hour?

Price Ceilings

A price ceiling is an upper limit on the price of a good or service. A price ceiling sets the maximum amount that can be charged for a good or service.

Restrictions that place an upper limit on the price that can be charged for a good or service are called **price ceilings**. Examples include rent controls that limit the amount of rent that can be charged for an apartment, limits on the prices that utility companies can charge for electricity or natural gas, and executive pay caps.

Figure 4.5 illustrates the impact of a price ceiling in our market for tutoring services. If the market is in equilibrium, the price of tutoring is $30 per hour and 3 tutoring hours are sold per week. At this equilibrium, economic surplus is $45.

Figure 4.5 **Impact of a Price Ceiling for Tutoring Services**

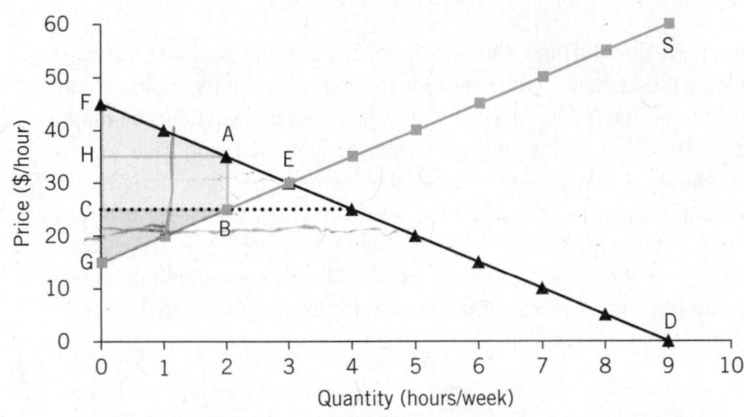

If a price ceiling is set at $25 per hour, 2 hours of tutoring services will be traded. Consumer surplus will be the area ABCF and producer surplus will be the area BCG. The deadweight loss from the price ceiling will be ABE.

Now suppose that some students protest that the $30 per hour rate for tutoring is too expensive. As a result, the administrators at your school impose a price ceiling on tutoring services, limiting the maximum price that can be charged to $25 per hour. At this price, quantity supplied is 2 hours per week and quantity demanded is 4 hours per week. Because quantity demanded is greater than quantity supplied, a market shortage of tutoring results, and we would expect to see wait lists for tutoring.

How does the price ceiling impact social welfare? When P = $25, producer surplus is the shaded triangle BCG in Figure 4.5:

$$½ * (\$25 - \$15) * 2 = \$10 \text{ per week}$$

Consumer surplus is the area of the shaded triangle AFH plus the area of the shaded rectangle HABC

$$[½ * (\$45 - \$35) * 2] + [(\$35 - \$25) * 2] = \$10 + \$20 = \$30 \text{ per week}$$

The economic surplus after the imposition of the price ceiling is $40 per week. Because the economic surplus fell from $45 to $40 when the price ceiling was imposed, we can say that society as a whole is made worse off by the price ceiling. Why? Although the price ceiling increased consumer surplus from $22.50 to $30 per week, it reduced producer surplus from $22.50 to $10 per week. The amount by which consumers are made better off by the price ceiling ($7.50 per week) is less than the amount by which producers are made worse off ($12.50 per week). In addition, $5 per week in economic surplus, shown by triangle ABE, is the amount of the deadweight loss generated by the price ceiling. It represents the value of trades that *could* occur but *do not* occur because of the price ceiling's restriction on the market.

THINK FOR YOURSELF

What would be the deadweight loss generated if the price ceiling were set at $20 per week?

JUAN BARRETO/AFP/ Getty Images, Inc.

Price Ceilings and Food Shortages in Venezuela

Venezuelan President Hugo Chavez, infamous for his socialist policies nationalizing oil, cement, and other industries in the country, is also a fan of price controls. Beginning in 2003, he established price ceilings on many basic food items, including milk and rice, to combat rising food prices in Venezuela. As a result, supermarket shelves have become increasingly bare, citizens engage in hoarding food when they can obtain it, and rice producers cut their production because they could not cover their costs of production at the lower prices. In 2009, Chavez's government seized and took over several privately-owned rice and pasta-making plants because they were not meeting state-imposed production levels.

Sources: Morsbach, Greg (1/10/2006), "Venezuelan shoppers face food shortages," BBC News. http://news.bbc.co.uk/2/hi/business/4599260.stm; CNN.com (updated 5/15/2009) "Venezuela seizes U.S.-owned food plant." http://www.cnn.com/2009/WORLD/americas/05/15/venezuela.cargill .plant.seizure/index.html.

Price Floors

*A **price floor** is a lower limit on the price of a good or service. It sets the minimum amount that can be charged for a good or service.*

Like price ceilings, price floors are restrictions on the price of goods and services. **Price floors** place a lower limit on the price of a good or service by establishing a minimum price that can be charged for a good or service. The minimum wage is one example of a price floor. The minimum wage sets a minimum price that can be paid to most types of labor per hour. Some agricultural markets also operate with price floors.

Figure 4.6 illustrates the impact of a price floor in our market for tutoring services. Suppose a price floor is set at $40 per hour. At that price, quantity supplied is 5 hours per week and quantity demanded is 1 hour per week. This generates a market surplus of tutoring services of 4 hours per week.

Consumer surplus will now be the triangle AFH, and producer surplus will be the area of the triangle BGC plus the rectangle ABCH. The price floor will generate a deadweight loss equal to the triangle AEB.

Figure 4.6 **Impact of a Price Floor for Tutoring Services**

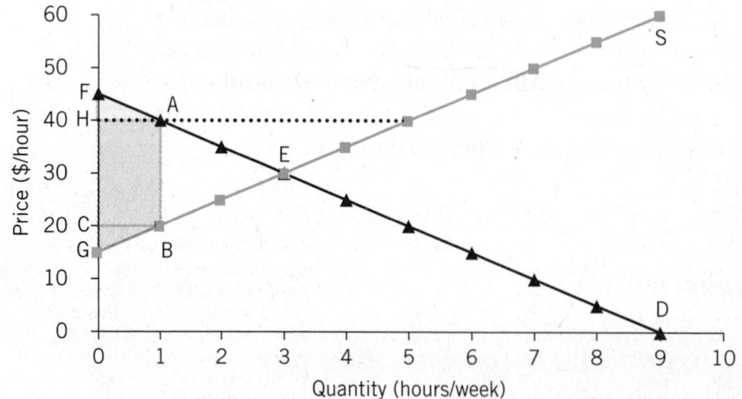

If a price floor is set at $40 per hour, 1 hour of tutoring services will be traded. Consumer surplus will be the area AFH and producer surplus will be the area ABGH. The deadweight loss from the price floor will be ABE.

THINK FOR YOURSELF

Compute the value of producer surplus, consumer surplus, economic surplus, and the deadweight loss resulting from the $40 per hour price floor in the tutoring market shown in Figure 4.6.

As you might expect based on the examples above, price ceilings and price floors are highly controversial policies because they make some people better off while making other people worse off. They also introduce inefficiencies into the market, which we measure as the deadweight loss. Quotas, which we turn to next, also generate economic inefficiency.

Vilfredo Pareto (1848–1923) (b/w photo), French Photographer, (19th century)/ Archives Larousse, Paris, France / Giraudon/Bridgeman Art Library/NY

Vilfredo Pareto and Economic Efficiency

Vilfredo Pareto (1848–1923) was an Italian economist and philosopher whose ideas continue to influence the economics of social welfare today. His notion of efficiency, called *Pareto efficiency*, is that an outcome is efficient when no one can be made better off without making someone worse off. Output choices on an economy's production possibility frontier and market equilibriums are both Pareto efficient because movements away from the PPF or to disequilibrium prices help some groups but hurt others.

Quotas

A **quota** is used to restrict the production of goods and services or to limit the amount of imports of goods allowed into a country. Let's again use the tutoring services market to illustrate how quotas impact social welfare. In our original equilibrium, 3 hours of tutoring services were traded per week at P = $30 per hour. Consumer surplus and producer surplus were both equal to $22.50 per week.

A quota is a limit on the quantity of a good that can be sold.

Figure 4.7 illustrates the impact of a quota that limits the amount of tutoring services to 2 hours per week. At the quota quantity, suppliers of tutoring services will

Figure 4.7 **Impact of a Quota on Tutoring Services**

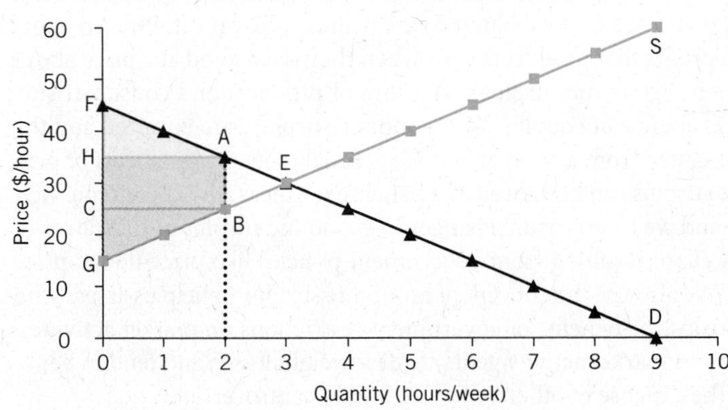

If the amount of tutoring is limited to 2 hours per week, the price will be $35 per hour, shown as point A on the demand curve. Consumer surplus will be the area AFH and producer surplus will be the area ABGH. The deadweight loss from the quota will be ABE.

have an incentive to charge as much as buyers are willing to pay for tutoring, which is $35 per hour, as shown by point A on the demand curve.

With the quota in place, consumers are able to buy fewer hours of tutoring services, and they have to pay a higher price to obtain tutoring. Consumer surplus, triangle AHF, is equal to

$$\tfrac{1}{2} * 2 * (\$45 - \$35) = \tfrac{1}{2} * 2 * \$10 = \$5 \text{ per week}$$

Consumers are clearly worse off as a result of the quota since their consumer surplus falls from $22.50 to $5 per week.

Producers could be made better or worse off by the quota. They are able to charge a higher price than in equilibrium, which would increase their producer surplus, but they sell fewer hours of tutoring than in equilibrium, which would reduce their producer surplus. Producer surplus is the area ABGH, equal to

$$(\tfrac{1}{2} * 2 * (\$25 - \$15) + ((\$35 - \$25) * 2) = \$10 + \$20 = \$30 \text{ per week}$$

Since producer surplus rises from $22.50 to $30 per week, producers are made better off as a result of the quota. Finally, overall economic surplus falls as a result of the quota, so economists would say that society as a whole is worse off as a result of the restriction. The deadweight loss is equal to triangle ABE in Figure 4.7.

Why would a society enact policies like price floors, price ceilings, or quotas that generate deadweight losses? Most often, the policies result from political pressure from the groups who gain producer or consumer surplus from the policies. In our tutoring market examples, consumer surplus increased when a price ceiling was imposed on the tutoring market, and producer surplus was increased by the quota on tutoring services. Groups that realize a net gain from price ceilings, price floors, or quotas have an incentive to pressure their government representatives to put these policies in place.

SUMMARY

Voluntary trades between buyers and sellers in markets generate benefits for both trading parties. Consumer surplus represents the net benefits that buyers receive when they obtain a good or service for less than they are willing to pay for it. Producer surplus represents the profits that producers earn when they sell a good at a price above its cost of production. Economic surplus is the sum of producer and consumer surplus. When markets operate at equilibrium, economic surplus is maximized and the marginal benefit obtained from a good or service is equal to its marginal cost of production. Economic surplus can be viewed as a benchmark measure of economic welfare or well-being, and we can measure changes in economic surplus as indicators of changes in social welfare resulting from government policies like price floors, price ceilings, or quotas. We also use the concept of economic surplus to help us assess who bears the costs or reaps the benefits of government restrictions on market activities. Because restrictions on market activity generate deadweight losses and tend to benefit some groups at the expense of others, they are highly controversial.

KEY CONCEPTS

- Consumer surplus
- Producer surplus
- Economic surplus
- Deadweight loss
- Price ceiling
- Price floor
- Quota

DISCUSSION QUESTIONS AND PROBLEMS

1. The following table shows the demand and supply of boxed lunch meals per day at a small local restaurant.

Boxed Lunches Per Day		
Q^S	P	Q^D
0	0	20
0	1	18
4	2	16
8	3	14
12	4	12
16	5	10
20	6	8
24	7	6
28	8	4
32	9	2
36	10	0

   a. Graph the demand and supply curves.
   b. Compute consumer surplus, producer surplus, and economic surplus at equilibrium.
   c. What is the marginal consumer's willingness to pay for the fourth unit of the good? What is the minimum price that the marginal producer would be willing to accept for the fourth unit of the good?
   d. Suppose a price ceiling of $3 per lunch is imposed on this market. What will be the quantity supplied, quantity demanded, market surplus or shortage, and amount of the good traded under this restriction? Compute the consumer surplus, producer surplus, and deadweight loss associated with this restriction.
   e. Suppose a price floor of $6 per lunch is imposed on this market. What will be the quantity supplied, quantity demanded, market surplus or shortage and amount of the good traded under this restriction? Compute the consumer surplus, producer surplus, and deadweight loss associated with this restriction.

2. Using the table in Problem 1, suppose the demand for boxed lunches falls such that Q^D is reduced by six lunches per day at each price.
   a. Describe two factors that could generate this change in demand.
   b. What is the new equilibrium price and quantity? What is the new value of economic surplus at this equilibrium?
3. The online auction site eBay allows buyers to enter a beginning bid on an item and then automatically increment their bids upward to some maximum bid level. Sellers are allowed to enter a minimum price that they will accept for their items, called a reserve price, below which the item will not be sold. Use the concepts of producer and consumer surplus to explain why this setup is attractive to buyers and sellers. Why does eBay promise that it will not reveal the seller's reserve price or the buyer's maximum bid to other users?
4. Suppose that a supplier of a good knew every customer's willingness to pay for the good. Would it be possible for buyers to obtain consumer surplus in this market? Why or why not?

MULTIPLE CHOICE QUESTIONS

1. On Friday night you dream about eating donuts with chocolate frosting and sprinkles. You wake up Saturday morning with a deep hunger for donuts with chocolate frosting and sprinkles, so you head down to Granny's Gourmet Donuts and see that each chocolate frosted sprinkled donut costs $0.50. You're willing to pay $5 for your first donut. You eat it, but you want more. So you pay another $0.50 for a second donut (which you would have been willing to pay $2 for). Two donuts still aren't enough, so you pay $0.50 for a third donut (exactly

the amount you are willing to pay for it). Assuming that Granny's Gourmet Donuts has an upward-sloping supply curve, which of the following is true?

a. You got a smaller amount of consumer surplus for each additional donut eaten Saturday morning.
b. You got the same amount of consumer surplus for each donut (otherwise you wouldn't have kept eating them).
c. Granny's Gourmet Donuts received a larger amount of producer surplus per donut for each donut you bought.
d. Granny's Gourmet Donuts received a smaller amount of producer surplus for each donut you bought.
e. Both a and d

2. You have a love of cinnamon bear gummies and are willing to pay $2.00/lb for them. The equilibrium price of cinnamon bear gummies is $2.25. Will you consume cinnamon bear gummies?

a. Yes
b. No
c. Not enough information
d. All of the above

3. You have a love of cinnamon bear gummies and are willing to pay of $2.00/lb for them. The equilibrium price of cinnamon gummies is $2.25. Which of the following could generate a price where you would buy cinnamon bear gummies?

a. An increase in supply
b. A decrease in supply
c. A decrease in market demand
d. Both a and c
e. Both b and c

4. When economic policies such as price floors or price ceilings generate nonequilibrium prices, which of the following can occur?

a. Market surplus
b. Market shortage
c. Deadweight loss
d. All of the above

5. Orangeland has a lot of orange groves and a high demand for oranges. Which of the following scenarios would make it difficult to find oranges in local Orangeland stores?

a. The government sets a price ceiling above equilibrium price.
b. The government sets a price ceiling below equilibrium price.
c. The government sets a price floor above equilibrium price.
d. The government sets a price floor below equilibrium price.

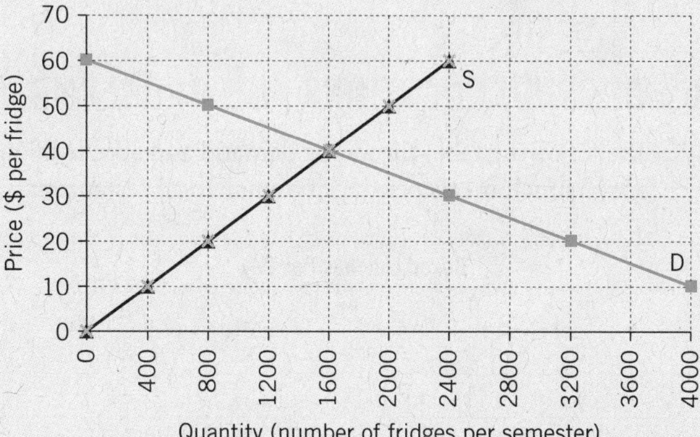

6. The accompanying graph shows the demand and supply of dorm-room-sized fridges sold in Collegetown per semester. At equilibrium, producer surplus is ______ per semester.

a. ½ * 1600 * $60 = $48,000
b. ½ * 1600 * $20 = $16,000
c. ½ * 1600 * $40 = $32,000
d. $40 * 1600 = $64,000
e. Unknown, since the price of fridges is unknown

7. The graph shows the demand and supply of dorm-room-sized fridges sold in Collegetown per semester. Suppose that the price is initially $50 each. At this price ___ fridges would be sold per semester. As the market adjusts to equilibrium, the quantity of fridges sold will ___ and the price will ____.

a. 2000; fall; fall
b. 800; fall; fall
c. 2000; fall; rise
d. 800; rise; rise
e. 800; rise; fall

8. The graph shows the demand and supply of dorm-room-sized fridges sold in Collegetown per semester. If the cost of shipping fridges to Collegetown falls, a possible new equilibrium price and quantity of fridges could be

a. P = $50; Q = 800.
b. P = $50; Q = 2000.

c. P = $40; Q = 1600.
d. P = $30; Q = 1200.
e. P = $30; Q = 2400.

9. The graph shows the demand and supply of dorm-room-sized fridges sold in Collegetown per semester. Given this information, the maximum amount that consumers are willing to pay for the 800th fridge per semester is _____.

a. $20.
b. $50.
c. $50 − $20 = $30.
d. $50 − $40 = $10.
e. Unknown, since the price of fridges is unknown.

10. The graph shows the demand and supply of dorm-room-sized fridges sold in Collegetown per semester. At equilibrium, consumer surplus is _____ per semester.

a. ½ * 1600 * $60 = $48,000
b. ½ * 1600 * $20 = $16,000
c. ½ * 1600 * $40 = $32,000
d. $40 * 1600 = $64,000
e. Unknown, since the price of fridges is unknown

ADDITIONAL READINGS AND WEB RESOURCES

Harford, Tim. (2005) *The Undercover Economist,* Oxford University Press.

Presents easily readable applications of economic theory, including why Starbucks prices its coffee the way it does, how used car markets work, and many other examples of gains from trade.

www.ebay.com

The Help menu presents a through explanation of the reserve price auction and the automatic bid increment process.

Landsburg, Steven "Taken to the Cleaners?," *Slate Magazine,* 7/3/1998. http://www.slate.com/id/2050/

Presents a discussion of the practice of price discrimination, the practice of sellers charging different prices to different consumers to extract the maximum consumer surplus possible.

© Katja Bone/iStockphoto

5 Elasticity

After studying this chapter, you should be able to:

- Define elasticity
- Classify elasticity values into inelastic and elastic categories
- Use the elasticity coefficient to assess the price elasticity of demand
- Assess the relationship between elasticity and total revenue
- Describe the factors that determine the price elasticity of demand

In many towns, the pet adoption fees charged by the local animal shelter are set by county commissioners. At a recent county commission meeting on the adoption fee issue in one town, the commissioners and the animal shelter workers were at odds. In the face of rising costs to run the shelter, the county commissioners proposed an increase in pet adoption fees. The commissioners argued that the fee increase was necessary in order to raise revenue at the shelter. Critics of the plan worried that the fee increase might decrease adoptions enough to actually lower the shelter's revenue. Who was right?

Suppose that you are the manager in charge of the men's shirt section of your locally owned clothing store. Your boss has told you that you need to increase revenues for your section, either by putting items on sale or by raising the amount that you mark up the prices. You understand that if you lower prices you'll sell more shirts. On the other hand, if you raise prices you'll earn more money per shirt sold. Should you raise prices or lower prices in order to increase revenues?

Research has shown that sales of gasoline do not change by very much when the price of gasoline rises. When gasoline prices go up, people tend to grumble about it, but they don't change their purchases of gasoline by very much, at least initially. Does the law of demand hold for gasoline purchases?

Finding the answers to these questions depends on understanding how much consumers respond to changes in the prices of goods and services. Elasticity is the concept economists use to assess this responsiveness.

WHAT IS ELASTICITY?

We learned in Chapter 3 that changes in the prices of goods or services cause changes in the quantity of those goods and services demanded and supplied. The law of demand asserts that, all else equal, when the price of a good rises, the quantity demanded of that good falls. The law of supply asserts that when the price of a good rises, the quantity supplied of that good rises, ceteris paribus. The concept of elasticity takes these laws one step further to assess *how large* changes in quantity demanded or supplied are. Elasticity helps us assess how responsive consumers or suppliers are to changes in the prices of goods or services.

Elasticity is a measure of responsiveness between any two variables. In the demand model, the **price elasticity of demand** measures how responsive quantity demanded is to a change in a good's price, ceteris paribus. In the supply model, the price elasticity of supply measures how responsive quantity supplied is to a change in a good's price. In this chapter we focus our discussion on the price elasticity of demand.

Elasticity is a measure of responsiveness between any two variables.

The price elasticity of demand measures the responsiveness of quantity demanded to changes in price.

"Wait a minute," you might be thinking, "we can already tell how much quantity demanded changes when the price of a good changes by looking at the demand curve. We did this when we looked at the demand for bread in Chapter 3. Why do we need a new measure?" This is a good question. An example can illustrate why using numerical changes in price and quantity demand—for example, a $1 change in price or a 1 loaf change in the quantity of bread demanded—does not provide a very useful measure of consumer responsiveness.

Suppose we are interested in two goods, gasoline and flat screen TVs. Suppose also that a price increase in gasoline from $3.00 per gallon to $3.75 per gallon causes a 10 million gallon decrease in quantity demanded per year. An increase in the price of flat screen TVs from $400 to $500 also causes a 10 million unit decrease in quantity demanded per year. Are these price and quantity changes big? Are consumers' responses to these price changes big or small?

If we just look at the raw numbers, the price of gasoline increased by 75 cents per gallon, while the price of TVs increased by $100 each. Although you might be tempted to say that the price increase in TVs was big and the price increase in gasoline was small, this would ignore the fact that the initial prices for the goods were vastly different. In fact, in both cases the price change represents a 25 percent price increase. Similarly, although the quantity demanded for both goods falls by the same numerical amount (10 million units) in response to the price increase, the relative sizes of these changes are very different. U.S. consumers buy about 140 billion gallons of gasoline each year, so a 10 million gallon decrease is a very small change in quantity demanded, only 0.007 percent of yearly sales. Sales of flat screen TVs are about 30 million units per year, so a 10 million unit decrease represents about 33 percent of total sales. The same percentage increase in price generates a relatively small percent change in the quantity of gasoline demanded, but a relatively large percent change in the quantity of flat screen TVs demanded. If we had just used the raw quantity changes, we would not see this difference.

The price elasticity of demand measures how quantity demanded responds to changes in price, but uses percentage changes rather than raw numerical changes. Percentage changes provide a consistent measure that we can compare across different variables such as price and quantity. Using percentage changes also allows us to compare responses across goods that are measured in different units, like gallons of gasoline and numbers of TVs.

CATEGORIES OF ELASTICITY

In the preceding example, when the price of TVs increased by 25 percent, consumers responded by reducing the quantity of TVs they demanded by 33 percent. When the price of gasoline increased by 25 percent, consumers reduced their quantity of gasoline demanded by only 0.007 percent. In other words, consumers were more responsive to the change in the price of TVs than they were to the change in the price of gasoline. Economists categorize the price elasticity of demand into two broad categories to describe the different levels of consumer responsiveness to changes in goods' prices: elastic demand and inelastic demand.

Elastic Demand and Inelastic Demand

Elastic demand: When a given percent change in the price of a good causes a larger percent change in the quantity demanded of the good.

When consumers respond to a change in the price of a good by changing their quantity demanded of the good by a relatively large amount, consumers have **elastic demand** for the good. In our example, consumers' demand for TVs is elastic because the 25 percent change in the price of TVs caused a relatively larger 33 percent change in the quantity of TVs demanded. When consumers have elastic demand for a good, they are relatively responsive to changes in that good's price, so that a given percent change in the good's price causes a larger percent change in the good's quantity demanded.

Inelastic demand: When a given percent change in the price of a good causes a smaller percent change in the quantity demanded of the good.

When consumers respond to a change in the price of a good by changing their quantity demanded by a relatively small amount, consumers have **inelastic demand** for the good. When consumers have inelastic demand for a good, they are relatively unresponsive to changes in that good's price. In our example, consumers' demand for gasoline is inelastic because the 25 percent change in the price of gasoline caused a relatively smaller 0.007 percent change in the quantity of gasoline demanded. When demand is inelastic, a given percent change in the good's price causes a smaller percent change in the good's quantity demanded.

Why the terms "elastic" and "inelastic"? It is helpful to translate the economic concept of elasticity into its physical sciences counterpart. When an object has elasticity in the physical sense, it changes shape when it is put under physical strain, the way a balloon collapses inward when you push on it with your hand. When an object is inelastic or lacks elasticity, it does not dramatically change shape when it is acted on by an outside force, the same way it takes lots of pressure to bend the cover of a hardcover book when you push on it with your hands.

Applying the physical science analogy to the elasticity of demand, if we imagine a change in the price of a good as the physical force acting on an object and the resulting change quantity demanded for the good as the object's response to the physical force, then elastic demand is like the balloon, since quantity demanded changes substantially in response to a change in the price of the good. Similarly, inelastic demand is like the hardcover book, since quantity demanded does not change by much in response to a change in the price of the good.

Perfectly Inelastic Demand, Perfectly Elastic Demand, and Unit Elastic Demand

Within the elastic and inelastic categories of elasticity are three important subcategories that represent the special cases of consumer responsiveness to price changes: perfectly inelastic demand, perfectly elastic demand, and unit elastic demand.

Perfectly Inelastic Demand

For some goods, quantity demanded does not respond at all when the price of the good changes, just like a rock's shape does not respond at all when we push on it. These goods have **perfectly inelastic demand**. For goods that have perfectly inelastic demand, changes in the price of the good do not cause changes in the quantity of the good demanded. When the demand for a good is perfectly inelastic, the demand curve is vertical, as in Figure 5.1. In Figure 5.1, changes in the price of the good do not generate any change in the quantity of the good demanded. Goods with perfectly inelastic demand are very rare. One could argue that drugs like insulin have perfectly inelastic demand because diabetics who take insulin have no choice but to take insulin as prescribed, regardless of insulin's price. At the same time, however, increases in the price on insulin could mean that some diabetics cannot afford it, which would decrease quantity demanded so that the demand curve is not perfectly inelastic.

Perfectly Inelastic Demand: The extreme subcategory of inelastic demand that describes the situation where quantity demanded does not change in response to a price change.

Figure 5.1 **Perfectly Inelastic Demand**

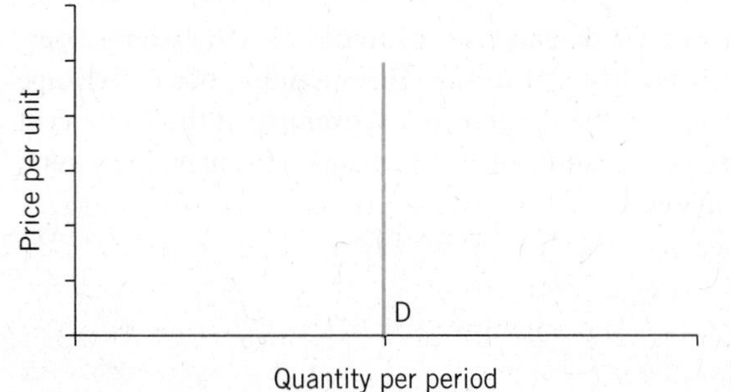

When demand is perfectly inelastic, the demand curve is a vertical line. In this case, changes in P do not generate changes in Q^D.

Perfectly Elastic Demand

At the other extreme of price elasticity is the case of the horizontal demand curve, as shown in Figure 5.2. When goods have a horizontal demand curve, they are classified to have **perfectly elastic demand.** In Figure 5.2, the price does not change along the demand curve D. If the price of the good increased, quantity demanded would fall to zero. If the price of the good fell, quantity demanded would be infinite. Because any change in price generates a change in quantity demanded that is the largest change possible, the change in quantity demanded in response to a price change is effectively infinite when demand is perfectly elastic.

Perfectly Elastic Demand: The extreme subcategory of elastic demand that describes the situation where quantity demanded changes by an infinite amount in response to a price change.

Firms that operate in markets that are very competitive, with lots of sellers of the same good, can be viewed as facing perfectly elastic demand for their product.

Figure 5.2 **Perfectly Elastic Demand**

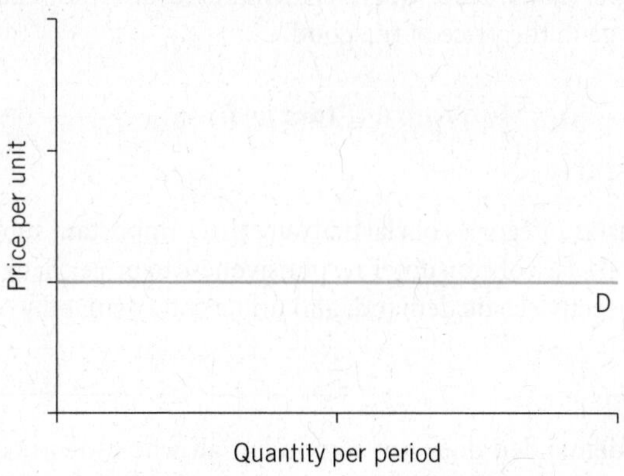

When demand is perfectly elastic, the demand curve is a horizontal line. In this case, any change in P would generate an infinitely large change in Q^D.

Think about egg production. For most consumers, eggs are pretty much the same regardless of which firms produce them, and it is easy for consumers to substitute among different brands of eggs in the supermarket. At the same time, there are lots of egg producers in the country competing for customers. This competitive situation implies that if one egg producer tries to raise the price of his eggs above the price charged by other producers, his consumers will simply shift their egg purchases to another brand. As a result, the quantity of eggs demanded from a high-price producer will fall to zero.

Unit Elastic Demand: When a given percent change in the price of a good causes an equal size percent change in the quantity of the good demanded.

Unit Elastic Demand

A final category of the price elasticity of demand is the unique situation where a percent change in a good's price is exactly equal to the corresponding percent change in quantity demanded for the good. In the flat screen TV example, if the 25 percent increase in the price of TVs caused the quantity of TVs demanded to fall by 25 percent, the demand for TVs would be unit elastic.

THE ELASTICITY COEFFICIENT

We can use the price elasticity of demand to assess the impact that changes in the price of a good have on the resulting changes in the quantity of the good demanded. Rather than comparing two numbers (the percent change in quantity demanded and the percent change in price) every time we want to assess consumers' responsiveness to price changes, we can use the **elasticity coefficient** (E) to indicate whether demand is elastic or inelastic. The elasticity coefficient is the percent change in quantity demanded divided by the percentage change in price. Using the delta symbol (Δ) as shorthand for "change in," the elasticity coefficient can be written as:

$$\text{Elasticity Coefficient} = E = \frac{\%\Delta Q^D}{\%\Delta P} = \frac{\text{percentage change in quantity demanded}}{\text{percentage change in price}}$$

In our original TV example, price increased by 25 percent and quantity demanded fell by 33 percent, so the elasticity coefficient is:

$$E = \frac{-33}{25} = -1.32$$

The elasticity coefficient tells us the percent change in quantity demanded that will result from a 1 percent change in the good's price. Since a 25 percent increase in the price of TVs caused a 33 percent decrease in the quantity of TVs demanded, a 1 percent increase in the price of TVs would cause a 1.32 percent decrease in the quantity of TVs demanded. Alternatively, a 1 percent decrease in the price of TVs would cause a 1.32 percent increase in the quantity of TVs demanded. Because the percent change in the price of TVs was smaller than the resulting percent change in quantity demanded, TVs would be classified as having elastic demand.

THINK FOR YOURSELF

Using the elasticity coefficient of –1.32, how much would the quantity of TVs demanded change if the price of TVs rose by 10 percent? How much would the quantity of TVs demanded change if the price of TVs fell by 20 percent?

The price of gasoline increased by 25 percent in our example, which caused the quantity of gasoline demanded to fall by 0.007 percent. The elasticity coefficient associated with this price and quantity change is:

$$E = \frac{-0.007}{25} = -0.0003$$

The 25 percent increase in the price of gasoline caused a 0.007 percent change in the quantity of gasoline demanded. The elasticity coefficient for this change implies that a 1 percent increase in the price of gasoline would cause a 0.0003 percent fall in the quantity of gasoline demanded. If the price of gasoline instead fell by 1 percent, the quantity of gasoline demanded would rise by 0.0003 percent. Because the percent change in the price of gasoline was greater than the resulting percent change in the quantity of gasoline demanded, gasoline would be classified as having inelastic demand.

The law of demand tells us that an increase in the price of a good (a positive percentage change in price) will cause a decrease in the quantity of the good demanded (a negative percentage change in quantity demanded). Alternatively, a decrease in the price of a good (a negative percent change in the good's price) will cause an increase in the quantity of the good demanded (a positive percent change in quantity demanded). Since the elasticity coefficient is the ratio of the $\%\Delta Q^D$ over the $\%\Delta P$, the law of demand implies that the elasticity coefficient will always be negative (or zero if demand is perfectly inelastic).

When we use the elasticity coefficient, we are primarily concerned with the relative sizes of the changes in price and quantity demanded, not with whether the changes are positive or negative. To compare magnitude of price and quantity demanded changes while ignoring whether they are positive or negative, we can use absolute values. The absolute value of a number is its value without regard to its sign. For example, the absolute value of −5 is 5 and the absolute value of +5 is also 5. The absolute value of a −25 percent change in price (a fall in price by 25 percent) is 25 percent. Similarly, the absolute value of a 25 percent increase in price is 25 percent. Vertical bars (| |) are placed around numbers to indicate absolute value.

When demand is elastic, the absolute value of the numerator of the elasticity coefficient, $|\%\Delta Q^D|$, will be greater than the absolute value of the denominator of the elasticity coefficient, $|\%\Delta P|$. When the numerator of a fraction is greater than the denominator of a fraction, the fraction's value is greater than 1. Correspondingly, when demand is elastic, the absolute value of the elasticity coefficient is greater than 1 ($|E| > 1$. When demand is inelastic, the absolute value of the elasticity coefficient is less than 1 ($|E| < 1$) because the numerator of E will be smaller than the denominator of E.

Table 5.1 summarizes all the possible price elasticity of demand coefficient values. When the demand for a good is inelastic, as it is for gasoline, consumers are relatively unresponsive to changes in the good's price. Consumers respond to a change in the price of a good by changing their quantity demanded by a relatively smaller amount, so $|\%\Delta Q^D| < |\%\Delta P|$ and $|E| < 1$. In the extreme case of perfectly inelastic demand, consumers do not change their quantity demanded at all when the good's price changes, so $|E| = 0$. When demand for a good is elastic, as it is for TVs, consumers are relatively responsive to changes in the price of the good, so $|\%\Delta Q^D| > |\%\Delta P|$ and $|E| > 1$. In the extreme case where demand is perfectly elastic, price does not change, so $|\%\Delta P| = 0$ and $|E| = \infty$. Finally, in the rare case where demand is unit elastic, the elasticity coefficient is equal to 1 in absolute value because the percent change in quantity demanded is equal to the percent change in price.

Table 5.1 Summary of Elasticity Coefficient Values

Inelastic Demand		Unit Elastic Demand	Elastic Demand	
Perfectly Inelastic	***Inelastic***		***Elastic***	***Perfectly Elastic***
$|\%\Delta Q^D| = 0$	$|\%\Delta Q^D| < |\%\Delta P|$	$|\%\Delta Q^D| = |\%\Delta P|$	$|\%\Delta Q^D| > |\%\Delta P|$	$|\%\Delta P| = 0$
$|E| = 0$	$|E| < 1$	$|E| = 1$	$|E| > 1$	$|E| = \infty$

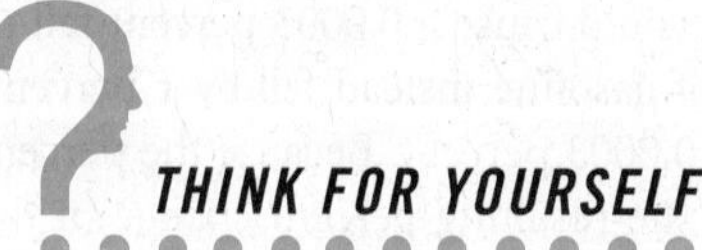

THINK FOR YOURSELF

Compute the elasticity coefficient for TVs if quantity demanded falls by 10 percent when price increases by 25 percent. Given your elasticity coefficient, how much would quantity demanded change if the price increases by 1 percent? Is the demand for TVs elastic or inelastic in this case?

ELASTICITY AND TOTAL REVENUE

We can now use the concept of elasticity to answer the questions raised in the scenarios described at the beginning of this chapter. In the first scenario, the opposing sides argued about whether the best way to raise money for the animal shelter was to

Total Revenue (TR) is the amount of money earned when a supplier sells a given quantity of a good.

increase or decrease the price of adoptions. The key to resolving this argument lies in understanding the relationship between elasticity and **total revenue.**

Total revenue (TR) is the amount of money earned when a supplier sells a given quantity of a good. Total revenue is equal to the price of the good multiplied by the quantity of the good sold. If you are selling shirts at P = $50 and you sell 20 shirts per day, your total revenue from selling shirts will be

TR = $50/shirt * 20 shirts/day = $100/day

TR = P * Q

By examining the calculation for total revenue, TR = P * Q, and also remembering that the law of demand implies an inverse relationship between price and quantity demanded, we can conclude that changes in price and quantity demand have opposing effects on total revenue. In the case of the animal adoption fee debate, the opposing effects of price and quantity demanded are what gave rise to the arguments about whether increasing or decreasing the price of adoptions would increase total revenues at the animal shelter. On the one hand, an increase in price causes total revenue to increase. On the other hand, the corresponding decrease in quantity demanded causes total revenue to fall. Similarly, a decrease in price causes total revenue to fall, but the corresponding increase in quantity demanded causes total revenue to rise. The net impact of a price change on total revenue depends on whether the price change is larger or smaller than the resulting change in quantity demanded. The elasticity of demand tells us just that.

Suppose that the adoption fee at the animal shelter is currently $15 and the quantity of animals adopted is 100 per week. Total revenue from adoptions at the shelter is

TR = $15/adoption * 100 adoptions/week = $1,500/week.

Now suppose that the adoption fee is increased to $25. What will happen to total revenue? It depends on whether demand is elastic or inelastic. If demand is elastic, consumers are relatively responsive to the higher adoption fee. Suppose consumers decrease their quantity demanded by half, to Q = 50 adoptions per week. In this case, total revenue would be

TR = $25/adoption * 50 adoptions/week = $1,250/week

When demand is elastic, the percent increase in price, which increases TR, is more than offset by the percent decrease in quantity demanded, which decreases TR. As a result, total revenue falls from $1,500 to $1,250 per week.

If demand is inelastic, consumers are not very responsive to the higher adoption fee. Suppose consumers reduce their quantity demanded by only 10 animals per week, to Q = 90 per week. The resulting total revenue would be

TR = $25/adoption * 90 adoptions/week = $2,250/week

When demand is inelastic, the percent increase in price is larger than the percent decrease in quantity demanded, and total revenue rises from $1,500 to $2,250 per week.

So who is right in the case of the animal shelter? If the demand for adoptions at the animal shelter is inelastic, the county commissioners who wanted to increase the adoptions fee would be right because raising prices would increase the total revenue of the shelter. If the demand for adoptions at the animal shelter is elastic, the workers who opposed the fee increase would be right because raising prices would reduce total revenue at the shelter.

THINK FOR YOURSELF

Suppose that the price of adoptions was reduced from $15 to $10. What category of demand (elastic or inelastic) would generate an increase in total revenue as a result of this price change? What category of demand would generate a decrease in total revenue as a result of this price change? What would happen to total revenue if demand were unit elastic?

In the second scenario described in the chapter introduction, your job as manager of the men's shirt section of a clothing store meant that you had to decide whether to increase or decrease the price of men's shirts. If the demand for men's shirts at your store is elastic, decreasing the price of shirts would increase total revenues for the store. Alternatively, if the demand for men's shirts is inelastic, you could increase total revenues for the store by increasing the price of men's shirts.

Table 5.2 summarizes the relationship between elasticity and total revenue. The case of inelastic demand is summarized in the first column of the table. When demand is inelastic, price changes are larger than quantity changes in percentage terms so any change in price generates a change in total revenue in the same direction. When demand is inelastic, a decrease in price causes an increase in quantity demanded, but a decrease in total revenue. This is expressed in shorthand in the table by ↓P→ ↑Q → ↓TR. When demand is inelastic, an increase in price causes an increase in total revenue.

Table 5.2 The Relationship Between Elasticity and Total Revenue

Inelastic Demand		*Elastic Demand*	
$|\%\Delta P| > |\%\Delta Q^D|$		$|\%\Delta P| < |\%\Delta Q^D|$	
↓P→ ↑Q → ↓TR	↑P→ ↓Q → ↑TR	↓P → ↑Q → ↑TR	↑P→ ↓Q → ↓TR

In the case of elastic demand, summarized in the second column of the table, price changes are smaller than quantity changes in percentage terms, so any change in price generates a change in total revenue in the opposite direction as the price change. When demand is elastic, a decrease in price causes an increase in total revenue, while an increase in price causes a decrease in total revenue.

THINK FOR YOURSELF

What do you think happens to total revenue in response to an increase in price if demand is unit elastic? What do you think happens to total revenue in response to a decrease in price if demand is unit elastic?

Understanding elasticity is very important to understanding and anticipating how policy changes will impact market outcomes. For example, when university administrators raise tuition in an attempt to increase revenues to the university, they are counting on their students having relatively inelastic demand for university courses. Policymakers often focus tax increases on goods like cigarettes or gasoline that have relatively inelastic demand because taxes on goods with inelastic demand will generate larger tax revenues than taxes on goods with elastic demand.

Francois Quesnay and the Impact of Taxes

Francois Quesnay (1694–1774) was a French economist whose 1758 book, *Tableau economique*, presented one of the first analytical discussions of the way economies work. Although many of Quesnay's ideas were refined by later economists, he was one of the first to discuss the relative impact of taxes on buyers and sellers. Economists now know that the burden of taxes does not depend on where the tax is imposed but instead depends in part on the elasticity of demand. When the demand for a good is inelastic, an increase in a tax on the good causes a large increase in the price of the good but only a small reduction on the quantity of the good demanded. In this case, consumers bear a large portion of the tax burden because the total spending on the good (the TR to suppliers) will rise. When the demand for a good is elastic, an increase in taxes causes total spending on the good to fall, and consumers bear a smaller portion of the tax burden.

Album / Oronoz/NewsCom

DETERMINANTS OF THE PRICE ELASTICITY OF DEMAND

Where does the price elasticity of demand come from? Why is the demand for some goods, like TVs, elastic and the demand for other goods, like gasoline, inelastic? These are questions about the determinants of the price elasticity of demand. There are four factors that impact the price elasticity of demand, discussed next.

The Availability of Substitutes

We learned about the consumer substitution effect in Chapter 3. The consumer substitution effect implies that, ceteris paribus, people respond to a higher price of one good by decreasing their quantity demanded of that good and substituting instead into goods whose prices have not changed. For example, you could respond to a higher price of bread by increasing the amount of bagels you buy. Because you can choose bagels (or croissants, or pitas, or tortillas), it is easy to respond to a price increase for bread by reducing the quantity of bread you demand and buying substitutes instead.

What about products with little or no substitutes available? There are very few substitutes for gasoline to power cars or insulin to help diabetics manage the disease. When the price of gasoline increases, consumers cannot easily respond by putting, say, milk or turpentine into their gas tanks. However, if consumers live in an area with public transportation, they could take the train or the bus as a substitute for gasoline. They could also choose to ride a bike or walk instead of driving. Even so, it is harder to substitute other goods for gasoline than it is to substitute bagels for bread. Because you can easily reduce the quantity of bread you demand when its price changes, the demand for bread will be relatively elastic compared to the demand for gasoline. Similarly, because it is difficult for diabetics to substitute into another drug when the price of insulin increases, the demand for insulin will be relatively inelastic compared to other goods.

THINK FOR YOURSELF

Public transportation is more widely available in urban areas than in rural areas. Ceteris paribus, who will have more inelastic demand for gasoline, those in rural communities or those in urban communities? Why?

Luxury versus Necessity Goods

For all of us, food and water are necessities. They are necessary for our survival. For most of us, however, foods like gourmet chocolates and designer bottled waters are luxuries. They are nice to have, but we could certainly survive without them. Do we respond differently when the prices of necessity and luxury goods rise? For necessities, our responses to price increases tend to be relatively small. When the price of food goes up, we can't very well cut our food consumption by much and still maintain our health. When the price of gourmet chocolates goes up, however, we can easily cut our quantity of gourmet chocolates demanded. All else equal, the demand for luxury goods is relatively elastic, while the demand for necessity goods is relatively inelastic. What makes something a luxury or a necessity? A good that is a luxury for one person may be a necessity for another person and vice versa. Because the classification of goods as luxuries or necessities is person-specific, economists use caution when comparing elasticity values across people.

The Length of Time Available to Adjust to a Price Change

We learned earlier that people tend to have relatively inelastic demand for gasoline. This stems in part because there are few substitutes for gasoline available. The price elasticity of demand for gasoline also depends on the amount of time people have to adjust to a change in the price of gasoline. For example, if when you went to bed you had an almost empty gas tank in your car, and then you woke up in the morning to find that the price of gasoline had risen by $2 per gallon, you would likely still put gasoline your car's tank because you need to get to work or school that day. Your immediate response to the price increase is very inelastic. However, if gasoline continues to cost $2 per gallon more than usual for several months or years, you might make more substantial changes in your driving behavior. You might organize a carpool or purchase a more fuel efficient car, each of which would reduce your quantity of gasoline demanded by more than it changed on the day after the price increase. As you have more time to adjust to any given price change, your response will be larger. For a given change in the price of a good, the price elasticity of demand will be more elastic over the long term than it is in the short term.

The Portion of Income Spent on the Good

You probably purchase a wide array of products in a given week or month. Some of these products, like food, tuition, gasoline, or rent, probably account for a large fraction of your income. Other products, like toothpicks, candy bars, or pencils, probably account for only a tiny fraction of your income. If the price of candy bars and the price of tuition both rose by 10 percent, for which good would your response be greater? Ceteris paribus, people tend be less responsive to price changes for items that account for only a small portion of their income. This is because increases in the price of goods that account for only a small portion of income don't tend to impact us as much as price changes for larger-budget goods. When tuition increases by 10 percent, you notice because tuition accounts for a large portion of your income. You might consider cutting back on the number of classes you take, attending a relatively cheaper university, or even dropping out. When the price of candy bars rises by 10 percent, you probably don't even notice since candy bars are small-budget items for most people. The price elasticity of demand tends to be larger for goods that make up a larger portion of people's incomes.

Be careful here. It is tempting to say, "Rent and tuition are necessities, that is why I spend so much money on them and their demand is more elastic." This thinking violates the ceteris paribus assumption. It is true that for many people rent and tuition are necessities, which would make their demand more inelastic relative to luxuries. However, even among goods that are necessities, those that account for larger portions of people's income tend to have more elastic demand than those for which the portion of income spent on them is small.

SUMMARY

In this chapter, we learned about the elasticity of demand, which measures how responsive consumers are to changes in the prices of goods and services. When changes in quantity demanded are relatively large in response to price changes, demand is elastic. When changes in quantity demanded are relatively small in response to price changes, demand is inelastic. Goods with few substitutes and goods that are necessities have relatively inelastic demand. Demand tends to be more elastic for goods when consumers have more time to adjust to price changes and when consumers spend larger fractions of their incomes on the goods.

How total revenue responds to price changes is influenced by the elasticity of demand. When the demand for a good is inelastic, sellers can increase total revenue by increasing the price of the good. When demand is elastic, sellers can increase total revenue by decreasing the price of the good.

KEY CONCEPTS

- Elasticity
- Price elasticity of demand
- Elastic demand
- Inelastic demand
- Perfectly inelastic demand
- Perfectly elastic demand
- Unit elastic demand
- Elasticity coefficient
- Total revenue

DISCUSSION QUESTIONS AND PROBLEMS

1. Suppose that the adoption fee at the animal shelter is initially $15.00 and the average number of animals adopted per week at that price is 100. In the face of rising costs, there is an increase in the pet adoption fees at the animal shelter from $15.00 to $22.50 (a 50 percent price increase). Proponents of the increase argue that it is necessary to raise revenues for the shelter. Critics of the plan worry that the fee increase might decrease adoptions enough to actually lower shelter revenues.
   a. What is the revenue earned by the shelter for animal adoptions before the fee increase?
   b. Suppose animal adoptions fall by 10 percent in response to the 50 percent fee increase (to 90 animals per week). What is the new level of total revenue earned from adoptions? What is the value of the elasticity coefficient for this price and quantity change? Is demand elastic or inelastic?
   c. Now suppose animal adoptions fall by 60 percent in response to the 50 percent fee increase (to 40 animals per week). What is the new level of total revenue earned from adoptions? What is the value of the elasticity coefficient for this price and quantity change? Is demand elastic or inelastic?
   d. Besides price, describe a factor that could influence the elasticity of demand for animals from the animal shelter.
2. Describe the relationship between price and total revenue when demand is elastic (when price rises and demand is elastic, what happens to total revenue?) Describe the relationship between price and total revenue when demand is inelastic.
3. For each of the choices (a–d) below, decide whether the choice is correct or incorrect and explain why. Ceteris paribus, a given decrease in the supply of a good will generate a larger decrease in the equilibrium quantity of the good traded when
   a. demand is perfectly inelastic.
   b. demand is relatively inelastic.
   c. demand is relatively elastic.
   d. demand increases at the same time that supply decreases.
4. If the demand for milk is inelastic, will a small reduction in the supply of milk result in an increase or a decrease in the total revenue earned by milk suppliers? Why?

MULTIPLE CHOICE QUESTIONS

1. Ceteris paribus, the demand for a product will be relatively elastic if
   a. there are no close-substitute products available.
   b. spending on the product constitutes a very small portion of consumer income.
   c. the product is considered to be a luxury.
   d. the consumer has very little time to adjust to a price change.
2. Ceteris paribus, when the supply of beef increases, beef prices will rise by a greater amount
   a. when the demand for beef is elastic.
   b. when the demand for beef is inelastic.
   c. when the demand for beef is perfectly elastic.
   d. when the demand for beef is unit elastic.
3. Ceteris paribus, when the supply of beef increases, the quantity of beef traded will rise by a smaller amount
   a. when the demand for beef is elastic.
   b. when the demand for beef is inelastic.
   c. when the demand for beef is perfectly elastic.
   d. when the demand for beef is unit elastic.
4. If the demand for a good is relatively inelastic, an increase in the price of the good will generate
   a. an increase in quantity demanded for the good and an increase in total revenue.
   b. an increase in quantity demanded for the good and a decrease in total revenue.
   c. a decrease in quantity demanded for the good and an increase in total revenue.
   d. a decrease in quantity demanded for the good and a decrease in total revenue.
   e. a decrease in quantity supplied and an increase in quantity demanded.
5. Marianne loves cinnamon rolls. Marianne always buys one cinnamon roll each morning, even when the price of a cinnamon roll increased from $1.50 to $2.50. Marianne's demand for cinnamon rolls is
   a. relatively elastic.
   b. perfectly inelastic.
   c. illustrated by a horizontal demand curve.
   d. unit elastic.
   e. relatively inelastic.

6. When the price of flour was $10 per unit, total spending on flour was $100,000 per day. When the price of flour fell to $8 per unit, total spending on flour rose to $125,000 per day. In this price range, the demand for flour is
   a. perfectly inelastic.
   b. inelastic.
   c. elastic.
   d. unitary elastic.
   e. perfectly elastic.

7. The price elasticity of demand is a measure of the
   a. relative change in the demand curve in response to a change in price.
   b. responsiveness of demand to a change in the price of a substitute good.
   c. responsiveness of consumers to changes in their incomes.
   d. responsiveness of quantity demanded to a change in price.

8. When the price of ski lessons rises by 1 percent, the quantity of ski lessons demanded falls by 3 percent. This implies that the price elasticity of demand for ski lessons is
   a. −1/3, elastic.
   b. −1/3, inelastic.
   c. −3, elastic.
   d. −3, inelastic.
   e. none of the above.

9. Name-brand medicines have fewer close substitutes than do generics. This means that the price elasticity of demand for generics is _______ the price elasticity of demand for name-brand medicines.
   a. more elastic than
   b. less elastic then
   c. the same as
   d. unrelated to

10. The price of corn in Mexico has fallen more than 70 percent 1994, which some attribute to an increase in the supply of corn from the U.S. to Mexico. If the incomes of corn farmers in Mexico have fallen as a result of this price decrease, the elasticity of demand for corn in Mexico must be ___
    a. relatively elastic.
    b. relatively inelastic.
    c. perfectly elastic.
    d. unknown, since we don't know the price of corn.

Chapter 5 Appendix Elasticity and the Slope of Demand

Sometimes it is easier to understand the price elasticity of demand if we use a graphical approach. We learned in this chapter that perfectly inelastic demand is represented by a vertical line. When demand is perfectly inelastic, at each of the possible prices quantity demanded is constant and unchanging. At the other extreme, when demand is perfectly elastic, price does not change, and demand is represented by a horizontal line. There is a relationship between the slope of a demand curve and the price elasticity of demand. For a given change in price, a steeper demand curve reflects more inelastic demand than a flatter demand curve.

Let's use the demand for bread to illustrate this relationship. Panel A of Figure A5.1 shows a relatively flat demand curve, whereas Panel B shows a relatively steep demand curve. As we move from point A to point B along each of the demand curves, the price of bread falls by $1, from $8 to $7 per loaf. Along the flat demand curve in Panel A, the quantity of bread demanded changes by 1 loaf per day, from 2 to 3 loaves per day. Along the steep demand curve in Panel B, the quantity of bread demanded changes by 0.5 loaves per day, from 1 to 1.5 loaves per day. For the same $1 price change, the quantity demanded response is bigger along the flatter demand curve than on the steeper demand curve. Along the flat demand curve, quantity demanded changed by 1 loaf per day while on the steep demand curve quantity demanded changed by only 0.5 loaves per day. The quantity demanded is more responsive along the flat demand curve than on the steep demand curve, which means that demand is more elastic on the flat demand curve than on the steep demand curve.

As a general rule, for the same price change, steeper demand curves reflect more inelastic demand, while flatter demand curves reflect more elastic demand. At the extremes, the steepest possible demand curve is vertical and reflects perfectly inelastic demand. The flattest possible demand curve is horizontal and reflects perfectly elastic demand.

Although there is a relationship between the price elasticity of demand and the slope of the demand curve, we cannot conclude that steep curves always represent inelastic demand and flat curves always represent elastic demand. We can use the demand curve in Panel A of Figure A5.1 to demonstrate the difference between elasticity and slope. Figure A5.2 repeats the graph from Panel A of Figure A5.1 but illustrates several price changes instead of just one. When we move from point A to point

Figure A5.1 **Elasticity on Flat and Steep Demand Curves**

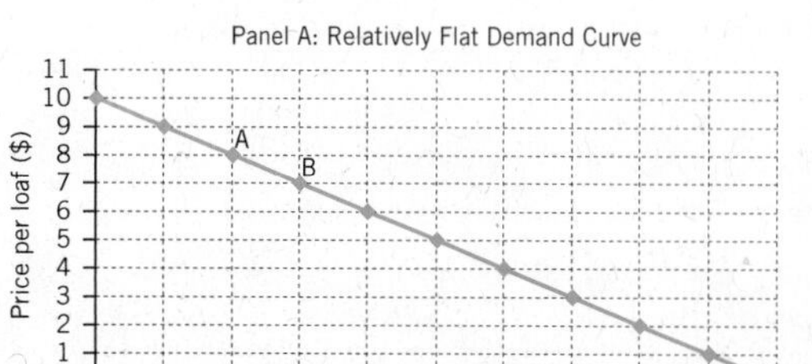

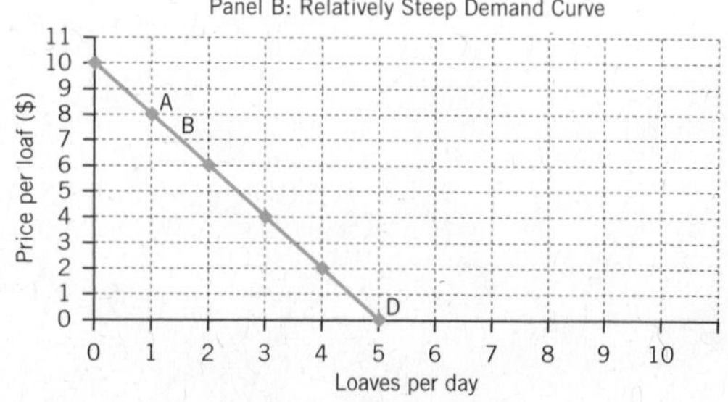

B in Figure A5.2, price changes by \$1, from P = \$9 to P = \$8, which is a roughly 11percent fall in price. In response to this price change, quantity demanded changes by 1 loaf per day, from $Q^D = 1$ to $Q^D = 2$, which is a 100 percent increase in quantity demanded. Based on the price and quantity demanded changes, as we move from point A to point B, the elasticity coefficient would be

$$E = 100/-11 = -9.1$$

Between point A and point B, each 1 percent change in price causes a 9.1 percent change in quantity demanded. Because the percent change in quantity demanded is larger than the percent change in price, demand is elastic between point A and point B.

Now consider the move from point E to point F in Figure A5.2. Price changes by \$1, from P = \$2 to P = \$1, which represents a 50 percent price decrease. In response, quantity demanded changes by 1 loaf per day, from $Q^D = 8$ to $Q^D = 9$, which is a roughly 12 percent increase. For this change in price

$$E = 12/-50 = -0.24.$$

Each 1 percent change in price between point E and point F causes a 0.24 percent change in quantity demanded. Because the percent change in quantity demanded is smaller than the percent change in price, demand is inelastic between point E and point F.

We obtain different elasticity coefficients as we move between different points along the demand curve in Figure A5.2. This happens along all linear demand curves. For points on the upper half of the linear demand curves, prices are relatively large, so movements from one point to another generate small percent changes in price. At the same time, quantity demanded is small, so movements from one point to another along the upper half of the linear demand curve cause large percent changes in quantity demanded. Between points on the lower half of linear demand curves, movements from one point to another cause large percent changes in price since price is small but cause small percent changes in quantity demanded because quantity demanded is large. In the middle of linear demand curves, demand switches from being elastic to inelastic. At the exact midpoint, demand is unit elastic.

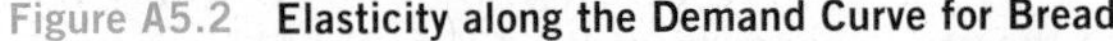

Figure A5.2 **Elasticity along the Demand Curve for Bread**

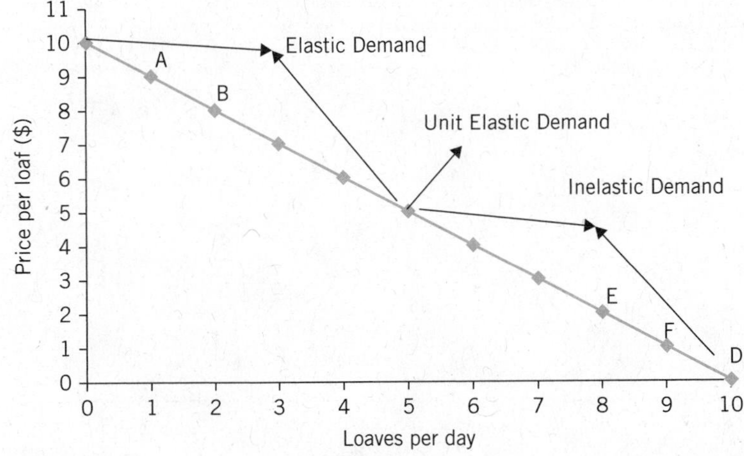

The elasticity of demand varies along a linear demand curve. Between points A and B, demand is elastic. Between points E and F, demand is inelastic.

DISCUSSION QUESTIONS AND PROBLEMS

Price ($ per TV)	Q^D (# TVs per semester)
250	0
200	10
150	20
100	30
50	40
0	50

1. The accompanying table illustrates the demand for TVs in a small college town.
   a. Compute total revenue at each of the P and Q^D combinations in the table.
   b. When price increases and demand is elastic, total revenue ___ (rises/falls).
   c. When price increases and demand is inelastic, total revenue ___ (rises/falls).
   d. When price decreases and demand is elastic, total revenue ___ (rises/falls).
   e. When price decreases and demand is inelastic, total revenue ___ (rises/falls).

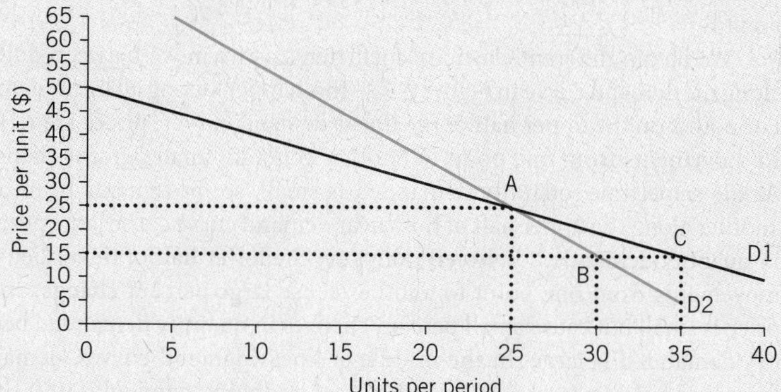

2. Which of the two demand curves in the accompanying graph (D1 or D2) has more elastic demand for the price change from P = $25 to P = $15 per unit? Why?

Fuse/Getty Images, Inc.

6

Measuring Economic Activity

After studying this chapter, you should be able to:

- Explain the circular flow model
- Define gross domestic product
- Describe differences in GDP across countries and time
- Describe what business cycles are and how they occur
- Illustrate the workings of the aggregate demand/aggregate supply model

As you have probably observed, economies are dynamic and in constant flux. The ongoing interactions between producers, sellers, transporters, and buyers of goods and services are continuously changing. Changes in expectations or incomes cause changes in demand for goods, and prices and quantities adjust. Changes in technology generate changes in supply, so prices and quantity adjust again. Interactions between workers and employers cause continuous adjustment in the labor market. Innovation and entrepreneurship, research and development, and international trade generate continuous ups and downs in economic activity. How does one keep track of it all? This chapter focuses on how economists measure economic activity.

THE CIRCULAR FLOW OF ECONOMIC ACTIVITY

Figure 6.1 presents a general model of the macroeconomy, gives an overview of the main sectors of the economy, and shows the flows of income and output between them. The model in Figure 6.1 is called the circular flow model because it illustrates that the exchange of resources and output between producers and consumers can be viewed as flows of products, inputs, and money between households and businesses.

Households are shown on the left side of the circular flow model. Households are the primary demanders of goods and services in the economy. They are also the primary suppliers of labor and other economic resources. Businesses are shown on the right side of the circular flow model. Business firms are the primary suppliers of output and the primary demanders of labor and other economic resources. The interactions between households and businesses take place in two types of markets: output markets and input markets.

The box at the top of Figure 6.1 represents the output markets in the economy. Output markets are where the food, cars, medical services, music downloads, books, and all the other goods and services produced in the economy are traded. In output markets, business firms are the suppliers of goods and services, and households are the demanders of goods and services. The interaction of demand and supply in output markets determines the quantity of goods and services sold in the economy and the prices at which the goods and services are traded. The outside arrows pointing away from households in the upper half of Figure 6.1 represent the flow of money spent on goods and services in output markets. The inner arrows pointing away from businesses in the upper half of Figure 6.1 represent the flow of goods and services from business firms to households.

Input markets are the other markets where trade between households and businesses take place. In input markets, businesses are the demanders of the land, labor, and capital inputs used to produce goods and services. Households are the suppliers of these inputs. The flows of resources and payments in input markets are represented in the bottom half of Figure 6.1. The outer arrows leading from households to businesses represent the trade of land, labor, and capital inputs. The inner arrows in the bottom half of Figure 6.1 represent the payments of rent, wages, and interest from businesses to households in exchange for inputs.

Figure 6.1 **Circular Flow Model**

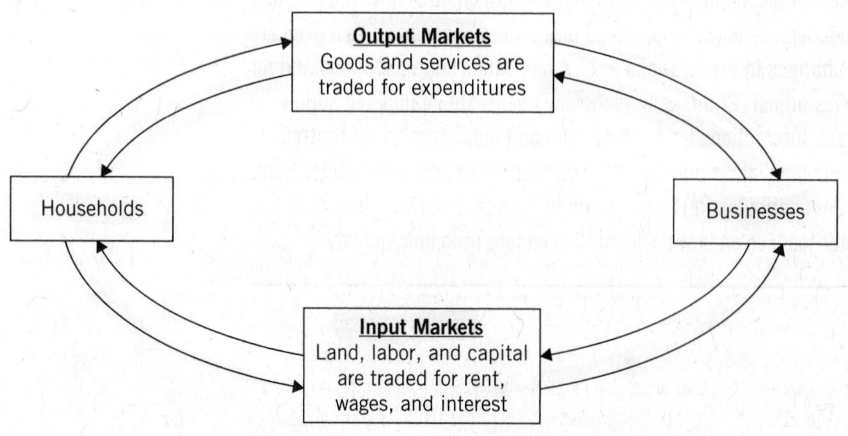

The circular flow model shows the movement of income and spending between households and businesses in the economy. In output markets, businesses trade goods and services for expenditures from households. In input markets, households trade their land, labor, and capital in exchange for income in the form of rent, wages, and interest.

THINK FOR YOURSELF

List three items that are traded in output markets. Who are the demanders and who are the suppliers in output markets? List three items that are traded in input markets. Who are the demanders and who are the suppliers in input markets?

Figure 6.1 represents a simple model of the economy, where households and businesses are the only entities that trade. When trades between households and businesses are the only exchanges taking place, the flows of income, resources, and products through the output and input markets capture all of the production and spending activity in the economy. If we wanted to measure how much production and trade are taking place in this economy, we could examine either the input markets or the output markets. Spending in input markets would provide a measure of all of the income that is being earned in the economy, whereas spending in output markets would provide a measure of all of the production that is taking place in the economy. In a simple economy like this, increases in income for households would cause increased spending on goods and services, and both the input and output markets would have increased levels of activity. Alternatively, if production slows down, firms will hire fewer inputs, and activity in input markets would decrease. In turn, households would have less income, which would be reflected by decreased demand for goods and services and reduced spending in output markets.

It is useful to think of the circular flow of income and spending as being like a bicycle tire. Air circulates around in the tire as the wheel spins, and the air pressure is similar at all the different points on the tire, just as the flow of income and spending is the same in either the input or output markets in the simple economy in Figure 6.1. If air is put into a bicycle tire, the tire will expand, just as increased income and production would expand the flow of economic activity between households and businesses. If air is let out of a bicycle tire, the air pressure will decrease. If income and production in an economy decrease, the amount of goods and services produced and incomes earned in the economy will shrink.

The economy depicted in Figure 6.1 is called a closed economy that has no government sector. A closed economy is one that does not engage in international trade. Most countries have open economies because they trade goods and services with other nations. In addition, most economies have a government that participates in the economy by buying goods and services and hiring employees to perform government work. Figure 6.2 depicts the circular flow model of a simple open economy with a government sector. To keep this figure from being cluttered, the sets of arrows from households and businesses to the input and output markets in Figure 6.1 have been replaced in Figure 6.2 with double-ended arrows. As before, these arrows represent the flows of goods and services and income.

The box in the middle of Figure 6.2 represents the government sector of the economy. The government is neither a household nor a business, but it shares characteristics with both. The government buys computers, tanks, office supplies, and an array of other goods and services in output markets. In this way, the government acts like a household because it is a demander of goods and services. The government acts like a business when it produces goods and services and sells them in output markets. For example, when the government supplies access to national parks in exchange for

Figure 6.2 **Circular Flow Model with Government and Foreign Sector**

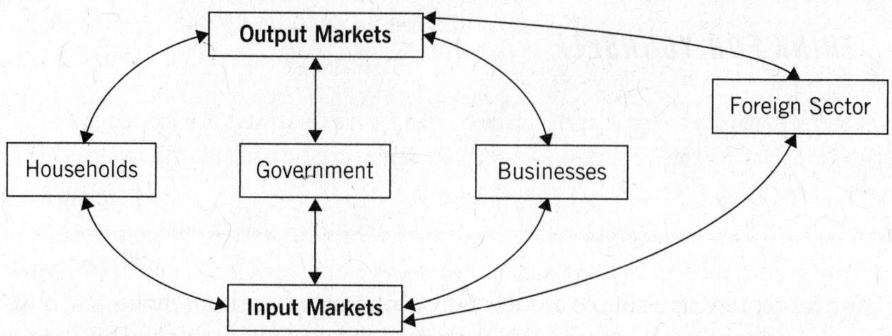

The government participates in input and output markets in the economy, as represented by the arrows between government and the output and input markets in the figure. The foreign sector buys outputs, called exports, from domestic producers and sells outputs, called imports, to domestic buyers. These flows are represented by the arrow between the foreign sector and the output markets. The foreign sector also buys and sells inputs in the economy, as illustrated by the arrow between input markets and the foreign sector.

entrance fees or provides higher education in exchange for tuition, it is acting like a supplier in output markets. The flow of goods and services and payments for goods and services is represented by the double-ended arrow between the government and output markets in Figure 6.2.

The government also participates in input markets in the economy. Government is a demander in input markets when it hires workers or buys land and capital. Government is a supplier in input markets when it sells or rents its resources to buyers. When the government sells permits for timber companies to harvest wood from national forests, for example, it is acting as a seller in input markets. The flow of inputs to the government and the payments for those inputs are represented by the double-ended arrow between government and input markets in Figure 6.2.

The foreign sector is also a participant in most economies. Foreign consumers buy U.S.-made goods and services in output markets, and foreign businesses sell their goods and services in U.S. output markets. The sale of goods and services to foreign buyers is called **exports**. The purchase of foreign-made goods and services by domestic buyers is called **imports**. Imports and exports are represented by the double-ended arrow between the output markets and the foreign sector in Figure 6.2. Foreign businesses and households also buy and sell resources in input markets, as illustrated by the double-ended arrow between the input markets and the foreign sector.

Exports are the sale of goods and services to foreign buyers.

Imports are the purchases of goods and services from foreign producers.

As was the case in the simple economy depicted in Figure 6.1, we can measure the flows of income and output in an economy by examining the input and output markets depicted in Figure 6.2. In the next section, we describe gross domestic product, which measures economic activity using the concepts in the circular flow model.

GROSS DOMESTIC PRODUCT

Gross Domestic Product (GDP) measures the dollar value of all final goods and services produced in an economy in a given time period.

Gross Domestic Product (GDP) is one of the most widely used indicators of economic activity. GDP measures the dollar value of all final goods and services produced in an economy during a given period (such as per quarter or per year). Final goods and services are goods that are sold to their end users and will not be sold again. A car produced by Ford and sold to a family in Michigan is a final good. The steel used by Ford to produce the car is an input or intermediate good. GDP counts only final goods and services to avoid double-counting inputs. If we counted the value of each of the parts of an automobile in GDP and then counted the value of the automobile itself, we'd double-count the automobile parts because the price of the automobile will include the cost of the inputs used to build it. GDP is called gross *domestic* product because it counts only production that occurs within a given economy's borders. U.S. GDP does not count goods produced abroad by U.S.-based companies (such as IBM computers assembled in Taiwan) but does count goods produced in the United States by foreign-based companies (such as Subaru cars assembled in Indiana).

As we saw in the circular flow diagrams in Figures 6.1 and 6.2, GDP can be measured using several methods. We could measure GDP by counting the incomes earned by the factors of production in input markets. This is called the **income approach** to measuring GDP. Alternatively, we could measure GDP as the value of total sales minus the value of inputs used to make those sales. This is the **value-added approach** to measuring GDP. Finally, we could measure GDP by counting the expenditures on final goods and services in output markets. This is the **expenditures approach** to measuring GDP.

*The **income approach** uses incomes earned by producers to measure GDP.*

*The **value-added approach** uses total sales minus the value of inputs to measure GDP.*

*The **expenditures approach** uses total expenditures on final goods and services to measure GDP.*

Table 6.1 illustrates how the income, value-added, and expenditures approaches can be used to calculate GDP in a simple economy made up of a farmer, a miller, and a baker. The farmer earns income by producing the wheat that he sells to the miller. The miller buys the wheat from the farmer, mills the wheat into flour, and sells it to the baker. The baker buys the flour from the miller and turns it into bread. Using the income approach, this economy's GDP is equal to the sum of the income earned by each of the producers in the economy

Table 6.1 Measuring GDP

Person	Product	Input Cost Per Period	Income Per period	Sales Revenue Per Period
Farmer	Wheat	$0	$2	$2
Miller	Flour	$2	$3	$5
Baker	Bread	$5	$4	$9
	Total	**$7**	**$9**	**$16**

Using the income approach, GDP is equal to the sum of the income earned by producers in the economy, or $2 + $3 + $4 = $9 per period. Using the value-added approach, GDP is equal to the sum of the sales revenue minus the input cost or ($2 – $0) + ($5 – $2) + ($9 – $4) = $9 per period. Using the expenditures approach, GDP is equal to the spending on final goods and services, or $9 per period.

$$\text{Income approach GDP} = \text{income earned by farmer} + \text{income earned by miller} + \text{income earned by baker}$$

$$\text{GDP} = \$2 + \$3 + \$4 = \$9 \text{ per period}$$

Using the value-added approach, GDP is equal to the sum of the sales revenue minus the input cost

$$\text{Value-added GDP} = (\text{farmer's sale revenue} - \text{farmer's input cost}) + (\text{miller's sales revenue} - \text{miller's cost}) + (\text{baker's sales revenue} - \text{baker's cost})$$

$$\text{GDP} = (\$2 - \$0) + (\$5 - \$2) + (\$9 - \$4) = \$9 \text{ per period}$$

Using the expenditures approach, GDP is equal to the spending on final goods and services, or $9 per period, since this is the amount spent on bread, the only final good produced in this economy.

The expenditures approach is the most commonly used measure of GDP. Using the expenditures approach, GDP can be divided into four basic components: consumption expenditure (C), private investment (I), government expenditure and investment (G), and net exports (exports [X] minus imports [M]). The expenditures approach measures GDP as

$$GDP = C + I + G + (X - M)$$

Table 6.2 presents the value of GDP in 2011 using the expenditures approach. The rest of this section summarizes each of the expenditure components of GDP.

Table 6.2 U.S. GDP in 2011

Component	Billions $
Consumption expenditure (C)	10,668.2
Private investment (I)	1,881.9
Government expenditure and investment (G)	3,030.9
Net exports (X – M)	−570.7
Exports (X)	2,020.0
Imports (M)	2,590.7
Gross domestic product (GDP)	15,010.3

Source: U.S. Bureau of Economic Analysis, U.S. Department of Commerce

Consumption (C)

Consumption (C) is household spending on final goods and services. Purchases of items like TVs, groceries, restaurant meals, and doctor and lawyer services are counted in consumption. Because the C component of GDP is a measure of household spending on final goods and services, it does not include the value of output produced at home but not sold in the market. For example, the value of childcare services produced by a stay-at-home parent is not counted as consumption because the childcare services are not purchased in output markets. The measure of consumption also excludes the value of other services that households produce for themselves, including housecleaning and cooking, but C does count the value of these services when they are purchased from others. Although some economists have developed consumption measures that include the value of home production activities, they are excluded from the official measure of GDP. Consumption is generally the largest component of GDP, accounting for about 71 percent of total GDP in 2011.

THINK FOR YOURSELF

Using what you learned in Chapter 3, which presented the demand and supply model, explain how consumer expectations could influence overall consumption in the economy. In particular, how would consumer expectations impact the consumption component of GDP?

Investment (I)

Private investment (I) is a measure of business spending on equipment used in production, spending on construction, and changes in business inventories. It is called private investment to distinguish it from government investment, which is included in G. Business spending on tools, computers, and buildings is investment, as is spending on new residential housing. Changes in businesses' inventories of goods are also counted as investment so that all of the goods that are produced in a given period are counted, even if they are not sold in the same period. Investment does not include the purchases of financial products like stocks and bonds, because stocks and bonds are not goods and services that are produced. Instead, stocks and bonds represent ownership of companies or loans to companies or the government. Investment accounted for about 13 percent of GDP in 2011.

Government Expenditure and Investment (G)

Government expenditure and investment (G) includes government spending on wages for government employees, government purchases of services, government purchases of final goods, and government investment in buildings and other capital. Not all government spending is included in GDP because spending on things such as social security, debt service, and unemployment insurance are not purchases of goods and services. Government expenditure and investment made up about 22 percent of GDP in 2011.

Net Exports (X – M)

Net exports is a measure of the difference between exports and imports. Exports are goods produced domestically but sold abroad, such as wheat grown in Montana and sold to consumers in Asia. Imports are goods that are produced abroad but purchased domestically, such as French wine purchased by a U.S. consumer. Exports are included in GDP because they are produced domestically but not captured in the other expenditure components of GDP. Because the measures of expenditures on consumption, investment, and government expenditure include spending on imported goods, we subtract off the value of imports from GDP to ensure that it only includes domestic production. America imported more than it exported in 2011, so U.S. net exports in 2011 were negative, accounting for about −4 percent of GDP.

Simon Kuznets and the Measurement of GDP

Simon Kuznets (1901–1985) is a Nobel-prize-winning economist widely credited with collecting, organizing, and standardizing the data used to measure GDP in the United States. His book *National Income and Its Composition, 1919–1938* was a meticulous work on measuring GDP. His measures of the production, income, and expenditure activities in an economy are called the national income accounts and form the basis for our measures of income and output in economies. Kuznets's work with the U.S. Department of Commerce to formalize the national income accounts set the standard for measuring GDP in the United States and across the world that is still used today.

AFP/Getty Images, Inc.

GDP Across Time

Figure 6.3 shows how the components of GDP have changed across time. In 1929, U.S. GDP was $103 billion per year. In 2011, GDP was $15 trillion per year. Some of the increase in GDP depicted in Figure 6.3 occurred because the U.S. produces more goods and services today than in the past, and some occurred because the prices of goods and services are higher today than in the past. Chapter 7 discusses how economists account for differences in prices over time. For this chapter, it is sufficient to focus on the overall level of GDP and the relative sizes of its components.

Consumption is consistently the largest component of GDP, as illustrated by the height of the C bars in Figure 6.3. The second largest components of GDP are I and G. Net exports have sometimes been positive and sometimes been negative since the 1930s. During the last decade or so, imports have consistently been larger than exports, meaning that net exports have been negative since the late 1990s.

Figure 6.3 U.S. GDP Over Time (billions of dollars)

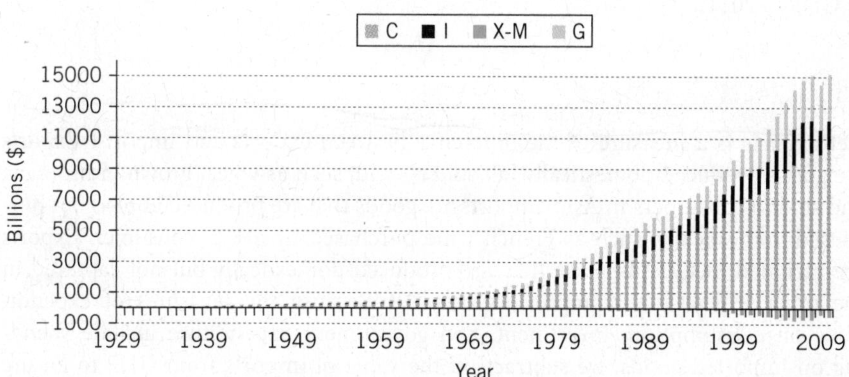

GDP is composed of C + I + G + (X-M). C is the largest component of GDP, followed by G and I. Net exports have sometimes been positive and sometimes been negative since the 1930s. Source: U.S. Department of Commerce Bureau of Economic Analysis.

International GDP Comparisons

GDP is often used to compare the relative productivity and output across countries. Table 6.3 presents 2010 GDP values for the 10 largest and 10 smallest GDP countries worldwide. Measured by GDP, the United States is the largest economy in the world, producing almost 50 percent more output than its closest competitor, China. The rest of the top 10 GDP countries are primarily large and highly developed nations. Countries with the lowest GDP are primarily smaller, with fewer natural or other resources to use in production.

Although international GDP comparisons can tell us the relative size of a country's economy, they are not very good indicators of the standard of living in the country. Countries like China and India, for example, have high GDP but also very high populations across which their GDP is spread. A better measure of the average standard of living in a country is GDP per capita, which divides GDP by the population of the country. Table 6.4 presents per capita GDP values for the countries with the highest and lowest per capita GDP in the world.

Table 6.3 International GDP Comparisons, 2010

Largest GDP		Smallest GDP	
Country	GDP $ billions/year	Country	GDP $ millions/year
United States	14,700	Tuvalu	36.0
China	10,100	Marshall Islands	133.5
Japan	4,310	Palau	164.0
India	4,060	Anguilla	175.4
Germany	2,940	Micronesia	238.1
Russia	2,230	Sao Tome and Principe	311.0
United Kingdom	2,170	Kiribati	618.0
Brazil	2,170	Saint Kitts and Nevis	684.0
France	2,150	Tonga	751.0
Italy	1,750	Dominica	758.0

Source: CIA World Factbook. GDP values are computed at purchasing power parity (PPP), which uses exchange rates to value each country's output using U.S. prices.

Table 6.4 International GDP Per Capita Comparisons, 2010

Largest GDP Per Capita Per Year			Smallest GDP Per Capita Per Year		
Country	Population	GDP Per Capita $ Per Year	Country	Population	GDP Per Capita $ Per Year
Qatar	848,000	179,000	Congo	71,713,000	300
Liechtenstein	35,000	141,100	Burundi	10,217,000	400
Luxembourg	503,000	82,600	Liberia	3,787,000	500
Bermuda (2004)	68,000	69,000	Zimbabwe	12,084,000	500
Singapore	4,741,000	62,100	Somalia	9,926,000	600
Jersey (2005)	94,000	57,000	Eritrea	5,939,000	600
Norway	4,691,000	54,600	Niger	16,469,000	700
Brunei	402,000	51,600	Central African Republic	4,950,000	700
United Arab Emirates	5,149,000	49,600	Malawi	15,879,000	800
Kuwait	2,596,000	48,900	Afghanistan	29,835,000	900

Source: CIA World Factbook. GDP values are computed at purchasing power parity (PPP), which uses exchange rates to value each country's output using U.S. prices.

Dominating the top 10 largest per capita GDP countries are developed nations with relatively small populations (6 of the 10 have less than 1 million people), plus the oil and natural resource–rich nations of Qatar, Kuwait, Norway, and the United Arab Emirates, and the highly developed economy of Singapore. African nations dominate the list of small per capita GDP countries (9 of the 10 are from the African continent).

Many of these nations are war-ravaged or highly governmentally controlled economies whose citizens depend primarily on subsistence agriculture.

Although per capita GDP can provide an average measure of the standard of living in a given economy, it can also be misleading. Because per capita GDP simply divides the total GDP by the total population of a country, it does not account for how that GDP is spread among the population. One country with GDP of $1,000 and 100 people sharing income equally will have the same per capita GDP as another country with GDP of $1,000 concentrated into the hands of one citizen. Chapter 19 will discuss issues related to the distribution of income within and among countries. In the next section, we use a demand and supply model to understand the factors that can cause changes in GDP.

AD/AS MODEL

Aggregate demand (AD) is the demand for all goods and services in an economy, ceteris paribus.

Aggregate supply (AS) is the supply of all goods and services in an economy, ceteris paribus.

In earlier chapters, we used the demand and supply model to understand how markets work. As the demand and supply of various goods and services change, their prices and quantities traded increase or decrease. Economies operate in a similar way, although on a much larger scale. We can use our demand and supply model to describe the activity of the economy as a whole if we modify the model slightly to capture the concepts of **aggregate demand** and **aggregate supply**.

Aggregate means to gather a set of items together to form a total or whole. Aggregate demand (AD) represents the whole of the demand for all goods and services of the economy at different price levels. Aggregate supply (AS) represents the whole of the supply of all the goods and services in the economy at different price levels.

Figure 6.4 illustrates the aggregate demand/aggregate supply (AD/AS) model. The curve AD represents aggregate demand, and AS represents aggregate supply. As in the usual demand and supply model, quantity is measured on the horizontal axis and price is measured on the vertical axis. The intersection of the AD and AS curves represents the point of equilibrium in the economy. At that intersection, the equilibrium level of output in the economy is shown on the horizontal axis as GDP*.

You should take note of three key differences between the AD/AS model and the usual demand and supply model. First, the price of a particular good or service is measured on the vertical axis in the usual supply and demand model. In the AD/AS model, the vertical axis measures the average prices for all goods and services in the economy. This measure is called the **price level**. The details of measuring the overall price level in an economy are presented in Chapter 7. For now, we can think of the price level as a measure of the average cost of the goods and services produced in the economy.

The price level is a measure of the average level of prices in an economy.

Figure 6.4 **Aggregate Demand/Aggregate Supply Model**

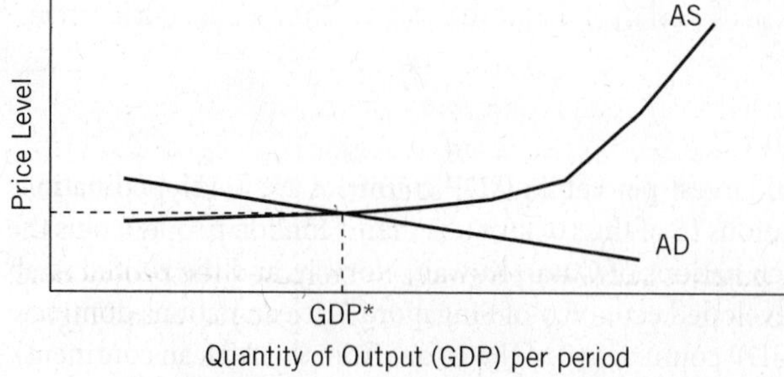

In the AD/AS model, the horizontal axis represents total output per period (GDP) and the vertical axis represents the price level in the economy. AD is the demand for all goods and services in the economy and AS represents the supply of goods and services in the economy. The intersection of AD and AS tells the equilibrium level of GDP and the equilibrium price level in the economy.

As the price level rises, businesses have an incentive to increase their production of goods and services, which will move the economy upward along the AS curve. When prices fall, businesses cannot afford to cover the cost of as much production, so they reduce their output levels and the economy moves down along the AS curve. On the demand side, increases in the price level reduce the amount of goods and services that consumers can buy, so the quantity of goods and services demanded falls and the economy moves upward along the AD curve. Alternatively, reductions in the price level increase the amount of goods and services that consumers can buy, which moves the economy downward along the AD curve.

A second difference between the AD/AS model and the usual demand and supply model is the shape of the supply curve. As in the usual model, the AS curve is positively sloped, indicating that the quantity of goods and services produced tends to increase as the prices of goods and services increase. In the AD/AS model, however, the AS curve becomes steeper as the quantity of output produced increases. The steep portion of the AS curve is meant to illustrate the idea that resources and technology place a limit on the amount of output that an economy can produce, ceteris paribus. It is helpful to think of the steep portion of the AS curve as a representation of the economy moving to a point on its production possibilities frontier. Ceteris paribus, because there is no increase in output possible beyond the PPF, points on the PPF would correspond to vertical portions of the AS curve. At low levels of output, the AS curve is relatively flat. The flat portion of the AS curve reflects the underutilization of resources relative to the economy's potential. At low levels of aggregate output, it is relatively easy to increase production without also having large increases in the price level. This is because at low levels of output there are many idle resources available that can be used in production at relatively low cost. As production expands and the economy moves closer to its full capacity, attracting additional resources into production becomes more expensive and the AS curve becomes steeper.

The final difference between the AD/AS model and the usual demand and supply model is that AD is not the demand for an individual good or service but instead is the sum of the demand for all goods and services in the economy. The circular flow diagram illustrates that the demand for goods and services comes from consumption, investment, government spending, and net exports. Thus, AD is the sum of C+I+G+(X-M). "Wait!" you might be protesting. "I thought GDP was the sum of C+I+G+(X-M)." In the AD/AS model, the intersection of AD and AS determines the level of GDP. At that equilibrium, the level of GDP and the level of AD are both equal to C+I+G+(X-M).

Shifts in AD and AS

As in the demand and supply model, shifts in either the AD or AS curves can cause changes in the quantity of output and the price level in the economy. Figure 6.5 illustrates the impacts of increases in AD and AS in the economy. Panel A of Figure 6.5 shows the impact of two different increases in AD. The first increase is from AD_1 to AD_2 along the relatively flat portion of the AS curve. The second increase is from AD_3 to AD_4 along the steeper portion of the AS curve. As in the usual demand and supply model, an increase in AD from AD_1 to AD_2 or from AD_3 to AD_4 generates a temporary shortage of goods and services at the old price level. This shortage puts upward pressure on prices and gives suppliers incentive to increase their production. As a result, the economy moves along the AS curve to a higher price level and higher amount of GDP than before.

The sizes of the increases in the price level and GDP that result from an increase in AD depend on the shape of AS. At relatively low levels of AS, the AS curve is relatively flat. Increases in AD like the increase from AD_1 to AD_2 result in relatively large increases in GDP but only modest increases in the price level. At higher levels of AS, the AS curve is steep, which means that increases in AD, from AD_3 to AD_4, for example, cause large increases in the price level but only small increases in GDP.

Panel B of Figure 6.5 illustrates the impact of an in increase in AS on the economy. Ceteris paribus, a shift in AS from AS_1 to AS_2 causes a temporary surplus of goods and services at the old price level. The surplus puts downward pressure on prices. As prices fall, the economy moves downward along the AD curve to a new equilibrium. An increase in AS causes an increase in economic output and a decrease in the price level.

What happens to GDP and the price level when there is a decrease in aggregate demand? What happens to GDP and the price level when there is a decrease in aggregate supply?

Figure 6.5 **Increases in AD and AS**

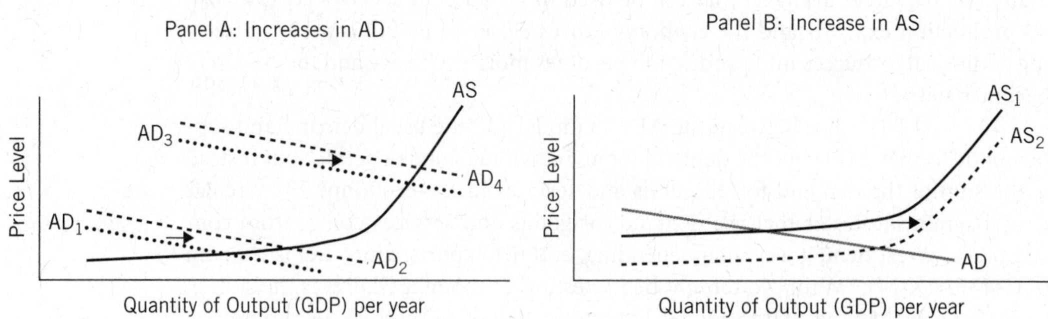

Increases in AD along the flat portion of the AS curve cause large changes in output but relatively small changes in the price level, as in the movement from AD_1 to AD_2 in Panel A. Increases in AD along the steep portion of the AS curve cause small changes in output but relatively large changes in the price level, as in the movement from AD_3 to AD_4 in Panel A. Increases in AS generate increases in output and reductions in the price level, as shown by the movement from AS_1 to AS_2 in Panel B.

Because changes in aggregate demand and supply generate changes in the price level and GDP in an economy, it is crucial to understand the factors that cause shifts in AD or AS. We turn to this topic next.

Factors That Shift AD

Aggregate demand is composed of all of the consumption, investment, government spending, and net export expenditures that make up GDP. Changes in any of these components of AD will cause shifts in AD. For example, if consumers suddenly decide to cut their savings and instead increase their spending on goods and services, consumption will increase and AD will shift outward. As a result, GDP will increase and the average prices of goods and services in the economy will rise. As was demonstrated in Figure 6.5, if the increase in AD occurs on the flat portion of the AS curve, the price increase will be relatively small and the output increase will be relatively large. If the increase in AD occurs when the economy is on the steep portion of the AS curve, output will not increase by much, but average prices will rise dramatically.

Alternatively, if people's expectations about the economy become more pessimistic, consumers and businesses will likely cut their consumption and investment, and the AD curve will shift inward. The reduction in household and business spending will generate a reduction in GDP and in the price level. The sizes of the GDP and price level changes will depend on where the economy is operating on the AS curve.

Changes in government spending or in exports and imports can also shift AD. If the government increases spending on things like roads, military equipment, and services, the G component of AD will increase and AD will shift outward. If foreigners increase their consumption of domestically made goods, exports will increase and AD will shift outward. If foreigners suddenly decrease their demand for U.S. goods and services, exports will fall and AD will shift inward. If U.S. consumers increase their demand for goods produced abroad, imports will increase and AD will fall, resulting in lower levels of GDP and average prices.

Factors That Shift AS

Aggregate supply represents the production of all final goods and services in the economy. Important shifters of AS include the prices of inputs needed to produce goods and services, the productivity of inputs, changes in technology used in production, and the cost of financing business activities. If the overall prices of widely used inputs increase, AS will shift inward. For example, rising oil prices generate increases in the costs of production across a wide array of industries. AS falls when oil prices increase, which in turn reduces GDP and increases the average price level in the economy. Alternatively, when inputs become more productive through education or technology, the AS of goods and services increases and the AS curve shifts outward. An increase in AS causes an increase in GDP and a reduction in average prices. Finally, an increase in interest rates makes it more expensive for firms to obtain loans to finance their operations. Higher-cost loans would cause firms to decrease their production of goods and services and generate a decrease in AS.

The AD/AS model illustrates how increases in AD and AS generate increases in the overall levels of output, income, and business activity in the economy. The model also illustrates how decreases in AD or AS cause reduced levels of output, income, and business activity. Increases and decreases in economic activity cause business cycles, the topic we turn to next.

BUSINESS CYCLES

Business cycles are recurring expansions and contractions in the level of aggregate economic activity. Figure 6.6 illustrates an example series of business cycles. The vertical axis in Figure 6.6 measures the level of GDP in the economy, and the horizontal axis measures time.

Business Cycles are recurring expansions and contractions in the level of aggregate economic activity.

Although they vary in length and intensity, each business cycle has distinct phases. **Business cycle expansions** are periods of increasing economic activity, rising production, and increasing employment.

Business cycle expansions are periods of increasing economic activity, rising production, and increasing employment.

Business cycle expansions are illustrated by the solid portions of the curve in Figure 6.6. Notice that although they are called business cycles, they are not consistent in length or size. The first business cycle expansion shown in Figure 6.6 is has

Figure 6.6 **Examples of Business Cycles**

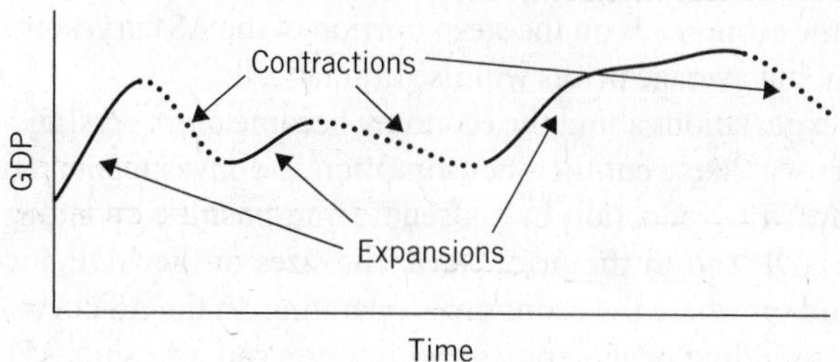

Business cycles are the recurring expansions and contractions in economic activity. Expansion periods are shown by the solid portions of the curve. During expansions, GDP grows. Contractions are illustrated by the dotted portions of the curve. During contractions, GDP falls.

a larger increase in GDP than the second expansion. The third expansion is longer than those in the other periods but is of inconsistent intensity, with rapidly increasing GDP at the beginning of the expansion but slower growth in GDP toward the end of the expansion.

Periods of declining economic activity are called **business cycle contractions** or **recessions**. Recessions are characterized by declines in economic activity and decreases in employment. The dotted portions of the curve in Figure 6.6 represent recession periods. As with expansions, recessions can vary in length and intensity. The first recession shown in Figure 6.6 has a more rapid decrease in GDP than the second recession, but it does not last as long.

Business cycle contractions or recessions are periods of decreasing economic activity, falling production, and falling employment.

Peaks in the business cycle are the times of change from expansions to recessions. Troughs in the business cycle are turning points between recessions and economic expansions. A full business cycle extends from the one trough to another trough. In the United States, the National Bureau of Economic Research (NBER) is the most-cited source that declares changes in the business cycle.[2]

Figure 6.7 presents data on U.S. GDP since 1930. The periods shown in dark shading are business cycle expansions, while those in light shading are recessions. Between 1929 and 2011, there have been 14 recessions.

There is a fairly steady upward trend in GDP in Figure 6.7. Although it is tempting to think that this long-term rise in GDP stems from general increases in the prices

Figure 6.7 **US GDP and Business Cycles**

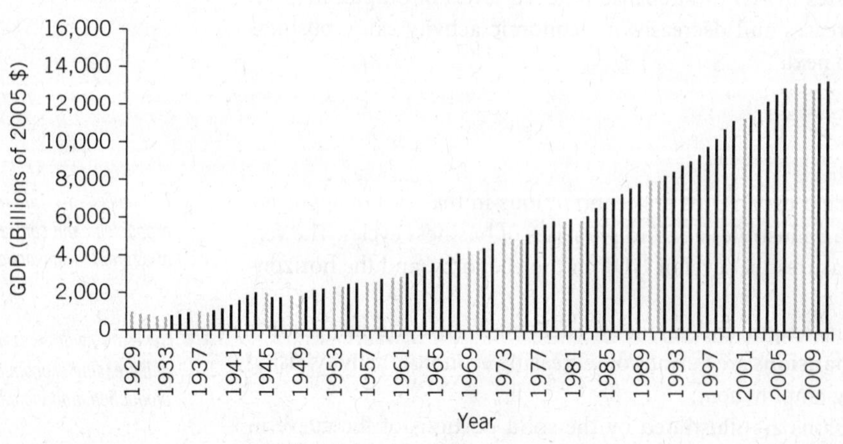

Although the level of economic output in the US has grown fairly steadily since the 1930s, GDP still exhibits expansionary and contractionary periods over time. Business cycle expansions are shown as dark bars, contractions as light bars. Sources: US Bureau of Economic Analysis and the National Bureau of Economic Research.

2 A complete listing of all of the US business cycles is available from the NBER at: http://www.nber.org/cycles/cyclesmain.html

of goods and services over time, the GDP values reported in Figure 6.7 reflect only changes in production and output, not changes in the overall price level.

Aggregate Demand and Aggregate Supply in Business Cycles

We can use the AD/AS model to illustrate the causes and impacts of business cycles. Figure 6.8 shows the changes in AD and AS than can generate business cycle contractions. Panel A illustrates a decrease in aggregate demand from AD_1 to AD_2. The decrease in AD generates a surplus of goods and services at the old price level. As the economy adjusts to this surplus, GDP and prices decline and the economy moves downward along the AS curve. As we learned in the previous section, any factors that generate declines in consumption, investment, government expenditures, or net exports can cause a decline in AD and move the economy into recession. For example, decreases in household income would lower consumption and cause AD to shift inward. Decreases in government spending on goods and services would have a similar impact on AD.

While business cycle contractions can be caused by reductions in AD, business cycle expansions could result from increases in AD. If households or businesses become more willing to spend their incomes on goods and services, consumption rises and AD shifts outward. Increases in government spending on goods and services or foreign purchases of U.S. exports also generate increases in AD and can cause business cycle expansions.

Panel B of Figure 6.8 shows how changes in aggregate supply can impact economic activity. When aggregate supply declines, the AS curve shifts inward from AS_1 to AS_2 and GDP declines, pushing the economy into a recession. Factors that can generate decreases in aggregate supply include increases in the prices of inputs or declines in productivity of those inputs. Increases in oil prices are one factor that causes decreases in AS and can push the economy into a recession. When oil prices increase, industries across the economy are impacted because oil is used not only to fuel factories but also to transport goods and services to and from markets. One of the longest periods of recession illustrated in Figure 6.7 occurred during the mid-1970s. During that time, the Organization of Petroleum Exporting Countries (OPEC) decreased its exports of oil to the United States in response to U.S. support of Israel. As a result, oil and gas prices increased dramatically, overall economic activity in the United States fell, and the average prices of goods and services rose. Chapters 21 and 22 highlight the different ways that governments respond to business cycles.

Figure 6.8 **Declines in AD and AS**

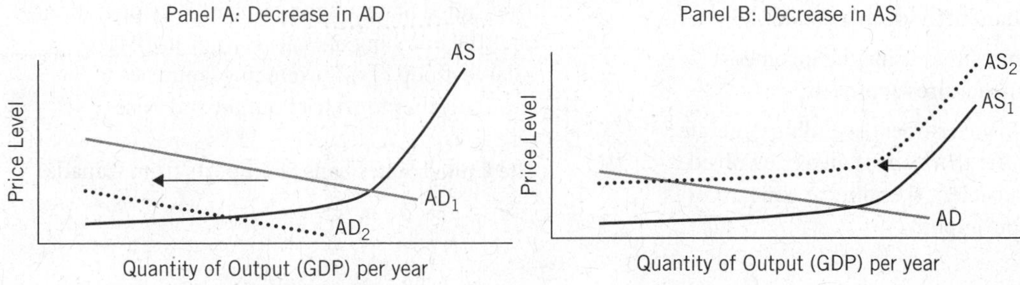

Decreases in AD, such as that shown in Panel A, generate reductions in GDP and the average price level and correspond to periods of recession. Decreases in AS, such as that shown in Panel B, also cause recessions because they generate decreases in output. Decreases in AS also cause increases in the price level.

SUMMARY

In the circular flow model of the macroeconomy, businesses, households, governments, and the foreign sector interact with one another in input and output markets. The flow of income and expenditures on goods and services in an economy is measured by GDP. GDP measures the value of all final goods and services produced in an economy during a given period. The primary components of GDP are consumption, investment, government spending, and net exports. GDP is sometimes used to compare the relative sizes of economies, and per capita GDP is frequently used as a gauge of the standard of living in an economy.

Business cycles are the recurring expansions and contractions in GDP over time. Business cycle expansions are characterized by increasing levels of employment, increased production, and increases in the average prices of goods and services in the economy. Business cycle contractions or recessions are periods of slowdown in economic activity, reduced employment, and declines in production. The AD/AS model can be used to show how changes in the behavior of buyers and sellers impact GDP. Increases in AD or AS cause increases in GDP and are associated with business cycle expansions. Decreases in AD or AS can cause business cycle contractions or recessions.

KEY CONCEPTS

- Exports
- Imports
- Gross domestic product
- Aggregate demand
- Aggregate supply
- Price level
- Business cycles
- Business cycle expansions
- Business cycle contractions
- Recessions

DISCUSSION QUESTIONS AND PROBLEMS

1. What are the major components of GDP? Provide an example of each.
2. Why are only final goods and services included in the computation of GDP?
3. Why can GDP per capita be a misleading indicator of the economic standard of living in a country?
4. Why can GDP be measured using the income approach or the expenditures approach?
5. Why do increases in government spending generate increases in GDP? Are there any tradeoffs involved with increased government spending as a means of increasing economic output?
6. How will each of the following affect the GDP and the price level of the U.S. economy?
   a. The government drastically cuts its spending on goods and services.
   b. The UK bans all U.S. imports.
   c. The United States expands its military operations after the bombing of Pearl Harbor in 1941.
   d. A large group of oil-producing countries band together to restrict output and raise oil prices.
   e. The United States bans all imports from Canada.

MULTIPLE CHOICE QUESTIONS

1. The calculation of gross domestic product would include
   a. the purchase of a new automobile.
   b. unemployment compensation benefits received by a former steel worker.
   c. the money Alice receives when she sells her used bicycle to Fred.
   d. the services of a lawyer when he cleans his own apartment.

2. If a newspaper headline indicates that U.S. net exports were $190 billion in 2011, it likely means that
   a. U.S. exports were $190 billion and U.S. imports were zero.
   b. U.S. imports were $190 billion and U.S. exports were zero.
   c. U.S. exports exceeded U.S. imports by $190 billion.
   d. U.S. imports exceeded U.S. exports by $190 billion.

3. In the calculation of GDP, which of the following purchases is included as household consumption expenditure?
   a. A new apartment building purchased by a landlord
   b. A new calculator required for a statistician's job
   c. A new computer purchased by a college student
   d. A new tractor purchased by a farmer

4. The value of the bricks purchased by a contractor to build a fireplace in a new home is *not* counted in GDP because
   a. business spending of any type is excluded from GDP.
   b. it would be double counting since the value of the home is already counted in GDP.
   c. the price of the bricks would not be known to the contractor.
   d. this is a purely financial transaction.

5. In the AD/AS model, an increase in aggregate demand will cause
   a. an increase in GDP and an increase in the price level.
   b. a decrease in GDP and an increase in the price level.
   c. an increase in GDP and a decrease in the price level.
   d. a decrease in GDP and a decrease in the price level.

6. Per capita GDP is criticized as a measure of the economic well-being in a country because
   a. it does not take the size of the country's population into account.
   b. it does not measure the level of production in a country.
   c. it does not measure the level of income in a country.
   d. it does not describe the distribution of income in a country.

7. In the AD/AS model, a decrease in aggregate supply will cause
   a. an increase in GDP and an increase in the price level.
   b. a decrease in GDP and an increase in the price level.
   c. an increase in GDP and a decrease in the price level.
   d. a decrease in GDP and a decrease in the price level.

8. In the circular flow model,
   a. households trade their income for goods and services in output markets.
   b. households trade their income for goods and services in input markets.
   c. businesses trade their goods and services for money in input markets.
   d. governments trade imports for exports with the foreign sector.

9. In the circular flow model,
   a. prices in input markets are determined by the government.
   b. prices in output markets are determined by the government.
   c. governments engage in both the input and output markets.
   d. the foreign sector engages only in input markets, not in output markets.

10. The expenditures approach calculation for GDP is
    a. $C + I - G + (X + M)$.
    b. $C + I + G + (X + M)$.
    c. $C + I + G + (X - M)$.
    d. $C - I - G - (X - M)$.

ADDITIONAL READINGS AND WEB RESOURCES

http://www.gpoaccess.gov/eop/

Economic Report of the President. An annual overview of U.S. economic activity. Includes extensive data of all components of GDP, published by the Council of Economic Advisors to the President.

http://www.census.gov/compendia/statab/

Statistical Abstract of the United States. An annual summary of social, political, and economic activity in the United States, published by the Census Bureau.

https://www.cia.gov/library/publications/the-world-factbook/

The CIA World Factbook. Presents information on economic, government, population, history, and other facts for countries throughout the world.

www.nber.org

The website of the National Bureau of Economic Research, home of the Business Cycle Dating Committee.

http://www.whitehouse.gov/briefing_room/

The White House Briefing Room. Includes links to information on an array of issues including the economy and government spending.

http://www.bea.gov/national/pdf/nipa_primer.pdf

The Bureau of Economic Analysis national income and product accounts primer. Presents an introduction to the basics of the U.S. national income and product accounts.

Public Domain image from wikipedia: http://en.wikipedia.org/wiki/File: Mugabecloseup2008.jpg

Inflation and the Measurement of Prices

After studying this chapter, you should be able to:

- Explain the difference between the face value of money and the purchasing power of money
- Describe inflation and calculate inflation across time periods
- Describe the winners and losers from inflation
- Distinguish the sources of inflation
- Illustrate the difference between real and nominal values

In 1980, the former British Colony of Rhodesia in south eastern Africa became Zimbabwe, led by Prime Minister (and now President) Robert Mugabe. Mugabe's policies and practices have been highly controversial, including land redistribution among citizens, accusations of electoral fraud, support and intervention in the Second Congo War, and the printing of hundreds of trillions of Zimbabwean dollars. As a result of this and other flawed economic policies, Zimbabwe's economy is in collapse and its citizens find themselves in the midst of one of the worst inflation periods in the history of the world. **Inflation**, the rise in the general level of prices in the economy, is estimated to be over 11.2 million percent per year in Zimbabwe. At levels this high, Zimbabwe's inflation can be classified as hyperinflation, or inflation that has gone out of control. At its worst, the hyperinflation meant a doubling of the prices of goods and services every 25 hours! Because the Zimbabwean currency was losing its usefulness for buying goods and services so quickly, the Reserve Bank

Inflation is the rise in the general level of prices in an economy.

of Zimbabwe was faced with frequently reissuing currency, with some bills taking on values of $100,000,000,000,000 (100 trillion). In 1980, one Zimbabwean dollar traded for about 1.59 U.S. dollars. At the peak of the hyperinflation in November 2008, it took 688 trillion Zimbabwean dollars to trade for 1 U.S. dollar. In July 2008, one egg cost 50 billion Zimbabwean dollars. Workers were always in need of salary increases to keep up with food and other costs, shops would have to constantly update their prices, and foreign businesses were extremely hesitant to invest in the Zimbabwean economy. Eventually, people gave up using Zimbabwean currency altogether, opting instead to trade using the more stable U.S. dollar and South African rand. Zimbabwe stopped printing its own money in April 2009. The Zimbabwean economy remains crippled, with approximately 80 percent of the workforce unemployed and one of the lowest levels of living standards in the world. This chapter focuses on inflation and the measurement of prices in an economy. Since inflation and prices are a reflection of the value of money, we start with an overview of the role that money plays in economies.

THE VALUE AND USES OF MONEY

The face value of money is determined by governments and printed on currency.

The purchasing power of money reflects the amount of goods and services that a given unit of money could be used to acquire.

As the introduction to this chapter illustrates, there can be a vast difference between the **face value of money**, which is the value declared by the government and printed on the currency, and the **purchasing power of money**, which is determined in the marketplace. As prices rise, the amount of goods and services that can be purchased with money of a given face value falls. When prices rise at the rates seen in Zimbabwe in 2008–09, economies can be devastated.

The Definition and Evolution of Money

What *is* money? Over time and in differing situations, many different things have been used to exchange goods and services. Early exchanges often relied on barter, which is the trading of goods or services directly for one another. In a barter system, a carpenter may trade his services to the farmer in exchange for chickens or grain. The local doctor may get paid in milk from the dairy farmer, honey from the beekeeper, and clothing from the seamstress. As you might expect, barter tends to be relatively time consuming because in order to trade, people must have a coincidence of wants. The carpenter has to find a farmer who needs carpentry work done, the beekeeper needs to find a doctor who needs honey, and so on.

Money's role as a medium of exchange means that it can be used as a means of payment for goods and services or repayment of debt.

Money's role as a unit of account means that it provides a common measure of the worth of goods or services.

As economies evolved, people began to use metals like gold and silver as a means of payment in trades. Because people could trade metals for a wide array of goods and services, it was no longer necessary to trade using a barter system. Using metals greatly reduced the cost of conducting economic transactions because the metals could be used to facilitate trades even when there was no coincidence of wants among the traders. This is one of the primary roles of money: as a means of payment or **medium of exchange**.

Money also serves as **unit of account** or a way to measure how much something is worth. Using money as a unit of account allows us to easily compare the relative costs of different goods. In a barter system, each good or service must be compared against all other goods or services for which it could trade. The price of three chickens, for example, could be ten pounds of flour or one sack of potatoes or one doctor appointment or one room swept by a maid, and so on. The unit of account function of money simplifies trades because it provides a common measure of worth. In our example, three chickens might be worth $10, which implies that 10 pounds of flour and one sack of potatoes are also worth $10.

Money also serves as a **store of value**. Money allows us to hold and retrieve purchasing power over time. When you put your money into a piggy bank or savings account, you are holding on to its purchasing power to use at a later time. Some things serve as a better store of value than others. Suppose, for example, that our economy used milk as money. Milk could be used as a medium of exchange to facilitate trades. Because we can value all items relative to the amount of milk they are worth, milk could also serve as a unit of account. However, milk would not be a good store of value because it is perishable. We could not use milk that we had put away as savings two years ago to purchase things today because no one will want to trade with us for rotten milk.

Money's role as a store of value means that it can be saved and used to purchase goods and services at a future time.

Because perishable items do not serve well as a way to store value over time, people sometimes hold on to purchasing power by buying stocks, real estate, precious metals or stones like gold and diamonds, and art or antiques. Items like real estate or art generally have to be exchanged for money before they can be used to purchase other goods and services. Money is more convenient as a store of value than art or real estate because money can be used directly to purchase goods and services.

Why were metals attractive as one of the first forms of money? Metals are durable, can be divided into parts, are in limited supply, and have value in their own right (to make jewelry, dishes, and so on). Money that has use and value apart from that stemming from its role as money is called **commodity money**. In addition to gold and silver, shells, stones, decorated belts, cigarettes, and alcohol have all been used as commodity money. Most paper currency in world is **fiat money**, which is valuable because of government declaration rather than because it can be used for other purposes besides money. In the United States, all paper currency includes the statement, "this note is legal tender for all debts, public and private," which means that paper U.S. currency has been decreed as a means of payment by the government.

Commodity money has value for its own sake, in addition to its value as money.

Fiat money has value because of government law or regulation.

Although the government declares the legality of money as a medium of exchange, the purchasing power of the money is determined in markets. When the prices of goods and services rise, the quantity of goods and services that can be purchased with money of a given face value falls. The falling purchasing power of money in the face of rising prices implies that money is a poor store of value when prices rise. When prices increase like they did in Zimbabwe during the 2008–2009 period, all three functions of money can collapse. The Zimbabwean dollar could no longer serve as a store of value because prices were eroding its purchasing power at phenomenal rates. Its usefulness as a unit of account became limited because it was produced in denominations of hundreds of trillions, amounts hard to imagine, let alone to serve as a useful frame of reference for value. Eventually, the Zimbabwean dollar's use as a medium of exchange collapsed and Zimbabweans turned to other countries' currencies instead. Although instances of hyperinflation such as Zimbabwe's are relatively rare, inflation as an ongoing and continual increase in the prices of goods and services is a common phenomenon in most economies. The next section describes how inflation is measured.

MEASURING PRICES AND INFLATION

Inflation is the general, ongoing rise in the prices of goods and services in an economy. Having inflation does not mean that the prices of each and every good in an economy are rising but rather that the average level of prices in the economy is increasing. Economists use a price index to measure the average level of prices in an economy.

Price Index

Measures of the average price level take the form of an index, which is a series of numbers that track the rise and fall of a variable over time. We can use an index to measure changes in any variable, from crime rates to the cost of college tuition to the prices of a set of stocks. An index establishes a relative value of a variable across time. If the value of an index in March is higher than its value in February, the value of the variable measured by the index increased between February and March. Economists use a **price index** to track the value of prices over time.

A price index is a measure of the average prices of a given set of goods or services across time.

THINK FOR YOURSELF

One of the most famous index measures is the Dow Jones Industrial Index, which tracks the value of a set of stock prices over time. Can you think of other index variables?

The Consumer Price Index (CPI) is the most widely used measure for tracking prices in the United States. The CPI is compiled and reported by the Bureau of Labor Statistics (BLS) to provide an aggregate measure of the prices faced by the typical American consumer. The CPI is computed by tracking changes in the cost of purchasing a fixed set of goods and services over time. The fixed set of goods and services is called the **market basket**, and it includes the types and amounts of goods commonly bought by a typical consumer in a specified time period. When computing the CPI, workers at the BLS use a market basket consisting of thousands of goods and services, including an array of food and beverages, housing, fuel and utilities, household furniture and supplies, clothing, transportation, medical care, and education expenses. When the price of the market basket of goods and services increases, we can deduce that the average price of U.S. goods and services has risen.

A market basket is a fixed set of goods or services whose prices are tracked across time.

To compute the CPI, economists measure the cost of the market basket of goods and services for several time periods (usually quarters or years) and examine how the cost of the market basket changes over time. Economists start with a reference, base year and compare the cost of the market basket over time against its cost in the base year. The CPI measures the cost of the market basket in the current year as a percentage of the cost of the same basket of goods and services in the base year. The CPI is the ratio of the cost of the market basket in one year over the cost of the market basket in the base year multiplied by 100:

$$\text{Price Index in Current Year} = \frac{\text{cost of market basket in current year}}{\text{cost of market basket in base year}} * 100$$

We can build a hypothetical example to illustrate how to compute a price index. Let our market basket contain one dozen eggs and two gallons of milk. To build our price index, we first need to track the prices of milk and eggs across time. Hypothetical price data for eggs and milk are reported in Table 7.1. The price of a dozen eggs was $1.30 in 1980 and 1990, $1.25 in 2000, and $1.50 in 2010. The price of a gallon of milk rose from $1.60 in 1980 to $3.00 in 2010.

We use the prices of the items in each year to compute the cost of the market basket in each year. Our market basket consists of one dozen eggs and two gallons of

Table 7.1 Prices of Goods in Market Basket

Item	Price in 1980	Price in 1990	Price in 2000	Price in 2010
Dozen eggs	$1.30	$1.30	$1.25	$1.50
Gallon of milk	$1.60	$2.15	$2.75	$3.00

To compute a price index, we begin by finding the prices of each of the items in the market basket in each year. One dozen eggs cost $1.30 in 1980 and $1.50 in 2010. One gallon of milk cost $2.15 in 1990 and $3.00 in 2010.

milk. Table 7.2 shows the cost of this market basket in each year. In 1980, the cost of the market basket was $4.50. In 2010, the cost of the market basket was $7.50.

To compute the price index, we compute the ratio of the cost of the market basket in each year over its cost in the base year and multiply by 100. Let's set 1990 as the base year. This means that 1990 is the benchmark year against which we will compare prices in 1980, 2000, and 2010.

Table 7.2 Cost of Market Basket in Each Year

Year	Cost
1980	$1.30 + 2($1.60) = $4.50
1990	$1.30 + 2($2.15) = $5.60
2000	$1.25 + 2($2.75) = $6.75
2010	$1.50 + 2($3.00) = $7.50

To determine the cost of the market basket in each year, we multiply the cost of each set of items by their prices in that year. In 1980, the market basket of one dozen eggs and two gallons of milk cost $4.50. In 2010, the same market basket cost $7.50.

Table 7.3 Price Index for Each Year

Year	Price Index
1980	(4.50/5.60) * 100 = 80.4
1990	(5.60/5.60) * 100 = 100
2000	(6.75/5.60) * 100 = 120.5
2010	(7.50/5.60) * 100 = 133.9

The price index is the ratio of the cost of the market basket in the current year divided by the cost of the market basket in the base year, multiplied by 100.

Table 7.3 shows the price index values for each year. In 1980, the cost of the market basket was $4.50. The cost of the market basket in the base year (1990) is $5.60, so the price index in 1980 is

$$\text{Price Index in 1980} = \frac{\text{cost of market basket in 1980}}{\text{cost of market basket in base year}} * 100$$

$$= (\$4.50/\$5.60) * 100$$

$$= 80.4.$$

THINK FOR YOURSELF

What would be the total cost of the market basket in each year if we used three gallons of milk instead of two? What would be the total cost of the market basket in each year if one dozen eggs cost $2.00 in 2010? How would the price index values in Table 7.3 change given these two scenarios?

The values of the price index tell us whether prices are higher or lower in one year relative to the base year. The value of a price index in the base year is always 100 because we divide the cost of the market basket by itself in the base year. If the price index for a given year is less than 100, prices in that year are lower on average than they were in the base year. If the price index for a given year is greater than 100, prices in that year are higher on average than they were in the base year. In our example, the value of the price index in 1980 is less than 100, so the price of the market basket of goods was lower in 1980 than in 1990. The price index values in 2000 and 2010 are greater than 100, indicating that prices were higher in those years than in 1990.

The Consumer Price Index

Figure 7.1 presents the values of the U.S. Consumer Price Index since 1950. The base year used for these computations is 1982–84, highlighted by the dashed horizontal line at 100 on the vertical axis. In periods before 1982–84, the value of the CPI was less than 100, while in periods after 1982–84, the CPI was greater than 100.

What is the CPI used for? Governments, businesses, unions, and many others use the CPI as a guide in their decision making. If the CPI is increasing rapidly, policymakers tend to adjust the wages of government and military workers and the level of government payments to people receiving social security, food stamps, or welfare payments. The CPI is also used to adjust federal income tax rates to keep tax payments in line with inflation. In the private sector, several million workers are covered by union contracts that tie their wages to the level of the CPI. When businesspeople write contracts to buy and sell products over many years, they often include price adjustments tied to the CPI in the contracts.

We can deduce from Figure 7.1 that prices were lower on average before 1982–84 than they were after 1982–84. However, if we look more closely, it appears that the CPI did not rise very much between 1950 and 1960 but rose fairly steadily after about 1965. Economists would argue that inflation was very low during the 1950s and was relatively high in the 1970s. How do they know this? In the next section, we'll learn how to use the price index to determine the inflation rate.

Figure 7.1 **US Consumer Price Index Values**

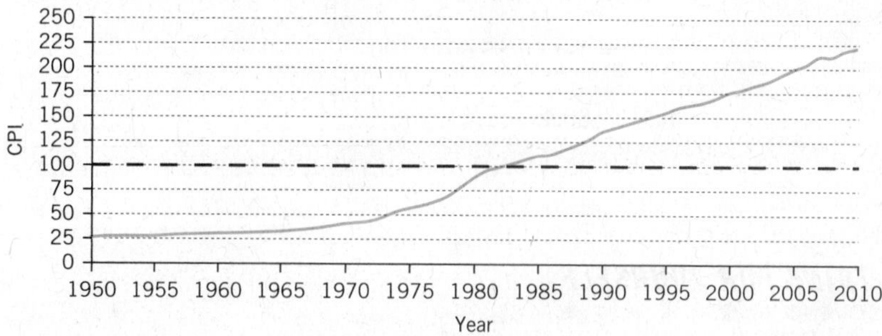

The CPI tracks the average price level for a typical set of goods and services purchased in the U.S. over time. CPI values less than 100 imply that prices in that year are lower than in the base year. CPI values greater than 100 imply that prices in that year are greater than in the base year. *Source*: www.bls.gov. Chart reports seasonally adjusted December U.S. city average CPI values for each year, using 1982–84 as the base year.

Irving Fisher and Price Indexes

Irving Fisher (1867–1947) was an American economist who focused on monetary economics. Monetary economics is the branch of economics that analyzes the functions of money, types of monetary systems, and the regulation of money and financial institutions. His book, *The Making of Index Numbers*, is an influential work in the measurement of the price level and inflation, and Fisher's ideas are still used today.

The Granger Collection, NYC — All rights reserved

The Inflation Rate

A price index allows us to establish an average level of prices at a given point in time. To assess how much prices change across time, we compute the percentage change in the price index over time. For example, if the price index is 100 in the base year (1982–84) and 110 in the following year (1985), prices rose by an average of 10 percent between 1984 and 1985. Similarly, if the price index was 220 in 2000 and 200 in 2010, prices fell by an average of 10 percent between 2000 and 2010.

The inflation rate is the percentage change in the price level over time. It is measured as the percent change in the price index (PI) between two periods.

Computing the percent change in the price index is the way to measure inflation. The **inflation rate** between two time periods is simply the percentage change in the price index between the periods.

$$\text{Inflation rate from period 1 to 2: } \frac{PI_2 - PI_1}{PI_1} * 100$$

Table 7.4 shows the inflation rates for our hypothetical market basket of eggs and milk. The inflation rate between 1980 and 1990 was 24.4 percent, meaning that the prices of the goods in our market basket increased by 24.4 percent on average over the 10-period. Between 2000 and 2010, prices rose less dramatically, by only 11.1 percent over the period.

Although inflation rates can be computed for any time period, they are usually reported as monthly or annual percent changes. Figure 7.2 reports annual inflation rates for the United States from 1950 to 2010. The solid horizontal line in the figure

Table 7.4 Inflation Rates over Time

Years	Inflation Rate
1980–1990	[(100 − 80.4)/80.4] * 100 = 24.4%
1990–2000	[(120.5 − 100)/100] * 100 = 20.5%
2000–2010	[(133.9 − 120.5)/120.5] * 100 = 11.1%

The inflation rate is computed as the percentage change in a price index across time. Between 1980 and 1990 the price index rose from 80.4 to 100. This represents a 24.4 percent increase in the price level, or a 24.4 percent rate of inflation over the decade.

Figure 7.2 **U.S. Annual Inflation Rates**

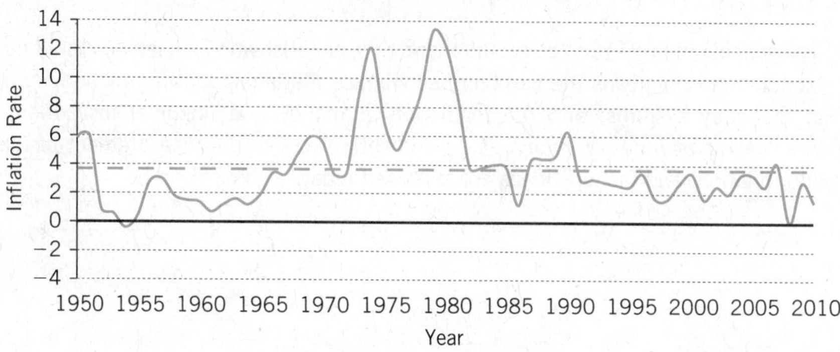

Source: Author's calculations from BLS data. Values represent December–December changes. The dashed line represents the average inflation rate over the period (3.8 percent).

represents a zero rate of inflation, while the dashed horizontal line shows the average inflation rate over the period. Inflation in the United States has ranged from 0 percent to over 12 percent since 1950. At the same time, inflation has tended to fluctuate around an average rate of 3.8 percent per year.

If we compare Figure 7.2 with Figure 7.1, you can see that inflation during the 1950s was close to zero in many years during that period. The low level of inflation corresponds to the relatively flat portion of the CPI during those years shown in Figure 7.1. During the 1970s and 1980s, the CPI rose rapidly, and inflation was much higher, reaching above 12 percent per year in some years. During 1990 to 2010, inflation was again relatively low, close to 2 percent per year.

Disinflation is a period of positive but falling inflation. Disinflation indicates a slowing of the rate of price increase in the economy.

Notice that although inflation itself goes up and down over time, it is almost always positive. Even though inflation *fell* from almost 13 percent in 1980 to just below 4 percent in 1983, inflation was still *positive*. Prices were still rising during 1980–83; they were just rising by less in the mid-1980s than they had in the late 1970s. This type of price change is called **disinflation**. During disinflation, prices are rising, but they are rising more slowly than before.

Deflation is negative inflation. Deflation indicates a period of declining prices of goods and services.

Only rarely has inflation been negative in the United States. Negative inflation, or **deflation**, indicates a general *decline* in the prices of goods and services. The recession that began in 2008 was the first period of deflation in the United States since the mid-1950s. Figure 7.2 shows that the annual change in the CPI between 2007 and 2008 was 0 percent, but during several months of 2008 the inflation rate fell below zero, indicating that U.S. prices were falling on average.

Although on the surface falling prices may seem like a good thing to consumers, deflation is actually problematic for economies. When the prices of goods and services are continually falling, consumers have an incentive to delay their purchases in order to obtain goods and services more cheaply by waiting until prices fall. Delayed purchases will cause a decline in aggregate demand in the current period, which in turn generates reductions in production and output that can push an economy into recession. During the Great Depression, for example, the price level declined by an average of 10 percent per year. In the face of falling prices for their products, many producers could not afford to continue production. In the agricultural sector, the prices of food and grain fell so much and so quickly that many farmers found that it was not even worthwhile to have their crop harvested. Instead, many of the crops were left to whither.

Deflation in the Housing Market

© Andy Dean/iStockphoto

In the mid-2000s, the United States saw a dramatic change in housing prices. After rising steadily for many years, U.S. home prices took a dramatic downward turn. By 2010, one in four U.S. homeowners was "upside down" in their mortgage, meaning they owed more on their home loan than what their homes were worth. Such a situation provides strong incentives for homeowners to enter foreclosure, meaning they default on their mortgage and let the bank take possession of their house. Banks prefer to sell foreclosed houses rather than hold them, which increases the supply of homes for sale on the market. The increase in home supply causes a further reduction in home prices, causing even more homeowners to be upside down in their mortgages. Because most Americans hold the majority of their wealth in their homes, the fall in home prices reduced people's wealth and their demand for other goods and services. This decline in aggregate demand was an important factor that pushed the economy into a deep recession.

Although the United States has managed to keep inflation fairly steady over time, many other countries in the world struggle with high and volatile inflation rates. Figure 7.3 illustrates annual inflation rates by country in 2008. North America and Greenland, Western Europe, Australia, Japan, and several countries in Northeastern Africa had inflation rates below 5 percent in 2008. Alternatively, Venezuela, Iran, Ukraine, Burma, and several African nations faced inflation above 25 percent, including Zimbabwe's 11.2 million percent inflation rate for the year.

Figure 7.3 **World Annual Inflation Rates in 2008**

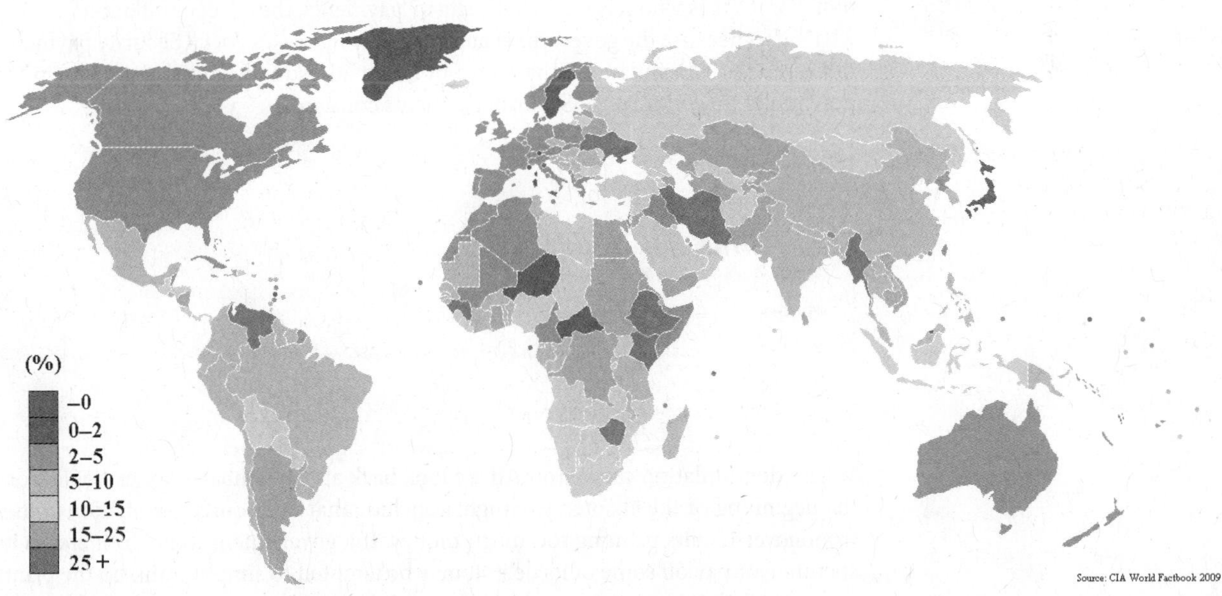

Inflation rates vary across the world. In North America, Europe, Australia, and North Africa, inflation rates were below 5 percent in 2008. In Venezuela, Central Africa, and Ukraine, inflation was above 15 percent. *Source*: Author Sbw01f at Wikipedia.com. Data from CIA World Factbook. http://en.wikipedia.org/wiki/File:World_Inflation_rate_2007.PNG. GNU Free Documentation License.

WINNERS AND LOSERS FROM INFLATION

Does inflation make everyone worse off? No. Inflation can benefit some people at the same time it hurts others. This section describes the winners and losers from inflation.

Savers and Borrowers

When inflation occurs, money that you have saved loses its purchasing power and becomes a poor store of value. Suppose you decide to save money by putting $100 into a locked box under your bed. At the time you put the $100 under your bed, it could purchase $100 worth of goods and services. If you pull the $100 out of its box in, say, five years, it will not purchase the same amount of goods and services that it could have purchased initially. Inflation has eroded the purchasing power of the $100. Money's decline in purchasing power during times of inflation means that inflation hurts savers. Suppose instead that you put your $100 into a savings account at a bank. Inflation will continue to erode the purchasing power of your money, and you will be worse off for saving it unless the interest rate you earn on the savings account is more than the rate of inflation.

Borrowers, on the other hand, benefit from inflation. Suppose you borrow $100 today in order to purchase a given amount of goods and services. Unless you have to pay an interest rate on that loan that is greater than the rate of inflation, you are better off than if you waited to purchase the goods and services. You can buy the goods and services for the $100 today, but they would cost more than $100 in the future.

People on Fixed Incomes

People on fixed incomes lose purchasing power in the face of inflation. Many retirees, for example, receive a fixed monthly payment from their retirement plan. Over time, that fixed payment can purchase fewer and fewer goods and services because of inflation. For retirees who rely on Social Security payments, the effect of inflation is somewhat offset because the government automatically increases Social Security payments to keep pace with inflation. These cost of living adjustments are meant to keep the purchasing power of Social Security payments constant.

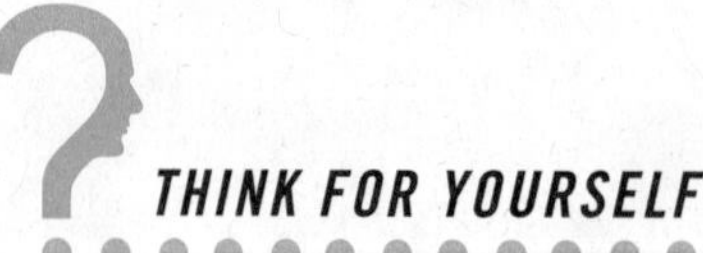

Who would be the winners and losers from deflation? Why?

THE SOURCES OF INFLATION

Where does inflation come from? If we look back at the Zimbabwean example from the beginning of the chapter, we might conclude that one source of inflation comes from governments printing too much money. If a government wants to increase its spending or pay off some of its debt, it may be tempted to simply crank up the printing press and print more money. Unfortunately, printing more money will not by itself generate increases in the output of goods and services in a country and instead will result in inflation. This is what happened in Zimbabwe, where the government fueled inflation by printing Zimbabwean dollars at increasing rates. Because the output of Zimbabwe did not increase, the government printing more money simply caused more dollars to be spent to purchase the same amount of goods. Not all inflation results from governments printing more money, however. Inflation can arise from increases in the costs of resources used in production or from increases in the demand for goods and services. We can use the aggregate demand–aggregate supply model we learned in Chapter 6 to help identify sources of inflation.

Aggregate Demand and Aggregate Supply

Aggregate demand (AD) represents the whole of the demand for all goods and services of the economy. Aggregate supply (AS) represents the whole of the supply of all the goods and services in the economy. The AD/AS model shows the level of economic output per year (GDP) on the horizontal axis, and the price level on the vertical axis. Increases in the price level can arise from factors that either increase AD or decrease AS. Inflation that arises from increases in AD is called **demand-pull inflation**, while inflation that stems from decreases in AS is called **cost-push inflation**.

Demand-pull inflation arises from increases in aggregate demand.

Cost-push inflation arises from decreases in aggregate supply.

Demand-Pull Inflation

Figure 7.4 illustrates demand-pull inflation. An increase in any of the components of AD (consumption, investment, government spending, or net exports) can cause an outward shift in the AD curve and a corresponding increase in the price level. In Figure 7.4, the shift from AD to AD′ generates a relatively small increase in the price level from P to P′. The small price change results because the economy is far from its productive capacity so that it can generate increases in output by using relatively cheap idle resources. The shift from AD″ to AD‴ occurs on the steeper section of the AS curve, where aggregate output is closer to the limit that the economy can produce with its available resources and technology. Increases in aggregate demand in this area of the AS curve generate much larger increases in the price level, from P" to P"' because there are very few underutilized resources in the economy at this level of output.

The AD/AS model implies that we can expect inflation to result from policies that increase any of the components of aggregate demand. As an example, if consumer

Figure 7.4 **Demand-Pull Inflation**

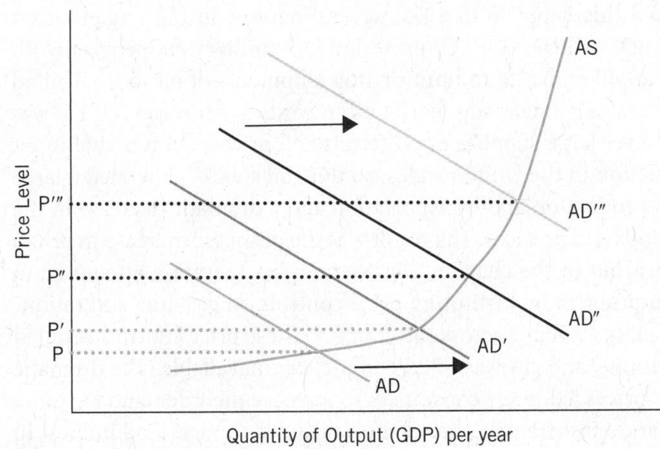

Increases in AD from AD to AD′ along the flatter portion of the AS curve generate small increases in demand-pull inflation. Increases in AD from AD″ to AD‴ generate large increases in demand-pull inflation.

incomes or business investment rise, we would expect an outward shift in the AD curve and a corresponding increase in the price level. Positive changes in consumer expectations or increases in government spending also increase aggregate demand. Although increases in aggregate demand are beneficial because they increase GDP, they can also cause inflation. The degree to which increases in aggregate demand generate inflation depends on where the economy is operating on the AS curve. The closer we are to our potential output level, the more inflation we will see from a given increase in aggregate demand. The further we are inside our production possibilities frontier, the smaller the impact an increase in AD will have on inflation.

Cost-Push Inflation

Cost-push inflation comes from reductions in aggregate supply like the one illustrated in Figure 7.5. With cost-push inflation, increases in the costs of inputs into production

Figure 7.5 **Cost-Push Inflation**

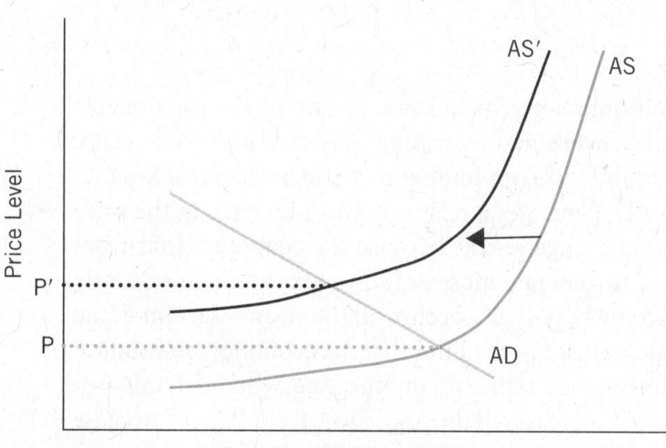

Decreases in AS from AS to AS' cause cost-push inflation. When aggregate supply falls, the price level rises and GDP falls.

cause decreases in the aggregate supply of goods and services, as shown by the inward shift in the aggregate supply curve from AS to AS'. The decrease in aggregate supply puts upward pressure on the overall price level, and prices rise from P to P'.

The high inflation experienced by the United States during the 1970s resulted from cost-push inflation. During the 1970s, average prices increased as much as 13% per year. Why did this happen? In 1973, several nations in the Organization of Petroleum Exporting Countries (OPEC) protested U.S. military cooperation with Israel by engaging in an oil embargo to limit or stop shipments of oil to the United States. Because OPEC was a primary supplier of oil to western countries, OPEC was able to use its control over large supplies of oil to raise oil prices. Oil is a vital input for much of the production in the United States, so this "oil shock" generated a large increase in the cost of production and transportation and a dramatic decrease in the aggregate supply of goods and services. The result was the dramatic increase in prices we saw in Figure 7.2 earlier in the chapter. The Nixon administration attempted to deal with the inflation problem by instituting price controls on gasoline and rationing the amount of gasoline available across the country. These price controls resulted in long lines at gas stations, and gas was often completely unavailable. The dramatic increase in oil and gas prices led many consumers to increase their demand for more fuel efficient vehicles and mass transit. The oil shock also led to increased interest in alternative forms of energy, including wind and solar power.

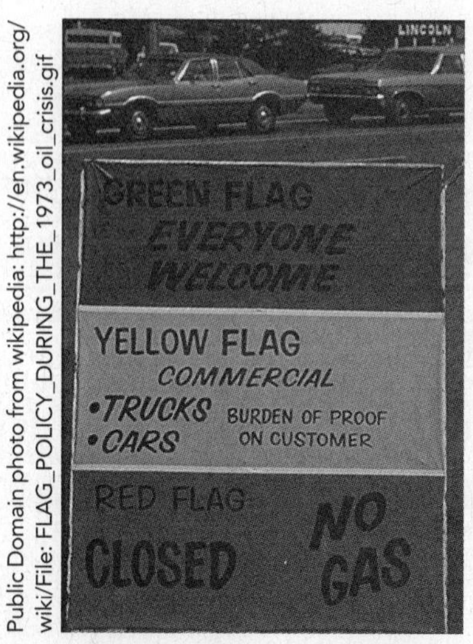

Public Domain photo from wikipedia: http://en.wikipedia.org/wiki/File: FLAG_POLICY_DURING_THE_1973_oil_crisis.gif

Sign explaining the gasoline rationing in 1974.

MEASURING NOMINAL AND REAL VALUES

We learned at the beginning of this chapter that inflation, particularly high levels of inflation like those experienced in Zimbabwe in 2008–09, erode the purchasing power of money. Perhaps you've heard your grandparents or great-grandparents talk about buying a new house for $10,000 or earning a salary of $6,500 per year in 1960. Average salaries are closer to $45,000 today. So did your grandparents earn more money than the average person today? In order to answer that question, we need to assess the purchasing power of money across time. In other words, we need to adjust the face value of the $6,000 your grandparents earned in 1950 in order to account for inflation.

We can use price index measures to translate **nominal values** to **real values**. Nominal values or nominal prices are not adjusted for inflation. Nominal values are sometimes called *current values* or *face values* because they express prices using the value of the money of the time. Expressing prices in nominal values would use the 1950 costs of goods and services to measure 1950 prices and would use 2010 costs to measure 2010 prices. The market basket prices in Tables 7.1 and 7.2 and the grandparents' $10,000 home price are both expressed in nominal values.

Real values are values that have been adjusted for inflation.

Nominal values are values that have not been adjusted for inflation.

Real values are adjusted for inflation. Real values are sometimes called *constant values* because they use a constant level of purchasing power to measure prices and output. Expressing prices in real values would use 2010 costs of goods and services to measure the prices of goods and services in both 1950 and 2010.

Suppose that it is 2010 and you are considering taking a job as a teacher. The job pays $45,000 per year. Your grandmother informs you that she earned $6,500 per year in her job as a teacher in the same town in 1960. Will you make more than she did in real earnings? In other words, would $45,000 in 2010 allow you to purchase more or fewer goods and services than your grandmother was able to purchase with $6,500 in 1960? To answer this question, we can compare the values of the CPI during the two time periods. In 1960, the CPI was 29.6. In 2010, the CPI was 220.2. This means that prices in 2010 were 7.4 times higher in 2010 than in 1960 because

$$\text{CPI in 2010/CPI in 1960} = 220.2/29.6 = 7.4$$

If you accept the teaching job, your earnings in 2010 will be 6.9 times higher than your grandmother's were in 1960 since

$$\$45{,}000/\$6{,}500 = 6.9$$

Prices were 7.4 times higher and teacher earnings were 6.9 times higher in 2010 than in 1960. Prices rose faster than teachers' earnings between 1960 and 2010. In terms of purchasing power, your grandmother made more than you will in the teaching job. Stated differently, your grandmother's real income was higher in 1960 than your real income was in 2010.

THINK FOR YOURSELF

Would your real income be greater than that of your grandmother if your job paid $47,500 instead of $45,000? What if your job paid $50,000?

More generally, we can compute the real value of any economic variable by dividing its nominal value by the CPI and multiplying the result by 100:

$$\text{Real value in base year} = (\text{nominal value in current year}/\text{CPI in current year}) * 100$$

For example, the real value of your grandmother's earnings of $6,500 in 1960 is

$$(\$6{,}500/29.6) * 100 = \$21{,}959 \text{ in 1982–84 dollars.}$$

We use 1982–84 dollars because that is the base year we used to compute the CPI. The real value of your $45,000 earnings in 2010 is

$$(\$45{,}000/220.2) * 100 = \$20{,}436 \text{ in 1982–84 dollars.}$$

Since your real earnings are $20,436 and your grandmother's real earnings are $21,959, we have illustrated again that your grandmother's earnings had more purchasing power than yours. The real value of your grandmother's income was greater than the real value of your income.

If the CPI in 2010 is 220.2, what is the real value of $47,500 in terms of its purchasing power in 1982–84? What is the real value of $50,000?

SUMMARY

Inflation is a general, ongoing increase in the price level in an economy. In the presence of inflation, the purchasing power of money declines. A price index is used to measure the general level of prices in an economy and can be used to compare the real value of money over time. Inflation can be caused by governments engaging in excess printing of currency, as in the case of Zimbabwe in 2009. Inflation can also arise from demand-side factors, including increases in consumption or government spending and from supply-side factors including broad increases in the cost of inputs. Price indices can be used to translate nominal values into real values that allow us to compare the purchasing power of money over time by adjusting for inflation.

KEY CONCEPTS

- Inflation
- Face value of money
- Purchasing power of money
- Medium of exchange
- Unit of account
- Store of value
- Commodity money
- Fiat money
- Price index
- Market basket

- Inflation rate
- Disinflation
- Deflation
- Demand-pull inflation
- Cost-push inflation
- Nominal values
- Real values

DISCUSSION QUESTIONS AND PROBLEMS

1. The following table presents prices and quantities consumed by a typical college student.

Year	Price Per Book	Quantity of Books	Price Per Pen	Quantity of Pens	Price Per Notepad	Quantity of Notepads
2010	50	10	2.00	20	1.00	30
2011	60	12	2.50	30	1.50	50
2012	75	12	3.00	30	1.00	50

a. Assuming that the purchases in year 2010 are chosen as the relevant market basket for all years, complete the following table:

Year	CPI Base 2010	CPI Base 2011	CPI Base 2012
2010			
2011			
2012			

b. Using 2010 as the base year, compute the inflation rate from 2010 to 2011.

c. Using 2010 as the base year, compute the inflation rate from 2011 to 2012.

2. How are savers hurt and borrowers helped by inflation?
3. What are the functions of money? Why is each important?
4. What is the difference between demand-pull and cost-push inflation?
5. During 2011, many citizens in the Middle East called for governmental reform. In some countries, oil production was reduced in the face of protests. Use an AD/AS diagram to illustrate the potential impact of these outcomes on inflation in the United States.

MULTIPLE CHOICE QUESTIONS

1. Inflation occurs when
   a. the purchasing power of money is increasing.
   b. some prices are increasing but most other prices are decreasing.
   c. the average level of prices is increasing.
   d. the purchasing power of money remains unchanged.

2. Demand-side or demand-pull inflation would be the result of a(n)
   a. increase in the economy's level of total spending.
   b. increase in the economy's level of employment.
   c. decrease in the economy's productivity.
   d. decrease in the resource prices of the economy.

3. Suppose the price level (as measured by the CPI) in four successive years is 100, 90, 85, and 80. Which of the following is true?
   a. The economy is experiencing rising inflation.
   b. The economy is experiencing misinformation.
   c. The economy is experiencing deflation.
   d. The economy is experiencing constant inflation.

4. Suppose the price level (as measured by the CPI) in four successive years is 100, 110, 130, and 160. Which of the following is true?
   a. The economy is experiencing rising inflation.
   b. The economy is experiencing misinformation.
   c. The economy is experiencing deflation.
   d. The economy is experiencing constant inflation.

5. Inflation is important because
   a. it affects the value of one's income.
   b. it affects the real return one earns on investments.
   c. it affects the real interest rate.
   d. it often affects the negotiation of wage contracts and the size cost of living allowances.
   e. all of the above.

6. Which of the following is not a function of money?
   a. Unit of account
   b. Store of value
   c. Protection against inflation
   d. Medium of exchange

7. If the CPI in a given year is 300, this means that
   a. prices are 200 percent higher than in the base year.
   b. prices have fallen since the base year.
   c. prices are three times higher than in the base year.
   d. the economy is experiencing hyper inflation.

8. The CPI was 220.2 in December 2010 and 174.6 in December 2000. This means that the inflation rate between 2000 and 2010 was
   a. 21 percent.
   b. 26 percent.
   c. 46 percent.
   d. 79 percent.

9. Your income was $25,000 in 2009 and $25,500 in 2010. The CPI was 217.2 in 2009 and 220.2 in 2010. This means that
   a. your real income has fallen.
   b. your real income has risen.
   c. your real income has not changed.
   d. there is not enough information to determine what happened to your real income.

10. The CPI was 217.2 in December 2009 and 220.2 in December 2010. This means that the inflation rate between 2000 and 2010 was
   a. 3 percent.
   b. 1.38 percent.
   c. 1.36 percent.
   d. 2 percent.

ADDITIONAL READINGS AND WEB RESOURCES

The Bureau of Labor Statistics website www.bls.gov includes current and historical data on the Consumer Price Index and related inflation rates.

Milton Friedman, the 1977 Nobel-prize winning economist, gave his Nobel lecture on inflation and unemployment. Friedman, Milton (1977) "Nobel Lecture: Inflation and Unemployment," *The Journal of Political Economy* 85(3) (June): 451–472.

Friedman, Milton and Anna Jacobson Schwartz (1963) *A Monetary History of the United States 1867–1960.* Princeton University Press.

The Federal Reserve Board produces reports on inflation. www.federalreserve.gov

© Anna Zielińska/iStockphoto

8 The Power and Limits of Markets

After studying this chapter, you should be able to:

- Describe the resource allocation and resource ownership decisions facing societies
- Classify the basic types of economic systems
- Describe the differences in types of ownership of resources
- Describe the differences in types of decision making about resource allocation
- Evaluate the tradeoffs between efficiency and equity; security and liberty
- Understand the concept of market failure

People's wants and needs tend to far outstrip their available resources. Because of this, people are destined to constantly make choices at both the individual and the societal level. At the individual level, we face choices about how to allocate our time, money, and other resources. We face similar choices at the societal and global levels because there are millions of alternative uses for the land, labor, and capital resources of a society. Societies also face choices about the ownership of resources. Resources could be owned as a group or owned individually by the members of a society. Choices about what to do with resources are **resource allocation** decisions. Choices about who owns resources are **resource ownership** or property rights decisions.

The resource allocation decisions of a society determine how the resources are shared among society's citizens.

The resource ownership decisions of a society determine the property rights over the resources in a society.

In this chapter, we focus on resource allocation and resource ownership decisions. These are the big questions about how societies organize themselves and divide up their land, labor, and capital resources. Resource allocation and resource ownership choices include decisions about what outputs a society will produce with its resources, how it will produce this output, and to whom the output will be distributed. Choices about resource allocation and resource ownership are how societies answer these basic economic questions.

As an analogy to the resource allocation and resource ownership decisions, think of all of a society's resources being used to make an economic output "pie." We don't have the resources to produce all the kinds of pie everyone wants and needs, so we must ration the resources among the different choices we could make. What type of pie will be baked? How big will it be? What kind of ingredients and efforts will be used to make it? Who will own the resulting slices and how big will each slice be? If one person's slice is thought to be too small, will we take slices from others to make up for it?

Public Domain image from Wikipedia: http: //en.wikipedia .org/wiki/File:RationingBoardNOLAVachonC.jpg

An alternative analogy would describe resource allocation as a rationing process. In this view, societies have to parcel out or ration their resources because people have more wants and needs than resources available. Societies utilize many types of rationing systems. One system is the rationing provided by market prices. A system of ration books and stamps was used by the United States and other countries during World War II to distribute sugar, gasoline, tires, shoes, coffee, meat, cheese, and many other items made scarcer because of the war. Sometimes rationing is done via queues or lines, as in the case of people lining up to ride the lifts at ski resorts or see a Broadway show. Sometimes rationing is done using a first come, first served method, which is likely the method used to ration the desks during your economics class. Sometimes rationing is done via a lottery, which is how many hunters obtain permits to hunt wild game, how recreationalists obtain permits to float down the Colorado River in the Grand Canyon, and how some universities allocate prime parking spaces on campus.

SYSTEMS OF RESOURCE ALLOCATION AND RESOURCE OWNERSHIP

Choices about the methods of resource allocation and types of resource ownership are among the most important choices a society must make. These choices are deeply interwoven into all aspects of our lives. They affect how people spend their time, how they choose their careers, and whether or not they can easily trade to obtain the goods and services they want and need.

The array of different resource allocation methods can be classified along a spectrum running from command to market methods. The different types of resource ownership can also be classified along a spectrum running from private ownership to public ownership. The combination of the resource ownership and the resource allocation methods used in a society determines the society's type of economic system.

Resource Allocation: Command and Market Systems

Command systems use governmental regulation or central planning to allocate resources.

At one end of the resource allocation spectrum is the **command system**, where rationing is done through a public, centralized planning, or communal method. In a command system, choices about how to allocate land, labor, and capital resources are made by citizens together as a group, through elected officials, or through social leaders, and the decisions are decreed or commanded by government or community agencies. Examples of the command system include decisions about how and where roads and schools get built, government regulations regarding how safe products or working environments must be, laws about the lowest wage allowed in certain jobs, and regulations about the appropriate prices for electricity.

At the other end of the resource allocation spectrum is a private, decentralized, or individual-based system. This is called a **market system** because markets frequently evolve to coordinate resource allocation in these systems. Examples of the market, system include the market where you purchased this textbook, the labor market, and the markets for music, art, food and a wide array of other goods and services. Through prices, markets allocate resources from those most willing and able to sell them to those most willing and able to buy them.

Market systems use decentralized interactions between buyers and sellers to allocate resources.

THINK FOR YOURSELF

Provide an example of a command system of resource allocation that you have observed. Provide an example of a market system of resource allocation that you have observed. What are the characteristics of command systems? Of market systems?

Resource Ownership: Socialist and Capitalist Systems

Having ownership of a resource or output means having the right to consume it, keep it, or sell it to another. At one end of the resource ownership spectrum are **socialist systems**, which are also known as public property or communal ownership systems. In most socialist systems, resources are jointly owned by the public and are held by the government. Under socialism, individuals cannot trade the right of ownership away because resources and outputs are publicly owned. Examples of publicly owned resources include public parks, public schools, government buildings, military equipment, public libraries, and public roads.

Socialist systems use public property ownership.

At the other end of the resource ownership spectrum is **capitalism**, which entails private property ownership. In capitalist systems, individual people, households, or businesses have tradable ownership rights to resources. Examples of privately owned property include the clothes you are wearing, cars, computers and equipment owned by individuals or businesses, and the pen or pencil you use to take notes during your economics class.

Capitalist systems use private property ownership.

THINK FOR YOURSELF

Provide an example of a socialist system of resource ownership that you have observed. Provide an example of a capitalist system of resource ownership that you have observed. What are the characteristics of socialist systems? Of capitalist systems?

Market capitalism is an economic system that uses private property ownership and private resource allocation decisions.

Command socialism is an economic system that uses public property ownership and public resource allocation decisions.

Market socialism is an economic system that uses public property ownership and private resource allocation decisions.

Command capitalism is an economic system that uses private property ownership and public resource allocation decisions.

TYPES OF ECONOMIC SYSTEMS

In Table 8.1, the categories of resource allocation and resource ownership are used to classify different types of economic systems. Private resource allocation systems are market systems, and private resource ownership systems are capitalist systems, so the combination of private property ownership and private resource allocation decisions is called **market capitalism**. The combination of public property ownership and public resource allocation decisions is called **command socialism**. **Market socialism** utilizes public property ownership but private resource allocation decisions, whereas **command capitalism** utilizes private property ownership and public resource allocation decisions.

Table 8.1 Types of Economic Systems

		Resource Allocation	
		Private	Public
Resource Ownership	Private	Market Capitalism	Command Capitalism
	Public	Market Socialism	Command Socialism

The mixture of resource allocation and resource ownership systems used in a society determine a society's economic system.

Examples of Economic Systems

Where do the different societies in the world fall in terms of these categories of economic systems? There is no society that uses only one type of economic system. Instead, societies tend to use a mixture of economic systems with varying degrees of command versus market allocation and public versus private ownership.

The United States is one of the most well-known examples of a society that relies primarily on the market capitalist economic system, which is distinguished by relatively minimal government regulation, minimal government involvement in the economy, and extensive private property. Based on these criteria, Hong Kong, Singapore, Australia, Ireland, New Zealand, the United States, and Canada are the most market capitalist countries in the world.

France and Sweden are examples of societies that rely more on command capitalism, distinguished by high levels of government regulation and involvement in the economy. In the United States, many utility companies are privately owned but face regulations regarding the prices they can charge, which is a characteristic of command capitalism.

Market socialism is characterized by public or governmental ownership of resources but a market allocation system. In the United States, logging permits in National Forests are allocated using a market socialist system, since the forests are publicly owned and logging permits are auctioned to bidders using a market process.

Command socialist systems are characterized by governmental ownership of resources and governmental control of how the resources are used. Examples of this economic system include the Marxist-Leninist societies of the former Union of Soviet Socialist Republics, the People's Republic of China under the leadership of Mao Zedong, and present day North Korea. An example of command socialism in the United States includes military bases and military equipment, as the use of military bases is determined by the government and military bases are owned by the taxpayers.

Roger Viollet Collection/Getty Images, Inc.

Karl Marx and Command Socialism

Karl Marx (1818–1883) is a German philosopher often viewed as the father of *communism*. Communism is a classless society based on cooperation among its citizens, the absence of private ownership of society's resources, and without distinctions of income or social status. Societies organized under this design allocate resources based on Marx's principle "from each according to his ability, to each according to his need." Such systems rely heavily on command socialism, with communally-owned resources that are allocated based on government decisions. Marx believed that class struggles within capitalism would lead to its self-destruction and that capitalism would eventually be replaced by a communist society. Marx's tombstone is engraved with the message: "WORKERS OF THE WORLD UNITE!," the final line of *The Communist Manifesto*, which Marx coauthored with Friedrich Engels. The book is one of the most influential political books of all time.

JUDGING AMONG ALTERNATIVE ECONOMIC SYSTEMS AND POLICIES

Which economic system is best? There is no objective answer to that question, and societies have grappled throughout history with finding the system that works best for them. With the exceptions of the Great Proletarian Cultural Revolution in China in the 1960s and the Russian Revolution in the early 1900s, both of which moved their societies toward command socialist economic systems, it has not been the experience of recent history that societies make drastic changes in their degree of reliance on one economic system relative to another. Instead, government policies tend to emphasize one economic system or another at the margin. For example, the imposition of the minimum wage in the United States can be viewed as a movement from a market capitalist policy toward a command capitalist policy, since the minimum wage sets a regulation regarding the price that can be paid to labor, but individuals in the U.S. own the property rights to their labor.

Emphasizing more of one type of economic system over another involves tradeoffs. The primary tradeoffs that arise when we emphasize one economic system over another are between efficiency versus equity and between security versus liberty.

Efficiency

We examined the concept of economic efficiency in Chapters 2 and 4. In Chapter 2, we used the production possibilities frontier (PPF) to show that a combination of outputs that lies on an economy's PPF is an efficient outcome. An inefficient outcome was one lying inside the PPF, where resources were wasted or not put to their best use. In Chapter 4, we learned that markets can generate economic efficiency when they reach equilibriums that equate the marginal benefits and marginal costs of production of goods and services. Such equilibriums generate the maximum net benefit possible from a given set of resources.

Market capitalist economic systems are quite effective at generating efficient resource allocations because they tend to rely on comparative advantage. In market capitalist systems, prices provide individuals and businesses with incentives to specialize in production according to their comparative advantage and then trade with others who have comparative advantage in other goods or services. In market capitalist systems, the people who have the highest willingness and ability to pay for a good or service obtain the good or service from suppliers who have comparative advantage in its production and are able to produce at the lowest cost. Trades that generate equilibrium between buyers and sellers in market capitalist systems maximize the consumer and producer surplus derived from production and consumption.

*The **invisible hand** is the self-regulating mechanism of market systems that generates allocation of resources based on self-interest, competition, and comparative advantage.*

In his book *An Inquiry into the Nature and Causes of the Wealth of Nations*, Adam Smith noted that market capitalist systems can produce efficient resource allocations with very minimal government involvement. He called this self-regulating mechanism of allocation the **invisible hand**, saying

> *"[The individual decision maker], intends only his own gain; and he is in this, as in many other cases, led by an invisible hand to promote an end which was no part of his intention . . . By pursuing his own interest, he frequently promotes that of the society more effectually than when he really intends to promote it."*

Command socialist systems are not as well suited to generate economic efficiency. In command socialist economic systems, the prices and quantities of goods and services are determined through central planning, where government serves to coordinate the production and distribution of society's resources. Although it is feasible that central planning could coordinate production based on people's comparative advantage, the sheer amount of information necessary to determine who has comparative advantage in what and how resources should be allocated within the system implies that substantial social resources would need to be devoted to the information gathering, analysis, and regulation of activity in order to ensure that resources are allocated to their best use. Because market capitalist systems do not need to divert resources in order to plan and coordinate economic activities, market capitalist systems are more likely than command socialist systems to generate efficient resource allocations. In addition, resource prices and quantities that are set by the government are less likely to provide an incentive for producers or sellers to find the lowest cost method of producing goods and services.

Equity

Philosophers and economists have long struggled with defining the ideas of equity, fairness, and justice. In *The Republic*, Plato describes justice as a harmonious relationship between citizens and their government. The philosopher John Rawls has described a fair or just allocation system as one we would choose if we were making the rules of our allocation system behind a theoretical veil of ignorance where we did not yet know our future place in society. You might decide that the equitable way to split a pizza among your roommates is to give an equal number of slices to each person. Under this interpretation of equity, market capitalism is not equitable because market capitalism distributes goods and services based on willingness and ability to pay rather than on an equal distribution of goods and services among members of society. One criticism of market capitalist systems is that they are unlikely to produce many goods and services for the poor because the poor lack the ability to pay for goods and services. At the same time, market capitalism will produce luxury items like tanning booths, cosmetic surgery, $10,000 bottles of whisky, and full-size in-home movie theaters for the rich.

A further criticism of the inequity that can result from market capitalist systems arises because our individual opportunities for obtaining goods and services depend greatly on the resources we each have available to us, including our health, education, motivation, and value system. Because many of these attributes are innate, the resource allocation that results in a market system can depend greatly on the endowments each of us receives at birth. Our health and the class status of our parents are outcomes that are somewhat random and subject to luck rather than hard work. Indeed, it can be argued quite effectively that the most important decision someone in a market capitalist society makes is to "choose their parents wisely," since parental outcomes play such an important role in the outcomes of their children.

Command socialist economic systems are more likely than market capitalist systems to achieve an equitable resource allocation because they dictate the types of goods and services produced and their distribution to all members of society. Societies based on economic equity are also called egalitarian systems. Although it is difficult to find real-world examples of societies that reach an equal distribution of resources among their members, many societies have policies that tend to equalize the distributions of goods and services. A classic example from literature is Robin Hood. Hood's "take from the rich, give to the poor" motto equalized the distribution of resources around Nottingham. The U.S. income tax system is egalitarian because those earning more income pay higher income tax rates than those who earn less. The welfare system, inheritance taxes, Pell education grants, and subsidized student loans are all examples of U.S. programs that generate a more equitable distribution of income.

Describe ways that you have seen society trade efficiency for equity and vice versa.

Liberty

The term "liberty" has many interpretations, but in modern economics it is often used interchangeably with the term "individual freedom." Under this interpretation, liberty describes a situation in which an individual can act according to his or her own will and is free from outside compulsion. Indeed, one of the defining documents of the economic and governmental system of the United States, the preamble to the U.S. Declaration of Independence, states that "We hold these truths to be self-evident, that all men are created equal, that they are endowed by their Creator with certain unalienable rights, that among these are Life, Liberty and the pursuit of Happiness." Liberty in this context means freedom from coercion by government or other individuals. A similar phrase is included in the constitutions of Japan (1947) and Vietnam (1945). The United Nations Universal Declaration on Human Rights (1948) states in Article 3, "Everyone has the right to life, liberty, and security of person."

Because they rely on individual actors and individual decision-making, market-based systems tend to generate more personal liberty than do command-based systems. Similarly, because they rely on private rather than public property, capitalist systems tend to provide more liberty than do socialist systems.

John Stuart Mill, *On Liberty* and The Marketplace of Ideas

Rischgitz/Getty Images, Inc.

John Stewart Mill (1806–1873) was a moral and political theorist, economist, and one of the most influential philosophers of the nineteenth century. He wrote widely, including works on human rights and slavery, logic, women's rights, and religion. His book *On Liberty* sets forth his arguments for freedom of the individual and in particular freedom of thought and discussion. The ideas are of particular interest to economists. Mill is linked, along with other philosophers and thinkers, with promoting the "marketplace of ideas." According to Mill, people are individually responsible for their beliefs and actions, and the best beliefs and actions are those that can survive free and open critical assessment and debate. Just as the best goods can be produced through the competition of the marketplace, the best beliefs and actions will survive in the marketplace of ideas.

Security

In general terms, we can equate security with safety. We trade liberty for security when we enforce speed limits, require passenger and luggage screening at airports, and allow National Guard troops to exert military control in areas affected by natural disasters. We are not free to drive as fast as we might want or to carry particular items or substances on airplanes, but we comply with these restrictions on our freedom because we recognize that we are safer when we force people to drive at reasonable speeds and when we do not allow people to carry potentially explosive materials onto airplanes.

Economic security means having a stable standard of living. Economic security can come from having a steady source of income from employment, investments, savings, a retirement fund, or some other source. We trade away some of our economic liberty in order to increase our economic security through policies like mandatory unemployment insurance, mandatory Social Security taxes, worker's compensation insurance, and welfare programs that establish a minimum standard of living for people in society. Because command socialist economic systems tend to be more equitable, and because obtaining that equity involves redistribution of income from some groups to others through taxes or other policies, command socialist economic systems generate more economic security than do market capitalist economic systems.

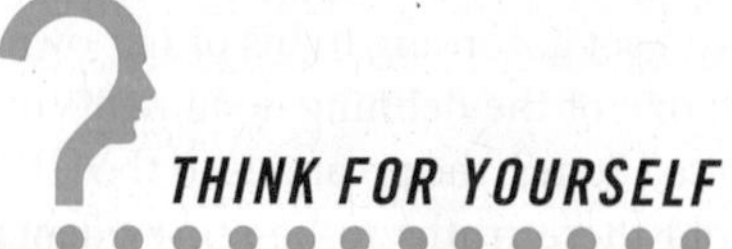

THINK FOR YOURSELF

Describe ways that you have seen society trade liberty for security and vice versa.

MARKET FAILURE AND THE LIMITS OF MARKET CAPITALIST ECONOMIC SYSTEMS

Market capitalist economic systems entail private property rights and private decision making and tend to generate relatively more efficiency and liberty compared to other economic systems. The combination of economic efficiency and personal liberty makes market capitalist systems powerful tools for achieving efficient resource allocations. However, there are limits to this power. In particular, market capitalist economic systems only generate economically efficient outcomes under a certain set of conditions. When these conditions are not met, market capitalist economic systems do not generate efficient outcomes and instead result in market failure.

Market failure describes situations when decision makers are not faced with the full costs or benefits of their actions, with the result that the market system will not generate an efficient allocation of goods or services for society.

Market Failure: When the market generates an inefficient allocation of goods or services.

Sources of market failure include monopolies, public goods, externalities, and imperfect information. We'll discuss each of these briefly in the following sections, but because market failures constitute an important part of economic and public policy decision making, they are described in more detail in several subsequent chapters.

Monopolies

A **monopoly** occurs when there is only one seller of a good or service in a given market. In a monopoly market, the seller has the ability to exert undue influence over the price of a good because there is no competition to push prices down to equate marginal benefits and marginal costs. A monopolist can instead set price above the good's marginal cost of production. When buying from a monopoly, buyers make choices about the quantity of the good to buy based on the high monopoly price rather than on the good's marginal cost of production, and the resulting allocation of resources is inefficient. Chapter 18 presents comparisons between monopoly and competitive markets.

A monopoly is a market with only one seller of a good or service.

Public Goods

When it is not possible for sellers to exclude nonbuyers from using a good, the good is called a **public good**. Public goods cause market failure because when people are able to get goods or services without paying for them (called free riding), sellers have no mechanism to recoup the costs of producing the good. When sellers can't cover their costs of production, they have no incentive to provide the good in the first place. Without government intervention, public goods will not be produced in a market capitalist system even though people would derive substantial marginal benefits if the public goods were produced.

A public good is one where the seller cannot exclude nonbuyers from using it.

National defense is an example of a public good. It is practically impossible to establish a U.S. national defense system that can exclude specific individuals from protection. A company that tried to establish a private national defense program in a market capitalist economic system would face free rider problems because there is no practical way to prohibit people who decide not to pay their national defense bill from enjoying national defense services. Even though people obtain benefits from national defense, the free rider problem would deter businesses from producing national defense in a market capitalist economic system.

Externalities

Externalities occur when some of the costs or benefits of a trade are imposed on people outside the trade. When a manufacturing company dumps its waste into a nearby river, for example, it generates costs that are borne by the people downstream. In a market capitalist economic system, the manufacturing company has no incentive to take these external costs into account when making its production decisions.

Externalities are costs or benefits of a trade that are imposed on people outside the trade.

As a result, the firm's output level will not reflect the full marginal costs to society that are generated by the firm's production, and the resulting allocation of resources will be inefficient. Chapters 15, 16, and 17 highlight the market failures that result from externalities.

Imperfect Information

Imperfect information occurs when the full costs or benefits of a trade are not known to all of the parties engaged in the trade. In the market for used cars, for example, sellers know the condition of the cars they are trying to sell. The cars may be defective lemons or may be in great shape. Buyers do not have enough information about all prospective cars to know whether or not a given used car is a lemon, so they tend to offer relatively low prices for used cars. This implies that sellers of high-quality used cars get relatively low prices for their cars because their good used cars are grouped with the lemons in buyers' minds. Faced with price offers that are lower than their cars' value, sellers of good used cars have incentives not to sell their cars at all, leaving only the lemons for sale in the used car market. Buyers who want high-quality used cars will understand that the used-car market consists primarily of lemons, and will thus prefer not to buy used cars. Imperfect information on the part of buyers can result in limited or nonexistent markets for high-quality used cars, even though mutually beneficial trades of high-quality used cars could occur. The implications of imperfect information are discussed in more detail in Chapter 15.

SUMMARY

This chapter has highlighted the intertwined relationships between resource ownership, resource use, and economic and political systems. Resource ownership systems can range from private property to public property. Private property ownership occurs in capitalist systems and public property ownership occurs in socialist systems. Decisions about resource use and resource allocation can be made privately, as in market systems, or publicly, as in command systems. Economic systems can be characterized by their degree of emphasis on different resource ownership and resource allocation systems.

Decisions about resource ownership and resource allocation involve tradeoffs between liberty and security and between efficiency and equity. Although most economies include elements of market and command resource allocation and capitalist and socialist resource ownership, societies like the United States tend to include more market capitalist elements. Market capitalist systems emphasize liberty and freedom and generate more efficient outcomes relative to other economic systems. Although market capitalist systems are powerful tools for achieving efficient resource allocations, they are limited in their ability to generate equitable outcomes and guaranteed minimum living standards. In addition, market capitalist systems do not generate efficient outcomes in the presence of market failures. In response to market failures and inequities inherent in market capitalist societies, policymakers often choose to engage in regulations, price controls, and other market interventions. We will examine the tradeoffs associated with market interventions as we assess policy responses to market failures and other economic issues throughout the text.

KEY CONCEPTS

- Resource allocation
- Resource ownership
- Command system
- Market system
- Socialist system
- Capitalist system
- Market capitalism
- Command socialism
- Market socialism
- Command capitalism
- Invisible hand
- Market failure
- Monopoly
- Public good
- Externalities

DISCUSSION QUESTIONS AND PROBLEMS

1. Make a list of three different ways to divide a bag of candy bars among a group. What are the pros and cons of each method you list? If this were the way that all resources in an economy were divided, what outcomes and responses might we anticipate among the members of society?
2. Describe how market capitalist systems tend to generate efficient allocations of resources. Is efficiency an important goal for economic systems and policy makers?
3. Why is equity not necessarily an outcome of market capitalist systems?
4. How does emphasizing security versus liberty affect the size of government? How does emphasizing efficiency versus equity affect the size of government?
5. China and many of the countries in Central and Eastern Europe are classified as "transition economies" because they are in the process of moving from centrally planned, command socialist economic systems toward market capitalist systems. What kinds of changes do you think take place for individuals and policy makers during this process?

MULTIPLE CHOICE QUESTIONS

1. Which of the following systems allows for the most liberty and more likely generates efficient outcomes?
   a. Market capitalist systems
   b. Command socialist systems
   c. Command capitalist systems
   d. Market socialist systems
2. The motto "take from the rich, give to the poor" is an example of which resource allocation priority?
   a. Equity
   b. Liberty
   c. Efficiency
   d. Austerity
   e. All of the above
3. An economic system characterized by private resource ownership and public resource allocation decisions is a ______ economic system.
   a. market capitalist
   b. market socialist
   c. command capitalist
   d. command socialist
4. Government-provided financial aid that is given to college students based on their income level would be an example of a ___ economic system.
   a. market capitalist
   b. market socialist
   c. command capitalist
   d. command socialist
5. A startup company developing and selling e-readers to customers is an example of a ___ economic system.
   a. market capitalist
   b. market socialist
   c. command capitalist
   d. command socialist

6. The members of a college fraternity pooling their money to buy and then share an economics textbook is an example of a ___ economic system.
   a. market capitalist
   b. market socialist
   c. command capitalist
   d. command socialist

7. Which of the following systems allows for the more equal distribution of goods and services among its citizens?
   a. market capitalist
   b. command socialist

8. Communism relies most heavily on a ___ economic system.
   a. market capitalist
   b. market socialist
   c. command capitalist
   d. command socialist

9. The United States relies most heavily on a ___ economic system.
   a. market capitalist
   b. market socialist
   c. command capitalist
   d. command socialist

10. An economic system characterized by public resource ownership and private resource allocation decisions is a ______ economic system.
   a. market capitalist
   b. market socialist
   c. command capitalist
   d. command socialist

ADDITIONAL READINGS AND WEB RESOURCES

Akerlof, George (1970) "The Market for Lemons: Quality Uncertainty and the Market Mechanism," *Quarterly Journal of Economics* 84(3): 488–500. The Nobel-prize-winning economist assesses the market failure of incomplete information using an analogy of the market for used cars.

Mill, John Stewart (2011) *On Liberty*, Simon & Brown Publishers. Presents Mill's arguments for individual moral and economic freedom.

Rand, Ayn (1957) *Atlas Shrugged*, Random House. Rand uses fiction to describe her interpretation of what happens when society moves away from the market capitalist economic system.

Rawls, John (2005) *A Theory of Justice*, Belknap Press of Harvard University. One of the most widely cited books on political philosophy and ethics.

Tanzi, Vito. (1999) "Transition and the Changing Role of Government," *Finance & Development Magazine* 36(2) (June). Describes the elements of a market economy and the economic changes that take place as centrally planned countries transition to market economies. Available at http://www.imf.org/external/pubs/ft/fandd/1999/06/tanzi.htm

Wilson, Fred (2007) "John Stuart Mill," *Stanford Encyclopedia of Philosophy*, presents a thorough overview of Mill's marketplace of ideas. Available at http://plato.stanford.edu/entries/mill/#SocPol

The Cato Institute Economic Freedom of the World Index annually measures several dimensions of economic freedom (institutions, policies, property rights) across countries. Available at http://www.cato.org/pubs/efw/index.html

United Nations Development Programme and the London School of Economics and Political Science newsletter on Development and Transition presents policy-oriented discussions on the challenges of development and transition toward market capitalist societies. Available at: http://www.developmentandtransition.net/

The PBS website that accompanies their *Liberty! The American Revolution* television documentary includes descriptions and links to writings of the time. Available at http://www.pbs.org/ktca/liberty/

The Equality Exchange is a website devoted to egalitarian theories and research. Available at http://mora.rente.nhh.no/projects/EqualityExchange/

Larry Eubanks, Economics Professor at the University of Colorado maintains a blog on Economics and Liberty at http://economicsandliberty.blogspot.com/

The Ludwig von Mises Institute website includes extensive resources and links related to libertarian political and social theory and the beginnings of the theory of marginal utility. Available at http://mises.org/

The Heritage Foundation ranks countries based on their emphasis on a market capitalist economic system. Available at http://www.heritage.org/index/Ranking.aspx

SECTION

Markets, Markets Everywhere

BARTON SILVERMAN/© The New York Times/Redux Pictures

9 Wage Determination and Superstar Salaries

After studying this chapter, you should be able to:

- Explain how buyers in the labor market make hiring and salary decisions
- Demonstrate the importance of the value of the marginal product of labor and the marginal cost of labor
- Explain why there are pay differences across occupations
- Explain why individual salary comparisons are not valid for determining how much society values different occupations

In 2001, Major League baseball player Alex Rodriguez signed a 10-year contract for $252 million with the Texas Rangers team. At the time, it was the richest contract ever for a professional athlete. Rodriguez now works for the New York Yankees, earning $33 million per year. In the summer of 2009, the association football (soccer) club Real Madrid paid Manchester United the equivalent of $136 million for the transfer of midfielder Cristiano Ronaldo. Ronaldo earns roughly $19 million per year at Real Madrid. Also in 2009, Eli Manning, an American football quarterback, signed a contract with the New York Giants worth roughly $15 million per year. Given the large salaries paid to many professional athletes, it is not uncommon to overhear fans (and nonfans) grumble that athletes and other entertainment superstars are overpaid.

Superstars certainly are highly paid. *Forbes* magazine reported that for 2011, pro golfer Tiger Woods's earnings were $75 million, entertainer Oprah Winfrey's earnings were $290 million, actor

Johnny Depp made $50 million, and singer Lady Gaga made $90 million. In that same year, the average annual earnings for registered nurses, elementary school teachers, and firefighters were $67,000, $56,000, and $47,000, respectively. To some observers, the incredible pay differences between superstars and "regular folk" seem to either reflect a problem with our labor markets or a distortion of our society's values. After all, school teachers are such an integral part of our society, while entertainers seem to be, well, less integral. In this chapter, we use the tools of economics to examine the market for labor. We'll gain an economic perspective of superstar (and mere mortal) salaries, and highlight the importance of market interactions in the process.

It is important to remember that the labor market is just that—a market. Markets serve to allocate resources through the interaction of the buyers and sellers of those resources. In the labor market, the demand and supply of labor determines worker earnings and the quantity of labor hired. Wages and other labor earnings are simply prices that are determined by the market interactions between buyers and sellers of labor.

THE BUYERS OF LABOR

The buyers of labor are business firms. In the labor market, buyers of labor include restaurants, accounting firms, banks, school districts, hospitals, and all the other producers of goods and services in the economy. When it comes to superstars, the buyers of their labor include movie studios, sports teams, and those hiring superstars for marketing or endorsement purposes.

A firm's profits can come from selling meals in a restaurant, selling loans or savings accounts to bank customers, or selling tickets and merchandise related to a baseball team. When hiring labor, firms face the choices of which workers to hire and how much to pay them. Profit maximizing firms will make their hiring and salary decisions by comparing the marginal benefits and costs of hiring their workers. A firm will only want to hire a worker if she adds more to the firm's revenues than she adds to the firm's costs.

An example can help to illustrate a firm's hiring decision. Imagine that you are the owner of Java, a small coffee shop where customers can purchase coffee drinks for $2 apiece. You currently run the shop yourself, but because business is growing, you are trying to decide whether to hire additional workers to help you. You know that adding a worker will increase your ability to produce drinks, but it will also increase your costs. The economic way of thinking about this choice involves comparing the marginal benefit that another worker brings to you against the marginal cost of hiring that worker.

The Marginal Cost of Labor

The marginal cost of hiring a worker is the increase in costs that businesses incur from hiring the worker. This cost includes the wages paid to workers and can also include nonwage costs like fees associated with advertising the open position, the opportunity cost associated with screening and interviewing job candidates, the cost of training new employees, taxes associated with hiring workers, and any benefits that are paid to employees. Because our analysis of the labor market does not depend on whether or not we include the nonwage costs of hiring as part of the marginal cost of labor, we'll keep things simple and just assume that the marginal cost of hiring a worker is the wage the worker is paid.

Suppose that a survey of similar coffee shops in your town reveals that coffee shop workers earn $15 per hour. Because you want to be competitive in hiring workers but do not want to pay more than you need to for labor, you decide to pay $15 per hour as well. Thus, the marginal cost of hiring a worker at Java is $15 per hour.

The Marginal Benefit of Hiring Labor

The marginal benefit of hiring an additional worker depends on the output that you gain by hiring the worker, which is described by a production function. A **production function** shows the amount of **total product** or total output than can be produced with different amounts of inputs. Table 9.1 illustrates Java's production function. If you are the only worker at Java, you can produce 50 drinks per hour, so Java's total product is 50 drinks per hour when one worker per hour is used. If you add a second worker, the two of you together are able to raise Java's total product to 80 drinks per hour. Adding a third worker raises Java's total product to 100 drinks per hour, and so on.

A production function shows the amount of output that can be produced with different amounts of inputs.

Total product is the total output produced at a given level of input use.

Figure 9.1 illustrates Java's production function graphically. The horizontal axis measures the number of workers employed per hour and the vertical axis measures the number of drinks produced per hour. As more workers are hired, Java's output increases, which is reflected by the upward-sloping total product (TP) curve. We would expect this pattern from any smart business owner, because you would not stay in business long if you hired additional workers and they cut into your firm's output.

Table 9.1 Java's Production Function

Workers/Hour	Total Product (Drinks/Hour)
0	0
1	50
2	80
3	100
4	110
5	115
6	118

A production function shows the amount of total output that can be produced with different amounts of inputs. When two workers are employed per hour, total product is 80 drinks per hour. When four workers are employed per hour, total product is 110 drinks per hour.

Figure 9.1 Java's Production Function

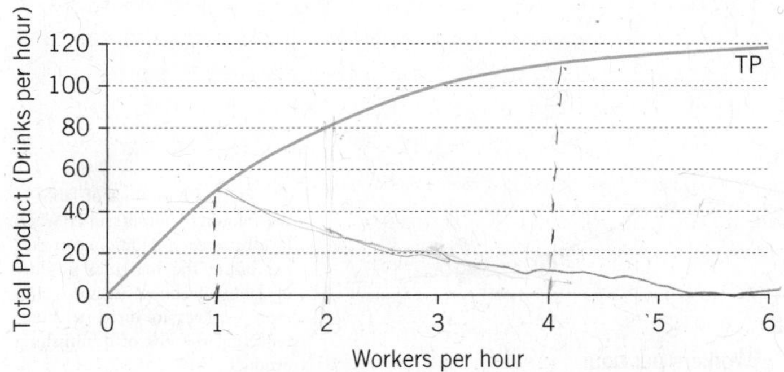

The total product (TP) is the amount of output produced per hour at different levels of input use. When Java hires 3 workers per hour, its total product is 100 drinks per hour. When Java hires 4 workers per hour, its total product is 110 drinks per hour. Total product increases as more workers are hired per hour.

Marginal Product of Labor

The marginal product of labor (MP_L) is the additional output gained from hiring an additional worker, ceteris paribus.

To compare the marginal benefit of hiring a second or third worker against the marginal cost of hiring him or her, you need to know how much output you gain when you hire each worker. The amount of output you gain when you hire an additional worker is called the **marginal product of labor** (MP_L).

Table 9.2 describes the marginal product of labor for Java. When you hire a second worker, Java's total product rises by 30 drinks per hour, since drink output is 50 drinks per hour when you are the only worker but is 80 drinks per hour when Java has two workers. The 30 drinks added to Java's total product by the second worker is the second worker's marginal product of labor. If after hiring the second worker you then decide to hire a third worker, Java's total product would rise from 80 to 100 drinks per hour. Thus, the third worker's marginal product of labor is 20 drinks per hour. Because output rises from 100 to 110 when you hire the fourth worker, his marginal product of labor is 10 drinks per hour, and so on, for the fifth and sixth workers.

Figure 9.2 shows a graph of the marginal product of labor at Java. The number of workers employed per hour is measured on the horizontal axis, and the marginal product of labor, measured as additional drinks produced per hour, is measured on the vertical axis. Because output is zero if you don't work at Java but is 50 drinks per hour when you are working, you generate a 50-drink-per-hour increase in total

Table 9.2 Java's Total Product and Marginal Product of Labor

Workers/Hour	Total Product (Drinks/Hour)	Marginal Product of Labor (Drinks/Hour)
0	0	-
1	50	50
2	80	30
3	100	20
4	110	10
5	115	5
6	118	3

The marginal product of labor is the amount of output gained when Java hires each additional worker. When the number of workers hired is two per hour, total product is 80 drinks per hour. When the number of workers hired is three per hour, total product is 100 drinks per hour, so the marginal product of the third worker hired per hour is 20 drinks per hour.

Figure 9.2 Java's Marginal Product of Labor

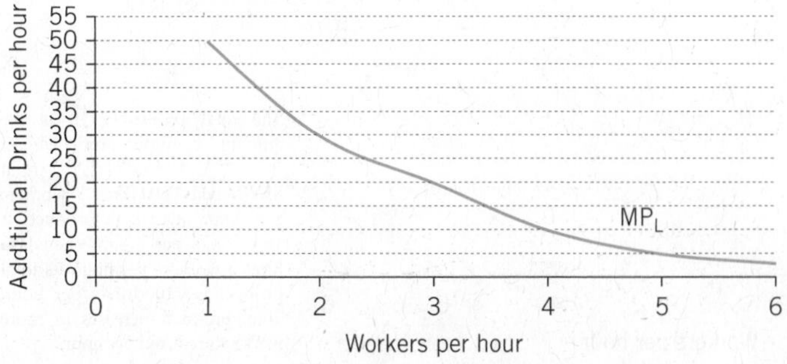

The marginal product of labor is the amount of output gained when Java hires each additional worker per hour. The marginal product of labor declines as more and more workers are hired per hour, reflecting the law of diminishing product.

product, so your marginal product of labor is 50 drinks per hour. The second worker generates 30 additional drinks per hour, and the third worker generates 20 additional drinks per hour.

Notice that the marginal product of each additional worker hired per hour is less than that of the previous worker hired per hour, as demonstrated by the downward-sloping marginal product of labor curve. The lower addition to total product by each additional worker hired is not an unusual situation; in fact, the phenomenon occurs so often that it is termed the **law of diminishing marginal product.**

Law of diminishing marginal product: Holding other inputs constant, as additional units of an input are added to a production process, at some point increases in total production occur at a decreasing rate.

In Java's case, the law of diminishing marginal product implies that each additional worker hired adds fewer drinks to Java's hourly output than the worker hired before. It is important to note that diminishing marginal product does not occur at the same rate for different firms. In some cases, marginal product will initially rise as more workers are hired because hiring additional workers allows each worker to specialize in different tasks. After some point, however, marginal product of labor falls because there is only so much space and equipment to share among the workers. Be careful not to think that *diminishing* marginal product implies *negative* marginal product. Total product rises as additional workers are hired at Java, so each worker has positive marginal product, but because each worker adds less to Java's output than the previous worker, Java's production function shows diminishing marginal product.

Marginal Product and Value of Marginal Product

The total product and marginal product columns of Table 9.2 show the benefits of hiring workers in terms of the number of drinks produced. Because the marginal cost of hiring a worker is measured in dollars per hour and the marginal product of each additional worker is measured in drinks per hour, we do not yet have enough information to decide whether or not the marginal benefits exceed the marginal costs of hiring a worker. In order to compare the marginal benefit of hiring an additional worker against the marginal cost of doing so, we need to use the marginal product of labor and the price of the drinks at Java to measure the marginal benefits of hiring a worker in dollars rather than units of output produced.

The price of each coffee drink at Java is \$2, so each coffee drink produced increases Java's revenues by \$2. If a worker's marginal product of labor is 10 drinks per hour, the additional revenue that Java earns by hiring that worker is to \$20 per hour, which is the worker's marginal product of labor multiplied by the price of Java drinks. The additional revenue earned by hiring an additional worker is called the **value of the marginal product of labor** (VMP_L).

The value of the marginal product of labor (VMP_L) is the increase in total revenue earned when the firm hires an additional worker. VMP_L is equal to the MP_L multiplied by the price of the output being produced (P_{output}). $VMP_L = MP_L * P_{output}$

Table 9.3 shows the total product, marginal product, and value of marginal product of labor for workers at Java. The marginal product of the second worker hired is 30 drinks per hour because total product rises from 50 to 80 drinks per hour when the second worker is hired. The value of the marginal product of labor for the second worker is \$60 per hour. In other words, the second worker hired produces 30 drinks, each worth \$2, and so adds \$60 to Java's revenues. Similarly, the third worker adds 20 drinks per hour to Java's output, which is the equivalent of \$40 per hour in revenues.

Figure 9.3 is a graph of the value of marginal product of labor at Java. The number of workers hired per hour is measured on the horizontal axis, and the additional revenue that each worker hired earns for Java is measured on the vertical axis. The VMP_L curve has the same shape as the MP_L curve in Figure 9.2, but VMP_L measures the additional revenue that each worker adds to Java's total revenue on the vertical

Table 9.3 Java's Marginal Product of Labor and Value of Marginal Product of Labor

Workers/Hour	Total Product (Drinks/Hour)	Marginal Product of Labor (Drinks/Hour)	Value of Marginal Product of Labor ($/Hour)
1	50	50	100
2	80	30	60
3	100	20	40
4	110	10	20
5	115	5	10
6	118	3	6

The value of the marginal product of labor is the increase in total revenue earned when the firm hires an additional worker. It is equal to the marginal product of labor multiplied by the price of the output. When the price of a drink is $2, the value of the marginal product of the second worker hired per hour is $60, and the value of the marginal product of the third worker hired per hour is $40.

Figure 9.3 **Java's Value of Marginal Product of Labor**

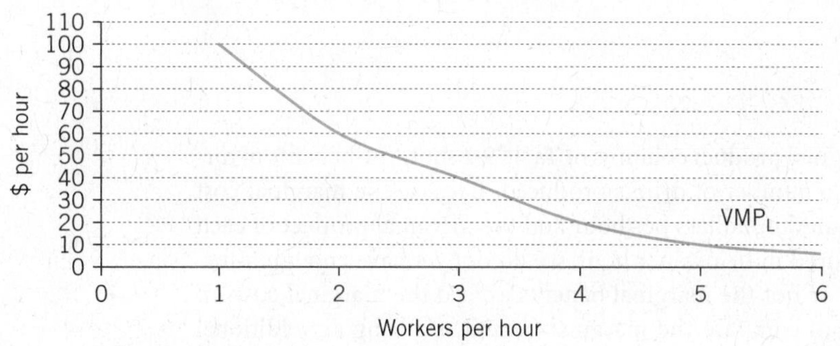

The value of the marginal product of labor is the amount of revenue gained when Java hires each additional worker. VMP_L is determined by the productivity of workers and the price of the output produced.

axis, whereas MP_L measures the additional output that each worker adds to Java's total product on the vertical axis.

Determinants of MP_L and VMP_L

What determines the size of a worker's MP_L and VMP_L? The marginal product of labor is a reflection of a worker's productivity, which is influenced by a wide array of factors. Workers who are more motivated tend to be more productive, so more motivated workers will have higher MP_L. Workers with more **human capital** also tend to be more productive. Human capital is the skills and knowledge workers acquire through education, experience, and training that makes them more productive in the workforce. The workers at Java gain human capital as they learn how to run the cash register and other equipment in the shop. As the owner of Java, you could increase your workers' human capital by providing them with customer service or other types training to increase their productivity. You are acquiring human capital by attending college. Alex Rodriquez and Cristiano Ronaldo acquire human capital when they train and practice with their teammates, and Johnny Depp acquires human capital when he attends acting school and practices for his movie roles.

Human capital: The acquired skills and knowledge that makes workers more productive.

A second factor that influences worker productivity is access to capital equipment and technology. The marginal product of labor for workers at Java would be substantially lower if they did not have access to espresso machines and computerized cash registers. Farm worker productivity is lower when farm workers do not have access to sophisticated tractors and harvesters. Office worker productivity is higher when office workers have access to computers and automated copy machines. Similarly, pro golfer Tiger Woods plays better golf when he uses specialized golf clubs and golf balls, and actor Johnny Depp is more productive at making movies when he has access to high-technology filming equipment that allows him to instantly assess the quality of each movie take.

Finally, the price of the output produced by workers is directly related to their VMP_L. For example, when the price of each drink at Java is $2, the VMP_L of the third worker hired per hour is $40 per hour. If the price of a Java drink rises to $3, the VMP_L of the third worker hired per hour would rise to $60 per hour. Because the VMP_L is determined in part by the price of output, anything that changes the price of output will change the VMP_L. If the demand for Java drinks falls, the VMP_L for workers at Java will also fall because a decrease in the demand for Java drinks will decrease the equilibrium price of Java drinks, ceteris paribus. Similarly, if the demand for Java drinks rises, the VMP_L of workers at Java will also rise because the price of Java drinks will increase.

How would an increase in the demand for movies impact the VMP_L of Johnny Depp? How would a decrease in the demand for football impact the VMP_L of Eli Manning?

The Firm's Profit Maximizing Hiring Decision

Because VMP_L is a dollar measure of the marginal benefit of each worker hired and the wage is a dollar measure of the marginal cost of each worker hired, we can now determine the profit-maximizing number of workers for Java to hire. We can also use the marginal benefit of each worker to determine the maximum that Java would be willing to pay each worker.

When we determine the profit-maximizing hiring decision for a firm, we are really finding the firm's demand for labor. We learned in Chapters 3 and 4 that it is useful to think about demand relationships using both horizontal and vertical interpretations. In a horizontal interpretation of a demand relationship, a demand curve describes how much of a good or service that buyers are willing and able to buy at a given price. A horizontal interpretation of the demand curve for labor describes how many workers a firm is willing and able to hire at a given wage. A vertical interpretation of a demand relationship describes the maximum amount that buyers are willing and able to pay to obtain a given amount of a good or service. A vertical interpretation of the demand curve for labor describes the maximum amount that a firm would be willing and able to pay each unit of labor, ceteris paribus. The firm's profit maximizing hiring decision can be found using either of these interpretations of the demand relationship, as we'll demonstrate next.

Optimal Number of Workers to Hire

In determining the optimal number of workers to hire in order to maximize Java's profits, we compare the marginal benefits and marginal costs of hiring each additional worker. It is only profitable to hire an additional worker if he or she adds more to Java's revenues than he or she adds to Java's costs. If a worker adds more to revenues than she adds to costs, Java's profits will increase by hiring that worker. If a worker adds more to costs than she adds to revenues, then Java's profits will fall if that worker is hired.

Table 9.4 presents the marginal benefits and marginal costs of hiring workers at Java. The marginal benefit is the VMP_L earned by hiring each worker, and the marginal cost is the wage. For Java, hiring the second worker will be profitable because the second worker's VMP_L is $60 per hour, which is greater than the $15 per hour wage. If you hire the second worker, Java's profits will rise by $45 per hour, the difference between the second worker's VMP_L and his wage. The third worker's VMP_L is $30 per hour, so hiring the third worker at a wage of $15 per hour will generate an additional $25 in profits per hour for Java. Similarly, hiring the fourth worker will increase Java's profits by $5 per hour because the fourth worker's VMP_L is $20 per hour and the wage is $15 per hour. Java would not maximize its profits by hiring the fifth worker per hour, however, because that worker would add $10 per hour to Java's revenues but add $15 per hour to Java's costs. It would also not be profit maximizing to hire the sixth worker per hour, because the sixth worker would add only $6 per hour to Java's revenues but would add $15 per hour to Java's costs.

Table 9.4 Java's Marginal Benefits and Marginal Costs of Labor

Workers/Hour	VMP_L ($/Hour)	Wage ($/Hour)
1	100	15
2	60	15
3	40	15
4	20	15
5	10	15
6	6	15

The marginal benefit of hiring a worker is the worker's VMP_L. The marginal cost of hiring a worker is the worker's wage. For workers 1-4, the $VMP_L >$ Wage, so hiring those workers increases Java's profits. For workers 5 and 6, $VMP_L <$ Wage, so hiring those workers would decrease Java's profits.

Table 9.5 presents the total product, total revenue, total cost, and profit values at different employment levels for Java. We learned in Chapter 5 that a firm's total revenue is equal to the price of its product times the quantity of the product sold. The price of Java drinks is $2, so Java's total revenue is equal to its total product times $2, as reported in the Total Revenue column of Table 9.5.

To keep the analysis simple, we can assume that wages are the only cost that Java faces in its business. Although this is not completely realistic, our analysis of Java's hiring decision would not change if we allowed Java to have other costs of production.[1]

The Total Cost column of Table 9.5 shows the total cost of hiring different numbers of workers per hour given the wage of $15 per hour. If Java hires one worker per hour, its total cost is $15 per hour. If Java hires two workers per hour, its total cost is

$$\text{Total Cost} = 2 \text{ workers} * \$15 \text{ per hour} = \$30 \text{ per hour}$$

1 Chapter 18 describes the decisions of firms that have other costs of production.

Table 9.5 Java's Profits

Workers/Hour	Total Product (Drinks/Hour)	Total Revenue ($/Hour)	Total Cost ($/Hour)	Profit ($/hour)
1	50	100	15	85
2	80	160	30	130
3	100	200	45	155
4	110	220	60	160
5	115	230	75	155
6	118	236	90	146

When the price of Java's drinks is $2, total revenue is $160 per hour when two workers are hired, and total cost is $30 per hour when two workers are hired, so profits are $130 per hour when two workers are hired. Java maximizes profits by hiring four workers per hour.

If Java hires three workers, its total cost is $45 per hour, and so on for four, five, or six workers hired per hour. Java's **profit** can be computed as its total revenues minus its total costs.

Profit = Total Revenue − Total Cost.

Java's profits are listed in the last column of Table 9.5. When Java hires only one worker per hour, profits are $85 per hour. When Java hires a second worker, profits rise to $130, since the second worker generates more revenue than cost for Java. Hiring the third worker also causes profits to increase since the VMP_L of the third worker is greater than the wage. The fourth worker is the last worker in Java's production function who has VMP_L greater than $15, so hiring the fourth worker maximizes Java's profits.

Maximum Wage to Pay a Given Worker

Instead of determining the optimal number of workers for Java to hire when the wage is $15 per hour, we could determine the maximum amount that Java would be willing and able to pay each additional worker hired. This is a more realistic scenario in the superstar labor market because although there is likely to be a going wage rate for baristas (workers who produce coffee drinks), welders, accountants, or workers in labor markets where there are lots of buyers and sellers of labor, it is unlikely that there is a going rate for elite baseball pitchers, pro golfers, or actors.

To determine the maximum amount that a firm would be willing and able to pay a worker, think of the worker's contribution to the firm's revenue. A firm will earn profit whenever it can pay a worker less than his or her value of marginal product of labor. A firm will break even if it pays the worker a wage equal to his or her VMP_L. In our Java example, the first worker hired adds $100 to Java's revenues, so Java would make a profit by hiring the worker at any wage less than $100 per hour. Thus, $100 is the very maximum that Java will be willing and able to pay the first worker. It would not make a profit by paying the second worker $100, however, since that worker's VMP_L is only $60 per hour. Instead, the maximum that Java would be willing and able to pay the second worker is $60 per hour. Similarly, the maximum that Java would be willing and able to pay the third worker is $40 per hour, and the maximum amount that Java would be willing to pay the sixth worker is $6 per hour.

The Firm's Demand Curve for Labor

Figure 9.4 illustrates the VMP_L and wage (W) for Java. The VMP_L curve shows the marginal benefits of hiring additional workers at Java, and the W line shows the marginal costs of hiring additional workers, which at Java is $15 per hour.

Figure 9.4 Java's VMPL and Demand Curve for Labor

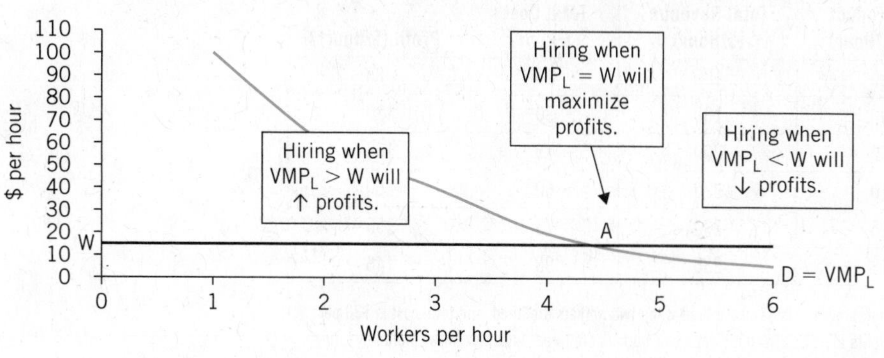

Java will hire a worker as long as his marginal benefit is greater than his marginal cost. If the wage is below the value of marginal product, as with workers 1–4, the worker's marginal benefit is greater than his marginal cost and the firm will increase its profits by hiring the worker. If the wage is above the VMP_L, as with workers 5–6, the firm will lose money by hiring the worker. Because the VMP_L curve illustrates both the quantity of workers to hire at a given wage and the maximum amount that a firm would be willing and able to pay each worker, the VMP_L curve is the demand curve for labor.

For workers 1–4, VMP_L is greater than W, so hiring these workers will increase Java's profits. For workers 5 and 6, the VMP_L is less than W, so hiring these workers will reduce Java's profits. Point A in Figure 9.4 shows the hiring level where the marginal benefit of hiring an additional worker is just equal to the marginal cost of hiring him. For Java, this happens at a hiring level of about 4.5 workers per hour. If it were possible for Java to hire 4.5 workers per hour, hiring that amount of labor would maximize profits. Splitting hiring into small units like this is easier for some firms than for others. Firms that can hire workers in smaller increments will maximize their profits by equating the VMP_L with the wage. Firms that can only hire whole units of labor (for example, either four workers per hour or five workers per hour) will maximize profits by hiring the last worker for which VMP_L is greater than W.

Recall that demand curves tell us the quantity of goods or services that consumers are willing and able to buy at different prices. Because the VMP_L curve tells us how many workers Java would be willing and able to hire at different wages, the VMP_L curve is the demand curve for labor for Java. Just as changes in the price of a good cause buyers to move along the demand curve for the good, when the wage changes we move along the VMP_L curve to determine the new optimal quantity of labor for Java to hire.

What would happen if the going wage rate for baristas were $8 per hour instead of $15 per hour? In this case, Java would maximize its profits by continuing to hire the first through fourth workers, because if they were worth hiring at $15 per hour, they must also be worth hiring at $8 per hour. Java will also increase its profits by hiring the fifth worker per hour because the fifth worker's VMP_L is $10, which is greater than the $8 per hour marginal cost of hiring him. If the wage were $25 per hour, Java would maximize its profits by hiring only three workers per hour, since the fourth worker's VMP_L is $20 per hour.

THINK FOR YOURSELF

How many workers would be optimal for Java to hire if the wage were $5 per hour? How many workers would be optimal to hire if the wage were $45 per hour? How many workers would be optimal to hire if the wage were $7.50 per hour?

Since the VMP_L curve is the demand curve for labor, we can also think about a firm's profit-maximizing hiring decision using the concept of consumer surplus. We learned in Chapter 4 that consumer surplus is the difference between the benefit that buyers receive from buying a good or service and the price that buyers pay for the good or service. In the labor market, firms are the buyers of labor and VMP_L is the benefit that firms receive by hiring workers; W is the price that firms pay to hire workers. Consumer surplus in the labor market is the difference between workers' VMP_L and wage, but it can also be viewed as the profit a firm earns by hiring workers. Applying the concept of consumer surplus to the labor market implies that a firm can maximize its profits by maximizing the amount of consumer surplus it obtains by hiring labor.

The comparison of the value of marginal product of labor against the marginal cost of labor is a generalizable profit-maximizing hiring rule for firms, which is summarized in Table 9.6. If a given worker's VMP_L is greater than his wage, the firm will increase its profits by hiring the worker. If a worker's VMP_L is less than his wage, the firm will lose profits if it hires the worker. The maximum profit for a firm can be obtained by hiring labor where the VMP_L is just equal to the wage.

SPL/Photo Researchers

William Stanley Jevons and the Marginal Revolution

William Stanley Jevons (1835–1882) was a British economist and logician who is often credited (along with his contemporaries Carl Menger and Léon Walras) with contributing to the marginal revolution in economics. The marginal revolution explained economic behavior in terms of diminishing marginal utility, noting that the value of an additional unit of a good to a consumer is negatively related to the amount of the good that the consumer already has. Although other economists had noticed the diminishing marginal productivity of inputs in production, Jevons, Menger, and Walras formalized and popularized the idea of examining values at the margin and set the stage for the marginal analysis at the core of economics today, including the marginal analysis of the firm's profit-maximizing hiring decision.

Table 9.6 Summary of the Profit-Maximizing Hiring Decision

If $VMP_L > W$ hiring the worker will increase profits	If $VMP_L = W$ hiring the worker will maximize profits	If $VMP_L < W$ hiring the worker will decrease profits

The Sellers of Labor

In the previous section, we learned about how the demand for labor comes from firms making profit-maximizing decisions about the number of workers to hire and how much to pay each worker. The supply of labor comes from workers who sell their time and effort to employers. The sellers of labor are individuals, like athletes Cristiano Ronaldo and Tiger Woods, actress Cameron Diaz, and you.

Individual sellers of labor face choices about how much to work, who to work for, and how much to invest in their human capital. Economists assume that individuals make their labor supply decisions based on the goal of maximizing their utility.

Just as is the case with other choices, supplying labor involves costs and benefits. The costs of working may include direct costs such as transportation, clothing, and childcare, as well as more indirect costs such as fatigue and stress. The benefit of supplying labor is the utility obtained from working in a job you like, from the satisfaction of job well done, and from using earnings from work to purchase goods and services.

Given these cost and benefit tradeoffs, workers will decide to work for a firm and at a given wage as long as the benefits exceed the costs. For most workers, increases in the wage provide an incentive for them to increase the quantity of labor they supply to the market, so that there is a positive relationship between the wage and the quantity of labor workers supply to the market.

LABOR MARKET EQUILIBRIUM

As in other markets, interactions between buyers and sellers determine the prices and quantities of labor services traded in the labor market. Figure 9.5 illustrates a typical market for labor. The demand for labor reflects the VMP_L, and the supply of labor reflects workers' willingness and ability to work at different wages. In equilibrium, the quantity of labor hired per hour is Q* and the equilibrium wage is W*.

Figure 9.5 **The Demand and Supply of Labor**

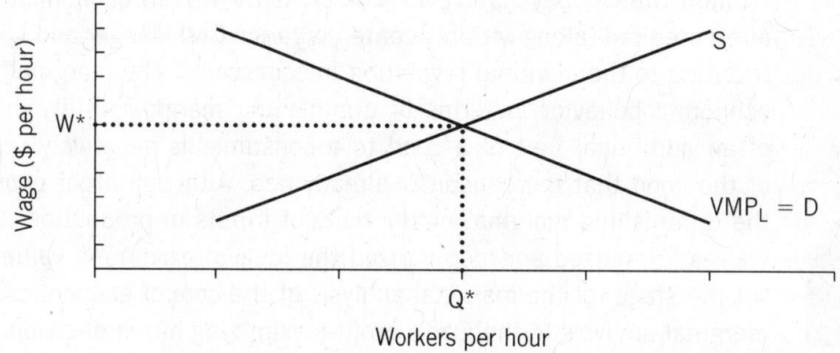

The demand for labor reflects the VMP_L and shows the number of workers the firm is willing and able to hire at each wage. The supply of labor reflects the number of workers willing and able to work at each wage. In equilibrium, the wage paid is W* and the quantity of workers hired is Q* per hour.

If the supply or demand for labor changes, the equilibrium wage and quantity of labor hired will also change. On the supply side, factors that could increase the supply of labor include the costs of working, the wages that workers could earn in other labor markets, worker expectations, and the total number of workers in the labor market.

An increase in childcare or transportation costs, for example, would decrease the supply of labor because increases in these costs make working outside the home more expensive. Figure 9.6 illustrates how this would impact wages and employment in the labor market. A decrease in the supply of labor is illustrated by the movement from S to S' in Figure 9.6. When the supply of labor falls, the wage increases from W* to W' and the quantity of workers hired per hour falls from Q* to Q'. Factors that increase the supply of labor, such as an influx of workers into an area, will increase the supply of labor, shown by the movement from S' to S in Figure 9.6. An increase in the supply of labor will increase employment but will also cause workers' wages to fall.

We learned in Chapter 3 that demand shifters include tastes and preferences, income, the prices of related goods, expectations, and the number of consumers in the market. These factors also shift the demand for labor. In the manufacturing industry,

Figure 9.6 **Shifts in the Demand and Supply of Labor**

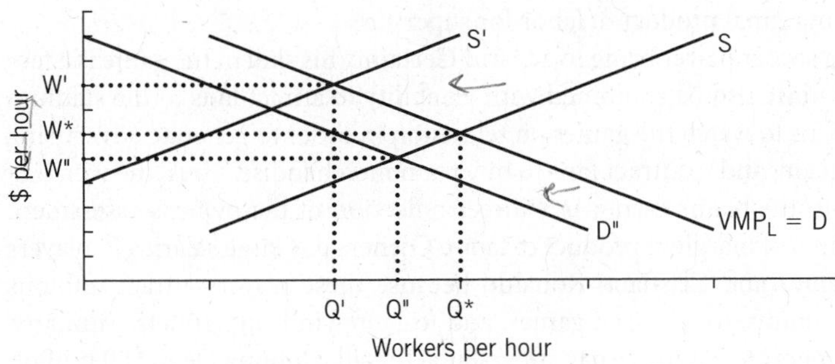

In the initial equilibrium, the wage paid is W* and the quantity of workers hired is Q* per hour. If the supply of labor falls to S', the wage rises to W' and the quantity of workers hired per hour falls to Q'. If the demand for labor falls to D", the wage falls to W" and the quantity of workers hired per hour falls to Q".

for example, assembly line workers and capital are substitute goods because cars, textiles, and other manufactured goods can be assembled by workers or by machines. When the price of capital falls, firms in this industry will increase the quantity of capital they demand and decrease their demand for labor. A decrease in the demand for labor is illustrated by the movement from D to D" in Figure 9.6. When the demand for labor falls, the wage falls from W* to W" and the quantity of labor hired per hour falls from Q* to Q".

The demand for labor can increase when there is a fall in the price of a complement to labor. Computer programmers and machinists are complements to capital in the manufacturing industry. If the price of capital falls, firms will increase their quantity of capital demanded and also their demand for computer programmers and machinists. An increase in the demand for these workers would be illustrated by a movement from D" to D in Figure 9.6, with the result that the wages and employment levels of computer programmers and machinists rise when the price of capital falls.

One factor that shifts demand differently in the labor market than in the market for TVs, cars, or other goods and services is the price of the good produced by labor. The VMP$_L$ is equal to the MP$_L$ times the price of the output produced by labor, so anything that causes a change in the price of the output will also cause a change in the demand for labor. A reduction in the demand for Java drinks will cause the price of Java drinks to fall. The fall in the price of Java drinks will reduce the VMP$_L$ for workers at Java. As a result, the demand for workers to make drinks at Java will fall.

THINK FOR YOURSELF

The pay of U.S. workers is higher than in many other less developed countries. Use the concept of VMP$_L$ and the differing availability of capital in the United States relative to capital availability in less developed countries to help explain why this is the case.

THE SUPERSTAR LABOR MARKET

Let's apply the concepts we've developed so far to the superstar labor market. Earlier in the chapter we learned that Cristiano Ronaldo earns $19 million and Johnny Depp earns $50 million per year. It is natural to wonder how a soccer player can be worth

$19 million to a club owner or how a movie star can be worth $50 million to a movie studio. We now have the tools to address these questions. The key is to think about the value of the marginal product of labor for superstars.

What does a soccer player bring to a team? Certainly his skill in the game is a factor. But his skill must also be combined with an ability to attract fans to the stadium seats, to attract fans to watch the games on television in order to generate advertising revenue for the team, and to attract fans to buy team merchandise. Thus, the worth of a soccer player to the team's owner is a direct reflection of the owner's assessment of the player's value of marginal product of labor. Owners pay large salaries to players like Alex Rodriguez and Cristiano Ronaldo because these players attract millions of fans to the stadiums, to televised games, and to merchandising outlets. Similarly, movie studio owners are willing to pay superstar actors like Johnny Depp $50 million because the studio owners expect that Johnny Depp will bring in at least $50 million in additional revenue for films in which he stars. Just as the most productive workers in the labor market can generate competing job offers from several business firms, superstars often attract job and salary offers from competing sports teams and movie studios. In order to be competitive in hiring superstars, team owners and movie studios must offer wages close to the stars' value of marginal product of labor or risk losing those stars to competing teams and studios.

But what is it that makes superstars have such high VMP_L? What determines how many fans go to see Cristiano Ronaldo or Johnny Depp? An obvious answer is that fans go to see the stars based on their own expected utility from watching the stars' games or movies. People pay $8 for a ticket to watch Johnny Depp in a movie because they expect to get at least $8 worth of enjoyment or utility from the experience. Thus, we could argue that Johnny Depp is "worth" $50 million per year if we are willing to accept the enjoyment people receive from him, as measured by their willingness to pay to watch him, as an indication of social value.

Lucy Nicholson/©AP/Wide World Photos

We can illustrate the importance of a superstar's value of marginal product in determining his or her earnings by comparing the earnings of male and female professional basketball players. When Lisa Leslie played professional basketball for the Los Angeles Sparks, she was one of the top players in the Women's National Basketball League (WNBA), and she earned the league's Most Valuable Player award several times. A counterpart to Lisa Leslie is Kobe Bryant, who also plays professional basketball for a Los Angeles team, the L.A. Lakers. Bryant is one of the top players in the National Basketball League (NBA) and was a nine-time NBA all-star and a two-time NBA scoring champion. Lisa Leslie and Kobe Bryant are both clearly among the top players in their sport. There is, however, a very wide discrepancy in their earnings. In 2009 Kobe Bryant earned $29 million from the Lakers, while Lisa Leslie earned only $100,000 from the Sparks ($100,000 is the maximum that players could earn in the WNBA at that time).

Why is there such a discrepancy in their earnings, when both players have very similar jobs? The answer can be found by considering the value of each player's marginal product of labor. The NBA has a much larger fan base than the WNBA, so Bryant's performance attracts many more fans than does Leslie's. Because their VMP_L is so different, it is not surprising that their earnings are different as well.

Endorsements

The superstar earnings we've discussed so far come from the stars' performances in games or movies. Superstars also earn substantial incomes from endorsements they provide to marketing all sorts of products. As one example, Kobe Bryant has had endorsement contracts with brands Nike, Sprite, Nutella, and McDonalds. It is hard to imagine that Bryant is better at making a McDonalds hamburger than another worker, so why would he be valuable to the company? The answer again comes from thinking about the value of the marginal product of labor. By paying a superstar for an endorsement, a firm expects that sales revenue will increase by at least as much as the star's compensation. Why else would a firm voluntarily enter into an expensive endorsement agreement?

Not surprisingly, when superstars are no longer expected to bring in additional revenues, their endorsement opportunities wane. This was certainly the case with Tiger Woods when it was revealed in 2009 that he had committed adultery and had multiple mistresses during his career as a professional golfer. Soon afterward, Accenture and Gillette, two of Woods's major sponsors, ended or limited their contracts with Woods, fearing that their association with him would cost them customers. In 2009, Olympic medalist and world-record-holding swimmer Michael Phelps lost his multimillion dollar endorsement contract with Kellogg's after a photograph of him smoking marijuana appeared in a British tabloid newspaper. Another example occurred with Michael Vick, former superstar NFL quarterback for the Atlanta Falcons. In 2005, *Forbes* magazine reported that Vick's earnings were $37.5 million and that he had endorsement contracts with Nike, Coca-Cola, Kraft, and several other firms. In 2007, Vick was accused and pleaded guilty to federal dog-fighting charges. He was suspended from the NFL and lost his endorsement contracts, as the NFL and other companies scrambled to distance themselves from him and the potential loss of revenues that an association with him was expected to cause.

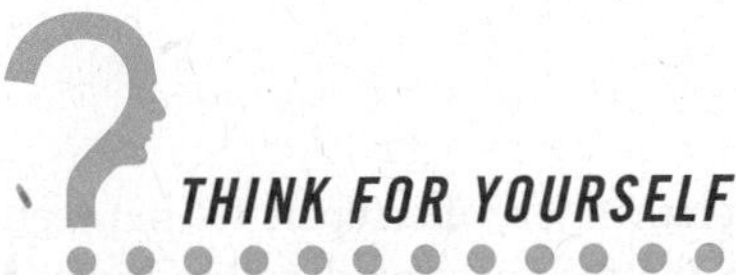

THINK FOR YOURSELF

Lance Armstrong is a world-famous cyclist. He retired from cycling in 2005 after winning the Tour de France seven consecutive times. He returned to the sport in 2009 and finished the Tour in third place. In 2010 he finished in 23rd place. In 2005, at the peak of his cycling career, he earned $28 million. In 2009 he earned $20 million. How might Armstrong's age have impacted his VMP_L?

THE IMPORTANCE OF THINKING AT THE MARGIN

When presented with information about the large discrepancies between entertainment superstars' salaries and those of the average nurse, teacher, or firefighter, people often question our society's values. It is common to interpret the pay discrepancy as an implication that our society values sports more than essential activities like education, nursing, or firefighting. The problem with this type of thinking is that it ignores the fact that salaries reflect the value of the *marginal* unit of labor hired, not the value of labor *in total.*

Look back at Table 9.4, where we determined that if the market wage for baristas was $15 per hour, Java would maximize its profits by hiring four workers. Because the VMP_L of the workers declines as more workers are hired, however, this $15 reflects neither the VMP_L of the first worker hired nor the value produced by the workers in total. To compute the value produced by workers in total, we would add up the VMP_L of each worker, not just examine the wage paid to the marginal worker hired.

Figure 9.7 illustrates the importance of thinking at the margin when inferring the value that society places on a given occupation. The demand curve for labor in the market is shown as the line $VMP_L = D$. When the wage is W, suppose that 100 workers will be hired per hour, since hiring more or fewer than Q workers would not maximize profits. The wage W is just equal to the VMP_L of the 100th worker hired, but it does not reflect the VMP_L of all 100 of the workers hired. To find the total value of the product of the workers, we would find the area beneath the VMP_L curve between 0 and 100, which is equal to the area 0ABQ. The area 0ABQ is much higher than the wage of the 100th worker hired.

Figure 9.7 **Marginal Value vs. Total Value of Labor**

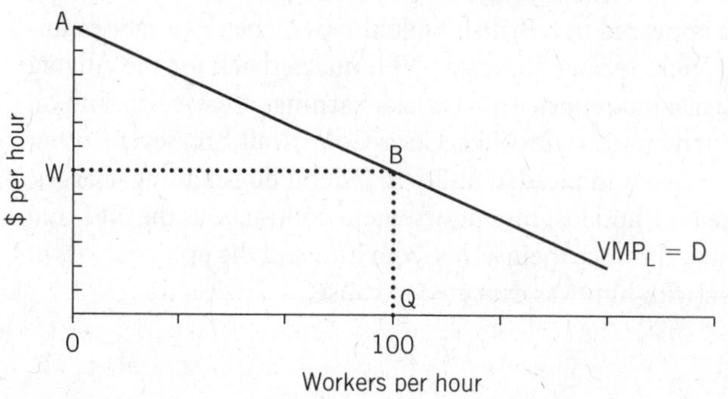

The wage W reflects the value of the marginal product of the 100th worker hired, but not the value produced by workers in total. The value produced by all the workers hired if the wage is W would be equal to the area 0ABQ, since that is the sum of the VMP_L for the workers.

How does thinking at the margin help explain salary discrepancies between superstars and "regular" workers? Let's compare the marginal worker hired in the nursing industry to that of a player in the NBA. At the margin, one more player like Kobe Bryant would increase the enjoyment of millions of NBA fans, so the demand for Kobe Bryant's labor is very high and his VMP_L is large. In addition, because basketball players with the level of skill needed to perform in the NBA are very rare, the supply of NBA-quality labor is relatively low. The high demand for superstar labor combined with the low supply of superstar labor results in a very high level of earnings for superstars.

At the same time, there are millions of nurses in the United States, and the demand for nurses is large. The skills needed to be a nurse, although important, are not as rare as the skills needed to be an NBA superstar, so the supply of nurses is relatively large compared to the supply of NBA superstars. At the margin, one more nurse is not likely to impact millions of people the way that one more Kobe Bryant would, so the VMP_L of the nurse hired at the margin will be lower than the VMP_L of the NBA superstar hired at the margin. A star NBA basketball player's salary or a mega-movie star's salary is larger than that of a nurse in part because the skills necessary to slam dunk a basketball or attract millions of fans to movie theaters are incredibly scarce, while the skills necessary to be an excellent nurse are not as scarce. However, adding up the VMP_L of each of these millions of nurses would generate a total value produced to society in the many billions of dollars, far more than the total value produced by Kobe Bryant or Johnny Depp. Using the same logic, because the skills necessary to serve food or clean buildings are not as scarce as the skills necessary to be a nurse, a nurse's salary is relatively larger than that of a waitress or custodian.

THINK FOR YOURSELF

The AFL-CIO labor union has an interesting website called Executive Pay Watch (www.aflcio.org/corporatewatch/paywatch/) that lists chief executive officer (CEO) compensation at dozens of large corporations. Among those listed for 2010: Ralph Lauren, the CEO of Polo Ralph Lauren, who earned $277 million, Robert Igen, CEO of Walt Disney Company, who earned $29.6 million, and K.I. Chenault, CEO of American Express, who earned $16 million. The AFL-CIO encourages visitors to the site to "Click on a company name to find the CEO's total compensation and to see how it compares to your and other workers' earnings." Using the concepts we've learned in this chapter, provide an economic explanation for the difference in between Ralph Lauren's compensation as CEO of Polo Ralph Lauren and "other workers' earnings" at the company.

SUMMARY

Like other prices, wages and salaries result from interactions between buyers and sellers in markets. Wages and salaries signal workers' relative scarcity and allocate workers to the firms most willing and able to pay for them. Firms determine how many workers to hire and what wages to pay workers by comparing workers' marginal benefits and marginal costs. The marginal benefit of hiring a worker is equal to his value of marginal product, which is determined by the worker's motivation and human capital, the capital and technology available for use by the worker, and the price of the product that the worker produces.

The demand for superstar labor is relatively high because there are millions of fans willing to pay to see sports and movie stars in action. In addition, there are relatively few people with the elite level of skill necessary to win an NBA championship or sell out multiplex movie theaters around the world, so the supply of superstar labor is relatively small. The combination of high demand and low supply helps to explain superstars' high salaries. "Regular" workers like firefighters, nurses, and teachers also have high demand for their labor. At the same time, however, there are millions of workers with the skills necessary to be firefighters, nurses, and teachers, so the supply of labor to those occupations is relatively high. The combination of high demand and high supply helps explain why the salaries earned by most workers are relatively lower than those earned by superstars.

It is a misconception to assume that the high pay of superstars implies that our society values superstar labor more than it does the work of firefighters, nurses, or teachers. The wages that we observe in labor markets reflect the value of the marginal product of the worker hired at the margin, not the total value produced by workers in the market. Rather than examining the wage paid to the marginal worker hired, we would more accurately determine how much society values the output of a set of workers in a particular job by adding up the VMP_L of all the workers in the job.

KEY CONCEPTS

- Production function
- Total product
- Marginal product of labor
- Law of diminishing marginal product
- Value of the marginal product of labor
- Human capital
- Profit

DISCUSSION QUESTIONS AND PROBLEMS

Workers/Hour	Total Product (Wuzzies/Hour)
0	0
1	19
2	36
3	51
4	62
5	72
6	79
7	84

1. The accompanying table shows the production function for WAS corporation, which sells wuzzies.
   a. Suppose the equilibrium price of a wuzzy is \$2. Given this output price, what is the VMP_L of the fourth worker hired per hour? What is WAS's total revenue at that level of production? What is the VMP_L of the sixth worker hired per hour? What is WAS's total revenue at that level of production?
   b. What is the maximum amount WAS should pay the fifth worker per hour? If labor is WAS's only cost and all workers are paid the same wage as the fifth worker, how much profit will WAS earn if it hires five workers per hour?
   c. What is the maximum amount WAS should pay the sixth worker per hour? If labor is WAS's only cost and all workers are paid the same wage as the sixth worker, how much profit will WAS earn if it hires six workers per hour?
   d. Suppose the price of a wuzzy rises to \$4, ceteris paribus. What is the maximum amount WAS should pay the fifth worker per hour? If labor is WAS's only cost and all workers are paid the same wage as the fifth worker, how much profit will WAS earn if it hires five workers per hour?
2. Professional U.S. soccer players earn much less than professional U.S. baseball players. Using economic reasoning, explain why.
3. From an economic perspective, are professional sports players worth their multimillion-dollar salaries? Explain why or why not.

Workers/Week	Total Product (Boxes of Apples/Week)	Price ($/Box)
0	0	10
1	90	10
2	170	10
3	240	10
4	300	10
5	355	10
6	400	10

4. Suppose that the Mt. Pleasant Apple Company has the production function shown in the accompanying table.
   a. What is the MP_L of the fourth worker hired per week?
   b. What is the VMP_L of the second worker hired per week?
   c. If the company wants to maximize profit, what is the maximum amount that it should pay the fourth worker per week?
5. In 2009, Alex Rodriguez admitted to using steroids in earlier baseball seasons. What would you expect to happen to his opportunities for endorsements as a result of this revelation?
6. How does an increase in the demand for a product influence the demand for workers who produce that product?
7. Use a graph to illustrate how an increase in the supply of workers in a given labor market impacts wages and employment levels in that market.

MULTIPLE CHOICE PROBLEMS

Workers/Hour	Total Product (Dogs Walked/Hour)	Price ($/Walk)
0	0	5.00
1	6	5.00
2	11	5.00
3	15	5.00
4	18	5.00
5	20	5.00
6	21	5.00

1. Terrier Touring is a dog-walking service with the production function shown in the accompanying table. What is the marginal product of the third worker hired per hour?
   a. $4.00 per hour
   b. 15 dogs walked per hour
   c. 4 dogs walked per hour
   d. $20.00 per hour
   e. $5.00

2. Terrier Touring is a dog-walking service with the production function shown in the accompanying table. If the wage is $12 per hour, Terrier Touring would want to
   a. hire the first but not the second worker.
   b. hire the second but not the third worker.
   c. hire the third but not the fourth worker.
   d. hire the fourth but not the fifth worker.
   e. hire the fifth but not the sixth worker.

3. Terrier Touring is a dog-walking service with the production function shown in the accompanying table. What is the total revenue earned if Terrier Touring hires four workers per hour?
   a. $18 per hour
   b. $20 per hour
   c. $90 per hour
   d. $15 per hour
   e. $70 per hour

4. When we draw a supply and demand diagram describing the labor market, the supply curve ______ and the demand curve ______.
   a. represents employers, represents employees
   b. represents employees, represents employers
   c. is drawn on the *x*-axis, is drawn on the *y*-axis
   d. is drawn on the *y*-axis, is drawn on the *x*-axis

5. By hiring workers based on their marginal benefits and marginal costs, the buyers in the labor market can
   a. maximize the amount of labor hired.
   b. minimize the amount of capital used.
   c. maximize their profits.
   d. both a and c
   e. all of the above

6. A decrease in the supply of fast-food restaurant workers could be the result of
   a. higher wages paid to workers in other types of restaurants
   b. lower wages paid to fast-food restaurant workers
   c. lower wages paid to workers in other types of restaurants
   d. decreased demand for fast-food
   e. higher wages paid to fast-food restaurant workers

Workers/Day	Marginal Product (Snoodles/Day)
1	22
2	25
3	20
4	18
5	15
6	10
7	8

7. The accompanying table shows production figures for Snoodle Corporation, which sells snoodles. Labor is Snoodle's only input, and wages make up Snoodle's only cost. If the equilibrium price of a snoodle is $10.00 and the wage paid to labor is $175.00 per day, the optimum number of workers to hire is ______ per day. At that level of employment, total costs are ______ per day.
   a. 2 workers; $120.00
   b. 2 workers; $256.00
   c. 4 workers; $180.00
   d. 4 workers; $40.00
   e. 4 workers; $700.00

8. Suppose that a film studio expects that hiring comedian Chris Rock to star in its next film will generate $50 million in extra revenue relative to hiring comedian Eddie Murphy to star in the film. Chris Rock demands $100 million to star in the film. Eddie Murphy demands $75 million to star in the film. Ceteris paribus, based on this information, the film studio will earn the highest profits by
   a. hiring Eddie Murphy.
   b. hiring both stars.
   c. hiring Chris Rock.
   d. none of the above.

9. Your friend tells you that our society has sick values because teachers make significantly less than sports stars like Alex Rodriguez. Applying the economic way of thinking, you argue that
   a. sports stars have more expensive tastes than teachers and must make more to live comfortably.
   b. comparing the salary of a teacher against the salary of Alex Rodriguez confuses total value with marginal value.
   c. this is because there is a larger demand for teachers than for sports stars like Alex Rodriguez.
   d. this is because there is a smaller supply of teachers than for sports stars like Alex Rodriguez.

10. When hiring workers, it is **only** profit maximizing for firms to hire additional workers when
   a. the marginal benefit of each worker hired is positive.
   b. the marginal cost of each worker hired is above zero.
   c. the marginal benefit of each worker hired is less than the marginal cost of each worker hired.
   d. the marginal benefit of each worker hired is greater than the marginal cost of each worker hired.
   e. each worker hired is productive.

ADDITIONAL READINGS AND WEB RESOURCES

Fort, Rodney D. (2003) *Sports Economics.* New Jersey: Prentice Hall. Applies economics to the business of sports, including professional sports and college sports.

Zimbalist, Andrew (2004) *May the Best Team Win: Baseball Economics and Public Policy.* Examines the economics of baseball, including unionization, stadium building, and competition.

The U.S. Bureau of Labor Statistics website includes information and data on earnings, employment, and other labor market outcomes in the United States. www.bls.gov

The Sports Economist blog includes economic commentary on sports and society. www.thesportseconomist.com

The *Forbes* magazine website includes economic news plus annual lists of salaries for celebrities, the richest American and world citizens, and many other economics-related topics. www.forbes.com

© David Levenson/Alamy Limited

10

The Minimum Wage

After studying this chapter, you should be able to:

- Define the minimum wage
- Describe the history of the minimum wage
- Describe the difference between the real and nominal values of the minimum wage
- Assess the theoretical impacts of the minimum wage on the labor market
- Explain why minimum wage laws are controversial
- Describe research findings regarding impacts of the minimum wage

In 2010, policymakers in Colorado were faced with an unusual problem. The state's voters had passed a law in 2006 that automatically adjusted Colorado's minimum wage to keep pace with the prices of food, housing, and other goods and services. The goal at the time was to automatically adjust the earnings of minimum wage workers as the cost of living in Colorado increased, which would reduce the need for future contentious legislative debates regarding whether or not to increase Colorado's minimum wage. The recession that started in 2007, however, resulted in a lower cost of living in Colorado as home prices fell and jobs disappeared during the economic downturn. The net impact was that Colorado policymakers were bound by law to lower the minimum wage from $7.28 to $7.24 per hour. Although this reduction is small, it generated substantial controversy and lower pay for the affected workers.

Minimum wage laws have a long and controversial history in the United States. This chapter introduces the economics of the minimum wage, presents a history of minimum wages, and illustrates the cost and benefit tradeoffs that minimum wage policy generates.

WHAT ARE MINIMUM WAGES?

The minimum wage is the lowest wage that employers can legally pay workers.

The **minimum wage** is the lowest wage that employers can legally pay workers. Most countries have some sort of minimum wage policy. In the United States, Canada, Australia, and many European nations, the minimum wage is set on an hourly basis. The minimum wage is set on a per month basis in Chile and China, and on a per day basis in India.

Regardless of the time period over which it is calculated, the minimum wage is a price floor. As we learned in Chapter 4, price floors set lower limits on prices. The minimum wage is a floor on the price of labor.

History of Minimum Wages

Minimum wages in the United States were first established in 1938 as part of the Fair Labor Standards Act (FLSA). The FLSA was the first major piece of U.S. worker protection legislation at the federal level. The FLSA also includes provisions mandating time and one-half overtime pay and restrictions on the use of child labor. Since its inception, the FLSA has been amended many times, including several amendments that increased the minimum wage. Figure 10.1 shows the changes in the federal minimum wage over time.

The nominal value of the minimum wage is expressed in current dollar values and is not adjusted for inflation.

The real value of the minimum wage is expressed in constant dollar or inflation-adjusted values.

Figure 10.1 includes two curves that depict the minimum wage. The solid curve shows the **nominal value of the minimum wage** over time, and the dotted curve shows the **real value of the minimum wage** over time. As we learned in Chapter 7, nominal values are values that have not been adjusted for inflation, so the

Figure 10.1 **Federal Minimum Wage, 1938–2011**

The federal minimum wage has been increased many times since it was introduced in 1938, as shown by the solid nominal minimum wage curve. Because rising prices erode the purchasing power of the minimum wage, the real value of the minimum wage has fallen since its peak in 1968, as shown by the dotted real minimum wage curve. Data source: Author's calculations based on data from U.S. Department of Labor Bureau of Labor Statistics (http://www.bls.gov). Real values are expressed in 2011 dollars.

nominal value of the minimum wage is expressed in the dollar values of each year. The nominal minimum wage of $0.25 in 1938 reflects the value of money in 1938, and the nominal minimum wage of $1.60 in 1968 reflects the value of money in 1968. In terms of real values, the $0.25 nominal minimum wage in 1938 is worth $4.00 in 2011 dollars, and the nominal minimum wage of $1.60 in 1968 is worth $10.39 in 2011 dollars. Between 1997 and 2006, the nominal value of the minimum wage was $5.15 per hour, as shown by the flat portion of the nominal minimum wage curve for those years. During those nine years, inflation affected the purchasing power of the $5.15 nominal wage, so the real value of the minimum wage fell between 1997 and 2006. The declining real value of the minimum wage between 1997 and 2006 is illustrated by the downward slope of the real minimum wage curve for those years. Because the real minimum wage values in Figure 10.1 are expressed in 2011 dollars, the nominal and real values of the minimum wage are equal in 2011.

The Fair Minimum Wage Act of 2007 amended the FLSA to raise the minimum wage in a series of three increments from $5.15 in 2006 to $7.25 per hour by 2009. In 2011, the nominal value of the minimum wage was still $7.25 per hour, but because inflation occurred between 2009 and 2011, the real value of the minimum wage fell during that period. The real value of the minimum wage reached its peak in 1968, and although the nominal value of the minimum wage has been increased many times since then, these increases have not kept pace with inflation.

State-level Minimum Wages

Some states also have their own minimum wage laws. Thirteen states have minimum wages that are higher than the federal level, five states have minimum wages that are lower than the federal level, and other states have minimum wages that are the same as the federal level. When state and federal minimum wages are different, workers are entitled to whichever minimum wage is higher. Some states, including Colorado, have laws that automatically adjust the state minimum wage to keep pace with inflation. As described in the introduction to this chapter, such laws open up the possibility that state-level minimum wages could be reduced during economic downturns. This is obviously a rare occurrence. It is more often the case that state-level minimum wages automatically adjust upward each year, depending on the level of inflation.

THINK FOR YOURSELF

What is the current minimum wage in your state? How does it compare with the federal minimum wage? How does the minimum wage compare with the average wages of workers in your state? What are the tradeoffs associated with having a minimum wage that is automatically adjusted for inflation?

THE THEORETICAL IMPACTS OF THE MINIMUM WAGE

Because the minimum wage is a type of price control, we can use the demand and supply model to assess how the minimum wage will affect the quantity of labor demanded and supplied.

Demand for Labor

Suppose that you are an employer. How will the amount of labor you demand be affected by an increase in the minimum wage? Figure 10.2 illustrates a hypothetical demand curve for labor. The vertical axis measures the price of labor, which is the wage per hour, and the horizontal axis measures the quantity of labor demanded per week. Suppose that before the most recent minimum wage increase the market was in equilibrium, and you were paying your workers $5.50 per hour. At that wage, your quantity of labor demanded was 60 hours per week. This is illustrated as point A in Figure 10.2.

Figure 10.2 **Demand for Labor**

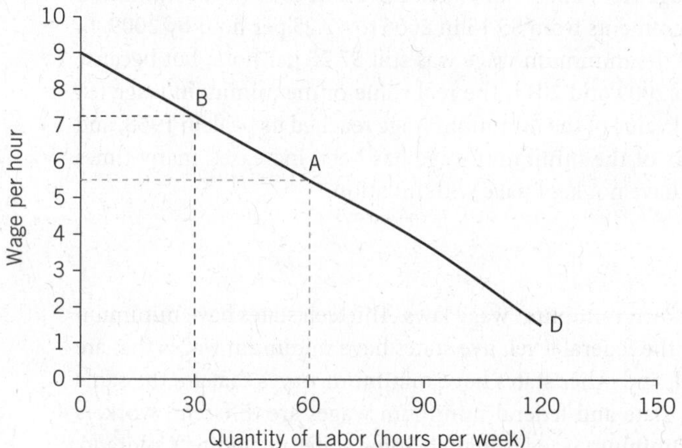

The demand curve for labor shows the price of labor, the wage per hour, and the quantity of labor demanded per period. When the price of labor rises from $5.50 to $7.25 per hour, the quantity of labor demanded falls from 60 hours per week (shown at point A) to 30 hours per week (shown at point B).

Now suppose that the minimum wage increases to $7.25 per hour, as it did in 2007–09. What might you do to deal with the higher cost of workers? Business firms typically respond to increased costs of labor by hiring fewer workers, cutting back on hours of operation, raising the prices of the goods they sell, or in some cases going out of business altogether. Each of these responses entails a decrease in the quantity of labor demanded. Just like buyers of other goods and services who decrease their quantity demanded when their prices rise, business firms respond to increases in the price of labor by decreasing the quantity of labor they demand. The movement from point A to point B in Figure 10.2 shows a decline in the quantity of labor demanded from 60 to 30 hours per week when the wage increases from $5.50 to $7.25 per hour.

Supply of Labor

How do workers respond to changes in the minimum wage? Suppose that you are a worker in the labor market. Before the minimum wage increase, you are supplying your labor to the market at a wage of $5.50 per hour. At that wage, the market is in equilibrium so that you and any other workers are able to supply all the labor you want at the $5.50 per hour wage. If there were two workers at your firm and each of you wanted to work 30 hours per week at a wage of $5.50, 60 hours of labor would be supplied per week at that wage. This combination of wage and quantity of labor supplied is shown as point A in Figure 10.3.

Figure 10.3 **Supply of Labor**

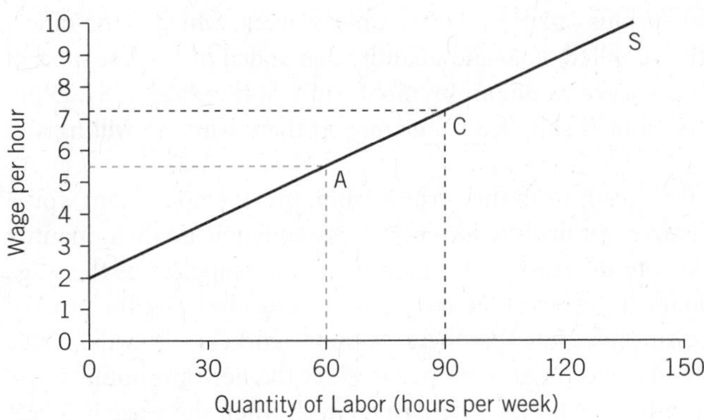

The supply of labor shows the quantity of labor supplied per period at each wage. An increase in the wage from \$5.50 to \$7.25 per hour would increase the quantity of labor supplied from 60 to 90 hours per week, as shown by the movement from point A to point C.

If the minimum wage increases to \$7.25 per hour, how might you respond? For many workers, an increase in their wage provides an incentive for them to want to work more hours per week. In addition, there may be people who were not willing to work at all when the wage was \$5.50 per hour, but who do want to work when the wage is \$7.25 per hour. Both of these factors will generate an increase in the quantity of labor supplied when the wage increases. The movement from point A to point C reflects an increase in the quantity of labor supplied from 60 to 90 hours per week in response to the increase in the wage from \$5.50 to \$7.25 per hour.

Above-equilibrium Minimum Wage

Increases in wages cause the quantity of labor demanded to decrease and the quantity of labor supplied to increase. Figure 10.4 combines the demand and supply of labor to illustrate how an increase in the minimum wage impacts the labor market. At the original wage of \$5.50, the market was in equilibrium at point A, with the quantity of labor demanded per week equal to the quantity of labor supplied per week. When the wage increases to \$7.25, the quantity of labor demanded falls to 30 hours per week (point B), while the quantity of labor supplied rises to 90 hours per week (point C).

Figure 10.4 **The Impact of a Minimum Wage in the Labor Market**

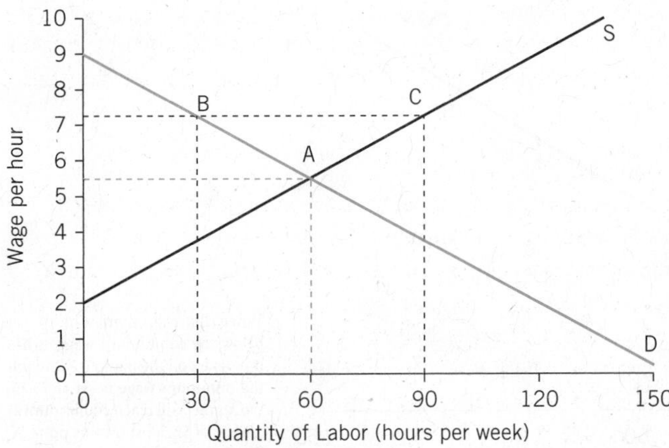

When the labor market is in equilibrium at point A, the quantity of labor demanded is equal to the quantity of labor supplied. An increase in the minimum wage above the equilibrium wage causes the quantity of labor demanded to fall from point A to point B and the quantity of labor supplied to rise from point A to point C. The above-equilibrium minimum wage causes a surplus of labor in the market.

Because firms will not want to hire more than 30 hours of labor per week, 30 hours per week is the amount of labor that will be employed in the market. The wage of $7.25 generates a market surplus of labor of 60 hours per week, which is the difference between the quantity supplied of 90 and quantity demanded of 30. A surplus of labor in the market is also known as **unemployment**, since at the wage of $7.25 per week a higher quantity of labor is supplied to the market than firms are willing and able to hire.

Unemployment occurs when there is a surplus of labor in the market.

If the market were free to adjust to the surplus labor, the unemployment would be eliminated by the incentives for firms to lower the wage and increase their quantity demanded and for workers to decrease their quantity of labor supplied as the wage falls. As with all price floors, however, the market cannot adjust to lower the price of labor, and it is left with a surplus. Note that there are some workers who will be able to keep their jobs and level of hours of work per week at the new minimum wage, because firms will want to hire 30 hours of labor per week when the wage is $7.25. For workers who are able to keep their jobs and level of hours per week, an increase in the minimum wage generates an increase in their earnings.

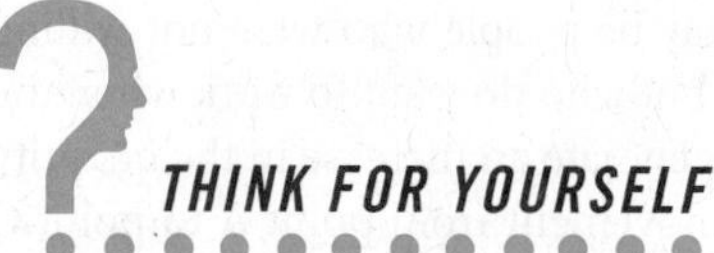

Would the amount of unemployment be larger or smaller if the minimum wage in Figure 10.4 was $8 per hour instead of $7.25 per hour? What if the minimum wage was $6 per hour?

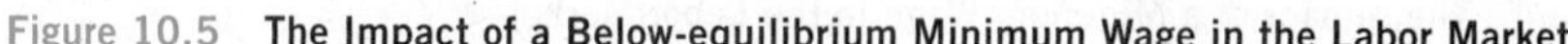

Below-equilibrium Minimum Wage

In the example illustrated in Figure 10.4, the minimum wage was set above the equilibrium wage. Figure 10.5 illustrates what happens if the minimum wage is set below the equilibrium wage. Suppose again that the equilibrium wage in the labor market is $5.50 and the equilibrium amount of labor employed is 60 hours per week, shown at point A in Figure 10.5. If a minimum wage of $3.75 is imposed on the market, what

Figure 10.5 **The Impact of a Below-equilibrium Minimum Wage in the Labor Market**

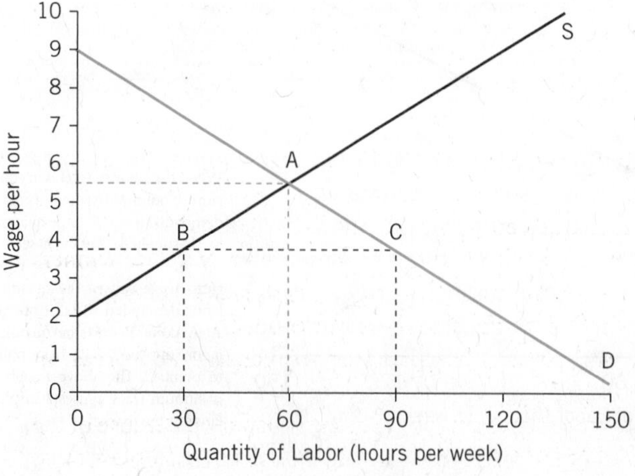

When the minimum wage is set below the equilibrium wage, it has no impact on the market. Although the minimum wage is set at $3.75, the market will reach equilibrium at a wage of $5.50, shown as point A. The below-equilibrium minimum wage is not binding.

will happen? When the wage is \$3.75, the quantity of labor demanded is 90 hours per week, as shown at point C in Figure 10.5. The quantity of labor supplied when the wage is \$3.75 is 30 hours per week, as shown at point B. If the wage were \$3.75 per hour, there would be a shortage of labor in the market, which would provide an incentive for employers to raise their wages. Because the \$3.75 wage is a minimum, there is no restriction that prevents employers from increasing wages above that level. As employers increase wages, the quantity of labor supplied will rise and the quantity of labor demanded will fall until the market reaches the equilibrium wage of \$5.50 and equilibrium quantity of labor traded of 60 hours per week. The below-equilibrium minimum wage has no impact on the labor market at all, since it does not impact either the equilibrium wage or quantity of labor hired.

Why is the situation in Figure 10.5 different from the one depicted in Figure 10.4? Remember that the minimum wage is a price floor, which means it places a restriction only on downward movements in the wage. When the wage is below equilibrium as in Figure 10.5, market forces will cause the wage to rise, which is not prohibited by minimum wage laws. However, when the wage is above equilibrium as in Figure 10.4, market forces put downward pressure on the wage, but the minimum wage law prohibits the market from adjusting to these forces.

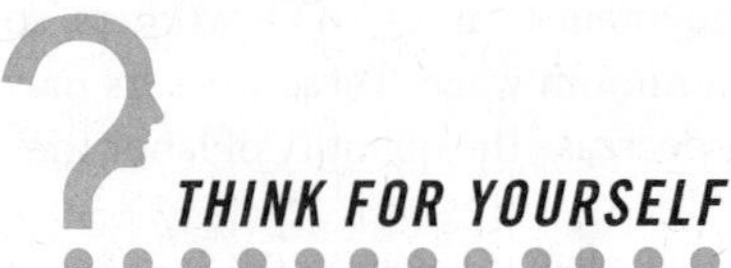

Suppose that the equilibrium wage in a local labor market is \$7.50 per hour. What impact would a minimum wage of \$10 per hour have on the market? What impact would a minimum wage of \$6.00 per hour have on the market?

THE WINNERS AND LOSERS FROM THE MINIMUM WAGE

Like any public policy decision, the imposition of minimum wages generates tradeoffs. In addition, the costs imposed by the minimum wage tend to be borne by different groups than those who reap the benefits of the minimum wage. Not surprisingly, this situation generates controversy, disagreement about the effectiveness of minimum wages, and heated debates over minimum wage policy. This section highlights some of the groups who win and some who lose when minimum wages are increased.

Workers

Figure 10.6 illustrates several changes that occur with the imposition of an above-equilibrium minimum wage in the labor market. The labor market is initially in equilibrium at point A, with Q_0 workers hired per hour at wage W_0. When a minimum wage of W_1 is imposed on the market, employment falls from Q_0 to Q_1.

The Q_1 workers who remain employed at the new minimum wage are winners from the minimum wage because the minimum wage causes their incomes to rise. One could argue that firms who sell products to these workers will also win from the minimum wage because the workers' increased incomes will generate an increase in their demand for normal goods.

Although the Q_1 workers who keep their jobs are clearly better off because of the minimum wage, the net impact of the minimum wage on workers overall is less clear.

Figure 10.6 The Winners and Losers from the Minimum Wage

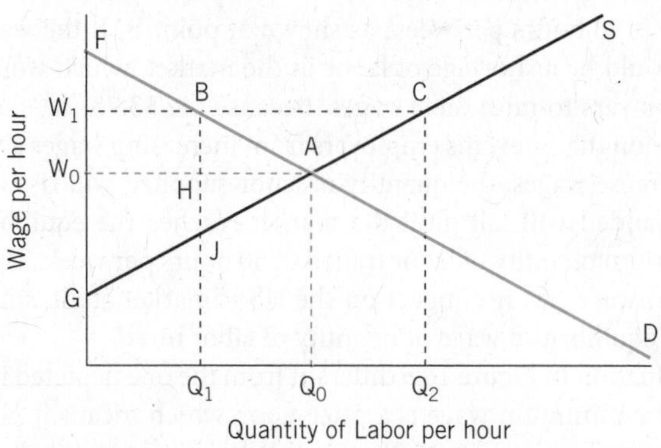

The minimum wage results in a drop from Q_0 to Q_1 hours of labor employed per hour. With the minimum wage in place, producer surplus changes from area W_0AG to area $GJBW_1$. Workers who are able to keep their jobs and hours of work are "winners" from the minimum wage because their earnings rise, but other workers are "losers" from the minimum wage because they lose their jobs, cannot find jobs, or see their hours of work cut. Firms are "losers" from the minimum wage because consumer surplus falls from area W_0AF to area W_1BF. The deadweight loss from the minimum wage is area BJA.

The minimum wage generates a decrease in employment from Q_0 to Q_1 workers, so workers between Q_0 and Q_1 are losers from the minimum wage. These workers may be laid off or see their work hours cut when firms decrease the quantity of labor they demand in response to the higher wage.

Because workers are the producers in the labor market, we can use the concept of producer surplus to measure the overall impact of the minimum wage on workers in the labor market. We learned in Chapter 4 that producer surplus is the area above the supply curve but below the price of the good or service in the market. At the initial equilibrium, producer surplus is equal to the area W_0AG. With the minimum wage in place, producer surplus changes to area $GJBW_1$.

Are workers better off or worse off as a result of the minimum wage? On the one hand, producer surplus rises by area W_0HBW_1 when the minimum wage is in place. On the other hand, producer surplus falls by area HAJ. Whether the increase in producer surplus is larger than the decrease in producer surplus depends on the elasticity of the demand and supply curves, so we cannot make a clear theoretical prediction about the net impact of the minimum wage on workers in the labor market.

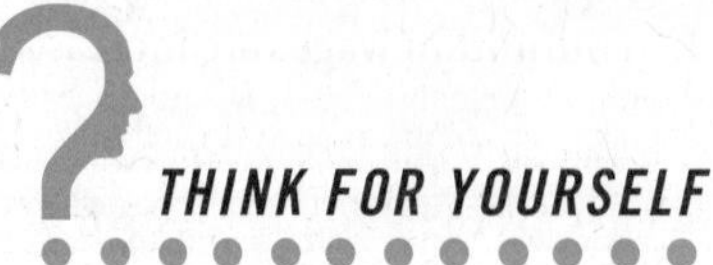

THINK FOR YOURSELF

How would the size of unemployment generated by an increase in the minimum wage differ if the demand for labor were relatively elastic versus relatively inelastic?

In addition to workers Q_1 to Q_0, another set of workers is also impacted by the minimum wage. When the wage increases from W_0 to W_1, the quantity of labor supplied rises from Q_0 to Q_2. The increase in the quantity of labor supplied arises because the increased wage encourages some workers to supply more hours of work to the market, and because some workers who were not willing to work at wage W_0 enter the labor market to find work at wage W_1. Because the quantity of labor demanded is only Q_1, however, many of the new labor market entrants will not be able to find jobs and will instead be unemployed. These workers are also losers from the minimum wage.

Finally, although it is not illustrated in Figure 10.6, the minimum wage may also cause some firms to cut funding for employee benefits such as employee health insurance, paid sick leave, employee training, or other benefits. Employees who face these types of cuts are also losers from the minimum wage.

Businesses & Consumers

How are business firms affected by the minimum wage? Businesses are the consumers in the labor market, so we can use the concept of consumer surplus to summarize the impact of the minimum wage on businesses. In the initial equilibrium shown in Figure 10.6, consumer surplus is area W_0AF, which is the area below the demand curve for labor and above the equilibrium wage W_0. With the minimum wage W_1 in place, consumer surplus falls to area W_1BF. Because consumer surplus falls when the minimum wage is imposed, businesses are losers from the minimum wage. In addition, the minimum wage generates a deadweight loss in the labor market equal to area BJA.

How are customers affected by the minimum wage? An increase in the cost of labor to business firms will cause firms to decrease the supply of their product. The decrease in supply will cause an inward shift in the supply curve for the product, an increase in the equilibrium price of the product, and a decrease in the equilibrium quantity of the product sold. So consumers will face higher prices for products and find fewer products available when the minimum wage is imposed. The degree to which prices rise depends on the size of the supply shift and the elasticity of demand for the good. Goods that have more elastic demand will have relatively small price increases, whereas those that have more inelastic demand will have relatively large price increases. Either way, consumers are losers from the imposition of the minimum wage.

The Granger Collection, NYC—All rights reserved.

John Kenneth Galbraith and Guaranteed Minimum Income

John Kenneth Galbraith (1908–2006) was an economist, author, economic advisor to several American presidents, including Roosevelt, Truman, Kennedy, and Johnson, and was the U.S. Ambassador to India from 1961–1963. In 1968, he and many other economists called on Congress to introduce a guaranteed minimum income in the United States, which would include the minimum wage, student grants and loans, and income transfers to the poor. He was awarded the Presidential Medal of Freedom twice for his work in economics, and his many books, including *The Affluent Society* and *The New Industrial State*, remain influential today.

WHY ARE MINIMUM WAGES CONTROVERSIAL?

As the previous section illustrates, there are winners and losers from the minimum wage. Winners include those who keep their jobs, hours of work, and benefits when the minimum wage rises. Losers include those who lose their jobs, see their work hours cut, or are not hired into jobs at the minimum wage. Businesses and customers also lose from the imposition of the minimum wage. The fact that there are winners and losers from minimum wages makes them controversial policy tools.

To understand the controversy surrounding minimum wages, it is important to consider the purpose of minimum wage laws. Minimum wage laws are most often touted as antipoverty policies. Most workers affected by minimum wage laws are in low-paying jobs and have relatively low levels of labor market experience. Indeed, the majority of those employed at or near the minimum wage are young workers ages 16 to 24, workers in part-time jobs, and relatively low-skilled adult workers. Proponents of minimum wages argue that minimum wages help the poor by raising their incomes. This is true for workers who are able to keep their jobs and level of employment when the minimum wage rises. Proponents of the minimum wage also note that the increase in worker incomes does not come at the direct expense of taxpayers, because the minimum wage is paid by employers rather than the government. Proponents of the minimum wage also argue that because the minimum wage only raises the incomes of those who are working, it provides better employment incentives than do welfare or other government income transfer programs to the poor.

Opponents of the minimum wage argue that because minimum wages benefit relatively few poor workers at the expense of other poor workers, businesses, and consumers, minimum wages do not reduce poverty and instead reduce overall social welfare. Although some workers are able to keep their jobs when the minimum wage increases, others see their employment opportunities reduced because firms decrease the quantity of workers they demand. The minimum wage may also discourage firms from investing in training for their workers. In addition, opponents argue, the minimum wage provides incentives for businesses to raise the prices of their products, generating increased costs for consumers. Opponents of the minimum wage also argue that by raising the cost of labor, minimum wages provide incentives for some businesses to use substitute inputs like machines or lower-cost workers in foreign countries instead of domestic workers.

MINIMUM WAGE RESEARCH

In debates over minimum wage policy, those from divergent points on the political spectrum tend to emphasize the winners or the losers differently, depending on whether it helps support their arguments for or against the minimum wage. The politically charged debate surrounding the minimum wage highlights the importance having access to unbiased research on sensitive economic issues. Such research can come from many sources, but peer-reviewed research is less likely to be subject to political bias than research published by one side or the other in the minimum wage debate. When researchers submit their work to peer-reviewed publications, it is intensely scrutinized and must be able to withstand criticism by other experts before it is published. This section highlights some of the peer-reviewed research on the impacts of the minimum wage.[1]

Research on the impacts of the minimum wage has focused primarily on poverty, employment, and school enrollment. Because teenagers are the group most affected by minimum wage changes, teens are frequently studied to assess the impacts of the minimum wage. Teenagers are most affected by minimum wages because they have among the lowest education and experience levels of workers in the labor force.

---

1 Full citations for this research plus additional readings on the impacts of the minimum wage are listed at the end of the chapter.

With respect to employment, researchers have found somewhat mixed impacts of the minimum wage. Some researchers have found no impacts of the minimum wage on teenage employment, and others have found increases in teenage employment resulting from the imposition of minimum wages (see, for example, Card and Krueger, 1995). Most research in this area, however, finds that the minimum wage causes a small reduction in employment opportunities for low-skilled workers and teenagers (Neumark and Wascher, 2008). The relatively small impacts of the minimum wage on employment stem from the relatively inelastic demand and supply of labor in minimum wage labor markets. Recall from Chapter 5 that when demand and supply are relatively inelastic, changes in the price of goods cause only small changes in the quantity demanded and supplied of the good.

Other researchers have focused on how minimum wages affect students' choices to remain in school (Neumark and Wascher, 1995). Because most teens are low skilled and have low levels of experience, the minimum wage is a good estimate of what they earn in their jobs. When the minimum wage increases, the opportunity cost of staying in school rises, so students on the margin of staying in school face increased incentives to drop out of school to work or look for a job. Other teens might choose to stay in school but increase the amount of hours they work when the minimum wage increases, which may in turn affect their school performance. The research findings in this area indicate that increases in the minimum wage are associated with increased high school dropout rates.

With respect to research on the impacts of the minimum wage on poverty, research indicates that minimum wages do increase the incomes of some poor families, which would imply that the minimum wage is associated with decreases in poverty (Neumark and Wascher, 2002). At the same time, however, minimum wages cause decreased employment among the poor and among the near-poor, which increases poverty. The net effect of these two opposing impacts of the minimum wage is that increases in the minimum wage are associated with increases in the proportions of families that are poor and near-poor. In other words, it appears that minimum wages are associated with slight increases rather than decreases in poverty.

SUMMARY

The minimum wage is a form of price control in the labor market because it sets a legal minimum that can be paid to workers. Standard demand and supply analysis indicates that minimum wages are associated with increased quantity of labor supplied and decreased quantity of labor demanded. Minimum wages that lie above equilibrium wages generate decreased employment among affected workers. Although the minimum wage helps some workers by increasing their incomes, the minimum wage hurts other members of society by generating unemployment, reduced profits, and higher prices. Research evidence indicates that the minimum wage is not effective at reducing poverty.

KEY CONCEPTS

- Minimum wage
- Nominal value of the minimum wage
- Real value of the minimum wage
- Unemployment

DISCUSSION QUESTIONS AND PROBLEMS

1. Why has the real value of the minimum wage declined since 1968, even though the nominal value of the minimum wage has increased several times since then?
2. Are teenagers better off when a higher minimum wage enables some to get higher wages but causes others to lose their jobs?
3. Why do you think that businesses would generally be opposed to increases in the minimum wage?
4. Would you be likely to leave school if the minimum wage were increased to $15.00 per hour? Why or why not? What types of students would be most likely to leave school as a result of a minimum wage increase?
5. Suppose the demand and supply of labor in your town is given in the accompanying graph.
   a. What is the equilibrium wage per hour and quantity of workers hired per month?
   b. What is the value of consumer surplus, producer surplus, and economic surplus in equilibrium?

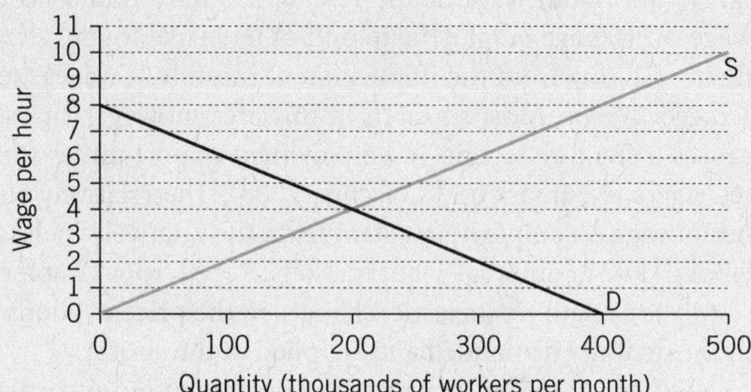

   c. Suppose the government institutes a minimum wage of $7.00 per hour in this market. What will be the new quantity of labor demanded, quantity of labor supplied, and quantity of labor hired in this market?
   d. What is the value of consumer surplus, producer surplus, economic surplus, and deadweight loss when the minimum wage is imposed on this market?
   e. Which parties in the market win and which lose from the imposition of the new wage?

MULTIPLE CHOICE QUESTIONS

1. Those that lose when the minimum wage is increased include
   a. employers only.
   b. all workers.
   c. no workers.
   d. some workers.
2. One effect of the minimum wage is
   a. higher unemployment among teenagers.
   b. higher incomes for all workers.
   c. an overall reduction in poverty.
   d. more on-the-job training offered to workers.
3. The real value of the minimum wage
   a. is set by employers.
   b. is set by lawmakers.
   c. is impacted by inflation.
   d. is always the same as the nominal value of the minimum wage.
4. Those that win when the minimum wage is increased include
   a. buyers of goods produced using minimum wage workers.
   b. workers who lose their jobs.
   c. employers.
   d. workers who keep their jobs.
5. When the government sets out to help low-income people by establishing a minimum wage
   a. increased unemployment may occur.
   b. a shortage of labor may occur because there will not be enough workers to fill existing jobs.
   c. many workers will leave the work force.
   d. all poor people will definitely be helped by the minimum wage.
6. An increase in the minimum wage
   a. makes all poor people better off by increasing their incomes.
   b. does not make anyone better off because employers won't hire people if they have to pay them more.
   c. makes everyone better off by increasing the average wages in the economy.
   d. makes some workers better off by compelling their employers to pay them more.
   e. makes all of those willing to work at the minimum wage better off.
7. When the demand for labor is very elastic, a given increase in the minimum wage will

generate _____ relative to when the demand for labor is very inelastic.

a. a larger decrease in the quantity of labor demanded
a. a smaller decrease in the quantity of labor demanded
b. the same size decrease in the quantity of labor demanded
c. a larger increase in the quantity of labor demanded

8. Suppose the elasticity of demand for low-skill labor is −1.0. Currently, the minimum wage keeps the price of low-skill labor 20 percent above the equilibrium wage. If the minimum wage is removed, how much more low-skill labor will be hired?
   a. 40 percent
   b. 30 percent
   c. 20 percent
   d. 10 percent
   e. not enough information to answer this question

9. If the demand for labor is inelastic then
   a. any unemployment caused by raising the minimum wage is less than if demand were elastic.
   b. any unemployment caused by raising the minimum wage is the same as if demand were elastic.
   c. any unemployment caused by raising the minimum wage is more than if demand were elastic.
   d. there will be no change in unemployment by raising the minimum wage.

10. If an individual suggests that any decision regarding an increase in the minimum wage should only be made after objectively comparing the costs and benefits of the increase,
   a. that individual must not care about the well-being of the poor.
   b. that individual is engaging in the economic way of thinking.
   c. that individual should not be elected to public office.
   d. that individual is not being fair.

ADDITIONAL READINGS AND WEB RESOURCES

Card, David and Krueger, Alan B. (1995) *Myth and Measurement: The New Economics of the Minimum Wage*, Princeton University Press. Presents research that finds increased employment resulting from increases in the minimum wage.

Ehrenreich, Barbara (2001) *Nickel and Dimed: On (Not) Getting By in America*. New York: Henry Holt and Company http://www.henryholt.com/holt/nickelanddimed.htm Describes the author's experience with living on the minimum wage for one year.

Miller, Roger, Benjamin, D. and North, D. (2003) *The Economics of Public Issues*, Boston: Addison Wesley. Includes a chapter on the minimum wage and several other chapters on public policy issues.

Neumark, D., and Wascher, W. (1995) "Minimum Wage Effects on School and Work Transitions of Teenagers," *American Economic Review* 85(2): 244–249. Presents research on the impact of minimum wages on high school dropout rates.

Neumark, David, and Wascher, W. (2002) "Do Minimum Wages Fight Poverty?" *Economic Inquiry* 40(3) (July):315–33. Presents research on the impact of minimum wages on poverty rates.

Neumark, David, and Wascher, W. L. (2008) *Minimum Wages*, Cambridge, MA: The MIT Press; Sowell, Thomas (2007) *Basic Economics: A Common Sense Guide to the Economy*, New York: Basic Books. Presents an academic overview of the research on the impacts of the minimum wage.

The International Labour Organization, Conditions of Work and Employment Programme database includes descriptions of minimum wage laws in many different countries. Available at www.ilo.org/public/english/protection/condtrav/index.htm

The U.S. Department of Labor FLSA website presents historical information on the minimum wage and other labor-related laws. http://www.dol.gov/esa/whd/flsa/

The Economic Policy Institute's "Minimum Wage Issue Guide" presents an overview of the impacts of the minimum wage from the perspective of an organization with the mission to "achieve shared prosperity by raising the economic status of low- and middle-income Americans." It is available at http://www.epi.org/publications/entry/issue_guide_on_minimum_wage/

The Heritage Foundation presents an overview of the impacts of the minimum wage from the perspective of an organization whose mission is to "formulate and promote conservative public policies based on the principles of free enterprise, limited government, individual freedom, traditional American values, and a strong national defense." It is available at http://www.heritage.org/research/testimony/the-economic-effects-of-the-minimum-wage

© Lee Pettet/iStockphoto

International Trade of Goods

After studying this chapter, you should be able to:

- Discuss the extent of U.S. international trade
- Explain the concepts of comparative advantage and absolute advantage
- Analyze the costs and benefits of international trade
- Describe the distribution of the costs and benefits from international trade
- Assess the arguments for and against limiting international trade
- Describe the costs, benefits, and mechanisms of limiting international trade
- Describe some of the forms of trade liberalization

If you are like many students, you had coffee to drink this morning. Where did your coffee come from? There are many sources of coffee, but it is unlikely that your coffee was grown in the United States. Most coffee producers are located in the warm climates of Central America, South America, and parts of Africa, Asia, and Indonesia. Your iPhone and iPad were manufactured by a company based in Taiwan, your laptop was probably manufactured in China, and your Toyota could have easily been manufactured in Mexico. A large percent of the goods and services that you use every day were produced abroad.

This chapter highlights the extent of international trade and the underlying economic factors that drive international trade. We'll review the concepts of comparative and absolute advantage from Chapter 2. We'll highlight the costs and benefits of international trade, as well as the distribution of those costs and benefits within an economy. Finally, we'll discuss the incentives, impacts, and controversies surrounding international trade agreements and policies.

THE EXTENT OF INTERNATIONAL TRADE

International trade is the exchange of goods and services between countries. It is composed of **exports** and **imports**. Exports are goods produced domestically but sold abroad, such as wheat grown in Montana and sold to consumers in Europe. Imports are goods that are produced abroad but purchased domestically, such as Columbian coffee or French wine purchased by an Australian. When the amount of a country's exports exceeds the amount of its imports, the country has a **trade surplus**. When the amount of a country's imports exceeds the amount of its exports, the country has a **trade deficit**.

Exports Goods or services produced domestically but sold abroad.

Imports Goods or services produced abroad but sold domestically.

Trade surplus When a country's level of exports exceeds its level of imports.

Trade deficit When a country's level of imports exceeds its level of exports.

Although all of the countries in the world have at least some amount of international trade, most international trade is concentrated among relatively few countries. Table 11.1 shows the levels of imports and exports for the 10 leading importing and exporting countries in the world. Not surprisingly, the list includes the largest economies in the world. The top 10 exporting countries account for 77 percent of total world exports, and the top 10 importing countries account for 81 percent of total world imports. The United States is the world's third largest exporter and the world's second largest importer.

International trade has been a part of economies throughout history. One example is the set of Silk Road trade routes across Asia, Africa, and the Mediterranean, where traders of silk, spices, jewels, and other merchandise connected people and cultures from widely scattered parts of the world. The development of China, India, Egypt, Rome, Arabia, and many other civilizations was dramatically influenced by

Table 11.1 Leading Exporters and Importers, 2010

Exports				Imports			
Rank	Exporters	Value ($ Billions U.S.)	Percent of Total Exports	Rank	Importers	Value ($ Billions U.S.)	Percent of Total Imports
1	Extra-EU*	1,788	15.1	1	Extra-EU*	1,991	16.5
2	China	1,578	13.3	2	United States	1,969	16.4
3	United States	1,278	10.8	3	China	1,395	11.6
4	Germany	1,269	10.7	4	Germany	1,067	8.9
5	Japan	770	6.5	5	Japan	694	5.8
6	Netherlands	573	4.8	6	France	606	5.0
7	France	521	4.4	7	United Kingdom	560	4.7
8	South Korea	466	3.9	8	Netherlands	517	4.3
9	Italy	448	3.8	9	Italy	484	4.0
10	Belgium	412	3.5	10	Hong Kong	442	3.7
	Top 10 Total	**9,103**	**76.7**		**Top 10 Total**	**9,725**	**80.8**
	World Total	11,872	100		**World Total**	12,037	100

*Extra-EU trade does not include trade among European Union nations (e.g., between Italy and Germany).
Source: World Trade Organization "International Trade Statistics 2011, available at http://www.wto.org/english/res_e/statis_e/its2011_e/its11_appendix_e.htm

international trade. From this historical perspective, international trade is a growing, evolutionary process. More recently, rapid increases in technology have decreased the costs of transporting goods and services and have resulted in increased international trade and globalization in the world.

Although international trade and economic globalization are increasingly spread among nations across the world, most international trade takes place locally because, ceteris paribus, trading with neighboring countries has lower costs than trading with countries farther away. Table 11.2 lists the top international U.S. trading partners. Neighboring countries Canada and Mexico are the top U.S. trading partners in part because of their geographic proximity.

Table 11.2 Top U.S. International Trade Partners, January–March 2012

Rank	Country	Percent of Total U.S. Trade
1	Canada	16.5
2	Mexico	13.1
3	China	13.0
4	Japan	5.9
5	Germany	4.1
6	United Kingdom	3.1
7	South Korea	2.7
8	Brazil	2.0
9	Saudi Arabia	1.9
10	France	1.7
Top 15 countries % of total value of U.S. trade		72.1

Source: U.S. Census Bureau Top Trading Partners – Total Trade, Exports, Imports. Available at U.S. http://www.census.gov/foreign-trade/statistics/highlights/toppartners.html

WHY DO WE TRADE?

Countries trade goods and services for the same reasons that individual consumers and producers trade goods and services, namely because trade generates benefits to the trading partners. We learned in Chapter 2 that people are better off if they buy goods and services from others who have comparative advantage in production.

Countries benefit from trade with one another as well. Figure 11.1 illustrates daily production possibilities frontiers (PPFs) for two hypothetical countries, Landia and Seavia, who produce shoes and computers. For simplicity, we can assume constant opportunity costs of production for both countries. In Chapter 13 we'll learn about the economics of international money exchange, but we can ignore this and other costs related to international trade for now because these factors will not affect the conclusions in this chapter.

If Landia devotes all its resources to computer production, the maximum number of computers that Landia could produce in a given day is 3,000. If all Landia's

Figure 11.1 **Production Possibilities for Landia and Seavia**

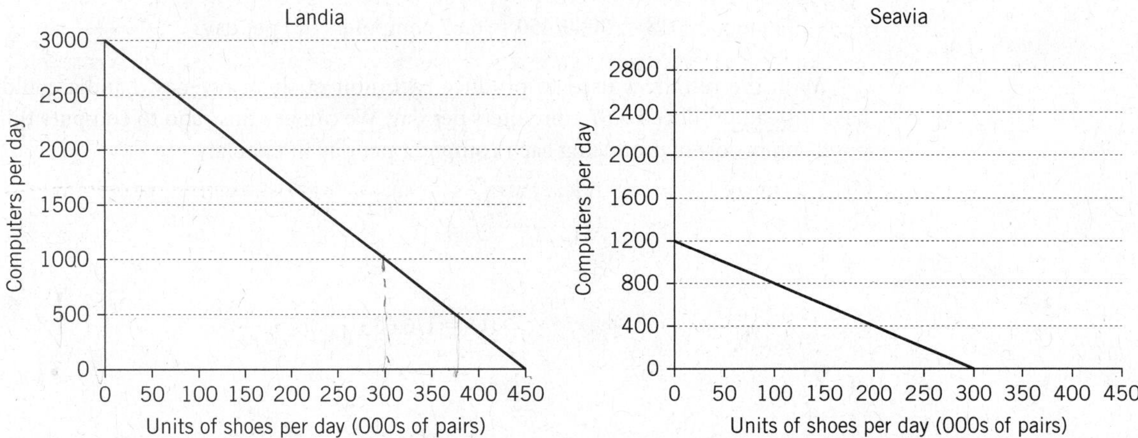

Using all of its available resources, Landia can produce either 3,000 computers per day or 450 units of shoes per day. Seavia can produce either 1,200 computers per day or 300 units of shoes per day. The opportunity cost of each computer produced per day in Landia is 6.67 units of shoes per day. The opportunity cost of each computer produced in Seavia is 4 units of shoes per day. Because it has lower opportunity cost of producing computers, Seavia has comparative advantage over Landia in producing computers.

resources are instead devoted to shoe production, Landia could produce 450 units (450,000 pairs) of shoes per day.

If Seavia devotes all its resources to computer production, 1,200 computers could be produced each day. If Seavia devotes all its resources to shoe production, 300 units (300,000 pairs) could be produced per day.

We learned in Chapter 2 that having the ability to produce more of a good than another producer means having absolute advantage in production of the good relative to the other producer. In our example, Landia has absolute advantage in the production of both computers and shoes relative to Seavia since Landia can produce more computers and shoes than Seavia. Remember, however, that it is *comparative advantage*, not *absolute advantage*, which is important for generating benefits from trade. Having comparative advantage in the production of a good or service means being able to produce the good or service at a lower opportunity cost than another producer.

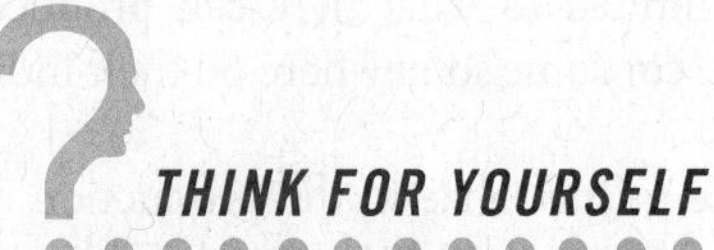

What is absolute advantage? What is comparative advantage? Which is more important in determining whether it is beneficial for countries to engage in international trade?

To determine which country has comparative advantage in producing shoes and which has comparative advantage in producing computers, we need to know the countries' opportunity costs of production. The slope of the PPF is equal to the opportunity cost of the good measured on the horizontal axis, so the opportunity cost of producing 1 unit of shoes (S) per day for Landia is

$$1S = 3000/450 = 6.67 \text{ computers (C) per day}$$

With the resources used to produce each unit of shoes per day, Landia could have instead produced 6.67 computers per day. We can use this ratio to compute the opportunity cost of producing each computer per day in Landia:

$$1S = 6.67C$$

so

$$1C = 1/6.67S$$

or

$$1C = 0.15S$$

For Seavia, the opportunity cost of 1 unit of shoes per day is

$$1S = 1200/300 = 4C \text{ per day}$$

The production of 4 computers per day is foregone each time 1 unit of shoes is produced per day in Seavia. Alternatively, the production of 0.25 units of shoes per day is foregone for each computer produced per day in Seavia:

$$1S = 4C$$

so

$$1C = 0.25S$$

The opportunity cost of producing shoes is lower in Seavia than it is in Landia because the opportunity cost of producing 1 unit of shoes in Seavia is 4 computers, whereas the opportunity cost of producing 1 unit of shoes in Landia is 6.67 computers. Because Seavia can produce shoes at a lower opportunity cost than Landia, Seavia has comparative advantage relative to Landia in producing shoes. Because the cost of producing a computer in Landia is lower than it is in Seavia, Landia has comparative advantage relative to Seavia in producing computers.

When people, firms, and even countries trade according to their comparative advantage, both trading parties can be made better off. If Landia and Seavia do not trade with one another, their consumption is limited to what they can produce. Without trade, Landia and Seavia are restricted to consume somewhere on their individual PPFs shown in Figure 11.1.

Now suppose that Landia and Seavia decide to specialize in the production of the good in which they each have comparative advantage and then trade with one another. Landia will specialize in producing computers and Seavia will specialize in producing shoes. If Landia devotes all its resources to producing computers, Landia will produce 3,000 computers and no shoes. If Seavia specializes in producing shoes, it will produce 300,000 pairs of shoes and no computers.

The terms of trade describes the price or rate of exchange of one good for another. In order for two countries to be better off by trading, the terms of trade need to be between the two countries' opportunity costs of production.

How do the countries decide how much of each good to trade? The rate of exchange or **terms of trade** of one good for another will depend on many factors, including the countries' bargaining power and the demand for each good in each country. The terms of trade arrangement will describe the number of computers to be traded for each unit of shoes and vice versa. There is an infinite number of possible terms of trade that will generate mutual gains for Landia and Seavia, but each of the terms of trade will set the price for each good between the two countries' opportunity costs of producing the good.

In our example, Seavia will produce shoes and exchange them for computers. Since the opportunity cost of a computer in Seavia is 0.25S, Seavia will need to obtain each computer from Landia at a price lower than 0.25S in order to be better off. Landia produces each computer at an opportunity cost of 0.15S. To be better off by trading with Seavia, Landia will need to sell each computer to Seavia at price higher than 0.15S. These two conditions imply that the price of each computer needs to be between 0.15S and 0.25S:

$$0.15S < 1C < 0.25S$$

We can also determine the terms of trade for each unit of shoes produced. Since Seavia has comparative advantage in producing shoes, Seavia will produce and sell shoes to Landia for computers. To be better off, Seavia will need to at least cover its opportunity cost of production for shoes, so Seavia will need to obtain at least 4C for each unit of shoes it sells. For Landia to be better off by buying shoes from Seavia, Landia needs to obtain shoes for less than its opportunity cost of producing shoes, 6.67C. Thus, the terms of trade will set the price of shoes will between 4C and 6.67C, or

$$4C < 1S < 6.67C$$

An infinite number of possible prices that will fit these terms of trade. One potential fit is

$$1C = .2S$$

or

$$1S = 5C$$

Figure 11.2 illustrates the production possibilities frontiers and consumption possibilities frontiers for Landia and Seavia when the terms of trade are 1S = 5C. The solid lines in Figure 11.2 represent the PPFs for Landia and Seavia, and the dotted lines show the consumption possibilities for each country.

If Landia trades away 1,000 computers at these terms of trade, it will gain 200 units of shoes in return. This trade will leave Landia with 2,000 computers. This combination of 2,000 computers and 200 units of shoes is point A on Landia's consumption possibilities frontier in Figure 11.2. When Seavia trades its 200 units of shoes to Landia for 1,000 computers, Seavia can move to a point A on its consumption possibilities frontier. Specialization and trade allows both countries to move beyond the confines of their production possibilities.

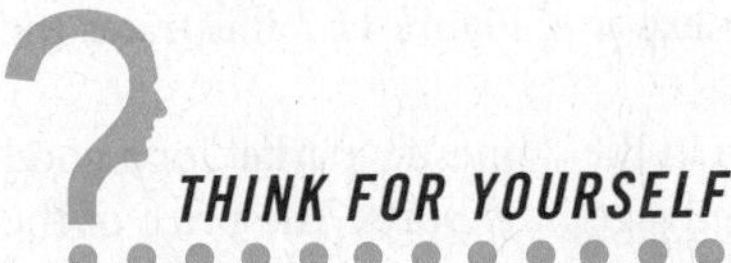

THINK FOR YOURSELF

Draw consumption possibilities frontiers for Landia and Seavia if the terms of trade are 1S = 4.5C.

Figure 11.2 **Production and Consumption Possibilities Frontiers**

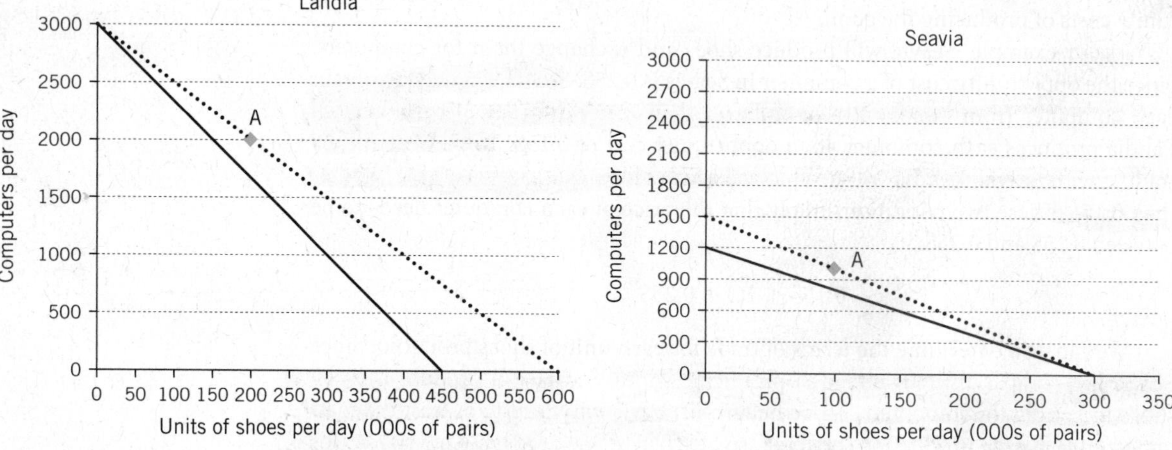

The solid lines represent the PPFs for Landia and Seavia. If Landia produces only computers and Seavia produces only shoes and the two countries trade with one another at the rate of 200 units of shoes for 1,000 computers, or 1S = 5C, the two countries can consume at levels outside their PPF, as shown by the dotted consumption possibilities curves. Point A illustrates one possible consumption level for the two countries, if Landia trades 1,000 computers to Seavia for 200 units of shoes.

Understanding the concept of comparative advantage helps illuminate why the coffee you drink comes from somewhere outside the U.S., since countries in South and Central America, Asia, and Indonesia have comparative advantage relative to the United States in producing coffee. The fact that the largest category of U.S. goods exported is capital goods—machines, equipment, industrial and aircraft engines—tells us that the U.S. has comparative advantage relative to many other countries in producing these goods.

THE "WINNERS" AND "LOSERS" FROM INTERNATIONAL TRADE

We have learned that specialization and trade according to comparative advantage can benefit both trading partners. A natural question then is why international trade and globalization are so controversial. Meetings of groups that seek to encourage international trade, such as the World Trade Organization, are often sites of large protests and demonstrations against international trade. Debates in Congress over whether the U.S. should restrict its engagement in trade with other nations take place frequently. One reason that international trade is controversial is that it involves costs and benefits. Although most economists would agree that the overall benefits of free trade outweigh its overall costs, the distribution of these costs and benefits is unequal.

The supply and demand model can help us understand the impacts of international trade in domestic markets. Let's start with exports. Figure 11.3 illustrates the impact of exports on a domestic market.

Panel A of Figure 11.3 illustrates equilibrium in the domestic market for a good or service, assuming that the supplier does not engage in exports. The price of the good is P_0 and the quantity of the good traded is Q_0.

Entering the international export market is similar to increasing the number of consumers of the good or service, which causes an increase in demand. Panel B illustrates that, ceteris paribus, if the supplier decides to enter the international export

Figure 11.3 **Impact of Exports on the Domestic Market**

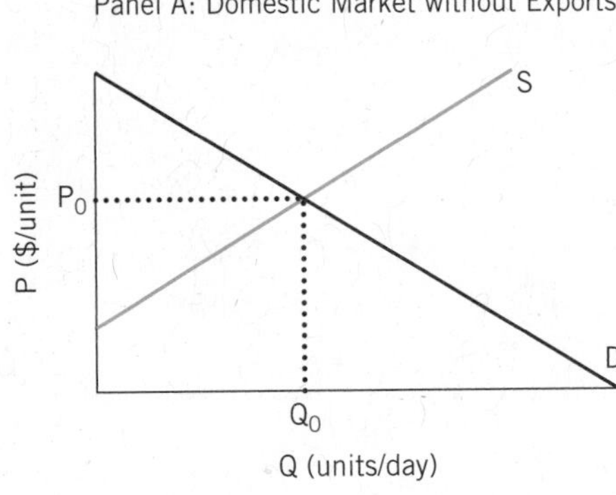

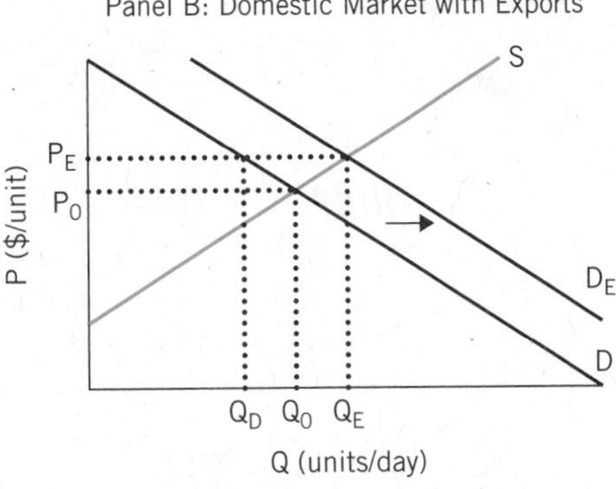

In Panel A, the supplier of the good does not engage in exporting, so the domestic demand for the good (D) is the supplier's only demand. The equilibrium price of the good is P_0 and the equilibrium quantity of the good is Q_0. In Panel B, the demand for the good shifts from D to D_E as the seller exports some of its product. The higher demand generates an increase in the price of the good to P_E and an increase in the quantity of the good sold to Q_E. Q_D of the good is sold domestically and $Q_E - Q_D$ of the good is sold as exports.

market, he faces not only the domestic demand (D) but also international demand for the good or service, shown by the increase in demand from D to D_E. As a result of this increase in demand, the price of the good rises domestically, from P_0 to P_E. The quantity traded domestically falls from Q_0 to Q_D, since Q_D is the quantity demanded at price P_E on the domestic demand curve. The quantity supplied rises to Q_E, with the difference between Q_E and Q_D being the amount of exports. Thus, exporting goods and services generates an increase in demand and higher prices for suppliers but at the same time causes a decrease in quantity demanded and higher prices for domestic consumers.

Figure 11.4 illustrates the impact of imports on a domestic market. Panel A illustrates the initial equilibrium in the domestic market. Domestic demand is given by curve D, and domestic supply is shown as curve S. As before, equilibrium price is P_0 and the equilibrium quantity traded is Q_0.

Allowing imported goods into the market generates an increase in the supply of those goods and services, as shown in Panel B. The curve S_I represents the new supply curve, which includes both domestic and imported goods. The increase in supply causes a decrease in the price of the good from P_0 to P_I. As a result of the price change, domestic quantity demanded rises from Q_0 to Q_I. Domestic quantity supplied falls to $Q_{D,}$ which is the quantity corresponding to P_I on the domestic supply curve. The difference between Q_I and Q_D is the quantity of imports. Thus, imports of

Figure 11.4 **Impact of Imports on the Domestic Market**

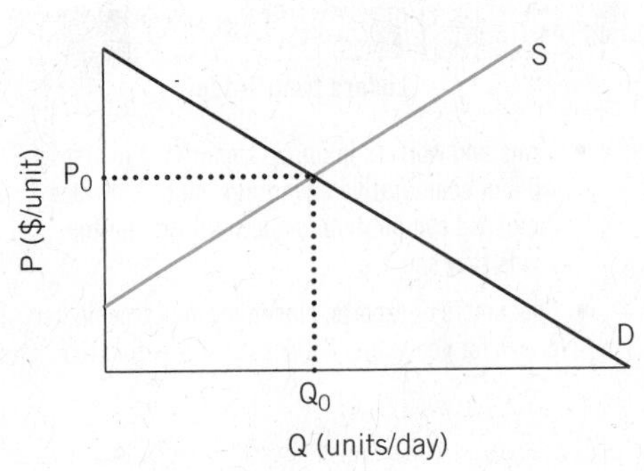

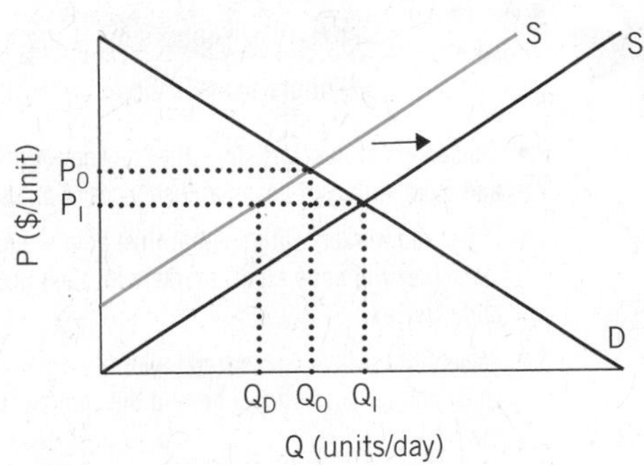

In Panel A, there are no imports, so the domestic supply (S) and domestic demand for the good (D) determine the equilibrium price of the good P_0 and the equilibrium quantity of the good Q_0. In Panel B, the supply of the good shifts from S to S_I as foreign suppliers sell some of their goods in this market. The increase in supply causes a decrease in the price of the good to P_I and an increase in the quantity of the good sold to Q_I. Q_D of the good is produced by domestic suppliers and $Q_I - Q_D$ of the good is sold by foreign suppliers.

goods and services generate an increase in supply and lower prices for consumers but at the same time cause a decrease in quantity supplied and lower prices for domestic producers.

How is the elasticity of demand related to the size of the price change that occurs when an economy allows imports into its markets?

Photo by Yale Joel/Time & Life Pictures/Getty Images, Inc.

Paul Samuelson and International Trade Theory

Paul Samuelson (1915–2009) was a professor of economics at MIT and the first American to win the Nobel Prize in Economics. He wrote a weekly column for *Newsweek* magazine and provided economic policy advice to Presidents Kennedy and Johnson, the U.S. Treasury, and the U.S. Council of Economic Advisors. Samuelson's contributions to economics are far reaching, with important applications to international trade. The Stopler-Samuelson theorem, for example, describes the relationship between the prices of economic inputs (i.e., land, labor, capital) across trading countries. The theorem predicts that when international trade increases, the prices of inputs will tend to equalize across countries.

The examples in Figures 11.3 and 11.4 illustrate that international trade involves costs and benefits and generates winners and losers from the trade. Table 11.3 presents a summary of the "winners" and "losers" from free international trade.

In the case of imports, firms and workers in import-competing industries lose because increased supply and increased competition from imports lower the price that domestic producers are able to receive for their good. On the other hand, domestic consumers of imports are winners from the lower prices and higher variety available when goods are imported.

Table 11.3 Summary of Winners and Losers from Free Trade

Winners from Trade	Losers from Trade
• Consumers of imports, since they face lower prices and more variety of goods and services available • Firms and workers with comparative advantage, since they will have export markets for their goods and services • Society as a whole, since trade allows consumption possibilities beyond the confines of the PPF	• Firms and workers in import-competing industries without comparative advantage, since they face increased competition and lower prices for the goods they sell • Consumers of exports, since they may face higher prices for goods and services that are exported

In the case of exports, firms and workers with comparative advantage in production win because the increased demand from foreign consumers generates increased prices for their products, ceteris paribus. Domestic consumers of exports, on the other hand, are losers because they face higher prices for goods and services than they would have faced otherwise.

Overall, economists conclude that societies as a whole benefit from free trade because trade allows them to reach consumption levels beyond the confines of the PPF. In other words, the overall benefits of free trade exceed the overall costs of free trade. Nonetheless, when countries engage in international trade, firms and workers who produce in import-competing industries face competition from foreign producers. If domestic producers do not have comparative advantage in production, they will lose because they will be unable to compete as effectively in international markets. Domestic producers will also likely struggle in domestic markets as foreign-produced goods and services generate increased domestic competition. Because they stand to lose when faced with international competition, domestic producers often push policymakers to enact limits on international trade. The next sections highlight the arguments for and against limiting trade and present an overview of the methods used to limit trade.

INTERVENING IN INTERNATIONAL TRADE

From a purely efficiency-based perspective, it is difficult to justify intervening in international trade. Countries gain from trade because it allows them to consume at a point outside their PPFs. Most arguments for **protectionism**, which involves placing limits to free trade, are not based on efficiency but rather on other concerns, detailed next.

Protectionism is the limiting of free trade between countries by using tariffs, quotas, or other regulations.

Protecting Jobs

Opponents of free trade sometimes argue that it is important to protect the jobs of workers in industries facing competition from imports. While it is true that restricting the imports of certain goods and services does protect jobs in those areas, this protection comes at a very high cost for a large number of other consumers, households, and businesses in the economy.

Table 11.4 summarizes the costs of protecting jobs in several U.S. industries. Researchers have found that the average cost per job saved from protecting industries from import competition is $231,289 per year. These costs come in the form of higher prices for the protected goods and services themselves and from higher prices for the products that use protected goods as inputs.

Using sugar as one example, because domestic candy makers face higher prices for sugar as a result of protectionist policies, the price of candy rises in the United States. Protections on the sugar industry not only raise prices for consumers but also reduce the quantity of candy demanded, which in turn reduces the quantity of labor that candy makers employ. Higher sugar prices also affect firms and workers that produce soda, cereal, and many other goods that use sugar as inputs.

National Security

Some goods and services are important for national defense. For these goods and services, free international trade could reduce national security. Although it might make economic sense to have the missiles used on U.S. military aircraft produced abroad, for example, it may not be politically prudent.

Table 11.4 Costs of Protectionist Policies in the U.S.

Protected industry	Jobs Saved	Total Cost (in $ millions)	Annual Cost per Job Saved ($)
Benzenoid chemicals	216	297	1,376,435
Luggage	226	290	1,285,078
Softwood lumber	605	632	1,044,271
Sugar	2,261	1,868	826,104
Polyethylene resins	298	242	812,928
Dairy products	2,378	1,630	685,323
Frozen concentrated orange juice	609	387	635,103
Ball bearings	146	88	603,368
Maritime services	4,411	2,522	571,668
Ceramic tiles	347	191	551,367
Machine tools	1,556	746	479,452
Ceramic articles	418	140	335,876
Women's handbags	773	204	263,535
Canned tuna	390	100	257,640
Glassware	1,477	366	247,889
Apparel and textiles	168,786	33,629	199,241
Peanuts	397	74	187,223
Rubber footwear	1,701	286	168,312
Total	191,764	$44,352	
Average (weighted)			$ 231,289

Source: 2002 Annual Report, Federal Reserve Bank of Dallas www.dallasfed.org/fed/annual/2002/ar02f.cfm

Differences in Environmental or Labor Policy

Another argument for limiting free trade stems from the sources of comparative advantage in production by other countries. If, for example, a foreign producer has comparative advantage because it faces much more lax policies regarding pollution, child labor, or worker safety, policymakers often use these factors to justify restricting imports from these producers.

FORMS OF TRADE RESTRICTIONS

Restrictions on international trade generally take the form of tariffs, quotas, and regulatory actions.

Tariff

A tariff is a tax on imported goods or services.

A **tariff** is a tax on imported goods. The U.S. has imposed tariffs on a wide variety of goods and services over time. The Hamilton Tariff Act of 1789, for example, was the second statute ever enacted by the U.S. federal government and imposed tariff rates of between 5 and 10 percent on imported goods. The Smoot-Hawley Tariff Act of 1930

Figure 11.5 **Impact of a Tariff on Steel**

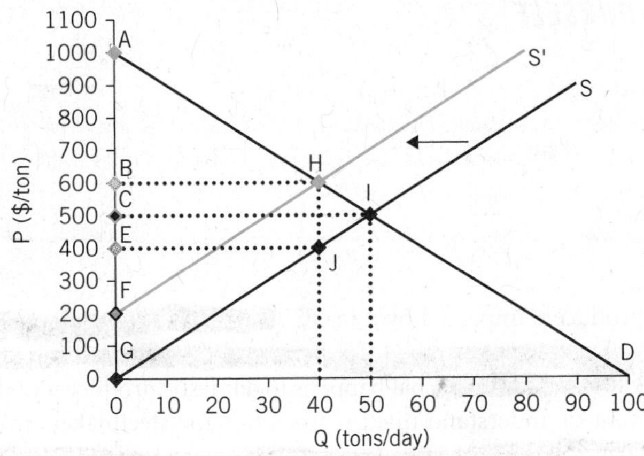

A tariff on foreign steel causes a reduction in the supply of imported steel from S to S'. The price of foreign steel rises from $500/ton to $600/ton and the quantiy of foreign steel sold falls from 50 tons/day to 40 tons/day. Producer surplus falls from area CGI to area EGJ. Consumer surplus falls from ACI to ABH. The tax revenue from the tariff is equal to BEJH. Foreign producers and domestic consumers are worse off because of the tariff.

raised taxes on over 20,000 imported goods and services in the U.S. In response to the Act, many U.S. trading partner countries retaliated with tariffs on U.S. products that substantially reduced exports from the U.S. to other countries.

In 2002, President Bush imposed a tariff of up to 30 percent on imported steel, citing the need protect steel workers and towns from competition from imports. Did this policy make U.S. producers and consumers better off? We can answer this question by examining what happens to consumer and producer surplus when a tariff is imposed on a market.

Figure 11.5 illustrates the impact of a tariff on the domestic market for steel rebar, which are the tube-shaped rods of steel used in many construction projects. Suppose that the initial supply of imported steel rebar is shown by curve S and the domestic demand for imported rebar is shown by curve D. At this level of supply and demand, the price of rebar is $500/ton and the quantity traded is 50 tons per day. At the initial equilibrium, producer surplus is the area of the triangle CGI and consumer surplus is the area of the triangle ACI.

If a tariff of $200/ton, or 40 percent of the original equilibrium price, is imposed on this market, the supply of rebar is effectively reduced from S to S', with the vertical distance between S and S' equal to the size of the tariff. This reduction in supply causes a movement to a new equilibrium price of $600/ton and equilibrium quantity traded of 40 tons per day.

How are consumer surplus and producer surplus affected by this policy? Consumer surplus falls from ACI to ABH. Because consumer surplus is lower after the tariff, consumers are worse off as a result of the policy. With the tariff in place, producer surplus falls from CGI to EGJ, so sellers of imported rebar are also worse off. The rectangle BEJH is the per-day tax revenue paid to the government by foreign suppliers.

Overall, foreign producers and domestic consumers of rebar are worse off as a result of the policy, while the government is better off in the form of increased tax revenues. In addition, the triangle HJI represents a deadweight loss to society resulting from the tariff. Because of pressure from consumer groups, foreign steel producers, and U.S. trading partners, the steel tariff was lifted 21 months later.

THINK FOR YOURSELF

What is the dollar value of consumer and producer surplus in Figure 11.5 before the tariff is enacted? What is the dollar value of consumer and producer surplus after the $200/ton tariff is in place? How much money in tax revenue will be collected from the tariff? What is the dollar value of the deadweight loss that results from the tariff?

How are domestic producers impacted by a tariff? In the short term, domestic producers will be better off as a result of the policy because they will experience an increase in the demand for their product. What happens to domestic producers in the longer term? It is important to understand that by protecting the steelmakers from lower cost imports, the tariff provides incentives against innovation and cost-cutting action on the part of domestic producers. When producers are protected from competition, whether it is domestic or international competition, domestic producers face reduced incentives for producing efficiently. As a result, tariffs and other protectionist policies may actually reduce the competitiveness of domestic producers in the global marketplace in the long term.

Quota

A quota is a restriction on the quantity of imported goods or services in a country.

A **quota** is a restriction on the quantity of a good that can be imported into a country. The United States imposes quotas on a variety of items ranging from dairy products to tobacco to peanut butter to cotton. The U.S. Customs Service and the U.S. Department of Agriculture (for dairy products) are the agencies primarily responsible for administering U.S. import quota laws.

In the early 1980s, imported Japanese cars became increasingly popular, which threatened the profitability of U.S. carmakers. In response to pressure from domestic producers, the U.S. imposed a quota limiting the number of Japanese cars that could be imported to 1.68 million per year.[1]

Figure 11.6 illustrates the impact of a quota in the domestic car market. The initial equilibrium in the market is at P_0 and Q_0. Because the quota sets a limit on the quantity of a good or service that can be supplied by foreign producers, the quota generates a perfectly inelastic supply of the good at the quota level, as shown by S'.

With the quota in place, the price of Japanese cars rises to P_Q and quantity of Japanese cars traded in the U.S. falls to Q_Q. Consumers are made worse off by the quota, and their consumer surplus falls from triangle AP_0G to triangle AP_QE. It is theoretically unclear whether Japanese producers are helped or hurt by the quota because although producers receive a higher price for their cars with the quota in place, they sell fewer cars. In our example, producer surplus changes from triangle P_0CG to the area P_QCFE in Figure 11.6.

Economists who examined the impact of the quota found that the quota raised the prices of Japanese cars sold in the U.S. by about 14 percent. The reduced sales and higher prices just offset one another for Japanese car makers, leaving their profits largely unchanged. American automakers, however, saw higher demand and higher

1 The policy was technically called a "voluntary export restraint," but it operated as an import quota.

Figure 11.6 **Impact of a Quota on Japanese Cars**

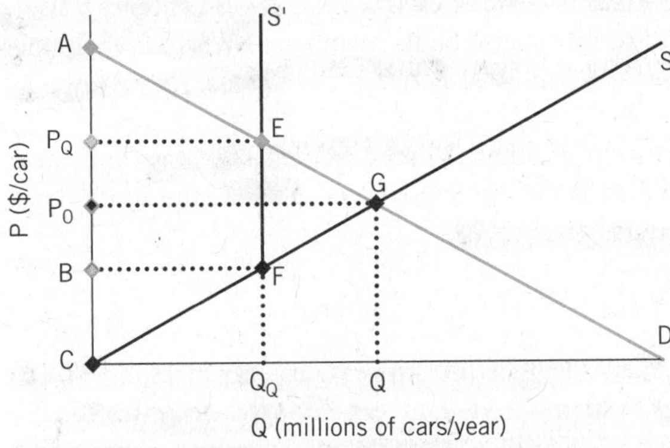

A quota causes the supply of Japanese cars to change from S to S' since only Q_Q cars can be imported per year. Producer surplus changes from P_0CG to P_QCFE when the quota is imposed. Consumer surplus falls from AP_0G to AP_QE, and there is a deadweight loss to the economy of EFG. Economists estimated that the dollar value of the deadweight loss to the U.S. economy from the quota was $3 billion.

prices for their cars when the quota was in place, and the profits of U.S. carmakers rose by about $2 billion per year because of the quota. Economists estimate that American car buyers lost about $13 billion from the quota because of the higher car prices. Finally, the deadweight loss from the quota, which is equal to area EFG in Figure 11.6, was estimated at $3 billion. The quota was ended in 1994.

Regulations

Regulations that either directly or indirectly restrict trade can take many forms, including technical or content requirements placed on imports as well as subsidies for domestically produced goods. In 2003, for example, many countries banned the import of U.S.-produced beef because of fears that U.S. beef inspection processes were inadequate to detect the presence of BSE ("Mad Cow" disease) in cattle. Exports of U.S. beef fell dramatically as a result. Governments can also impose minimum local content restrictions that require a certain amount of the content of the good or service be produced locally. In 2001, the U.S. and several European nations alleged that India had imposed local content restrictions that required Indian car manufacturers to use no more the 50 percent imported content in their passenger cars. The restriction made it harder for countries to export car parts to India.

FORMS OF TRADE LIBERALIZATION

Although countries engage in restricting international trade, they also engage in agreements to reduce trade barriers between one another. Trade liberalization activities take on many forms, primarily including regional trade agreements and participation in the World Trade Organization's international trade agreements.

Regional Trade Agreements

Regional trade agreements are agreements by countries in a region to reduce trade restrictions among themselves.

Regional trade agreements arise when countries in a region join together to reduce trade restrictions among their members. Trade barriers between the members of regional trade agreements are eliminated or greatly reduced. Examples include the European Union (EU) and the North American Free Trade Agreement (NAFTA). The EU is a set of European nations that engage in free trade among the members and collectively negotiate trade agreements with non-EU nations. Most members also utilize a common currency, the Euro. Because there are no significant barriers to trade among the members, the EU is a single economic market with relatively unrestricted movement of goods and services between its members. NAFTA is a regional trade liberalization agreement formed in 1994 between the United States, Canada, and Mexico.

There is a virtual alphabet soup of other regional trade agreements, including CAFTA (the Central American Free Trade Agreement) and SAFTA (the South Asian Free Trade Agreement), both similar to NAFTA.

World Trade Organization

The World Trade Organization is an international organization with the goal of reducing trade barriers throughout the world.

The **World Trade Organization** (WTO) is an international organization of 153 member states with the goal of reducing trade barriers throughout the world. The WTO acts as the official arbiter of trade disputes between countries and is the negotiator and administrator of WTO trade agreements ratified by its members. In addition to these primary activities, the WTO engages in research on the extent and impacts of trade on various outcomes.

So what are the impacts of trade liberalization? Like any economic choice, reducing trade barriers involves costs and benefits. Moving toward a system of freer international trade means moving toward a trading system where comparative advantage plays an increasingly important role. Not surprisingly, firms and workers in protected industries are likely to incur costs when protectionist trade policies are lifted. On the other hand, firms and workers that had faced barriers to their exports under protectionist policies will benefit from trade liberalization.

Research on the impacts of free trade agreements tends to focus on specific industries or sectors of the economy. For example, the U.S. Department of Agriculture Economic Research Service (USDA ERS) has conducted extensive analysis on the impacts of NAFTA on international trade in agricultural products. Researchers at the USDA ERS conclude that U.S. exports of beef, rice, dairy products, potatoes, apples, pears, and corn increased markedly as a result of NAFTA. NAFTA also generated increased U.S. imports of peanuts, wheat, and calves. Research that looks more broadly finds that NAFTA has had a small, positive overall impact on the U.S. economy, and large, positive impacts on the Mexican economy.

SUMMARY

International trade is an important part of most economies in the world. Although all countries participate to some extent in international markets, the largest 10 economies generate more than half of all international exports and imports. Like individual consumers and producers within those economies, countries engage in international trade because trading according to comparative advantage generates benefits for both buyers and sellers in international markets. Nonetheless, international trade can generate costs for workers and firms who do not have comparative advantage in production. Businesses who face losses from international trade are often strong supporters of trade restrictions or protectionist policies, which can include tariffs, quotas, and other regulations.

KEY CONCEPTS

- Exports
- Imports
- Trade surplus
- Trade deficit
- Terms of trade
- Protectionism
- Tariff
- Quota
- Regional trade agreements
- World Trade Organization

DISCUSSION QUESTIONS AND PROBLEMS

Person	Production Per Day
Tommy Trout	10 lb trout or 2 lb coffee
Coleen Coffee	2 lb trout or 5 lb coffee

1. The accompanying table shows the daily production possibilities for two individuals, Tommy Trout from Alaska and Coleen Coffee from Columbia. Use the table to answer the following questions.
   a. What is the opportunity cost of producing 1 lb of trout for Tommy Trout? What is his opportunity cost of producing 1 lb of coffee?
   b. What is the opportunity cost of producing 1 lb of trout for Coleen Coffee? What is her opportunity cost of producing 1 lb of coffee?
   c. Who has comparative advantage in producing trout? Who has comparative advantage in producing coffee?
   d. Will both producers be better off if they specialize and trade according to the terms of trade: 1 trout = 1 lb coffee? Graph each producer's PPF and CPF to illustrate your answer.
2. It takes country A 2 units of labor to produce 1 computer and 2 units of labor to produce 1 TV. It takes country B 3 units of labor to produce 1 computer and 4 units of labor to produce 1 TV.
   a. Which country has absolute advantage in producing TVs?
   b. Which country has absolute advantage in producing computers?
   c. Which country has comparative advantage in producing TVs?
   d. Which country has comparative advantage in producing computers?
3. What are some of the costs of protectionism? In your opinion, is it worth it to restrict trade to protect jobs?

MULTIPLE CHOICE QUESTIONS

1. Determining the comparative advantage of a country requires that you look at the economic notion of
   a. opportunity cost.
   b. ceteris paribus.
   c. accounting and economic profit.
   d. external costs.
2. It takes country X 1 unit of labor to produce either a computer or a TV and it takes country Y 2 units of labor to produce a computer and 1 unit of labor to produce a TV. Based on this information, country X has
   a. a comparative advantage in producing both goods.
   b. an absolute advantage in producing both goods.
   c. a comparative and absolute advantage in producing both goods.
   d. an absolute and comparative advantage in producing computers.
   e. a comparative and absolute advantage in producing TVs.
3. In 1 year, the U.S. can produce 10 units of computer software or 5 units of computer hardware. In 1 year, China can produce 3 units of software and 3 units of hardware. Based on this information,
   a. the U.S. has comparative and absolute advantage in producing both goods.
   b. China has comparative and absolute advantage in producing both goods.
   c. China has comparative advantage in producing hardware and the U.S. has comparative advantage in producing software.

d. the U.S. has comparative advantage in producing both goods.
e. the U.S. has comparative advantage in producing hardware and China has comparative advantage in producing software.

4. If new international trade markets for tractors are opened up and U.S. workers have comparative advantage in producing tractors, U.S. workers are likely to be
   a. worse off because demand for tractors will fall.
   b. worse off because their wages may fall.
   c. better off because demand for tractors will rise.
   d. better off because demand for tractors will fall.

5. U.S. and Indian workers are substitutes. What effect would an increase in the wages of Indian workers have on the demand for U.S. workers, ceteris paribus?
   a. No effect on demand, because price changes affect quantity demanded, which would fall.
   b. The demand would decrease.
   c. The demand would increase.
   d. No effect on demand, because price changes affect quantity demanded, which would rise.
   e. We cannot tell unless we know what happened to the price of U.S. workers.

6. Those that "lose" from international trade include
   a. all workers.
   b. workers who have comparative advantage in production.
   c. exporting firms.
   d. import-competing firms.

7. A tariff implemented to reduce international imports to the U.S. will typically
   a. raise the price received by U.S. sellers.
   b. raise the price paid by U.S. consumers.
   c. lower the price received by U.S. sellers.
   d. increase consumer and producer surplus.
   e. both a and b are correct.

8. A reasonable argument *against* increased international trade is that
   a. international trade hurts U.S. consumers.
   b. international trade hurts U.S. producers.
   c. some goods are important for national security and are better produced domestically.
   d. international trade reduces U.S. employment.

9. Those that "win" from international trade include
   a. all workers.
   b. workers who have comparative advantage in production.
   c. employers in import-competing industries.
   d. consumers of domestically produced exported goods.

10. Suppose that the United States Organization of Movie Actors successfully negotiates for tariffs on movies imported to the U.S. As a result, we would expect to see
   a. a decrease in the equilibrium price and an increase in the equilibrium quantity of movies in the U.S.
   b. an increase in the equilibrium price and a decrease in the equilibrium quantity of movies in the U.S.
   c. a decrease in the equilibrium price and quantity of movies in the U.S.
   d. an increase in the equilibrium price and quantity of movies in the U.S.
   e. none of the above

ADDITIONAL READINGS AND WEB RESOURCES

Benjamin, Daniel K. (1999) "Voluntary Export Restraints on Automobiles," PERC Reports 17(3). Summarizes the research on the impact the quota on Japanese car imports had on U.S. producers and consumers and on Japanese automakers. Available at: http://www.perc.org/articles/article416.php

Burfisher, Mary E., Robinson, Sherman, and Thierfelder, Karen (2001) "The Impact of NAFTA on the United States," *The Journal of Economic Perspectives*, 15(1): 125–144. Presents research on the impact of NAFTA on the U.S. and Mexican economies.

Davis, Lance, and Engerman, Stanley. (2003) "History Lessons: Sanctions—Neither War nor Peace," *Journal of Economic Perspectives*, 17(2):187–197. Discusses the use and impact of trade sanctions over the past century.

Roberts, Russell (2007) *The Choice: A Fable of Free Trade and Protectionism*. Upper Saddle River, New Jersey: Prentice Hall. A "whimsical" novel that looks at global economic issues without excessive economic jargon.

Tokarick, Stephen (2008) "Dispelling Some Misconceptions about Agricultural Trade Liberalization," *Journal of Economic Perspectives*, 22(1):199–216. Discusses the impacts of trade liberalization in agriculture, particularly on low-income countries.

Zahniser, Steven (2002) "NAFTA's Impacts on US Agriculture: Trade & Beyond," USDA ERS Agricultural Outlook. Available at http://www.ers.usda.gov/publications/agoutlook/oct2002/ao295i.pdf Presents research on the impact of NAFTA for the U.S. agriculture industry.

The Organisation for Economic Co-operation and Development. The OECD "brings together the governments of countries committed to democracy and the market economy from around the world." www.oecd.org

The CIA World Factbook. Includes information on economic conditions and many other characteristics of countries throughout the world. https://www.cia.gov/library/publications/the-world-factbook/

The USDA Economic Research Service. Provides economic information and research on U.S. agriculture, including export and import information. www.ers.usda.gov

The World Trade Organization. A global international organization dealing with the rules of trade between nations. www.wto.org

The U.S. House of Representatives Committee on Foreign Affairs often has hearings related to international trade, where competing views on international trade are presented. The transcript of one such hearing presents competing views from Lou Dobbs, a conservative reporter for CNN, and Carla Hills, a former U.S. Trade Representative under President G.W. Bush. Available at http://foreignaffairs.house.gov/110/34484.pdf

Mills, Richard (2001) "US Wins WTO Case on Indian Auto Restrictions," available at http://www.ustraderep.gov/Document_Library/Press_Releases/2001/December/US_Wins_WTO_Case_on_Indian_Auto_Restrictions.html. Highlights the minimum local content case that the U.S. and other nations brought against India at the World Trade Organization.

OMAR TORRES/AFP/GettyImages, Inc.

Immigration and the International Trade of Labor

After studying this chapter, you should be able to:

- Describe the extent of international migration
- Assess the costs and benefits of migration for migrants
- Assess the costs and benefits of migration for host and home countries
- Define and describe the extent of outsourcing and offshoring

In 2010, the state of Arizona passed SB 1070, the toughest anti-illegal immigration law in the United States at that time. The law requires police to ask about the immigration status of anyone they encounter if there is any suspicion that the person is unlawfully in this country. The law makes it a crime to be unable to prove lawful U.S. residence; failure to present proof means being subject to arrest without warrant, so people need to carry immigration documents at all times. In most other states at that time, laws did not make it mandatory for police to inquire about immigration status, in part because of worry that such a law would make legal and illegal immigrants hesitate to report crimes or otherwise interact with law enforcement. Proponents of the law argue that Arizona has a very fast-growing illegal immigrant population, which puts increasing pressure on governmental resources devoted to law enforcement and public programs. Opponents of the law worry that it will result in civil rights violations, including harassment and racial and ethnic profiling of Hispanics. Volatile political debates tend to focus on illegal immigration, but the political, social, and economic issues surrounding legal immigration are also controversial.

This chapter focuses on the economics of immigration without making a distinction between legal and illegal immigration.

THE EXTENT OF U.S. AND INTERNATIONAL IMMIGRATION

An **immigrant** is someone who migrates to live in a **host country**. An **emigrant** is someone who has left his or her **home country** to live in a host country. Someone who was born and grew up in Australia but now lives in the United States is an immigrant to the U.S. and an emigrant from Australia.

An immigrant is someone who migrates into a host country.

An emigrant is someone who migrates out of their home country.

Figure 12.1 shows the trends in international migration for different regions of the world. In 2010, about 3 percent of the world's population were immigrants, a level that has remained steady since 1990. The percent of populations who are immigrants in the more developed regions of Europe, North America, Australia, New Zealand, and Japan rose from 7 to 10 percent between 1990 and 2010. The percent of the population in North America who are immigrants rose from 10 to 14 percent between 1990 and 2010. In the less developed regions of the world, only 2 percent of the population were immigrants in 2010, a figure that was unchanged since 1990.

Figure 12.1 **International Migrants as a Percentage of the Population**

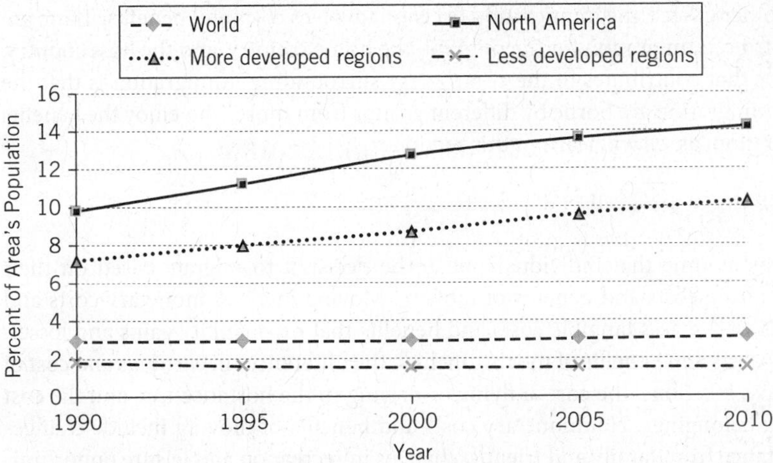

The percent of the world's population who are migrants has remained steady at 3 percent since the 1990s, but the percent of populations who are immigrants has grown in more developed regions of the world. *Source:* United Nations, Department of Economic and Social Affairs, Population Division (2009). "Trends in International Migrant Stock: The 2008 Revision."

Within the United States, the percent of the population who are immigrants varies widely across states and regions. Figure 12.2 illustrates the immigrant population among the states in 2010. The coastal states of California, New York, Texas, Arizona, and Florida have large immigrant populations. More rural states like West Virginia, Mississippi, the Dakotas, and Montana have fewer than 2 percent immigrant populations. Many of the patterns of international immigration and immigration within the U.S. can be explained by assessing the costs and benefits of immigration.

Figure 12.2 **Immigrant Population by State, 2010**

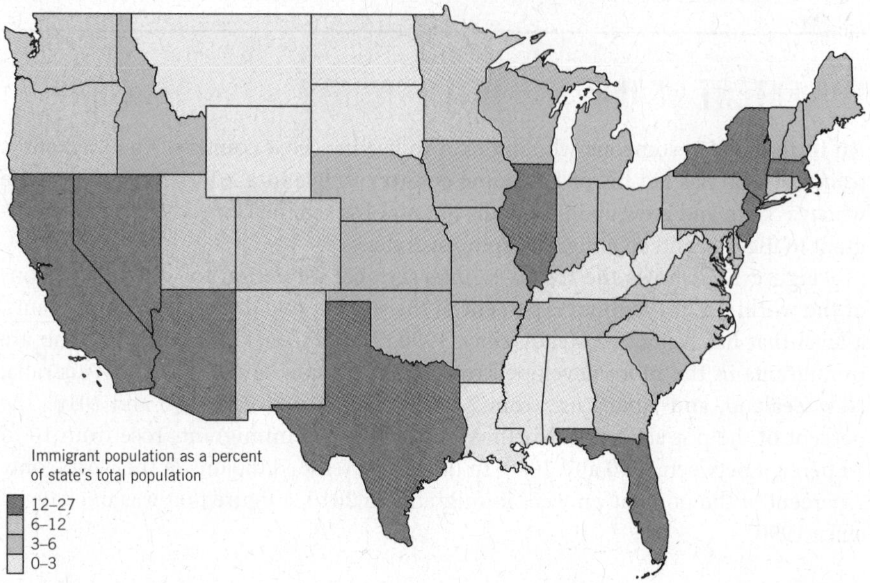

Immigrant population as a percent of state's total population

- 12–27
- 6–12
- 3–6
- 0–3

THE COSTS AND BENEFITS OF IMMIGRATION

Like any other choice, the immigration decision involves costs and benefits. There are tradeoffs from immigration for the migrant, the home country, and the host country. One factor that contributes to the controversy surrounding immigration is that the costs of immigration are borne by different groups from those who enjoy the benefits of immigration, as we will learn in this section.

Costs and Benefits for Immigrants

Economists assume that individuals make the decision to migrate based on their weighing of the costs and benefits of moving. Moving involves monetary costs and benefits as well as less tangible costs and benefits that cause utility gains and losses. Monetary costs and benefits of moving include the differences in earnings and cost of living across locations, the cost of flying or driving to the host location, and the cost of moving belongings. Nonmonetary costs and benefits of moving include changes in the distance from family and friends, changes in recreation and leisure opportunities, as well as language, cultural, and governmental differences in the two locations. If someone decides to migrate, he must expect that his utility will be higher in the host country than in his home country. If someone decides not to migrate, she must expect that her utility will be higher in her home country than in the host country.

Viewing the immigration decision using a simple cost verses benefit framework leads to several predictions about immigration. First, an improvement in earnings opportunities in the host country increases the benefits to migration and raises the likelihood that someone immigrates. Periods of economic expansion in a host country are associated with increased immigration because earnings opportunities improve. Alternatively, when a home country has an expansion of jobs and other opportunities, the opportunity cost of migrating increases and fewer people emigrate. As an example, the United States experienced lower rates of immigration during the post-WWII versus pre-WWII era in part because of improving economic and social conditions in Europe after the war. Today, roughly 60 percent of the world's migrants reside in the more developed regions of the world, and the U.S. is home to roughly 20 percent of the world's migrants. The relatively better earnings opportunities in the more developed regions of the world provide an incentive for immigrants to move there.

Second, an increase in the monetary or other costs of moving reduces the likelihood of immigration. All else being equal, a host country's immigrants are more likely to come from nearby countries because of the smaller costs of moving shorter distances. Table 12.1 shows the most common home regions of immigrants to the U.S. The largest proportion of migrants to the U.S. comes from Mexico. The Caribbean, Central America, and South America are also home regions for many U.S. immigrants, reflecting the relatively lower costs of migrating from nearby countries.

Table 12.1 Region of Birth of U.S. Foreign Born Population

Country	Percent of U.S. Foreign Born Population, 2009
Mexico	30
South and East Asia	24
Caribbean	9
Central America	8
South America	7
Middle East	4
All other	18

Source: Pew Hispanic Center tabulations of 2009 American Community Survey

Third, ceteris paribus, individuals who are more financially secure and have more labor market skills are more likely to migrate than others, since having more wealth or access to money makes it easier to cover the costs of moving. This does not mean that host countries do not attract relatively poor or low-skilled immigrants. Rather, those who immigrate are likely to have more access to wealth and resources than their nonimmigrant counterparts, ceteris paribus.

Finally, younger individuals are more likely to migrate than older individuals, as younger individuals will have more time to reap the benefits of immigration and recover the up-front costs of migrating. Indeed, the majority of immigrants in the world are under 35 years old.

Why are younger individuals more likely to migrate than older individuals? Other things equal, why would those who choose to immigrate be more financially secure than their non-migrating counterparts? How would a decrease in transportation costs impact a person's decision to immigrate? How would a decline in potential earnings in the host country impact a person's decision to immigrate?

Costs and Benefits of Immigration for Host Countries

Immigration impacts the host countries in many ways. Immigrants produce benefits for host countries in the form of increased output, tax revenues, and participation in the political process. Host countries also benefit from immigrant expertise and entrepreneurship. Immigrants are more likely to be business owners than natives with similar characteristics, and 40 percent of Ph.D. scientists working in the U.S. are immigrants. At the same time, immigration imposes costs on some native workers and increases the demand for resources, public programs, and other goods and services in host countries.

Impacts of Immigration on Host Country Labor Markets

Immigration causes an increase in the supply of labor in the host country. Whether native workers are better off or worse off from immigration depends on whether native workers are substitutes or complements to immigrant labor. We can use measures of consumer and producer surplus to measure the impacts of immigration on native workers and employers. We learned in Chapter 4 that consumer surplus is the net benefit that buyers get from buying a good or service. Since employers are the buyers in the labor market, consumer surplus measures the net benefit that firms earn from hiring labor. Producer surplus is the net benefit that sellers earn from selling a good or service. As workers are the suppliers in the labor market, producer surplus measures the net benefit that workers gain from working.

Impact on Substitutes Substitutes are things that can be used in place of one another, like Coke and Pepsi or butter and margarine. If immigrants are relatively low skilled, they are substitutes for other low-skilled native workers. If immigrants have high skill levels, they are substitutes for highly-skilled native workers.

Figure 12.3 illustrates the impact of immigration in the market when native workers are substitutes for immigrant labor. The native labor supply is illustrated

Figure 12.3 **The Impact of Immigration on Substitute Labor**

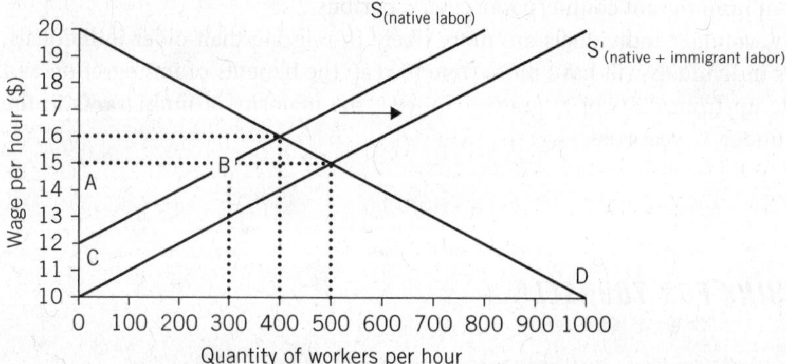

Immigration causes an increase in the supply of labor in markets where immigrants and native workers are substitutes. Before immigration, the supply of labor is shown by curve S. The equilibrium wage is \$16 per hour and the equilibrium employment level is 400 workers per hour. Producer and consumer surplus are both \$800 per hour before immigration. After immigration, the supply of labor increases to S'. The increase in supply causes wages to fall to \$15 per hour, employment to rise to 500 workers per hour, and consumer and producer surplus to each rise to \$1250 per hour. Native workers' producer surplus at the new equilibrium is area ABC, which is \$450 per hour. Because their producer surplus falls after immigration, native workers who are substitutes for immigrant labor are worse off after immigration.

by the supply curve $S_{(\text{native labor})}$, and curve D represents the demand for labor. Before immigration, the equilibrium wage is $16 per hour, and the equilibrium quantity of labor hired is 400 workers per hour. At this equilibrium, consumer surplus is

$$CS = .5 * 400 * \$(20-16) = \$800 \text{ per hour}$$

and producer surplus is

$$PS = .5 * 400 * \$(16-12) = \$800 \text{ per hour}$$

Now suppose that 200 immigrants move into this labor market. The immigration shifts the labor supply curve rightward by 200 workers at each wage, to $S'_{(\text{native + immigrant labor})}$. The market will adjust to a new equilibrium wage of $15 per hour and a new equilibrium quantity of labor hired of 500 workers per hour. Producer surplus at the new equilibrium rises to

$$PS = .5 * \$5 * 500 = \$1250 \text{ per hour}$$

The rise in producer surplus implies that workers are made better off as a result of immigration. Although this is true for workers as a whole, it is not necessarily true for native workers. To assess the impact of immigration on native workers, we can compare the producer surplus earned by native workers before and after immigration. At the $15 per hour wage, the quantity of labor supplied by native workers is 300 per hour, shown as point B in Figure 12.3. At the new equilibrium, producer surplus for native workers can be measured as the area of triangle ABC, which lies above the native labor supply curve $S_{(\text{native labor})}$ and below the new equilibrium wage:

$$PS_{(\text{native labor})} = .5 * \$(15-12) * 300 = \$450 \text{ per hour}$$

which is lower than the producer surplus that native workers earned before immigration. Thus, immigration generates a lower wage, reduced employment, and a reduction in producer surplus for substitute native workers in the labor market. At the same time, however, immigration generates benefits for employers, since they can now hire more workers and at lower wages than before. If the labor cost savings are passed on from businesses to customers, consumers will also see benefits in the form of lower prices for the goods or services they buy.

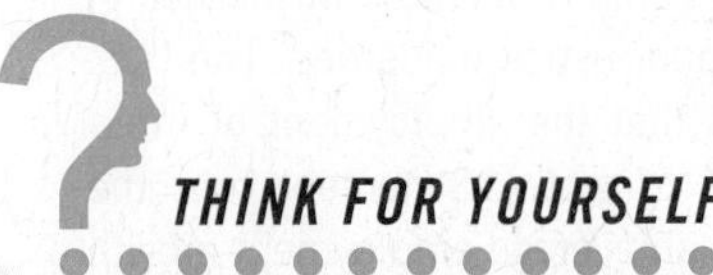

THINK FOR YOURSELF

Who are the winners and losers from immigration when immigrants are substitutes for native workers in the labor market?

Impact on Complements The impacts of immigration on the labor market are different when immigrants and native workers are complements. Recall that complements are things that go together, like peanut butter and jelly or iPods and iTunes downloads. In labor markets, native workers who are complements to immigrant workers have productivity and income gains from immigration. Complements to lower-skilled or non-English-speaking immigrants include skilled craftsmen, supervisors, and managers, as well as interpreters and employee trainers. Complements to highly skilled immigrants include lower-skilled native workers.

Figure 12.4 illustrates the impact of immigration in the labor market for workers who are complements to immigrant labor. Suppose that before immigration, the supply of labor is S and the demand for labor is D. The equilibrium wage is $14 per hour, and 200 workers are hired per hour. Immigration will cause an increase in the demand for complement workers from D to D'. As a result, the wage for complement workers rises to $16 per hour, and employment rises to 400 workers per hour. Workers who are complements to immigrants gain from immigration because their wages and employment levels rise.

Immigration generates both winners and losers in the labor market in the host country. Winners include the immigrants themselves, firm owners who employ immigrants, consumers that pay lower prices for goods and services, and native workers who are complements to immigrant workers. Native workers who are substitutes for immigrant workers tend to lose from immigration since their wages fall.

Figure 12.4 The Impact of Immigration on Complement Labor

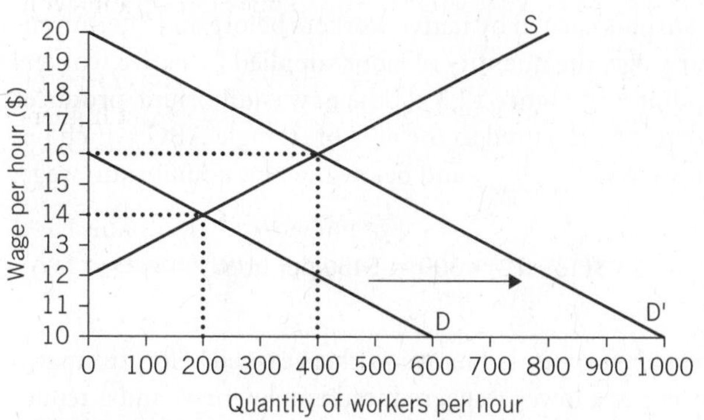

Immigration generates an increase in the demand for native labor in markets where immigrants and native workers are complements. The increase in demand causes a rise in the wages and employment of native workers who are complements to immigrant labor.

The Charlotte Observer,Diedra Laird/©AP/WideWorld Photos

Interpreter Services and the Immigrant Population

In the United States, individuals who work as language interpreters are complements to immigrants who speak a language other than English. Interpreter services are particularly valuable in the health care, conference services, and law and justice industries. The U.S. Bureau of Labor Statistics predicts that the employment of interpreters and translators is expected to grow 22 percent over the 2008–2018 decade, much faster than average employment growth in the U.S.

Source: http://www.nycourts.gov/courtinterpreter/pdfs/WR_CISBrochure.pdf

THINK FOR YOURSELF

Who are the winners and losers from immigration when immigrants are complements to native workers in the labor market?

The Importance of Immigrants' Skills The impact of immigrants on local labor markets depends on whether immigrants are complements or substitutes for native workers, which in turn depends on the level of training and skills that immigrants bring to the labor market. Because the skills necessary to perform a job vary across occupations, economists tend to use educational attainment as a rough measure of a worker's skill level. Using this metric, low-skill workers are those without a high school diploma, high-skill workers are those with at least a college degree, and mid-skill workers are those with at least a high school diploma but less than a college degree. Low-skill immigrants make up large portions of the construction, grounds keeping, farm worker, and food service industries. High-skill immigrants make up large portions of the information technology, engineering, scientific research, and health care industries.

Figure 12.5 presents trends in the skill level of U.S. immigrants. In 1980, about 40 percent of immigrants had less than a high school diploma, while fewer than 20 percent of immigrants had a college degree. Between 1980 and 2010, the proportion of immigrants with low skill fell to 28 percent while the portion of immigrants with high-skill rose to 30 percent.

The distribution of immigrant skills is not uniform across the U.S. Larger metropolitan areas, including San Francisco and Washington, DC, tend to attract higher-skilled immigrants, while Arizona, California, Texas, and the Great Plains states tend to attract immigrants with lower levels of education. The changing mix of immigrant skill level and the diverse geographic location of immigrants with different skills have led in recent years to a changing mix of native workers who are complements or substitutes for immigrant labor.

Figure 12.5 **Skill levels of Immigrant Population in the U.S.**

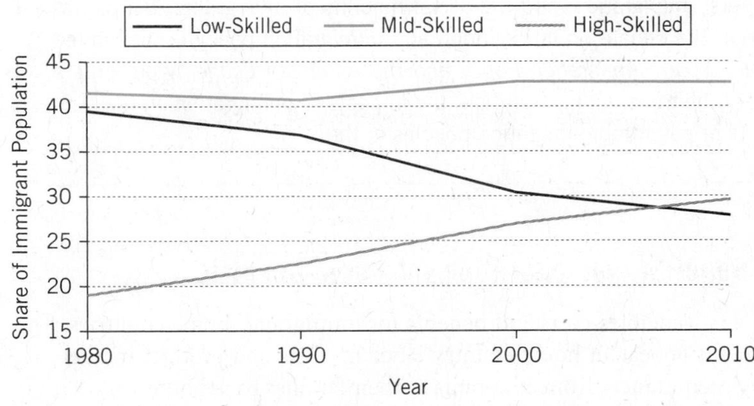

Low-skilled immigrants are those without a high school diploma, high-skilled immigrants are those with at least a college degree. The share of low-skilled immigrants in the U.S. has fallen since 1980 and the share of high-skilled immigrants in the U.S. has risen. *Source:* Hall, et al (2011).

Impacts of Immigration on Product Markets

Immigration has impacts on product markets in both host and home countries because changes in the size of a population generate changes in the demand for goods and services. When immigrant populations increase, demand for the goods and services that immigrants buy increases. As a result, sales of those goods expand and the demand for workers to produce those goods and services rises. For example, the Tortilla Industry Association estimates that U.S. tortilla sales revenue grew from $300 million to over $1.5 billion per year between 1980 and 1990. Although tortillas are traditionally made by hand, many small firms have had to automate to keep up with the growth, thereby expanding their demand for mechanical and technical workers. The increase in tortilla sales has been fueled in part by increased immigration to the U.S. from Mexico and in part by changing U.S. tastes and preferences.

Impacts of Immigration on Host Country Resources

Some of the controversy surrounding immigration involves questions about whether the costs that immigrants impose on host country resources, including public schools, roads, and other government services, are offset by the tax revenues immigrants generate. The impact of immigration on public budgets is complex and plays out over long periods of time. To assess the fiscal impacts of immigration, economists make projections based on the mix of immigrants' skills, employment patterns, childbearing, demographic trends, and expected tax and government spending policies. A comprehensive study by the National Research Council estimated that over the course of a lifetime, the average U.S. immigrant pays about $115,000 more in taxes (in 2011 dollars) than he uses in public resources. Because people with higher incomes tend to use fewer public resources, high-skilled immigrants pay about $285,000 more in taxes than they use in public services. Alternatively, immigrants with less than a high school diploma use an average of $19,000 more in services than they pay in taxes over the course of a lifetime.

George Borjas

George Borjas and the Economics of Immigration

George Borjas, a professor of public policy at Harvard University, has written extensively on the economics of immigration. His research has focused on the degree of substitution between immigrants and natives in the U.S., the impact of immigration on wages, the labor market impact of high-skill workers' immigration, and the social mobility of immigrants. Borjas has played an important role in the debate on immigration and immigration policy in the United States. His book *Heaven's Door: Immigration Policy and the American Economy* presents a comprehensive overview of the trends in immigration, the impacts of immigration on the U.S. economy, and the impacts of potential immigration policies in the U.S.

Costs and Benefits of Immigration for Home Countries

Immigration also generates costs and benefits for immigrants' home countries. The costs and benefits appear in home country labor markets and product markets, as well as through remittances from emigrants to their families back home.

Figure 12.6 **The Impact of Emigration on Home Country Labor Markets**

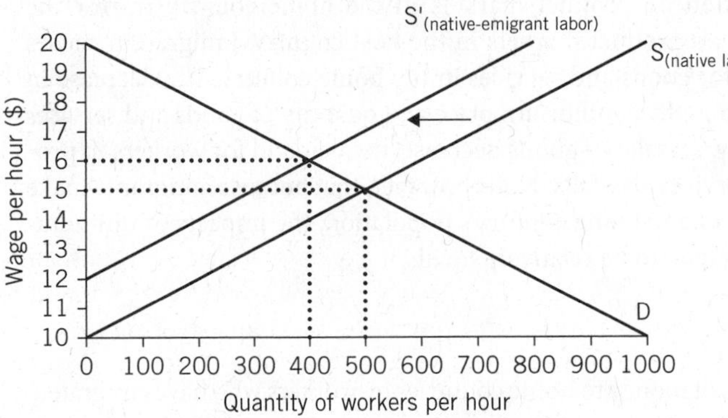

Emigration causes a decrease in the supply of labor in the home country. The decrease in supply causes wages to rise and employment to fall.

Impacts of Emigration on Labor Markets

Figure 12.6 illustrates the impact of emigration on the home country labor market. The supply of labor is originally $S_{(\text{native labor})}$, and reflects the labor supply of native workers in the home country prior to emigration. In the initial equilibrium, the wage is \$15 per hour, and employment is 500 workers per hour. The producer surplus and consumer surplus in the labor market each equal

$$.5 * \$5 * 500 = \$1{,}250 \text{ per hour}$$

If 200 workers in the labor market decide to emigrate to another country, the supply of labor in the home country shifts inward to $S'_{(\text{native − emigrant labor})}$. The new equilibrium wage is \$16 per hour, and the new employment level is 400 workers per hour. The reduction in the supply of labor in the home country generates increases in wages for the workers who remain.

THINK FOR YOURSELF

Using Figure 12.6, compute the producer surplus at the original and post-emigration equilibriums for native workers who do not emigrate. Are the native workers better or worse off after the emigration?

The reduction in the supply of labor affects companies hiring labor because the higher equilibrium wage raises production costs. The firms' consumer surplus after 200 workers emigrate is

$$CS = .5 * \$(20-16) * 400 = \$800 \text{ per hour}$$

Since their consumer surplus is lower after some workers emigrate from the home country, firms in the home country lose when workers emigrate.

Impacts of Emigration on Product Markets

The impacts of emigration on product markets in the home country mirror the impacts of immigration on product markets in the host country. Emigration causes a decrease the demand for goods and services in the home country. The decrease in demand causes a decline in the equilibrium price and quantity of goods and services sold in the home country. As sales of goods decrease, the demand for workers to produce those goods and services also falls. Note, however, that because emigrants make up only a small fraction of any home country's population, the impacts of immigration on product markets tend to be relatively small.

Remittances

Remittances are transfers of money to home countries by workers who have emigrated. In many developing countries, remittances are an important source of income for emigrants' family members who remain in the home country. Because they raise people's incomes, remittances generate increases in the demand for normal goods and services in the home country. The World Bank estimates that remittance flows to developing nations exceed $300 billion annually. In Tajikistan, for example, remittances account for 45 percent of the country's gross domestic product (GDP). Remittances account for 20 percent of Haiti's GDP. Remittances by emigrants from developed countries are much smaller, accounting for less than 1 percent of GDP in the U.S. and the UK.

OUTSOURCING AND OFFSHORING AS INTERNATIONAL TRADE IN LABOR

Outsourcing occurs when someone hires another person or firm to produce a good or service.

Offshoring is the movement of a firm's production from one country to another.

During his 2004 presidential campaign, U.S. Senator John Kerry called firms that outsource their jobs to international markets Benedict Arnold corporations, likening them to the U.S. Revolutionary War general who betrayed his military comrades and defected to the British army. What is outsourcing, and why is it so controversial? **Outsourcing** occurs when someone hires another person or firm to produce a good or service. **Offshoring** refers to the movement of work from within one country to a location outside of that country. Outsourcing and offshoring rose to prominence in the political arena in the United States in the early part of the 2000s as increasing global competition among workers caused some U.S. firms to use international rather than native labor.

In Chapter 2 we learned that when people, firms, and even countries trade according to their comparative advantage, both trading parties can be made better off. Because none of us has comparative advantage in producing everything, we all outsource. You probably don't grow the grain used to make your bread, and you probably don't run a power plant to produce your own electricity. Instead, you outsource these tasks to farmers and power companies that have comparative advantage in producing bread and electricity. When a company outsources labor services, it hires workers outside the company to perform the company's work. For example, some business firms find it more profitable to outsource their tax and payroll work to specialty accounting firms rather than do that work in-house. Many companies use advertising agencies to conduct their marketing for them. When viewed from this perspective, outsourcing is just an example of the law of comparative advantage at work, and most economists agree that outsourcing generates net benefits to the economy.

So why is outsourcing controversial? Part of the controversy surrounding outsourcing arises because the distribution of the costs and benefits of outsourcing are not equally shared. Some people lose and others gain when firms outsource.

Figure 12.7 illustrates the impact of outsourcing on the home country labor market. Before outsourcing occurs, the demand for labor is D and the supply of labor is S. The equilibrium wage is W, and the equilibrium level of employment is Q workers per hour. When jobs that were previously performed by native workers are outsourced or moved overseas, the demand for native workers to do those jobs falls to D'. The decline in demand generates a new equilibrium wage of W' and a new equilibrium employment level of Q' workers per hour. Workers whose jobs are outsourced face lower wages and fewer job opportunities and thus lose from outsourcing or offshoring.

Figure 12.7 **The Impact of Outsourcing on Home Country Labor Markets**

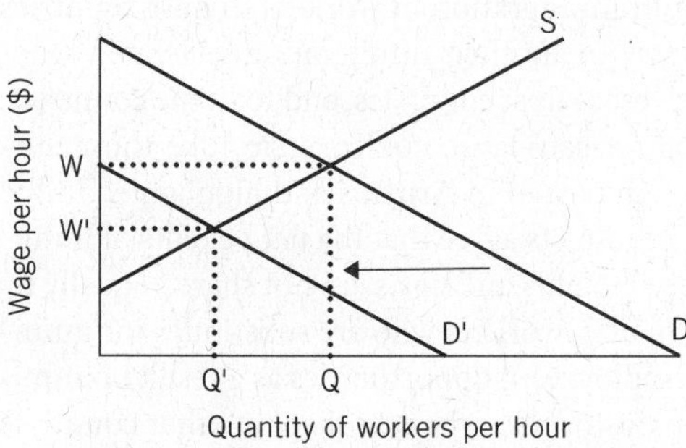

When firms outsource jobs to other locations, the demand for labor in the home country falls from D to D'. The employment of workers in the home country falls from Q to Q' and wages fall from W to W'.

Firms and consumers benefit from outsourcing. Figure 12.8 shows the impact of outsourcing on a typical home country product market. Before work is outsourced, the supply is equal to S, the equilibrium price of the product is P, and Q units of the good are traded per period. Firms that outsource their work do so because other workers are either less expensive or more productive, both which lower firms' costs of production. The lower cost of production causes the supply curve to shift outward to S'. The new equilibrium price of the product is P' and the new equilibrium quantity sold is Q' per period. Firms benefit from outsourcing because it lowers their costs of production, and consumers benefit because outsourcing results in lower prices of goods and services.

Figure 12.8 **The Impact of Outsourcing on Home Country Product Markets**

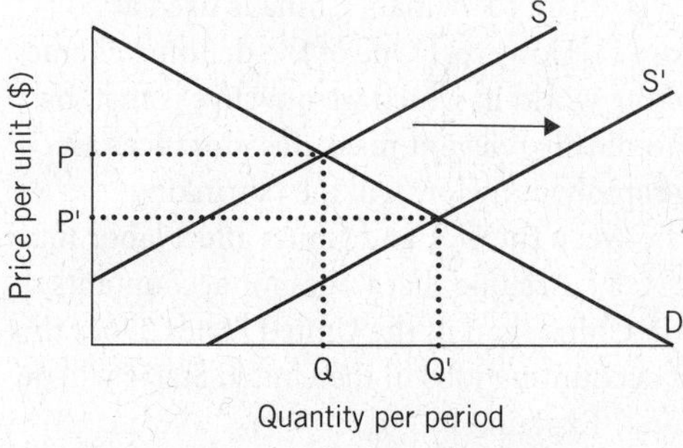

When firms outsource jobs to other locations, their costs of production fall and their supply of products increases from S to S'. The price of their product falls from P to P' and the quantity traded rises from Q to Q' per period. Firms benefit from increased production and sales and consumers benefit from lower prices for goods and services.

Apart from erecting barriers to international trade in labor, how can domestic workers negatively affected by outsourcing or immigration adjust to an increasingly globalized labor market?

SUMMARY

International trade in labor involves both immigration of workers to host countries and outsourcing of jobs from one country to another. Immigration generates benefits and costs to the immigrants themselves, to host countries, and to home countries. The tradeoffs associated with immigration can cause controversies like those surrounding the strict immigration legislation passed in Arizona and highlighted in the chapter introduction. Although most economists agree that the net benefits of immigration exceed the costs it imposes, these benefits and costs are not shared equally by those impacted by immigration. In particular, workers who are substitutes for immigrant labor face reduced earnings and employment opportunities as a result of immigration. Outsourcing and offshoring of jobs occurs when workers in other countries gain comparative advantage over native workers in producing goods and services. The benefits of outsourcing and offshoring come to firms in the form of higher profits and consumers in the form of lower prices. The costs of outsourcing and offshoring tend to be borne by workers who are substitutes for foreign labor.

KEY CONCEPTS

- Immigrant
- Emigrant
- Outsourcing
- Host country
- Home country
- Offshoring

DISCUSSION QUESTIONS AND PROBLEMS

1. What are some of the benefits of immigration? What are some of the costs?
2. Suppose a worker is deciding whether to move from one country to another. Describe three economic factors that are likely to influence his decision.
3. Why do more developed nations have larger immigrant populations than less developed nations?
4. What factors would a firm consider when deciding whether to move production overseas?
5. In a recent speech, a U.S. government official stated, "The physical distance along a great circle from Wausau, Wisconsin to Wuhan, China is fixed at 7,020 miles . . . [However] One of the defining characteristics of the world in which we now live is that, by most economically relevant measures, distances are shrinking rapidly. . . ." How will the "shrinking distance" between the U.S. and China affect labor markets in the U.S.? Assume that wages for accountants are lower in China than in the United States. Does this mean that accounting jobs in the United States will be lost to China? Explain.

MULTIPLE CHOICE QUESTIONS

1. A local labor market for lawn-mowing workers is initially in equilibrium. If there is an influx of low-skill immigrants to the area, which of the following is likely to occur in the market for lawn-mowing workers?
   a. Both labor demand and labor supply will decrease, leading to higher wages
   b. Both labor demand and labor supply will increase, leading to lower wages
   c. Labor demand will decrease, leading to lower wages
   d. Labor supply will increase, leading to lower wages

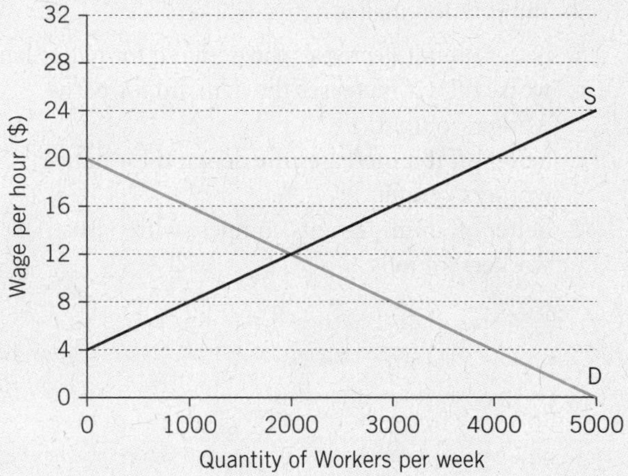

2. The accompanying graph shows the demand and supply for computer support workers in the U.S. At equilibrium, producer surplus is ________ per week.
   a. $12
   b. $2,000
   c. $24,000
   d. $16,000
   e. $8,000

3. The accompanying graph shows the demand and supply for computer support workers in the U.S. If there is an influx of 1,000 immigrants with computer support skills to the U.S., the new equilibrium would be
   a. Wage = $14; Q = 1,500 workers per week
   b. Wage = $14; Q = 2,500 workers per week
   c. Wage = $10; Q = 2,500 workers per week
   d. Wage = $10; Q = 1,500 workers per week

4. If a foreign firm outsources its computer support work, and workers in the U.S. have comparative advantage in producing computer support, the U.S. workers in this market are likely to be
   a. worse off because the demand for their output will fall.
   b. worse off because their wages will fall.
   c. better off because the demand for their output will rise.
   d. better off because the demand for their output will fall.

5. What effect would an increase in the wages of Indian workers have on the demand for American workers, ceteris paribus?
   a. No effect on demand, because price changes affect quantity demanded, which would fall
   b. The demand for American workers would decrease
   c. The demand for American workers would increase
   d. No effect on demand, because price changes affect quantity demanded, which would rise

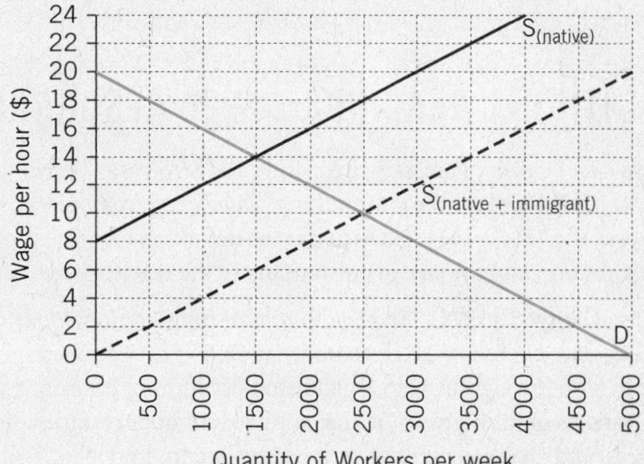

6. The accompanying graph shows the demand and supply of workers in a given market. The curve $S_{(native)}$ represents the supply of native workers in the market and $S_{(native + immigrant)}$ represents the supply of workers in the market after immigration. As a result of immigration, the wages of native workers ________, implying that native and immigrant workers are ________ in this market.
   a. rose; complements
   b. fell; complements
   c. rose; substitutes
   d. fell; substitutes

7. The graph shows the demand and supply of workers in a given market. The curve $S_{(native)}$ represents the supply of native workers in the market and $S_{(native + immigrant)}$ represents the supply of workers in the market after immigration. Before immigration, the producer surplus to native workers is ______ per week.
   a. $4,500
   b. $3,000
   c. $500
   d. $12,500

8. The graph shows the demand and supply of workers in a given market. The curve $S_{(native)}$ represents the supply of native workers in the market and $S_{(native + immigrant)}$ represents the supply of workers in the market after immigration. After immigration, the producer surplus to all workers is ______ per week.
   a. $4,500
   b. $3,000
   c. $500
   d. $12,500

9. The graph shows the demand and supply of workers in a given market. The curve $S_{(native)}$ represents the supply of native workers in the market and $S_{(native + immigrant)}$ represents the supply of workers in the market after immigration. After immigration, the producer surplus to native workers is ______ per week.
   a. $4,500
   b. $3,000
   c. $500
   d. $12,500

10. Which of the following statements is true? An increase in immigration makes native workers
   a. better off if it decreases the demand for native labor.
   b. worse off if it increases the demand for native workers' output.
   c. better off if it increases the demand for native workers' output.
   d. better off if immigrants compete with native workers for jobs.

ADDITIONAL READINGS & WEB RESOURCES

Bhagwati , Jagdish , Panagariya, Arvind , and Srinivasan, T. N. (2004) "Th Muddles over Outsourcing," *Journal of Economic Perspectives,* 18(4): 93–114. Discusses the definition of "outsourcing" and the size of outsourcing in the U.S.

Borjas, George J. (1994) "The Economics of Immigration," *Journal of Economic Literature* 32(December):1667–1717. Describes research on immigrant performance in host country economies, the impacts of immigrants on the employment opportunities of natives, and an assessment of various immigration policies.

Brown, Sharon P., and Siegel, Lewis B. (2005) "Mass Layoff Data Indicate Outsourcing and Offshoring Work," *Monthly Labor Review* 128(8)(August). Presents research and data on the relationship between outsourcing, offshoring, and layoffs in local labor markets. Available at http://www.bls.gov/opub/mlr/2005/08/art1full.pdf

Caratora, Steven A. (1997) "Immigrants in the United States, 2007: A Profile of America's Foreign-born Population" Center for Immigration Studies. Available at http://www.cis.org/articles/2007/back1007.html. Presents an overview of the number of legal and illegal immigrants in the U.S., as well as a detailed description of the socio-economic status of immigrants.

Freeman , Richard, B. (2006) "People Flows in Globalization" *Journal of Economic Perspectives,* 20(2): 145–170. Focuses on international trade in labor, including policy impacts of immigration restrictions

Friedberg, R. and Hunt. J. (1995) "The Impact of Immigrants on Host Country Wages, Employment, and Growth," *Journal of Economic Perspectives* 9(2): 23–44. Presents an overview of the economics research on the impacts of immigration.

Friedman, Thomas L. (2005) The *World Is Flat: A Brief History of the Twenty-First Century*, Farrar, Straus & Giroux. Friedman, the Nobel-prize-winning economist and *New York Times* columnist, presents an overview and history of the globalization of the world economy and describes what it means for societies, governments, and individuals.

Mosisa, Abraham T. (2002) "The Role of Foreign-born Workers in the U.S. Economy," *Monthly Labor Review* (May): 3–14. Reviews the history of immigration to the U.S., compares the demographics of the foreign-born population to the native population, and examines immigrants' contributions to labor force growth from 1996–2000. Available at http://www.bls.gov/opub/mlr/2002/05/art1abs.htm

Smith, J. and Edmonston, B. (eds.) (1997), *The New Americans: Economic, Demographic, and Fiscal Effects of Immigration*, Washington DC: National Research Council, National Academy Press.

Hall, Matthew, Singer, Audrey, De Jong, Gordon F., and Roempke Graefe, Deborah (2011) "The Geography of Immigrant Skills: Educational Profiles of Metropolitan Areas," Brookings Institution Metropolitan Policy Program paper. Presents an overview of the skill and geographic distribution of immigrants in the U.S. http://www.brookings.edu/~/media/Files/rc/papers/2011/06_immigrants_singer/06_immigrants_singer.pdf

The Department of Homeland Security Immigration page has information on immigration statistics in the U.S. (http://www.dhs.gov/files/immigration.shtm)

The U.S. Census Bureau Immigration Page includes information on international migration in the U.S.: http://www.census.gov/population/www/socdemo/immigration.html

The U.S. Citizenship and Immigration Service presents extensive information on immigration policy. http://www.uscis.gov/

The Pew Hispanic Center presents nonpartisan research on Latino issues in the U.S., including extensive information on immigration. http://pewhispanic.org/

The United Nations Department of Economic and Social Affairs, Population Division does extensive research on international migration worldwide. http://www.un.org/esa/population

The World Bank People Move: A Blog about Migration, Remittances, and Development presents data, research, and other information about international immigration. http://blogs.worldbank.org/peoplemove

The U.S. Council of Economic Advisors under President G.W. Bush prepared a review of the research on the economic impact of immigration in 2007. http://georgewbush-whitehouse.archives.gov/cea/cea_immigration_062007.html

© MARIA TOUTOUDAKI/iStockphoto

Foreign Exchange and the International Trade of Money

After studying this chapter, you should be able to:

- Understand how foreign exchange markets operate
- Demonstrate how foreign exchange rates are determined
- Describe how foreign exchange rates influence international trade

Suppose you are headed on a vacation this year. You are going to Europe to visit various sites in France, Italy, and Germany. When you arrive in France, one of the first things you need to do is head to a local bank to exchange your U.S. dollars for Euros, the currency used in France, Italy, Germany, and most other European countries. The teller at the bank informs you that the exchange rate is currently 0.71 Euros (EUR) per U.S. dollar (USD). She also frowns and lets you know that if you had arrived yesterday, you would have benefited from a better exchange rate of 0.75 EUR per USD. What does this mean? Where did this exchange rate come from? Why did it change from one day to the next? In this chapter, we'll learn about the international trade of money.

FOREIGN EXCHANGE MARKETS

To purchase goods and services in France, you need to be able to pay in Euros. Foreign exchange markets facilitate the trade of one currency for another. Even if you use a credit card, your dollars will ultimately need to be converted to Euros in order to pay for your purchases. The rate at which one currency can be exchanged for another is called the **exchange rate**, and it is usually stated in terms of how many units of one currency can be bought with one unit of a different currency.

The exchange rate is the rate at which one currency can be exchanged for another. It is usually stated in terms of how many units of one currency can be bought with one unit of a different currency.

In our example, the exchange rate was 1 USD for 0.71 EUR. This implies that each U.S. dollar can be traded for 0.71 Euros. Alternatively, each Euro can be traded for 1/0.71 U.S. dollars (about $1.40). Suppose you want to buy a bottle of fancy French perfume to take home. If the perfume sells for 100 Euros, it will cost you the equivalent of about $140 if the exchange rate is 1 USD for 0.71 EUR. If you had bought the perfume yesterday, when the exchange rate was 1 USD for 0.75 EUR, the perfume would have been cheaper, since it would have cost you the equivalent of $133. At an exchange rate of 1 USD for 0.75 EUR, each Euro costs 1/0.75 U.S. dollars, or about $1.33.

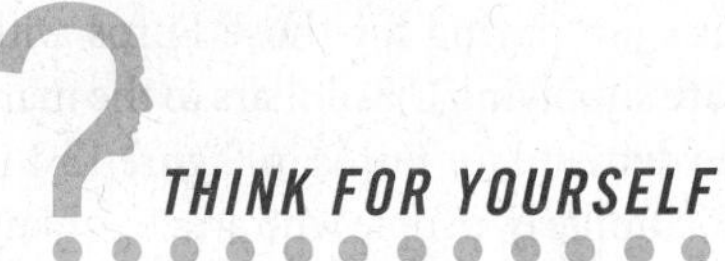

THINK FOR YOURSELF

How much would a bottle of French perfume priced at 100 Euros cost in U.S. dollars if the exchange rate were 1 USD for 2 EUR? What if the exchange rate were 1 USD for 0.5 EUR?

DEMAND AND SUPPLY OF FOREIGN CURRENCIES

Exchange rates are determined in foreign exchange markets through the interaction between the buyers and sellers of different currencies. Figure 13.1 represents the foreign exchange market for U.S. dollars and Euros. The demand for Euros comes from people who need to exchange U.S. dollars for Euros. The demanders of Euros include U.S. importers of French wine or other products, tourists like you, and U.S. investors who want to invest in French companies.

The demand curve for Euros illustrates the quantity of Euros that buyers are willing and able to purchase at different exchange rates. The downward slope of the demand curve shows that as the price per Euro rises, the quantity of Euros demanded falls, ceteris paribus. In other words, when buyers have to pay more U.S. dollars to obtain each Euro, the quantity of Euros demanded falls. When Euros are cheaper, people have to pay fewer U.S. dollars to obtain each Euro, and the quantity of Euros demanded rises.

The supply of Euros in this market comes from people and firms who want to buy U.S. dollars. If French citizens or businesses want to purchase U.S. goods and services or travel to the U.S., they need to exchange their Euros for U.S. dollars.

Figure 13.1 **Market for Euros**

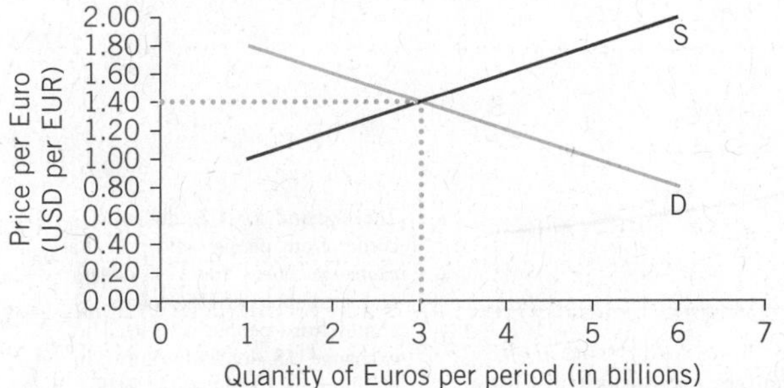

The demand for Euros (D) comes from people who need to exchange U.S. dollars for Euros and the supply of Euros (S) comes from people who need to exchange Euros for U.S. dollars. In equilibrium, 1 EUR = 1.4 USD.

The supply curve in Figure 13.1 illustrates the quantity of Euros that sellers are willing and able to sell at different exchange rates. The supply curve is upward-sloping, so when the price of Euros is low, the quantity of Euros supplied is low. When each Euro trades for fewer U.S. dollars, fewer people want to trade Euros for U.S. dollars. When the price of Euros rises, each Euro is traded for more U.S. dollars and the quantity of Euros supplied rises. In our example in Figure 13.1, the equilibrium price of Euros is 1 EUR = 1. 4 USD. This means that each Euro costs $1.40 At that price, 3 billion Euros are exchanged for U.S. dollars each period.

If we assume that Euros and U.S. dollars are the only currencies trading for one another, the market for Euros and the market for U.S. dollars mirror each other. Figure 13.2 presents the market for U.S. dollars. If Euros and dollars are the only currencies being traded, people demanding Euros are paying for those Euros with U.S. dollars. In other words, demanders of Euros are supplying U.S. dollars to the market in order to exchange them for Euros. Thus, the demand for Euros in Figure 13.1 is reflected as the supply of U.S. dollars in Figure 13.2. Similarly, people who are supplying Euros in exchange for U.S. dollars are demanding U.S. dollars in exchange for Euros, so the supply of Euros in Figure 13.1 is shown as the demand for U.S. dollars in Figure 13.2. In the equilibrium depicted in Figure 13.1, each Euro traded for 1.4 USD. This means that each U.S. dollar trades for 0.71 Euros; if

$$1 \text{ EUR} = 1.4 \text{ USD}$$

then

$$1/1.4 \text{ EUR} = 1 \text{ USD}$$

and

$$1 \text{ USD} = 0.71 \text{ EUR}$$

In addition, in the equilibrium in Figure 13.1, 3 billion Euros are traded. Since each Euro traded for 1.4 USD,

$$3 \text{ billion EUR} * 1.4 \text{ USD}/1 \text{ EUR} = 4.2 \text{ billion USD}$$

are traded in equilibrium, which is the equilibrium quantity of U.S. dollars depicted in Figure 13.2.

Figure 13.2 **Market for U.S. Dollars**

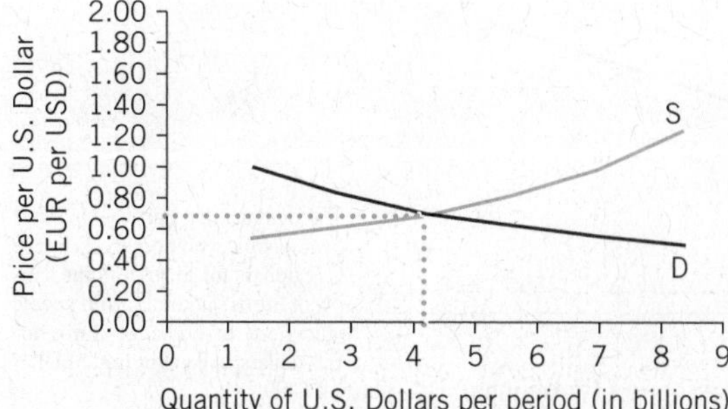

The demand for U.S. dollars (D) comes from people who need to exchange Euros for U.S. dollars and the supply of U.S. dollars (S) comes from people who need to exchange U.S. dollars for Euros. In equilibrium, 1 USD = 0.71 EUR.

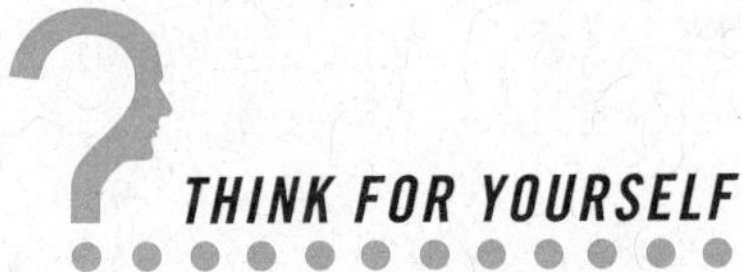

THINK FOR YOURSELF

What would be the equilibrium price of dollars (EUR per USD) if the equilibrium exchange rate were 1 USD for 2 EUR? What if the exchange rate were 1 USD for 0.5 EUR?

Changes in Demand and Supply

Now that we understand how the foreign exchange market functions, we can assess how factors that change the demand and supply of different currencies impact equilibrium exchange rates.

Figure 13.3 illustrates the impact of an increase in the demand for Euros. In our original equilibrium, the price of Euros was 1.4 USD per EUR. At that price, 3 billion Euros were traded per period. If the demand for Euros increases from D to D', the equilibrium price of Euros increases and the equilibrium quantity of Euros traded increases. In Figure 13.3, the equilibrium price of Euros rises to 1.6 USD per EUR, so buyers of Euros have to pay more for each Euro they buy. As the number of dollars paid per Euro rises, sellers of Euros are willing to increase the quantity of Euros supplied, and there is an upward movement along the supply curve for Euros. In the market for U.S. dollars shown in Figure 13.4, the increase in demand for Euros is mirrored by an increase in the supply of U.S. dollars. As the supply of U.S. dollars increases, the price of U.S. dollars falls and the quantity traded increases. At the new equilibrium in Figure 13.3, 4 billion Euros are traded per period at a price of 1.6 USD per Euro. This exchange rate implies that

$$4 \text{ billion EUR} * 1.6 \text{ USD/EUR} = 6.4 \text{ billion USD}$$

are traded, which is the equilibrium quantity shown in Figure 13.4.

When the price of Euros increases, so that it takes more U.S. dollars to obtain each Euro, the Euro has **appreciated** against the dollar. When the price of U.S. dollars falls, so that it takes fewer Euros to buy each U.S. dollar, the U.S. dollar has **depreciated** against the Euro.

When the price of currency A rises relative to currency B, currency A has appreciated.

When the price of currency A falls relative to currency B, currency A has depreciated.

Figure 13.3 **An Increase in the Demand for Euros**

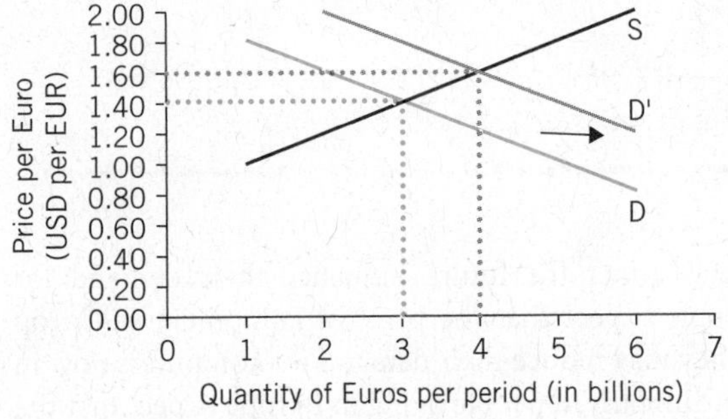

An increase in the demand for Euros from D to D' causes an increase in the price of Euros. In the initial equilibrium, 1 EUR = 1.4 USD. After the increase in demand for Euros, 1 EUR = 1.6 USD.

Figure 13.4 **An Increase in the Supply of U.S. Dollars**

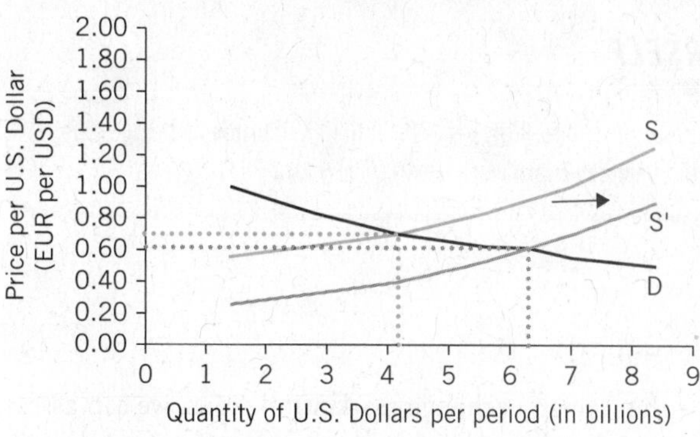

An increase in the supply of U.S. dollars from S to S' causes a decrease in the price of U.S. dollars. In the initial equilibrium, 1 USD = 0.7 EUR. After the increase in the supply of U.S. dollars, 1 USD = 0.6 Euros.

Shifters in the Demand for Euros and the Supply of Dollars

What kinds of factors can cause the shifts illustrated in Figures 13.3 and 13.4? Many of the same factors that shift demand for "regular" goods and services are demand shifters in foreign exchange markets. These include tastes and preferences, income, and expectations. Changes in the relative interest rates, risk, or relative price levels across countries can also cause shifts in the demand for foreign currency.

Tastes and Preferences Changes in tastes and preferences for a certain country's goods and services can change the demand for that country's currency. For example, if Americans develop an increasing preference for French wine, Americans will increase their demand for French wine. As a result, importing companies will need to increase their demand for Euros in order to pay French winemakers for their products. This increase in demand for Euros will result in an appreciation of the Euro relative to the dollar.

Income Assuming that foreign goods and services are normal (rather than inferior) goods, increases in people's incomes in one country can increase their demand for foreign goods and services. The increased demand for foreign goods and services will cause an increase in demand for foreign currency as well. As an example, if the economies of Europe enter into a growth period and European incomes rise, Europeans may increase their demand for American products. This will in turn increase the demand for U.S. dollars. At the new equilibrium, the U.S. dollar will have appreciated against the Euro.

How would a decrease in incomes in the U.S. affect the price of U.S. dollars relative to the Euro? Will the U.S. dollar appreciate or depreciate against the Euro?

Expectations People's expectations about the future influence their demand for goods and services today. If people expect that the price of computers will drop in the near future, for example, they may reduce their demand for computers now in order to wait for the lower prices. Similarly, if people living in Europe expect that the

U.S. dollar will appreciate against the Euro in the future, they may increase their demand for U.S. dollars now in order to obtain U.S. dollars at lower prices.

Interest rates and Risk Business firms and individuals are increasingly able to borrow and lend money across international borders. If the interest rate in Europe is higher than the interest rate in the United States, potential lenders and investors will want to increase the amount of lending and investing they do in Europe relative to the U.S. They may buy European government bonds instead of U.S. government bonds and invest in European companies rather than U.S. companies, for example. This will increase the demand for Euros in the market. The higher interest rate in Europe will also provide an incentive for Europeans to invest more in European companies and less in U.S. companies, which will reduce the supply of Euros in the market.

The risks associated with lending also play a role in foreign exchange. If lending in Europe becomes more risky, perhaps due to a recession or an increase in the rate of bankruptcies in Europe, potential lenders will want to decrease the amount of lending and investing they do there. This will decrease the demand for Euros in the market.

Government Debt and the Eurozone Crisis

Milos Bicanski/Getty Images, Inc.

The recession that began in 2007 had wide-ranging impacts throughout the world. During the recession, unemployment increased and incomes fell. As a result, government revenues from taxes fell and government spending on unemployment and other social programs rose. Many countries, including the United States and its European counterparts, turned to increased governent borrowing to cover the shortfall between government spending and government revenues. In Greece, for example, government borrowing rose to record levels, raising concern that Greece would not be able to make payments coming due on its debt and would instead default on its loans. The increased riskiness of loans to Greece caused investors to charge higher interest rates on loans to Greece and to decrease their lending to Greece. This in turn contributed to a decrease in the demand for Euros. The price of Euros fell by about 15 percent against the U.S. dollar between 2010 and the end of 2011. Other EU countries have stepped in to help Greece with its debt, on the condition that the Greek government drastically cut its spending. Greek citizens have protested these spending cuts, which are called "austerity packages," since they involved cuts to employee salaries and pensions paid to retirees, as well as cuts in government programs. The demonstrations have resulted in widespread social unrest throughout Europe.

FOREIGN CURRENCY VALUATION AND INTERNATIONAL TRADE

The value of a country's currency affects its level of international trade, and vice versa. Goods produced domestically but sold abroad are **exports**, while goods that are produced abroad but purchased domestically are **imports**. When the amount of a country's exports exceeds the amount of its imports, the country has a **trade surplus**. When the amount of a country's imports exceeds the amount of its exports, the country has a **trade deficit**.

Exports: Goods or services produced domestically but sold abroad.

Imports: Goods or services produced abroad but sold domestically.

Trade surplus: When a country's level of exports exceeds its level of imports.

Trade deficit: When a country's level of imports exceeds its level of exports.

When the price of the U.S. dollar appreciates against the Euro, the cost of U.S.-made goods becomes relatively more expensive since it takes more Euros to buy each dollar. When U.S.-made goods become more expensive relative to European-made goods, the demand for U.S.-made goods will fall relative to the demand for European-made goods. In other words, the appreciation of the U.S. dollar relative to the Euro will lead to a reduction in U.S. exports to Europe.

The appreciation of the U.S. dollar against the Euro simultaneously involves a depreciation of the Euro against the U.S. dollar, making Euro-denominated goods relatively cheaper. The depreciation of the Euro will lead to an increase in European exports to the U.S. Ceteris paribus, these changes would cause a decrease in the trade surplus or an increase in the trade deficit between the U.S. and Europe.

Alternatively, when the U.S. dollar depreciates against the Euro, U.S.-made goods become relatively cheaper and the demand for U.S.-made goods rises. A depreciation of the U.S. dollar against the Euro will lead to an increase in U.S. exports to Europe and a decrease in U.S. imports from Europe. Ceteris paribus, a depreciation of the U.S. dollar against the Euro would cause an increase in the trade surplus or decrease in the trade deficit between the U.S. and Europe.

Universal History Archive/ Getty Images, Inc.

David Hume and the Flow of Currency

David Hume (1711–1776), a Scottish philosopher and historian, is considered to be one of the most important figures in Western philosophy. His ideas about experience and observation influenced scientists such as Albert Einstein and Charles Darwin, as well as economists Adam Smith and John Maynard Keynes. Hume's ideas on private property, inflation, and foreign trade are still influential in economics. He was the first to assert that international trade and flows of international currency tend to offset one another by influencing the prices of goods and services in trading countries. When a country has a trade surplus, Hume argued, currency flows into that country in an amount equal to the surplus. The increased supply of currency causes the prices of goods and services rise, making the country's exports more expensive and in turn reducing its trade surplus or increasing its trade deficit.

FIXED AND FLEXIBLE EXCHANGE RATES

Our discussion so far has assumed that exchange rates are able to adjust to changes in the demand and supply of currencies over time. We have assumed that exchange rates are flexible. Under a **flexible or floating exchange rate system**, the interaction of demand and supply determines the exchange rate for a given currency.

*In a **flexible or floating exchange rate system**, exchange rates are determined by demand and supply.*

Some countries do not use a flexible exchange rate system and instead keep the rate of exchange between their currency and the currency of other countries at a fixed rate. This is called a **fixed or pegged exchange rate system**. In a fixed exchange rate system, government agencies or central banks intervene in foreign exchange markets in order to increase or decrease the demand and supply of their currency and keep exchange rates at the fixed level.

*Under a **fixed or pegged exchange rate** system, exchange rates are kept constant through government action in foreign exchange markets.*

Several countries in West Africa have fixed or pegged their currency values relative to the value of the Euro. Mali, for example, uses the West African CFA franc as its currency. The CFA franc has been pegged to the Euro at a rate of just over 650 CFA francs per Euro since 1999. Figure 13.5 illustrates how a fixed exchange rate between CFA francs and the Euro operates.

Suppose the equilibrium exchange rate is 675 CFA francs per Euro. At that equilibrium, the 3 billion Euros would be traded for CFA francs per period, and there would be no pressure on the exchange rate to move from that equilibrium, ceteris paribus. Now suppose the Malian government wants to keep the exchange rate fixed at 650 CFA francs per Euro.

Figure 13.5 A Fixed Exchange Rate System

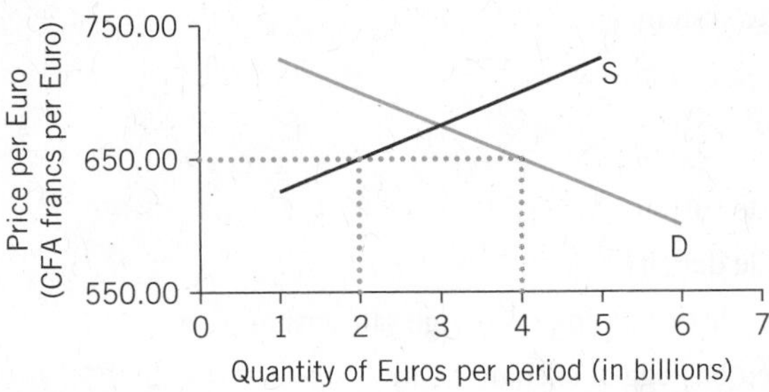

Under the fixed exchange rate system used by Mali, the price of CFA francs is fixed relative to the Euro at a rate of 1 EUR = 650 CFA francs. If the equilibrium price of Euros is above this fixed exchange rate, the Malian government must intervene in the foreign exchange market to decrease the demand for Euros by buying CFA francs or increase the supply of Euros by selling Euros in order to move the exchange rate down to the desired level.

At 650 CFA francs per Euro, the quantity of Euros demanded is 4 billion per period while the quantity supplied is 2 billion per period, so there would be shortage of 2 billion Euros in the market each period. To keep the exchange rate at the target of 650 CFA francs per Euro, the Malian government will need to increase the supply or decrease the demand for Euros by 2 billion each period. The government would likely sell some of its holdings of Euros and also buy CFA francs. The increased supply of Euros and increased demand for CFA francs will keep the Euro from appreciating against the CFA franc.

THINK FOR YOURSELF

Suppose the equilibrium exchange rate is 675 CFA francs per Euro. What action would the Malian government need to take if it wanted the exchange rate fixed at 700 CFA francs per Euro?

Why would a country want to have a fixed exchange rate system? The primary argument for a fixed exchange rate system is that by keeping exchange rates stable, currencies are less susceptible to the risk and uncertainty that arise in markets. By pegging the value of CFA francs to the value of the Euro, trade between Mali and the European Union is more predictable. Note, however, that if the value of the Euro changes, so will the value of the CFA franc, since it is pegged to the Euro. The primary criticism of a fixed exchange rate system is that it requires the use of substantial government resources to maintain. In our example in Figure 13.5, the Malian government needed to hold large reserves of Euros and CFA francs to keep the exchange rate stable. Very few large countries in the world use a fixed exchange rate system.

SUMMARY

The currencies of different countries are traded back and forth in order to facilitate the international trade of goods, services, workers, and investments. The rate at which one country's currency trades for another country's currency is called the exchange rate. Flexible exchange rates are determined in markets through the interaction of supply and demand. All else equal, if the demand for a given currency rises, it becomes more expensive or appreciates against other currencies. If the supply of a given currency rises, that currency becomes less expensive or depreciates against other currencies. In a fixed exchange rate system, central banks or governments intervene in foreign exchange markets in order to keep exchange rates stable. Most countries use a flexible exchange rate system.

KEY CONCEPTS

- Exchange rate
- Appreciated
- Depreciated
- Exports
- Imports
- Trade surplus
- Trade deficit
- Flexible or floating exchange rate system
- Fixed or pegged exchange rate system

DISCUSSION QUESTIONS AND PROBLEMS

1. What are the costs and benefits having a fixed exchange rate system?
2. What are some factors that would cause an increase in the demand for Mexican Pesos relative to U.S. dollars?
3. The accompanying figure shows the foreign exchange market between the South African Rand (ZAL) and the Mexican Peso (MXN).

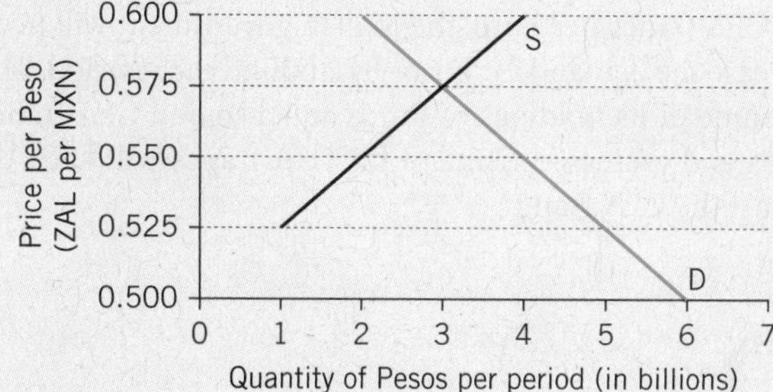

   a. What is the price of each Peso in terms of Rand?
   b. What is the price of each Rand in terms of Pesos?
   c. What quantity of Pesos is traded in the market each period?
   d. What quantity of Rand is traded in the market each period?
   e. Suppose that the demand for Pesos increases. Will the Peso appreciate or depreciate against the Rand? Will the Rand appreciate or depreciate against the Peso?

MULTIPLE CHOICE QUESTIONS

1. If the U.S. dollar appreciates against the Canadian dollar,
   a. it costs more U.S. dollars to obtain each Canadian dollar.
   b. it costs fewer U.S. dollars to obtain each Canadian dollar.
   c. it costs fewer Canadian dollars to obtain each U.S. dollar.
   d. if costs more Canadian dollars to obtain each U.S. dollar.
   e. a and c are correct.
   f. b and d are correct.
2. If the U.S. dollar depreciates against the Canadian dollar,
   a. it costs more U.S. dollars to obtain each Canadian dollar.
   b. it costs fewer U.S. dollars to obtain each Canadian dollar.

c. it costs fewer Canadian dollars to obtain each U.S. dollar.
d. if costs more Canadian dollars to obtain each U.S. dollar.
e. a and c are correct
f. b and d are correct

3. If there is an increase in the demand for Canadian dollars relative to U.S. dollars,
   a. the price and quantity of Canadian dollars traded will fall.
   b. the price and quantity of Canadian dollars will rise.
   c. the Canadian dollar will appreciate against the U.S. dollar.
   d. the Canadian dollar will depreciate against the U.S. dollar.
   e. a and d are correct
   f. b and c are correct

4. If there is a decrease in the demand for Canadian dollars relative to U.S. dollars,
   a. the price and quantity of Canadian dollars traded will fall.
   b. the price and quantity of Canadian dollars will rise.
   c. the Canadian dollar will appreciate against the U.S. dollar.
   d. the Canadian dollar will depreciate against the U.S. dollar.
   e. a and d are correct
   f. b and c are correct

5. Suppose that China maintains a fixed exchange rate for its currency (the Yuan) against the U.S. dollar. If the equilibrium price of Yuan in the foreign exchange market is below the government's target price of Yuan, the Chinese government will need to ________ in the market in order to maintain the target price of Yuan.
   a. buy Yuan
   b. sell Yuan
   c. buy dollars
   d. sell dollars
   e. a and d are correct
   f. b and c are correct

6. Suppose that China maintains a fixed exchange rate for its currency (the Yuan) against the U.S. dollar. If the equilibrium price of Yuan in the foreign exchange market is above the government's target price of Yuan, the Chinese government will need to ________ in the market in order to maintain the target price of Yuan.
   a. buy Yuan
   b. sell Yuan
   c. buy dollars
   d. sell dollars
   e. a and d are correct
   f. b and c are correct

7. Suppose that in equilibrium, the price of U.S. dollars (USD) relative to Canadian dollars (CAD) is 1 USD = 1. 5 CAD. This means that it takes ________ USD to buy 1 CAD.
   a. 1.5
   b. 1
   c. 0.667
   d. 6.67

8. Ceteris paribus, if the USD appreciates against the Euro,
   a. U.S. exports to Europe will increase.
   b. U.S. imports from Europe will increase.
   c. European exports to the U.S. will increase.
   d. European imports from the U.S. will increase.
   e. a and d are correct
   f. b and c are correct

9. Ceteris paribus, if the USD depreciates against the Mexican peso,
   a. U.S. exports to Mexico will increase.
   b. U.S. imports from Mexico will increase.
   c. Mexican exports to the U.S. will increase.
   d. Mexican imports from the U.S. will increase.
   e. a and d are correct
   f. b and c are correct

10. An increase in the demand for Euros relative to Mexican pesos will
   a. increase the price of Euros.
   b. decrease the price of Euros.
   c. increase the price of pesos.
   d. decrease the price of pesos.
   e. a and d are correct
   f. b and c are correct

© AVTG/iStockphoto

Farm Policy

After studying this chapter, you should be able to:

- Describe the history and evolution of government agricultural policy
- Demonstrate how inelastic demand influences agricultural goods' prices
- Describe the main components of U.S. farm policy
- Demonstrate the impacts of price supports in agriculture
- Illustrate the impacts of supply restriction policies
- Illustrate the impacts of demand enhancement policies
- Asses the costs and benefits of recent U.S. farm policy

In 2008, despite a presidential veto and criticism from the United Nations, the World Trade Organization, and several other international and national organizations, a new U.S. farm bill was passed. The bill, formally known as the Food, Conservation, and Energy Act of 2008, is a $288 billion program that finances direct payments, loan and insurance programs, and a wide variety of other supports for agricultural producers. Although it was new legislation, the 2008 farm bill continued a long tradition of government intervention in agricultural markets, dating back to the Agricultural Adjustment Act of 1933. A new farm bill is slated to be sent to the president in 2012.

The arguments for why governments intervene in agricultural markets range from food security, to preserving family farms and rural communities, to ensuring economic competitiveness, and finally to political pressure. In this chapter we use the economics toolkit to understand how U.S. farm programs developed and how they impact the agriculture industry and economy more broadly.

CHARACTERISTICS OF AGRICULTURE

Two characteristics have contributed to government's long-standing involvement in agricultural markets. The first is the long-term decline in agricultural employment; the second is the inelastic nature of the demand for agricultural products.

Declining Employment and Increased Concentration

Farmers have been called, "the founders of human civilization."[1] Although this may be true historically, in most countries economic development is accompanied by a movement of resources out of agricultural production and into other uses. Figure 14.1 illustrates the trends in farm labor and farm numbers in the United States since 1910. In 1910, about 13.5 million people were farm workers, which represented about 15 percent of the 92 million people in the U.S. at that time. By 2000, less than 1 percent of the 281 million U.S. population were farm workers.

Figure 14.1 **U.S. Farms and Farm Workers**

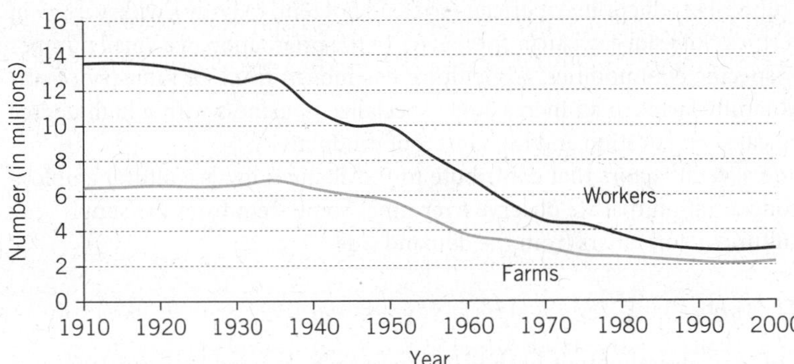

The number of farms and farm workers in the U.S. has declined steadily since the 1900s. *Source:* Author's graph based on USDA National Agricultural Statistics Service Data.

Accompanying the decline in employment in agriculture is a change in the concentration of agricultural production away from small family farms and toward larger-scale commercial producers. Figure 14.1 highlights this change in the agricultural sector. In 1910, there were approximately 6.5 million farms in the U.S. The average farm size at that time was 150 acres. The number of American farms peaked at almost 7 million in the late 1930s and fell continuously before leveling off at around 2 million farms today. Today, the average farm size is about 450 acres.

The decline in agricultural employment is not limited to the United States. As shown in Figure 14.2, other developed and developing countries experience similar patterns as their economies grow. In 1950, almost 90 percent of China's population worked in agricultural production. Today, only 60 percent are employed in

---

1 Daniel Webster, a famous U.S. statesman and lawyer in the mid-1800s said, "When tillage begins, other arts follow. The farmers, therefore, are the founders of human civilization."

Figure 14.2 **Agricultural Population as percent of Total Population in Various Countries, 1950 and 2010**

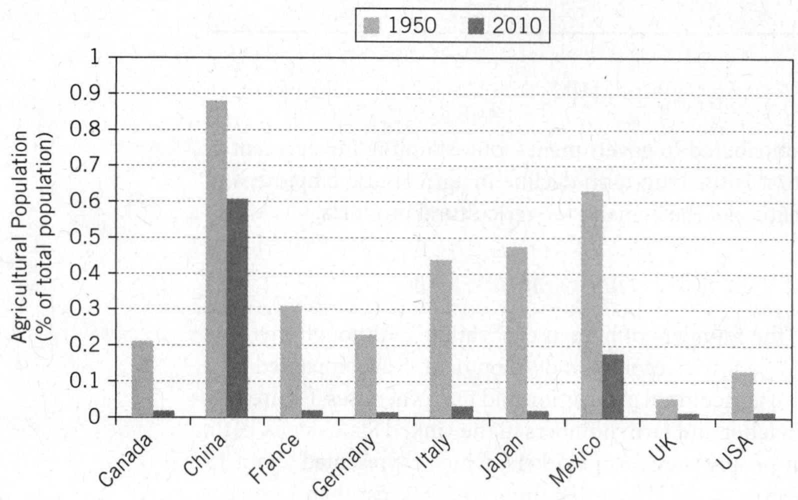

The U.S. and many other developed and developing countries experienced a decline in their agricultural population over the last half-century. *Source:* Author's graph based on United Nations Food and Agriculture Organization FAOSTAT database.

agriculture. Similarly, over 60 percent of Mexico's population worked in agricultural production in 1950, but fewer than 20 percent do so today.

The decline in the number of farms has been coupled with increased specialization in agricultural production. American farms do not tend to grow a wide variety of crops or livestock. Instead, each farm specializes in the production of a small number of relatively specific commodities. Agriculture has moved from an industry of primarily rural family farms to an increasingly specialized business with a high degree of technological sophistication and high levels of productivity.

There are several factors that contribute to the changes in agricultural employment and concentration that we observe over time. Some stem from the supply side of the agriculture sector, others from the demand side.

Supply-side Explanations: Technological Change and Increased Productivity

The supply of agricultural output in the U.S. more than doubled between 1950 and 2000. During the same period, agricultural labor use declined by over 30 percent, and the amount of land used in agriculture fell from 1.2 billion to 0.9 billion acres. Labor-saving processes including the use of fertilizer, improved crop and livestock breeding, machinery, and other technological innovations were the primary drivers of these trends. Economists estimate that between 1950 and 2000, the average amount of milk produced per cow in the U.S. increased from 5,314 pounds per year to 18,201 pounds per year; the average amount of corn produced per acre rose from 39 to 153 bushels; and the average amount of output per hour worked by a farmer was 12 times higher in 2000 than in 1950. These dramatic increases in productivity have generated tremendous increases in the supply of agricultural products.

Demand-side Explanations: Increased Incomes and Increased Population

Demand-side factors have also played a role in agricultural markets. Two demand shifters that changed markedly over the past century are the size of the population and the incomes of consumers. The U.S. population increased from around 75 million in 1900 to over 300 million in 2010. As we learned in Chapter 3, increases in population generate increases in demand, ceteris paribus.

Incomes in the U.S. have also risen. Since 1967, for example, the average amount of U.S. income earned per person has more than doubled, even after adjusting for inflation. This increase in income generates an increase in demand for agricultural output. Ceteris paribus, the increase in demand caused by population and income growth would cause an increase in agricultural output and an increase in agricultural goods' prices.

Combined together, the supply-side and demand-side factors at work in agriculture generate mixed predictions about outcomes in that sector. On the one hand, the increase in demand would cause higher prices and output of agricultural goods. At the same time, however, the increase in supply would lead to increased output but decreases in agricultural prices. Although both shifts generate increases in output, the demand and supply model cannot give us a clear prediction about the prices of agricultural output without more information. If the demand shift is larger than the supply shift, prices will rise. Alternatively, if the supply shift is larger, prices will fall.

Figure 14.3 An Increase in the Supply and Demand for Agricultural Output

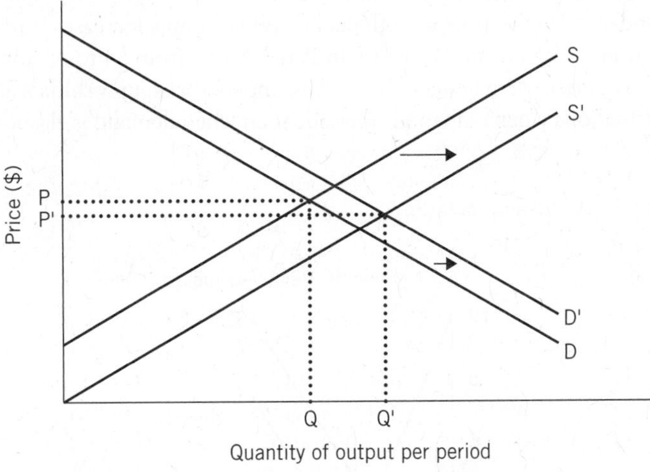

The increase in supply of agricultural output from S to S' causes a reduction in the price and increase in the quantity of output traded. The increase in demand for agricultural output from D to D' causes an increase in both price and quantity traded. Both shifts cause an increase in the quantity traded, from Q to Q'. Because the supply shift was larger than the demand shift, the price of output falls from P to P'.

Figure 14.3 illustrates the combined demand and supply shifts. The increase in supply is illustrated by the shift from S to S'. By itself, this shift in supply would generate increased output and decreased prices for agricultural goods. The demand shift, illustrated by the move from D to D', causes an increase in agricultural output and prices. The demand and supply shifts together cause agricultural output to increase from Q to Q'. The shifts have opposite effects on equilibrium prices. The fact that we have seen a decrease in the inflation-adjusted prices of agricultural goods and services over time implies that the supply shift must have more than offset the demand shift, as shown by the reduction in price from P to P' in Figure 14.3.

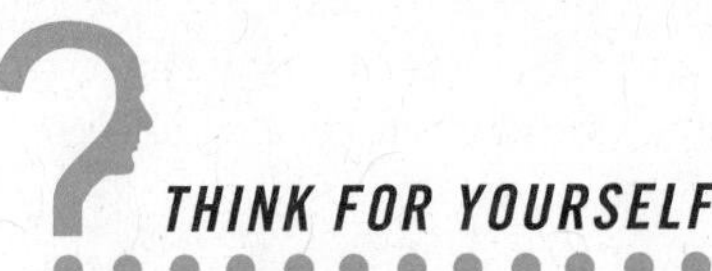

THINK FOR YOURSELF

Use the demand and supply model to determine what will happen to equilibrium prices and output when (a) a large increase in demand is accompanied by a small increase in supply; (b) a small decrease in demand is accompanied by a large decrease in supply; (c) a large decrease in demand is accompanied by a small decrease in supply.

Inelastic Demand

A second important economic characteristic of agriculture is the relatively inelastic demand for agricultural products. The U.S. Department of Agriculture (USDA) estimates that the elasticity of demand for agricultural commodities ranges from −0.04 for fluid milk to −0.7 for pork. Very few agricultural products have elastic demand. We learned in Chapter 5 that when a product has inelastic demand, a given change in the good's price will cause relatively small changes in the quantity of the good demanded. In addition, the demand curves for products with inelastic demand tend to be steep relative to the demand curves for goods with more elastic demand. The inelastic demand for agricultural products implies that changes in supply in agricultural markets do not cause large changes in equilibrium quantity but do cause large fluctuations in price.

Figure 14.4 illustrates the impact of a given increase in supply when demand is elastic and when demand is inelastic. The demand curve in Panel A is flatter and reflects more elastic demand than the demand curve in panel B. The supply curves S and S' are the same in both panels, and the initial equilibrium price of $4 and equilibrium quantity of 2 units per period are also the same in both panels. When supply increases from S to S', the equilibrium price falls from $4 to $3.5 in Panel A and from $4 to $2.5 in Panel B. The larger drop in price when demand is inelastic implies that supply shifts will causes larger price fluctuations when demand is inelastic than when demand is elastic.

Figure 14.4 Changes in Supply When Demand Is Elastic and Inelastic

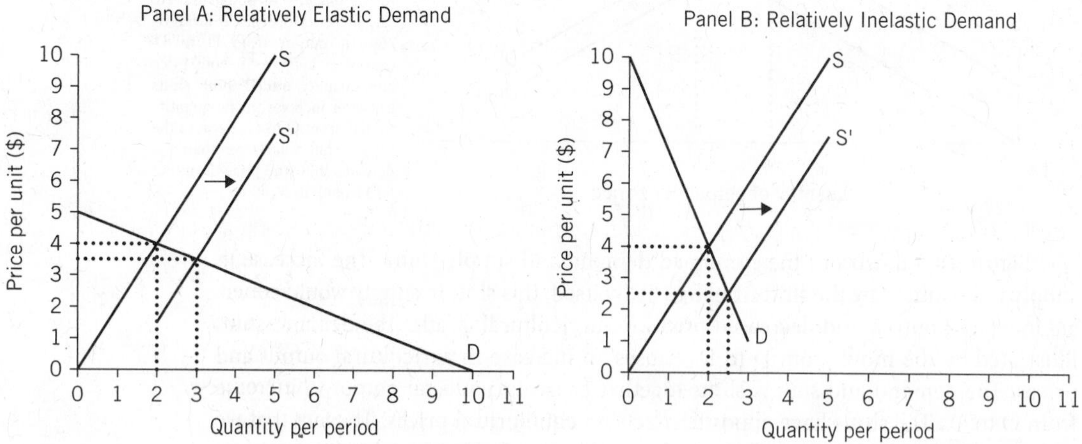

When demand is relatively elastic, as in Panel A, a shift in supply from S to S' causes a small change in the equilibrium price (from $4 to $3.5) but a relatively large change in the equilibrium quantity (from 2 to 3 units per period). When demand is relatively inelastic, as in Panel B, the same size supply shift (from S to S') causes a relatively large change in the equilibrium price (from $4 to $2.5) and a relatively small change in the equilibrium quantity (from 2 to 2.5 units per period).

THINK FOR YOURSELF

How would a decrease in supply impact the equilibrium price and quantity of a good when demand is relatively inelastic? When demand is relatively elastic?

Why does the elasticity of demand matter for agriculture? We noted earlier that agriculture is characterized by relatively inelastic demand. Because agriculture is also subject to relatively large changes in supply across time due to bumper crops, drought, disease, and other factors, the prices of agricultural goods tend to be more volatile than prices in other industries.

Figure 14.5 illustrates price fluctuations in several agricultural commodities, as well as in the Consumer Price Index (CPI), a measure of the average price level in the economy across a wide spectrum of goods and services. The average prices of eggs, milk, and beef show larger variation over time, which would be expected based on their relatively inelastic demand.

Figure 14.5 Price Changes in Agricultural Commodities

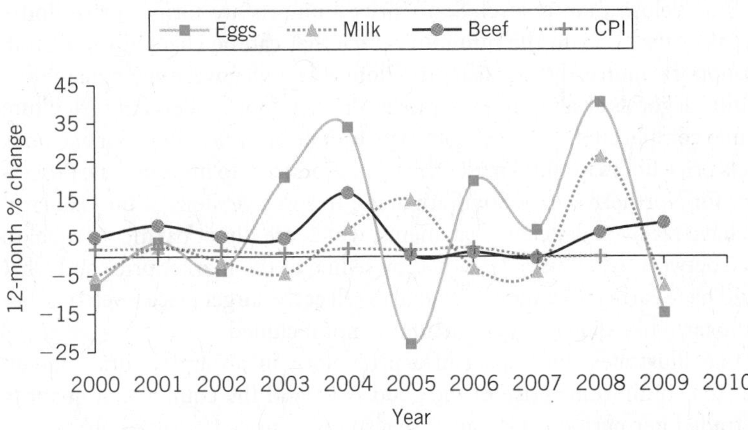

The prices of agricultural commodities like eggs, milk, and beef fluctuate much more than the prices of consumer goods generally, as shown by the smaller changes in the CPI relative to the prices of eggs, milk, and beef.

AGRICULTURAL POLICY

Wide swings in prices in agriculture, decreasing employment, and unpredictable changes in supply make the agriculture sector relatively risky, and many U.S. agricultural policies are aimed at reducing this risk. Much of the extensive governmental involvement in the industry that we see today originated in the Great Depression Era of the 1930s. At that time, demand fell domestically in response to high unemployment and falling incomes. Demand also fell internationally as many other countries imposed restrictions on imports from the U.S. in a misguided attempt to keep the depression outside their borders. As a result, prices for farm products fell dramatically, often to the point that it became too expensive to harvest crops, and they were left to rot in the fields. Not surprisingly, bankruptcies among farmers skyrocketed. It is in this arena that the first comprehensive farm legislation was passed in 1933 to provide subsidies to the agricultural industry. A **subsidy** is a program of financial or other assistance given to a business or industrial sector.

A subsidy is a program of financial or other assistance given to a business or industrial sector.

There are a wide array of provisions and programs covered under the titles, "Farm Policy" and "Farm Subsidy." Some programs focus on research and education, others on energy and nutrition, still others on trade and taxes. Some policies are explicitly designed to raise farmers' incomes and stabilize agricultural product markets; other policies reach these outcomes less directly.

Agricultural policies have evolved from relatively narrow income and commodity price support programs enacted during the Great Depression to the incredibly complicated programs of today, including direct payments, soil conservation payments, food distribution, crop insurance, access to credit, and marketing support. At times, farm policies seem at odds with one another, since they can encourage farming and encourage decreased farmland use at the same time. Some policies reduce the prices of agricultural commodities, whereas other policies cause increases in commodity prices.

It is helpful to group agricultural policies into four main categories: price supports, supply restrictions, demand enhancement, and income supports. Although many agricultural programs are much more wide-ranging and complex than this simple grouping implies, most have impacts that fit into each of these areas.

Price Supports

A price support is a policy aimed at preventing the price of a given good or service from falling below a target level.

A price floor is minimum amount that can be legally charged for a good or service.

A **price support** is a policy aimed at preventing the price of a given good or service from falling below a target level. Some price supports are formal **price floors** that place legal restrictions on the minimum price that can be charged for a good. Other price supports indirectly establish price floors through government guarantees to buy agricultural goods at set minimum prices. Price support policies in agriculture tend to be quite complicated and vary from state to state and over time. For example, California sets price floors for fluid milk sales from producers to intermediate processors that vary for Northern versus Southern areas. In some versions of the U.S. farm bill, farmers have received deficiency payments, which are direct payments equal to the difference between what farmers earned by selling at the market price and what farmers would have earned had they been able to sell at the target price level. In other versions of the farm bill, deficiency payments are not included.

Figure 14.6 illustrates the impact of a price floor in an agricultural market. Suppose that the equilibrium price of the good is P^* and the equilibrium quantity of the good traded per period is Q^*. Suppose also that a price floor is established at price P_F. At P_F, the quantity demanded is Q_D, the quantity supplied is Q_S, and there is a market surplus of $Q_S - Q_D$ of the good per period.

If the market were allowed to adjust to the surplus created at price P_F, the surplus would be eliminated as suppliers reduce the quantity of the good they supply and the price falls to P^*. In the case of a price floor, however, the price is prevented from falling below P_F, so the surplus will not eliminated by the market. Consumers will purchase Q_D of the good, but the rest of the good produced will remain as surplus, ceteris paribus.

Figure 14.6 **Impact of a Price Floor**

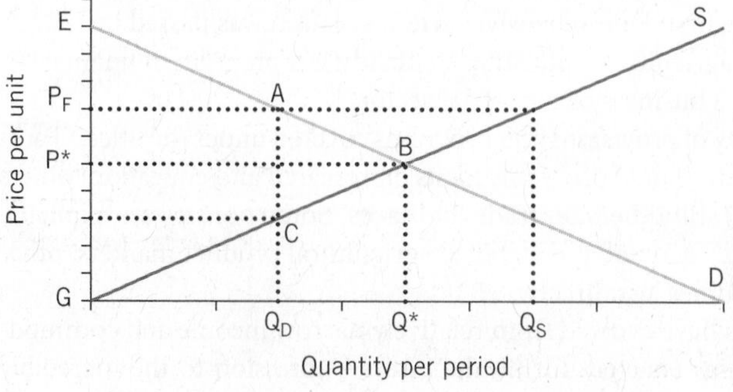

The equilibrium price and quantity are P^* and Q^*. A price floor of P_F increases the quantity supplied to Q_S and reduces the quantity demanded to Q_D. The price floor results in a surplus of the good and a deadweight loss equal to area of triangle ABC.

Are consumers and producers better off with the price floor in place? We can use the concepts of producer surplus, consumer surplus, and deadweight loss to measure the impacts of a price floor. Without the price floor in place, consumer surplus is equal to EBP*, which is the area below the demand curve and above the equilibrium price of the good in Figure 14.6. Producer surplus is equal to GBP*, the area above the supply curve and below the price P*. When the price is restricted to P_F, consumer surplus falls to EAP_F. Since consumer surplus is lower with the price floor in place, consumers are made worse off by the price floor. Producer surplus with the price floor in place is equal to the area $GCAP_F$, the area above the supply curve and below the price floor. Although producer surplus can theoretically rise or fall when the price floor is in place, it is difficult to imagine that the price floor would be implemented if it did not help producers. Finally, the price floor causes a deadweight loss of ABC.

Because of the persistent surpluses they generate, it is rare to enact price floors as stand-alone policies.[2] Price floors are usually coupled with other policies to reduce or prevent excess supply. One policy that complements a price floor is to decrease the supply of the good. A second complementary policy is to increase the demand for the good. These policies are described in the next section.

THINK FOR YOURSELF

How would a price floor that is set below the equilibrium impact the price and quantity of agricultural products?

Supply Restrictions

Supply restrictions raise the prices of agricultural goods by reducing their supply. Supply restriction programs have existed since the 1930s, appearing under titles including *acreage controls*, *soil conservation*, *soil bank*, and *set-aside*. Supply restriction programs pay farmers for limiting production by not planting on some of their acreage. Since the mid-1980s, supply restrictions have been accomplished through the Conservation Reserve Program (CRP), which provides payments to eligible farmers when they convert land from farming to conservation use. The 2008 Farm Bill allows payments for up to 32 million acres nationally through the CRP program. This represents a 50,000 square-mile area, a size roughly the equivalent of the state of Alabama. Payments under the CRP program are approximately $2 billion per year.

The impact of agricultural supply restriction policies is illustrated in Figure 14.7. Taking farmland out of production reduces the supply of agricultural commodities from S to S'. The reduction in supply causes an upward movement in the price of commodities from P* to P' and a reduction in the equilibrium quantity traded from Q* to Q'.

Given the relatively inelastic demand faced in the agriculture sector, supply restriction programs cause higher equilibrium prices but have only small impacts on equilibrium quantities traded in the agricultural sector. The inelastic nature of demand also implies that producers will earn higher total revenues after the supply restrictions are in place.

---

2 One exception is the minimum wage, which is discussed in Chapter 10.

Figure 14.7 **Impact Supply Restriction Policies**

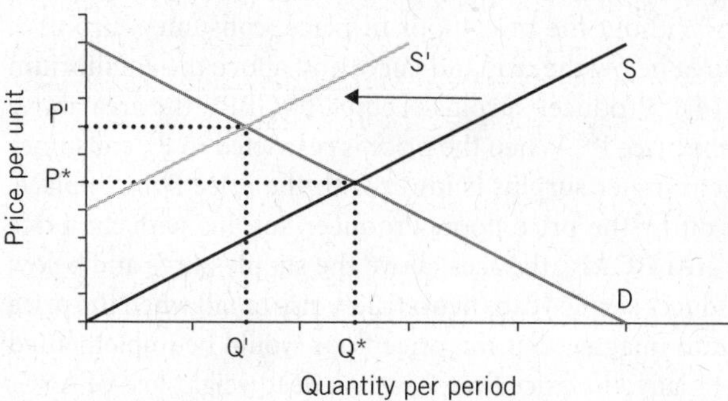

Supply restriction policies cause a reduction in supply from S to S'. This causes the price of output to rise from P* to P' and the quantity traded to fall from Q* to Q'. Because the demand for agricultural products is inelastic, the reduction in supply can increase producers' total revenues.

Demand Enhancement

Demand enhancement policies raise the prices of agricultural goods by increasing their demand. Demand enhancement policies are wide ranging, but they tend to be targeted toward low-income groups and foreign countries as well as agricultural producers. Food assistance programs, nutrition programs, international food aid programs, and government-supported school lunch programs all serve to increase the demand for agricultural products.

The impact of demand enhancement programs is shown in Figure 14.8. Government policies to buy agricultural products increase the demand for those products from D to D'. The increase in demand causes an increase in price from P to P' and an increase in the quantity traded from Q to Q'.

Figure 14.8 **Impact of Demand Enhancement Policies**

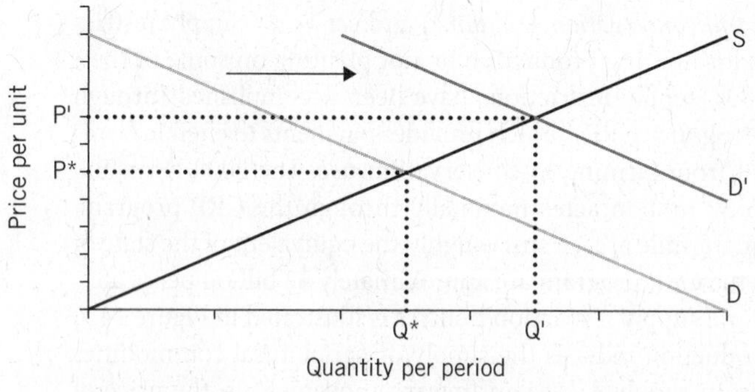

Demand enhancement policies cause the demand for agricultural output to increase from D to D'. The increased demand increases the price of agricultural output from P* to P' and increases the quantity traded from Q* to Q'.

One example of a demand enhancing farm policy occurred in the 1980s and 1990s. The U.S. government's Commodity Credit Corporation bought and stored surplus cheese that resulted from price supports to the dairy industry at that time. The cheese was later distributed directly to low-income welfare and food stamp recipients. The government's purchase and distribution of this "government cheese" generated higher prices and output in the dairy sector.

The United States also engages in demand enhancement through its Foreign Agricultural Service (FAS), which provides U.S. agricultural goods to millions of people throughout the world. One example of FAS activities that enhance the demand for agricultural output is the Food for Peace Act. The Food for Peace Act provides funding for government purchases and sales of U.S. agricultural commodities to developing countries. Food purchased with these funds has been distributed to over 3 billion people in 150 countries around the world since 1960.

Income Support

Income support programs include direct payments to producers of many agricultural commodities, subsidized crop insurance programs, disaster relief funds, and subsidized loan programs. Because they guarantee income support to farmers, income support programs provide incentives for continued or increased production of agricultural products. In this way, income support programs indirectly increase agricultural production, which in turn generates increases in the supply of agricultural products output and reductions in food prices, ceteris paribus.

© Everett Collection Inc/ Alamy Limited

Theodore Schultz and the Economics of Agriculture

Theodore Schultz (1902–1988) was awarded the Nobel Prize in Economics in 1979 for his work in development economics and the economics of agriculture. His research on the role of agriculture in the economy and the relationship between agriculture, technology, education, and economic development influenced U.S. policies toward many countries after World War II. He was particularly interested how the relationship between education and productivity influenced the post-war recovery in Japan and Europe. His work encouraged policymakers and others to increase their emphasis on education as a means of foreign aid.

THE COSTS AND BENEFITS OF AGRICULTURAL POLICY

Because agricultural policies and programs are varied, ranging from insurance to loans to food stamps and nutrition programs to foreign aid, it is difficult to quantify their full costs and benefits. We do know, however, that the programs generate benefits as well as costs for the economy.

Increased Incomes for Agricultural Producers

As described earlier, agricultural programs are largely designed to increase and stabilize the incomes of agricultural producers. This can happen overtly through direct payments and low-cost loans, or indirectly through price supports, supply restrictions, and demand enhancement. Approximately half of the agriculture industry in the U.S. receives support from governmental farm programs, and direct payments account for nearly 40 percent of net cash income for farmers.

Advocates of farm programs sometimes argue that the policies are necessary to preserve the incomes of traditional family farms and rural communities. In the 1930s, the incomes and wealth of U.S. farmers were lower than that of nonfarm households, which was one reason farm programs had strong support. In recent years, however, U.S. farm household income has exceeded the income of the average U.S. household. Figure 14.9 shows the average annual income of farm households and U.S. households

Figure 14.9 **Average Farm Operator Household Income and Average U.S. Household Income**

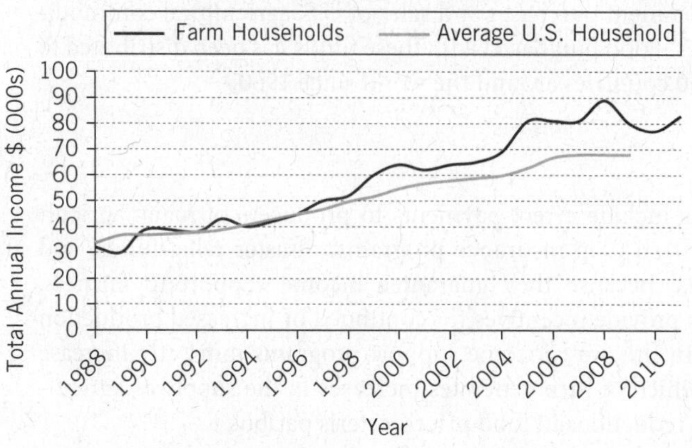

Average farm household incomes were lower than the income of the average U.S. household before the 1980s, but farm household incomes have been higher than average U.S. household incomes since the mid-1990s. *Source:* Author's chart based on USDA Economic Research Service, and National Agricultural Statistics Service Data.

more generally. In 1988, farm households earned an average of $32,000, while the average household earned $34,000. In 1996, farm household income was equal to that of the average household in the U.S. ($45,000). Since 1996, farm household income has exceeded average household income every year.

In addition, farm programs increasingly support large-scale rather than small-scale agricultural producers. The USDA Economic Research Service (ERS) reports that commodity program payments increasingly favor large and higher income farms. Between 1989 and 2002, for example, the share of commodity program payments that went to farms with at least $500,000 in annual sales increased from 12 percent to 27 percent. In 2002, half of the commodity program payments went to farms with household incomes over $60,000. That same year, the median U.S. household income was $42,000.

Higher Prices for Consumers

Farm programs that restrict supply, increase demand, or establish price floors raise the prices that consumers pay for agricultural goods. At the same time, farm programs that encourage increased production through low-cost loans or other subsidies generate reductions in agricultural goods' prices. Given these countervailing influences, there is some debate about the price impacts of farm programs. Economists estimate that if U.S. commodity protection and subsidy policies were eliminated, the prices of many commodities would drop only modestly—1 percent or less for milk, pigs, poultry, and soy, around 3 percent for beef and rice. Prices of fruit and vegetables are estimated to drop 5 percent, and the price of sugar is estimated to drop 15 percent.

THINK FOR YOURSELF

Would an agricultural policy that restricts supply generate a larger or smaller impact on price for pork, which has a price elasticity of demand of –0.7, or milk, which has a price elasticity of demand of –0.04?

Higher Taxes

Not only do consumers pay for farm programs through higher prices for agricultural products, they also pay for farm programs through their taxes. The 2008 Farm Bill cost $288 billion dollars, although the Congressional Budget Office estimates that the total spending for the bill will be closer to $307 billion.

Reduced Competitiveness

By protecting and subsidizing agricultural producers, farm policies reduce incentives for producers to obtain optimal levels of production, investment, and output. In addition, some farm policies make it difficult for domestic producers to compete in international markets without subsidies, restricting the competitiveness of U.S. producers relative to their foreign counterparts. At the same time, however, because many foreign governments also subsidize agriculture, unilaterally removing U.S. subsidies could reduce U.S. agricultural producers' competitiveness in some markets.

Higher Costs for Farmland

Because agricultural policies make farm earnings higher than they would be otherwise, they raise the relative price of agricultural land and other farm inputs. In real estate markets, the value of land depends in large part on the expected future income derived from the land. When farm policy payments make the land more valuable, land buyers must pay prices that cover this higher opportunity cost of the land. According to economists at the USDA, the value of agricultural land would be an average 15 to 20 percent lower in the absence of government payments.

Inefficient Use of Resources

We illustrated earlier in the chapter that agriculture has been characterized by incredible technological and productivity improvements over the last century. A natural consequence of being able to produce more and more output with fewer and fewer resources is the movement of the less productive resources into other areas of the economy. When farm programs prop up resources that would have otherwise moved into areas where they are more productive, the programs hamper the ability of the economy to produce on its PPF. Economists estimate that current commodity programs reduce U.S. net income by about $5 billion annually due to misallocated resources, including resources used for political lobbying, program administration, and market interventions.

SUMMARY

The agriculture industry has changed markedly over the last century. A much smaller portion of the U.S. population is involved in agricultural production today than in the 1900s. The U.S. government has been involved in the agriculture industry since the Great Depression, in part because of the dramatic decline in employment in the industry. In addition, the inelastic demand for agricultural output causes prices in the sector to be highly volatile. Government intervention in agricultural markets takes the form of price supports, supply restrictions, demand enhancement, and income support. Like all policy choices, farm programs involve costs and benefits. Although advocates of such policies emphasize that they preserve family farms and rural communities and ensure economic competitiveness, many economists argue that farm policies do not meet these goals.

KEY CONCEPTS

- Subsidy
- Price support
- Price floor

DISCUSSION QUESTIONS AND PROBLEMS

1. Given that they create deadweight loss and inefficiency, why do agricultural subsidies continue to exist?
2. When Hugo Chavez became the president of Venezuela in 1999, he promised his people lower food prices. He felt this would ensure that everyone would have enough to eat, and farmers and other food producers would not be lining their pockets with profits made off the poor. Chavez set a price ceiling on certain commodities and quotas on the amount that each producer had to produce. What does the demand and supply model predict would happen as a result of Chavez' policies?
3. A wheat producer is willing and able to sell her wheat at a price of $7 per bushel. This works well for her in the first year, but during the second year, the maximum price she is able to get for her wheat is $5 per bushel. Explain whether or not each of the scenarios a.-e. could be the reason behind this change.
   a. An increase in wheat production technology
   b. A price floor above the first year equilibrium price
   c. An increase in wheat consumers' incomes
   d. A decrease in population
   e. A price ceiling below the first year equilibrium price
4. Penelope's Pumpkin Patch produces and sells an average of 500 pumpkins per Halloween. This year, Penelope's fairy godmother visited her and turned all the worms in Penelope's garden into pumpkins, so now she has more pumpkins to sell than usual. This same year, a restaurant in Penelope's town began baking and shipping, "The Greatest Pumpkin Pie Ever Made" all over the country. This restaurant buys all its pumpkins from Penelope.
   a. If the demand for Penelope's Pumpkins increased by more than the supply, what would we expect to happen to the price of Penelope's Pumpkins?
   b. If supply and demand shifted by the same amount, what would we expect to happen to price?
   c. Now assume that the "Greatest Pumpkin Pie Ever Made" recipe was never discovered, and the restaurant had never caused an increase in demand for Penelope's Pumpkins. What would we have expected to happen to the price of pumpkins? Why? What do we expect will happen to the price of pumpkins next year, assuming that Penelope's fairy godmother does not return?
5. Almost all ethanol currently in production in the U.S. is made from corn. U.S. corn and ethanol producers are generally different entities. The government currently provides a subsidy of $0.51 per gallon to ethanol producers, which allows ethanol producers to charge a lower price for fuel mixes containing ethanol. How would the ethanol subsidy affect demand and supply in the corn market? How would the ethanol subsidy affect the supply of agricultural products that are production substitutes for corn (i.e., crops that corn producers could grow instead of corn)?
6. The accompanying table shows the quantity of cheese demanded by and supplied to a city in a given week.
   a. Compute the value of consumer surplus and producer surplus when this market is in equilibrium.
   b. Suppose a price floor of $1,000 per unit is imposed on this market. Compute the value of consumer surplus and producer surplus if the government takes no other action besides setting the price floor.
   c. Now suppose that the government supports the price floor by buying up the surplus cheese created by the price floor. How much would it cost the government to buy the surplus cheese? What would be the value of consumer surplus and producer surplus under this policy?
   d. Who is helped by the imposition of the price floor in this market?
   e. Who is hurt by the imposition of the price floor in this market?

Quantity Demanded (units per week)	Price Per Unit ($)	Quantity Supplied (units per week)
0	1,300	1,200
100	1,200	1,100
200	1,100	1,000
300	1,000	900
400	900	800
500	800	700
600	700	600

Quantity Demanded (units per week)	Price Per Unit ($)	Quantity Supplied (units per week)
700	600	500
800	500	400
900	400	300
1,000	300	200
1,100	200	100
1,200	100	0
1,300	0	0

MULTIPLE CHOICE QUESTIONS

1. You observe that the price of coffee has decreased and the quantity sold has increased. Ceteris paribus, this could result from
   a. a decrease in the demand for coffee.
   b. an increase in the supply of coffee.
   c. a decrease in the supply of coffee.
   d. an increase in the demand for coffee.

2. When the government pays Farmer Freddy to not plant corn on some of his land (and instead leave it empty), how does this affect Consumer Carrie?
   a. Consumer Carrie gets to pay a lower price for corn.
   b. Consumer Carrie must pay a higher price for corn.
   c. Some of Consumer Carrie's taxes go to Farmer Freddie to let his land go unplanted.
   d. Both a and c
   e. Both b and c

3. Farmer Fred is paid by the government to leave a fourth of his cropland unplanted during the next growing season. Farmer Fred's vegetables will probably be more expensive because of the reduced supply, so the government decides to give each villager in Fred's town a set of vouchers that can only be spent at Fred's farm. Farmer Fred can turn in the vouchers to the government later in exchange for cash. Which of the following agricultural policies has the government employed?
   a. Price supports
   b. Supply restrictions
   c. Demand enhancement
   d. Income support
   e. Both a and b
   f. Both b and c

4. Given that the demand for milk is relatively inelastic, an increase in the supply of milk would tend to generate
   a. a large fluctuation in price.
   b. a large fluctuation in quantity.
   c. a large fluctuation in both price and quantity.
   d. no change in price.

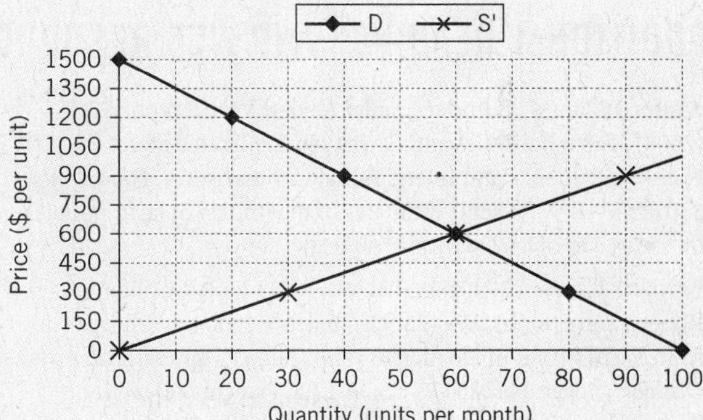

5. The accompanying figure depicts the market for milk in Sydney, Montana. If a late spring blizzard kills a large proportion of the dairy cows in Sydney, a possible new equilibrium price and quantity of milk could be
   a. P = $600; Q = 160.
   b. P = $900; Q = 90.
   c. P = $150; Q = 90.
   d. P = $300; Q = 30.
   e. P = $1050; Q = 30.

6. The figure depicts the market for milk in Sydney, Montana. If the price of Chips Ahoy Cookies (a complement good for consumers) falls, a possible new equilibrium price and quantity of milk could be
   a. P = $600; Q = 160.
   b. P = $900; Q = 90.
   c. P = $150; Q = 90.
   d. P = $300; Q = 30.
   e. P = $1050; Q = 30.

7. The figure depicts the market for milk in Sydney, Montana. Suppose the government imposes a price floor on milk of $900 per unit. At this price floor, the

quantity of milk sold will be ___ units per month and consumer surplus will be ___ per month.

a. 40; $12,000
b. 90; $27,000
c. 60; $36,000
d. 40; $36,000

8. The figure depicts the market for milk in Sydney, Montana. Suppose the government imposes a price floor on milk of $1,050 per unit. At this price floor, deadweight loss will be ___ per month.

a. $4,500
b. $27,000
c. $33,750
d. $11,250
a. $9,000

9. Ceteris paribus, when the supply of beef increases, the quantity of beef sold will change by a smaller amount

a. the more elastic is the demand for beef.
b. the more inelastic is the demand for beef.
c. the flatter is the supply curve.
d. the flatter is the demand curve.
e. Both a and d are correct.

10. Ceteris paribus, when the supply of beef increases, beef prices will change by a greater amount

a. the more elastic is the demand for beef.
b. the more inelastic is the demand for beef.
c. the flatter is the supply curve.
d. the flatter is the demand curve.
e. Both a and d are correct.

ADDITIONAL READINGS AND WEB RESOURCES

Alston, Julian M., Sumner, Daniel A., and Vosti, Stephen A. (2008) "Farm Subsidies and Obesity in the United States: National Evidence and International Comparisons," *Food Policy* 33(6):470–479. Presents estimates of the impact of farm policies on the prices of agricultural products.

Barnard, Charles, Nehring, Richard, Ryan, James, Collender, Robert, and Quinby, Bill (2001) "Higher Cropland Value from Farm Program Payments: Who Gains?" *Agricultural Outlook*, November: 26–30 USDA ERS. Presents research on the relationship between agricultural subsidies and the price of farmland.

Fuglie, Keith O., MacDonald, James M., and Ball, Eldon (2007) Productivity Growth in U.S. Agriculture. EB-9, U.S. Dept. of Agriculture, Econ. Res. Serv. Documents the increase in agricultural productivity in the U.S. over time.

MacDonald, James, Hoppe, Robert, and Banker, David (2005) "Growing Farm Size and the Distribution of Commodity Program Payments," *Amber Waves: The Economics of Food, Farming, Natural Resources, and Rural America.* February. http://www.ers.usda.gov/AmberWaves/February05/DataFeature/ Presents information on the recipients of farm subsidies.

Mercier, Stephanie, and Smith, Vince (2006) "Domestic Farm Policy for 2007: Forces for Change," *Choices* 21(4):209–214. Presents an easy to read overview of recent farm policy.

Orszag, Peter. Congressional Budget Office Director's Blog, "Farm Bill Cost Estimate," May 13, 2008, http://cboblog.cbo.gov/?p=99 Presents estimates of the cost of the 2008 farm bill.

Ryan, James, Barnard, Charles, Collender, Robert, and Erickson, Ken (2001) "Government Payments to Farmers Contribute to Rising Land Values," USDA ERS Agricultural Outlook. June/July 2001. Summarizes research on the relationship between farm subsidies and agricultural land values.

Steinbeck, John (1939) *The Grapes of Wrath*, Penguin Classics. Stienbeck's Pulitzer Prize–winning novel provides a timeless fictional account of the experiences of farm workers during the Depression era.

Tweeten, Luther (1995) "The Twelve Best Reasons for Commodity Programs: Why None Stands Scrutiny," *Choices* 10(2):4–7 & 43–44. Presents arguments for and against farm subsidy programs.

USDA ERS, "Diet Quality and Food Consumption: Price Elasticity Estimates" http://www.ers.usda.gov/Briefing/DietQuality/Data/table1.htm. Updated July 16, 2008. Presents estimates of price elasticity values for agricultural products.

The USDA Economic Research Service is a primary source of economic information from the USDA, including research on economic and policy issues involving food, farming, natural resources, and rural development. http://www.ers.usda.gov/

The USDA National Agricultural Statistics Service provides data, statistics, and publications related to U.S. agriculture. http://www.nass.usda.gov

The California Department of Food and Agriculture provides information on the bimonthly announcement of the minimum prices allowable for milk in California. http://www.cdfa.ca.gov/dairy/

Daniel Grill/Getty Images, Inc.

15

The Economics of Illegal Drugs

After studying this chapter, you should be able to:

- Describe the incidence of drug use
- Model the externalities associated with drug use
- Describe the incomplete information problem associated with drug use
- Appraise the policy responses to drug use
- Analyze supply and demand issues in regulation policy
- Analyze the impacts of drug legalization

In April 2010, the former dictator of Panama, Manuel Noriega, was extradited from the United States to a prison in France. Noriega was captured in Panama during a U.S. invasion of the country in 1989 and had been imprisoned in the U.S. for 17 years for drug trafficking, racketeering, and money laundering. The capture of Noriega was part of the continuing U.S. "War on Drugs," a set of policies and activities undertaken by the U.S. government to reduce the use and trade of illegal drugs. The War on Drugs began in the 1970s under the Nixon administration in response to rising recreational drug use in this country and by U.S. servicemen in Vietnam. The War on Drugs has been waged in particular against heroin, cocaine, crack, marijuana, methamphetamine, and pharmaceutical drug abuse. Federal funding for drug control programs is approximately $15.5 billion annually, and roughly 2 million Americans are arrested for drug-related offenses each year.

The War on Drugs is a highly controversial set of policies, often pitting politicians against one another and legalization advocates against the U.S. Drug Enforcement Agency. The War on Drugs is an area ripe for economic analysis because of its impacts on the demand and supply of drugs and on the marginal benefits and marginal costs of drug use and drug reduction activities. This chapter presents the economics of illegal drugs, but many of the concepts here easily translate into other activities that have the potential to negatively impact people.

THE INCIDENCE OF DRUG USE IN THE U.S.

It is difficult to obtain information about the exact amount of drug use in the United States. The illegal nature of drug use makes people understandably reluctant to honestly respond to surveys about their drug use. Nonetheless, various sources allow researchers to estimate the extent of U.S. drug use. These sources include direct surveys, data from drug seizures, and arrest and other law enforcement data. Figure 15.1 presents estimates of the use of illicit drugs in the United States over time.

Drug use in America was much higher in the 1970s than it is today. In 1979, approximately 14 percent of the U.S. population over age 12 reported using illegal drugs during the past month. Drug use fell dramatically during the 1980s and 1990s, in part because of the increased efforts in the War on Drugs during the Reagan and George H.W. Bush administrations. Drug use appears to have leveled off during the 2000s, with about 8 percent of the U.S. population over age 12 reporting using illegal drugs.

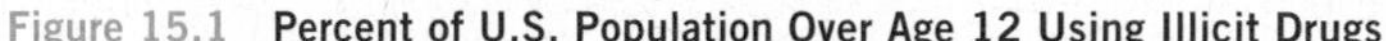

Figure 15.1 **Percent of U.S. Population Over Age 12 Using Illicit Drugs**

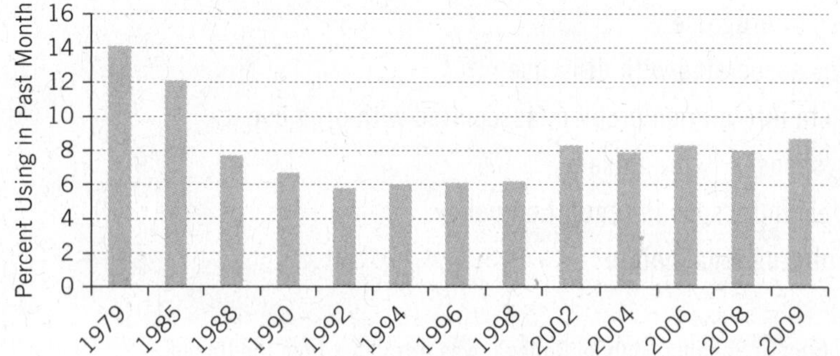

The trends in drug use over time reflect increased emphasis on the War on Drugs in the 1980s. Illicit drug means marijuana, cocaine, heroin, hallucinogens, inhalents, or nonmedical use of sedatives, tranquilizers, stimulants, or analgesics. *Sources:* National Household Survey on Drug Abuse (1979–1991), Substance Abuse and Mental Health Services Administration (1992–1998) National Drug Control Strategy: Annual Report, Results from 2008 National Survey on Drug Use and Health: National Findings.

Statistics on average rates of drug use like those in Figure 15.1 hide widely variable patterns in terms of the types of drugs used and the demographics of those who use drugs. The most commonly used illicit drug is marijuana, which is used by roughly 76 percent of illicit drug users. The rate of drug use tends to be higher among the unemployed than among those with jobs. Drug use also tends to be higher among 18- to 25-year-olds than among other age groups. The rate of drug use is lower for college graduates than for those with lower levels of education. There are many reasons why the rate of drug use changes over time and differs among different demographic groups. Economics can help explain these differences and can help assess the potential impacts of policies designed to reduce drug use.

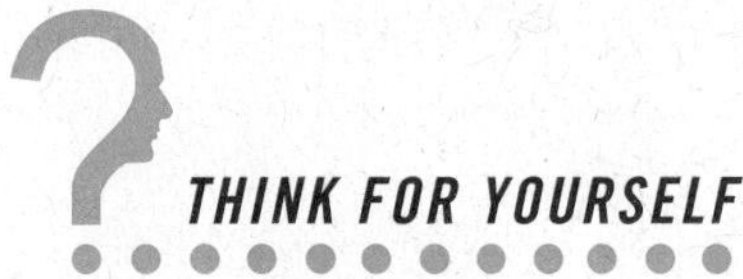

What are some of the benefits associated with drug use? What are some of the costs? Why might the costs and benefits of drug use differ among those of different ages, education levels, or among the employed versus the unemployed?

THE MARKET FOR DRUGS

Like any other good, drugs are traded in markets where the interactions between demand and supply determine drug prices and the incidence of drug use. Figure 15.2 depicts the market for a hypothetical drug, Huxsoma.[1] The demand curve D(MB) represents consumers' willingness to pay or marginal benefit from consuming Huxsoma. We learned in Chapter 3 that for most goods, the downward slope of the demand curve reflects the inverse relationship between the price of the good and the quantity demanded. As the price of Huxsoma increases, the quantity of Huxsoma demanded falls for several reasons. A rising price makes Huxsoma harder to afford, so the income effect generates a reduction in the quantity of Huxsoma demanded as its price increases. The substitution effect implies that as the price of Huxsoma increases, consumers will instead purchase substitute goods that are now relatively cheaper. Finally, the law of diminishing marginal utility implies that consumers' willingness pay for Huxsoma falls as the quantity of Huxsoma consumed rises.

Figure 15.2 **The Market for Huxsoma**

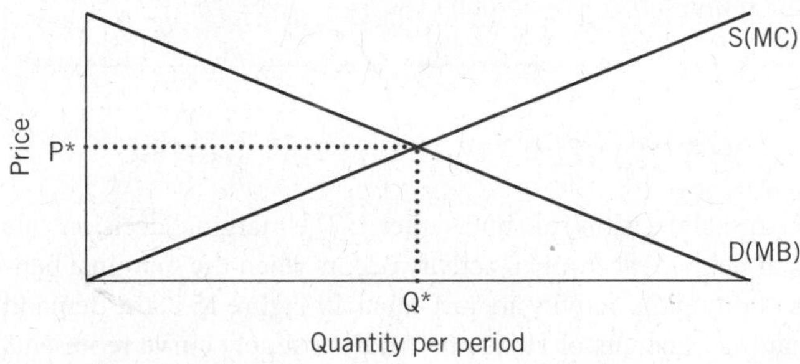

The demand curve for Huxsoma D(MB) depicts consumers' marginal benefits from consuming the drug. The supply curve S(MC) represents the marginal cost of producing and selling Huxsoma. In equilibrium Q* units of Huxsoma are traded per period at price P*.

The supply curve for Huxsoma, S(MC) shows the relationship between the price of Huxsoma and the quantity of Huxsoma supplied. The supply curve also represents the marginal cost of producing and selling Huxsoma. As we learned in Chapter 3, the supply curve is upward sloping because of the scale effect, the substitution effect, and the law of increasing marginal costs. At equilibrium, Q* units of Huxsoma are traded per period at price P*. In addition, the marginal benefit of consuming Huxsoma is just equal to the marginal cost of producing Huxsoma at equilibrium.

1 This name is a portmanteau of the words "Huxley" and "soma." In Aldous Huxley's 1932 novel *Brave New World*, soma is a legal drug whose use is strongly encouraged by the government.

THINK FOR YOURSELF

What factors would shift the demand curve for Huxsoma? What factors would shift the supply of Huxsoma?

© kzenon/iStockphoto

Alcohol and Marijuana: Complements or Substitutes?

The high prevalence of alcohol use on college campuses is problematic, causing alcohol-related accidents, alcohol poisoning, increased crime, and increased fatalities. In response, many colleges have policies targeted at reducing drinking and binge drinking among college students. Research has shown that such policies have been relatively effective at reducing binge drinking. Economists, however, wonder about unintended consequences of these policies. If marijuana is a substitute for alcohol, when policymakers act to raise the cost of using alcohol, they may inadvertently generate an increase in marijuana use. Alternatively, if marijuana is a complement to alcohol, policies that raise the cost of using alcohol will have the added benefit of decreasing marijuana consumption. Researchers have investigated the relationships between alcohol policy, alcohol and marijuana prices, and the subsequent use of alcohol and marijuana to assess whether alcohol and marijuana are complements or substitutes among college students. Their findings indicate that the two goods are complements among college students. The implication of the research is that recent efforts to reduce college students' access to alcohol have not contributed to a rise in marijuana use.[2]

MARKET FAILURES ASSOCIATED WITH ILLEGAL DRUGS

We learned about the marginal decision rule in Chapter 1. The marginal decision rule asserts that the maximum net benefit from an activity occurs when the marginal benefits and marginal costs of doing the activity are just equal. In Figure 15.2, the demand curve represents the marginal benefits of Huxsoma, and the supply curve represents its marginal costs, so the market equilibrium is also the point where the net benefits of Huxsoma are maximized. All else equal, the equilibrium quantity Q* and price P* would be the efficient and optimal quantity and price of Huxsoma in society. Consuming and producing any quantity below Q* would result in foregone net benefits, and consuming and producing a quantity above Q* would generate net costs for society.

Unfortunately, the consumption and production of drugs like Huxsoma are associated with at least two market failures that make the P* and Q* outcomes in Figure 15.2 undesirable from a social efficiency perspective. We learned in Chapter 8 that market failures occur when markets generate inefficient allocations of goods and services. In the case of drugs, externalities and imperfect information give rise to market failure.

2 Williams, Jenny, Pacula, Rosalie Liccardo, Chaloupka, Frank J., and Wechsler, Henry (2004) "Alcohol and Marijuana Use Among College Students: Economic Complements or Substitutes?" *Health Economics* 13:9 (September):825–843.

Externalities

Externalities occur when some of the costs or benefits of a trade are imposed on people outside the trade. People outside a trade are called third parties to the trade. For example, when a drug user's habit affects his or her family, the family members are third parties to the trade between the drug user and the drug supplier. When a paper mill emits pollution into a local neighborhood, the people living in the neighborhood are third parties to the trade between the paper mill and paper consumers. **Negative externalities** are costs that are imposed on third parties. **Positive externalities** are benefits received by third parties.[3] The market for drugs tends to generate negative externalities. Drug use is associated with increased rates of automobile accidents, drug-related theft and other crimes, marital problems and family turmoil, poor work performance, negative health impacts on the unborn, and increased health care costs.

Negative externalities are costs that are imposed on third parties.

Positive externalities are benefits that are imposed on third parties.

The marginal cost–marginal benefit framework can help us assess how negative externalities impact the market for drugs. Figure 15.3 presents a graphical description of the market for Huxsoma that incorporates negative externalities. Because negative externalities impose costs on others, we need to consider private marginal costs and social marginal costs in the market for drugs. **Private marginal costs** are marginal costs that accrue only to the producers of Huxsoma. In Figure 15.3, private marginal costs are labeled $S(MC_{private})$.

Private marginal costs are marginal costs that accrue only to the producers of a good or service.

Social marginal costs are marginal costs that accrue to society as a whole.

Social marginal costs are marginal costs that accrue to society as a whole. In our example, the curve $S(MC_{social})$ reflects the social marginal costs of Huxsoma. Social marginal costs include private marginal costs plus the negative externality imposed on others. The negative externality is shown as the vertical distance between $S(MC_{private})$ and $S(MC_{social})$ in Figure 15.3.

$$MC_{social} = MC_{private} + \text{Negative Externality}$$

In an unregulated market, demanders and suppliers of Huxsoma only have incentives to consider the costs they incur ($MC_{private}$) and the benefits they receive (MB). Based on this comparison, the optimal level of production and consumption of Huxsoma is $Q^*_{private}$ and the optimal price is $P^*_{private}$.

Figure 15.3 **Externalities Associated with Huxsoma**

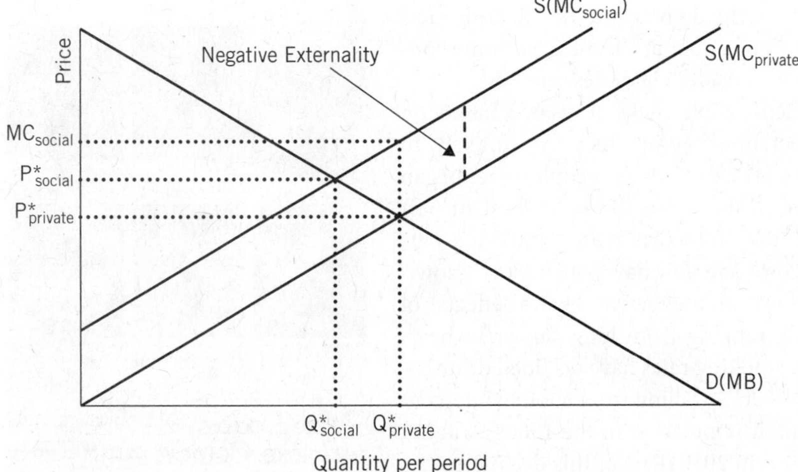

Negative externalities are costs imposed on third parties. The difference between $S(MC_{private})$ and $S(MC_{social})$ represents the negative externality associated with Huxsoma. If there were no negative externality, $Q^*_{private}$ and $P^*_{private}$ would be the optimum quantity and price of Huxsoma. With the negative externalities considered, the socially optimal level of Huxsoma is Q^*_{social}. Since producers and consumers do not have incentives to consider externalities when they buy and sell Huxsoma, without intervention the market equilibrium amount of Huxsoma would be $Q^*_{private}$. Thus, the market would produce too much Huxsoma from a social efficiency perspective.

3 Positive externalities are covered in Chapter 17.

Are the price and quantity $P^*_{private}$ and $Q^*_{private}$ best for society overall? To determine the socially optimal quantity of Huxsoma, we need to compare social marginal costs (MC_{social}) against marginal benefits (MB). Point Q^*_{social} illustrates the level of production and consumption where the marginal benefits associated with Huxsoma are equal to its social marginal costs. At Q^*_{social}, the marginal benefits attained from Huxsoma are just equal to the marginal social costs incurred to get those benefits. At output levels above Q^*_{social}, society incurs higher marginal costs than marginal benefits from Huxsoma. At output level $Q^*_{private}$, for example, the private marginal cost of Huxsoma is $P^*_{private}$, but the social marginal cost of Huxsoma is MC_{social}, so the social marginal costs exceed marginal benefits. In the presence of negative externalities, an unregulated market produces more than the socially optimal level of Huxsoma.

THINK FOR YOURSELF

Are the negative externalities associated with marijuana production and consumption likely to be larger or smaller than those associated with tobacco use? Alcohol use? Methamphetamine use? How would the level of negative externality associated with a drug relate to the difference between the socially optimal quantity of the drug and the quantity that would be traded in an unregulated market?

Imperfect Information

Imperfect information occurs when demanders or suppliers do not know the true costs and benefits associated with a good or service.

A second market failure associated with drugs is imperfect information. In a market plagued by **imperfect information**, producers or consumers have only limited information about a good or service, and they may not be aware of the full costs and benefits of producing or consuming the good.

An example of imperfect information comes from the cigarette industry. In the 1950s, cigarette companies touted the health benefits of smoking in their advertising. Ads included statements like, "More doctors smoke Camels than any other cigarette," and "Chesterfield gives you the scientific facts in support of smoking." The ads led some consumers to consider cigarettes safe.

When people make decisions based on imperfect information, they are unlikely to choose optimally. Many people who began smoking in the 1950s did so at least in part because they underestimated smoking's true health costs. We now have much more knowledge about the negative health effects of smoking, ranging from lung cancer to heart disease. Smoking rates have declined dramatically in the U.S., falling from about 45 percent of the adult population in the 1960s to about 20 percent in 2010. Part of this decline comes from people having more complete information about the true costs of smoking.

The Granger Collection, NYC—All rights reserved.

Because of the market failures associated with drugs, unregulated markets for drugs will likely result in too much production and consumption from a social efficiency perspective. In part because of these market failures, countries around the world have engaged in a wide array of activities to reduce drug use. The next section presents an overview of some of these efforts.

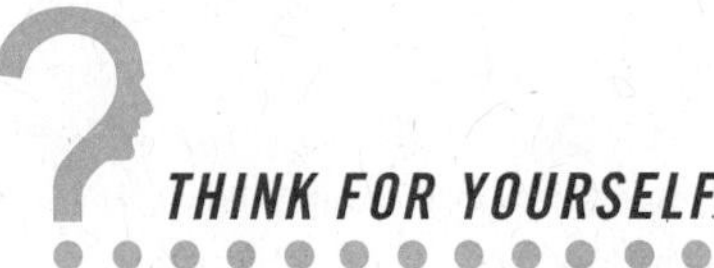

One way to get around the problem of imperfect information is through "learning by doing." For example, people who do not know the benefits and costs they may incur from rock climbing could try it out and then decide if it is an activity they want to repeat. Would "learning by doing" be an effective way for someone to gain information about the costs and benefits of using addictive drugs? Why or why not?

MONICA M. DAVEY/ AFP/ NewsCom

George Akerlof and the Economics of Information

George Akerlof (1940–) is an American economist and professor at the University of California, Berkeley. Along with economists Michael Spence and Joseph Stiglitz, he was awarded the Nobel Prize in Economics in 2001 for work on the impact of imperfect information on market outcomes. In his paper, "The Market for Lemons: Quality Uncertainty and the Market Mechanism," Akerlof describes a market in which sellers know more about product quality than buyers. In some situations, Akerlof demonstrates, imperfect information can result in high-quality products and honest producers being driven out of the market by low-quality products and dishonest suppliers.

REDUCING DRUG USE

Because drugs are bought and sold in markets like the one depicted in Figure 15.3, policy makers have two basic tools at their disposal to reduce drug use: policies to reduce the demand for drugs or policies to reduce the supply of drugs. U.S. lawmakers have used both demand-side and supply-side policies as part of the War on Drugs.

Demand-side Policies

Demand-side policies in the War on Drugs aim to reduce drug use by reducing the demand for drugs. We learned in Chapter 3 that factors that can shift the demand for a good or service include changes in income, changes in the prices of substitute or complement goods, changes in tastes and preferences, changes in expectations, and changes in the number of consumers in the market. It is unlikely that policymakers could reasonably reduce the demand for drugs by enacting policies to manipulate incomes or the number of consumers in the market. Policymakers' ability to alter the prices of substitute and complement goods is also limited. For example, since marijuana and alcohol are complements, an increase in the price of alcohol could reduce the demand for drugs. Alcohol producers, however, are unlikely to support such a policy. Instead, demand-side policies have predominately aimed at changing expectations and reducing people's tastes and preferences for drugs.

Suppose that drugs and alcohol are substitutes for consumers. What action could policymakers take in the market for alcohol in order to reduce the demand for drugs?

Laws that make it illegal to consume or possess a drug are aimed at the demand side of the market. By targeting consumers rather than suppliers, such laws reduce the demand for illicit drugs. Programs aimed at the prevention and treatment of drug abuse are also demand-side policies. In the 1970s, the majority of funding in the War on Drugs went to treatment programs, including extensive support of methadone clinics geared toward reducing drug use among heroin addicts. In the 1980s, the "Just Say No" advertising campaign was implemented to discourage young children from using drugs. The Drug Abuse Resistance Education (D.A.R.E) program is an educational program in which police officers go into schools to teach children ways to avoid involvement in drugs, gangs, and violence. Founded in 1983, the D.A.R.E. program is now in place in 75 percent of U.S. schools and in more than 43 countries around the world. D.A.R.E. is primarily a demand-side program, designed to reduce the demand for drugs by teaching children about the dangers of drug use. Another example of a demand-side policy is the Montana Meth Project (MMP). The MMP is a large-scale marketing campaign that presents very graphic images depicting the results of methamphetamine use. MMP television and print ads include pictures of meth users in the hospital, on the street, and in other situations designed to show the devastating impacts of meth use.

Figure 15.4 illustrates the impact of an effective demand-side drug use reduction policy for Huxsoma. Prior to a demand-side policy implementation, the market for Huxsoma was in equilibrium at Q units traded per period at a price of P per unit. An effective demand-side policy would reduce the demand for Huxsoma from D to D'. As a result, the quantity of Huxsoma traded would fall from Q to Q' and the price of Huxsoma would fall from P to P'.

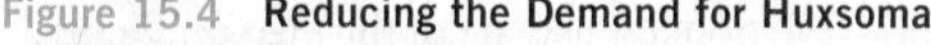

Figure 15.4 **Reducing the Demand for Huxsoma**

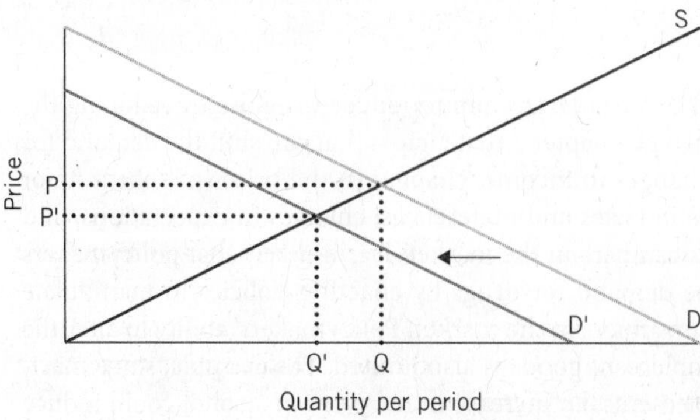

Programs like D.A.R.E. and the Montana Meth Project are designed to reduce the demand for drugs. When demand falls from D to D', the quantity of drugs used falls from Q to Q'.

Supply-side Policies

Although there are several examples of demand-side actions to reduce drug use, the majority of the efforts of the War on Drugs have been aimed at drug suppliers. Supply-side policies involve interdiction (disrupting the transport of drugs), destroying drug production facilities, eradicating crops, and pressuring governments in other countries to help reduce exports of drugs to the U.S.

According to the Congressional Budget Office, the federal government allocates nearly 2.5 billion dollars per year for drug interdiction and related international activities. Because the War on Drugs tends to focus on restricting the supply of drugs produced abroad and imported into the U.S., many operations occur across international borders and include military training and equipment for foreign governments.

The impacts of supply-side policies to reduce drug use are illustrated in Figure 15.5. The market for Huxsoma is originally in equilibrium with Q units trading per period at price P. Now suppose that a shipment of Huxsoma is seized. The seizure will reduce the supply of Huxsoma from S to S'. As the market adjusts to a new equilibrium, the quantity of Huxsoma traded falls from Q to Q' and the price of Huxsoma rises from P to P'.

Figure 15.5 Reducing the Supply of Huxsoma

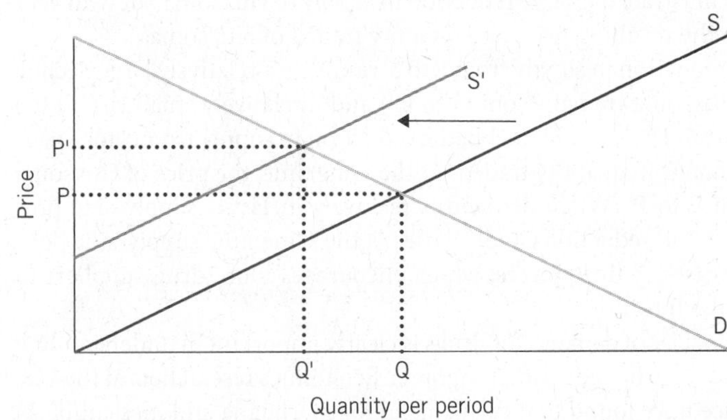

Supply-side policies are designed to reduce the supply of drugs. The decrease in supply from S to S' causes the quantity of drug use to fall from Q to Q', but also causes the price of drugs to rise from P to P'.

Supply-side policies generate a costly tradeoff in the War on Drugs. On the one hand, the higher price created by the reduction in supply decreases the quantity of drugs traded and used in the current period. On the other hand, higher drug prices mean increased incentives for new drug dealers to enter the market in later periods. Higher prices may also generate increases in drug-related theft and other crimes as users must now find more money than before to fuel their habit.

The Importance of Elasticity

It is important to note that the sizes of the changes in the prices and quantity of drugs traded that result from supply-side policies depend on the elasticity of demand for drugs. In Chapter 5 we learned that the elasticity of demand tells us how responsive quantity demanded is to a change in a good's price. When demand is relatively elastic, changes in the price of the good generate relatively large changes in the quantity of the good demanded. When demand is relatively inelastic, changes in price cause relatively small changes in the quantity of the good demanded.

Figure 15.6 **Reducing the Supply of Huxsoma**

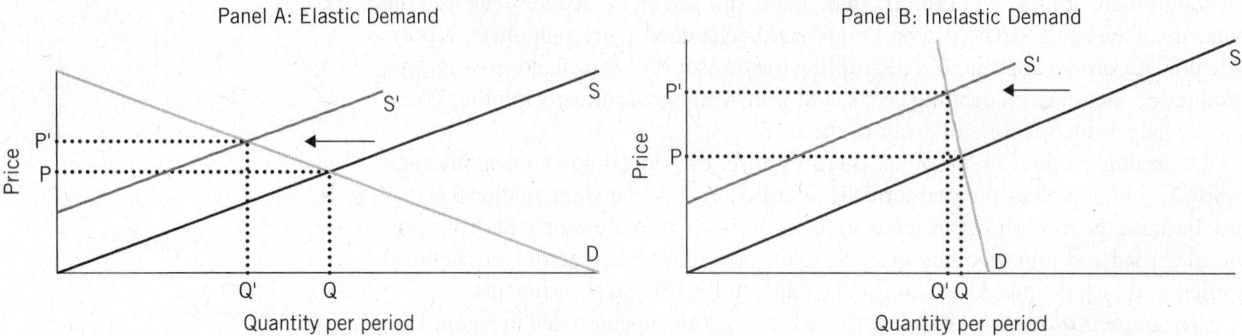

When the demand for drugs is relatively elastic, as in Panel A, supply-side policies cause the quantity of drugs used to fall dramatically from Q to Q'. When the demand for drugs is relatively inelastic, as in Panel B, supply-side policies do not generate very large reductions in drug use but do cause large increases in drug prices.

Why does the elasticity of demand play a role in the War on Drugs? Figure 15.6 illustrates how supply-side policies generate very different outcomes, depending on the elasticity of demand. In Panel A, the demand for Huxsoma is shown to be relatively elastic when compared to the demand for Huxsoma illustrated in Panel B. Panels A and B both illustrate the same reduction in supply of Huxsoma but with very different impacts on the resulting price and quantity traded of Huxsoma.

In Panel A, the reduction in supply from S to S' results in a relatively large decline in the quantity of Huxsoma traded (from Q to Q') and a relatively small rise in the price of Huxsoma (from P to P'). In Panel B, the reduction in supply from S to S' generates only a small change in quantity traded. At the same time, the price of Huxsoma rises markedly, from P to P'. When demand is relatively inelastic, supply-side programs generate only small reductions in drug use. At the same time supply-side policies cause large increases in drug prices, which encourages more drug suppliers to enter the market in the future.

Knowing the elasticity of demand for drugs is clearly important in understanding the effects of supply-side drug reduction programs. Economics researchers at the U.S. Department of Justice have found that the demand for marijuana and methamphetamine are relatively elastic, while the demand for heroin and cocaine are relatively inelastic. These elasticities imply that supply-side programs to reduce the supply of marijuana tend to generate relatively large reductions in quantity and small increases in price. Alternatively, programs to reduce the supply of cocaine and heroin generate relatively large increases in price but only small reductions in quantity traded. The researchers estimate that if supply-side programs were not in place for drugs like cocaine and heroin, the drugs would sell for prices that are comparable to aspirin!

THE ECONOMICS OF LEGALIZATION

An additional approach to the War on Drugs is legalization, a highly controversial approach to the issue of drug use. In 2009, more than a dozen members of the U.S. House of Representatives sponsored the Personal Use of Marijuana by Responsible Adults Act, which would decriminalize the possession of small amounts of marijuana. At least 16 states allow for the legal use of marijuana for medical purposes. Arguments against the legalization of marijuana include its potential to be more easily accessible to children and its use as a gateway to more dangerous drugs.

What impact would legalizing a drug such as marijuana have? This section examines the economic impacts of legalization of drugs.

The United States has historical experience with the consequences of making certain goods and services illegal and then legalizing them again later. Abortion was illegal in 30 states in the U.S. prior to the 1973 Roe v. Wade Supreme Court case, and alcohol was illegal in the U.S. during the Prohibition period (1920–1933). During Prohibition, a large illegal market for alcohol flourished, earning millions of dollars for organized crime groups and generating increased crime and corruption related to the illegal alcohol trade. With the repeal of Prohibition in 1933, the production and distribution of alcohol were again legal.

As was the case with the repeal of Prohibition, making a drug like marijuana legal would likely impact both its demand and its supply. The demand for marijuana would likely rise because the potential costs of using it, including fines and imprisonment, would fall. All else equal, the increased demand would increase marijuana prices and use.

The supply of marijuana would likely also increase with legalization because the risk of fines and imprisonment for producers would fall. Production and transportation costs would likely also fall because producing and transporting marijuana on the black market is likely more expensive than producing and transporting it legally. One could even imagine better production technology contributing to an increase in supply as researchers find improved crop varieties, better fertilizer, and improved agricultural techniques for growing marijuana. Advocates of marijuana legalization also argue that the safety of drugs would improve if they were legalized, since they could be regulated in the same way as other agricultural products. All else being equal, the increased supply would decrease marijuana prices.

Figure 15.7 illustrates the potential impacts of legalizing the hypothetical drug Huxsoma. Before legalization, the demand for Huxsoma is D and the supply of Huxsoma is S. The equilibrium price of Huxsoma is P and the equilibrium quantity is Q. After legalization, the demand for Huxsoma rises to D' and the supply of Huxsoma increases to S'. The increases in demand and supply cause the quantity of Huxsoma traded to rise. The effect of legalization on the price of Huxsoma depends on the relative sizes of the shifts in supply and demand. If the supply increases by more than demand does, as depicted in Figure 15.7, the price of Huxsoma will fall from P to P'. If the demand shift is larger than the supply shift, the price of Huxsoma would rise.

Figure 15.7 An Increase in the Supply and Demand for Huxsoma

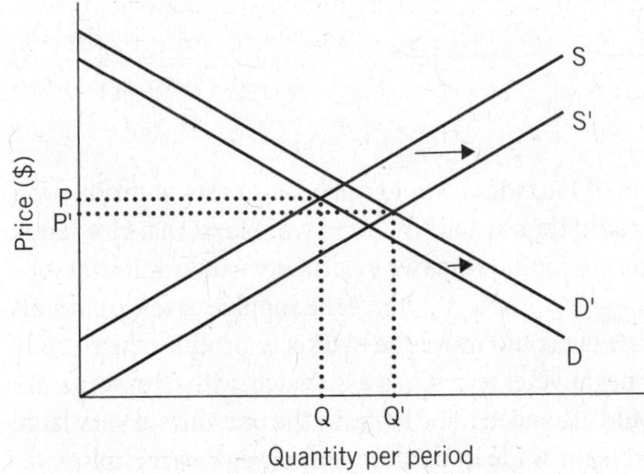

The increase in supply of Huxsoma from S to S' causes a reduction in the price and increase in the quantity traded. The increase in demand for Huxsoma from D to D' causes an increase in both price and quantity traded. Both shifts cause an increase in the quantity traded, from Q to Q'. If the supply shift is larger than the demand shift, the price of Huxsoma will fall from P to P'. If the demand shift were larger, the price of Huxsoma would rise.

THINK FOR YOURSELF

What would be some of the costs of marijuana legalization? What would be some of the benefits? Do you believe the benefits would outweigh the costs? Why or why not?

Negative Externalities

Even if drugs like marijuana were legal, many of the negative externalities associated with drugs would still exist. Those who advocate legalization argue that the problems associated with these negative externalities can be solved by taxation similar to the taxes on businesses that emit pollution. Legalization advocates also argue that legalization would help mitigate the market failure of imperfect information associated with marijuana because more research and information on the costs and benefits of marijuana use would be available.

Figure 15.8 illustrates the impact of a tax on Huxsoma. Suppose that Huxsoma is legal. The supply of Huxsoma is $S(MC_{private})$, the social marginal cost of Huxsoma is $S(MC_{social})$ and the demand is D(MB). Without government intervention in the Huxsoma market, the level of Huxsoma traded is $Q^*_{private}$ and the price is $P^*_{private}$. Because of the negative externalities associated with Huxsoma, the optimal level of trade for society is Q^*_{social}, where the social marginal costs of Huxsoma are equal to its marginal benefits.

Figure 15.8 **Taxing Huxsoma**

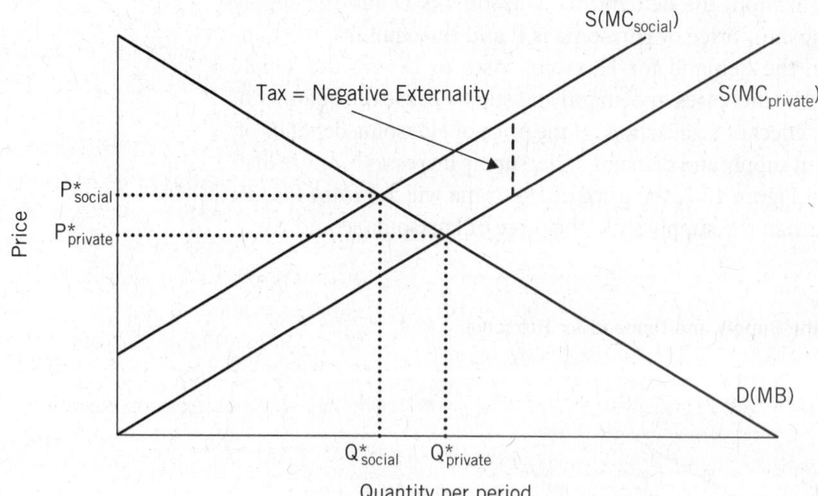

A tax set equal to the value of the negative externality will move the amount of Huxsoma used from $Q^*_{private}$ to Q^*_{social}.

A tax charged to the producers of Huxsoma would raise their costs of production by the amount of the tax. The tax would thus reduce the supply of Huxsoma. How large should the tax be? A tax equal to the size of the negative externality would shift the supply curve for Huxsoma from $S(MC_{private})$ to $S(MC_{social})$, since the supply curve would shift upward by the amount of the tax. The tax could move the market to produce the socially optimal level of Huxsoma. If the negative externalities associated with Huxsoma are very large, the tax on Huxsoma would also need to be large. In the presence of very large taxes, there may still be black markets for trade in untaxed and unregulated Huxsoma.

SUMMARY

Drugs present an economic problem largely because of the market failures of negative externalities and imperfect information associated with their production and use. Like other goods and services, using drugs involves both costs and benefits. Because drug use imposes costs on third parties, the interactions between drug buyers and sellers are unlikely to result in the socially optimal level of drug use. Because of the market failure, it is possible to intervene in the drug market and improve social welfare. Policies like the War on Drugs are designed to reduce the supply and demand for drugs to move drug use toward a socially optimal level. Other approaches to the market failure, such as legalization combined with a tax, could also alleviate the market failures associated with drugs.

KEY CONCEPTS

- Negative externalities
- Positive externalities
- Private marginal costs
- Social marginal costs
- Imperfect information

DISCUSSION QUESTIONS AND PROBLEMS

1. The accompanying table shows the marginal benefits and costs of beer production and consumption per week:

Quantity Produced/ Consumed (# six-packs per week)	Private Marginal Costs (supply)	Private Marginal Benefits (demand)
200	5	9
400	6	8
600	7	7
800	8	6
1000	9	5

   a. Based on these private costs and benefits, what will be the equilibrium price of a six-pack?
   b. Based on these private costs and benefits, what will be the equilibrium quantity of six-packs sold per week?
   c. Are there likely to be negative externalities associated with beer production and consumption? If so, describe some of them. If not, why not?
   d. Is the equilibrium quantity of six-packs sold per week the socially optimal quantity? Why or why not?
   e. Suppose that an economist estimates that the negative externalities associated with beer production and consumption average $2.00 per six-pack of beer sold. She also concludes that there are no positive externalities associated with beer production and consumption. Based on the social marginal costs, what is the socially optimal price of a six-pack? What is the socially optimal quantity of six-packs sold per week?
   f. Propose a method to get from the market equilibrium level of beer consumption to the socially optimal level of beer consumption.
2. Alcohol is legal in the U.S. but marijuana is not. Why is this?
3. In 2011, 16 states had enacted laws legalizing medical marijuana. How would the legalization of medical marijuana affect the market for illegal marijuana?
4. Would legalizing drugs reduce crime? Why or why not?

5. Figure A and Figure B represent two hypothetical demand curves for cocaine.

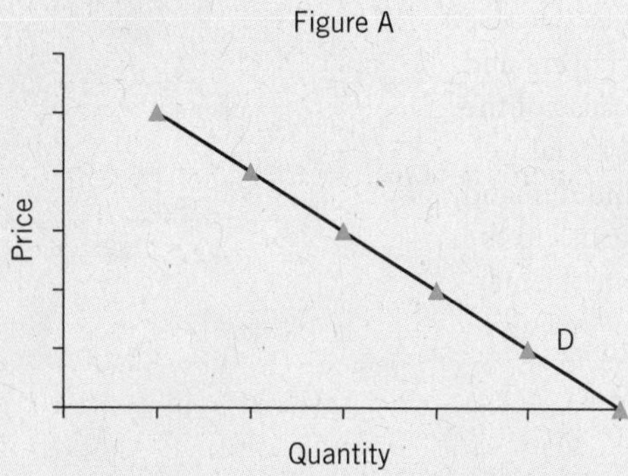

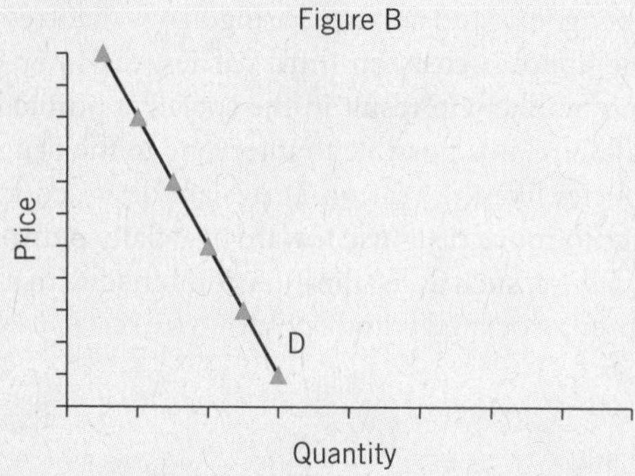

a. Which demand curve would more likely reflect the demand of people who are addicted to cocaine, and which would reflect the demand of casual users? Explain.

b. Assume that legalizing cocaine does not change the demand for cocaine. In which figure would legalizing cocaine cause the largest increase in its use? Explain.

MULTIPLE CHOICE QUESTIONS

1. When production of a product causes negative externalities, we know that in the absence of government intervention, the producer's decision
   a. will result in economic equity.
   b. will result in economic efficiency.
   c. will result in economic inefficiency.
   d. will result in an underproduction of the product from a social efficiency perspective.
2. Legalization of drugs would most likely ____ the supply of drugs in the market
   a. increase
   b. decrease
   c. not change
   d. shift backwards
3. Legalization of drugs would most likely ____ the demand for drugs in the market.
   a. increase
   b. decrease
   c. not change
   d. shift backwards
4. In general, drug prohibition
   a. tends to increase drug use as drug pushers entice customers into drug use.
   b. tends to decrease drug use as drug prices increase.
   c. tends to cause drug prices to fall as a result of increased demand for drugs.
   d. tends to make drugs more attractive to adults because of the psychological need for adults to rebel against established societal norms.
5. In the case of addicts (whose demand is relatively inelastic), drug prohibition will
   a. tend to increase the revenues of drug dealers due to increased expenditures on drugs.
   b. tend to decrease the revenues of drug dealers due to decreased expenditures on drugs.
   c. cause a relatively large decrease in the output that drug dealers are able to sell.
   d. reduce crime rates as users have less need to steal to finance their drug habit.
6. Suppose the price elasticity of demand for marijuana is −4. If the price of marijuana increased by 2 percent, the quantity demanded will
   a. decrease by 8 percent.
   b. decrease by 0.5 percent.
   c. increase by 8 percent.
   d. decrease by 2 percent.

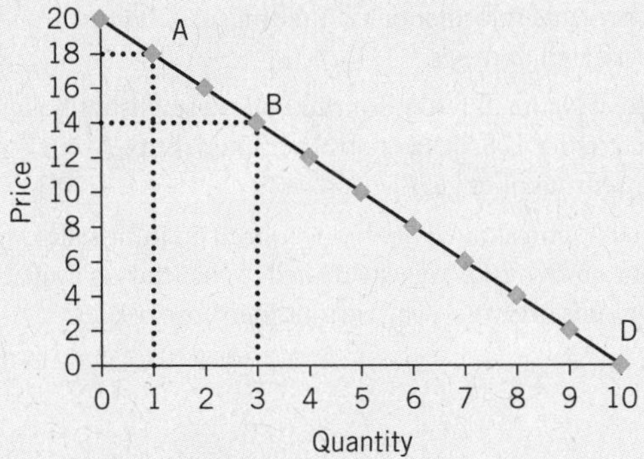

7. In the demand curve shown, the price elasticity of demand between point A and point B is
   a. elastic.
   b. inelastic.
   c. unit elastic.
   d. perfectly inelastic.
   e. perfectly elastic.

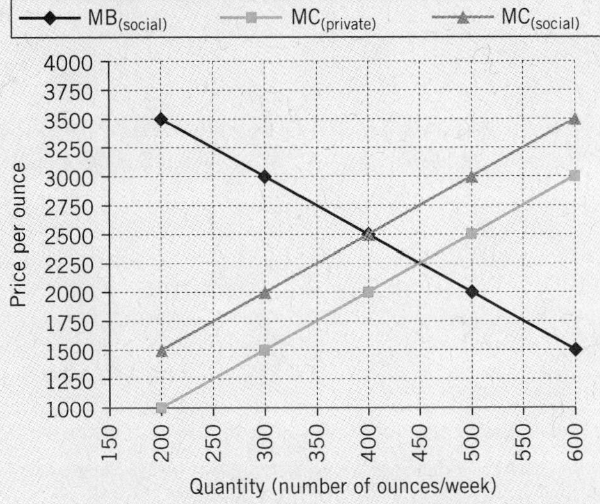

8. Suppose that the market for marijuana is shown in the accompanying graph, where $MC_{(private)}$ represents the private supply curve and $MC_{(social)}$ represents the social supply curve that reflects the full social marginal costs of marijuana. $MB_{(social)}$ is the demand curve and represents the private and social marginal benefits of marijuana. The gap between $MC_{(social)}$ and $MC_{(private)}$ represents
   a. the difference between the private and social benefits of marijuana production and consumption
   b. the negative externalities associated with marijuana production and consumption
   c. the difference between the market price of marijuana and the actual private cost involved in producing marijuana
   d. producer surplus
   e. consumer surplus
9. Suppose that the market for marijuana is shown in the graph, where $MC_{(private)}$ represents the private supply curve and $MC_{(social)}$ represents the social supply curve and reflects the full social marginal costs of production. $MB_{(social)}$ is the demand curve and represents the private and social marginal benefits of marijuana production. From an efficiency standpoint, the socially optimal level of production is _____ounces per week at a price of_____ per ounce.
   a. 450; $2,750
   b. 400; $2,000
   c. 400; $2,500
   d. 450; $2,250
   e. 400; $2,250
10. Suppose that Medical Marijuana, Inc. is currently producing at a point where its private marginal cost of production is $15.00. At this level of production, social marginal cost is $25.00. At the current production level, marginal social benefit is $15.00. Thus, the negative externality associated with Medical Marijuana Inc.'s level of production is
   a. $0 because marginal private cost and marginal social cost are equal.
   b. $0 because marginal private cost and marginal social benefit are equal.
   c. $25.00 per unit.
   d. $15.00 per unit.
   e. $10.00 per unit.

ADDITIONAL READINGS AND WEB RESOURCES

Akerlof, George (1970) "The Market for Lemons: Quality Uncertainty and the Market Mechanism," *Quarterly Journal of Economics* 84(3):488–500. A Nobel-prize winning economist describes one potential outcome of imperfect information.

Huxley, Aldous (1932) *Brave New World*, Harper Perennial Modern Classics. This novel presents a fictional future where citizens are required to consume daily doses of soma, an antidepressant.

Rhodes, William, Johnston, Patrick, Song, Han, McMullen, Quentin, and Hozik, Lynne (2002) "Illicit Drugs: Price Elasticity of Demand and Supply," Department of Justice document number 191856. Presents information on the elasticity of demand for various drugs. http://www.ncjrs.gov/pdffiles1/nij/grants/191856.pdf

Thornton, Mark (2007) "The Economics of Prohibition," Ludwig von Mises Institute. Presents an economic examination of prohibition and links it to U.S. drug policy.

The U.S. Drug Enforcement Administration enforces laws and regulations regarding U.S. drug control policies. http://www.justice.gov/dea/index.htm

The National Institute on Drug Abuse presents scientific research on drug abuse and addiction. http://www.drugabuse.gov/

U.S. Bureau of Justice Statistics, Drugs and Crime Facts, http://bjs.ojp.usdoj.gov/content/dcf/dcb.cfm and Crime in the United States, annual, Uniform Crime Reports, U.S. Bureau of Justice Statistics presents information on funding, expenditures, and outcomes related to drugs.

The Office of National Drug Control Policy establishes policies and objectives for U.S. drug control activities. http://www.whitehousedrugpolicy.gov/

The PBS television show *Frontline* produced an informative special on the War on Drugs. A website related to the study is available at http://www.pbs.org/wgbh/pages/frontline/shows/drugs/

© RelaxFoto.de/iStockphoto

16

Pollution, The Environment, and Global Warming

After studying this chapter, you should be able to:

- Describe the benefits and costs of pollution
- Model the externalities associated with pollution
- Describe the policy responses to pollution
- Assess methods to address pollution problems

In 2007, former U.S. Vice President Al Gore shared the Nobel Peace Prize with hundreds of scientists on the Intergovernmental Panel on Climate Change (IPCC) for work related to increasing awareness of global warming. Although concern about the environment and the conservation of natural resources is longstanding, rising international awareness of climate change has caused increasing concern about pollution and the environment in recent years. Environmentally friendly products and services are commonplace, and advice on living a "sustainable" lifestyle or being more "ecofriendly" is ubiquitous. Indeed, U.S. President Barak Obama has promoted "green jobs" as part of a set of programs designed to stimulate economic growth.

Ask yourself the following question: "Should there be zero pollution?" Invariably, some readers will enthusiastically answer, "Of course!" However, chances are these same folks (like most of us) use cars, public transportation, or bikes, eat food purchased at grocery stores and transported there by truck or train, heat or cool their living spaces, and bathe in water processed by a municipal water treatment plant. All of these activities generate pollution. Indeed, even as you read this sentence, you are breathing out carbon dioxide, a greenhouse gas. Even the most environmentally conscious among us generate some amount of pollution.

Pollution is contamination of the environment that causes instability, harm, or disruption to ecosystems. Pollution can be naturally occurring or human-induced.

But what *is* pollution? **Pollution** is contamination of the environment that causes instability, harm, or disruption to ecosystems. Pollution can be naturally occurring or anthropogenic (human-induced), although scientists, environmental groups, and policymakers place primary emphasis on understanding and reacting to human-induced pollution. Prior to the more recent focus on potential responses to climate change, many early debates centered on whether global warming was a naturally occurring or anthropogenic phenomenon. The IPCC has concluded that most of the observed rise in global temperatures since the 1950s has very likely resulted from anthropogenic causes.

Pollution and the use of natural resources are necessary byproducts of human existence. Given this fact, environmental economics is not focused on reducing pollution to zero. Instead, the focus is on assessing what the optimal level of pollution might be and determining how to get to that level most efficiently. As with other applications of economics, the economics of pollution, the environment, and global warming involves an assessment of the costs and benefits of alternative choices.

THE COST-BENEFIT APPROACH TO ENVIRONMENTAL PRESERVATION

The marginal benefit—marginal cost framework we learned about in Chapter 1 is a useful way to think about pollution. The marginal cost–marginal benefit framework can also be used to assess the likely impacts of pollution regulations, environmental regulations, and policies designed to mitigate global warming. Identifying the benefits and costs of pollution is crucial to applying the marginal cost–marginal benefit framework to the problem of environmental preservation.

Benefits of Pollution

It may seem odd to assert it, but there are many benefits of pollution. Using cars, trains, and airplanes generates such benefits as faster transportation from place to place, face-to-face communication, and increased ability to trade goods and services with others. It is difficult to imagine the increases in technology, health care, communication, and general quality of life achieved in the last 150 years had we not had large-scale electricity generation.

Recall that the marginal benefit of a choice is the additional or incremental benefit associated with the choice. The marginal benefit of driving is the amount of additional benefit attained from choosing to drive one more mile. The marginal benefit of watching TV is the additional benefit attained from watching TV for one more hour. We learned in Chapter 3 that we can conceptualize marginal benefits in terms of the amount someone is willing to pay for an additional unit of a good. Using a willingness to pay framework for marginal benefits allows us to compare benefits and costs using dollars as a common measure.

Let's use electricity generation to illustrate the marginal benefits and costs of pollution. Suppose that you are the first person in your area to open up a power plant and generate electricity to sell. Your first customers will most likely be those that place the highest value on electrical service. You could provide basic electric services to light homes and businesses in highly populated areas, for example. This is likely to generate very high revenues for you because people will have high willingness to pay for the ability to keep their homes and businesses lit.

The MB curve in Figure 16.1 illustrates the marginal benefits associated with electricity generation. Point A represents the marginal benefits associated with your first units of electricity generated per period. Point A lies high up on the MB curve, reflecting the high marginal benefit associated with the first units of electricity produced per period.

Figure 16.1 Marginal Benefits from Electricity Generation

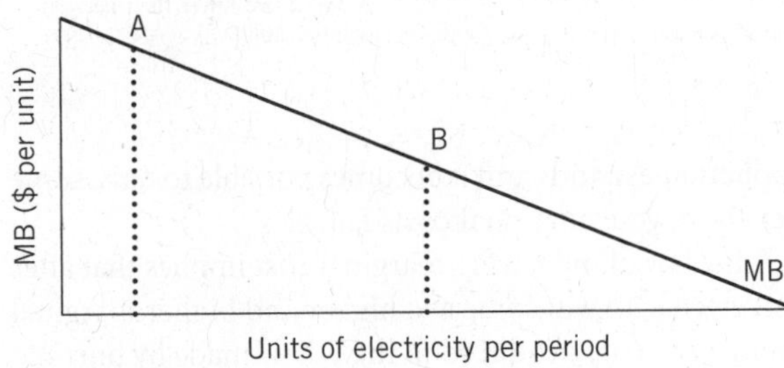

The marginal benefits (MB) from electricity generation include revenue to electricity producers and utility to electricity consumers. Production at point A generates more marginal benefit than the production at point B. The marginal benefits decline as more and more electricity is generated, reflecting the law of diminishing marginal benefits.

You might next provide electricity for the town's streetlights. People value this use of electricity as well, but are not willing to pay as much for streetlight as for lighting their own homes and businesses. As a result, the marginal revenue you earn from selling the second unit of electricity per period is less than that earned from the production of electricity for homes and businesses. As you generate more electricity, your customers will have lower willingness to pay for electricity, and you will earn lower marginal revenues than you did for the first and second units of electricity you produced. Uses of electricity produced between points A and B might include electricity for refrigeration, ovens, or washing machines, or electricity for more rural areas with fewer potential customers. Electricity produced beyond point B might be used for things like lighting nighttime little league baseball games, electricity for heated driveways so people don't have to shovel snow in the winter, or power for midnight movie premier parties. These uses of electricity generate marginal benefits, but these marginal benefits are lower than the marginal benefits of having electricity for refrigeration or washing machines.

Is the marginal benefit curve likely to be the smooth, straight line depicted in Figure 16.1? Probably not, since some activities will cause relatively large changes in marginal benefits, while others will cause relatively small changes. Thus MB curves are likely to be less smooth than the one in Figure 16.1. Regardless of the shape of the MB curve, however, electricity production is subject to the law of diminishing marginal benefits, so the MB curve for electricity is downward-sloping.

Costs of Pollution

The costs of pollution include negative health impacts, climate change, changes in wildlife habitat, environmental degradation, and changes in property values. When your company produces electricity, you pay for coal, hydroelectric dams, nuclear reactors, or wind turbines. You also have to pay the costs of labor to run your plant and install and service your power lines. Figure 16.2 presents the marginal cost curve (MC) for your electricity company. Your initial development of technology and equipment to generate electricity is likely very high, so your MC curve intersects the *y*-axis

Figure 16.2 **Marginal Costs from Electricity Generation**

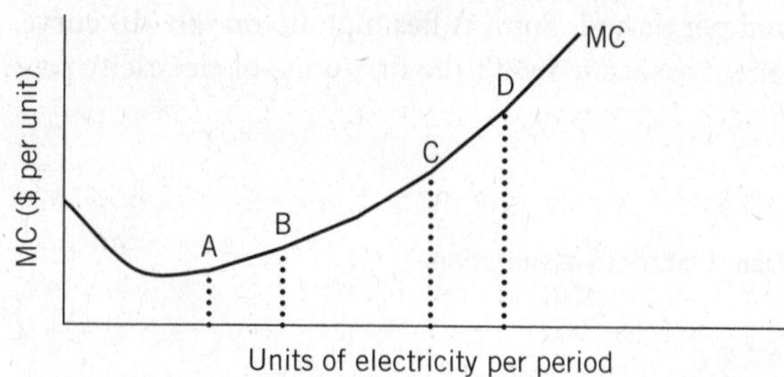

MC represents the marginal cost of generating electricity. The declining marginal costs at low levels of production reflect the impact of specialization. After point A, the law of increasing marginal costs takes hold and marginal costs rise. The marginal costs between points A and B are lower than between points C and D.

at a relatively high level. As production expands and it becomes possible to have some of the tasks of production specialized, your marginal costs fall.

As we learned in Chapter 1, the law of increasing marginal cost implies that after some point, more production of electricity will come at a higher and higher marginal cost. Approximately 45 percent of electricity produced in the U.S. is made by burning coal, so let's assume that you use coal as well. At points A and B, the marginal costs of additional power generation are likely to be small because coal is relatively cheap. As you produce more and more electricity, you move from point B to point C to point D, and the marginal costs rise because the coal you use to generate electricity will be more costly to attain. You might need to dig deeper or more complicated coal mines, for example. Beyond point D, you may need to use more expensive methods of electricity generation like hydro, solar, or nuclear technology, which would further increase the marginal costs of power generation.

The Optimal Level of Pollution in the Market

To determine the optimal level of electricity to produce, you compare the marginal benefits from electricity generation against the marginal costs of electricity generation. The level of electricity you produce will determine the amount of pollution you emit from your power plant. Figure 16.3 combines your marginal benefits and marginal costs of producing electricity. At levels of production below Q*, the marginal benefits gained from producing more electricity exceed the marginal costs incurred, so additional electricity generation increases in your firm's profit. At production levels above Q*, the marginal costs of additional electricity generation are higher than the marginal benefits, so you would lose profits by producing output above Q*.

Figure 16.3 **Marginal Benefits and Costs of Electricity Generation**

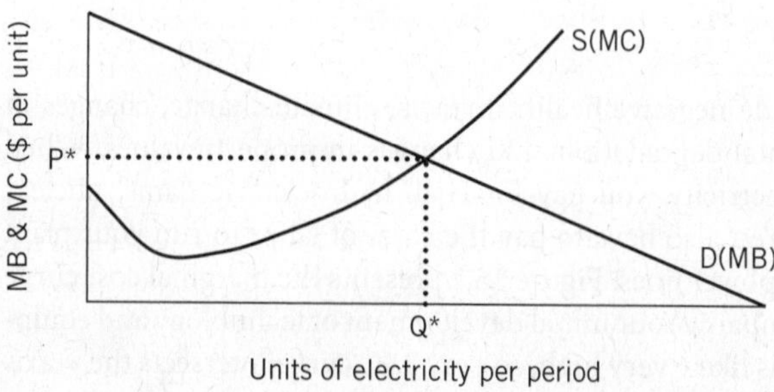

The optimal level of electricity generation for your power plant is Q* since Q* is the output level that equates the marginal benefits and marginal costs of producing electricity for your company. When output is Q*, the price of electricity is P*.

In Chapter 3 we learned that the supply curve for a good or service reflects the marginal cost of producing that good or service, while the demand curve reflects the marginal benefit derived from the good or service. Thus, the marginal benefit and marginal cost curves for electricity in Figure 16.3 represent the demand and supply for electricity. The market equilibrium amount of electricity is Q* and the market price for electricity is P*.

In the traditional marginal benefit-marginal cost model illustrated in Figure 16.3, markets can generate optimal outcomes efficiently by providing incentives for production to occur where marginal benefits equal marginal costs. If you produce too much electricity, your company's profits will fall because you won't sell enough electricity to cover your costs of production. If you produce too little electricity, you'll forego profits that you could earn by producing more electricity.

Unfortunately, activities that cause pollution are associated with a type of market failure that makes the P* and Q* outcomes in Figure 16.3 undesirable from a social efficiency perspective. We learned in Chapter 8 that market failures occur when markets generate inefficient allocations of goods and services. In the case of activities that generate pollution, externalities give rise to market failure.

EXTERNALITIES

Externalities occur when some of the costs or benefits of a trade are imposed on people outside the trade. People outside a trade are called third parties to the trade. For example, when a drug user's habit affects his or her family, the family members are third parties to the trade between the drug user and the drug supplier. When a paper mill emits pollution into a local neighborhood, the people living in the neighborhood are third parties to the trade between the paper mill and paper consumers. **Negative externalities** are costs imposed on third parties. **Positive externalities** are benefits bestowed on third parties.[1]

Negative externalities are costs imposed on third parties.

Positive externalities are benefits bestowed on third parties.

Negative externalities from pollution include negative health impacts and associated health care costs resulting from pollution for those living downstream or downwind from pollution-emitting firms, reductions in property or product value, limits on views because of smog, smoke or exhaust, as well as impacts on climate change.

Negative externalities are not limited to pollution-related situations. For example, noise and traffic from airports or roads can be considered a negative externality by those in affected neighborhoods. Your neighbor's unsightly yard or constantly barking dog, a new building that impedes your view of the mountains or sea, and your wild, older sibling whose reputation made your school teachers apprehensive about you before they even met you are all examples of negative externalities.

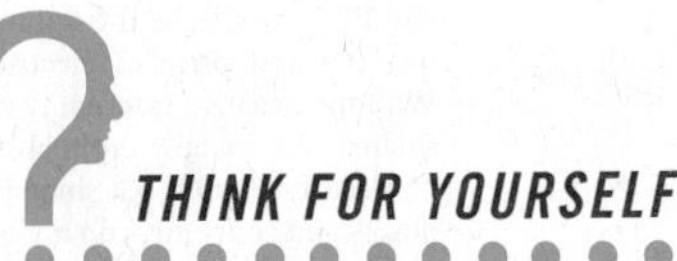

THINK FOR YOURSELF

The use of cell phones while driving is illegal in many locations. Use the concept of negative externalities to explain why. What are some examples of negative externalities arising from cell phone use?

1 Positive externalities are covered in Chapter 17.

We can use your power plant to illustrate the impact of negative externalities. When you burn coal to generate electricity, you emit pollutants through your power plant's smokestack. These pollutants travel downwind to a nearby town. Because the town residents inhale the pollution, consume fish from nearby waters, and consume agricultural products grown on land where the pollutants settle, they are exposed to an array of health problems. The pollution also causes a relative decline in the value of homes in town, because people prefer to live in less polluted areas, all else being equal. On a wider scale, the emissions from your power plant contribute to global climate change.

Because negative externalities impose costs on others, we need to consider those costs in order to determine the optimal level of electricity generation for society as a whole. In Figure 16.3, the optimal level of pollution for your company was found by comparing your company's marginal costs and marginal benefits of electricity production. The marginal costs illustrated in Figure 16.3 do not account for the negative externalities imposed on others. Instead, they are your plant's private marginal costs. **Private marginal costs** ($MC_{private}$) are marginal costs that accrue only to the producers of a good or service. **Social marginal costs** (MC_{social}) are marginal costs that accrue to society as a whole. Social marginal costs include private marginal costs plus the negative externality imposed on others. Mathematically,

Private marginal costs are marginal costs that accrue only to the producers of a good or service.

Social marginal costs are marginal costs that accrue to society as a whole.

$$MC_{social} = MC_{private} + \text{Negative Externality}$$

Figure 16.4 illustrates the impact of negative externalities in our electricity example. The supply curve $S(MC_{private})$ reflects only the marginal costs you bear for electricity production. The supply curve $S(MC_{social})$ reflects your private marginal costs plus the negative externality caused by your power plant.

The difference between $S(MC_{private})$ and $S(MC_{social})$ represents the negative externality generated by electricity production. At low levels of production, the negative

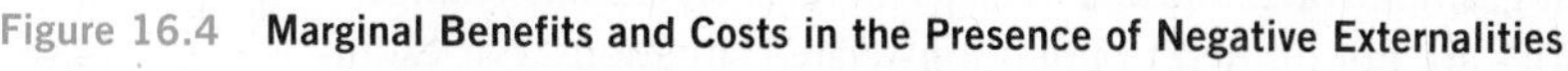

Figure 16.4 **Marginal Benefits and Costs in the Presence of Negative Externalities**

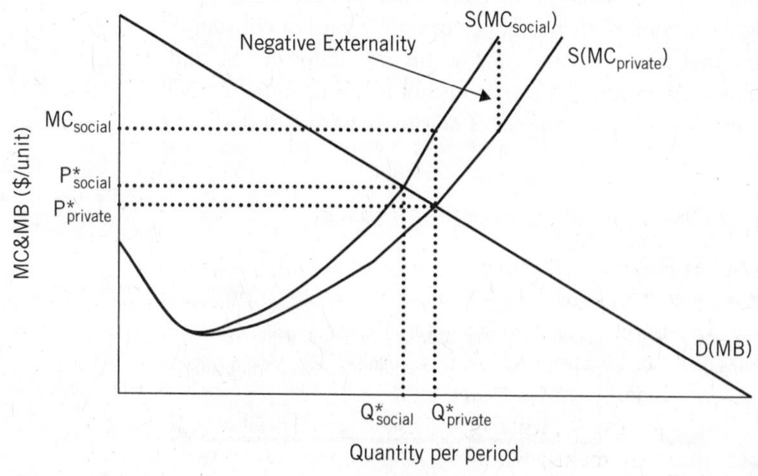

Negative externalities are costs imposed on third parties. The difference between $S(MC_{private})$ and $S(MC_{social})$ represents the negative externality associated with electricity generation. If there were no negative externality, $Q^*_{private}$ and $P^*_{private}$ would be the optimum quantity and price of electricity. With the negative externality considered, the socially optimal level of electricity is Q^*_{social}. Since producers and consumers do not have incentives to consider negative externalities when they buy and sell electricity, the market equilibrium amount of electricity would be $Q^*_{private}$. Without intervention, the market will produce too much electricity from a social efficiency perspective.

externality may be small because the people in nearby towns and the local environment can absorb relatively low levels of pollution with minimal impacts. As your electricity production expands, the size of the negative externality grows because the environment becomes less able to absorb the power plant's emissions and because town residents begin to feel negative health effects at higher levels of pollution exposure.

As the producer of electricity, you have incentive to compare your marginal costs ($MC_{private}$) against your marginal benefits (MB). Given these comparisons, the optimal level of production for you is $Q^*_{private}$. At this level of production, you maximize your profits from electricity production because your marginal benefits of electricity generation are equal to your marginal costs of electricity generation.

Is the level of electricity generation that is optimal for you also optimal for society? To determine the socially optimal quantity of electricity, we need to compare social marginal costs (MC_{social}) against marginal benefits (MB). Point Q^*_{social} illustrates the level of production where the marginal benefits associated with electricity are equal to the social marginal costs. At output levels above Q^*_{social}, society incurs more costs than benefits from electricity production. At output level $Q^*_{private}$, for example, the private marginal cost of electricity is $P^*_{private}$, but the social marginal cost is MC_{social}, so the social marginal costs exceed marginal benefits. In other words, too much electricity is generated relative to the socially optimal amount because you make your production decision based only on private marginal costs rather than on social marginal costs. In the presence of negative externalities, the market produces more than the socially optimal level of pollution. This is why negative externalities represent a type of market failure.

In the real world, the socially optimal level of pollution-generating activities is determined through a combination of science and politics. Much of the work done by the IPCC, for example, seeks to quantify the impact that various levels of greenhouse gas emissions will have on ecosystems as we move into the future. Policymakers use this information to assess the benefits and costs of the array of policies they could enact to reduce greenhouse gas emissions. As one example, climate change was a main topic of discussion of the 2009 G8 Summit. The Group of Eight (G8) consists of Canada, France, Germany, Italy, Japan, Russia, the United Kingdom, the United States, and representatives of the European Union. Representatives meet throughout the year, and leaders of G8 governments attend an annual summit to discuss issues of mutual and global interest. At that meeting, leaders announced a commitment to reduce their greenhouse gas emissions by 80 percent by 2050. However, few developing nations were willing to agree to such cuts as doing so would reduce production and incomes.

APPROACHES TO ENVIRONMENTAL PRESERVATION

We have demonstrated that when the production of goods or services causes negative externalities, a market failure occurs and markets will produce too much pollution than is socially optimal. As a result, we often are faced with choices about how to decrease pollution and preserve the environment. Not surprisingly, engaging in environmental preservation activities generates costs as well as benefits. These costs and benefits do not tend to be distributed evenly, which gives rise to substantial controversy and debate when it comes time to make environmental policy choices.

Command-and-control methods of pollution reduction involve direct government regulation of pollution through taxes or emissions limits.

We can classify environmental policy choices into two primary groups, although they are often used in conjunction with one another. The first, called **command-and-control**, involves direct government regulation of pollution through taxes or emissions limits. The second policy choice is the assignment of property rights to environmental resources.

Command-and-Control

Command-and-control methods of pollution reduction involve the use of pollution taxes and fees as well as quotas or limits on pollution emissions. We discuss each of these pollution reduction methods in the following sections.

Taxes and Fees

The imposition of taxes or fees on polluters is a common method of command-and-control regulation in markets with externalities. Taxes and fees increase production costs so that producers take negative externalities into account when making their production decisions. Ideally, a pollution tax would be set just equal to the negative externality. A tax of that size would make a producer's private marginal cost of production plus the tax equal to the social marginal cost of production.

Figure 16.5 shows the impact of a pollution tax on your power plant. If your marginal cost of producing electricity is $S(MC_{private})$, a tax equal to the negative externality would shift your supply curve upward by the amount of the tax. Your new marginal cost curve would be equal to $S(MC_{social})$. You would then choose to produce Q^*_{social} electricity per period, because that level of output equates your marginal costs and marginal benefits.

Examples of pollution taxes include U.S. federal taxes of about 18 cents per gallon on gasoline and state taxes that average about 30 cents per gallon on gasoline (although a portion of these taxes are for road maintenance). Sweden imposes

Figure 16.5 **Impact of a Pollution Tax on a Market with Negative Externalities**

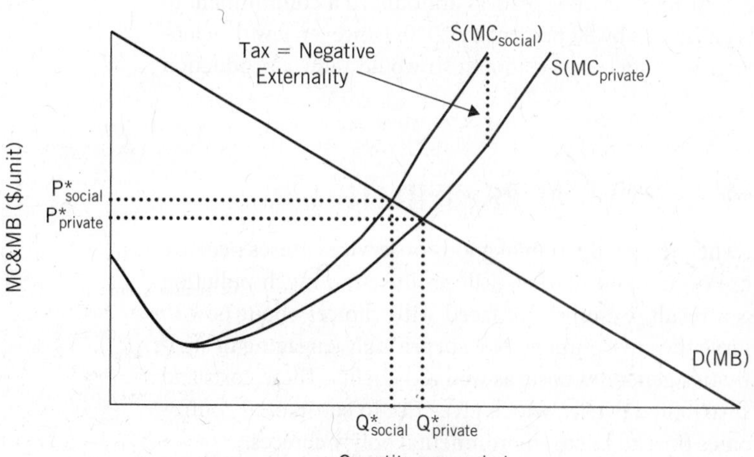

A tax that is equal to the negative externality will cause producers to produce where social marginal costs and marginal benefits are equal. Rather than producing at $Q^*_{private}$, the tax results in Q^*_{social} amount of electricity being produced.

pollution taxes on coal, oil, natural gas, petroleum gas, and aviation fuel. British Columbia imposed a carbon tax on gasoline in 2008.

Emissions Limits

A second command-and-control method is to ban pollutants altogether or to impose emission limits. **Emissions limits** place controls or restrictions on specific sources of pollutant. As one example, the pesticide DDT was widely used during and after World War II to control the spread of malaria, typhus, and other diseases transmitted to humans and livestock by mosquitoes and other insects. Despite its success in disease prevention, growing concern emerged in the 1960s regarding the environmental and human health impacts of widespread DDT use. In 1962, the publication of Rachel Carson's bestselling book, *Silent Spring*, brought widespread attention to negative impacts of DDT. Investigation and congressional hearings on the impacts of DDT ensued, and between 1968 and 1972 DDT was banned from most uses in the United States and other developed nations. Although many public health agencies support the use of DDT as part of malaria prevention in developing nations, DDT use remains highly controversial.

Emissions limits place controls or restrictions on specific sources of pollutants.

Figure 16.6 illustrates the impact of emission limits in our electricity market. Without intervention, you would produce $Q^*_{private}$ electricity per period. If an emissions limit is imposed, you would be required to produce no more than Q_{limit} electricity per period. Ideally, Q_{limit} would be set at the socially efficient level of production. If $Q_{limit} = Q^*_{social}$, the socially optimal amount of electricity would be produced. If the limit is anywhere below Q^*_{social}, as in the case in Figure 16.6 where $Q_{limit} < Q^*_{social}$, society will not maximize the net benefits of electricity generation because we would forego production levels between Q_{limit} and Q^*_{social} where the marginal benefits to society exceed the marginal costs to society. Much of the current controversy over DDT, for example, stems from arguments that the DDT ban and its related policies may set the allowable DDT level too low relative to the socially optimum level.

Figure 16.6 **Impact of Emissions Limits on a Market with Negative Externalities**

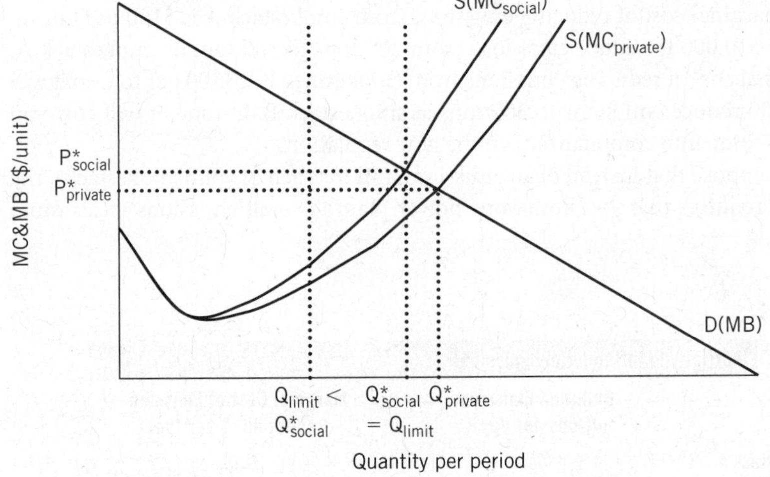

An emissions limit restricts the amount of output that a firm can produce. If the emissions limit (Q_{limit}) is set equal to Q^*_{social}, the socially optimal amount of electricity will be produced. If Q_{limit} is set below Q^*_{social}, too little electricity will be produced from a social efficiency perspective.

DDT Revisited

REUTERS/Roberto Escobar/Landov LLC

Residual Insecticide Spraying for Mosquitoes

According to the World Health Organization (WHO), there are approximately 1 million malaria-caused deaths per year worldwide, mostly among African children under age 5. The most commonly used methods to prevent malaria include the use of insecticide-treated nets and indoor residual spraying of insecticides (IRS). Although nets have demonstrated effectiveness against malaria, the WHO recognizes that nets are not sufficient to effectively combat malaria on their own. Among the 12 pesticides approved by the WHO for IRS use, DDT is generally considered the most cost effective at this time. The implementation of an IRS program using DDT in South Africa in 2000 resulted in a dramatic reduction of malaria cases, and several other African countries have implemented similar programs. The effective use of DDT for IRS has sparked renewed interest in DDT use and has also reignited the debate over whether or not DDT should have a more prominent place in malaria control.

Source: Centers for Disease Control

Even when emissions limits are set at the socially optimal level, it is important to meet those limits in the most cost effective way. Imagine, for example, that you have two smokestacks at your electricity plant, smokestack A and smokestack B. Smokestack A is newer and can be used with relatively cheap pollution control equipment, if necessary. Smokestack B is older and utilizes relatively expensive pollution control equipment.

Table 16.1 illustrates the amount of emissions and the marginal cost of emission reduction at your two smokestacks. At current production levels, your plant emits 400 tons of pollution per day from each smokestack, for a total of 800 tons of pollution emitted per day. Suppose that a new environmental regulation requires you to limit the amount of pollution emitted from each of your smokestacks to no more than 300 tons per day. How much will it cost you to comply with the regulation?

The marginal cost of reducing emissions from smokestack A is $100 per ton, so it will cost $10,000 to reduce emissions from 400 tons to 300 tons at smokestack A. The marginal cost of reducing emissions from smokestack B is $200 per ton, so it will cost $20,000 reduce emissions to 300 tons at smokestack B. In total, it will cost you $30,000 to come into compliance with the new regulation.

Now suppose that instead of an emission limit for each of your smokestacks, the regulation requires that you limit your power plant's overall emissions to no more

Table 16.1 Electricity Plant Pollution Emissions

	Pollution Emissions (tons per day)	Marginal Cost of Emission Reduction ($ per ton)
Smokestack A	400	$100
Smokestack B	400	$200

than 600 tons per day, but it does not specify how you should reach that limit. Given this flexibility, it will be cheaper for you to not buy the expensive pollution control equipment for smokestack B but instead to reduce your emissions by 200 tons per day from smokestack A. Your total cost to meet the more flexible regulation is $20,000. The more flexible regulation allows you to reach the overall emission target at a lower cost, which will translate into smaller price increases passed on to your customers. Setting an overall target or cap on emissions but allowing flexibility on how that target is met is effectively how cap and trade systems work, as we will see in the next section.

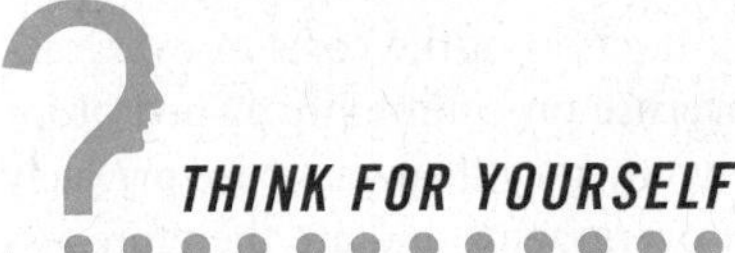

Electric cars are often touted as a means to reduce greenhouse gasses because electric cars tend to produce fewer emissions than traditionally fueled cars. What are the tradeoffs associated with electric cars? How is electricity generated in your area?

Album / Oronoz/NewsCom

Ronald Coase and the Coase Theorem

Ronald Coase (1910–) is a Nobel Prize–winning economist who studies the relationships between property rights and externalities. In 1960, he published "The Problem of Social Cost," in which he argued that the appropriate assignment of property rights can lead to efficient market outcomes in the presence of externalities. In the case of pollution, policymakers can establish either a property right to clean air or a property right to emit pollution. Regardless of how the property right is established, affected parties can then bargain with one another to reallocate resources to their mutual benefit. If the right to clean air is established, polluters can pay property right holders for the costs imposed by pollution. If the right to pollute is established, those desiring clean air can pay polluters to reduce their pollution output. Either way, a socially optimal level of pollution is achieved through bargaining between the affected parties.

Assignment of Property Rights

Property rights are important to environmental preservation for two primary reasons. First, environmental outcomes tend to be different for private versus common property resources. Second, the assignment of tradable property rights to pollute is a means to reduce pollution in a relatively low cost way.

Common Property Resources versus Private Property Resources

Common property resources are resources that are collectively owned. Examples of common property resources include public lands and parks, the air we breathe, much of the Earth's oceans, and the wildlife and other resources contained in these common areas.

Common property resources are resources that are collectively owned.

In a 1968 issue of *Science* magazine, Garrett Hardin published his famous essay, "The Tragedy of the Commons." The essay describes how collective ownership of a resource can lead to overuse and destruction of the resource. The term "**tragedy of the commons**" is now normally used to describe the overuse of common property resources, and Hardin's arguments are frequently applied to environmental preservation issues.

The tragedy of the commons describes how collective ownership of a resource can lead to overuse and destruction of the resource.

Key to understanding the tragedy of the commons is realizing that the benefits and costs of using common property resources are shared among many people. In Hardin's example, a set of cattle owners have access to a common grazing area. Each individual cattle owner has the incentive to put as many cows on the commons as possible, because the cattle owner will receive all of the benefits from having his cows on the commons but will bear only a small fraction of the costs of overgrazing the commons. To prevent overgrazing and overuse on commonly owned property, the government must intervene. Alternatively, when cattle owners use privately owned grazing land, they bear the full burden of overgrazing and are therefore less likely to overgraze the land.

THINK FOR YOURSELF

African elephants are listed as an endangered species, but environmental groups are at odds about how best to preserve the elephants. In particular, People for the Ethical Treatment of Animals supports complete bans on elephant hunting, while the World Wildlife Fund supports safari hunting of elephants. In places where elephant hunting is banned, rural African landowners have a strong incentive to turn to agriculture rather than habitat and species protection. Could allowing elephant hunting be a way to increase the elephant population?

The tragedy of the commons suggests a method of environmental preservation that does not rely on continual government intervention. By moving away from common property resources and toward private property resources, it is possible to move to the socially optimal levels of environmental use. For example, many commercial ocean fisheries use a "race to fish" or "fishing derby" method to manage fish populations. Under this method, legal fishing seasons close once a specific amount of fish is harvested industry-wide. The race to fish encourages individual fishers to harvest as many fish as possible as quickly as possible. Fishers are rewarded for using larger and larger boats, and they have strong incentives to lobby for larger and larger harvest quotas, both of which result in reduced populations of fish. An alternative commercial fishing system allocates an individual transferable quota (ITQ) to harvesters that guarantees the property right to a specified share of the total catch. Fishers can then harvest their quota or sell their ITQ to lower cost producers. According to research published in *Science* magazine, the fraction of fisheries that suffers from fish population collapse is half as large in ITQ-managed fisheries as it is in non-ITQ fisheries.

Dr. Scott M. Lieberman/©AP/ Wide World Photos

The Deadliest Catch

In 2005, the Discovery Channel premiered a new documentary series, *Deadliest Catch.* The show documents the lives of several crab fishing boat crews working in the Bering Sea during two crab fishing seasons each year. The title of the show highlights the extremely dangerous nature of Alaskan crab fishing. Between 2005 and 2008, for example, three of the fishing vessels featured on the show were lost at sea. During the first season of *Deadliest Catch,* fishers operated under fishing derby management, and each boat raced to catch as much crab as possible during the short season. During later seasons, fishing was regulated under an ITQ system. In these later seasons, many small crabbers sold their ITQs to larger producers.

Tradable Pollution Rights

Since 1992, many members of the United Nations have entered into an international treaty on the greenhouse gas emissions, now known as the Kyoto Protocol. In addition to restrictions on emissions, the Kyoto protocol includes an emissions trading or **cap and trade system** for greenhouse gas reduction. Under a cap and trade system, an upper limit or "cap" on total emissions is established. Ideally, this cap is set where the marginal social costs of emissions are just equal to the marginal benefits of emissions. Polluters or other groups are then issued **tradable pollution rights** that give the right to emit a specific amount of pollutant. The total amount of pollution rights issued is equal to the established emissions cap level. If a firm emits more pollution than it has a right to, the firm must buy pollution rights from others. If a firm emits less pollution than it has a right to, it can sell the excess pollution rights to other firms or groups. Through trades of pollution rights, the cap on emissions is reached in a low-cost manner, as those who can reduce emissions cheaply can earn profits by selling their pollution rights to firms with higher costs of reducing emissions. This is similar to the example in Table 16.1, where your power plant reduced pollution more cheaply when it was allowed to choose which smokestack to use to reduce emissions.

In a cap and trade system of pollution reduction, polluters can buy tradable pollution rights that give the right to emit a specific amount of pollutant. The amount of tradable pollution rights issued is capped at the desired pollution level.

The United States has not ratified the Kyoto Protocol. However, tradable pollution rights have existed in the U.S. since the early 1990s, when the Clean Air Act included provisions for sulfur dioxide emissions trading to control Acid Rain. Under the Acid Rain Program, the U.S. Environmental Protection Agency (EPA) held annual auctions of sulfur dioxide pollution permits. At these auctions, pollution rights could be purchased by electric utilities and other producers of air pollution. The permits could then be traded on the Chicago Board of Trade, a commodities exchange similar to the New York Stock Exchange. Researchers estimate that the cost of reducing sulfur dioxide emissions to target levels under the Acid Rain Program was reduced by approximately 80 percent relative to setting emissions limits on individual polluters. In addition, it is common for environmental or community groups to purchase pollution permits but not use them, which reduces pollution levels even further.

The Chicago Climate Exchange is another effort to reduce pollution and greenhouse gas emissions through tradable pollution rights. The Chicago Climate

Exchange assists with the exchange of tradable pollution permits and carbon offsets among individuals and firms that are committed to reduce greenhouse gas emissions. **Carbon offsets** are reductions in emissions of carbon dioxide in one place that offset or replace emissions of carbon dioxide elsewhere. Examples of carbon offsets include investments in wind farms, energy efficiency projects, and reforestation projects. Because there is currently no regulatory cap on carbon emissions, however, demand for carbon emissions permits and carbon offsets is very low. When the Chicago Climate Exchange stopped trading carbon permits at the end of 2010 due to lack of trading volume, the price of a permit to emit 1 ton of carbon dioxide was $0.05.

Carbon offsets are reductions in emissions of carbon dioxide in one place that offset emissions of carbon dioxide made elsewhere.

THINK FOR YOURSELF

One response to global warming has been to promote the use of biofuels like ethanol over traditional fossil fuels. Producers of ethanol, which is primarily made from corn, receive billions of dollars in tax breaks in the U.S. How would a tax break to producers of ethanol affect food prices?

SUMMARY

Economists assess pollution and environmental preservation activities using a cost-benefit framework. Socially optimal levels of pollution occur when the marginal benefits of pollution are equal to the marginal social costs of pollution emission. Because pollution generates externalities, however, markets alone are unlikely to generate socially optimal levels of pollution. Pollution reduction policies include command-and-control methods involving taxes and emissions limits, as well as the assignment of rights to pollute coupled with markets for tradable pollution rights.

KEY CONCEPTS

- Pollution
- Negative externalities
- Positive externalities
- Private marginal costs
- Social marginal costs
- Command-and-control
- Emissions limits
- Common property resources
- Tragedy of the commons
- Cap and trade system
- Tradable pollution rights
- Carbon offsets

DISCUSSION QUESTIONS AND PROBLEMS

1. The accompanying table shows the marginal benefits and costs of paper production and consumption per week:

Quantity Produced/ Consumed (# boxes per week)	Private Marginal Costs (supply)	Private Marginal Benefits (demand)
100	3	7
200	4	6
300	5	5
400	6	4
500	7	3

   a. Based on these private costs and benefits, what will be the equilibrium price of paper?
   b. Based on these private costs and benefits, what will be the equilibrium quantity of paper sold per week?
   c. Are there likely to be negative externalities associated with paper production? If so, describe some of them. If not, why not?
   d. Is the equilibrium quantity of paper sold per week the socially optimal quantity? Why or why not?
   e. Suppose that an economist estimates that the negative externalities associated with paper production average $2.00 per box. She also concludes that there are no positive externalities associated with paper production. What is the socially optimal price of paper? What is the socially optimal quantity of paper sold per week?
   f. Propose a method to get from the market equilibrium level of paper production to the socially optimal level of paper production.

2. Suppose that the electric power industry is made up of two power plants. Each power plant has three smokestacks that emit sulfur dioxide. The accompanying table shows the emissions for the smokestacks at each plant. Suppose also that the EPA wants to decrease total sulfur dioxide emissions from the plants by 1,200 tons per day.

	Emissions (tons per day)	Marginal Cost of Emission Reduction ($ per ton)
Plant 1		
Smokestack 1A	400	$100
Smokestack 1B	400	$200
Smokestack 1C	400	$300

	Emissions (tons per day)	Marginal Cost of Emission Reduction ($ per ton)
Plant 2		
Smokestack 2A	400	$75
Smokestack 2B	400	$125
Smokestack 2C	400	$175

   a. If the sulfur dioxide reduction occurs at the lowest possible cost, what is the total cost of reducing sulfur dioxide emissions by 1,200 tons per day?
   b. If the EPA orders each plant to reduce the amount of emissions from each of their smokestacks by 200 tons per day, what is the total cost of reducing sulfur dioxide emissions by 1,200 tons per day?
   c. If the EPA orders each plant to reduce their total pollution emissions by 600 tons per day but allows each plant to choose how to accomplish this reduction, what is the total cost of reducing sulfur dioxide emissions by 1,200 tons per day?

3. In the mid-19th century, before they were pushed to the brink of extinction, there were between 60 and 100 million American Bison in the U.S. There are an estimated 350,000 American Bison in the wild today, located primarily in a few national parks and other reserves. There are currently about 100 million cattle in the U.S. Using the notion of property rights, can you explain why these populations are so different?

4. "Fair-trade" coffee is sold with a certification that the coffee growers receive a "fair" price for their coffee crop. In order to pay growers more, fair trade coffee is sold at higher prices than "regular" coffee. Using a demand and supply model, describe the tradeoffs associated with fair trade coffee.

5. What are some of the costs and benefits of recycling as a means of environmental preservation?

6. One method of environmental preservation is the use of *moral suasion*. Moral suasion occurs when people are put under pressure to act in a "morally responsible" way in order to reach a particular goal. Can you think of examples of moral suasion being used for environmental preservation? How effective do you think moral suasion is as an environmental policy tool?

MULTIPLE CHOICE QUESTIONS

1. When production of a product causes pollution, in the absence of government intervention the producer's decision
   a. will result in economic equity.
   b. will result in economic efficiency.
   c. will result in economic inefficiency.
   d. will result in less than the socially optimal amount of the good being produced.

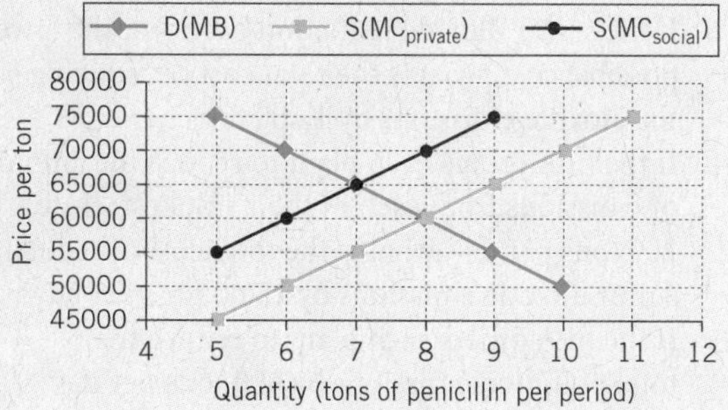

2. Suppose that the production of penicillin generates pollution of the Columbia River, which is gradually killing a valuable fish population. Among other problems, fishermen in the area are experiencing a decline in their incomes. Suppose that the demand and supply of penicillin is shown in the accompanying graph, where $S(MC_{private})$ reflects the private marginal costs of production and $S(MC_{social})$ represents the social marginal costs of production. Based on this information, the size of the negative externality from penicillin production is:
   a. $65,000.
   b. $60,000.
   c. 8 tons.
   d. $70,000.
   e. $10,000.

3. Suppose that the production of penicillin generates pollution of the Columbia River, which is gradually killing a valuable fish population. Among other problems, fishermen in the area are experiencing a decline in their incomes. Suppose that the demand and supply of penicillin is shown in the accompanying graph, where $S(MC_{private})$ reflects the private marginal costs of production and $S(MC_{social})$ represents the social marginal costs of production. Based on this information, without government intervention in the market the equilibrium price and quantity of penicillin produced will be:
   a. $65,000 per ton; 7 tons per period.
   b. $65,000 per ton; 8 tons per period.
   c. $60,000 per ton; 8 tons per period.
   d. $60,000 per ton; 7 tons per period.
   e. $70,000 per ton; 8 tons per period.

4. Suppose that the production of penicillin generates pollution of the Columbia River, which is gradually killing a valuable fish population. Among other problems, fishermen in the area are experiencing a decline in their incomes. Suppose that the demand and supply of penicillin is shown in the accompanying graph, where $S(MC_{private})$ reflects the private marginal costs of production and $S(MC_{social})$ represents the social marginal costs of production. Based on this information, the socially optimal quantity and price of penicillin is:
   a. $65,000 per ton; 7 tons per period.
   b. $65,000 per ton; 8 tons per period.
   c. $60,000 per ton; 8 tons per period.
   d. $60,000 per ton; 7 tons per period.
   e. $70,000 per ton; 8 tons per period.

5. Suppose that Mercury Thermometers, Inc. is currently producing at a point where its private marginal cost of production is $15.00. At this level of production, social marginal cost is $25.00. At the current production level, marginal social benefit is $15.00. Thus, the negative externality associated with Mercury Thermometer, Inc.'s level of production is
   a. $0 because marginal private cost and marginal social cost are equal.
   b. $0 because marginal private cost and marginal social benefit are equal.
   c. $25.00.
   d. $15.00.
   e. $10.00.

	Marginal Cost of Methane Reduction ($)		
Quantity of Methane Reduction (tons/day)	Eddie's Electric Eel Company	U.S. Power and Pollution	Skittish Petroleum
1	0	50	100
2	25	100	150
3	50	150	200
4	75	200	250
5	100	250	300
6	125	300	350
7	150	350	400
8	175	400	450
9	200	450	500
10	225	500	550

6. The accompanying table describes an electric power industry made up of three firms. The numbers in the table show the marginal cost of reducing each ton of methane for each of the three firms. If the EPA reduces total methane emissions for the industry by 6 tons at the lowest possible cost, the cost of methane reduction for the industry would be ______ per day.
   a. $0
   b. $275
   c. $400
   d. $600
   e. $300

7. The table describes an electric power industry made up of three firms. The numbers in the table show the marginal cost of reducing each ton of methane for each of the three firms. The total cost of reducing methane by 3 tons per day for Eddie's Electric Eel Company is ______.
   a. $0.
   b. $50
   c. $75
   d. $150
   e. $300

8. The table describes an electric power industry made up of three firms. The numbers in the table show the marginal cost of reducing each ton of methane for each of the three firms. If the EPA requires each firm to reduce its daily emissions by 2 tons, the total cost of pollution reduction for the whole industry would be ______ per day.
   a. $425
   b. $275
   c. $2,425
   d. $2,605

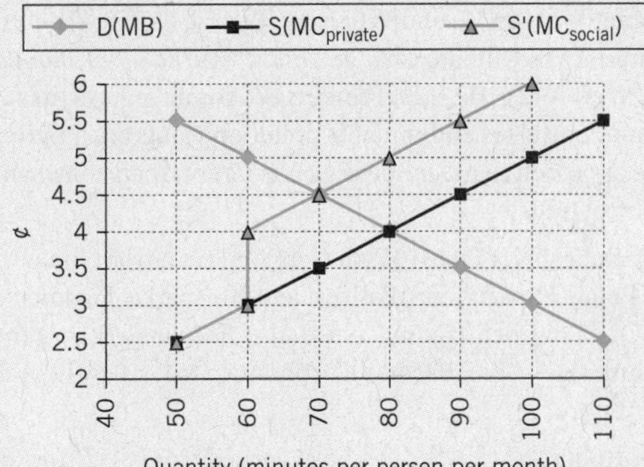

9. Suppose that the accompanying graph illustrates the marginal benefits and costs of cell phone use. $S(MC_{private})$ reflects the private marginal costs of cell phone use and $S(MC_{social})$ represents the social marginal costs of cell phone use. D(MB) represents the marginal benefits of cell phone use. Suppose consumers are currently using 100 minutes per month. The negative externality is
   a. $.01.
   b. $.02.
   c. $.03.
   d. $.04.
   e. $0.00.

10. Suppose that the graph illustrates the marginal benefits and costs of cell phone use. $S(MC_{private})$ reflects the private marginal costs of cell phone use and $S(MC_{social})$ represents the social marginal costs of cell phone use. D(MB) represents the marginal benefits of cell phone use. In the absence of government intervention cell phone use will be
   a. 60 minutes per person per month.
   b. 70 minutes per person per month.
   c. 80 minutes per person per month.
   d. 90 minutes per person per month.
   e. between 70 and 80 minutes per person per month.

ADDITIONAL READINGS AND WEB RESOURCES

Carson, Rachel (1962) *Silent Spring* Houghton Mifflin Company. One of the most popular books of the environmental movement. Presented an investigation of the impact of insecticides and weed killers on the environment and human health.

Coase, Ronald (1960) "The Problem of Social Cost," *Journal of Law and Economics*, 3(2) (October):1-44. Presents Coase's analysis of how property rights can generate socially optimal outcomes in the presence of externalities.

Costello, Christopher, Gaines, Steven D., and Lynham, John (2008) "Can Catch Shares Prevent Fisheries Collapse?" *Science* 321(September):1678–1681. Describes how ITQ fishery management impacts fish populations.

Hardin, Garrett (1968) "The Tragedy of the Commons" *Science* 162(3859):1243–1248. http://www.sciencemag.org/content/162/3859/1243.full. Presents an assessment of how individuals sharing a common resource have less incentive to preserve the resource than if it were owned privately.

Intergovernmental Panel on Climate Change "Climate Change 2007: Synthesis Report Summary for Policymakers." http://www.ipcc.ch/pdf/assessment-report/ar4/syr/ar4_syr_spm.pdf summarizes the IPCC work on climate change.

McKibbin, Warwick J., and Wilcoxen, Peter J. (2002) "The Role of Economics in Climate Change Policy," *Journal of Economic Perspectives*, 16(2):107–129. Presents economic arguments for why emissions taxes and tradable pollution rights are a more feasible approach to greenhouse gas reduction than command-and control policies.

Stavins, Robert N. (1998) "What Can We Learn from the Grand Policy Experiment? Positive and Normative Lessons from SO_2 Allowance Trading." *Journal of Economic Perspectives*, 12(Summer):69–88. Presents an economic analysis of the Acid Rain Program.

Stavins, Robert N. (2005) "Lessons Learned from SO2 Allowance Trading" *Choices Magazine* http://www.choicesmagazine.org/2005-1/environment/2005-1-11.htm. Presents an economic analysis of the Acid Rain Program.

The Intergovernmental Panel on Climate Change website includes climate change assessment reports, data, presentations, and speeches, and other links to climate change information. http://www.ipcc.ch/

The World Health Organization website on the Global Malaria Programme. Includes information on research and control of malaria. World Health Organization, *World Malaria Report 2008*. http://apps.who.int/malaria/

The World Health Organization's position statement on malaria prevention is available at *Global Malaria Programme Position Statement on ITNs*. http://apps.who.int/malaria/docs/itn/ITNspospaperfinal.pdf http://apps.who.int/malaria/mediacentre/wmr2008/

© Catherine Yeulet/iStockphoto

The Economics of Education

After studying this chapter, you should be able to:

- Describe the level and changes in educational attainment over time
- Describe the costs and benefits of education
- Define human capital
- Model the positive externalities associated with education
- Evaluate why some education is publicly provided
- Describe some of the issues surrounding education reform

The typical level of education in the United States has increased markedly over the past half century. Table 17.1 shows that in 1948, only one in three people over 25 years old had completed high school, and only one in 20 had four or more years of college. By 2008, almost a third of those over age 25 had four or more years of college, and only 13 percent had not completed high school.

Why has there been such a change in educational attainment in the U.S.? The answer comes from thinking about costs and benefits. In the 1940s, many well-paying entry-level jobs were available for people with only a high school diploma or less education. Over the past 50 years there has been a decrease in the demand for entry-level workers in well-paying jobs that do not require substantial levels of formal education. At the same time, the demand for more-educated workers has increased relative to the demand for less-educated workers. These demand and supply changes have increased the incentives to obtain higher levels of formal education.

Table 17.1 Highest Level of Educational Attainment of U.S. Population

	1948	1968	1988	2008
Not a high school graduate	65.9%	47.4%	23.7%	13.4%
High school graduate	20.5%	32.5%	38.9%	31.2%
Some college	6.7%	9.6%	17.0%	26.0%
4 or more years college	5.4%	10.5%	20.3%	29.4%

Data includes persons 25 years and older. *Source*: U.S. Census Bureau, Statistical Abstract of the United States.

In addition, the opportunity costs of going to school, which economists measure as the earnings foregone to attend school, fell when well-paying jobs for those with low levels of formal education became less available. In other words, since the 1940s the benefits of increased educational attainment have increased while the opportunity costs of additional educational attainment have decreased.

THE COSTS AND BENEFITS OF EDUCATION

Like any choice, the decision to pursue education involves both costs and benefits. We can use the marginal cost-marginal benefit framework we learned in Chapter 1 to determine the optimal level of education for an individual.

Costs of Education

The costs of education include opportunity costs and direct costs. The opportunity costs of education can be most easily measured as the value of foregone earnings, since time spent in school could have instead been spent working. For those pursuing primary and secondary education (i.e., kindergarten through high school, or K-12 education), the opportunity costs of going to school are low since there are not many jobs for people with less than a high school education. For those pursuing post-secondary education (i.e., vocational school, college, or university), the opportunity costs of going to school tend to be larger since job opportunities and average earnings increase with education.

The direct costs of education include tuition, fees, books, supplies, and other items necessary to attend school. For those in grades K-12, the direct costs of education are very small since education is publically provided free of charge and approximately 90 percent of students in the U.S. attend public K-12 schools.

Table 17.2 summarizes the average costs of attending a U.S. college. The average cost of tuition and fees differs at two-year versus four-year colleges and at public versus private schools. At public two-year colleges, the average annual cost for tuition and fees during 2011–2012 was $2,963. At public four-year colleges, tuition and fees costs were $8,224; they were $28,500 at private four-year colleges. Nationwide, books and supplies cost around $1,200 per year in 2011–2012. The largest cost of attending college is foregone earnings. For those in the first two years of college, foregone earnings are best approximated by the earnings of high school graduates. Adding foregone earnings to the tuition and other costs implies that the total costs for the average student attending a public two-year college are just over $52,000 per year. For those in their third and fourth year of college, foregone earnings are best estimated

Table 17.2 Average College Costs, 2011–2012

	Public Two-Year	Public Four-Year (years 1–2)	Public Four-Year (years 3–4)	Private Four-Year (years 3–4)
Tuition & Fees ($)	2,963	8,224	8,224	28,500
Books & Supplies ($)	1,182	1,168	1,168	1,213
Foregone Earnings ($)	48,332	48,332	58,685	58,685
Total ($)	52,477	57,724	68,077	88,398

Foregone earnings are the largest costs of attending college. Tuition is much higher at private than at public colleges.
Source: The College Board, "2011 Trends in College Pricing." Foregone earnings for 2-year and years 1–2 use high school graduates as comparators. Foregone earnings for years 3–4 use people with some college as comparators.

by the earnings of those with some college but no degree. Those at public four-year colleges give up an average of $68,077 per year during their third and fourth years of school. For those at private four-year colleges, the cost of attendance is almost $90,000 per year.

Marginal Costs

In order to determine the optimal level of schooling for an individual, we need to know the marginal costs of education. The marginal costs of education are the incremental costs associated with obtaining an additional year of education. Figure 17.1 illustrates the marginal costs of education. At low levels of education, the direct cost of additional education is very small, since public K-12 schooling is freely available. The opportunity cost of K-12 education is also relatively low since the job opportunities for workers with low levels of education are limited and do not tend to pay well. Thus, the marginal costs of education at low levels of education like point A in Figure 17.1 are relatively small.

As someone's educational attainment increases, his marginal cost of education also increases. For example, Table 17.2 showed that the foregone earnings for years 1–2 of college were lower than the foregone earnings for years 3–4 of college. Because more education is associated with more job opportunities and higher wages, the more

Figure 17.1 Marginal Costs of Education

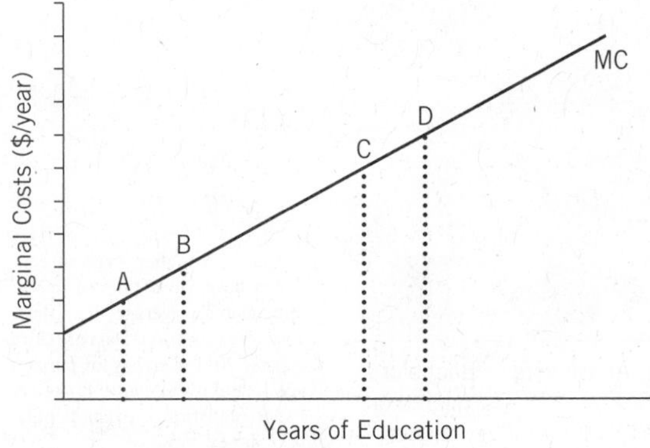

The marginal costs of education (MC) include the direct costs of education (tuition, books, etc.) plus the opportunity costs of education. At low levels of education, such as at points A and B, the marginal cost of education is low since job opportunities are limited. As education level increases, as between points C and D, the marginal cost of education rises, reflecting the law of increasing marginal costs.

education you have, the more earnings you forego to go to school. Beyond the K-12 level, individuals also face the tuition, fees, and other direct costs associated with college or vocational school. Thus, the marginal cost of education between points C and D in Figure 17.1 are higher than the marginal costs between points A and B.

The Benefits of Education

There is a wide array of benefits of increased educational attainment, ranging from job opportunities to pay to health outcomes. Education is one way to increase your human capital. **Human capital** is the acquired skills and knowledge that make you more productive. The demand for workers with more human capital and higher levels of productivity tends to be higher than the demand for workers with less human capital. As a result, workers with more education and human capital tend to have more job opportunities and higher average earnings.

Human Capital: The acquired skills and knowledge that make people more productive.

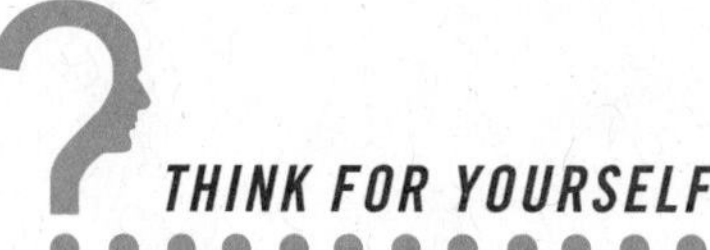

Formal schooling is one way to increase your human capital. What are some other ways to increase your human capital?

Figure 17.2 shows the rates of unemployment for people with different levels of education. The unemployment rate of those with less than a high school diploma was over 14 percent in 2011. High school graduates had lower unemployment rates than high school dropouts. For those with a bachelor's degree or more education, the unemployment rate was 4 percent, or less than one-third as high as those who did not complete high school. Figure 17.2 illustrates that on average, more education is associated with a lower chance of being unemployed.

Figure 17.2 **Educational Attainment and Unemployment**

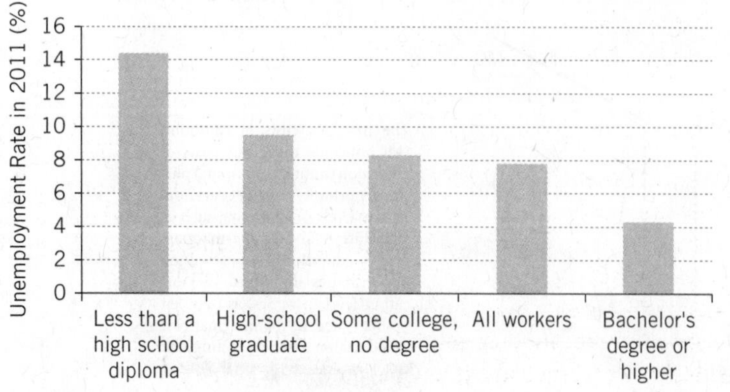

People with higher levels of education have lower rates of unemployment on average than those with less education. Data are third quarter 2011 averages for persons age 25 and over. *Source:* Bureau of Labor Statistics, Current Population Survey.

Figure 17.3 summarizes average earnings by education level. The median weekly earnings of those with a bachelor's degree or more education was over $1,100 in 2011, while high school dropouts' median earnings were under $500 per week and high school graduates' median earnings were about $600 per week. People with less education tend to have lower earnings than people with more education.

Figure 17.3 Education and Earnings

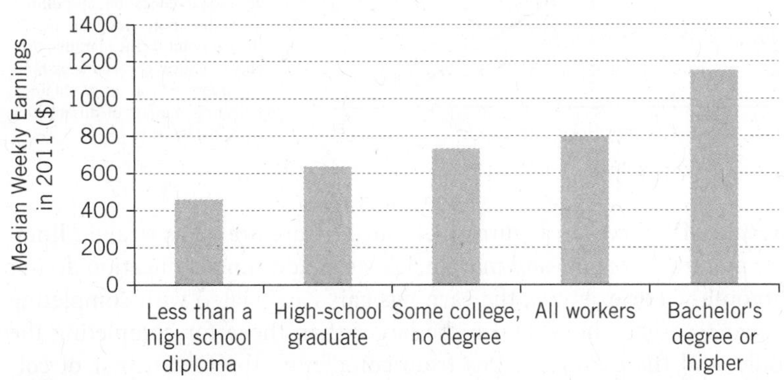

People with higher levels of education have higher earnings than those with less education. Data are third quarter 2011 averages for persons age 25 and over. Earnings are for full-time wage and salary workers. *Source:* Bureau of Labor Statistics, Current Population Survey.

More-educated workers also tend to have higher average nonmonetary compensation than those with less education. Nonmonetary compensation includes things like employer-paid retirement benefits, health insurance, life insurance, and long-term disability insurance. Individuals with higher levels of education also report better health outcomes than those with less education. Those with bachelor's degrees or more education have smoking rates that are less than half of those of their high school graduate peers (10 percent versus 30 percent). People with more education also report higher rates of engaging in exercise than those with lower rates of education. Research also shows that those with higher education are more likely to be employed in jobs where the rates of job satisfaction are high, whereas people with less education are more likely to work in jobs with lower rates of job satisfaction.

The children of people with more education also tend to fare better than their peers. Higher percentages of preschool children of mothers with higher levels of education can recognize their letters, count to 20, write their name, and read storybooks than children of mothers with lower levels of education. Children of parents with higher levels of education are also more likely to participate in after-school activities like sports, scouting, arts, or community service. Clearly the benefits of formal education extend beyond higher average pay and job opportunities.

Marginal Benefits

Figure 17.4 illustrates the marginal benefits of education. The marginal benefits (MB) of additional education when one has low educational attainment are large since learning how to read or do arithmetic, for example, causes drastic improvements in productivity. As additional education is obtained, the marginal benefits are still positive, but are smaller. The marginal benefits of additional education at point A are higher than the marginal benefits of education at point B, which reflects the law of diminishing marginal benefits that we learned about in Chapter 1.

Figure 17.4 **Marginal Benefits of Education**

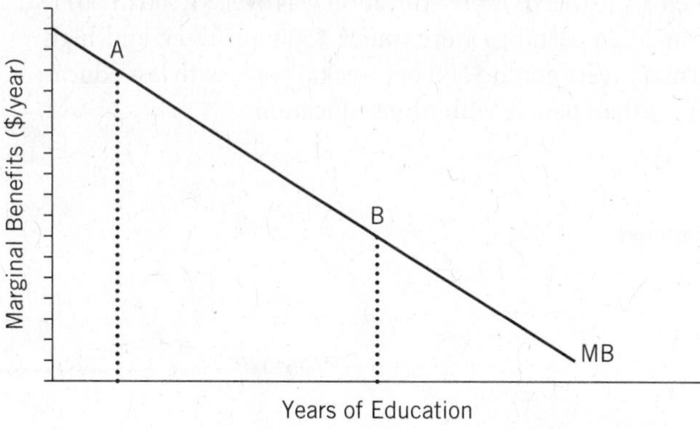

The marginal benefits of education (MB) include the increase in utility, earnings, and job opportunities associated with higher educational attainment. Obtaining additional education at point A generates more marginal benefit than at point B. The marginal benefits of education decline as more and more education is obtained, reflecting the law of diminishing marginal benefits.

The MC and MB curves in Figures 17.1 and 17.4 are drawn as straight lines. In reality, the marginal benefits and marginal costs of additional education do not change so smoothly. For example, the earnings gains associated with completing the twelfth year of high school tend to be larger than those for completing the eleventh grade, and the earnings gains from completing the fourth year of college tend to be higher than those from completing the third year of college. As a general rule, however, the upward slope of the MC curve and the downward slope of the MB curve are reflective of average changes in benefits and costs associated with additional education.

What are the marginal benefits and marginal costs of attending graduate school? What are your plans for after graduation, and how do they relate to these marginal benefits and marginal costs?

THE OPTIMAL LEVEL OF EDUCATION

To determine the optimal level of education, we compare the marginal benefits against the marginal costs of educational attainment. Figure 17.5 combines the marginal benefit and marginal cost curves for education. At levels of education below Q*, such as Q_1, the marginal benefits of more schooling (MB_1) are more than the marginal costs (MC_1), so more schooling would result in increased net benefits from education. At levels of education above Q*, the additional costs incurred from additional schooling are higher than the benefits gained, so a person would be made worse off by additional education. Thus, the optimal level of education is Q*, where the marginal benefits and marginal costs of education are equal to one another.

People make their educational investment decisions by weighing the marginal costs of additional education against the marginal benefits of additional education.

Figure 17.5 **Marginal Costs and Benefits of Education**

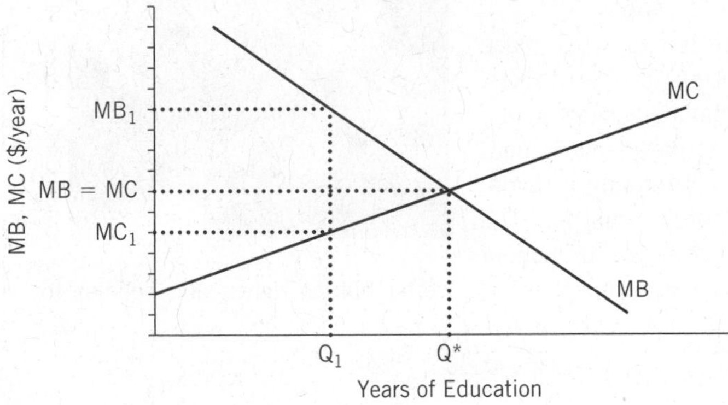

The optimal level of education is Q* since that level of education is where the marginal benefits of education are equal to the marginal costs of education. At levels of education below Q*, such as Q_1, the marginal benefits of additional education (MB_1) are higher than the marginal costs of additional education (MC_1). At education level Q_1, net benefits would be increased by obtaining more schooling.

If you undertake more than Q* education, your well-being will decline because you will not have high enough earnings and utility to cover the marginal costs you incur to obtain more education. If you undertake too little education, you would forego earnings and utility that you could obtain for less than the cost of the educational investment.

The education choice illustrated in Figure 17.5 considers only the individual or private marginal costs and benefits of education. Although this framework for understanding individual education decisions is useful, most economists would argue that it does not account for the impacts of education on society more broadly because education is associated with externalities.

EXTERNALITIES

Externalities occur when some of the costs or benefits of a trade are imposed on people outside the trade. People outside a trade are called "third parties" to the trade. For example, when a parent obtains a college education and as a result her children have better health outcomes, the children are third parties to the trade between the college and the parent. When a paper mill emits pollution into a local neighborhood, the people living in the neighborhood are third parties to the trade between the paper mill and paper consumers. **Positive externalities** are benefits received by third parties, and **negative externalities** are costs imposed on third parties.[1] Education is associated with positive externalities.

Positive externalities are benefits received by third parties.

Negative externalities are costs imposed on third parties.

In addition to the positive externalities associated with education that accrue to children of more educated parents, positive externalities from education include lower crime rates, reduced dependence on welfare and other publicly provided income programs, lower probability of reliance on unemployment compensation, increased rates of voter participation, and the increased social stability that comes with a more educated citizenry.

1 Negative externalities are covered in Chapters 15 and 16.

Education and the Arab Spring

© Joel Carillet/iStockphoto

The Arab Spring was a series of revolutionary protests that took place across the Arab world beginning in late 2010. The protests involved strikes, marches and rallies, and demonstrations against dictatorial governments. Revolutions in Egypt and Tunisia led to the departure of presidents in both countries, to civil war in Libya, and to calls for political reforms in Syria, Yemen, and many other Middle Eastern and North African countries. The underlying reasons for the uprisings are complex, but a large portion of the protesters are well-educated young people calling for government reform, better human rights, and policies to contribute to economic growth in the region.

THINK FOR YOURSELF

What are some activities besides education that generate positive externalities?

Private marginal benefits are marginal benefits that accrue only to individual decision makers.

Social marginal benefits are marginal benefits that accrue to society as a whole.

The marginal cost–marginal benefit framework can help us assess how positive externalities impact education decisions and education policy. Figure 17.6 presents a graphical description of the education decision that incorporates positive externalities. Because positive externalities bestow benefits on third parties, we need to consider the private marginal benefits and social marginal benefits of education. **Private marginal benefits** are marginal benefits that accrue only to the individuals obtaining education. In Figure 17.6, private marginal benefits are labeled $MB_{private}$.

Social marginal benefits are marginal benefits that accrue to society as a whole. In Figure 17.6, the curve MB_{social} reflects the social marginal benefits of education. Social marginal benefits include private marginal benefits plus the positive externality bestowed on others. The positive externality is shown as the vertical distance between $MB_{private}$ and MB_{social} in Figure 17.6.

$$MB_{social} = MB_{private} + \text{External Benefits}$$

Notice that the size of the positive externality changes as the level of education changes. At low levels of education, the positive externality is likely to be large because having basic literacy and social skills has the largest impact on crime rates, job readiness, and social stability. As educational attainment expands, the positive externality from education becomes smaller because the reduction in crime and increases in social stability are greater for completing lower levels of education than for completing higher levels of education. For example, the crime rate among high school dropouts is much higher than among high school graduates, but the crime rate among high school graduates is not much higher than among those who attend college.

When deciding on how many years of education to pursue, individuals have incentives to compare only the private marginal benefits of education ($MB_{private}$)

Figure 17.6 **Marginal Costs and Benefits in the Presence of Positive Externalities**

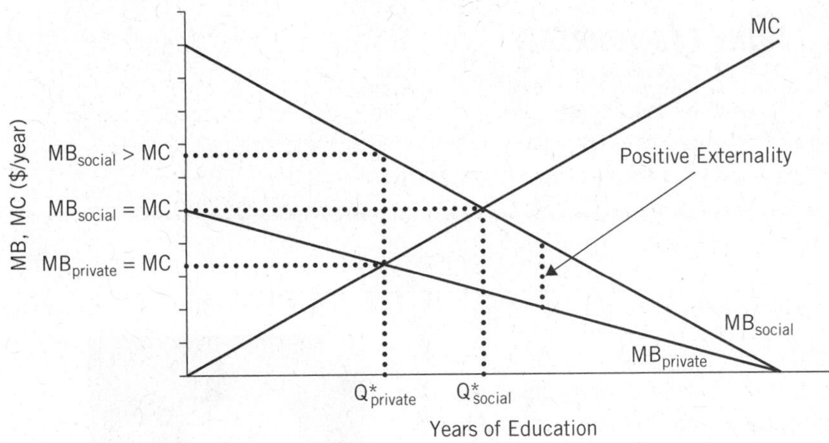

Positive externalities are benefits received by third parties. The difference between MB_{social} and $MB_{private}$ represents the positive externality associated with education. If there were no positive externality, $Q^*_{private}$ would be the optimal quantity of educational attainment. With the positive externalities considered, the socially optimal level of education is Q^*_{social}. Since people do not have incentives to consider positive externalities when they obtain education, the market-determined amount of education would be $Q^*_{private}$. Without intervention, people will undertake too little education from a social efficiency perspective.

against the marginal costs of education (MC). Using this comparison, the optimal level education for a given individual is $Q^*_{private}$ because that is the level of education where $MB_{private}$ = MC.

Is $Q^*_{private}$ the optimal level of education for society overall? To determine the socially optimal level of education, we need to compare the social marginal benefits of education (MB_{social}) against the marginal costs (MC). Point Q^*_{social} illustrates the level of education where the social marginal benefits of education are equal to the marginal costs of education. At levels of education below Q^*_{social}, the social marginal benefits of additional schooling are more than the marginal costs, so more schooling would result in increased net benefits for society. At education level $Q^*_{private}$, for example, the social marginal benefits of education are more than the marginal costs of education. At levels of education above Q^*_{social}, the marginal costs of education are higher than the social marginal benefits of education.

The positive externalities associated with education imply that a purely private market for education would generate a market failure. At the optimal level of education for you as an individual ($Q^*_{private}$), the social marginal benefits of more education exceed the marginal costs of more education. In other words, in the presence of positive externalities, too little education will be chosen relative to the socially optimal amount. Left to its own devices, a purely private market for education will result in less education than is socially optimal.

Why Is Education Publicly Provided?

Economists and policymakers have long recognized the positive externalities and resulting market failure associated with purely private educational markets. Because the optimal private level of educational attainment is lower than the socially optimal level of educational attainment, many societies provide incentives to encourage people to pursue education. Governments subsidize education by providing free primary and secondary schooling, by funding low-interest student loan programs, and by providing grants and other financial aid to decrease the private costs of attending college. The fact that the amount of subsidy for university-level education is smaller than for K-12 education reflects the relatively smaller size of the positive externality from university-level education relative to primary and secondary education.

THINK FOR YOURSELF

Why is the positive externality associated with education smaller for university-level education than for K-12 education? Use your answer to explain why attending a public K-12 school is free, but attending a public university involves paying tuition.

Arthur Cecil Pigou and Externalities

Arthur Cecil Pigou (1877–1959) was a British economist who helped establish the school of economics at the University of Cambridge. He was highly influential in developing the idea of market failure and in the study of welfare economics, the branch of economics that focuses on economic well-being and social welfare. Pigou developed the concept of economic externalities. A tax that is imposed on a market with negative externalities in order to move the market to the social optimum is called a Pigouvian tax. In a market with positive externalities, a Pigouvian subsidy can be used to move to the socially efficient outcome. Pigou's ideas continue to influence economists and policymakers around the world on issues such as financial regulation, environmental economics, health care, and education policy.

© Mary Evans Picture Library/The Image Works

EDUCATION SPENDING AND EDUCATION OUTCOMES

Education generates positive externalities for society. As a result, many governments allocate large budgets to education at K-12 and university levels in order to increase people's incentives to obtain more schooling. In this section, we examine the levels and changes in spending on public education in the United States and ask the natural question of whether we are getting the maximum benefit from this spending.

Education Spending

Spending per student in the U.S. has risen rapidly over the last 50 years. Figure 17.7 shows the spending on public K-12 education over the past half century, adjusted to 2011 dollar values. In 1961, the U.S. spent the equivalent of $3,000 per student per year for public education expenses, including classrooms and buildings, salaries, and maintenance. In 2011, the amount spent per student was nearly $12,000. Even after adjusting for inflation, we spend almost four times more per student today than we did 50 years ago.

Why has school spending increased so rapidly? There are several explanations. In 1960, average class sizes in public schools in the U.S. were close to 30 students per teacher. Today, the average class size is closer to 15 students per teacher. Smaller classes mean more spending on teacher salaries, classrooms, and associated support personnel. A second explanation for the increase in spending is the increased integration of special needs students into public schools. In the mid-1970s, only 8 percent of students enrolled in U.S. primary and secondary schools were served in special needs programs. Today, that number is closer to 14 percent. Because special needs students tend to require additional resources and support, increased integration of

Figure 17.7 **Inflation-adjusted U.S. Per Pupil Spending on K-12 Public Education**

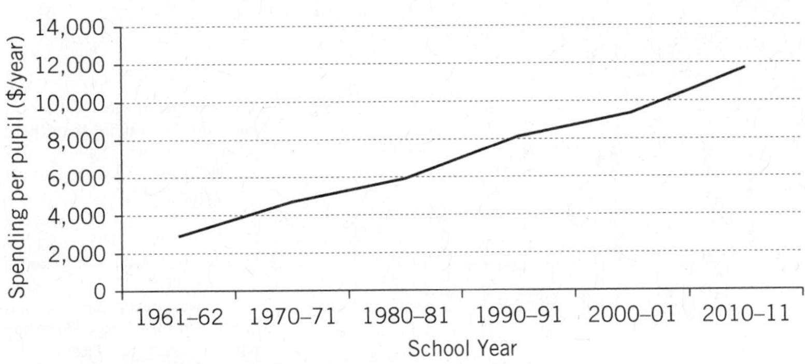

U.S. per-pupil spending on education has risen steadily since the 1960s. After adjusting for inflation, the U.S. spent an average of $3,000 per pupil per year for K-12 public education in 1961, but spent $12,000 per pupil per year for K-12 public education in 2011. *Source:* National Center for Education Statistics. Spending is for public elementary and secondary schools and is measured in inflation-adjusted dollars (2011 $ values).

special needs students generates additional education costs. A third explanation for the increase in spending comes from increased expenditure on administrators and support personnel in the public school system. In 1960, the percent of total spending on public K-12 education that went to administration was 3.4 percent; today that figure is closer to 7 percent.

Education Outcomes

People sometimes argue that we need to spend more on public education in the U.S. in order to generate better outcomes for students and improve their educational competitiveness in the global economy. This raises a natural question of whether increased spending on education in the U.S. over the past 50 years has generated improved student outcomes.

Research does not uniformly support the idea that more spending on education generates better student performance. Various measures of student performance, including graduation rates and standardized test scores, indicate very little, if any, improvements in student performance since the 1970s. Researchers who have studied the effect of increased per-pupil spending on education outcomes have found inconsistent results.

Figure 17.8 shows the average test scores for standardized tests of reading skills over time for U.S. 9-, 13-, and 17-year-olds. Despite the large increase in spending

Figure 17.8 **U.S. Student Reading Test Scores**

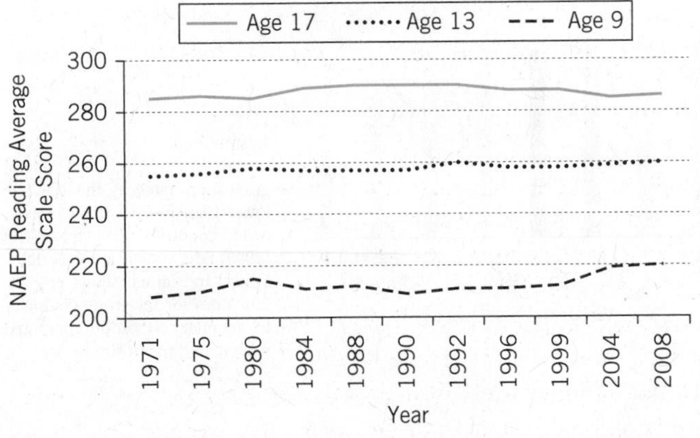

Average test scores in reading have been steady since the 1970s despite increased spending on education. *Source:* U.S. Department of Education, Institute of Education Sciences, National Center for Education Statistics, National Assessment of Educational Progress (NAEP), various years, 1971–2008 Long-Term Trend Reading Assessments.

Figure 17.9 **International Comparisons of Spending on Education (2006)**

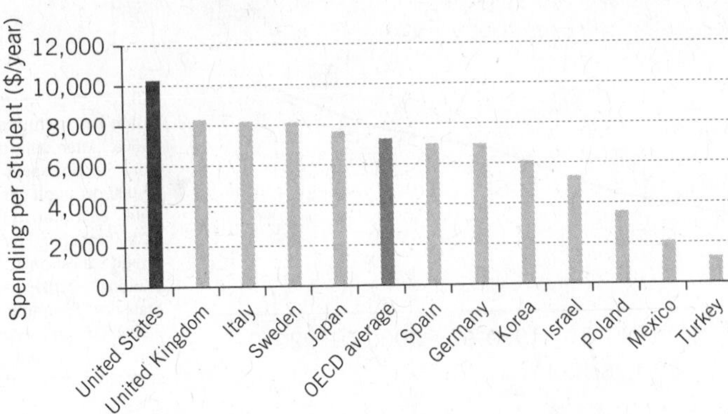

The U.S. spends more money per pupil for education than most other developed nations. The average spending per student per year among OECD countries was $7,000 in 2006. That same year, the U.S. spent over $10,000 per student *Source:* OECD (2009) Education at a Glance 2009: OECD Indicators. Shows average expenditure per student for primary, secondary, and post-secondary non-tertiary education in U.S. dollar equivalents.

per student since 1970, student performance on standardized tests of reading has not changed. Slightly better results hold for mathematics performance, with unchanged performance on standardized math tests for 17-year-olds, slightly higher scores for 13-year-olds, and higher scores for 9-year-olds since 1970.

International comparisons of student performance also indicate that the U.S. educational system may not be delivering the most value for our money. Figure 17.9 shows average per-pupil spending per year for several developed countries in the Organization for Economic Cooperation and Development (OECD). The OECD is a group of democratic and market-based economies. Spending on primary and secondary education in the U.S. is much higher than in similar countries. In 2006, the average amount spent per pupil in OECD countries was $7,000. That same year, U.S. spending per pupil was over $10,000. The U.S. spends roughly 30 percent more per student per year than the average OECD country.

At the same time, student performance in the U.S. is worse than in similar countries. U.S. fourth and eighth grade students in math and science perform worse than students in many Asian and European nations, and graduation rates are lower in the U.S. than in other developed nations. Figure 17.10 shows the high school graduation

Figure 17.10 **International High School Graduation Rates (2007)**

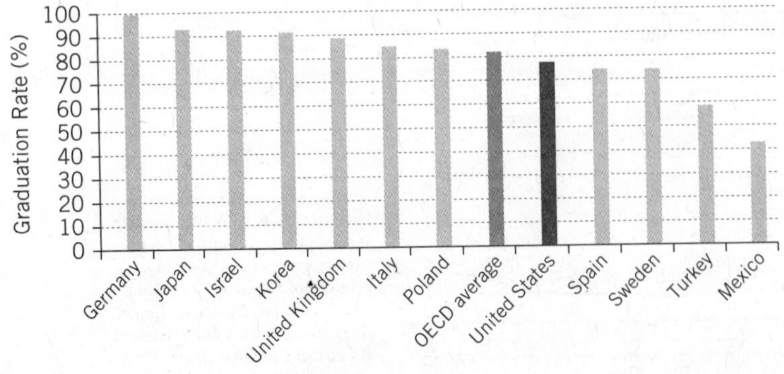

Despite higher spending on education in the U.S., high school graduation rates in the U.S. are lower than in many other developed countries. *Source:* OECD (2009) Education at a Glance 2009: OECD Indicators. Shows graduation rates for first-time graduates of secondary education, computed relative to those of similar age.

rates in several OECD countries in 2007. The U.S. graduation rate of 78 percent is lower than the OECD average of 82 percent and is much lower than in countries like Germany, Japan, Korea, and the United Kingdom.

EDUCATION REFORM

Given that increased spending has not seemed to generate better educational outcomes, the educational system in the U.S. is widely criticized and calls for reform are common. Two types of school reform frequently proposed are changes in the degree of choice that parents have over where their children attend public school and changes in pay structures for teachers.

School Choice

Reform programs that focus on school choice emphasize the value of competition in providing incentives for teachers and administrators to be as productive as possible with their resources. When parents have a choice about where their children attend school, schools must compete for those students and the resources that come with them, presumably by increasing school quality.

Two widely used school choice programs are vouchers and charter schools. Voucher programs provide parents with a voucher worth the cost of educating their student in a public school. Parents can use the vouchers to move their children from a failing public school into another school. Charter schools provide increased competition and choice by allowing parents or other groups to develop new schools in their school district using the resources that would have otherwise gone to regular public schools. Because charter schools are run by private citizens or citizen groups, charter schools are similar to private schools except that they are funded by the government.

How effective have these school choice programs been? Because the programs are relatively new and have been implemented on a small scale, data on their effectiveness is still somewhat limited. Researchers who have investigated the programs have found mixed results. Some studies find that voucher programs improve students' test scores; others find little evidence that the programs generate any systematic academic benefit. Research shows that schools with choice-based programs tend to place more value on teacher effort, teacher independence, the quality of teachers' education, and teachers' math and science skills.

THINK FOR YOURSELF

Many economists study peer effects in education. Peer effects are the positive or negative impacts of students' peers on their own academic performance. Students with high-achieving classmates tend to perform better than students with low-achieving classmates. How might school choice programs influence peer effects?

Changes in Teacher's Pay

A second set of school reform proposals focuses on pay levels and pay structures for teachers. Teachers' pay tends to be much lower than that of other professionals with similar levels of education. Low teacher's pay raises the opportunity cost of being a teacher, since the pay in the next best alternative job is relatively higher. As the opportunity cost of entering the teaching profession rises, people with better options will choose not to be teachers. People with better options are likely to be those that, on average, have higher quality training. Thus, when we expand the hiring of teachers to generate smaller class sizes but do not concurrently increase teacher's pay, we actually generate a shortage of high-quality teachers.

Many economists have examined the labor market choices and characteristics of teachers and potential teachers. Their research indicates that average teacher quality, as measured by undergraduate college selectivity, experience, and subject matter expertise, has fallen since the 1970s. Part of this decline in teacher quality comes because people with better training and higher skills appear to be opting for other, higher-paying professions instead of teaching. When public schools have increased teacher salaries in an effort to recruit better teachers, they tend to attract higher quality applicants. Given these outcomes, reform proposals often call for increased pay for teachers in order to attract the best and brightest into the profession.

Some calls for reforms in teacher's pay also include a structure to pay teachers based on individual merit rather than on seniority or education level. However, teachers' unions tend to favor pay structures based on seniority. Seniority-based pay structures can generate perverse outcomes where weak but more experienced teachers are paid more than better teachers with less experience. As you might guess, changes in teachers' pay structures are highly contentious, and large-scale pay reform has not been implemented.

SUMMARY

Educational attainment is one of the most important investments that individuals, families, and societies make. More education is associated with higher productivity, more job opportunities, and higher earnings. Like any choice, the decision to invest in education involves costs as well as benefits. Because education is associated with positive externalities, a purely private educational system would result in too little educational attainment from a social efficiency perspective. Governments around the world subsidize education in order to move toward socially optimal levels of educational attainment.

Student performance and achievement in the U.S. have not systematically improved since the 1970s, despite dramatically increased spending per student. Indeed, student performance in the U.S. has fallen below that of our peers internationally, raising concern about our ability to compete in an increasingly global marketplace. Proposals for education reform include school choice programs, raising teachers' pay, and instituting merit-based rather than seniority-based pay systems.

KEY CONCEPTS

- Human capital
- Positive externalities
- Negative externalities
- Private marginal benefits
- Social marginal benefits

DISCUSSION QUESTIONS AND PROBLEMS

1. Would a purely private market for education be socially efficient? Why or why not?
2. Will we improve K-12 education if we increase spending on K-12 education? Why or why not?
3. Using the concept of positive externalities, explain why most students are required to obtain vaccinations before they are allowed to attend public school.
4. Why is obtaining a private college education more expensive on average than obtaining a public college education?
5. The accompanying table shows the marginal private benefit, marginal social benefit, and marginal private cost for you to attend a local university.

Years of University Education	Marginal Costs (MC)	Private Marginal Benefits ($MB_{private}$)	Social Marginal Benefits (MB_{social})
0	2000	17000	29000
1	3000	15000	24000
2	4000	13000	20000
3	5000	11000	17000
4	6000	9000	14000
5	7000	7000	11000
6	8000	5000	8000
7	9000	3000	5000
8	10000	1000	2000

a. Why does the marginal private cost of education rise as years of education rises?
b. Why does the marginal private benefit fall as years of education rises?
c. Why do the private marginal benefits of education differ from the social marginal benefits of education?
d. What happens to the size of the positive externality associated with education as years of education increases? Why?
e. If this education market were purely private, what would be the optimal number of years of education for you to obtain?
f. What is the socially optimal number of years of education for you to obtain?
g. What are some methods that society uses to get from the private optimum level of education to the socially optimum level of education?

MULTIPLE CHOICE QUESTIONS

1. The economic argument that it is in society's best economic interest for taxpayers (even those without children) to pay for the education of other people's children is
   a. the positive marginal benefit argument.
   b. the positive externalities argument.
   c. the positive marginal cost argument.
   d. the moral obligation argument.
2. From an economics perspective,
   a. there should be no government intervention in the education market.
   b. government involvement in education is often justified because education is associated with positive externalities.
   c. we should not strive for efficiency when evaluating education activities.
   d. government involvement in education helps eliminate the negative externalities associated with education.

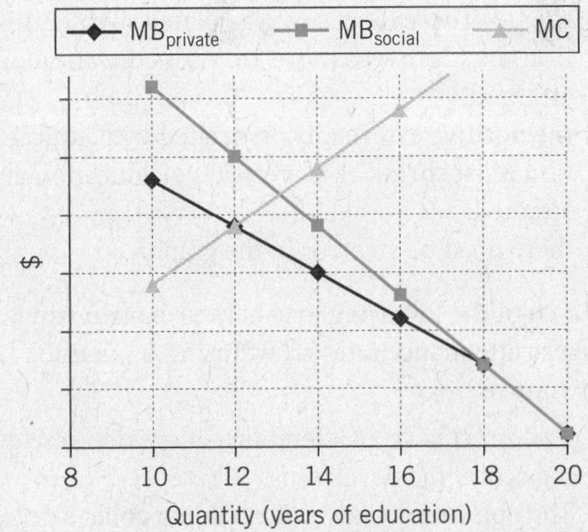

3. The accompanying graph shows the market for education, where MC represents marginal costs of education, $MB_{private}$ is the private marginal benefits of education, and MB_{social} is the social demand curve and represents the social marginal

benefits of education. Given the situation depicted in the graph,

a. without intervention, the market will generate the socially optimal level of education.
b. without intervention, the market will generate too great a level of education from a social efficiency perspective.
c. without intervention, the market will generate too low a level of education from a social efficiency perspective.
d. without intervention, the market won't generate any education production.

4. Using the graph above,

a. the private optimal level of education is 12 years.
b. the private optimal level of education is 13 years.
c. the private optimal level of education is 18 years.
d. the private optimal level of education is 20 years.
e. the private optimal level of education cannot be determined without knowing the dollar values on the vertical axis.

5. Using the graph above, the closing gap between $MB_{private}$ and MB_{social} as years of education increases implies that

a. the negative externality associated with education must grow as more years of education are attained.
b. the negative externality associated with education must shrink as more years of education are attained.
c. the positive externality associated with education must grow as more years of education are attained.
d. the positive externality associated with education must shrink as more years of education are attained.
e. there must be an error in the graph.

6. Which of the following may help to explain why college attendance rates grow during economic downturns?

a. The direct costs of attending college decrease during economic downturns.
b. The opportunity costs of attending college decrease during economic downturns.
c. The probability of being unemployed for college grads is lower than for noncollege graduates.
d. Both a and c
e. Both b and c

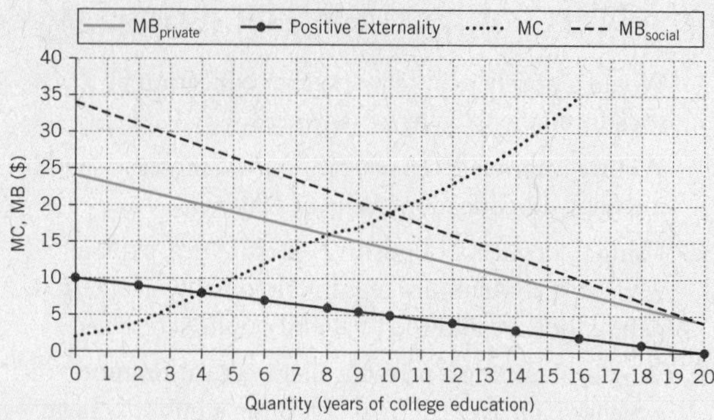

7. Cameron is a bright high school senior who is thinking about going to college. The accompanying figure illustrates the marginal benefits and marginal costs of going to college. Cameron's community derives benefits from Cameron's education, as illustrated by the positive externality curve above. Given this information, the socially optimal amount of college for Cameron to attain is

a. 0 years.
b. 4 years.
c. 8 years.
d. 10 years.
e. 20 years.

8. Cameron is a bright high school senior who is thinking about going to college. The figure illustrates the marginal benefits and marginal costs of going to college. Cameron's community derives benefits from Cameron's education, as illustrated by the positive externality curve above. Given this information, the privately optimal quantity of college for Cameron to attain is

a. 0 years.
b. 4 years.
c. 8 years.
d. 10 years.
e. 20 years.

9. Cameron is a bright high school senior who is thinking about going to college. The figure illustrates the marginal benefits and marginal costs of going to college. Cameron's community derives benefits from Cameron's education, as illustrated by the positive externality curve above. Given this information, if the community wants Cameron to obtain the socially optimal quantity of college, they could

a. impose a tax on Cameron to help pay for his schooling.

b. provide a subsidy to Cameron to help pay for his schooling.
c. impose a restriction on the number of years that Cameron can attend school.
d. do nothing, because Cameron will choose with the socially optimal quantity of education without their intervention.

10. Which of the following scenarios would you expect to yield the greatest private marginal benefit?
a. Bob, who is a slob, takes a class in organization.
b. Art, who is smart, returns to school to obtain his second Bachelor's degree.
c. Suzy Q, who is two, learns to talk.
d. Little Pete, who is sweet, learns to cook from his grandma.
e. Your future spouse, who lays around the house, learns to do laundry.

ADDITIONAL READINGS AND WEB RESOURCES

Bryner, Jenna (2007) "Survey Reveals Most Satisfying Jobs," presents a summary of the job satisfaction responses from 2006 General Social Survey (GSS) at the National Opinion Research Center at the University of Chicago. Available at: http://www.livescience.com/health/070417_job_satisfaction.html

Cullen, Julie Berry, Jacob, Brian A., and Levitt, Steven (2006) "The Effect of School Choice on Participants: Evidence from Randomized Lotteries," *Econometrica* 74(5) (September):1191–1230. Presents research evidence on the impact of school choice programs.

Figlio, David N. (1997) "Teacher Salaries and Teacher Quality," *Economics Letters* 55(2) (August): 267–271. Presents research on the relationships between teacher pay and teacher quality.

Hanushek, Eric A., and Jorgenson, Dale W., ed. (1996) *Improving America's Schools: The Role of Incentives*, Washington DC: National Academy Press. A compilation of research papers focusing on educational outcomes and education reform.

Hanushek, Eric A. (1996) "School Resources and Student Performance," in Gary Burtless, ed., *Does Money Matter? The Effect of School Resources on Student Achievement and Adult Success*, Washington, DC: Brookings Institution Press. Presents information on the relationship between school spending and educational outcomes.

Hedges, Larry V., and Greenwald, Rob (1996) "Have Times Changed? The Relation Between School Resources and Student Performance," in Gary Burtless, ed., *Does Money Matter? The Effect of School Resources on Student Achievement and Adult Success*, Washington, DC: Brookings Institution Press. Presents information on the relationship between school spending and educational outcomes.

Hoxby, Caroline M. (2002) "Would School Choice Change the Teaching Profession?" *The Journal of Human Resources*, 37(4) (Autumn):846–891. Presents research on whether school choice policies impact the demand for teachers and the types of teachers demanded.

Rouse, Cecilia Elena (1998) "Private School Vouchers and Student Achievement: An Evaluation of the Milwaukee Parental Choice Program," *The Quarterly Journal of Economics*, 113(2) (May): 553–602. Presents research on the impacts of school voucher programs on student educational outcomes.

Stoddard, Christiana (2003) "Why Has the Number of Teachers Per Student Risen While Teacher Quality Has Declined?: The Role of Changes in the Labor Market For Women," *Journal of Urban Economics*, 53(3) (May):458–481. Presents research on how the opportunity cost of being a teacher influences who selects into the teaching profession.

Stoddard, Christiana (2009) "Why Did Education Become Publicly Funded? Evidence from the Nineteenth Century Growth of Public Primary Schooling in the United States," *Journal of Economic History*, 69(1) (March):172-202. Presents evidence on the growth in public schooling in the U.S.

The College Board's "Education Pays" website includes information on the earnings and other benefits associated with higher education. http://trends.collegeboard.org/education_pays

The Institute of Education Sciences is the research arm of the U.S. Department of Education. Their mission is to provide data and research for those interested in education policy. http://ies.ed.gov/

The U.S. Department of Education website provides information on education legislation, outcomes, and policies for all levels of education in the U.S. www.ed.gov

The Koret Task Force on K-12 Education at the Hoover Institution of Stanford University focuses on education policy. Their website includes many presentations on education policy. http://www.hoover.org/taskforces/education

The National Center for Education Statistics is the primary federal entity for collecting and analyzing data related to U.S. and international education. www.nces.ed.gov.

The National Center for Education Digest of Education Statistics presents data on student enrollment, teacher/student ratios, and spending on public schools in the U.S. http://nces.ed.gov/programs/digest

The Organization for Economic Cooperation and Development (OECD) Education at a Glance reports include annual comparisons of spending on education and educational outcomes among OECD member countries. http://www.oecd.org/dataoecd/42/21/43638321.pdf

Chapter 17 Appendix

Education as an Investment: Present and Future Values

Investments involve costs borne today in exchange for benefits received in the future.

Now that we have an overview of the costs and benefits of additional educational attainment, we need to understand that obtaining additional education represents an investment. **Investments** involve costs that are borne in the present in exchange for benefits that come in the future. When you attend college, you pay tuition, buy books, and give up earnings that you could have had otherwise in order to obtain increased job opportunities, potential earnings, and other benefits that come in the future.

Present value tells us what a payment in the future is worth today.

How do we compare benefits and costs today against benefits and costs in the future? The concept of **present value** allows us to do this. Present value tells us what a payment in the future is worth today, after taking into account inflation, interest, and other factors that affect the value of money over time.

Time preference describes the idea that people prefer money in the present more than money in the future.

Which of the following would you prefer: $1,000 today or $1,000 one year from now? The $1,000 today is more valuable for several reasons. First, you could put the $1,000 in a savings or other investment account and earn interest on it so that in one year you would have more than $1,000. Second, inflation will erode the purchasing power of $1,000 over the course of a year so that $1,000 can buy less in a year than it can buy today. Third, it is risky to wait for the payment. Finally, the degree to which you prefer consumption in the present more than in the future will influence your present value calculations. Economists use the term **time preference** to describe the notion that people prefer money in the present more than in the future. Indeed, many of us are willing to pay for our time preference by borrowing to have access to money today and paying interest in exchange for it. Economists tend to use the interest rate as an indicator of the average person's degree of time preference.

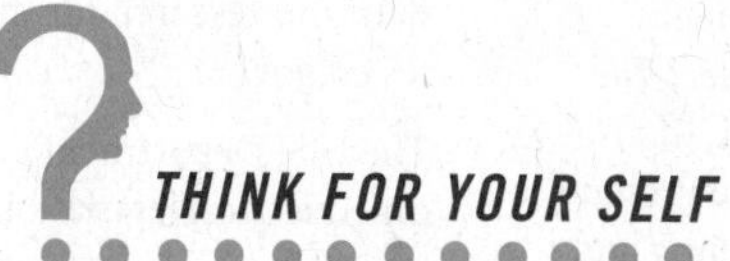

THINK FOR YOUR SELF

Do you have a time preference for money? Do you have any evidence of your time preference?

So how do we compare monetary values at different points in time? Suppose you put $1,000 into a savings account that earns 5 percent interest per year. In one year, you will have your original $1,000 plus $50 in interest. In other words, the value in the future of $1,000 today if the interest rate is five percent is

$$\$1{,}000\,(1 + .05) = \$1{,}050$$

If you left this amount in the savings account for another year, you'd earn another 5 percent interest on it, or an additional $52.50 in interest since

$$\$1{,}050 * .05 = \$52.50$$

In more general terms, if the interest rate is 5 percent, a payment of $1,000 today is worth:

$$\$1{,}000\ (1 + .05) \text{ after one year}$$

and

$$\$1{,}000\ (1 + .05)\ (1 + .05) = \$1{,}000\ (1 + .05)^2 \text{ after two years}$$

and

$$\$1{,}000\ (1 + .05)^t \text{ after } t \text{ years}$$

For any payment and interest rate, we can use this method to compute what the payment is worth in the future. Let the payment today be called *PV*, the interest rate be called *i*, and the number of periods into the future be called *t*. The value of the payment in the future, that is, its **future value** (FV) is

*The **future value** is the value of a payment at a time in the future.*

$$\text{FV} = \text{PV}(1 + i)^t$$

We can also use this formula to compute how much a payment in the future is worth today. For any payment *t* years in the future (FV) and interest rate *i*, its value in the present (i.e., its present value, PV) is:

$$\text{PV} = \text{FV}/(1 + i)^t$$

Using our example, a payment of $1,050 one year in the future is equivalent to a payment of $1,000 in the present if the interest rate is 5 percent because

$$\$1{,}000 = \$1{,}050/1.05$$

Understanding the tradeoff between present and future costs and benefits helps us understand many aspects individuals' education decisions. When the present value of an educational investment is higher, individuals will be more likely to invest in their education. What things make the present value of an educational investment higher? One factor would be the difference in the relative earnings available in careers that do and do not require education. The higher the earnings gain from investing in education, the more likely someone will be to make the educational investment.

A second factor that influences whether someone makes an educational investment is the cost of the investment. When tuition, fees, and the cost of books grow, ceteris paribus, the net benefit of the investment in education shrinks.

A third factor that influences whether someone invests in education is the length of time they have to earn the benefits of their investment. When you are young, there are many years left after college for you to reap the benefits of your college investment. The older you are, the less time you have to obtain those gains. This is one reason why the typical college student is in his or her early 20s rather than his or her early 50s.

A fourth factor that influences whether someone invests in education is their intensity of time preference. Those who are more present-oriented place a very high value on present benefits and as a result are less likely to make an investment in education (because it involves costs today for benefits in the future). Those who are more future-oriented are more likely to invest in education because they place a relatively high value on future benefits.

SUMMARY

Education is an investment because it involves costs paid in the present in exchange for benefits that come in the future. The value of costs and benefits that occur at different points in time can be analyzed using the concept of present value.

KEY CONCEPTS

- Investments
- Present value
- Time preference
- Future value

APPENDIX 17 DISCUSSION QUESTIONS AND PROBLEMS

1. If you invest $100 today at an interest rate of 3 percent per year, how much money will you have in five years?
2. Suppose someone offers to give you $1,000 in three years. If the interest rate is 5 percent per year, how much would that be worth today?
3. In the Aesop fable of the ant and the grasshopper, the grasshopper spends the summer relaxing, singing, and playing. The ant spends the summer working and saving up food for winter. When winter comes, the ant is prepared and comfortable while the grasshopper faces starvation. Economists would say that the grasshopper shows a high degree of time preference. He prefers to consume now, not to save, and not to plan for the future. The ant, however, is more future-oriented. He saves more and consumes less today in order to have more in the future. Do you know people who tend to act like the ant? Like the grasshopper? Do their educational attainment decisions reflect their time preferences?
4. In 2010, 63-year-old Joan Ginther of Texas won more than $1 million in the Texas Lottery for the fourth time. She opted to have the $10 million she won in 2010 paid out in a lump sum, which will total about $7.5 million. Why is the lump sum payout in the lottery less than the actual winnings?

Daniel Acker/Bloomberg via Getty Images

18

Competition and Monopoly

After studying this chapter, you should be able to:

- Understand how firms determine the optimal level of output
- Demonstrate the differences in output choices between firms in perfect competition and monopoly
- Compare profits for perfectly competitive firms and monopolies
- Assess the economic efficiency of firms in perfect competition versus monopolies
- Understand why some economists argue for regulation of monopoly power

Throughout the 20th century, the De Beers Company has been the dominant diamond producer and seller in the world. In the early 1900s, De Beers controlled roughly 90 percent of the world's diamond mines and diamond production. Because De Beers was effectively the only seller of diamonds in the world, it could keep the supply of diamonds artificially low and the prices for diamonds artificially high. By the turn of the century, other sources of diamonds were discovered, and De Beers's power over the diamond market diminished. As competition in the diamond industry grew, the supply of diamonds increased and the prices of diamonds fell. When De Beers was effectively the only seller of diamonds, it was a monopoly. A **monopoly** is a market with only one seller of a good or service.

A monopoly is a market with by only one seller of a good or service.

This chapter examines the impacts of monopolies on markets. We first examine how firms make decisions about the price and output level of their products. We then show how these decisions differ for competitive firms and monopolies. Finally, we assess the economic inefficiency of monopolies and learn why most economists argue that the regulation of monopolies can promote economic efficiency.

OUTPUT, PRICES, REVENUES, COSTS, AND PROFITS

Profit is the difference between total revenue and total cost.

How do firms determine the amount of output to produce and the price to charge for that output? Economists assume that the driving force behind firms' decision making is the goal of maximizing profit. **Profit** is the difference between a firm's total revenue and its total cost.

The total revenue earned by a firm comes from the sale of the firm's goods or services. The total cost for a firm comes from expenses that a firm must pay in order to produce its products. Total cost includes spending on resources like labor and materials plus the opportunity cost of the firm owner.

Output and Cost

Total costs of production include the direct costs and opportunity costs associated with producing a given level of output.

Suppose that you run Econoweb, a consulting business that produces reports on website traffic for your clients. Table 18.1 illustrates the costs involved in producing Econoweb's reports. The first column of Table 18.1 lists the number of reports Econoweb can produce per hour. The second column shows the total cost incurred to produce that output. These **total costs of production** include direct spending on hiring labor and materials, spending on utilities, computer upkeep, and the cost of a subscription to an Internet

Table 18.1 Econoweb's Costs of Production

Quantity of Output (Q) (reports per hour)	Total Cost (TC) ($ per hour)	Marginal Cost (MC) ($)
0	10	–
1	40	30
2	65	25
3	85	20
4	100	15
5	120	20
6	145	25
7	175	30
8	210	35
9	250	40
10	300	50

Total cost includes the cost of spending on labor and materials plus the opportunity cost associated with producing each possible quantity of output. Marginal cost is the change in total cost that arises from each increase in the quantity of output.

provider. Total cost also includes your opportunity cost as the owner of Econoweb. Your opportunity cost is the amount you could earn in your next best alternative job. When Econoweb's output is 5 reports per hour, for example, total cost is $120 per hour. When output is 4 reports per hour, total cost is $100 per hour.

Marginal Cost

The third column of Table 18.1 shows the marginal cost of production for Econoweb. The **marginal cost of production** is the additional cost that Econoweb incurs when it produces one more report per hour. Marginal cost is computed as the change in total cost for each additional unit of output produced. The Greek letter delta (Δ) is commonly used as shorthand for "the difference in" or "the change in." To compute marginal cost, we divide the change or difference in total cost by the change in the quantity of output produced as we move from one output level to another.

Marginal cost of production is the change in total cost incurred when an additional unit of output is produced. $MC = \Delta TC/\Delta Q$

When Econoweb's output is 2 reports per hour, total cost is $65 per hour. When Econoweb's output is 3 reports per hour, total cost is $85 per hour. The total cost changes from $65 to $85 per hour when Econoweb increases its production from 2 to 3 reports per hour, so its change in total cost is $20 per hour,

$$\Delta TC = \$85 - \$65 = \$20$$

and its change in output is 1 report per hour,

$$\Delta Q = 3 - 2 = 1$$

Thus, Econoweb's marginal cost of the third report produced per hour is

$$MC = \Delta TC/\ \Delta Q = \$20/\ 1 = \$20$$

THINK FOR YOURSELF

How would Econoweb's marginal costs change if total costs were $5 higher at each output level? If Econoweb's total cost at each level of output were $15, $50, $83, $113, $146, $181, $224, $274, $331, $396, $469, what are Econoweb's marginal costs of production?

Output and Revenue

To determine Econoweb's profits, we need to compare costs against revenues. Econoweb earns revenues by producing and selling website traffic reports to its clients. Suppose that you charge each client $37 to produce a report. Table 18.2 presents a summary of Econoweb's revenues. Column 1 lists the number of reports Econoweb can produce per hour. Column 2 lists the price per report ($37), and column 3 lists the total revenue that Econoweb will earn per hour if charges $37 per report. **Total revenue** is the amount of money earned by selling a given quantity of a good. Total

Total revenue (TR) is the amount of money earned when a supplier sells a given quantity of a good. It is equal to the price of the good (P) multiplied by the quantity of the good sold (Q). $TR = P * Q$

Table 18.2 Econoweb's Revenues

Quantity of Output (Q) (reports per hour)	Price Per Report (P) ($)	Total Revenue (TR) ($ per hour)	Marginal Revenue (MR) ($)
0	37	0	–
1	37	37	37
2	37	74	37
3	37	111	37
4	37	148	37
5	37	185	37
6	37	222	37
7	37	259	37
8	37	296	37
9	37	333	37
10	37	370	37

Total revenue is equal to the price of output times the quantity of output sold. Marginal revenue is the change in total revenue that arises from each increase in the quantity of output sold.

revenue is equal to the price of the good multiplied by the quantity of the good sold. For example, when Econoweb produces 3 reports per hour, its total revenue is equal to

$$TR = \$37/\text{report} * 3 \text{ reports/hour} = \$111 \text{ per hour}$$

Marginal Revenue

Marginal Revenue (MR) is the change in total revenue earned when an additional unit of output is produced and sold. $MR = \Delta TR/\Delta Q$

The last column of Table 18.2 shows the marginal revenue that Econoweb earns from its clients. **Marginal revenue** is the additional revenue that Econoweb earns when it produces and sells an additional report per hour. Marginal revenue is computed as the change in total revenue earned for each additional unit of output produced.

When Econoweb's output is 4 reports per hour, its total revenue is $148 per hour. When Econoweb's output is 5 reports per hour, total revenue is $185 per hour. Since total revenue increased from $148 to $185 per hour when Econoweb increased its production from 4 to 5 reports per hour, its change in total revenue is

$$\Delta TR = \$185 - \$148 = \$37$$

and its change in output is 1 report per hour

$$\Delta Q = 5 - 4 = 1$$

Thus, Econoweb's marginal revenue for the fifth report produced per hour is

$$MR = \Delta TR/\Delta Q = \$37/1 = \$37$$

Because Econoweb charges a fixed price for each report, its marginal revenue is $37 is per report. It is not always the case that the price of a good is equal to the marginal revenue earned for the good. We'll describe those situations in more detail later in this chapter.

THINK FOR YOURSELF

How would its marginal revenue change if Econoweb charged its clients $40 per report?

THE PROFIT-MAXIMIZING OUTPUT LEVEL

Econoweb's cost and revenue structures in Tables 18.1 and 18.2 provide the information needed to find the level of output that will maximize Econoweb's profits. The marginal benefit–marginal cost framework we learned in Chapter 1 is useful for finding Econoweb's profit-maximizing level of production. The marginal decision rule in Chapter 1 states that you can maximize the net benefit you receive from an activity when you engage in that activity until the marginal benefit is just equal to the marginal cost.

Applying the marginal decision rule implies that Econoweb can maximize its profits by producing up to the point where the marginal benefit of producing reports is equal to the marginal cost of producing reports. In other words, Econoweb should produce additional reports for its clients as long as the marginal revenue earned for each report produced is greater than the marginal cost incurred to produce the report. If the marginal revenue gained from producing an additional report is greater than the marginal cost of producing that report, Econoweb's profits will increase if it produces the report. If the marginal revenue gained from producing an additional report is less than the marginal cost incurred to produce the report, Econoweb's profits will fall if it produces the report.

Table 18.3 presents Econoweb's revenues, costs, and profits at different levels of production. When output is 0, Econoweb's total cost is $10 and its total revenue is $0, so profit is −$10 per hour.

The marginal revenue earned from producing the first report per hour is $37, and the marginal cost of producing the first report is $30 per hour, so MR > MC for the first report produced per hour. For the second report produced per hour, marginal revenue is $37 and marginal cost is $25. Because MR > MC, for the second report produced per hour, Econoweb's profit will rise if it produces 2 reports per hour. The marginal revenue earned from producing a third report per hour is $37, and the marginal cost of producing a third report per hour is $20, so Econoweb's profits rise by producing a third report per hour, and so on.

Econoweb's profits reach their highest point when Econoweb produces 8 reports per hour. For the eighth report produced per hour, marginal revenue is $37 and marginal cost is $35. The marginal revenue for the ninth report produced per hour is $37, but the marginal cost of the ninth report produced per hour is $40, so Econoweb's profits fall if it produces the ninth report per hour. For levels of output below 8 reports per hour, the marginal revenue earned from producing an additional report per hour is greater than the marginal cost of producing an additional report per hour. At levels of output above 8 reports per hour, the marginal cost of additional production is greater than the marginal revenue of additional production.

Figure 18.1 illustrates Econoweb's marginal revenues and marginal costs graphically. At levels of output below 8 reports per hour, the marginal revenue curve (MR)

Table 18.3 Econoweb's Marginal Revenues, Marginal Costs, and Profits

Quantity of Output (Q) (reports per hour)	Marginal Revenue (MR) ($)	Marginal Cost (MC) ($)	Total Revenue (TR) ($ per hour)	Total Cost (TC) ($ per hour)	Profit (TR – TC) ($ per hour)
0	–	–	0	10	-10
1	37	30	37	40	-3
2	37	25	74	65	9
3	37	20	111	85	26
4	37	15	148	100	48
5	37	20	185	120	65
6	37	25	222	145	77
7	37	30	259	175	84
8	37	35	296	210	86
9	37	40	333	250	83
10	37	50	370	300	70

When MR > MC, Econoweb can increase profit by expanding output. When MR < MC, Econoweb can increase profit by reducing output. Econoweb's maximum profit occurs when it produces 8 reports per hour.

Figure 18.1 Econoweb's Marginal Costs and Marginal Revenues

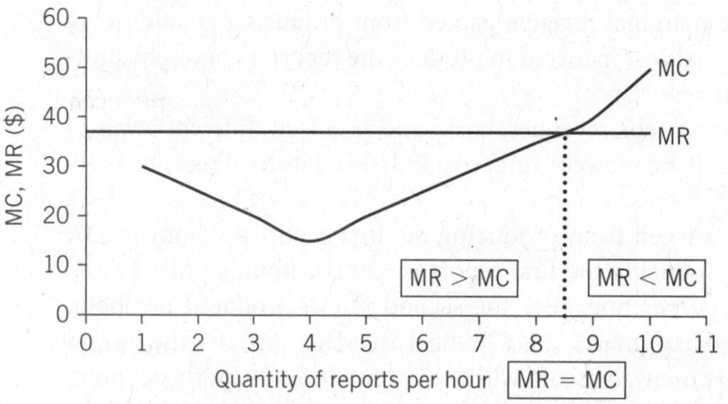

When MR > MC, profits can be increased by increasing output. When MR < MC, profits can be increased by decreasing output. The profit-maximizing level of output occurs where MR = MC.

lies above the marginal cost curve (MC). At those levels of production, marginal benefits of increased production are greater than the marginal costs of increasing production, so Econoweb can increase profits by expanding output. At levels of output above 9 reports per hour, the marginal cost of increasing output is higher than the marginal revenue earned from increasing output, so MR< MC. Producing above 9 reports per hour causes Econoweb's profits to fall.

When production is equal to 8.5 reports per hour, the marginal cost of production is just equal to the marginal benefit of production, so MR = MC. If it were possible for Econoweb to produce 8.5 reports per hour, that level of output would maximize profits. Splitting production into small units like this is easier for some firms than for others. For firms that can produce smaller increments of output, the **profit-maximizing output level** will be where the marginal revenue and marginal

*The **profit-maximizing output level** for a firm occurs where MR = MC. If MR > MC, increasing output will increase profits. If MR < MC, decreasing output will increase profits.*

cost of production are equal. Firms that can only produce whole units of output (i.e., either 8 reports per hour or 9 reports per hour) will maximize their profit by producing the highest level of output where marginal revenue is still greater than marginal cost.

It is profit-maximizing for a firm to produce the level of output where marginal revenue is equal to marginal cost. Different types of firms, however, have different marginal revenue structures. The next sections describe two types of firms, perfectly competitive firms and monopoly firms, and illustrate how the differences in their marginal revenue structures affect their profit-maximizing output levels and prices.

PERFECT COMPETITION

Although it wasn't noted explicitly, the presentation so far in this chapter has assumed that Econoweb operates in a market with perfect competition. **Perfect competition** is a type of market that has several distinguishing characteristics: identical products, complete information, many buyers and sellers, and easy entry and exit from the market. We discuss each of these characteristics in turn.

Perfect competition is a market characterized by many firms producing identical products for a large number of buyers. Buyers and sellers have complete information about prices, and firms can easily enter or exit the market.

Identical Products

Each firm in a perfectly competitive market produces a product that is identical to that produced by all the other firms in the market. The products produced by perfectly competitive firms are indistinguishable from one another as far as the buyer is concerned. As an example, producers of durum wheat, a species of wheat commonly used to make flour for pasta, obtain their seed from the same suppliers and grow their crops under similar conditions. Once those crops are delivered to the local grain elevator, one farmer's wheat is indistinguishable from that of his or her neighbor. Because firms in perfect competition make identical products, consumers can easily substitute one firm's product for another's if one firm tries to charge a higher price than another firm.

Complete Information

A second characteristic of perfect competition is that buyers and sellers have complete information about the prices charged by each firm. If one firm is charging more than another firm, buyers will know about it and will move their business to the lower-priced firm. When buyers have complete information about each firm's prices, any one firm will not be able to charge more for their product without losing customers to competitors. In our example, suppose that Econoweb tried to charge $45 for its reports but WebEcon, a rival firm, charged only $37 for the same reports. Because Econoweb's customers have complete information about the prices at both firms, Econoweb's customers would move their business to WebEcon.

Many Buyers and Sellers

A third characteristic of perfect competition is that perfectly competitive markets are made up of many buyers and sellers of a good or service. When there are many sellers of a product, each individual seller plays too tiny a role in the market to have any influence on the product's price. Each firm's supply is only a small part of the overall market supply, so changes in one firm's supply do not cause a change in the market supply or price of the good.

Figure 18.2 **Competitive Market Demand and Supply and the Output Choice of an Individual Firm**

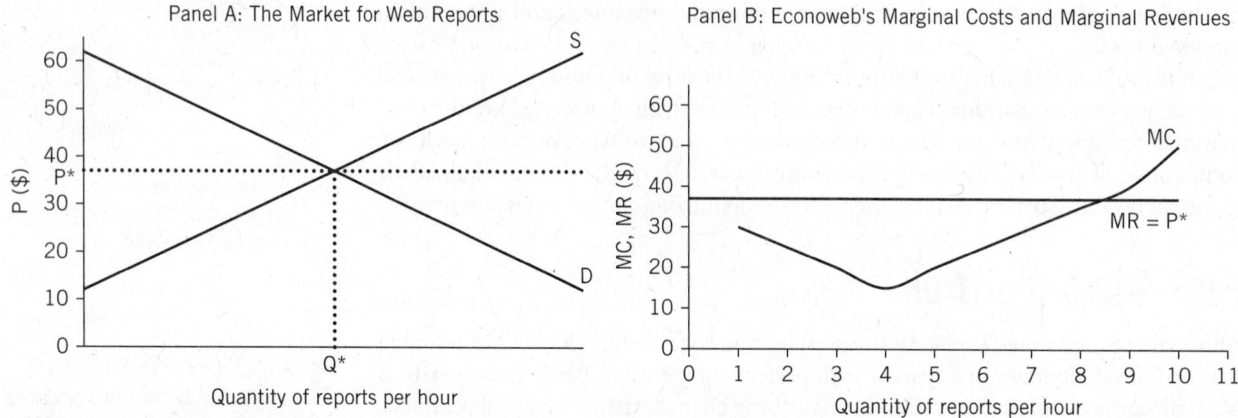

Panel A shows the market supply and demand for web reports. The intersection of the market supply and demand determines the market price for web reports, P* ($37). In Panel B, the market price for web reports becomes the marginal revenue curve for Econoweb. If Econoweb charges more than $37, its customers will take their business to other firms. If Econoweb charges less than $37, it will forego profits and eventually be outcompeted in the market. Thus, Econoweb is a price taker; it cannot set the price of its product. Instead, the price is set in the broader market for web reports.

In our example, Econoweb charged its clients $37 for each report produced. In a perfectly competitive market, this price would have come from the intersection of the market supply and demand for web reports. Figure 18.2 illustrates the relationship between the market demand and supply and the price that Econoweb can charge for its reports.

Panel A of Figure 18.2 shows the market demand and supply of web reports. The intersection between the demand and supply curves generates an equilibrium price of $37 per report. At the equilibrium price P*, a total of Q* reports are sold. Because there are a large number of firms in the market, each firm produces a small fraction of this total equilibrium quantity of reports.

Panel B of Figure 18.2 shows Econoweb's marginal cost and marginal benefit curves. The price that Econoweb charges for its web reports is P* = $37, which is exactly the same price charged by the other firms in the market. If Econoweb tried to charge more than $37, its customers would simply move their business to another firm. If Econoweb tries to charge less than $37 for its reports, it would lose revenues to other competitors. The reduction in revenues would reduce Econoweb's profits and make it less competitive than other firms. Over time, Econoweb's competitors could use their higher profits to drive Econoweb out of the market. They may be able to invest in faster Internet servers or better technology than Econoweb, for example. In a perfectly competitive market, each firm must take the market equilibrium price of its good as a given. Economists use the term **price takers** to describe this outcome.

Price takers are firms that cannot set the price of their good, but instead must take the market price as given.

Each time Econoweb sells an additional report, it earns the market price (P*). and its total revenues rise by P*. Because marginal revenue is the change in total revenue obtained by producing one more unit of the good, price and marginal revenue are the same for perfectly competitive firms. Thus Econoweb's marginal revenue curve is labeled MR = P* in Panel B.

Ease of Entry and Exit

A final characteristic of perfectly competitive markets is ease of entry and exit from the market. New firms can easily enter perfectly competitive markets when they see profits being made, and old firms can easily exit the market when profits fall.

Economists make a distinction between **economic profit** and **normal profit** to describe what happens to firms in perfect competition. **Normal profit** is the profit that business owners could earn if they applied their resources and skills in their next best business alternative. Normal profit is equal to total revenue minus total costs, including opportunity costs for the firm owner.

Normal profit is the profit that business owners could earn if they applied their resources and skills in their next best business alternative. Normal profit is total revenue minus total cost, including opportunity cost.

Economic profit occurs when a firm earns more than zero normal profits. A firm owner earning an economic profit is earning more than she would if she chose the next best alternative to owning the business. The ability of firms to enter and exit means that economic profits are eventually competed away in perfectly competitive markets. Why? If firms in a perfectly competitive industry are earning economic profits, other firms will enter the market. The increase in the number of firms in the market will cause an increase in the supply of the good, which will in turn reduce the good's equilibrium price. When the price falls, firms' profits also fall, and some firms will exit the market. The exit of some firms will cause a decrease in the supply of the good and an increase in profits. In equilibrium, firms have no incentive to either enter or exit a perfectly competitive market, which means than economic profits are zero.

Economic profit occurs when a firm earns more than $0 in normal profits. A firm owner earning economic profit earns more than she would if she chose her next best alternative.

Suppose that when you opened Econoweb, your next best job offer was at Microsoft. If Econoweb earns zero normal profit, you can expect to earn just as much at Econoweb as you would have earned at Microsoft. In other words, earning zero normal profit means that you just cover your opportunity costs. If Econoweb earns more than zero normal profit, other rival firms will enter the market and the competition will drive the economic profits to zero.

THINK FOR YOURSELF

Suppose your friend is thinking of opening a coffee shop in your town. In order to open the shop, she has to quit her $30,000 per year job. Suppose the total revenue earned by the coffee shop is $60,000 per year, and the total cost of space, equipment, and ingredients at the coffee shop are $30,000 per year. What is the normal profit earned by your friend per year? Is she earning economic profit? How would your answers change if the costs stayed the same but the total revenue at the coffee shop was $100,000 per year?

MONOPOLY

A monopoly is a market with only seller of a good or service. Monopolies arise because barriers to entry keep other firms out of the market. **Barriers to entry** are obstructions that make it difficult for new firms to enter a market. Barriers to entry can include control over resources, high startup costs, government regulations, and patents.

Barriers to entry are obstructions that make it difficult for new firms to enter a market.

As highlighted at the beginning of the chapter, the De Beers diamond company had a monopoly in the diamond industry for many years because it owned nearly all the worlds' diamond mines. When it takes a substantial amount of money to buy the equipment, materials, or other resources necessary to start up a business, new firms are less likely to enter the market, so high startup costs are another barrier to entry. Government regulations can pose barriers to entry by requiring firms to buy expensive licenses and permits before they can open for business. In some cases, government regulations establish monopolies more directly. For example, utility companies are often given monopoly power by governments to be the only sellers of electrical power in an area. If a firm has a patent on a product, it has a legal right to be the exclusive seller of a product until the patent expires. When a pharmaceutical company invents a new drug, for example, it usually gains the patent right to be the only seller of the drug. Until the patent expires, the company is a monopoly seller of drug.

THINK FOR YOURSELF

People often complain because brand-name drugs cost much more than generic drugs, but generic drugs are not generally available as substitutes for new brand-name drugs. It costs about $800 million in research and development to bring a new prescription drug to the market. How would the incentives for developing new drugs change if pharmaceutical companies were not allowed to patent new drugs that they develop?

Demand, Price and Marginal Revenue for Monopoly Firms

Would Econoweb behave differently if it were a monopoly instead of a perfectly competitive firm? Yes. The first difference is that if Econoweb were a monopoly, the market demand for web reports would be the same as the demand for Econoweb's web reports. The market demand for web reports is shown in Table 18.4. The first two columns show the price and corresponding quantity of reports demanded per hour. The third column shows the total revenue associated with each of the various points along the demand curve. For example, if Econoweb charges $52 per report, it can sell 2 reports per hour and earn $104 in total revenues per hour. If Econoweb charges $32 per report, it can sell 6 reports per hour and earn total revenues of $192 per hour.

Table 18.4 illustrates an important difference between perfectly competitive firms and monopolies. Each firm in a perfectly competitive market can sell all of the output it chooses to at the market equilibrium price. For perfectly competitive firms, the equilibrium price of the good is the marginal revenue that firms earn when they sell the good. If a monopoly firm wants to sell more output, it has to lower the price of its good. For monopolies, marginal revenue is less than the price of the good.

Econoweb's marginal revenues are illustrated in the last column of Table 18.4. When Econoweb produces 1 report per hour, it can sell that report for $57 and earn $57 in total revenue. Because total revenue is $0 when Econoweb does not produce any reports, the MR and TR are the same for the first report sold per hour. In order to sell 2 reports per hour, Econoweb must price its reports at $52 each. Econoweb's total revenue when it sells 2 reports per hour is $104 per hour. The marginal revenue for the second report per hour is

$$MR = \Delta TR/\Delta Q = (\$104 - \$57)/1 = \$47$$

Table 18.4 Market Demand and Marginal Revenue under Monopoly

Price ($ per report)	Quantity Demanded (reports per hour)	Total Revenue ($ per hour)	Marginal Revenue ($)
62	0	0	–
57	1	57	57
52	2	104	47
47	3	141	37
42	4	168	27
37	5	185	17
32	6	192	7
27	7	189	−3
22	8	176	−13
17	9	153	−23
12	10	120	−33

Econoweb's total revenue is equal to the number of reports sold per hour multiplied by the price of each report. Marginal revenue is the change in total revenue that Econoweb earns when it expands its output by one report per hour. Because a monopoly must lower the price of its reports in order to sell more output, its marginal revenue is less than the price of its product.

If Econoweb price its reports at $47 each, it can sell 3 reports per hour and earn total revenue of $141 per hour. The marginal revenue earned from producing the third report per hour is

$$MR = \Delta TR/\Delta Q = \$141 - \$104/1 = \$37$$

Figure 18.3 illustrates Econoweb's demand and marginal revenue curves if it operates as a monopoly. The demand curve D is the market demand for web reports. The marginal revenue curve (MR) shows the change in total revenue earned when Econoweb expands its output. For monopoly firms, marginal revenue is less than price. Why? Unless a monopoly can discriminate among its buyers and charge them each different prices, when a monopoly tries to sell a higher quantity of its good, it has to lower its price for all the units it sells.

Figure 18.3 Demand and Marginal Revenue under Monopoly

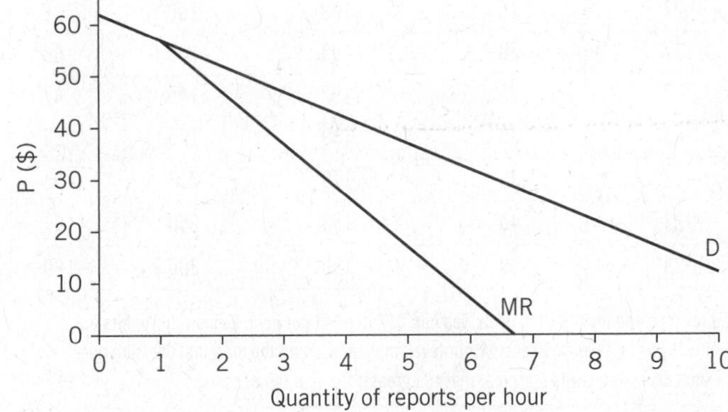

The demand curve for a monopoly firm (D) is the same as the market demand curve for the product. In order to sell more output, a monopoly must lower the price of its good. The lower price for each unit of the good sold means that marginal revenue is less than price for a monopolist. The marginal revenue curve (MR) for a monopolist lies below the demand curve (D).

Profit-Maximizing Output for Monopoly Firms

Given Econoweb's demand, marginal revenues, and marginal costs, we can determine Econoweb's profit-maximizing level of output using the marginal decision rule. Econoweb will want to increase its output as long as marginal revenue is greater than marginal cost. Its profit-maximizing level of output will occur where marginal revenue is just equal to marginal cost. Table 18.5 shows Econoweb's demand, marginal revenue, and marginal cost. Table 18.5 also shows Econoweb's total revenue, total cost, and profit at each level of output.

Using the marginal decision rule, the profit-maximizing level of output for Econoweb is 4 reports per hour. Producing 4 reports per hour is the highest level of output for which Econoweb earns marginal revenue greater than marginal cost. If Econoweb produced only 3 reports per hour, it would forgo profit from expanding its production. If Econoweb produced 5 reports per hour, it would incur more additional costs per hour than it would gain in revenues, so its profits would fall.

When Econoweb produces 4 reports per hour, it can charge $42 for each report. The $42 is the price that corresponds to 4 reports per hour on Econoweb's demand curve. Unlike perfectly competitive firms that have to accept market prices as a given, when Econoweb operates as a monopoly, it can set the price of its reports based on the price and quantity demanded combinations on the demand curve. While perfectly competitive firms are price takers, monopolies are **price setters** because they are able to set the prices for their products.

Price setters are firms that are able to set the prices for their products.

If Econoweb is a price setter, why doesn't it charge more than $42 per report? Even though Econoweb does not face competition from other firms, it cannot set whatever price it wants because it is constrained by the demand curve. If Econoweb tries to charge more than $42, the quantity of reports demanded will fall below 4 reports per hour.

Table 18.5 Market Demand, Revenue and Cost under Monopoly

Price ($ per report)	Quantity Demanded (reports per hour)	Marginal Revenue ($)	Marginal Cost ($)	Total Revenue ($ per hour)	Total Cost ($)	Profit ($)
62	0	–	–	0	10	−10
57	1	57	30	57	40	17
52	2	47	25	104	65	39
47	3	37	20	141	85	56
42	4	27	15	168	100	68
37	5	17	20	185	120	65
32	6	7	25	192	145	47
27	7	−3	30	189	175	14
22	8	−13	35	176	210	−34
17	9	−23	40	153	250	−97
12	10	−33	50	120	300	−180

If Econoweb produces 1 report per hour, it will earn $57 in total revenue and incur $40 in costs, leaving $17 in profit per hour. Econoweb's profits are highest when it produces 4 reports per hour, which is consistent with the profit-maximizing output level implied by using the marginal decision rule. Producing 4 reports per hour is the highest level of output for which Econoweb earns marginal revenue greater than marginal cost.

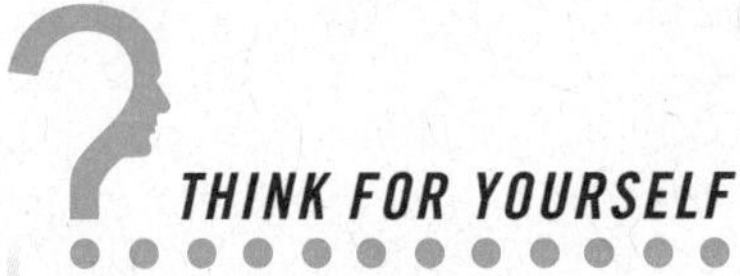

THINK FOR YOURSELF

What is the difference between a price taker and a price setter?

Photo by Express Newspapers/Getty Images, Inc.

Joan Robinson and the Economics of Imperfect Competition

Joan Robinson (1903–1983) was a British economist and one of the first women to rise to international prominence in the field of economics. One of her main contributions was in the study of market structures. Because they represent the most and least competitive markets, perfect competition and monopoly represent two extremes in market structures. In her 1933 book, *The Economics of Imperfect Competition*, Robinson expanded the models of perfect competition and monopoly to introduce and analyze "monopolistic competition" and "oligopoly," the market structures that lie between these two extremes. Her book was a major contribution to our understanding of market structures, as few firms fit completely into the perfectly competitive or monopoly models. She was also among the first economists to analyze markets where there is only one buyer of a good or service; these markets are called "monopsony" markets. Although many people expected Robinson to win the Nobel Prize for Economics in 1975, it is widely speculated that her gender and her left-wing political views (she was an outspoken supporter of the Chinese Cultural Revolution and other socialist policies) affected her chances of winning.

COMPARING PERFECT COMPETITION AND MONOPOLY

Our analysis so far has shown how Econoweb would choose its profit-maximizing output level if it were a perfectly competitive firm or if it were a monopoly. In this section, we compare the output, price, profit levels, and economic efficiency for perfectly competitive firms and monopolies.

Output and Prices under Perfect Competition and Monopoly

As a perfectly competitive firm, Econoweb took the market equilibrium price of reports ($37) as given and used a marginal revenue–marginal cost comparison to find its profit-maximizing output level (8 reports per hour). As a monopoly, the profit-maximizing level of output for Econoweb was 4 reports per hour, and the profit-maximizing price was $42 per report. Thus, Econoweb produced less output and charged higher prices when it operated as a monopoly than when it operated as a perfectly competitive firm.

This result, that monopolies produce less output and charge higher prices than similar firms operating in perfect competition, is a general characteristic of monopolies. Figure 18.4 illustrates the price and output levels for monopolies and perfectly

Figure 18.4 **Price and Output under Monopoly vs. Perfect Competition**

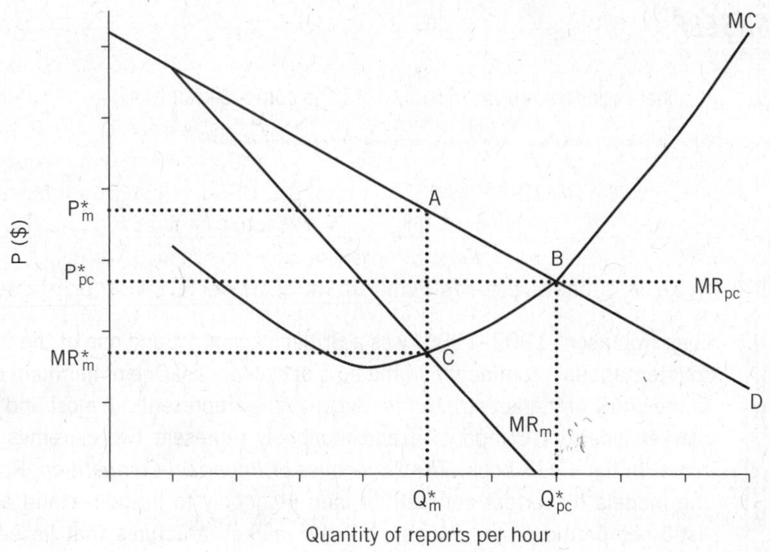

Perfectly competitive firms and monopolies both produce where MR = MC. For a perfectly competitive firm, MR_{pc} is equal to P^*_{pc}, and the profit-maximizing level of output is Q^*_{pc}. For a monopoly, the profit-maximizing output level is Q^*_m, where MR^*_m = MC. The price of a monopoly good is determined from the point on the demand curve that corresponds with Q^*_m. Because monopolies produce less output and charge a higher price than perfectly competitive firms, they are associated with market failure and a deadweight loss equal to area ABC.

competitive firms more generally. The demand curve for reports is shown by D, and marginal costs are shown by curve MC. If Econoweb were operating as a perfectly competitive firm, the marginal revenue curve MR_{pc} would be the same as the market equilibrium price of reports, P^*_{pc}. The marginal revenue curve MR_{pc} intersects the marginal cost curve at point B, so the optimal level of output for the perfectly competitive firm is $Q^*_{pc.}$ The price of reports is P^*_{pc}.

If Econoweb operates as a monopolist, MR_m represents its marginal revenue curve. MR_m intersects the marginal cost curve at point C, so the profit-maximizing level of output for the monopolist is Q^*_m. At this level of output, Econoweb will determine the price of reports by finding the price on the demand curve D that indicates how much consumers are willing and able to pay for Q^*_m reports. Point A on the demand curve shows the price that corresponds to Q^*_m, so the monopolist's profit-maximizing price is P^*_m. When Econoweb operates as a monopoly, its level of output is lower and the price it charges is higher than when it operates as a perfectly competitive firm.

Profit under Perfect Competition and Monopoly

When perfectly competitive firms earn economic profits, there are incentives for other firms to enter the market and drive the price down. The lower prices that result from entry mean reduced profits for perfectly competitive firms. In equilibrium, the price will come to rest at the point where firms in perfectly competitive industries earn zero economic profits.

In monopoly industries, outside firms do not have the ability to enter the market. Barriers to entry make it possible for a monopoly firm to earn economic profit over a long period of time, because it is firm entry that pushes prices down and erodes profits. Overall, monopoly firms will tend to earn higher economic profits than perfectly competitive firms.

Majid Saeedi/Getty Images

OPEC and Monopoly Power in the Oil Industry

The Organization of Petroleum Exporting Countries (OPEC) is a group of 12 developing countries that collectively control about 80 percent of the world's oil reserves and almost half of the world's oil production. OPEC is composed of many countries and firms, so it is not technically a monopoly. Instead, OPEC operates as a cartel, which is a group of manufacturers that agree to control the supply of their product in order to raise its price above competitive levels. During 1973, for example, OPEC stopped shipping oil to the U.S. and other nations that supported Israel. The reduction in supply caused oil prices to rise by over 400 percent and resulted in gasoline rationing throughout the U.S. As other sources of oil have been discovered throughout the world, OPEC's monopoly power has decreased.

Perfect Competition, Monopoly, and Efficiency

We learned in Chapter 1 that efficient outcomes are generated when all opportunities to generate marginal benefits greater than marginal costs are taken. When we forego choices that generate more marginal benefit than marginal cost, we make ourselves less well off than we could be. When we engage in activities that generate more marginal cost than marginal benefit, we make ourselves worse off. We can use this notion to assess the economic efficiency of perfectly competitive and monopoly firms.

In Figure 18.4, the perfectly competitive firm produces Q^*_{pc}, the level of output that equates marginal revenue and marginal cost. The price charged by the perfectly competitive firm, P^*_{pc}, is also equal to marginal revenue and marginal cost. Monopoly firms also equate marginal revenue and marginal cost to determine the profit-maximizing level of output Q^*_m, but monopolies charge a price P^*_m that is higher than marginal revenue MR_m. Although the price P^*_m is optimal for the monopoly, it is not socially efficient. Why? At levels of output between Q^*_m and Q^*_{pc}, consumers are willing and able to pay the marginal costs of increasing output. We know this because the demand curve, which illustrates the marginal benefit that consumers obtain from the good, lies above the marginal cost curve, which illustrates the cost of producing additional units of the good. Monopoly firms do not undertake all opportunities to produce units of output that generate higher marginal benefit than marginal cost, so monopoly firms do not produce the socially optimal level of output. Because the level of output chosen by a monopoly is not socially efficient, monopolies are a form of market failure.

Another way to understand the inefficiency generated by monopoly is to use the concept of deadweight loss that we learned in Chapter 4. In Figure 18.4, the area ABC represents the deadweight loss caused by the monopoly. If the market operated under perfect competition, society would have access to the producer and consumer surplus in area ABC because Q^*_{pc} units of the good would be produced. Under monopoly, only Q^*_m units of the good are traded so the producer and consumer surplus in ABC are foregone.

MONOPOLY REGULATION

Antitrust laws are laws that promote competition between businesses and prohibit anti-competitive behavior by firms with large control over markets.

Because monopoly firms produce less output and charge higher prices than is socially optimal, they tend to be heavily regulated and subject to antitrust laws. **Antitrust laws** are laws that promote competition between businesses and prohibit anti-competitive behavior by firms with large control over markets. Between 1870 and 1890, a series of court cases and the Sherman Anti-Trust Act led to federal regulation to ensure that firms charged "just and reasonable" rates and to prevent the formation of monopolies. The Federal Trade Commission was created in 1914 by the Clayton Anti-Trust Act to "prevent the unlawful suppression of competition."

Activities to regulate monopolies include setting limits on the prices that monopolies can charge, breaking large firms up into smaller components, and public ownership of monopoly firms. Occasionally, the government brings lawsuits against firms that are perceived to have monopoly power. The computer firm IBM, for example, one of the largest computer companies in the world, controlled a large share of the computer market throughout the 1960s. In 1969 the U.S. Department of Justice sued IBM under antitrust laws, claiming that IBM was a monopoly. The case was later dropped, in part because IBM began to sell its computer software and hardware separately and also because IBM's share of the market fell dramatically during the 1970s. In the 1990s, the Department of Justice sued Microsoft Corporation for maintaining a monopoly over the personal computer operating system market. In particular, the government argued that because Microsoft bundled its Windows operating system with its Internet Explorer web browser, it suppressed competition from other web browsers. The court found, however, that Microsoft had not violated any laws.

SUMMARY

Firms determine their profit-maximizing level of production by comparing their marginal costs of production against the marginal revenues they earn from producing and selling their output. Producing the level of output that equates marginal revenue and marginal cost generates the maximum profits. In perfectly competitive markets, there are many buyers and sellers, and the price for the good is determined by the intersection of the market demand and supply for the good. Firm entry and exit into perfectly competitive markets means that economic profits are difficult to sustain, so over the long term, perfectly competitive firms earn just enough to cover their opportunity costs. For monopoly firms, the optimal level of output also occurs where marginal revenue is equal to marginal cost, but monopoly firms can charge a higher price for their good than perfectly competitive firms can. The profit-maximizing level of output produced by a monopoly is lower than what would be produced by a competitive firm. Because monopoly firms generate deadweight losses, they are a form of market failure.

KEY CONCEPTS

- Monopoly
- Profit
- Total costs of production
- Marginal cost of production
- Total revenue
- Marginal revenue
- Profit-maximizing output level
- Perfect competition
- Price takers
- Normal profit
- Economic profit
- Barriers to entry
- Price setters
- Antitrust laws

DISCUSSION QUESTIONS AND PROBLEMS

1. Why is the price for a perfectly competitive firm equal to marginal revenue but the price for a monopoly firm greater than marginal revenue?
2. Can a monopolist charge whatever it wants for its product? Why or why not?
3. Why is monopoly associated with deadweight loss?
4. What is the difference between normal profit and economic profit?

Units of Output Per Period	Total Cost ($ per period)	Price ($ per unit)
0	50	350
1	150	350
2	300	350
3	500	350
4	750	350
5	1050	350
6	1400	350
7	1800	350
8	2250	350

5. Assume that the costs and revenues in the accompanying table apply to a perfectly competitive firm.
   a. Find the marginal cost, total revenue, marginal revenue, and profit associated with each level of output for the firm.
   b. What is the profit-maximizing level of output for this firm? What are the firm's profits at this level of output?
   c. Suppose that the price of the output rises to $400 per unit. Given this price, what is the profit-maximizing level of output for this firm? What are the firm's profits at this level of output?
   d. Suppose that the price of the output falls to $250 per unit. Given this price, what is the profit-maximizing level of output for this firm? What are the firm's profits at this level of output?

Quantity Demanded Per Period	Price ($ per unit)	MC($)
0	20	–
1	19	11
2	18	8
3	17	7
4	16	9
5	15	11
6	14	14
7	13	18
8	12	22
9	11	27
10	10	33

6. The table shows the demand and marginal costs for a monopolist.
   a. Find the total revenue, marginal revenue, total cost, and profit associated with each level of output for the firm.
   b. Graph the demand, marginal revenue, and marginal cost curves.
   c. What is the profit-maximizing level of output and price for this firm? What are the firm's profits at this level of output?

MULTIPLE CHOICE QUESTIONS

1. Total revenue minus total cost is equal to
   a. the rate of return.
   b. marginal revenue.
   c. profit.
   d. net cost.
2. The profit maximizing level of output for firms occurs where
   a. TR = MC.
   b. P = MC.
   c. Q = P.
   d. MC = MR.
   e. TR = MR.
3. At Elliott's dog-walking service, the only input is labor. Elliott's labor costs are $300 per day and his service walks 30 dogs per day. To walk 31 dogs per day, his labor costs would increase to $305 per day. The marginal cost of walking the thirty-first dog is _____ per day.
   a. $5
   b. $9.83
   c. $19.52
   d. $305
   e. $300
4. For Amelia's Recycling, the marginal cost of producing the first unit of output is $20, the marginal cost of

producing the second unit of output is $16, and the marginal cost of producing the third unit of output is $14. Amelia's total cost of producing three units of output is

a. $16.67.
b. $42.
c. $50.
d. $60.

Quantity of Output Per Period	Total Cost ($ per period)
0	11
1	15
2	19
3	22
4	24
5	27
6	31
7	36
8	42
9	49
10	57

5. The accompanying table shows costs for a perfectly competitive firm. The marginal cost of producing the sixth unit of output is _______.
   a. $31
   b. $36
   c. $5.16
   d. $5
   e. $4
6. The table shows costs for a perfectly competitive firm. If the market price of the output is $7.00, the profit-maximizing quantity of output is ____ units per period and profits at that level of output are ____ per period.
   a. 9; $54.00
   b. 3; $14.70
   c. 7; $13.00
   d. 9; $14.00d.
7. A monopolist observes that at a given output level, marginal cost exceeds marginal revenue but total revenue exceeds total cost. To maximize profit, the monopolist should:
   a. go out of business.
   b. reduce the level of production.
   c. expand the level of production.
   d. maintain the current production level.
8. One feature of monopoly that leads to unfavorable consequences for society is that monopolies tend to
   a. set marginal cost equal to price.
   b. produce more output than would a perfectly competitive firm.
   c. charge a higher price than would a perfectly competitive firm.
   d. devote too many resources to production.

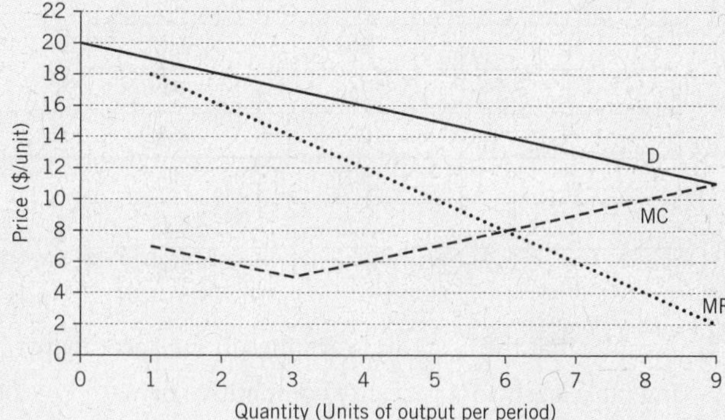

9. In the monopoly described in the accompanying graph, the profit-maximizing quantity of output is ____ per period, and the profit-maximizing price is ____ per unit.
   a. 9; $11
   b. 3; $15
   c. 6; $8
   d. 6; $14
   e. 9; $2
10. In the monopoly described in the graph, the deadweight loss from the monopoly is _____ per period.
   a. $0
   b. $4.50
   c. $9.00
   d. $13.50

ADDITIONAL READINGS AND WEB RESOURCES

Robinson, Joan (1969) *The Economics of Imperfect Competition*, London: Macmillan, 2nd ed. Describes the workings of the market structures between perfect competition and monopoly.

SECTION

Social Issues

© Jacob Wackerhausen/iStockphoto

19

The Economics of Labor Market Discrimination

After studying this chapter, you should be able to:

- Describe the sources of earnings differences among people
- Define discrimination
- Summarize the predominant economic models of discrimination
- Model the effects of discrimination
- Discuss the main antidiscrimination policies in the U.S. and the research findings on the effectiveness of these policies

Since the U.S. Bureau of Labor Statistics began tracking the relative earnings of men and women in 1979, the earnings of full-time working women have consistently been lower than the earnings of their male counterparts. Similarly, the average earnings of blacks and Hispanics are lower than the average earnings of whites. Job applicants with names more common among African Americans are significantly less likely to land job interviews than applicants with white-sounding names. Married women earn less than single women, but married men earn more than single men. Men are more likely than women to be hired as waiters at expensive restaurants, but women are more likely than men to be hired as waitresses at low-end restaurants.

Labor market discrimination can take many forms. Employment discrimination involves not hiring, promoting, or retaining workers because of their race, sex, or other demographic characteristics. Allowing men but not women in the same jobs access to overtime work or providing flexible schedules to young but not older workers in the same jobs are also examples of employment discrimination. Wage discrimination occurs when equally productive workers in the same job are paid different wages based on a characteristic unrelated to productivity.

Why are there pay and employment differences among race and gender groups? What is discrimination, and why do people discriminate? How effective are the laws that prohibit employment discrimination? This chapter investigates pay and employment differences among racial and gender groups, presents models of employment discrimination, and reviews some of the research on the impacts of antidiscrimination policy.

RACE AND GENDER IN THE U.S. WORKFORCE

The U.S. workforce has become more racially and gender diverse over the past 30 years. Hispanic men comprised 4 percent of the workforce in 1986 and are expected to make up 10 percent of the workforce by 2016. The percentage of Hispanic women in the workforce is expected to grow from 3 percent to 7 percent over the same period. By 2016, white non-Hispanic men are expected to account for only 35 percent of the workforce, compared to 45 percent in 1986. The trend of increasing diversity is expected to continue into the foreseeable future. As the U.S. workforce becomes more diverse, understanding and designing effective policies to combat employment and wage discrimination will become increasingly important.

*An **earnings ratio** measures the earnings of one group as a percentage of the earnings of another group.*

Figure 19.1 shows the earnings ratios of various demographic and gender groups relative to white males. An **earnings ratio** measures the earnings of one group as a percentage of the earnings of another group. In 2011, the median weekly earnings of white males were \$909, and the median weekly earnings of white females were \$735. The female/male earnings ratio was

$$\$735/\$909 = 0.81$$

which implies that women earned 81 percent as much as men.

Figure 19.1 Earnings Ratios Relative to White Males, 2011

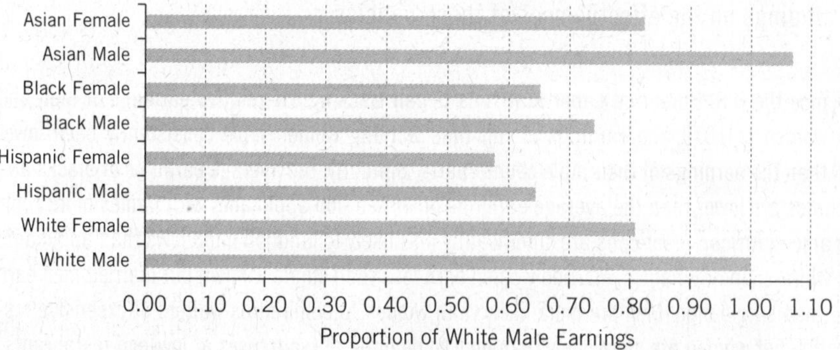

An earnings ratio shows the earnings of one group as a percentage of the earnings of another group. The median earnings of Asian males are higher than those of white males, so the earnings ratio for Asian males is greater than 1. The median earnings of other groups are lower than those of white males, so their earnings ratios are less than 1. *Source:* BLS Current Population Survey Data. Includes ages 16+ employed full-time wage and salary workers across all industries and all occupations, excluding incorporated self-employed. Hispanic male and female values are computed for any race. White, Black, and Asian values are computed for any ethnicity.

When females earn less than males, the female/male earnings ratio is less than 1. If male and female earnings were the same, the female/male earnings ratio would equal 1. Asian men earned more than white men in 2011, so the Asian male/white male earnings ratio was greater than 1. That same year, Asian females earned 82 percent as much as white males, Hispanic females earned 58 percent as much as white males, and Hispanic males earned 64 percent as much as white males.

Earnings ratios can be used to compute the **pay gap** between two groups. The pay gap is the percentage difference in earnings between groups. If the white female/white male earnings ratio is 0.81, the white male/white female earnings ratio is

The pay gap is the percent difference in earnings between two groups.

$$1/0.81 = 1.24$$

and the pay gap between white females and white males is 0.24. In other words, white men earn 24 percent more than white women. Figure 19.1 shows that the Hispanic female/white male earnings ratio is 0.58, so the white male/Hispanic female earnings ratio is 1.72, and white males earn 72 percent more than Hispanic females.

THINK FOR YOURSELF

Using the data in Figure 19.1, estimate the pay gaps between black females and white males and between black males and white males.

WHY ARE THERE PAY GAPS AMONG PEOPLE?

Given the data presented in Figure 19.1, it is natural to wonder what causes the pay gaps among the different racial, ethnic, and gender groups. Since worker pay is determined in labor markets, we can use the demand and supply model to help understand the sources of pay gaps among groups. As in other markets, the interactions between buyers and sellers determine the prices and quantities of labor services traded in the labor market. The demand for labor comes from businesses, including restaurants, accounting firms, banks, school districts, hospitals, and all the other producers of goods and services in the economy. The supply of labor comes from workers who sell their time to employers in exchange for wages. The equilibrium quantity and price of labor are determined by the demand and supply of workers in that particular market.[1]

The demand and supply model implies that one source of wage differences between groups is their relative supply of labor in high-paying versus low-paying jobs. If different demographic groups tend to be overrepresented or underrepresented in high-paying or low-paying jobs, the average wages of the groups as a whole will be different. For example, because the percent of physicians who are female is roughly 30 percent and the percent of female childcare workers is virtually 100 percent, we would expect females as a group to have lower average earnings than males as a group.

1 Chapter 9 presents a detailed description of how wages are determined in labor markets.

We should also expect to see earnings differences among workers based on their levels of education and training, whether they work full-time or part-time, whether they live in high or low cost-of-living areas, whether their jobs are particularly risky, and so on. To illustrate one source of pay gaps, Figure 19.2 shows the level of educational attainment by various demographic groups.

Figure 19.2 **Education Attainment by Race and Ethnicity**

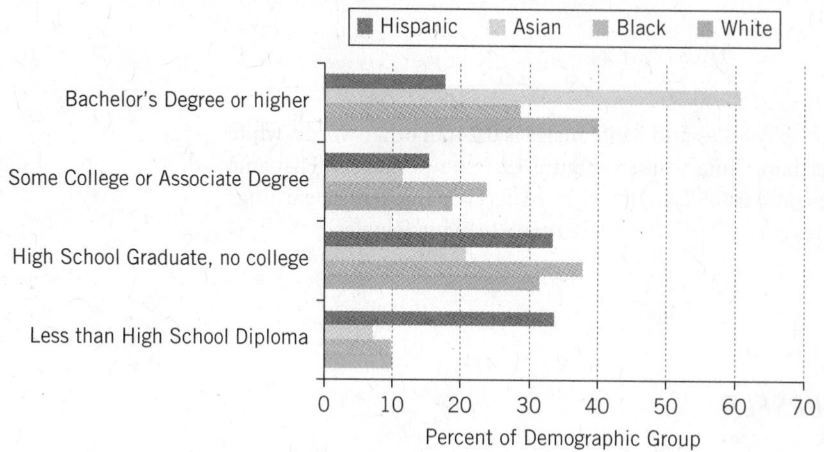

Educational attainment differs among various race and ethnic groups. Over 60 percent of Asians over age 25 who are in the labor force hold a Bachelor's degree or higher; less than 20 percent of Hispanics with the same characteristics hold a Bachelor's degree or higher. *Source:* Author's calculations based on 2011 BLS data for people age 25 or older in the civilian labor force.

One striking difference among the groups is the high proportion of Asians who hold a Bachelor's degree or higher level of education relative to the other demographic groups. Given this difference in education, it is not surprising that Figure 19.1 showed high earnings ratios for Asian workers relative to others. Similarly, the relatively small proportion of Hispanics who have earned a Bachelor's degree or higher and the relatively large proportion of Hispanics with less than a high school diploma helps to explain the relatively low earnings ratios of Hispanics in Figure 19.1.

Economists have estimated how much of the pay gap between groups can be explained by productivity-related characteristics, like education. About one-third of the pay gap between males and females can be explained by differences in the education, age, location, industry, and occupations of males and females. The remaining two-thirds of the gender pay gap stems from other factors. About half of the pay gap between black and white workers is explained by differences in the education, age, sex, location, occupation, and industry characteristics. The remaining half of the black/white pay gap cannot be explained by these characteristics.

THINK FOR YOURSELF

Suppose you learn that male college professors are paid more than female college professors. What information would you require before judging this to be evidence of pay discrimination?

WHAT IS DISCRIMINATION?

Discrimination in the labor market occurs when workers who are equally productive are treated differently based on characteristics that are not related to productivity, or when workers who are not equally productive are treated the same because of some arbitrary characteristic. In other words, when we compare basically identical workers in terms of their productivity and other labor market characteristics but we still see pay gaps between them, discrimination may be the cause.

Discrimination in the labor market occurs when workers who are equally productive are treated differently based on characteristics that are not related productivity, or when workers who are not equally productive are treated the same because of some arbitrary characteristic.

Discrimination happens when characteristics such as race, gender, age, marital status, national origin, sexual orientation, weight, or height are unrelated to productivity but are used as a basis for treating workers differently. There are cases, however, where seemingly arbitrary characteristics are related to worker productivity. For example, one would not expect a short male to be as effective at professional basketball as a tall male, so the fact that professional basketball teams tend to hire tall males is not evidence of discrimination against short males. Similarly, we would not expect a cosmetics company to hire male models to sell women's makeup. Because men and women can be equally productive as childcare workers, health care workers, or auto mechanics, however, it would be discrimination to preferentially hire women rather than equally qualified men to be childcare workers or nurses or to preferentially hire men rather than women to be auto mechanics.

© Everett Collection Inc/Alamy Limited

Education Discrimination and *Brown v. Board of Education*

Education discrimination occurs when certain groups are prevented from having access to the same level or quality of education as other groups. In the United States, the 1896 landmark Supreme Court decision *Plessy v. Ferguson* legitimized the doctrine of "separate but equal" concerning segregation of public facilities, including separate schools for whites and blacks. It was not until the 1954 Brown v. Board of Education Supreme Court case that the doctrine of "separate but equal" was reversed. The desegregation of schools in the U.S. was highly controversial. The famous photo here shows Elizabeth Eckford attempting to enter Little Rock High Central School through a crowd of angry white students in 1957. Because formal schooling and on-the-job training can increase people's productivity and wages, education discrimination can be a source of pay gaps between groups.

ECONOMIC MODELS OF DISCRIMINATION

Why do people discriminate? What impacts does discrimination have on its victims and perpetrators? Economists have developed several theories to answer these questions. The predominant economic theories of discrimination fall into two broad categories: personal prejudice or taste-based models of discrimination, and incomplete information or statistical discrimination models.

Taste-based Models of Discrimination

In **taste-based models of discrimination**, people are assumed to have preferences not to work with, hire, or buy from the discriminated group. These personal preferences impact how workers are treated in the labor market.

In taste-based models of discrimination, people are assumed to have preferences not to work with, hire, or buy from the discriminated group.

For example, let's assume that people are prejudiced against females. People who have prejudice against females have a "taste" for discriminating against them and feel lower utility if they have to work with females, buy goods or services from females, or hire female workers. Economists incorporate people's taste for discrimination into the demand and supply model by assuming that prejudiced people perceive their costs to be higher when they interact with the discriminated group. In this section, we illustrate how taste-based discrimination by employers and customers can impact labor market outcomes.

Gary Becker and the Economics of Discrimination

Gary Becker (1930–) is one of the first economists to study the economics of discrimination, and he developed the taste-based models of discrimination presented in this chapter. He was awarded the Nobel Prize in Economics in 1992 for his work in expanding the field of economics into examinations of discrimination, crime and punishment, educational investments, and the allocation of time between work and family. In all of these areas, Becker argued, people's behavior can be analyzed using the cost-benefit framework central to economics. In 2007, Becker was awarded the U.S. Presidential Medal of Freedom, the nation's highest civilian honor.

Photo by Robert Galbraith/ Bloomberg via Getty Images

THINK FOR YOURSELF

Do you exhibit taste-based discrimination against certain groups? For many people, the first response to this question is, "Of course not!" Upon further reflection, however, you may discover that you do have preferences for certain groups in certain situations. When you take your car for repairs, do you prefer to have a male mechanic or a female mechanic? Would you prefer to have a male doctor or a female doctor? Would you prefer to have a male babysitter or a female babysitter for your child? Would you vote for an atheist to be president of the United States? Your answers should give you an indication of whether you have discriminatory preferences in these situations.

Employer Discrimination

Employer discrimination occurs when employers base their employment decisions on prejudice against certain workers.

Employer discrimination occurs when employers base their employment decisions on prejudice against certain workers. We can use the demand model to show how this prejudice affects employers' hiring and pay decisions.

Figure 19.3 presents an example of the impacts of employer discrimination against women. As in the real world, some firms discriminate against women but other firms do not. Nondiscriminatory firms do not consider workers' gender when making employment decisions. Instead, they only hire workers based on their productivity. Firm A, a nondiscriminatory firm, will hire workers depending on the wage and quantity demanded combinations that lie on its demand curve

Figure 19.3 **Hiring Decisions for Discriminatory and Nondiscriminatory Firms**

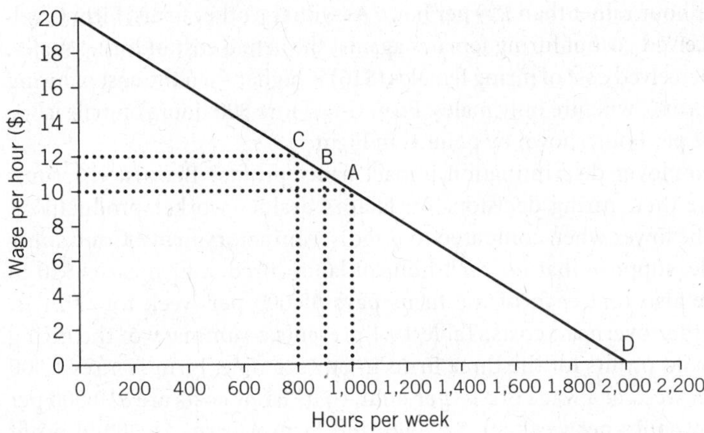

A nondiscriminating firm only considers productivity-related characteristics in its hiring decisions, so workers are hired based only on the wage and quantity demanded on the firm's labor demand curve D. When the wage is $10 per hour, the nondiscriminating firm hires 1,000 hours of labor per week (point A). A discriminatory firm hires workers based in part on its degree of prejudice. If a firm discriminates against females, it perceives the cost of hiring females to be higher than their actual market wage. Firm B acts as if the female wage is $11 per hour (point B). Firm B hires fewer females than is profit-maximizing. Firm C acts as if the wage for females is $16 per hour. Since $16 is higher than the male wage ($12), the firm hires only male workers (point C).

for labor. If the wages of male and female workers are both $10 per hour, Firm A will hire 1,000 hours of labor per week, shown by point A in Figure 19.3. The 1,000 hours of labor hired could be supplied by male workers, female workers, or some combination of both.

Now suppose, however, that discrimination against female workers by other firms causes females to have lower wages than males. When this happens, the nondiscriminatory firm faces an incentive to hire a different mix of workers. For example, if discrimination by other firms causes the wage for male workers to be $12 per hour and the wage for female workers to be $10 per hour, Firm A has an incentive to hire only females. Why? Female workers are just as productive as males, but female workers cost $10 per hour while male workers cost $12 per hour. Given this difference in costs, Firm A will hire 1,000 female worker hours at the wage of $10 per hour and will not hire any male workers. The counterintuitive result that a nondiscriminatory firm hires a female-only workforce rather than a mix of male and female workers is caused by the different market wages of male and female workers.

What do discriminatory firms do in this market? Discriminatory firms have prejudice against female workers. Because of their preferences against females, discriminatory firms act like the cost of hiring females is higher than it actually is. Suppose the market wage for females is again $10 per hour and the market wage for males is $12 per hour. Suppose also that Firm B, a discriminatory firm, acts like the cost of hiring females is $11 rather than $10. When hiring, Firm B compares its perceived cost of hiring female workers ($11) against the actual cost of hiring male workers ($12). Since female workers are still cheaper from Firm B's perspective, Firm B will hire only female workers. Unlike Firm A, however, Firm B will choose its quantity of labor demanded based on a wage of $11 per hour rather than $10 per hour. The quantity of female labor demanded by Firm B is 900 hours per week, shown by point B in Figure 19.3. Now imagine a firm with much stronger prejudice against female workers, Firm C. Because of its preferences, Firm C acts like the cost of hiring females is $16 per hour rather than $10 per hour. As with the other firms, Firm C will compare the perceived cost of hiring females against the actual cost of hiring males. For Firm C, the perceived cost of hiring females ($16) is higher than the cost of hiring males ($12), so Firm C will hire only males. Firm C will hire 800 hours of male labor at the wage of $12 per hour, shown by point C in Figure 19.3.

How does employer discrimination impact firms' profits? Because discriminatory firms base their hiring decisions on factors besides worker productivity, their profits will be lower when compared to nondiscriminatory firms. Continuing with our example, suppose that for each hour of labor hired, a firm earns $20 in revenue. Assume also that each of the firms pays $5,000 per week for utilities, insurance, and other overhead costs. Table 19.1 presents a summary of the hiring decisions, costs, and profits for the three firms in our example. Firm A hires 1,000 hours of labor per week at a wage of $10 per hour, so its labor costs are $10,000 per week. Firm A's revenues per week are $20,000, and Firm A earns $5,000 in profit per week.

Table 19.1 Relative Profits of Discriminatory and Nondiscriminatory Firms

	Firm A (non-discriminating firm)	Firm B (mildly discriminating firm)	Firm C (strongly discriminating firm)
Hours of labor hired per week (Q_{hours})	1,000	900	800
Wage paid per hour (W)	$10	$10	$12
Total Costs per week ($TC = (Q_{hours} * W) + \$5,000$)	(1,000 * 10) + $5,000 = $15,000	(900 * 10) + $5,000 = $14,000	(800 * 12) + $5,000 = $14,600
Total Revenue per week ($TR = Price * Q_{hours}$)	1,000 * $20 = $20,000	900 * $20 = $18,000	800 * $20 = $16,000
Profits per week (Profit = TR – TC)	$20,000 – $15,000 = $5,000	$18,000 – $14,000 = $4,000	$16,000 – $14,600 = $1,400

Firm B hires 900 hours of labor per week and pays its workers $10 per hour. Although Firm B makes its hiring decision as if the wage is $11 per hour, the actual wage it has to pay is $10 per hour. Firm B's total costs per week are $14,000, and its total revenues per week are $18,000. Firm B earns $4,000 per week in profits. Firm C hires 800 workers per week at the $12 per hour wage. Firm C's total costs are $14,600 per week, and its total revenues are $16,000 per week. Firm C earns $1,400 per week in profits.

This example illustrates an important impact of employer discrimination: it is costly. The nondiscriminatory firm hired labor at the lower wage and hired the profit-maximizing quantity of labor. The discriminatory firms did not hire the profit-maximizing amount of labor, and the most discriminatory firm, Firm C, paid more for labor than its competitors did. The more discriminatory a firm is, the more it "pays" for its prejudice through lower profits. One implication of employer discrimination is that if firms have to compete with one another for customers and profits, a nondiscriminatory firm should eventually be able to use its higher profits to drive its discriminatory competitors out of business. Indeed, many economists argue that one way to combat employers' labor market discrimination is to encourage more competition among firms.

© Andrew Rich/iStockphoto

The Cost of Discrimination in Major League Baseball

The economics prediction that discrimination is costly for firms is difficult to test in the real world. Firms' revenues, costs, and profits vary for reasons apart from discrimination, and data on firm hiring and cost structures are difficult to access. In an attempt to test whether the performance of discriminatory employers is different from that of nondiscriminatory employers, economist Andrew Hanssen turned to Major League baseball. Using data on teams' win-loss records after the color barrier was broken by black player Jackie Robinson, Hanssen examined whether teams that integrated more quickly won more games than other teams. Hanssen found that baseball teams with fewer black players lost substantially more often than more integrated teams. In other words, team owners who did not integrate their teams paid for it in terms of weaker win-loss records.

Customer Discrimination

Customer discrimination occurs when customers base their purchasing decisions on the race, sex, or other demographic characteristics of the workers with whom they interact.

In the **customer discrimination** model, employers are not discriminatory but customers are. For example, parents may have a preference for female childcare givers, patients might prefer a doctor of their own sex, and homeowners might prefer female maids. Prejudiced customers act as if the price of a good or service is higher than it actually is if they must deal with the discriminated group. Suppose that customers are prejudiced against women. If the actual price of a good is $100, discriminatory customers might act as if the good costs $110 and will thus have lower quantity demanded for the good if they have to buy the good from women.

Businesses can respond to customer discrimination in two ways. If employers can place the disfavored workers into jobs where there is no customer interaction, customer discrimination will lead to a segregated work force. If employers cannot put workers to positions that do not involve customer interaction, customer discrimination will have a negative effect on the wages of the discriminated group. Firms that hire females in customer service positions, for example, will have to lower the price of their good in order to compensate customers for their lost utility. Female wages would then have to be lower for firms to stay profitable.

Customer Discrimination in Professional Basketball

Harry How/Getty Images

Most of the fans of professional basketball are white, but most professional basketball players are black. These differences make professional basketball a good industry to use to study the impact of customer discrimination. Economists Larry Kahn and Peter Sherer have examined whether the racial composition of the National Basketball Association (NBA) teams affects game attendance. If white basketball fans prefer to watch white rather than black players, teams with more white players would have better game attendance, ceteris paribus. Customer discrimination would lower the relative salaries of black players, because team owners who want to cater to white fans would compete for the few white players available. Based on this hypothesis, Kahn and Sherer examined player productivity in the NBA and found results that are consistent with customer discrimination. Their research indicated that replacing one black player with an identical white player generated roughly 8,000 to 13,000 additional fans attending games per season. As a result, equally productive black players earned about 20 percent less than white players.

Incomplete Information Models

Taste-based discrimination models are based on people having prejudice against or preference for certain groups of workers. In incomplete information models of discrimination, differences in labor market outcomes arise because membership in a group conveys information about a person's potential skills and productivity. Incomplete information gives rise to **statistical discrimination** when wages and hiring are based in part on group characteristics. Statistical discrimination in employment happens because employers do not have complete information about the productivity of individual workers. In the absence of information on individual workers' productivity, employers sometimes use the characteristics of workers' demographic groups to predict potential productivity.

__Statistical discrimination__ occurs when people use information about the average characteristics of a group when making decisions about an individual member of that group.

THINK FOR YOURSELF

Automobile insurance companies routinely charge younger drivers higher rates than older drivers and charge single drivers higher rates than married drivers. Do automobile insurance companies engage in statistical discrimination?

Suppose you are an employer looking to hire someone to work with your company. It is critical that the worker be with your firm continuously for many years in order to establish long-term relationships with important clients. You are facing the choice between two 20-year-old applicants with essentially the same credentials, skills, and experience. The only difference between the two applicants is that one is a married female while the other is a married male. When compared to young married males at your company, young married females have tended to quit more often or have been more likely to take long leaves of absence for childbearing. Because of the long-term commitment needed for this particular position, you use this information about male and female employees when you decide to hire the male instead of the female. You do not necessarily know that this particular female candidate will leave the position, but you base at least some of your decision on the characteristics of her demographic group. This is statistical discrimination.

Racial Profiling and "Driving While Black"

Racial profiling is a form of statistical discrimination in which law enforcement or other security personnel target people for investigation because of their race or ethnicity. Higher rates of intense airport security screening for those of Middle Eastern descent, higher rates of traffic stops among black drivers, increased surveillance of minorities in shopping centers, and relatively more immigration audits of businesses that employ Latino workers are all examples of racial profiling. The term "driving while black" is a play on words for the phrase "driving while intoxicated," implying that black motorists are more likely to be pulled over simply because of their race.

ANTIDISCRIMINATION POLICIES IN THE UNITED STATES

In response to discriminatory practices in the labor market and other sectors of society, the United States has a long history of antidiscrimination legislation. At the state level, Michigan and Montana passed laws requiring equal pay for male and female workers in the same job back in 1919. Several states passed similar equal pay laws in the late 1940s. The earliest state laws prohibiting discrimination on the basis of race were passed in the 1930s in Illinois, Kansas, New York, and Pennsylvania.

At the federal level, President Roosevelt enacted an executive order prohibiting racial discrimination by federal contractors in 1941, but it was not until 1964 that a federal antidiscrimination law was enacted. The **1964 Civil Rights Act** was the first federal legislation to prohibit employment discrimination on basis of race, color, religion, sex, or national origin. The Civil Rights Act forms the cornerstone of federal antidiscrimination policy in the U.S. The Equal Employment Opportunity Commission is the agency that monitors compliance and enforces the Civil Rights Act.

*The **1964 Civil Rights Act** was the first federal legislation to prohibit employment discrimination.*

Other federal legislation aimed at discrimination includes the 1967 Age Discrimination in Employment Act, which prohibits discrimination in employment on the basis of age and eliminated mandatory retirement in most occupations. The 1990 American's With Disabilities Act prohibits discrimination in employment on the basis of disability and requires firms to make "reasonable accommodations" for disabled workers. In addition to the federal laws, a separate set of executive orders addresses the issue of **affirmative action**. President Kennedy's 1961 executive order requires federal contractors to take "affirmative action to ensure that applicants are employed, and that employees are treated during employment, without regard to their race, creed, color, or national origin." Later executive orders by Presidents Johnson and Nixon aimed to "correct the effects of past and present discrimination" by requiring certain organizations that accept federal funds to take action to increase employment of underrepresented groups.

__Affirmative action__ is a set of policies that mandate taking action to ensure the equal treatment of people regardless of their race, creed, color, or national origin. Affirmative action requires some organizations to take action to increase the representation of women and minorities.

THINK FOR YOURSELF

From the late 1800s until about 1950, many states had laws that restricted the employment of married women in some sectors of the labor market. Some of these laws prohibited married women from working in teaching and clerical jobs but allowed them to work as waitresses, domestic servants, and in manufacturing. Use a demand and supply model to illustrate how the laws affected employment and wages in teaching and clerical occupations. In a separate graph, illustrate how the laws affected employment and wages in waitress, domestic servant, and manufacturing jobs.

The Theoretical Impacts of Antidiscrimination Laws

The broad goal of antidiscrimination policies as they apply to the labor market is to reduce discrimination and encourage employment and pay based on ability rather than on other characteristics. In the case of affirmative action policy, the goal also includes increased employment of minority and women workers. The supply and demand model can be used to predict how antidiscrimination laws and affirmative action policies might impact the employment and wages of protected and unprotected groups.

Figure 19.4 shows one potential impact of antidiscrimination laws. Suppose initially that the demand for female workers is illustrated by the demand curve D. At that level of demand, the equilibrium wage for female workers is \$10 per hour, and the equilibrium level of employment is 1,000 hours per week. If antidiscrimination and affirmative action policies cause an increase in the demand for female workers, the demand curve shifts outward to D' The increase in demand causes an increase in the wages for females from \$10 to \$12, and an increase in female employment from 1,000 to 1,200 hours per week.

What happens to male workers as a result of these laws? It depends. If male and female workers are substitutes for one another, the increase in demand for female

Figure 19.4 **Potential Impact of Antidiscrimination Policies on Protected Workers**

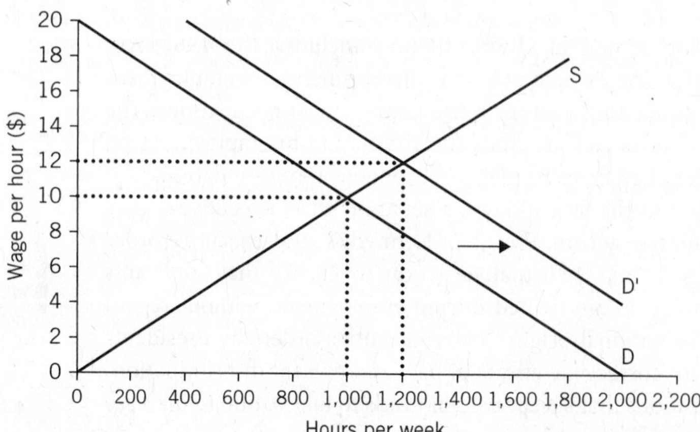

One goal of antidiscrimination laws is to increase the demand for protected workers. The demand for female workers is initially D, but after the antidiscrimination law is passed, the demand rises to D'. The increase in demand causes wages to rise from \$10 to \$12 per hour and increases employment from 1,000 to 1,200 per week.

workers may be accompanied by reduction in demand for male workers, ceteris paribus. If male and female workers are complements to one another, the increase in demand for female workers would cause an increase in the demand for male workers.

Female workers may also adjust their supply of labor in response to antidiscrimination policy. When faced with labor market discrimination, some women may reduce their labor supply, restrict the set of occupations they enter, or choose to leave the workforce altogether. When antidiscrimination policy and employment practices change, females may increase their labor supply and enter a broader set of occupations. The increased supply of labor would cause an increase in female employment. The net impact of the demand and supply changes on female wages would depend on the relative sizes of the demand and supply shifts. If the increase in demand for female workers is greater than the increase in supply of female workers, wages for females would rise. If the increase in supply is greater than the increase in demand, wages for females would fall.

The simple demand and supply model predicts that antidiscrimination laws would cause increased employment among the protected groups of workers. Unfortunately, the laws may also have unintended negative consequences for protected workers. For example, because antidiscrimination laws increase the chances that an employer can be sued for dismissing a female worker, the laws cause an increase the relative costs of hiring female workers. At the margin, the increase in costs could actually *decrease* the hiring of female workers. The conflicting predictions on the impacts of antidiscrimination laws have prompted economists to conduct research on the laws' actual impacts. The next section highlights some of the research findings regarding the impacts of antidiscrimination laws on minority and women workers.

Economics Research on the Effects of Antidiscrimination Laws

Economists and other social scientists have investigated the impacts of antidiscrimination laws for many years. Their research points to several general conclusions about how antidiscrimination laws have impacted protected groups.

Race

If antidiscrimination laws improve labor market opportunities and outcomes for blacks, we would expect the earnings ratios and employment of blacks to have risen after the laws were passed. Figure 19.5 shows how black/white earnings ratios in the U.S. changed after the passage of the Civil Rights Act. The black/white earnings ratios rose dramatically in the late 1960s and through the 1970s, which is consistent with the Civil Rights Act having a positive impact on black workers, particularly black females. Researchers have been cautious about attributing all of these earnings gains to antidiscrimination laws, however, because other factors have also contributed to the increase in black relative earnings over time. In particular, blacks had increased educational attainment and better quality of schools as a result of desegregation over this same time period. After controlling for all of these changes, researchers have found that antidiscrimination laws contributed to economic gains for blacks, with the largest gains occurring for black women.

Gender

Figure 19.6 shows the trend in female/male earnings ratios over time. Unlike the case for blacks relative to whites, there are no dramatic jumps in the female/male

Figure 19.5 **Black/White Earnings Ratios**

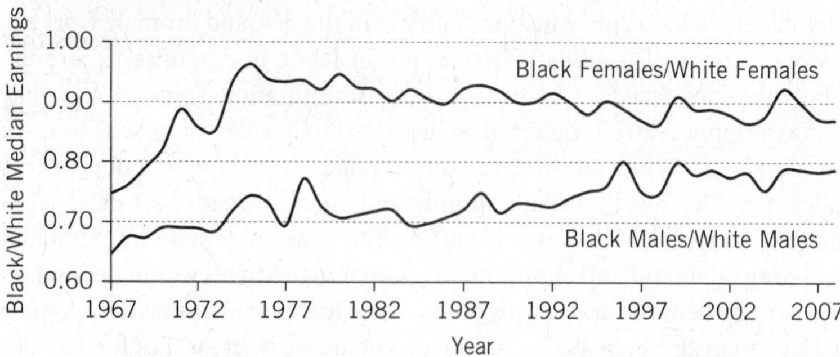

If laws prohibiting race discrimination are effective, black/white earnings ratios should increase after the laws are passed, ceteris paribus. The black/white earnings ratios increased after the mid-1960s, particularly for women. The black/white earnings ratios for men have remained fairly steady since the mid-1990s, but they declined slightly for women after the 1970s. *Source:* Author's computations based on U.S. Census Data. Includes median earnings of full-time year round workers 15 years old and over beginning in 1980, and 14 years old and over for previous years. Before 1989 earnings are for civilian workers only.

Figure 19.6 **Female/Male Earnings Ratios**

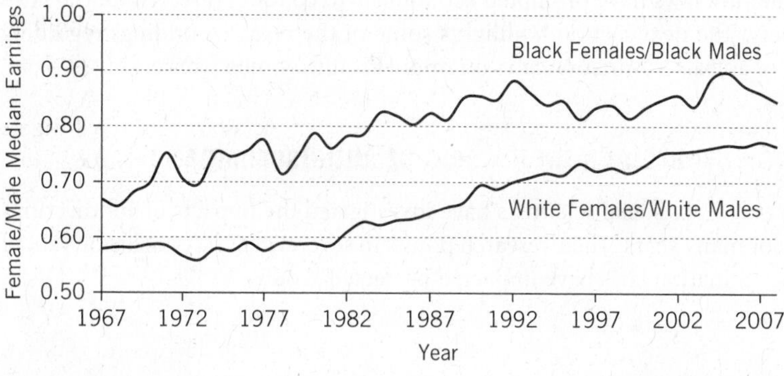

If laws prohibiting sex discrimination are effective, the female/male earnings ratios should increase after the laws are passed, ceteris paribus. The female/male earnings ratios for blacks increased after the mid-1960s, but have flattened or declined since the early 1990s. The female/male earnings ratios for whites have risen fairly steadily since the mid-1980s. *Source:* Author's computations based on U.S. Census Data. Includes median earnings of full-time year round workers 15 years old and over beginning in 1980 and 14 years old and over for previous years. Before 1989 earnings are for civilian workers only.

earnings ratios that coincide with passage of federal antidiscrimination laws in mid-1960s. The white female/white male earnings ratio remained flat during the 1960s and 1970s at about 0.60. The black female/black male earnings ratio did not jump dramatically after the Civil Rights Act was passed but instead increased slowly throughout the 1970s and 1980s. After controlling for changes in education and other factors, researchers have concluded that the labor market progress made by women after 1965 would probably have been of comparable magnitude even without affirmative action. In addition, some research has found that laws requiring equal pay for men and women were associated with *decreased* women's employment, which is consistent with the prediction that the laws raised the relative the cost of employing women.

Age and Disability

There is a much smaller body of research on the impact of age and disability discrimination laws than on race and sex discrimination laws. The research indicates that age discrimination laws are associated with increased employment of older workers. The general consensus from research on the impact of disability discrimination laws is that the ADA is associated with *lower* levels of employment of disabled workers. This finding is consistent with the idea that the reasonable accommodation clause in the ADA has the unintended consequence of making it more expensive to hire disabled workers.

SUMMARY

There are many explanations for the pay gaps that we observe between workers of different race, ethnicity, and gender. In particular, workers' education, occupation, location, and other choices can affect their productivity and wages. Pay gaps may also result from discrimination. Discrimination in the labor market occurs when workers who are equally productive are treated differently based on characteristics not related to that productivity. Discrimination can stem from taste-based factors including prejudice by employers, or customers. Statistical discrimination occurs when people use information about the average characteristics of a group to make decisions about an individual member of that group. Both types of discrimination can negatively impact the employment, earnings, and other labor market outcomes of discriminated groups.

The cornerstone of antidiscrimination policy in the U.S. is the 1964 Civil Rights Act, which prohibits employment discrimination on the basis of race, color, religion, sex, or national origin. Economic reasoning predicts that antidiscrimination policies can have both positive and negative impacts on protected groups of workers, and much economic research has sought to isolate the impacts of the laws.

KEY CONCEPTS

- Earnings ratio
- Pay gap
- Discrimination
- Taste-based models of discrimination
- Employer discrimination
- Customer discrimination
- Statistical discrimination
- 1964 Civil Rights Act
- Affirmative action

DISCUSSION QUESTIONS AND PROBLEMS

1. List and explain three reasons why we observe a wage differential when comparing the average wages of males and females.
2. What is an earnings ratio? What does it mean if the female/male earnings ratio is equal to 1? What does it mean if the black/white earnings ratio declines?
3. How has the black/white earnings ratio changed since the Civil Rights Act was passed? How has the female/male earnings ratio changed? Offer some possible explanations for these changes.
4. In their research paper "Beauty, Productivity, and Discrimination: Lawyers' Looks and Lucre" [*Journal of Labor Economics*, 16(1) (January 1998):

172–201], economists Jeff Biddle and Daniel Hamermesh examined the earnings and job placement of a large sample of lawyers. Their research data included objective ratings of the lawyers' looks. The research found that attractive lawyers earned more than other lawyers. Why might better-looking attorneys earn more?

5. In the early 1900s, many states passed legislation designed to "protect" women workers. In California, for example, a 1916 law prohibits women from employment in jobs that involve lifting "any excessive burden," cleaning moving machinery, work on moving abrasives, work in core making rooms, manufacture of nitro compounds, handling of any dry substance with specified amount of lead, employment in work environments that are not sufficiently lighted, ventilated, or sanitary, messenger service, bell boy, trucking, gas/electric meter reader, taxi cab driver, elevator operator, guard on streets or subways, work in pool hall/bowling alley, delivery service, or "employing women under any conditions detrimental to their health or welfare." How would these protective laws affect the employment and wages of women and men workers?

6. Suppose a commonly held but unfounded belief is that people with blue eyes are not as smart as people with brown eyes. What would you expect to happen to the relative wages between the two groups as a result of this belief?

Wage ($/hour)	Quantity of Workers Demanded (millions of workers/year)
17	6
15	8
13	10
11	12
9	14
7	16

7. Assume there are 24 million workers in the economy. Half are men and half are women. The workers supply their labor to three occupations (A, B, and C). Occupations A and B are men's occupations (they only employ men). Occupation C is a women's occupation (it only employs women). Otherwise, the occupations are the same. The accompanying demand schedule for workers is the same in all occupations.
   a. Give two examples of possible occupations for A and B. Give two examples of possible occupations for C.
   b. Assume that the labor supply to each occupation is perfectly inelastic. What will be the men's equilibrium wage? The women's?
   c. If an antidiscrimination law is passed that forces equal employment of men and women in all three occupations, what would be the equilibrium wage rate in the occupations? Who would gain and who would lose as a result of the law?

MULTIPLE-CHOICE QUESTIONS

1. An employer who is willing to pay higher wages to avoid employing persons from some group that he is prejudiced against is said to have
   a. a taste for discrimination.
   b. no business sense.
   c. a taste for justice.
   d. a mean personality.

2. The taste-based discrimination model implies that employer discrimination could be reduced if
   a. it is against the law.
   b. discriminating employers are at a cost disadvantage when compared to nondiscriminatory employers.
   c. firms cannot accurately predict the characteristics of an individual by looking at the group the individual belongs to.
   d. customers prefer to buy from whites instead of blacks.

3. The effects of discrimination include
   a. lower incomes for minorities, but not women.
   b. lower incomes for men, but not Hispanics.
   c. higher profits of discriminating employers.
   d. lower profits for discriminatory employers.

4. Among the following, which is *most likely* an instance of discrimination?
   a. A male orthopedic surgeon earns more than a female pediatrician.
   b. The university president's male secretary earns more than the economics department's female secretary.
   c. A white worker earns more than a black worker performing the same job at the same level.
   d. Women earn less than men, on average.
   e. All of the above represent discrimination.

5. Data comparing average earnings by gender and race
   a. provide proof that discrimination exists
   b. provide proof that no discrimination exists
   c. must be interpreted cautiously because people's choices may explain some of the observed differences
   d. must be interpreted cautiously because they are politically sensitive

6. Statistical discrimination
   a. is clearly illegal and almost never practiced.
   b. involves judging people on the basis of group rather than individual characteristics.
   c. increases the costs to the discriminator.
   d. benefits individuals from groups with low average values of characteristics that are valued by employers.
   e. all of the above

Use the following information to answer Questions 7–10. Suppose that labor market experience is the only characteristic that influences wages. Suppose also that males and females have different levels of experience and have different "wage functions" (equations that show relationship between wages and experience). The male and female wage functions are given by the following:

Males	Females
Wage = 10 + .5 * Experience	Wage = 9 + .25 * Experience

For example, males with 5 years of experience have hourly wages of W = 10 + .5(5) = $12.50 per hour.

7. Based on the given information, if the average number of years of experience for males is 20 years and the average number of years of experience is 16 years, the average male wage will be ____ per hour and the average female wage will be ____ per hour.
   a. $20; $16
   b. $16; $20
   c. $16; $13
   d. $20; $13

8. Based on the given information, if the average number of years of experience for males is 20 years and the average number of years of experience is 16 years, the pay gap between men and women will be __ per hour.
   a. $3
   b. $4
   c. $7
   d. $16
   e. $20

9. Based on the given information, the wage for a male with 10 years of labor market experience is __ per hour and the wage for a female with 10 years of labor market experience is __ per hour.
   a. $15; $15
   b. $11.50; $11.50
   c. $15; $11.50
   d. $11.50; $15

10. Based on the given information, if men and women had the same labor market experience,
   a. men's and women's pay would be the same.
   a. men's pay would be higher than women's pay.
   b. women's pay would be higher than men's pay.
   c. firms would treat men and women the same.

ADDITIONAL READINGS AND WEB RESOURCES

Arrow, Kenneth J. (1998) "What Has Economics to Say About Racial Discrimination?" *Journal of Economic Perspectives*, 12 (Spring):91–100. Presents an overview of the scope and limits of economics for understanding racial discrimination in labor markets.

Beller, A. H. (1979) "The Impact of Equal Employment Opportunity Laws on the Male-Female Earnings Differential," in *Women in the Labor Market*, edited by C. Lloyd, E. Andrews, and C. Gilroy. New York: Columbia University Press: 203–230. Presents research on the impact of antidiscrimination laws on the relative earnings of males and females.

Betrand, Marianne, and Mullainathan, Sendhil (2003) "*Are Emily and Greg More Employable Than Lakisha and Jamal?: A Field Experiment on Labor Market Discrimination*," NBER working paper series no. 9873; Cambridge: National Bureau of Economic Research. Presents research on the relationship between applicants' names and their subsequent job market opportunities.

Darity, W. A., and Mason, P. L. (1998) "Evidence on Discrimination in Employment: Codes of Color, Codes of Gender," *Journal of Economic Perspectives*, 12 (2):63-90. Presents an overview of the economic research on race and gender discrimination in the labor market.

Goldin, C. (1991) *Understanding the Gender Gap*, New York: Oxford University Press. Presents a history of women's employment in the U.S., including research on the impact of antidiscrimination laws on women's economic progress.

Hanssen, Andrew (1998) "The Cost of Discrimination: A Study of Major League Baseball," *Southern Economic Journal*, 64(3) (January):603–627. Presents research on the impact of racial integration on the win-loss records of baseball teams.

Heckman, James J. (1998) "Detecting Discrimination," *Journal of Economic Perspectives*, 12 (Spring):101–116. Presents an overview of the methods that economists use to disentangle the portions of wage gaps due to discrimination and portions due to differences in worker productivity.

Holzer, H., and Neumark, D. (2000) "Assessing Affirmative Action," *Journal of Economic Literature*, 38(3):483–568. Presents a comprehensive overview of the effects of affirmative action on the employment of women and minorities, as well as a review of the impact of affirmative action on economic efficiency.

Kahn, Lawrence M., and Sherer, Peter D. (1988) "Racial Differences in Professional Basketball Players' Compensation," *Journal of Labor Economics*, 6(1) (January):40–61. Presents research on the impact of consumer discrimination in the NBA.

Loury, Glenn C. (1998) "Discrimination in the Post-Civil Rights Era: Beyond Market Interactions," *Journal of Economic Perspectives*, 12 (Spring 1998):117–126. Presents evidence on the impact of differences in workers' skills on the wage gap.

Neumark, David, and Stock, Wendy A. (2006) "The Labor Market Effects of Sex and Race Discrimination Laws," *Economic Inquiry*, 44(3) (July):385–419. Presents research on the impact of antidiscrimination laws on the relative employment and earnings of blacks and women.

Smith, J. P., and Welch, F. (1977) "Black-White Wage Ratios: 1960–70." *American Economic Review*, 67(3):232–238. Presents evidence on changes in the black:white earnings ratio after the Civil Rights Act, and assess the contribution of educational attainment and educational quality to the narrowing of the black-white wage gap.

Vstock LLC/Getty Images, Inc.

Poverty and the Distribution of Income

After studying this chapter, you should be able to:

- Describe the distribution of income in the U.S. and the global distribution of income
- Explain various measures of income inequality
- Describe various measures of poverty
- Summarize the issues surrounding global poverty and inequality
- Describe some of the primary causes of poverty
- Describe the impacts of various poverty policies

In 2010, over 43 million of the 328 million people in the United States were living in poverty, the highest level of poverty in over a decade. That same year, 12 of the 25 richest people in the world lived in the U.S. How much money does it take to be rich in the U.S.? What does it mean to be "in poverty"? What policies can we use to fight poverty? Are the rich getting richer and the poor getting poorer?

How a country divides its income and other resources is a fundamental question for policymakers and citizens. Unfortunately, it appears that many people do not have a clear sense of how income is divided within and across countries. For example, Figure 20.1 presents data from a nationally representative sample of over 5,000 Americans who were polled in 2005 and asked to describe the division of wealth in the U.S. Wealth, which is closely related to income, is the total value of everything someone owns minus any debt he or she owes.

The "Estimated" bar at the top of the figure shows people's estimates of how the wealth in the U.S. is divided among quintiles or fifths of the population. The "Actual" bar in the middle of the figure shows how the wealth in the U.S. is actually divided. The top 20 percent of households own over 80 percent of the nation's wealth. The bottom 40 percent of households combined own less than 1 percent of the nation's wealth. People estimate that the division of wealth in America is more equal than it actually is.

Finally, survey respondents were also asked what they thought the division of wealth in the U.S. should be. The bar at the bottom of Figure 20.1 shows people's "Ideal" division of wealth. People's ideal division of wealth is much more equal than either the actual or estimated division of wealth in the U.S. Understanding how incomes are distributed is important, whether your goal is to move society closer to the "Ideal" distribution in Figure 20.1 or whether you would prefer not to redistribute income across groups. This chapter covers the interrelated issues of poverty and the income distribution.

INCOME DISTRIBUTION

In general, a distribution shows the values of a variable and the percentage of observations that take on those values. You've likely seen distributions before. As one example, some professors use distributions to curve grades in their courses. They might assign A grades to 10 percent of the students, B grades to 20 percent of the students, C grades to 40 percent, and so on. An **income distribution** shows the levels of income in an economy and the percentage of individuals or households earning those income levels. There are many ways to illustrate income distributions. Some show the distribution of income at a given time, others track changes across time.

An ***income distribution*** *shows the levels of income in an economy and the percentage of individuals or households earning those income levels.*

Figure 20.1 The Division of Wealth in the U.S.

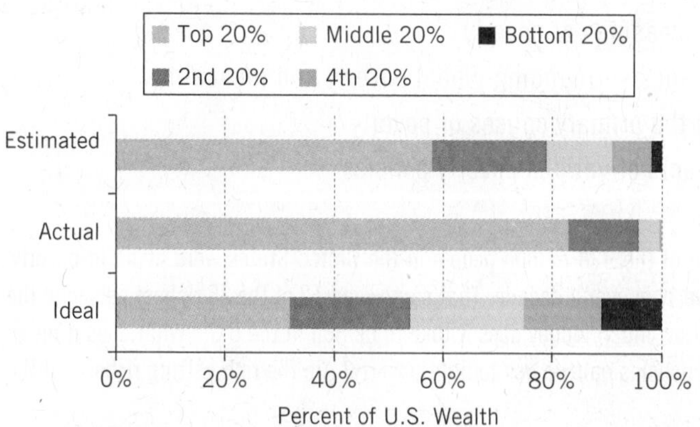

The actual division of wealth in the U.S. is very different from what people think it is or what they think it should be. Wealth is the total value of everything someone owns minus any debt he or she owes. The "Actual" bar shows how the wealth in the U.S. was divided in 2005. The top 20 percent of households own over 80 percent of the nation's wealth. The bottom 40 percent of households have less than 1 percent of the nation's wealth (the values for the 4th 20 percent and bottom 20 percent are too small to appear in the "Actual" bar). The "Estimated" bar shows people's estimates of how the wealth in the U.S. is divided. The "Ideal" bar shows how people think the wealth in the U.S. should be divided. *Source:* Author's chart based on Figure 20.2 of Michael I. Norton and Dan Ariely (2011) "Building a Better America—One Wealth Quintile at a Time," *Perspectives on Psychological Science* 2011 6(1):9–12.

U.S. Income Distribution

Figure 20.2 illustrates the U.S. income distribution in 2010. The height of the bars shows the percentage of households earning the annual income levels listed on the horizontal axis. At the bottom or left end of the distribution, roughly 25 percent of U.S. households have annual incomes between $0 and $24,999. At the top or right end of the distribution, roughly 2 percent of U.S. households earn $250,000 per year or more. The U.S. income distribution is a skewed income distribution, which means that a large percentage of U.S. households earn relatively low income, while a small percentage of households earn very high income. Most economies have income distributions with this skewed shape.

Figure 20.2 **U.S. Income Distribution, 2010**

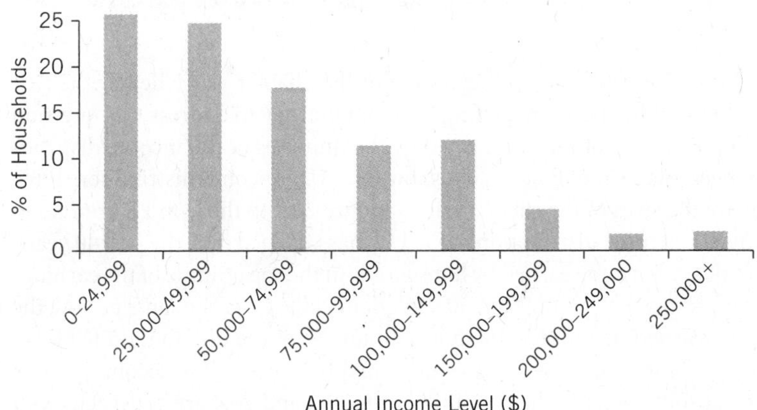

The U.S. income distribution shows the percent of households earning various levels of annual income. It is a skewed income distribution since a very small percentage of households earn very high incomes and a large percentage of households earn low incomes. *Source:* Author's chart based on U.S. Census data.

Figure 20.3 is another illustration of the U.S. income distribution. Each slice of "pie" in the chart represents the income share earned by each quintile of U.S. households in 2009. The lowest-earning quintile earned 3 percent of U.S. income. The average income for households in this quintile was $11,500 per year. Alternatively, the top-earning quintile earned 50 percent of U.S. income and had an average income of $171,000.

Figure 20.3 **Division of U.S. Income by Quintile, 2009**

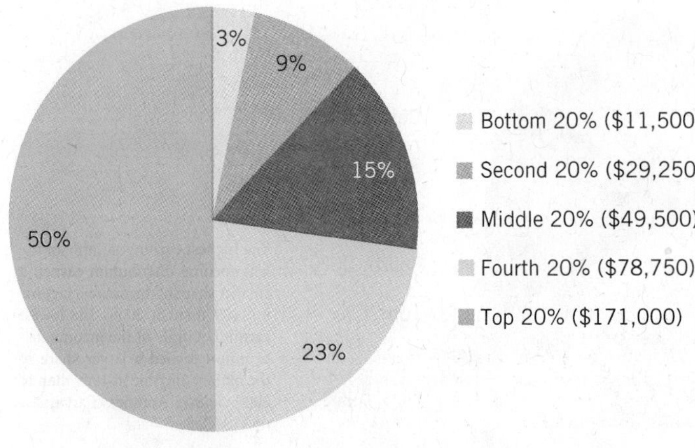

The highest earning quintile of the U.S. income distribution earns 50 percent of the nation's income. The lowest earning quintile of the income distribution earns 3 percent of the nation's income. The numbers in parentheses are the average household incomes for each quintile. *Source:* Author's chart based on U.S. Census data.

Figures 20.2 and 20.3 can be used to answer one of the questions posed at the beginning of the chapter: How much money does it take to be rich in the United States? If by rich we mean being in the top fifth of households, then it takes an average of $171,000 per year to be rich in the United States. If by rich we mean being in the top 2 percent of households, it takes $250,000 per year.

What are some of the costs and benefits associated with having an unequal income distribution?

A second question raised at the beginning of the chapter was whether the rich are getting richer and the poor are getting poorer. One way to address this question is to track whether shares of income earned by the quintiles of the income distribution have changed over time. Figure 20.4 shows the U.S. income distribution 1969. We can compare the sizes of the slices of pie in Figure 20.4 to those in Figure 20.3 to determine how the income distribution in the U.S. has changed over the past 40 years.

The share of total income earned by households in the top quintile of the earnings distribution was 43 percent in 1969 and 50 percent in 2009. Over the same period, the share of income earned by those in the bottom quintile of the distribution fell from 4 percent to 3 percent. The share of income earned by those in the second quintile also fell, from 11 to 9 percent. The data in Figures 20.3 and 20.4 are consistent with the idea that the rich are getting richer, since the share of income earned by the top quintile has grown over the last 40 years. In other words, the rich are getting richer.

However, we cannot conclude that the poor are getting poorer based on these data. The overall size of the income pie in the U.S. more than tripled between 1969 and 2009, even after adjusting for inflation. In other words, the rich did get richer over the past 40 years, but the poor got richer as well.

Figure 20.4 **Division of U.S. Income by Quintile, 1969**

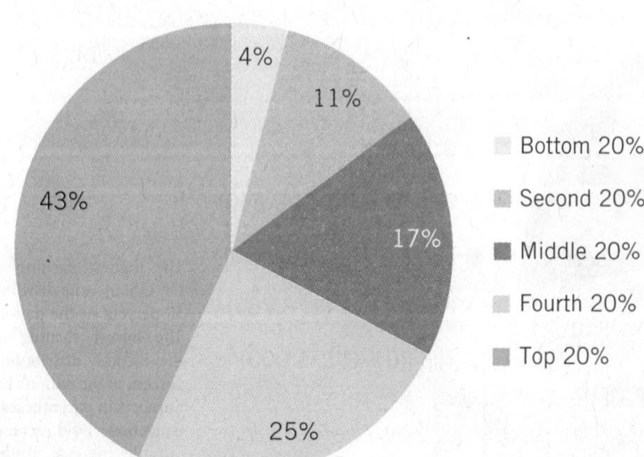

The highest earning quintile of the U.S. income distribution earned a smaller share of the nation's income in 1969 than in 2009. The lowest earning quintile of the income distribution earned a larger share of the nation's income in 1969 than in 2009. *Source:* Author's chart based on U.S. Census data.

Global Income Distribution

Measuring the global distribution of income is much trickier than measuring the income distribution within a given economy. This is primarily due to differences in data collection methods, available resources, and currency values across countries. Despite these difficulties, there is a growing body of research focused on the distribution of world income among countries and across time.

Figure 20.5 illustrates world distribution of income in 2010. Almost two-thirds of the world's income is earned by a few large economies. The 12 countries listed in Figure 20.5 earned 65 percent of the world's income in 2010, while the remaining 184 countries in the world earned about 35 percent of the world's income. The United States earned one-fifth of the world's income in 2010. The next largest economies were China, which earned 13 percent of the world's income, and Japan, which earned 6 percent of global income in 2010.

Figure 20.5 **Division of Global Income, 2010**

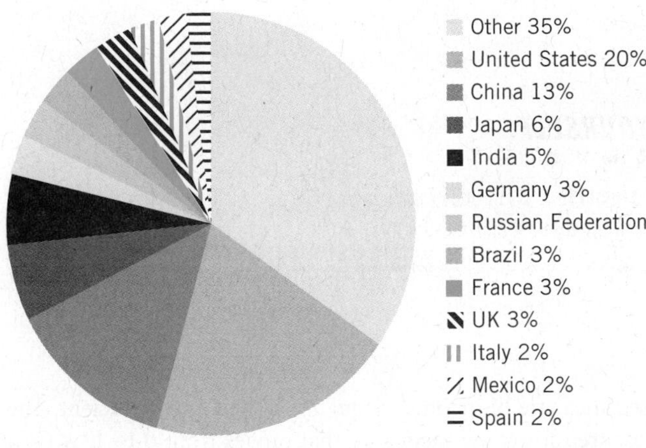

The largest 12 economies in the world earn roughly two-thirds of the world's income, while the other 184 countries combined earned 35 percent of the world's income. The United States earned one-fifth of the world's income in 2010. *Source:* Author's graph based on the CIA World Factbook 2010.

MEASURING INCOME INEQUALITY

The figures presented earlier in the chapter indicate that there is substantial inequality in the distribution of U.S. income and across the globe. There are several standard measures of income inequality that economists use to assess the income distributions within or across economies. These measures include income ratios and Gini coefficients, described in the next sections.

Income Ratios

Income ratios are measures of income inequality that compare the earnings of those at one point in the income distribution to the earnings of those at another point in the income distribution.

Income ratios are a commonly used measure of income inequality. An **income ratio** compares the incomes of those in the upper end of an income distribution to the incomes of those in the lower end of the income distribution. The 80:20 ratio, for example, compares the earnings of households at the 80th percentile of the income distribution to the earnings of households at the 20th percentile of the distribution. The 90:10 ratio compares the income of households at the 90th percentile to households at the 10th percentile. For example, if the income of households at the

80th percentile of the income distribution in the U.S. was $100,000 per year and the income of households at the 20th percentile of the income distribution was $25,000 per year, the 80:20 ratio would be

$$80{:}20 \text{ ratio} = \$100{,}000/\$25{,}000 = 4$$

An 80:20 ratio value of 4 indicates that the incomes of those at the 80th percentile of the income distribution are 4 times as large as the incomes of those at the 20th percentile of the income distribution.

Figure 20.6 shows U.S. 80:20 and 90:10 ratios over time. The 80:20 ratio was 4 throughout much of the 1960s and 1970s, but it rose to roughly 5 by 2010. The 90:10 ratio was 9 in 1967, meaning that households at the 90th percentile of the income distribution earned 9 times as much as those at the 10th percentile of the distribution. By 2010, the 90:10 ratio had increased to roughly 11. The increase in the income ratios indicates that there has been increasing income inequality in the U.S. over the past 40 years.

Suppose the 90:10 ratio is equal to 8. What does this imply about the earnings distribution? What would be happening to the income distribution if the 80:20 ratio were falling over time?

Gini Coefficient

*The **Gini coefficient** measures income inequality on a scale from 0 to 1, with higher values indicating more income inequality.*

A second commonly used measure of income inequality is the Gini coefficient. The **Gini coefficient** is a measure of income inequality that ranges from 0 to 1. A Gini coefficient value of 0 indicates perfect equality of income in an economy. A Gini coefficient value of 1 indicates perfect inequality of the income distribution, which means that one person in an economy has all the income, while the rest of the people have zero income.

Figure 20.6 **U.S. Income Ratios 1967–2010**

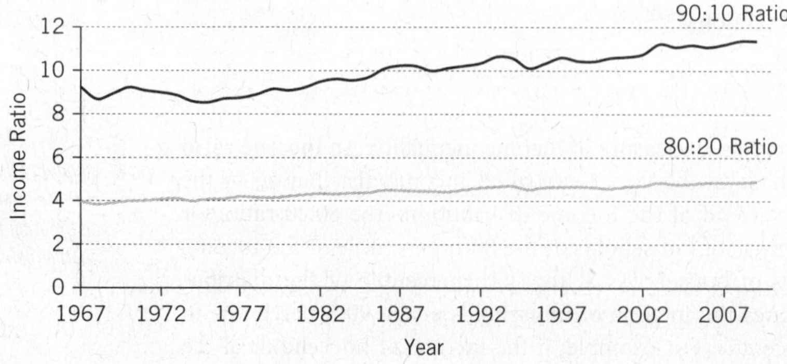

The U.S. 90:10 ratio has increased from 9 to 11 over the past 40 years. Those at the 90th percentile of the U.S. income distribution earned about 11 times more than those at the 10th percentile in 2010. The 80:20 ratio has risen from 4 to 5 over the same period. *Source:* Author's chart based on U.S. Census data.

The value of the Gini coefficient is not very useful on its own but is instead used to compare inequality across places or across time. Because higher values of the Gini coefficient indicate higher inequality, increasing Gini coefficients over time for a given country would imply that the country's income is becoming less equally distributed. Gini coefficients can also be compared across countries to gauge their relative income inequality.

Figure 20.7 presents Gini coefficients for the world in 2009. Areas with relatively low Gini coefficients, and thus relatively more equal income distributions, include Western Europe, Canada, and Australia. Areas with the highest Gini coefficients, and thus the highest degree of income inequality, include Brazil, Colombia, Bolivia, Sierra Leone, South Africa, and the Central African Republic.

Figure 20.7 **International Gini Coefficients, 2009**

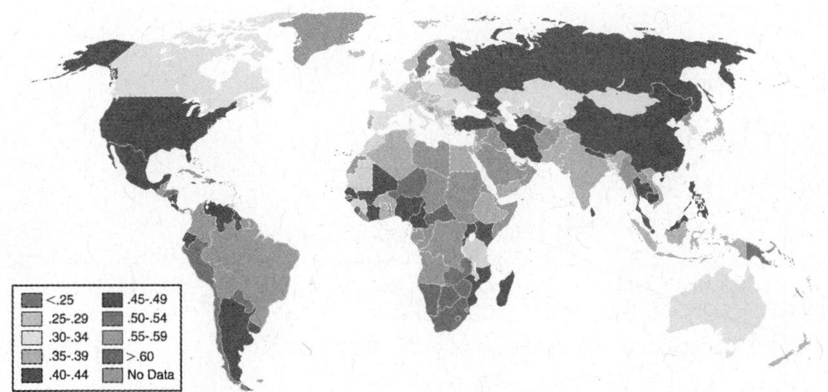

Gini coefficients measure income inequality, with higher values indicating more income inequality. Several countries in South America and parts of southern Africa have relatively high income inequality. Canada, Australia, and most countries in Europe have relatively low income inequality. *Source:* http://upload.wikimedia.org/wikipedia/commons/5/59/Gini_Coefficient_World_CIA_Report_2009-1.png. Public Domain based on CIA World Factbook data.

Gini coefficients can also be used to compare income inequality across time. Figure 20.8 presents Gini coefficients for selected countries between 1960 and 2010. Some countries, like China, India, the United Kingdom, and the United States, have had rising Gini coefficients. These countries have experienced increasing income

Figure 20.8 **Countries' Income Inequality Over Time**

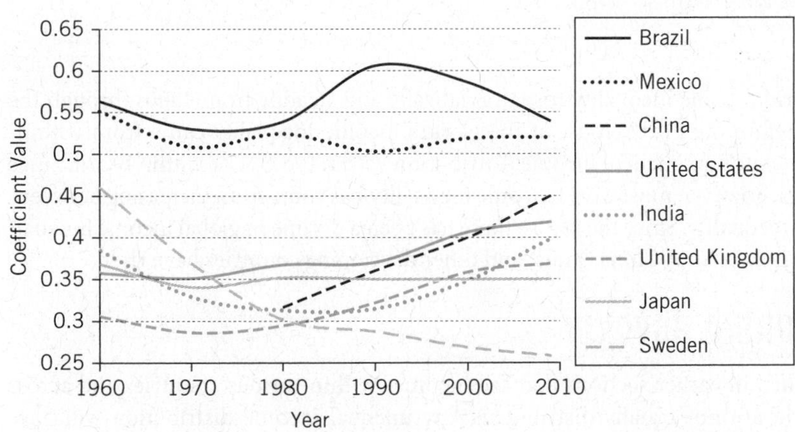

An index value of 0 represents perfect equality. A value of 1 represents perfect inequality (i.e., one person has all the income). Brazil and Mexico are among countries with the highest income inequality. Sweden and Japan have more equal distributions of income. The income inequality in the U.S. has increased since the 1970s. *Source:* Author's compilation of World Bank data and adjusted from William Easterly (1999) "Life During Growth," *Journal of Economic Growth* 4(3) (September): 239–275. Some values for 2010 are estimated.

inequality over time. Other countries, including Sweden, Japan, and Mexico, have had their income distributions grow more equal over time.

Figures 20.7 and 20.8 illustrate within-country income inequality measures for countries across the world. They indicate, for example, that Brazil has a relatively unequal income distribution when compared to other countries, but that Brazil's income inequality has been declining since 1990.

Figure 20.9 illustrates how the world's income distribution has changed over time. The vertical axis uses an index of inequality similar to the Gini coefficient in that higher values represent more inequality and lower values represent a more equal income distribution. The figure measures world income inequality from two sources: inequality that occurs within countries and inequality that occurs between countries. Within-country inequality comes from unequal income distributions within countries. Between-country inequality comes from an unequal distribution of world income among countries. Total inequality is the sum of between-country inequality and within-country inequality.

Figure 20.9 **World Inequality Over Time**

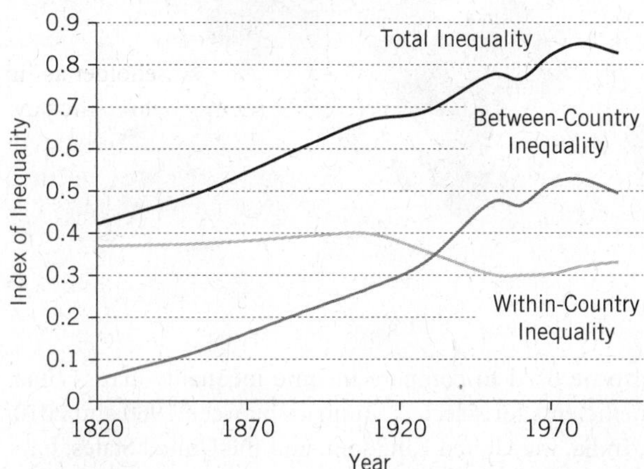

A higher index of inequality implies a less equal income distribution. Within-country inequality comes from unequal income distributions within countries. Between-country inequality comes from unequal income distribution of the world's income among countries. Total inequality comes from within-country inequality and between-country inequality. The largest source of increases in world inequality over this time period is between-country inequality. *Source:* Author's chart based on data in Bourguignon, F. and C. Morrisson (2002) "Inequality among World Citizens: 1820–1992," *American Economic Review* 92(4) (September): 727–744.

World income inequality rose dramatically and steadily from 1800s through the 1970s. Before the 1920s, most of the world's income inequality came from within-countries, such an unequal distribution within the U.S. or within Brazil. Since the 1920s, however, most world income inequality has come from increasing between-country inequality. Since the 1980s, there has been a decline in global income inequality as the incomes of China, India, and other developing countries have risen.

MEASURING POVERTY

We learned in earlier sections that the incomes within various countries and across the world are not equally distributed. Any unequal income distribution will have people at the lower end of that distribution—the poor. But what does it mean to be poor or "in poverty"? Is it an absolute, income-based concept that can be applied similarly throughout the world? Is it a relative concept that depends on one's place in the income distribution? Any understanding of poverty must start with a clear definition before policymakers and concerned citizens can design and assess the effectiveness of poverty reduction programs.

Poverty has traditionally been measured using income- or consumption-based guidelines. Examples of traditional measures of poverty include the amount of income earned or the ability to earn enough to meet a certain standard of living. Newer measures of poverty attempt to capture its multidimensionality by including indicators of educational attainment, measures of health outcomes, and measures of access to safe drinking water, or other services and infrastructure. All poverty measures set criteria or thresholds to determine who is in poverty and who is not.

Poverty Lines

A **poverty line**, poverty threshold, or poverty guideline is a specific level of income or consumption below which a person is classified as being in poverty. Poverty thresholds tend to vary by time, place, and family size. U.S. poverty lines are published annually in the Federal Register and on the Department of Housing and Human Services website. In 2011, U.S. poverty guidelines defined a single householder as "in poverty" if his or her annual income was below $10,890. For a family of four, the poverty line was $22,350. These thresholds are used to establish eligibility for Head Start, food stamps, free and reduced-price school lunch, and many other income-based assistance programs. For measuring poverty on a global level, the most commonly used poverty line is $1.25 per day in U.S.-equivalent income.

*The **poverty line** is the income or consumption level below which a person is considered to be in poverty.*

©AP/Wide World Photos

"Miss Poverty" and the Origin of the Official U.S. Poverty Thresholds

Mollie Orshansky, a statistician and economist working for the Social Security Administration in the early 1960s, developed the poverty thresholds still used by the U.S. government. In part based on her prior work at the U.S. Department of Agriculture, Ms. Orshansky assessed the cost of nutritionally adequate food plans for families of different sizes. Based on the costs of the food plans and data showing that families spent roughly one-third of their incomes on food in the 1960s, the cost of the food plans were multiplied by three to set poverty lines. Because of her work on measuring poverty levels and setting poverty thresholds, Ms. Orshansky was sometimes called "Miss Poverty."

Do you think that the poverty lines in the U.S. are set, too high, too low or at the right level? Explain your answer.

Poverty Rates

*The **poverty rate** is the percentage of people with incomes below the poverty line.*

The **poverty rate** is the percentage of people with incomes below the poverty line. Poverty rates vary across time, place, and demographic factors. Figure 20.10 presents U.S. poverty rates over time.

Figure 20.10 **U.S. Poverty Rate Over Time**

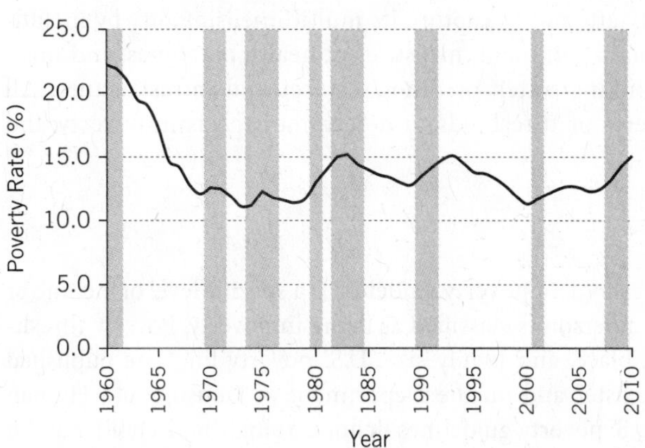

The U.S. poverty rate declined rapidly in the 1960s, but has remained steady at about 12–15 percent since the 1970s. The shaded areas represent economic downturns. *Source:* Author's chart based on U.S. Bureau of the Census, Current Population Survey, Annual Social and Economic Supplements data.

The U.S. poverty rate was over 20 percent in 1960, but fell rapidly during the early 1960s and has been between 10 and 15 percent since 1965. The shaded areas in Figure 20.10 represent periods of economic downturns. The poverty rate tends to rise during economic downturns and decline during economic expansions, which provides a clue into one of the causes of poverty.

Figure 20.10 summarizes changes in the overall U.S. poverty rate over time, but poverty varies widely among different educational and demographic groups. Table 20.1 presents poverty rates for several demographic groups.

In terms of family structure, poverty rates are lowest among married couple families. Poverty rates are particularly high among households headed by single women. Poverty rates are also higher among people under age 18, and roughly one in five U.S. children lives in poor families. Not surprisingly, poverty rates are much higher among people with relatively low levels of education, and poverty rates decline as educational attainment increases. Poverty rates tend to be lower among non-Hispanic whites and among Asians and higher among Hispanics and among non-Hispanic blacks. The race and ethnicity differences stem in part from differential levels of educational attainment and the higher rates of households headed by single women across racial and ethnic groups.

Global poverty rates are generally measured using a poverty line of $1.25 per day. Using this poverty threshold, Figure 20.11 shows poverty rates among the world's countries in 2008. Poverty rates based on the $1.25 per day threshold are under 2 percent for North America, Europe, Australia, and Russia. Poverty rates are between 2 and 5 percent in Argentina, Turkey, Kazakhstan, Morocco, and Tunisia. Alternatively, more than 60 percent of the populations of several Central and East African nations live on less than $1.25 per day.

Table 20.1 U.S. Poverty Rates by Demographic Characteristics, 2010

Group	Poverty Rate (%)
All people	15.1
All families	13.2
Married couples	5.8
Female householder families, no husband	31.6
Male householder families, no wife	15.8
Age	
Under 18	22.0
Age 18–64	13.7
Age 65+	9.0
Education	
Less than high school	24.9
High school diploma	22.6
Some college	15.5
Four year degree or more	6.5
Race & Ethnicity	
White, non-Hispanic	9.9
Black, non-Hispanic	27.4
Asian	12.1
Hispanic	26.6

Source: Author's chart based on U.S. Bureau of the Census, Current Population Survey, Annual Social and Economic Supplements. Rates by education are for 2009.

Figure 20.11 Percentage of Population Living on Less than $1.25 Per Day, 2008

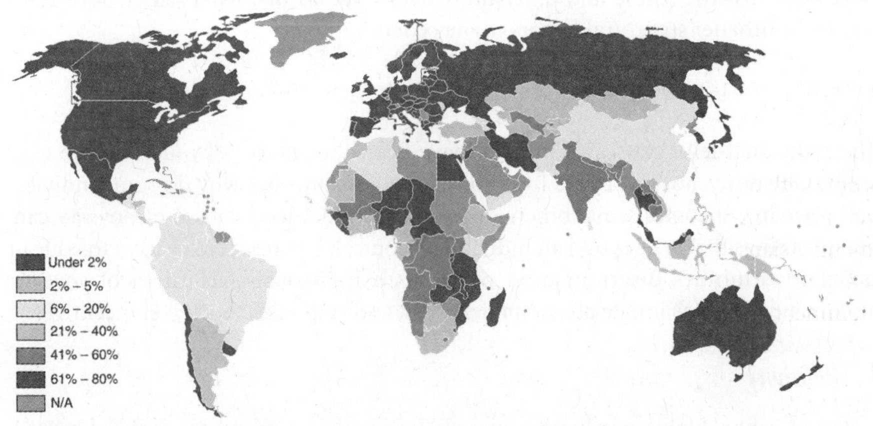

Less than 2 percent of those in North America, Europe, Australia, and Russia live on less than $1.25 per day. The percent of the population living on less than $1.25 per day is also relatively low for much of South America, China, Turkey, Morocco, and Kazakhstan. Alternatively, more than 60 percent of the populations of several Central and East African nations live on less than $1.25 per day. *Source:* http://en.wikipedia.org/wiki/File:Percentage_population_living_on_less_than_1_dollar_day_2007-2008.png. Data are from UN Human Development Statistics, licensed under the Creative Commons Attribution ShareAlike 3.0 and from the CIA World Factbook.

Relative versus Absolute Poverty Lines

*An **absolute measure of poverty** uses a fixed income or consumption level rather than an underlying income distribution to set the poverty line.*

*A **relative measure of poverty** uses position in the income distribution to determine the poverty line.*

The poverty thresholds and poverty rates described so far have been **absolute measures of poverty**. Absolute poverty measures do not refer to any underlying income distribution to set poverty thresholds. A **relative measure of poverty** uses the income distribution to set poverty thresholds. Relative poverty thresholds are always set in comparison to the income of others in the economy. One example of a relative poverty measure would be to set the poverty line to include households in the bottom 5 percent of the U.S. income distribution. A relative poverty threshold could also be set at half of the median income of a country. If the median income in a country rises, the relative poverty threshold would also rise.

THINK FOR YOURSELF

Suppose you are a policymaker with the task of designing U.S. poverty policy. To gauge the success of your policies, would you use an absolute poverty measure or a relative policy measure? Explain your answer.

CAUSES OF POVERTY

Understanding the causes of poverty is essential for policymakers and citizens hoping to alleviate poverty. Isolating factors that cause poverty is very difficult, however, since people fall into poverty for a wide variety of reasons. Some individuals facing a divorce, job loss, bad health, or poor educational opportunities may end up in poverty while others in the same situations escape poverty. Nonetheless, there are patterns of poverty by demographic, family, and educational characteristics. Some poverty stems from these and other individual-level factors, while other poverty is caused by broader structural factors in the economy.

Individual-level Causes of Poverty

The individual-level causes of poverty have been the subject of much debate and study. Obviously, poverty arises from low earned income, but why do some individuals have low incomes while others do not? Individual-level causes of poverty can include things that are beyond an individual's control, like restricted access to educational opportunities, discrimination, or bad luck. Individual-level causes of poverty also include people's innate ability, preferences, and responses to market incentives.

Productivity

Ceteris paribus, highly productive workers face higher demand for their labor and tend to have higher incomes. Worker productivity is a function of intelligence, education, motivation, and other characteristics. Some productivity-related characteristics are inherited from parents. Other productivity-related characteristics result from environment, upbringing, and investment in skills and education. In Table 20.1, for example, the poverty rate among people with four or more years of education is much lower than the poverty rate among people with only a high school diploma.

Restricted Opportunities

Some poverty stems from restricted opportunities faced by individuals or families. Restricted opportunities can arise because of discrimination, physical or mental health problems, or bad luck. Individuals with restricted access to high-quality education, for example, have fewer opportunities to increase their productivity than others. On the other end of the income distribution, individuals with the luck to inherit income from their families have more economic opportunities than those without such luck.

Incentives and Preferences

Although the perceptions have waxed and waned over time, public sentiment toward the poor often includes the notion that poverty is self-inflicted and results at least in part because of personal choice and motivation. As one example of this sentiment, 1996 legislation implementing large-scale U.S. welfare reform was called the "Personal Responsibility and Work Opportunity Act" to reflect the notion that some poverty results from personal choice. In reality, it is difficult to assess the extent to which people's responses to economic incentives and personal preferences and choices influence poverty.

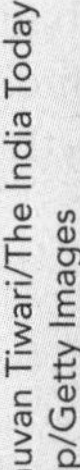

Tirbhuvan Tiwari/The India Today Group/Getty Images

Amartya Sen and the Causes of Poverty

Amartya Sen (1933–) is an Indian economist who was awarded the 1998 Nobel Prize in Economics for his work on the economics of poverty. When he was 9 years old, Sen witnessed a famine in Bengal that took the lives of 3 million people. Investigating the cause of the famine later, Sen concluded that declining wages, rising food prices, hoarding, and poor food-distribution systems, rather than a lack of food in Bengal at the time, led to the mass starvation. His work has renewed interest in finding practical methods to limit food shortages and famines. His ideas about poverty and economic development led *Time* magazine to list Sen as one of the 100 most influential persons in the world in 2010.

Structural Causes of Poverty

Some poverty stems from broad structural factors rather than individual-level choices and outcomes. Structural factors associated with poverty include macroeconomic downturns, resource availability, and governmental institutions.

Macroeconomic Downturns

Figure 20.10 illustrated that poverty rates tend to increase during economic downturns and fall during economic expansions. During the Great Depression in the 1930s, for example, the number of Americans living below the poverty threshold increased dramatically. Even people with high levels of skill and productivity can be pushed into poverty during economic downturns. In most cases however, the highly skilled more easily move out of poverty as economic conditions improve.

Resource Availability and Resource Use

Many of the poor in developing nations depend on agriculture for subsistence and income. Harsh environments, inadequate rainfall, and animal disease all contribute to poverty vulnerability among these groups. Many of the poor are in remote locations. The lack of access to roads or other infrastructure exacerbates their great distance from markets where they can buy and sell goods and services or obtain education and health resources. Lack of access to credit and other financial resources reduces opportunities for individuals to invest in education and to trade goods and services with others. In some countries, resources are abundant, but are used inefficiently, are concentrated among relatively few families or in few industries, or are allocated to military or other conflict uses.

Governmental Institutions

Some governmental institutions and structures impede economic growth and its accompanying declines in poverty. Governmental instability decreases the attractiveness of investments by foreign producers, an important source of growth and income. Governments that do not operate under the rule of law constrain economic growth and development by fostering bribery, unstable banking systems, and unsafe transportation systems.

Disease

Many of the world's poor are particularly vulnerable to diseases such as AIDS, malaria, and tuberculosis, which together account for 10 percent of all deaths globally. The diseases are both a cause and consequence of poverty. Malnourishment and inadequate access to clean water or reasonable health care contribute to vulnerability to these diseases. In turn, the declines in health associated with disease affect an individual's ability to work. When family members must also take time from other activities to care for the ill, family incomes fall even further.

POVERTY POLICY

Imagine that you are in charge of poverty policy. What would be your goals for dealing with individual-level causes of poverty? How would you deal with structural causes of poverty? On the one hand, your goal might be to provide income and other support to help the poor meet a certain standard of living. On the other hand, if you provide too much assistance, you will create disincentives for people to increase their productivity and work effort. Finding the balance between assistance and work disincentives is a constant struggle for policymakers. Dealing with global poverty adds additional complexity to poverty policy because of differences in governmental institutions, the interconnectedness of poverty and disease, and international trade issues.

U.S. Poverty Policy

The United States spends hundreds of billions of dollars annually on poverty programs. Although people generally think of food stamps or direct payments when they envision U.S. welfare programs, U.S. poverty programs are actually much broader in scope. The poverty policy includes direct payments, housing and insurance programs, tax policies, and labor market regulations.

Direct Payments

Programs that provide direct cash payments to the poor include the Temporary Assistance to Needy Families (TANF) program and the Supplemental Security Income (SSI) program. The TANF program is for qualifying families with children and with little wealth from cars, a house, or other assets. TANF payments are limited to 60 months within one's lifetime, although some states have shorter time limits. SSI provides payments to families with disabled or deceased spouses or parents.

Food, Health, and Housing and Education Programs

Programs that provide food assistance include the Women, Infants, and Children (WIC) program and the food stamp program. The School Lunch program provides free or reduced price lunch and breakfast for low income families. The governmental health care program for the poor, Medicaid, provides health and dental payments, and the State Children's Health Insurance Program (SCHIP) provides health insurance to low-income families with children who do not qualify for Medicaid. Housing programs for the poor provide reduced rent or low-cost housing. Education programs for the poor include Head Start, which provides education and other support for families of preschool children. The Pell Grant program provides tuition assistance for financially needy college students.

Tax Policy and Regulation

The Earned Income Tax Credit (EITC) is a refundable tax credit for low-income families with children. Because it is an income tax credit, only those who are working are eligible for the program. Minimum wage and living wage laws are also poverty prevention policies. Although they vary by location and wage level, living wage and minimum wage laws are similar in that they set a minimum price that can be paid to workers. Both are controversial, in part because researchers have not found clear evidence that they generate reductions in poverty.

THINK FOR YOURSELF

The majority of U.S. poverty assistance is spent on Medicaid, WIC, food stamps, Head Start, and other in-kind programs rather than on direct cash payments to the poor. Because providing cash payments requires less administration and bureaucracy, however, direct payments to the poor would be a less costly way to alleviate poverty. If providing direct cash payments to the poor is more efficient, why don't we spend a larger portion of poverty assistance on direct cash payments?

Global Poverty Policy

Global poverty policies differ widely across countries. Many organizations, such as CARE, Oxfam International, and Kiva have a global poverty focus, but they do not set specific poverty policies. Indeed, because the problem of global poverty cuts across geographical and governmental lines, there is no global institution that sets and enforces poverty policy. As a step toward global cooperation on the issue, the United Nations (UN) and other intergovernmental organizations have established a set of measurable Millennium Development Goals (MDG) and targets that member nations work toward achieving. These goals include eradicating extreme poverty and hunger, achieving universal primary education, promoting gender equality, reducing child mortality, improving maternal health, combating HIV/AIDS, malaria, and other diseases, and ensuring environmental sustainability.

To reach the goals, developing and developed nations are encouraged by the UN to develop effective, democratic governance, to invest in education and human capital development, and to encourage international trade and international investment.

It is difficult to assess whether the MDG program has been working, but there are some signs of improvement in global poverty over time. Figure 20.12 shows changes in poverty rates for several regions between 1990 and 2005. Based on the $1.25 poverty threshold, most regions of the world have experienced a decline in poverty rates since 1990. As one example, the percentage of people living on less than $1.25 per day in Eastern Asia was 60 percent in 1990, but fell to 15 percent by 2005. Despite this progress, the percentage of the developing world's population living in extreme poverty was still over 25 percent in 2005.

Figure 20.12 Percentage of People Living on Less than $1.25/Day

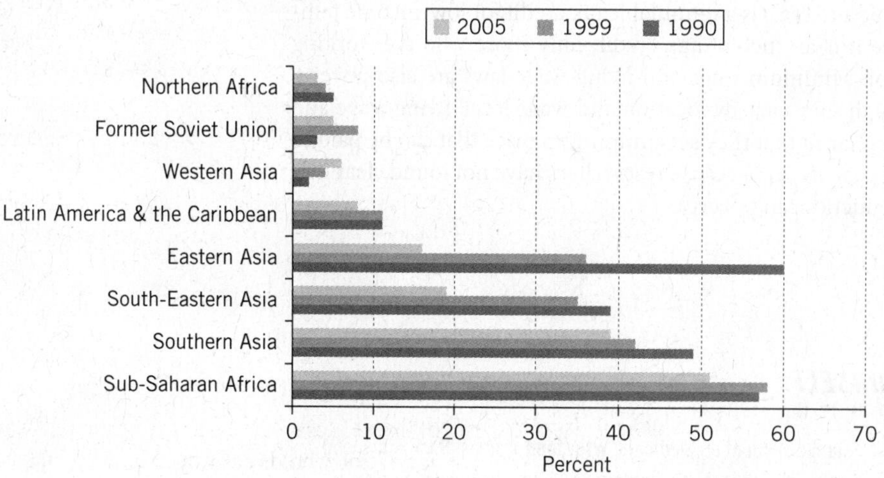

The percentage of people living on less than $1.25 per day has declined since 1990 in many regions. In Eastern Asia, the percent of people living on less than $1.25 per day fell from 60 percent in 1990 to 15 percent in 2005. Author's chart based on United Nations (2009) Millennium Development Goals Report 2009. http://www.un.org/millenniumgoals/pdf/MDG percent 20Report%202009%20ENG.pdf

SUMMARY

Income distributions describe how the resources and income of economies are divided among citizens. Income distributions can be used to describe how income is divided within a given country or how income is split among the countries of the world. Commonly used measures of income inequality include income ratios and Gini coefficients. Both measures indicate that U.S. income inequality has increased over the past 40 years.

There are several ways to measure poverty. The most widely used poverty thresholds are absolute thresholds that define poverty based on a specific income or consumption value. Relative poverty thresholds define poverty based on one's place in the income distribution. The causes of poverty include individual-level factors like productivity, opportunities, and preferences as well as structural factors like economic downturns and governmental institutions. Poverty policy involves a wide array of programs and actions.

KEY CONCEPTS

- Income distribution
- Income ratio
- Gini coefficient
- Poverty line
- Poverty rate
- Absolute measure of poverty
- Relative measure of poverty

DISCUSSION QUESTIONS AND PROBLEMS

1. Suppose that in country A the 90:10 ratio is 2, while in country B the 90:10 ratio is 4. Discuss the relative income inequality within the two countries. Do the 90:10 ratios tell you anything about the portion of global income earned by people in country A and country B?
2. What is the 80:20 ratio? What are the implications for income inequality when the 80:20 ratio increases within a country?
3. How do poverty rates differ across demographic and education groups in the Unites States? What are some possible sources of these differences?
4. Suppose that a direct payment welfare program provides a base payment of $10,000 per year to poor families. At the same time, however, the value of the base payment is reduced by $1.00 for every $1.00 of income the family earns. How would such a program affect a household's incentive to work? Would the effect on work incentives be different if the base payment were reduced by only $0.50 for each dollar of income earned?
5. Maria is a single mother of two living in San Francisco. She had her first child two weeks after graduating from high school and was unable to attend college due to lack of time and money. Dustin is married with one son. He and his wife live in a small town in Nebraska. Dustin, who also has only a high school education, is the sole breadwinner in his family. Both Maria and Dustin earn $18,000 per year. The U.S. poverty line for a family of three is $18,310.
   a. Which of these families would be considered poor by U.S. standards?
   b. Which family (Maria's or Dustin's) is likely to feel the effects of poverty more strongly? Why?

MULTIPLE CHOICE QUESTIONS

1. In 2009, those in the top 20th___ percentile of the U.S. income distribution earned about of the total U.S. income earned.
   a. 4 percent
   b. 20 percent
   c. 50 percent
   d. 75 percent
   e. 80 percent
2. The poverty rate is the
   a. percentage of rich people in the population divided by the percentage of poor people in the population.
   b. income of the poor divided by the income of the rich.
   c. percentage of the population with incomes below the poverty line.
   d. income level that marks the dividing line between poor households and those that are not poor.
   e. none of the above
3. The U.S. income distribution shows the
   a. different income levels in the U.S. and the percentage of households earning each income level.
   b. percentage of the population in poverty.
   c. value of output produced in the U.S. in a year.
   d. U.S. poverty rate.
   e. the income level at which a family is considered poor.
4. Over the past 40 years, the U.S. income distribution has
   a. become more equalized across income groups.
   b. become less equal across income groups.
   c. not really changed much.
   d. had a larger share of income going to the poor because of the expansion of U.S. poverty policy.
5. The portion of a given population that falls below the poverty line
   a. is called the poverty rate.
   b. does not change during economic downturns.
   c. is no different for populations with higher versus lower education levels.
   d. all of the above

6. Over the past 40 years, the richest 20 percent of the U.S. population has earned
   a. less income than the poorest fifth of the U.S. population.
   b. a declining share of total money income in the U.S.
   c. a constant share of total money income in the U.S.
   d. an increasing share of total money income in the U.S.
   e. none of the above

7. The major source of increased income inequality in the world over the past 100 years.
   a. within country inequality.
   b. between country inequality.
   c. increased world tax rates.
   d. increased agricultural production.

8. The town council of Glendale is considering a "living wage" law to raise the standard of living of all of its citizens. The new law will require businesses to pay each of their employees at least $14 per hour. The council also claims that the new wage will attract more productive workers to the town. The equilibrium wage in Glendale and neighboring Hilldale is $8 per hour. If the ordinance passes, what will happen to the wages in Hilldale, the next town over from Glendale?
   a. The wages in Hilldale will rise because the supply of workers in Hilldale will decrease.
   b. The wages in Hilldale will stay the same because Hilldale did not pass a living wage ordinance.
   c. The wages in Hilldale will fall because the supply of labor in Hilldale will decrease.
   d. The wages in Hilldale will fall because all of the Glendale businesses will move to Hilldale and there will be a higher demand for labor in Hilldale.

9. U.S. income inequality has
   a. decreased over the past 40 years.
   b. remained the same over the past 40 years.
   c. increased over the past 40 years.
   d. become similar to that of socialist countries over the past 40 years.

10. If the U.S. uses a relative poverty measure to determine its poverty rate
   a. poverty will be more easily eliminated.
   b. poverty will never be eliminated.
   c. poverty will be eliminated, but only after many years.
   d. none of the above, because the poverty rate does not depend on a poverty measure

ADDITIONAL READINGS AND WEB RESOURCES

Blank, Rebecca M. (2002) "Evaluating Welfare Reform in the United States," *Journal of Economic Literature* 40(4) (December):1105–1166. Reviews the literature on the impacts of U.S. welfare reform, summarizes the policy changes in welfare programs, and highlights some of the programs that have shown promising results in increasing work and earnings and reducing poverty.

Canning, David (2006) "The Economics of HIV/AIDS in Low-Income Countries: The Case for Prevention," *Journal of Economic Perspectives* 20(3) (Summer):121–142. Discusses some of the policy tradeoffs associated with reducing the burden of disease in low-income countries.

Cline, William R. (2004) *Trade Policy and Global Poverty,* Peterson Institute. Presents an overview of the relationships between free trade and poverty and offers suggestions for improving global development through free trade.

Deaton, Angus (2008) "Income, Health, and Well-Being around the World: Evidence from the Gallup World Poll," *Journal of Economic Perspectives* 22(2):53–72. Presents an analysis of data from a worldwide poll that included measures of life satisfaction and health satisfaction and how they relate to income.

Norton, Michael I., and Ariely, Dan (2011) "Building a Better America—One Wealth Quintile at a Time," *Perspectives on Psychological Science* 6(1):9–12. Presents research on people's perceptions of the actual and optimal level of U.S. wealth inequality.

Sachs, Jeffrey D. (2008) *Common Wealth: Economics for a Crowded Planet*, Penguin Press. Presents an overview of the poverty and other quality of life issues facing the world and suggests practical, low-cost methods to address some of these issues.

Steckel, Richard, H. (2008) "Biological Measures of the Standard of Living," *Journal of Economic Perspectives* 22(1) (Winter):129–152. Presents an overview of the benefits of using life expectancy, morbidity, stature, and other biological measures rather than monetary estimates to measure standard of living.

The PBS television program *The New Heroes* highlights social entrepreneurs, including those focused on problems of global poverty and disease. http://www.pbs.org/opb/thenewheroes/whatis/

The United Nations Millennium Development Goals program provides a framework for countries in the United Nations to work together to improve the standard of living in the less-developed regions of the world. www.undp.org

The U.S. Census Bureau annually summarizes poverty and income in the U.S. in the "Income, Poverty, and Health Insurance Coverage in the U.S." report. www.census.gov

The World Bank's annual *World Development Report* presents data and analysis of trends in global poverty and economic development. econ.worldbank.org

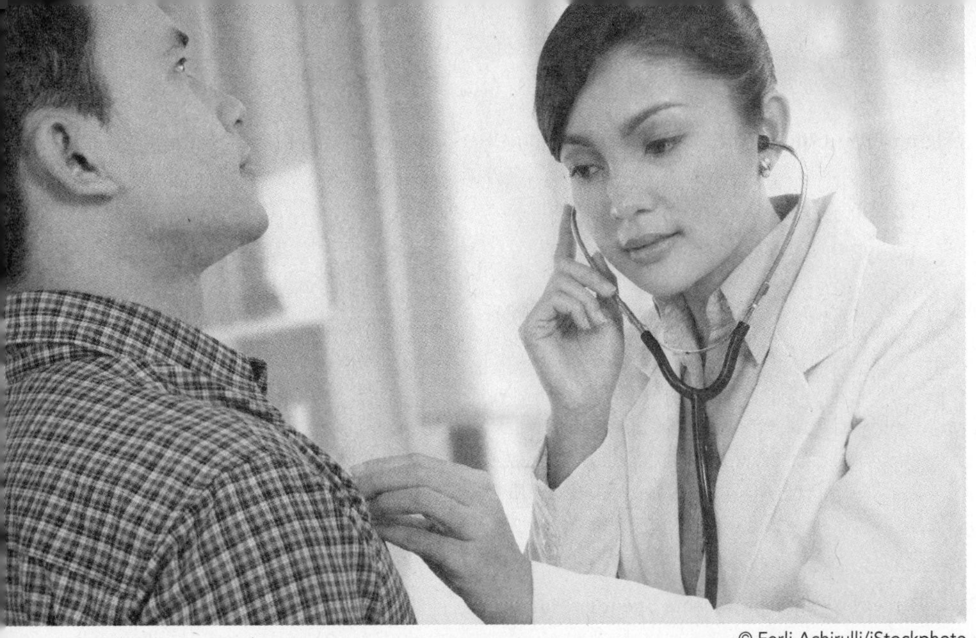

© Ferli Achirulli/iStockphoto

The Economics of Health Care

After studying this chapter, you should be able to:

- Describe the trends in costs and quality of U.S. health care
- Compare the cost and quality of U.S. healthcare relative to other developed nations
- Describe the factors that have contributed to the rising cost of health care
- Analyze the role that externalities play in the health care market
- Assess the potential impacts of healthcare reform proposals

How much did you spend last year on visits to the doctor, medication, and other healthcare costs? Chances are that you spent much more than your parents or grandparents did on their health when they were your age, even after adjusting for inflation. As Figure 21.1 illustrates, inflation-adjusted spending on U.S. health care has risen steadily over the last 50 years. Americans spent an average of $1,500 per person on health care in 1960, which represented about 5 percent of people's annual incomes. By 2020, Americans are projected to spend over $10,000 per person on health care, which represents over 15 percent of people's annual incomes.

Americans also spend more money on health care than any other nation in the world. Figure 21.2 shows trends in the percent of national income spent on health care for the U.S., UK, Canada, and Japan since 1960. In 1960, roughly 5 percent of U.S. national income was spent on health care. This level of spending as a percent of national income was similar among most other developed nations at the time. Spending on health care has increased among developed nations since

Figure 21.1 **Annual U.S. Healthcare Spending Per Capita**

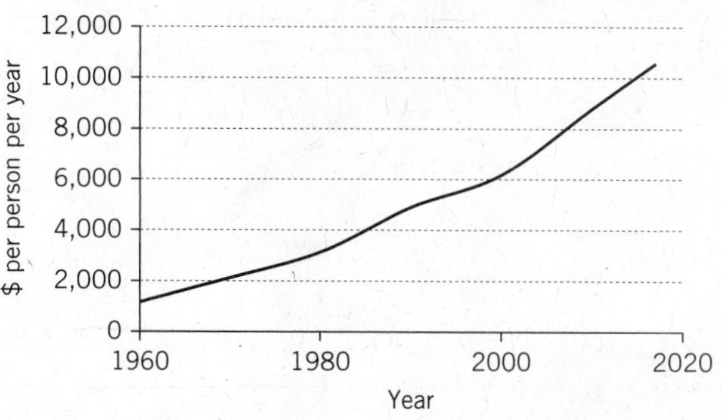

U.S. healthcare spending has risen from $1,500 per person per year to over $10,000 per person per year over the past 50 years, even after adjusting for inflation. *Source:* Statistical Abstract of the United States 2009. 2010 and 2020 are projected values. All values are in constant 2010 dollars.

Figure 21.2 **Percent of National Income Spent on Healthcare**

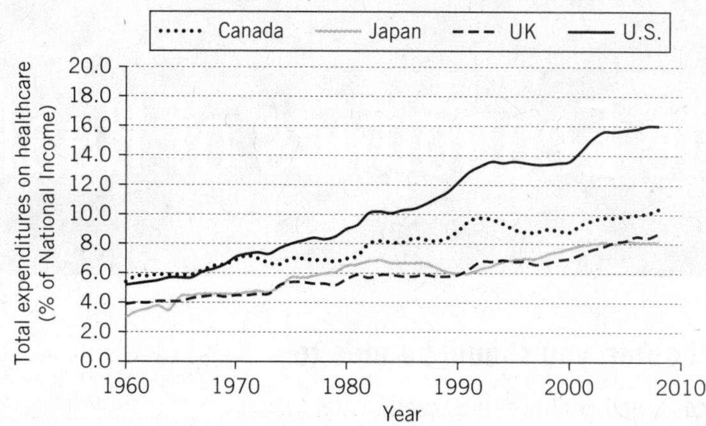

The U.S. spends a larger share of its national income on healthcare than any other nation in the world. The U.S. spends roughly double the percentage of national income on health than does the UK or Japan. *Source:* Author's chart based on "OECD Health Data 2010: Key Indicators" www.oecd.org

1960, but it has increased much faster in the United States than elsewhere. In 2010, spending on health care was approximately 16 percent of the U.S. total income but only 10 percent of total income in Canada and 8 percent of total income in the UK and Japan. The large increases in health care spending and the divergent patterns of spending between the U.S. and other nations is a key area of concern for policymakers, for employers who pay for health insurance for their employees, and for individuals as they pay for their health care.

In this chapter, we'll assess the cost and quality of U.S. health care and describe factors that contribute to the relatively high health care costs. Using the concepts of marginal benefit and marginal cost, we'll assess whether a privatized U.S. health care system is likely to generate the optimal level of health care. Last, we'll describe the key features of health care reform and evaluate their potential impacts.

THE COST AND QUALITY OF HEALTH CARE

When faced with evidence about increased spending on U.S. health care, you might respond, "Well of course we spend more than in the past and more than other nations. The quality of our medical care is much better now than in the past and is among the best and most technologically advanced in the world." You would be partially right.

Figure 21.3 **Infant Mortality Rates**

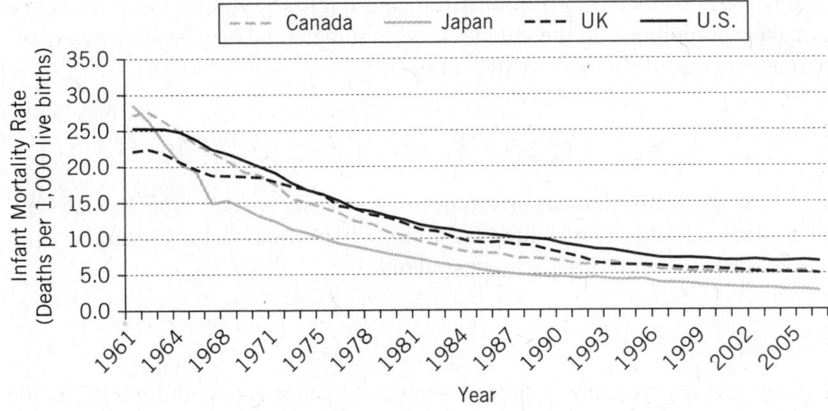

Infant mortality rates have fallen dramatically over the past 40 years. The U.S. has higher infant mortality rates than other similar nations. *Source:* Author's chart based on "OECD Health Indicators 2009" www.oecd.org

Figure 21.4 **Life Expectancy at Birth**

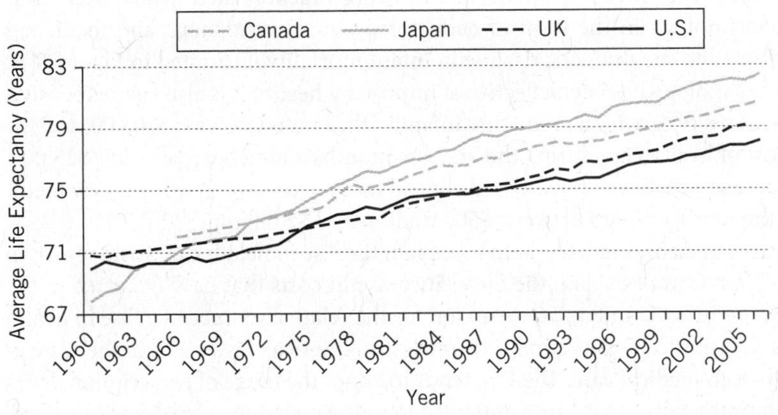

Lif expectancy has risen from 70 to over 80 years in many developed countries. The gains in life expectancy in the U.S. have been smaller than those in other developed nations. *Source:* Author's chart based on "OECD Health Indicators 2009" www.oecd.org

Figures 21.3 and 21.4 illustrate changes in health outcomes across time for the United States and other developed nations. Figure 21.3 shows infant mortality rates in the U.S., UK, Canada, and Japan since 1960. U.S. infant mortality has fallen from about 25 per 1,000 live births in 1960 to about 6 per 1,000 live births today. Figure 21.4 shows trends in average life expectancy. U.S. life expectancy has increased from less than 70 years of age in 1960 to almost 80 years of age today. These data are consistent with the idea that the quality of medical care is much better now than in the past.

Figures 21.3 and 21.4 also illustrate, however, that the improvements in health have been smaller in the U.S. than in other nations. In the 1960s, America was similar to other developed countries in terms of infant mortality and life expectancy. Today, the America has higher infant mortality rates and lower life expectancy than in other developed nations, despite spending dramatically more on health care.

The drastic increase in spending on U.S. health care raises many issues. Individuals who pay for their health care have seen a larger share of their income going to health spending, leaving less available to spend on other goods and services. Employers who pay health insurance for their employees have been faced with choices between cutting worker pay and cutting worker benefits. An increasing share of government spending has been devoted to health care over the past half-century, and that share is predicted to continue to increase into the future. Economists and policymakers grappling with these issues need to understand why health care expenditures have increased, an issue we turn to next.

WHY HEALTH CARE EXPENDITURES HAVE INCREASED

There is no single factor that has driven health care costs up over time. Instead, several factors are responsible including technology, behavioral factors, insurance, and our fee-for-service health care payment system.

Technology

Technology has dramatically improved health outcomes across the world. In the 1960s, for example, the common treatment for a heart attack included bed rest and morphine. This treatment was not very expensive, but it was not very effective either. Today, treatment for a heart attack can include medication, angioplasty surgery, bypass surgery, and heart transplants. These newer treatments are very effective and have contributed to the dramatic decline in heart attack–related deaths over time. Similarly, technology in the form of neonatology units, ventilators, and medicines has contributed to the dramatic decline in infant mortality illustrated in Figure 21.3. Although technology has been effective at improving health, it is also very expensive. The average cost of care for a premature infant in the United States is $70,000, and the average cost of health care during the first few months after a heart attack is $25,000. The cost of research, development, and clinical trials necessary to bring a new medication to the market ranges between $500 million and $2 billion.

Increases in technology can help to explain the rise in health care costs shown in Figure 21.2 but cannot explain the *larger* increase in costs that have occurred in the U.S. relative to other countries. One reason for the relatively larger increase in health care costs in America versus similar countries is America's faster and higher rate of use of high-tech medical care. The U.S. tends to adopt the usage of prescription drugs about 18 months faster than similar countries, and Americans use advanced laboratory and imaging facilities at higher rates. For example, about one in five U.S. births in the 1970s occurred by cesarean section (C-section). Today, about one-third of all U.S. births occur by C-section, a rate 30 percent higher than in similar nations. On average, C-sections cost about 2.5 times more than uncomplicated vaginal births. Americans also use more medical testing, such as fetal monitoring during childbirth, than mothers in other nations. Of course, health interventions like fetal monitoring and C-sections can result in improved health outcomes. At the same time, however, they come at a higher cost than lower-tech options.

Behavioral Factors

Behavioral choices have also contributed to high U.S. health care costs. Figure 21.5 shows rates of obesity, smoking, hypertension, and other diseases for Americans aged 50 to 53 and people in several European nations. By these measures, Americans are less healthy than similarly aged residents of other countries. Although the rate of smoking has dropped in the United States over time, U.S. obesity rates have been rising much more rapidly than in other countries. Americans also have higher rates of hypertension, heart disease, diabetes, stroke, lung disease, and cancer than people in Europe.

Figure 21.5 **Health Differences for Population Aged 50–53**

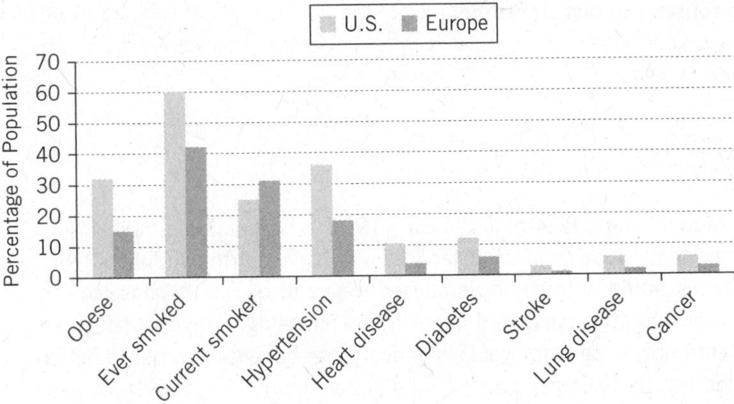

The U.S. has worse health outcomes along many dimensions than countries in Europe. *Source:* Health and Retirement Survey 2004, Survey of Health Aging and Retirement in Europe 2004. European countries include only Denmark, France, Germany, Italy, The Netherlands, Spain, Sweden.

Given this data, one reason for the relatively high U.S. health care spending is that our lifestyle choices make us more prone to disease than our European counterparts.

Mansell/Time Life Pictures/Getty Images

Thomas Robert Malthus, The Dismal Science, and the Principle of Population

Thomas Robert Malthus (1766–1834) was an English scholar and economist most famous for his theories about cycles of population growth and decline, sometimes called Malthusian catastrophes. Population growth occurs during times of plenty, Malthus argued, because resources are widely available and it is easy for families afford additional children. Eventually, however, increased population puts too much strain on the available resources, and population growth is reduced or reversed by disease, epidemics, and famine. In his famous book, *An Essay on the Principle of Population*, Malthus wrote, "The power of population is so superior to the power of the earth to produce subsistence for man, that premature death must in some shape or other visit the human race. The vices of mankind are active and able ministers of depopulation."[1] Malthus's dismal predictions about cycles of population growth and decline contributed to the branding of economics as "The Dismal Science," a nickname that persists today. Malthus had substantial influence on evolutionary biologist Charles Darwin, for whom Malthus's ideas helped lead to the theory of natural selection.

Insurance

About 84 percent of Americans use health insurance to cover all or some of their health care expenses. Most of this insurance is provided by private insurance companies, although about 25 percent have public health insurance coverage through governmental programs. Government insurance for individuals who are over 65 years

1 Malthus Thomas R. (1798) *An Essay on the Principle of Population*. Penguin Classics (1983 edition) p. 118.

old is provided by Medicare. Government insurance for the poor is provided by Medicaid. The government also provides health insurance and health care services for active and retired military personnel.

World War II and the Emergence of Employer-Provided Health Insurance

Although employer-provided health insurance existed in a limited form in the early 1900s, it expanded rapidly during World War II. At that time, the demand for workers to produce goods and services was high, but the supply of labor was low because of the war. Although market forces would normally have caused wages to rise in response to the shortage of workers, federally-imposed wage and price controls prevented wages from increasing. Fringe benefits like sick leave and health insurance were not considered wages, so employers expanded these benefits in order to better compensate and attract workers. Publicly provided health insurance coverage did not arise until 1965 with the passage of Medicare and Medicaid legislation.

Health insurance works by spreading risk among groups of people. Buyers of insurance pay a premium or fee for insurance coverage. In exchange for this premium, insurance companies pay for medical expenses (or portions of medical expenses) if and when they occur. Insurance buyers benefit from purchasing insurance because it reduces their risk of paying for all of their medical expenses out of their own pocket. Insurance sellers benefit from providing insurance because it is unlikely that all of their customers will need expensive medical procedures.

Health insurance is another factor that can help us to explain observed increases in U.S. health care spending. Because most people have health insurance coverage, they pay only a fraction of the cost when they get medical care. This fraction, called the co-payment, depends on the specific terms of their health insurance plan. The rest of the cost is paid by the insurer in the form of a **third-party payment**. A third-party payment occurs when the provider or seller of a good or service is paid by someone other than the buyer of the good.

*A **third-party payment** occurs when the provider or seller of a good or service is paid by someone other than the buyer of the good.*

We can use the concepts of marginal benefit and marginal cost to understand how having third-party payment affects the market for health care. Suppose that you wake up in the morning with a fever, aching neck, and headache. On the one hand, you may simply have a cold. On the other hand, you may worry that you have a more serious illness like influenza or meningitis. You are debating whether to see the doctor or wait a few days to see if your symptoms get worse. Suppose that your doctor charges a fee of $100 for an office visit, but if you have insurance you have a 20 percent co-payment for doctor visits. A 20 percent co-payment means that the insurance company pays for 80 percent of the cost of the visit and you pay only 20 percent. In this scenario, your marginal cost of the office visit is $20 if you have health insurance. If you do not have health insurance, you pay the full $100 cost of the visit yourself. Ceteris paribus, someone with insurance will be more likely to visit the doctor because their marginal cost per visit is much lower. Researchers have found that people with high co-payments use significantly less medical care than those with low co-payments.

*A **Moral hazard** occurs when people change their behavior to undertake more risk because they have insurance against that risk.*

Insurance can also introduce **moral hazard** into the health care market. Moral hazard occurs when someone changes their behavior because they are insured against risks associated with that behavior. We see the implications of moral hazard in many situations. For example, if you have car insurance and as a result drive more recklessly because you know any accident will be covered by your insurance, you exhibit moral hazard behavior.

Economist Sam Peltzman has studied moral hazard behavior extensively. He found that when the government passed the National Traffic and Motor Vehicle Safety Act of 1966, which mandated the installation of safety devices such as seatbelts, collapsible steering columns, and pop-out windshields in cars, some drivers responded by taking more risks when driving. As a result, although vehicle occupant deaths per accident fell, this was completely offset by more accidents in total and more fatalities to pedestrians, bicyclists, and motorcyclists, who are not protected by safety devices in cars.

Moral hazard in the health care market means that people with health insurance have an incentive to consume more health care services than may be optimal since, ceteris paribus, having insurance gives them incentives to engage in more risky health behaviors. Ceteris paribus, moral hazard generates an increase in health care demand and a resulting increase in health care costs. If moral hazard also provides an incentive for people with health insurance to engage in more risky health behaviors such as smoking, not eating right, or exercising less, its impact on health care cost increases is even larger.

THINK FOR YOURSELF

Use the concept of moral hazard to explain why many insurance companies do not cover experimental treatments or nonessential health services like cosmetic surgery.

Fee-for-Service

A final explanation for increased health care costs comes from the way we pay for health care. The U.S. health care system is primarily a fee-for-service system. In this type of system, doctors charge a fee for each visit or procedure, rather than being paid a fixed salary. When a patient visits a doctor, it is primarily the doctor who decides on the best course of treatment. Patients of course have the right to deny any treatment or procedure, but because most patients do not have extensive medical training, they frequently accept the doctor's recommendation. The fee-for-service system gives doctors considerable incentives regarding the treatments they recommend, because recommending additional visits or care will increase a doctor's income. This situation is called **physician-induced demand**, because doctors can increase the demand for their services by prescribing more treatment than is necessary.

Physician-induced demand occurs when doctors prescribe more treatment than is necessary in order to increase their own incomes.

THINK FOR YOURSELF

Do you think that the amount of physician-induced demand would fall if doctors were paid based on the health outcomes of their patients rather than on a fee-for-service basis? Why or why not?

EXTERNALITIES IN THE HEALTH CARE MARKET

When presented with information about rising health care costs and increased spending on health care, you might wonder why government is involved in health care at all. You might say, "I can make decisions about my own health like eating right or exercising. If I want to smoke or do other things that harm my health, that is my choice, not the government's business." Alternatively, you might argue that the government should be involved in health care and should regulate whether people can smoke, whether kids in public school need to take physical education classes, or whether people should be allowed to eat dangerous or fattening foods. Are there economic reasons for government intervention in health care? We can use the marginal benefit–marginal cost framework we learned about in Chapter 1 to address this question.

Marginal Benefits and Marginal Costs of Health

The marginal cost of doing activities to improve your health includes the time and effort involved in washing your hands before eating, in exercising, in eating healthy food, or in obtaining vaccinations. The marginal benefits of better health may include longer expected life, reductions in time off work for illness, and increased energy for daily activities.

Figure 21.6 provides an illustration of the marginal benefits and marginal costs of doing health-improving activities. The horizontal axis measures the quantity of health-improving activities per period. Health-improving activities include things like regular hand washing, getting vaccinations, healthy eating, and regular doctor visits.

Figure 21.6 **Marginal Costs and Benefits of Improving Health**

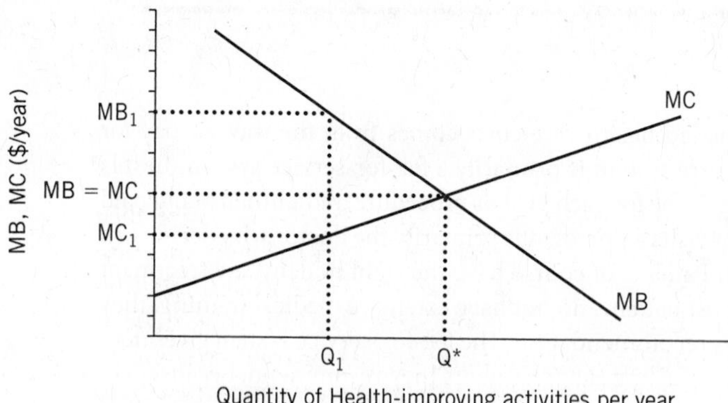

The optimal level of health-improving activity is Q* since that is where the marginal benefits of health improvments are equal to the marginal costs. At levels of health improvement below Q*, such as Q_1, the marginal benefits (MB_1) are higher than the marginal costs (MC_1). At activity level Q_1, net benefits would be increased by doing more health-improving activities.

The MC curve represents the marginal cost associated with health-improving activities. When people do low levels of health-improving activities, the marginal cost of additional health-improving activities is likely to be small. These marginal costs could include the time it takes to wash hands to remove germs or avoid consumption of obviously spoiled food. As more and more health-improving activities are done, the marginal costs of additional health improvements are likely to increase. Why? Once we improve our health through simple measures like washing hands or not eating spoiled food, additional health-improving activities are likely to involve more technology, including the development of vaccines, medicines, or improved food preservation methods. Further health improvements, such as those that come from intensive care or medical interventions, are likely to come at even higher marginal cost. These considerations give rise to the upward-sloping MC curve shown in Figure 21.6.

Figure 21.6 also illustrates how the marginal benefits of health-improving activities change as more health is obtained. When someone does not engage in healthy activities, the marginal benefits (MB) of doing things that improve health are likely to be large. For example, the reduction in illness from something as simple as hand washing is dramatic, with some studies finding that a simple hand washing regimen reduces doctor visits by 45 percent. As people become healthier, the marginal benefits of improving health are still positive but are smaller than the benefits obtained from the first healthy activities. The diminishing marginal benefit of health-improving activities generates the downward-sloping MB curve in Figure 21.6.

What is the optimal level of health improvement to undertake? At levels below Q*, the additional benefits gained from additional health improvement exceed the additional costs incurred, so that doing more health-improving activity results in net increases in well-being. At levels above Q*, the additional costs incurred from more health improvements are higher than the benefits gained, so that you would be made worse off by doing more health-improving activities. Thus, the optimal level of health-improving activities is Q*, where the marginal benefits and marginal costs of are just equal to one another.

What are the marginal benefits and marginal costs of using an exercise program to improve your health? Would the MB and MC curves from an exercise program have a shape similar to those in Figure 21.6? Why or why not?

Externalities

In the traditional marginal benefit–marginal cost model, people maximize their well-being by doing health-improving activities to the point where the marginal benefits and marginal costs are equal. If you do too much to gain health, you'll see your well-being decline. As an example, think of the joy you get from eating an occasional bag of potato chips even though you know they are bad for you! If you undertake too few activities to improve your health, you will forego utility that you could obtain for less than the cost of the health improvements. Although this simple framework for understanding individual health status decisions is useful, most economists would argue that it does not account for the impacts of individual health on society more broadly. Why? Because health improvements often generate a form of market failure known as externalities.

Externalities occur when some of the costs or benefits of a trade are imposed on people outside the trade. People outside a trade are called third parties to the trade. For example, when a parent obtains a college education and as a result her children have better health outcomes, the children are third parties to the trade between the college and the parent. When a paper mill emits pollution into a local neighborhood, the people living in the neighborhood are third parties to the trade between the paper mill and paper consumers. **Positive externalities** are benefits received by

Positive externalities are benefits received by third parties.

Figure 21.7 **Marginal Costs and Benefits in the Presence of Positive Externalities**

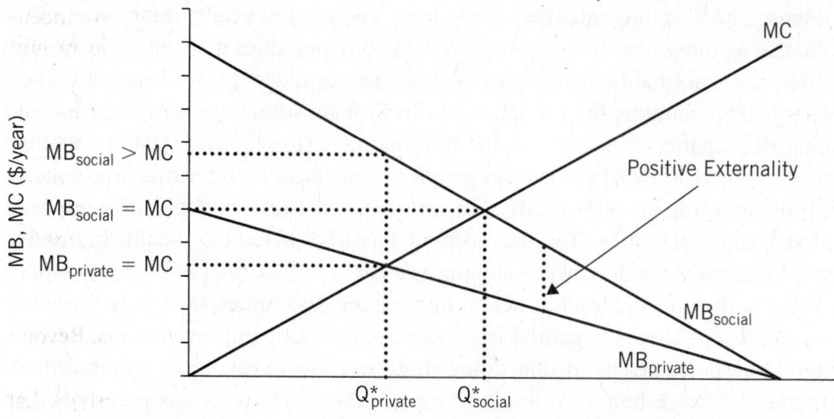

Positive externalities are benefits received by third parties. The difference between MB_{social} and $MB_{private}$ represents the positive externality associated with health-improving activities. If there were no positive externality, $Q^*_{private}$ would be the optimal quantity of health-improving activities. With the positive externality considered, the socially optimal level of health-improving activity is Q^*_{social}. Since people do not have incentives to consider positive externalities when they make choices about their health, the market-determined amount of health improvement would be $Q^*_{private}$. Without intervention, people will undertake too little action to improve their health from a social efficiency perspective.

Negative externalities are costs imposed on third parties.

third parties, and **negative externalities** are costs imposed on third parties.[2] Health improvements are associated with positive externalities.

The positive externalities associated with health improvements include things like a reduction in the transmission of disease to others when we take steps like hand washing or vaccination to prevent ourselves from getting sick. When you get a flu vaccine, your roommates benefit because they are less likely to get the flu from you. When your grandparents control their weight and blood pressure through exercise, you and other taxpayers benefit because Medicare costs are lower.

The marginal cost–marginal benefit framework can help us understand the role positive externalities play in health care decisions and health care policy. Figure 21.7 presents a graphical description of the health-improving activities decision that incorporates positive externalities. Because positive externalities bestow benefits on third parties, we need to consider the private marginal benefits and social marginal benefits of health-improving activities. **Private marginal benefits** are marginal benefits that accrue only to the individuals doing the activities. In Figure 21.7, private marginal benefits are labeled $MB_{private}$.

Private marginal benefits are marginal benefits that accrue only to individual decision makers.

Social marginal benefits are marginal benefits that accrue to society as a whole.

Social marginal benefits are marginal benefits that accrue to society as a whole. In Figure 21.7, the curve MB_{social} reflects the social marginal benefits of health-improving activities. Social marginal benefits include private marginal benefits plus the positive externality bestowed on others. The positive externality is shown as the vertical distance between $MB_{private}$ and MB_{social} in Figure 21.7.

$$MB_{social} = MB_{private} + \text{External Benefits}$$

Notice that the size of the positive externality changes as the level of health-improving activity changes. At low levels of health-improving activity, the positive externality is likely to be large because having basic sanitation and vaccinations has the largest impact on improving public health. As health improvements expand, the

2 Negative externalities are covered in Chapters 15 and 16.

positive externality becomes smaller because improvements in one individual's health are less likely to affect others as much.

When deciding on how much health to pursue, you as an individual have incentives to compare only the costs you incur (MC) against the benefits you receive ($MB_{private}$). Given this comparison, the optimal level of health improvements for you personally is $Q^*_{private}$. At this level, you maximize your net private benefits of health-improving activities.

Is $Q^*_{private}$ the optimal level of health improvement activity when it comes to costs and benefits for society at large? To assess the optimal level of health improvement for society at large, we need to compare the social marginal benefits against the marginal costs. Point Q^*_{social} illustrates the level of health-improving activity where $MC = MB_{social}$. This is the level where the extra social benefits attained from increases in your health are just equal to the extra costs incurred to get those benefits. Beyond that level, society gives up more than it gets from improvements in your health. At levels of activity below Q^*_{social}, you forego additional health improvements activity that would make society better off.

The different optimal levels of health-improving activity for you versus for society imply that a purely private market for health would generate a market failure. At the optimal level of health improvement for you as an individual ($Q^*_{private}$), the social marginal benefits exceed the marginal costs. In other words, in the presence of positive externalities, too few health-improving activities will be done relative to the socially optimal amount. This is the market failure generated by the positive externalities from health. Left to its own devices, a purely private market for health care will result in less health care than is socially optimal.

Why Is the Government Involved in the Health Care Market?

Economists and policymakers have long recognized the positive externalities and resulting market failure associated with purely private health care markets. Because the optimal private level of health-improving activities is lower than the socially optimal level, many societies provide incentives to encourage better health. Governments mandate childhood vaccinations for children entering public schools, provide extensive health education, fund health-related research for the development of medicines, and provide government-sponsored health insurance programs.

From the establishment of the Public Health Service and the Food and Drug Administration to providing funding of the Department of Health and Human Services and the Centers for Disease Control, U.S. government involvement in the health care industry has a long history. The government established hospital and health services for military soldiers as far back as 1798 and uses its power over the regulation of interstate commerce to include matters of public health. In the next section, we describe recent government action to reform U.S. health care.

THINK FOR YOURSELF

Why does the positive externality associated with health-improving activities fall as more health-improving activities are undertaken? Use your answer to explain why the government provides subsidies for childhood vaccinations but not for people to buy running shoes.

HEALTH CARE REFORM

Health care reform is not a new issue in America. National-level health care proposals date back to the early 1900s, when President Theodore Roosevelt supported universal U.S. government health care coverage. Failed efforts at universal health care coverage also occurred during the Great Depression and after World War II. In 1965, President Johnson introduced the Medicare and Medicaid systems, which cover hospital and medical care costs for senior citizens and the poor, respectively. In 1985, the Consolidated Omnibus Budget Reconciliation Act (COBRA) mandated the provision of health insurance to employees who leave their jobs. In 1997, the State Children's Health Insurance Program (SCHIP) was established to provide health insurance to children in poor families.

More recently, the high and rising cost of U.S. medical care relative to its peer nations is a driving force behind calls for reform of the healthcare system. Reform has also been spurred by the large number of Americans without health insurance coverage. The rest of this section describes the key features of the most recent U.S. health care reforms, the 2010 Patient Protection and Affordable Care Act and the Healthcare and Education Reconciliation Act of 2020. The primary pieces of this legislation expanded health insurance coverage and implemented substantial changes in government-provided health insurance.

Expanding Insurance Coverage

We learned earlier in the chapter that about 84 percent of Americans have health insurance coverage of some sort. The remaining 16 percent (roughly 46 million people) are without any form of health insurance. This obviously raises their health care costs and reduces the likelihood that they obtain medical care. At the same time, U.S. law requires hospitals and ambulance services to treat people regardless of their ability to pay, which imposes cost burdens on hospitals and other patients. Researchers have found that approximately 55 percent of U.S. emergency care is provided without compensation, amounting to over $30 billion per year. In the face of the mandate to provide services regardless of their ability to pay, health care providers have an incentive to charge higher fees to those who can pay in order to cover their costs. The average family pays an estimated additional $1,000 per year in health insurance costs in order to make up for the cost of providing health care to the uninsured.

Recent health care reform bills include several methods to expand insurance coverage. First, insurance companies are prohibited from ending coverage when people get sick. Second, children are now able to stay on their parents' health insurance plans until age 26 rather than age 19 or when they finish college. Third, small businesses have access to tax credits to help them provide health insurance for their employees. Fourth, health insurance companies will not be allowed to exclude people from coverage due to preexisting conditions.

Policies to expand health insurance coverage involve tradeoffs. Expanding insurance coverage to the previously uninsured will generate improved access to health care for that group. Mortality rates are higher for those without insurance, and people without insurance who have chronic health conditions are less likely to see a doctor, go to the hospital, and fill prescriptions than their counterparts with health insurance. The risk of losing health insurance keeps many workers from moving to another job that may be a better fit, so expanding coverage may generate more job mobility among workers. On the other hand, expanding coverage will involve costs to insurers and their customers.

THINK FOR YOURSELF

What are the costs and benefits of not having health insurance? Is it optimal for some people to choose to go without health insurance?

Government Insurance

Health care reform includes several changes in Medicare and Medicaid, the health insurance provided by the government to the elderly and the poor. Eligibility for Medicaid will be expanded to include a larger share of the poor in 2014. The payment rules for Medicare will be altered in 2015 to pay doctors based on quality of care rather than on the quantity of services that they provide. As described in the previous section, expanding health insurance coverage, including Medicaid coverage, can improve health care access for citizens. It also comes with a tradeoff of increased cost.

The government will also establish health insurance exchanges where individuals and small businesses can join together to purchase health insurance. Because purchasing individual-level insurance is very expensive, the exchanges are designed to help individuals and small employers to pool together to reduce costs by sharing risk across a wider group. Also by 2014, people may be required to obtain health insurance coverage or pay a tax penalty. This aspect of health care reform is highly controversial. Proponents of the policy argue that mandating that everyone must obtain health insurance is one way to reduce the costs that are passed on to others when an uninsured person seeks treatment in a hospital. Opponents argue that the policy impinges on individual freedom to choose whether or not to buy insurance.

SUMMARY

Health care in the United States involves a complex array of tradeoffs. Americans spend much more on health care than people in other developed nations, but U.S. health outcomes are not necessarily better. Economists predict that the costs of U.S. health care will continue to grow at a rapid pace, requiring us to spend larger and larger shares of our income on health care over time. Reasons for the increase in health care costs range from increased use of high-technology treatments to third-party payer system to people's own health behaviors. Because healthy activities generate positive externalities, it is unlikely that the private market sector will generate the optimal level of health care. Government involvement in the health care market primarily takes the form of regulation and the public provision of health insurance. Reform of the health care system is a longstanding issue, and recent changes in health care include expanding health insurance coverage to more people and using government insurance programs to alter the way that health care providers are paid.

KEY TERMS

- Third-party payment
- Moral hazard
- Physician-induced demand
- Positive externalities
- Negative externalities
- Private marginal benefits
- Social marginal benefits

DISCUSSION QUESTIONS AND PROBLEMS

1. How does having insurance through third parties affect people's incentives to visit the doctor?
2. Would people obtain the optimal amount of health care if the health care market were purely private and had no government intervention? Explain.
3. The accompanying table shows the marginal private benefit, marginal social benefit, and marginal private cost for you to exercise to improve your health.

Hours of Exercise per Week	Marginal Costs (MC)	Private Marginal Benefits ($MB_{private}$)	Social Marginal Benefits (MB_{social})
0	–	17	29
1	3	15	24
2	4	13	20
3	5	11	17
4	6	9	14
5	7	7	11
6	8	5	8
7	9	3	5
8	10	1	2

a. Why does the marginal private cost of exercise rise as hours of exercise per week rises?
b. Why does the marginal private benefit fall as hours of exercise per week rises?
c. Why do the private marginal benefits of exercise differ from the social marginal benefits of exercise?
d. What happens to the size of the positive externality associated with exercise as hours of exercise per week rises? Why?
e. If this market were purely private, what would be the optimal number of hours of exercise per week for you?
f. What is the socially optimal number of hours of exercise per week for you?
g. What are some methods that society uses to get from the private optimum level of exercise to the socially optimum level of exercise?

4. What are the costs and benefits of having employers pay part of the costs of health insurance coverage for employees?
5. What are the costs and benefits of requiring people to obtain health insurance or pay a tax penalty?

MULTIPLE CHOICE QUESTIONS

1. From an economics perspective,
   a. There should be no government intervention in the health care market.
   b. Government involvement in health care is often justified because health care is associated with positive externalities.
   c. We should not strive for efficiency when evaluating health care activities.
   d. Government involvement in health care helps eliminate the negative externalities associated with health care.
2. Ceteris paribus, if expanded health insurance coverage increases the demand for health care, we would expect to see the equilibrium price of health care _______ and the equilibrium quantity of health care _______.
   a. increase; increase
   b. increase; decrease
   c. decrease; increase
   d. decrease; decrease

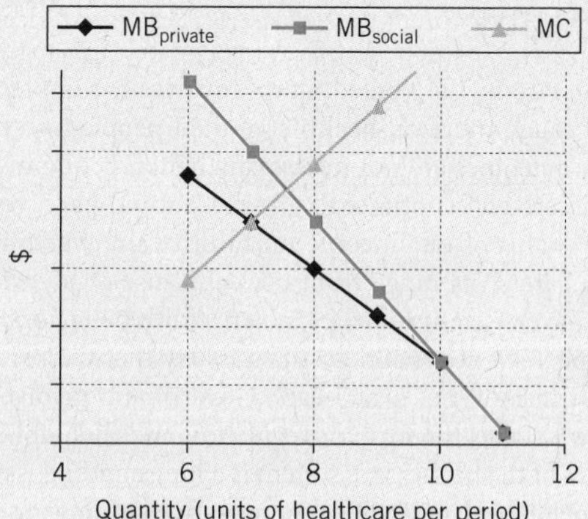

3. In the accompanying graph showing the market for health care, MC represents marginal costs of health care. $MB_{private}$ is the private marginal benefits of health care, and MB_{social} is the social demand curve and represents the social marginal benefits of health care. Given the situation depicted in the graph,

a. without intervention, the market will generate the socially optimal level of health care.
b. without intervention, the market will generate too great a level of health care from a social efficiency perspective.
c. without intervention, the market will generate too low a level of health care from a social efficiency perspective.
d. without intervention, the market won't generate any health care.

4. Using the graph in the previous Question,
a. the private optimal level of health care is 6 units.
b. the private optimal level of health care is 7 units.
c. the private optimal level of health care is 7.5 units.
d. the private optimal level of health care is 10 units.
e. the private optimal level of health care cannot be determined without knowing the dollar values on the vertical axis.

5. Using the graph, the closing gap between $MB_{private}$ and MB_{social} as years of health care increases implies that
a. the negative externality associated with healthcare must grow as more health care is obtained.
b. the negative externality associated with health care must shrink as more health care is obtained.
c. the positive externality associated with health care must grow as more health care is obtained.
d. the positive externality associated with health care must shrink as more health care is obtained.
e. there must be an error in the graph.

6. Ceteris paribus, if the supply of health care providers increases at the same time that there is an increase in the demand for health care, what can we predict about the equilibrium price and quantity of health care services?
a. Price and quantity will both increase.
b. Price and quantity will both decrease.
c. Price will increase, but the effect on equilibrium quantity is unknown.
d. Price will decrease, but the effect on equilibrium quantity is unknown.
e. Quantity will increase, but the effect on equilibrium price is unknown.

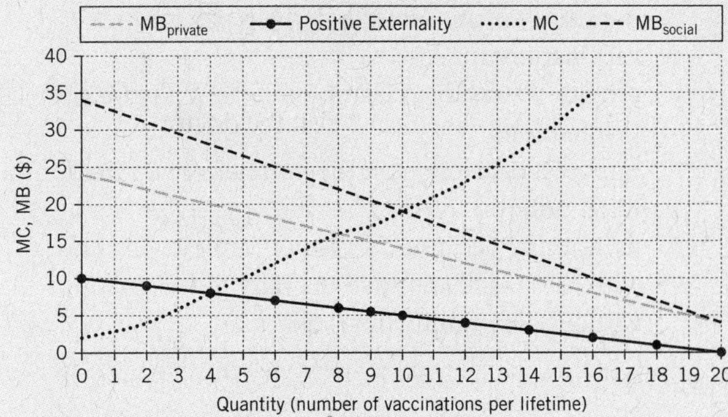

7. Cameron is a newborn baby whose parents are thinking about vaccinating him against disease. The accompanying figure illustrates the marginal benefits and marginal costs of vaccinations for Cameron. Cameron's community derives benefits from Cameron being vaccinated, as illustrated by the positive externality curve above. Given this information, the socially optimal number of vaccinations for Cameron to get is
a. 0.
b. 4.
c. 8.
d. 10.
e. 20.

8. Cameron is a newborn baby whose parents are thinking about vaccinating him against disease. The figure illustrates the marginal benefits and marginal costs of vaccinations for Cameron. Cameron's community derives benefits from Cameron being vaccinated, as illustrated by the positive externality curve above. Given this information, the privately optimal number of vaccinations for Cameron to get is
a. 0.
b. 4.
c. 8.
d. 10.
e. 20.

9. Cameron is a newborn baby whose parents are thinking about vaccinating him against disease. The figure illustrates the marginal benefits and marginal costs of vaccinations for Cameron. Cameron's community derives benefits from Cameron being vaccinated, as illustrated by the positive externality curve above. Given this information, if the community wants Cameron to obtain the socially optimal number of vaccinations, they could

a. impose a tax on Cameron to help pay for the vaccinations.
b. provide a subsidy to Cameron to help pay for the vaccinations.
c. impose a restriction on the number of vaccinations that Cameron can get.
d. do nothing because Cameron's parents will choose with the socially optimal quantity of vaccinations without community intervention.

10. Which of the following is an example of moral hazard?
a. Joey cheats on his third-grade spelling test.
b. Since her parents pay for her college, Sally does worse in her classes than she would if she were paying for college herself.
c. Jill has car insurance, so she drives more carefully.
d. Sam texts while driving even through it is against the law in his state.

ADDITIONAL READINGS AND WEB RESOURCES

Cutler, David M. (1995) "Technology, Health Costs, and the NIH," National Institutes of Health Roundtable on the Economics of Biomedical Research. http://www.economics.harvard.edu/faculty/cutler/files/Technology,%20Health%20Costs%20and%20the%20NIH.pdf. Presents an overview of how technology impacts healthcare costs.

DiMasi, J., Hansen, R., and Grabowski, H. (2003). "The price of innovation: new estimates of drug development costs," *Journal of Health Economics,* 22 (2):151–85. http://www.ncbi.nlm.nih.gov/pubmed/12606142. Presents a summary of the research and development costs of bringing a new drug to market in the U.S.

Gruber, Jonathan and David Rodriguez (2007). "How Much Uncompensated Care Do Doctors Provide?," *Journal of Health Economics,* 26(6):1151–1169. http://econ-www.mit.edu/files/6423. Presents research on the amount of uncompensated care that doctors in the U.S. provide to patients.

Manning, Williard et al. (1987) "Health Insurance and the Demand for Medical Care: Evidence from a Randomized Experiment," *American Economic Review,* 77(3): 251–277. http://www.jstor.org/stable/1804094. Presents research on how cost sharing affects the demand for medical services, including estimates of the price elasticity of demand for health care.

Michaud, Pierre-Carl, Goldman, Dana, Lakdawalla, Darius, Zheng, Yuhui, and Gailey, Adam (2009) "Understanding the Economic Consequences of Shifting Trends in Population Health," NBER Working Paper 15231. http://www.nber.org/papers/w15231. Presents research on the interrelationships between the decreased life expectancy associated with increases in obesity, diabetes, and other diseases and the increasing costs of caring and treating people with these diseases.

Newhouse, Joseph P. (1992) "Medical Care Costs: How Much Welfare Loss?," *Journal of Economic Perspectives,* 6(3):3–21. http://www.jstor.org/stable/2138297. Presents a nontechnical overview of the level of medical care spending in the U.S. and how containing those costs could impact social welfare.

Peltzman, Sam (1975) "The Effects of Automobile Safety Regulation," *The Journal of Political Economy,* 83(4):677–726. http://www.jstor.org/stable/1830396. Presents research on how moral hazard impacted people's driving behavior when automobile safety increased in the late 1960s.

Ringel, Jeanne S., Hosek, Susan D., Vollaard, Ben A., and Mahnovski, Sergej (2002) *The Elasticity of Demand of Healthcare: A Review of the Literature and Its Application to the Military Health System,* National Defense Research Institute, RAND. http://www.rand.org/pubs/monograph_reports/2005/MR1355.pdf. Presents estimates of the elasticity of demand for health care.

Ryan, M.A., Christian, R.S., and Wohlrabe, J. (2001) "Handwashing and Respiratory Illness Among Young Adults in Military Training," *American Journal of Preventative Medicine,* 21(2):79–83. http://www.ncbi.nlm.nih.gov/pubmed/11457626. Presents estimates of the relationship between handwashing and illness.

The Centers for Disease Control and Prevention (CDC) website includes a wide array of research on health-related topics. www.cdc.gov

The Organization for Economic Cooperation and Development (OECD) website includes pages on health policy, policy studies, and other health-related issues among its member nations. www.oecd.org

The American College of Emergency Physicians website includes information on access to health care among the uninsured, on universal health care, and other health care-related issues. www.acep.org

The Economix Blog at the *New York Times* includes several discussions of health insurance policy: http://economix.blogs.nytimes.com/2009/05/22/is-employer-based-health-insurance-worth-saving/

Camera Press/Redux Pictures

22 Monetary Policy and the Federal Reserve

After studying this chapter, you should be able to:

- Define the concept of money
- Explain how the fractional reserve banking system allows banks to create money
- Explain how the market for loans functions
- Describe the structure of the Federal Reserve System
- Summarize the roles of the Federal Reserve
- Explain how monetary policy takes place
- Illustrate the impact of monetary policy on the economy
- Assess the tradeoffs associated with monetary policy

Suppose you were a soldier in the Vietnam War. Chances are that you were issued meal, combat, individual (MCI) rations of portable food to eat when you were away from your base. Standard MCI rations included a meat item, a bread item, a spread, and a desert. On top of the rations was an accessory pack that included a spoon, salt, pepper, sugar, coffee, gum, cigarettes, and matches (at least until 1975 when concerns about health prompted the military to remove cigarettes from rations). But suppose you didn't smoke. Would it have been smart to keep your cigarette ration? Yes! Even if you didn't smoke, you could use the cigarettes to trade for other things you might want. At that time, cigarettes were commonly used like money among soldiers and were traded for all kinds of goods and services. Over time and in differing situations, many items have been used to exchange goods and services. In this chapter, we learn about money: how it serves as a means of exchange; how it is created; and how changes in policies related to money impact the economy.

THE EVOLUTION OF THE MONETARY SYSTEM

__Barter exchange__ is the trading of goods and services directly for other goods or services, without using money.

Our system of using money to exchange goods and services has a long history, and it begins with **barter exchange**. In barter exchange, goods and services are traded directly with one another. In a barter system, the farmer who needs to take his child to the doctor might bring along a few dozen eggs to use as payment. The doctor might also exchange his services for work from the carpenter, and so on. Although we tend to think of barter as an exchange system from the past, we still see it used fairly widely today. It is easy to find ads on Internet sites like Craigslist that include an offer to trade one type of good or service directly for other goods or services. For example, a bakery owner who needs her parking lot snowplowed might offer baked goods or bakery gift certificates in exchange for snow plow services, or an artist might trade art lessons for childcare services.

One downside of barter is that it tends to be time consuming. Suppose you want to use barter to trade your snowboard for a new pair of skis. First, you'll need to find someone with the skis you want and then hope that they want your snowboard. If they don't want your snowboard, you'll have to find someone else who wants your snowboard and has something the person with the skis wants, and so on. As you might expect, barter exchange can be very cumbersome.

A __medium of exchange__ is an item that is widely accepted as payment for goods and services.

One alternative to barter is to use a **medium of exchange** to facilitate trade. A medium of exchange is an item that is widely accepted as payment for goods and services. In the example of soldiers in Vietnam described earlier, cigarettes served as a medium of exchange because cigarettes could be traded for other goods and services. In the Micronesian Yap Islands, large stones called Rai are used to facilitate traditional or ceremonial exchange. In many countries, the U.S. dollar and the Euro are used as the medium of exchange.

Throughout history, metals like silver and gold have been used as a medium of exchange. Metals are durable, can be divided into parts, are in relatively limited supply, and have value in their own right for making jewelry, tools, or other items. As common measures and weights were developed over time, metals were measured into coins. Many coin edges were milled to include ridges around them because it made it more difficult for people to shave metal from the coins.

Despite its benefits, carrying around and storing silver or gold coins could be dangerous (think: Robin Hood), so people started to look for places to keep their precious metal safe. Village or town goldsmiths had facilities to store and secure precious metals, so villagers began to keep their coins at the goldsmith's. In exchange, the villagers would get a receipt. Soon the receipts began to circulate in exchange rather than the gold itself since trading the receipt saved the time and effort of going back and forth to the goldsmith. The trading of receipts for deposits at the goldsmith was the beginning of the type of monetary system that we have in place today.

The three __primary functions of money__ are (1) a medium of exchange, (2) a unit of account, and (3) a store of value.

A __unit of account__ is a standard measure of the value of goods and services.

The Functions of Money

There are three **primary functions of money**. First, as mentioned earlier, money serves as a medium of exchange. Second, money serves to establish a common **unit of account** or measure of how much goods and services cost. In a barter system, we might think, "a snowboard costs one pair of skis," or "a snowplowed parking lot costs 25 apple pies." In a monetary system, we think, "a snowboard costs $500" or "a snowplowed parking lot costs $50." If one good costs $100 and another costs $50 we know that the first good costs twice as much, without also having to consider the relative value of a bunch of other goods. Using money to value goods and services facilitates trade because it allows us to compare costs of different goods and services very easily.

The third function of money is as a **store of value**. A store of value is something that can be saved and used at a later time. If I am a farmer who uses eggs to trade for other goods and services, I have to worry about my eggs rotting. The short shelf life of my eggs might cause me to make exchanges sooner that I want to because I will need to get rid of the eggs before they spoil and lose their value. Because I can't save eggs for future use, using eggs as money will make it difficult for me to save up for big purchases. We don't need to worry about shelf life or storage problems when we use coins, paper, or electronic money. Using coins or paper rather than eggs or milk as our money allows us to save our earnings over time.[1]

*A **store of value** is something that can be saved and used at a later time.*

THE MONEY SUPPLY

So now we know what money is. But where does money come from? How is it regulated? What do banks do with it? How does it affect the economy? These are questions about the money supply and monetary policy.

The standard definition of the money supply is that it is money in circulation in the economy, moving back and forth between buyers and sellers and between lenders and savers. Money in circulation includes cash, demand deposits like checking accounts, traveler's checks, and other checkable deposits. All of these types of money are widely acceptable as payments for goods and services. You can use cash, checks, debit cards, and traveler's checks to buy things almost anywhere. Money in circulation is the **M1 money supply**.

*The **M1 money supply** includes money in circulation: cash, demand deposits, traveler's checks, and other checkable deposits.*

M1 excludes a lot of assets and other things people use as money, such as savings deposits and savings bonds. Other categories of the money supply, called M2 and M3, include these types of items. Although M2 and M3 are also measures of the money supply, it is enough to focus on M1 to gain an understanding of how money impacts the economy. Table 22.1 illustrates the size of the M1 money supply in the United States.

The total amount of M1 at the end of March 2012 was $2.2 trillion. About half of the M1 in the United States is in the form of cash. Demand deposits and other

Table 22.1 Components of the U.S. M1 Money Supply March 2012

Component	Amount ($ billions)
Currency (cash)	1,029
Traveler's checks	4
Demand deposits	763
Other checkable deposits	424
Total	2,220

The M1 money supply includes cash, traveler's checks, demand deposits, and checkable deposits.
Source: Federal Reserve Statistical Release, May 17, 2012. www.federalreserve.gov

1 Chapter 7 illustrates how inflation can impact the value of money over time.

checkable deposits account for about half of M1. Traveler's checks make up only a small percentage of the money supply.

THE BANKING SYSTEM

Almost half of the M1 in the U.S. is held as deposits in commercial banks or other depository institutions like credit unions or savings and loan associations. We can call all of these institutions "banks" to keep things simple. Banks issue checking or savings accounts and use the funds to make consumer, business, and mortgage loans. In this way, banks act as financial intermediaries or brokers between savers and borrowers. When you go to a bank and deposit money in your savings account, most of that money will in turn be loaned to other customers. As we will learn later, because banks serve this financial intermediary role, they exert substantial influence on the money supply of an economy.

Bank Balance Sheet

*A **balance sheet** is a statement of assets (things owned) and liabilities (things owed).*

One way to understand how banks influence the money supply is to examine how bank balance sheets change when banks make loans and accept deposits. A bank's **balance sheet** is a statement of its assets and liabilities.

Table 22.2 illustrates a simple balance sheet for a hypothetical bank, Econobank. The right-hand side of the balance sheet lists Econobank's liabilities. Liabilities represent the bank's obligations. When you deposit $100 in the bank, that $100 becomes a liability for the bank because you are now owed $100 should you decide to withdraw your money. In our example, Econobank has $100 million in checking deposits, and its total liabilities are $100 million.

The left of Econobank's balance sheet lists its assets. A bank's assets are things the bank owns that have value. Econobank has $10 million in cash in its vault, owns $10 million in securities (stocks or bonds), and has $100 million in loans to its customers. Econobank's total assets are $120 million.

*A bank's **total reserves** are deposits that it has received but not lent out.*

Econobank's cash holdings are its **total reserves**. Total reserves are deposits that banks have received but have not lent out. Total reserves can be held as either cash in the bank's vault or can be deposited at a Federal Reserve bank. We'll describe Federal Reserve banks in more detail later. For now, let's assume that Econobank keeps all of its total reserves as cash in the vault.

*The **required reserve ratio (rrr)** is the percentage of deposits that a bank must hold as reserves by law.*

*The dollar amount that a bank is required to hold as reserves is called its **required reserves**.*

Why would Econobank's want to hold reserves? Reserves are primarily held in case the bank needs extra cash on hand to cover the shortfall when withdrawals exceed deposits during a given period. There are also legal requirements that stipulate that banks must hold a certain percentage of their deposits as reserves. The **required reserve ratio (rrr)** is the percentage of deposits that a bank must hold as reserves by law. The dollar amount that a bank is required to hold as reserves is called its **required reserves**.

Table 22.2 Econobank Initial Balance Sheet

Assets ($ millions)		Liabilities ($ millions)	
Cash	10	Checking deposits	100
Securities	10		
Loans	100		

A bank balance sheet shows assets and liabilities. A bank's assets include cash, securities, and loans. A bank's liabilities include its customers' deposits.

Because banks are only required to hold a fraction of their deposits as reserves, the U.S. operates under a **fractional reserve banking** system. Different countries have different rules regarding reserve requirements. For large U.S. banks, the required reserve ratio for checkable deposit accounts is 0.10, which means that banks are required keep 10 percent of their checkable deposits as reserves.

Under a fractional reserve banking system, banks are required to hold only a fraction of their deposits as reserves.

Fractional reserve banking and a 10 percent required reserve ratio mean that Econobank is required to keep \$10 million as required reserves, since it has \$100 million in checkable deposits. Because Econobank is required to keep \$10 million in reserves, but is keeping \$10 million in reserves, Econobank has no **excess reserves**, which are reserves above the required reserve amount.

Excess reserves are the difference between a bank's total reserves and its required reserves.

A bank's total reserves are equal to its required reserves plus its excess reserves,

$$\text{Total reserves} = \text{required reserves} + \text{excess reserves}$$

THINK FOR YOURSELF

What would Econobank's required reserves be if it had \$200 million in checkable deposits? What would its required reserves be if the required reserve ratio were 0.05 instead of 0.10?

The Market for Loans

Lenders like Econobank do business with borrowers in the market for loans. Like markets for other goods and services, the market for loans can be illustrated using the demand and supply model that we learned in Chapter 3. Figure 22.1 illustrates the market for loans. The price of loans, measured on the vertical axis, is the interest rate that borrowers must pay in order to take out a loan. The quantity of loans, measured on the horizontal axis, reflects the amount of money borrowed and lent per period.

The supply of loans (S) comes primarily from savings accounts. As the interest rate increases, the amount of money people decide to save rises. Why? Because savings accounts pay interest on deposits, higher interest rates generate increased rewards for saving. As savings deposits increase, the quantity of money available to lend rises. The positive relationship between the interest rate and the quantity of loans supplied reflects the law of supply and is illustrated by the upward-sloping supply curve in Figure 22.1. As the interest rate increases, there is an increase in savings deposits which in turn generates an increase in the quantity of loans supplied to the market.

The demand for loans (D) comes from individuals and businesses who want to borrow money. When the interest rate that borrowers must pay on loans falls, the total cost of taking out a loan falls. Because loans are cheaper when the interest rate is lower, the quantity of loans demanded is negatively related to the interest rate. In other words, you are more likely to borrow money to buy a car or house when the interest rate on the car or home loan is low. When the interest rate on loans rises, loans become more expensive, and the quantity of loans demanded falls. The negative relationship between the interest rate and the quantity of loans demanded reflects the law of demand and is illustrated by the downward-sloping demand curve for loans in Figure 22.1.

Figure 22.1 The Market for Loans

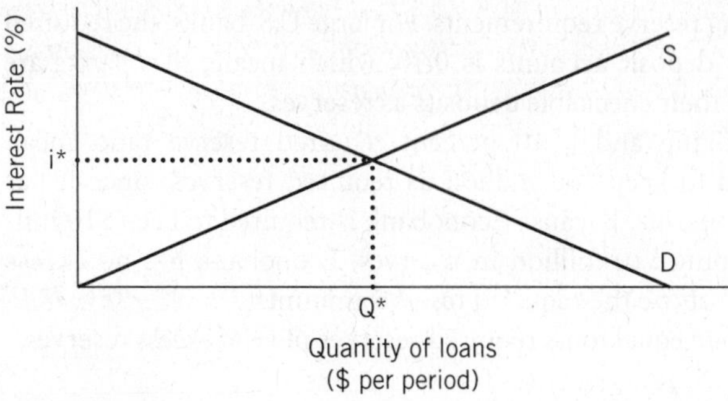

The supply of loans comes from savers. As the interest rate increases, the quantity of savings supplied rises, giving the supply curve (S) an upward slope. The demand for loans (D) comes from borrowers. As the interest rate rises, the quantity of loans demanded falls. The equilibrium interest rate is i* and the equilibrium quantity of loans is Q* per period.

The intersection of the supply and demand for loans determines the equilibrium interest rate (i*) and quantity of loans made in the market (Q*). At the equilibrium interest rate, all of the borrowers who are willing and able to take out loans at that interest rate are able to obtain loans, and all of the lenders who are willing and able to make loans at that interest rate are able to do so. If the interest rate is above equilibrium, the quantity of loans supplied will be higher than the quantity of loans demanded. A surplus of money available for loans means that banks will not be able to make as many loans as they would like to at the high interest rate. Ceteris paribus, banks will have an incentive to lower the interest rate they charge on loans in order to lend out their surplus money. As the interest rate falls, people will not want to hold as much money in savings, so the quantity of money available to loan out will fall and the market will move down along the supply curve for loans. The lower interest rate will also provide an incentive for individuals and businesses to increase their borrowing, and the market will move downward along the demand curve for loans. Ceteris paribus, a surplus in the lending market will be eliminated as the interest rate falls to its equilibrium level.

If the interest rate is below equilibrium, the quantity of loans demanded will be higher than the quantity of loans supplied, and there will be a shortage of loans available. At a below-equilibrium interest rate, potential borrowers will not be able to get the amount of loans that they demand because and banks will not find it as profitable to make loans at the low interest rate. The shortage will provide an incentive for lenders to increase interest rates. As interest rates rise, some potential borrowers will decide not to take out loans because they have become more expensive. At the same time, rising interest rates will give people an incentive to increase their savings, so the quantity of loans supplied will rise. The shortage will be eliminated as the interest rate rises to its equilibrium level.

THINK FOR YOURSELF

What happens to the interest rate and equilibrium quantity of loans when the demand for loans increases? What happens to the interest rate and equilibrium quantity of loans when the supply of loans increases?

Banks and Money Creation

We can use our understanding of bank lending and bank balance sheets to illustrate the influence that banks have on the money supply. Going back to our Econobank example, suppose that you inherit $10 million in cash from a long-lost relative, and you deposit that cash in your checking account at Econobank. Table 22.3 illustrates how Econobank's balance sheet changes as a result of this deposit.

Table 22.3 Econobank's Balance Sheet After $10 million Deposit

Assets ($ millions)		Liabilities ($ millions)	
Cash	20	Checking deposits	110
Securities	10		
Loans	100		

When a customer deposits $10 million into a checking account, the bank's liabilities rise by $10 million. The bank's cash assets also rise by $10 million.

When you deposit $10 million, Econobank's checking deposits increase from $100 million to $110 million. The cash you deposited goes into the bank's vault, raising Econobank's cash reserves from $10 million to $20 million. How do Econobank's required reserves change as a result of your deposit? Since Econobank must hold 10 percent of its checking deposits as required reserves, required reserves are now $11 million instead of $10 million. Notice that Econobank is holding a total of $20 million in total reserves, but its required reserves are only $11 million. This means that Econobank now has excess reserves of $9 million.

It is not profitable for Econobank to keep excess reserves on hand since they can be loaned out to earn interest or used to purchase securities that can increase in value over time. Suppose Econobank uses the $9 million in excess reserves to make a new $9 million loan to Techecon, a new technology company in town. Econobank makes this loan by crediting Techecon's checking account by $9 million. Econobank's new balance sheet is illustrated in Table 22.4. Econobank's checking deposits have risen to $119 million and its loans have risen to $109 million.

Recall that the definition of M1 includes cash and checkable deposits. This means that the additional $9 million in checking deposits at Econobank is newly created money. Techecon can use this money to purchase goods and services in the same way that you might use your checking account to make purchases. Issuing loans from excess reserves is how banks create money.

Now imagine another round in this process. In Table 22.4, Econobank's checking deposits are now $119 million, so Econobank's required reserves are now $11.9

Table 22.4 Econobank's Balance Sheet After Making $9 million in Loans

Assets ($ millions)		Liabilities ($ millions)	
Cash	20	Checking deposits	119
Securities	10		
Loans	109		

When a bank makes a $9 million loan, its assets rise by the amount of the loan. When the borrower deposits the loan in his checking account, the bank's liabilities increase by $9 million.

million. Econobank is holding $20 million in total reserves. Econobank again has excess reserves equal to its total reserves minus its required reserves, or

$$\text{\$20 million in total reserves} - \text{\$11.9 million in required reserves} = \text{\$8.1 million in excess reserves}$$

Econobank can loan this $8.1 million out to another customer, who will likely deposit it in the bank. The deposit will again increase checking deposits, required reserves, and excess reserves at Econobank, and the process will continue with new money being created by loans in each round. In the first round of loans, Econobank was able to make $9 million in loans. In the second round it was able to make $8.1 million in loans. Because banks keep a fraction of their checking deposits as required reserves, the amount of new loans they can make in each round of depositing and lending gets smaller and smaller.

THINK FOR YOURSELF

How much could Econobank lend out in the third round of deposits and lending? How much in the fourth round?

Of course, in reality deposits and loans do not occur at only one bank. In addition, bank customers may choose not to deposit all of their loan money into their checking account. Banks might find it more profitable to use some of their excess reserves to buy securities instead of making new loans. Each of these scenarios will change the amount that Econobank has available to loan out in each round of depositing and lending. Our example demonstrates the *maximum* amount that each deposit could potentially generate in new excess reserves, loans, and deposits again and again through this repeating cycle.

*The **money multiplier** (MM) tells the maximum amount that the money supply can increase for a given increase in deposits. It is equal to the reciprocal of the required reserve ratio. MM = 1/rrr*

If we track each round of new loans and their resulting deposits until there are no longer excess reserves to loan out, we can determine the maximum potential increase in checking deposits that can be generated by the initial $10 million deposit. Because checking deposits are part of the nation's money supply, this will tell us how much the money supply can potentially increase as a result of the initial $10 million deposit. Economists use the **money multiplier** (MM) to calculate this potential increase in the money supply. The money multiplier tells the maximum amount that the money supply can increase for a given amount of excess reserves loaned out. It is equal to the reciprocal of the required reserve ratio, 1/rrr.

For Econobank, the initial increase in deposits was $10 million. This means that up to

$$\text{\$10 million} * (1/.10) = \text{\$100 million}$$

in new money could be created through the rounds of loans and deposits that started from the initial deposit of $10 million. For a $10 million increase in deposits, the money supply can increase by up to $100 million.

It is important to note that the money multiplier tells us the *maximum* amount by which the money supply can increase as a result of an increase in deposits. If people hold some of their money as cash rather than depositing it in their checking accounts or if banks do not lend out all of their excess reserves, the actual increase in the money supply will be less than that predicted by MM.

THINK FOR YOURSELF

How much could the money supply increase if your inheritance were $5 million instead of $10 million, ceteris paribus? How much could the money supply increase if your inheritance was $10 million but the required reserve ratio was 0.20? 0.05?

Our Econobank example illustrates how an increase in deposits generates an increase in the money supply, but the money multiplier also works in reverse. Suppose that you decided to withdraw $5 million in cash from your checking account. Starting from Econobank's initial balance sheet in Table 22.2, Table 22.5 illustrates how the $5 million withdrawal will affect Econobank's balance sheet. First, checking deposits would fall from $100 million to $95 million. Second, Econobank's cash reserves would fall from $10 million to $5 million.

Table 22.5 Econobank's Balance Sheet After $5 million Withdrawal

Assets ($ millions)		Liabilities ($ millions)	
Cash	5	Checking deposits	95
Securities	10		
Loans	100		

When a customer withdraws $5 million, the bank's cash assets fall by $5 million and the bank's liabilities fall by $5 million.

How does the withdrawal affect Econobank's required reserves? With $95 million in checking deposits, Econobank is required to keep $9.5 million in reserves. However, since Econobank gave you $5 million in cash from its vault, its actual reserves are only $5 million. Econobank is now $4.5 million short of required reserves and must by law come up with that money. Econobank may have to sell some of its assets to cover its shortfall, or it may have to borrow money from another bank. Regardless of how it covers its reserve requirement, Econobank's its ability to make new loans will be cut. Just as your deposit at Econobank's expanded the money supply, your withdrawal will reduce the money supply.

Bank Regulation

We learned in the previous section that banks exert substantial influence over the money supply. A stable banking system is vitally important to a stable money supply and a stable economy. People's confidence in their bank's ability to provide them with their money on demand is crucial. Because banks hold only a fraction of their deposits as reserves, however, they can only function when their customers do not make substantial withdrawals. If a lot of customers withdraw all of their cash from a bank at one time, there is a potential for the bank to fail, meaning that it cannot pay its depositors their money on demand. This scenario is called a **bank run**.

*A **bank run** occurs when a large number of customers withdraw their deposits from the bank because they worry that their bank might fail.*

During the Great Depression of the 1930s, there were many bank runs and bank failures like the one pictured here. In 1933 alone, more than 4,000 U.S. banks failed. More than 9,000 banks failed between the stock market crash of 1929 and March 1933, when President Roosevelt declared a "bank holiday" that shut down all bank operations until the banking system could be stabilized.

Bank Runs and the 2007–2010 Financial Crisis

David McNew/Getty Images

Bank runs and bank failures are a fairly rare occurrence in this country. Indeed, fewer than ten banks per year closed between 1945 and 1970. Between 2008 and the end of 2010, however, a financial crisis caused 330 U.S. banks to fail. The accompanying photo depicts a run on California's IndyMac bank in July 2007. Economists and policymakers continue to debate the causes of the financial crisis, but most agree that a large contributing factor was a substantial increase in home loans made to borrowers without adequate resources to pay the loans back. When borrowers do not repay their loans, banks cannot provide their depositors with the money from their savings and checking accounts, and a bank run can occur. Fear of bank failures caused a significant decrease in the supply of loans, including loans to businesses. The decrease in available funding for businesses caused a decrease in production and a decrease in hiring. In turn, the decrease in demand for workers and the decreased availability of consumer credit caused a fall in consumer demand for all kinds of goods and services and a downward spiral in economic activity throughout the U.S. and the world.

Several safeguards were put in place during and after the Great Depression to enhance the stability of the banking system. One of the most prominent is the Federal Deposit Insurance Corporation (FDIC). Congress created the FDIC in 1933 to provide a federal government guarantee of bank deposits. Banks pay an insurance premium to the FDIC and the FDIC guarantees to reimburse bank deposits. For transaction accounts that do not pay interest (like many checking accounts) the FDIC guarantees full repayment of the account balance if the bank fails. For other accounts, the maximum amount insured is $250,000. In addition to insuring bank deposits, the FDIC also examines and audits banks to ensure they comply with required reserves and standard banking practices. When a bank fails, the FDIC is responsible for disbursing the bank's assets.

A second safeguard used after the Great Depression was increased reliance on the U.S. Federal Reserve System, a topic we turn to next.

THE FEDERAL RESERVE SYSTEM

The Federal Reserve System is the central bank of the U.S. Many other countries have a similar system, including the Deutsche Bundesbank in Germany, the European Central Bank for European Union member countries, and the Japanese Bank of Japan. The Federal Reserve, informally known as the "Fed," supervises and regulates banks, maintains the stability of the financial system, and provides financial services to banks and the federal government. Although its name sometimes confuses people into thinking that the Fed is a federal government agency, the Fed is not part of the federal government. Instead, the Fed operates independently in order to protect the banking system from political interference.

The Structure of the Federal Reserve System

The Federal Reserve is a network of 12 Federal Reserve District Banks that operate under the supervision of the Federal Reserve Board of Governors. There are seven members of the Board of Governors, each of whom is appointed by the president of the United States and confirmed by the U.S. Senate. Each member of the Board of Governors serves a 14-year term, and the terms are staggered so that one term expires every other year. The Board of Governors is led by the chairman and vice chair. The chairman and vice chair are members of the Board of Governors appointed to these leadership positions by the president and confirmed by the Senate to serve four-year terms, subject to reappointment as long as their term with the Board of Governors has not expired. Ben Bernanke is the current chairman, and Janet Yellen is the current vice chair of the Board of Governors.

The 12 Federal Reserve District banks are located throughout the U.S. In many ways, the Federal Reserve Banks provide commercial banks with the same services that commercial banks provide to their customers. Federal Reserve banks hold reserves on deposit and make loans to commercial banks in their district, move cash in and out of circulation, and collect and process checks. The Fed Banks also provide checking accounts for the U.S. Treasury, buy and sell government securities, and supervise commercial banks to make sure they are operating safely and within regulations.

U.S. currency includes the words Federal Reserve Note across the front of each bill. One dollar bills also include a symbol to the left of George Washington's image that tells which Federal Reserve Bank issued the bill. Investigate the dollar bills in your wallet and determine which of the Federal Reserve Banks issued them.

The Federal Open Market Committee (FOMC) is the policymaking arm of the Fed. The FOMC formulates Fed policies to promote economic growth, full employment, stable prices, and stability in the banking system. The FOMC consists of 12 members: the Board of Governors, the president of the Federal Reserve Bank of New York, and four other Federal Reserve Bank presidents, each serving rotating one-year terms.

Milton Friedman, Monetarism, and Free to Choose

HO/REUTERS//NewsCom

Milton Friedman (1912–2006) was an American economist, author, and economic advisor to President Reagan. Friedman was influential in developing the monetarist school of thought in economics, which focuses on the role of government and central banks in controlling the money supply through monetary policy. Friedman's best-selling book and 10-part PBS video series, *Free to Choose*, summarized his economic philosophy and strong support of the free market economic system and minimal government involvement in the economy. He won the Nobel Prize in economics in 1976 for his research on monetary history and monetary policy and his demonstration of the complexity of stabilizing the economy through policy actions. He was also very influential in eliminating U.S. military conscription and in promoting school choice policies. In his obituary, *The Economist* magazine described him as, "the most influential economist of the second half of the 20th century."

Federal Reserve and Monetary Policy

Monetary policy is the use of regulations or actions by the central bank to influence the money supply.

Two primary missions of the Federal Reserve are to promote price stability and to promote employment and economic growth. The Fed does this by conducting **monetary policy**, which includes actions that influence the availability of money and credit in the financial system.

The Fed uses monetary policy to balance the flow of money and credit to enhance the stability of the economy. If too much money is circulating in the economy, prices tend to rise rapidly. When too little money is available, consumers and businesses have less access to credit, which stifles economic activity. The Fed conducts monetary policy by influencing the ability of banks to create loans from their excess reserves. As we learned earlier, when banks' excess reserves grow, banks are able to produce more loans and the money supply increases. When banks' excess reserves fall, banks are able to make fewer loans and the money supply decreases. The Fed uses three tools to implement monetary policy: open market operations, the discount rate, and reserve requirements.

Open Market Operations

Open market operations are the purchases and sales of federal government securities by the Fed.

Open market operations is the buying and selling of federal government securities in financial markets. Conducting open market operations is the Fed's principal tool for carrying out monetary policy. The FOMC sets objectives for open market operations that ultimately increase or decrease the money supply.

If the Fed's objective is to increase the money supply, it will conduct open market purchases of securities from banks and investors. If the objective is to decrease the money supply, it will sell securities to banks and investors. We'll use our Econobank' example to illustrate how open market operations influence the money supply. Table 22.6 shows Econobank's initial balance sheet. Econobank initially has required reserves of $10 million and no excess reserves.

If the FOMC wants to increase the money supply, it can purchase $10 million in securities from Econobank. When this trade takes place, the Fed will deposit $10 million in Econobank's account at the Federal Reserve District Bank. Table 22.7 illustrates Econobank's new balance sheet after this sale.

Table 22.6 Econobank's Initial Balance Sheet

Assets ($ millions)		Liabilities ($ millions)	
Cash	10	Checking deposits	100
Securities	10		
Loans	100		

Table 22.7 Econobank's Balance Sheet After Sale of Securities to Fed

Assets ($ millions)		Liabilities ($ millions)	
Cash	10	Checking deposits	100
Securities	0		
Deposits at Federal Reserve	10		
Loans	100		

After a sale of $10 million in securities to the Fed, Econobank's securities fall by $10 million and Econobank's deposits at the Federal Reserve rise by $10 million.

Econobank's securities balance is now zero, and its balance of deposits at the Federal Reserve is now $10 million. Econobank now has $20 million in reserves but only needs $10 million to meet its reserve requirement. As a result, Econobank is likely to make loans of its $10 million in excess reserves. Given the required reserve ratio of 0.10, Econobank's $10 million new loans will generate a $100 million increase in the money supply.

The FOMC could also reduce the money supply by selling securities. The purchasing bank will see its account balance for deposits at the Federal Reserve decline, which will reduce its ability to make loans and result in a decrease in the money supply. Because the use of open market operations is very flexible and can be implemented easily, the Fed uses open market operations as its primary tool to influence the money supply.

THINK FOR YOURSELF

If the Fed wants to increase the money supply using open market operations, will it buy securities or sell them? What if the Fed wants to decrease the money supply?

The Discount Rate

A second tool of monetary policy is direct lending to banks by the Federal Reserve. The **discount rate** is the interest rate that Federal Reserve Banks charge commercial banks for loans.

The discount rate is the interest rate that the Federal Reserve charges banks for loans.

Banks can turn to the Fed for loans when they fall short of their required reserves. Loans to cover reserve shortfalls are generally very short term loans, usually just overnight. Banks also have the option to borrow directly from one another to cover required reserve shortfalls. The market for bank-to-bank loans to cover required

The ***federal funds rate*** *is the interest rate that banks charge one another for loans to cover required reserve shortfalls.*

reserve shortfalls is called the federal funds market, and the interest rate paid on those bank-to-bank loans is the **federal funds rate**. The Fed's discount rate is usually set just above the federal funds rate in order to encourage banks to use the Fed only as a last resort for borrowing.

Because the discount rate is the "price" that a bank must pay to borrow money from the Fed, the Fed's control over the discount rate can impact bank lending and borrowing. A higher discount rate discourages banks from borrowing from the Fed. As a result, banks that were intending to borrow from the Fed will instead turn to the federal funds market. More banks wanting to borrow in the federal funds market will increase the demand for loans in the federal funds market and increase the federal funds rate. Because an increase in the federal funds rate increases the cost of loans, banks will in turn have fewer excess reserves available to make loans to their customers. The final result from an increase in the discount rate will be a decrease in the money supply and fewer loans for bank customers.

THINK FOR YOURSELF

If the Fed wants to increase the money supply using its discount rate tool, will it lower or raise the discount rate? What if the Fed wants to decrease the money supply?

Although the discount rate can have a theoretically large impact on the money supply, in practice, the direct effect of changing the discount rate is fairly small. This is because most banks borrow in the federal funds market rather than directly from the Fed. The larger impact of the discount rate comes from its impact on *expectations* in financial markets. An increase in the discount rate, for example, is an indication that the Fed is moving to reduce the money supply. When the money supply falls, interest rates rise. When lenders see the Fed raising the discount rate, they form an expectation that interest rates are going to increase in the near future. As a result, they may reduce their lending now in order to wait for higher interest rates in the future. The reduction in the supply of loans will cause an increase in interest rates and a decrease in the money supply.

Reserve Requirements

A third tool of monetary policy is setting reserve requirements. The Board of Governors of the Fed has the authority to set the required reserve ratio. The required reserve ratio is different for different-sized banks. For example, banks with between $10.7 million and $58.8 million in checkable deposits have a required reserve ratio of 3 percent. The required reserve ratio for banks with more than $58.8 million in checkable deposits is 10 percent. For banks with less than $10.7 million in checkable deposits, the required reserve ratio is zero.

Increasing or decreasing the required reserve ratio instantly impacts banks' excess and required reserves. For example, if the required reserve ratio were increased from 3 to 5 percent for medium-sized banks, the amount of money they would be required to hold as required reserves would rise. This would decrease the amount of excess reserves they have available and would thus reduce the money supply. Similarly, decreasing the required reserve ratio has the effect of freeing up excess reserves, since the amount that a bank must hold as required reserves would be lower.

Changing the required reserve ratio has a direct impact on banks' required and excess reserves, but it has a larger impact on the money supply by changing the money multiplier. If the Fed increases the required reserve ratio from, say, 5 percent to 10 percent, the money multiplier falls from

$$1/.05 = 20 = MM$$

to

$$1/.10 = 10 = MM$$

A change in the required reserve ratio from 5 to 10 means that each dollar in excess reserves lent out will generate a smaller increase in the money supply. If the Fed decreases the required reserve ratio, the money supply will rise because banks can hold a smaller amount of their deposits as required reserves and because the money multiplier increases.

THINK FOR YOURSELF

What is the money multiplier when the required reserve ratio is 0.10? 0.03? How much could the money supply increase if a bank had excess reserves of $5 million and the required reserve ratio was 0.10? 0.03?

Monetary Policy and the Economy

As mentioned previously, the two primary missions of the Federal Reserve are to promote price stability and to promote employment. The Fed uses its tools of monetary policy to influence interest rates and expectations about interest rates, which in turn impact household and business borrowing and spending decisions. When the Fed needs to encourage spending to stimulate employment, the Fed undertakes **expansionary monetary policy**. Expansionary monetary policy involves actions to increase the money supply, including lowering the discount rate, buying securities, or reducing the required reserve ratio. Figure 22.2 illustrates the impact of expansionary monetary policy designed to promote employment.

Expansionary monetary policy involves Fed actions to increase the money supply.

Figure 22.2 **Impacts of Expansionary Monetary Policy**

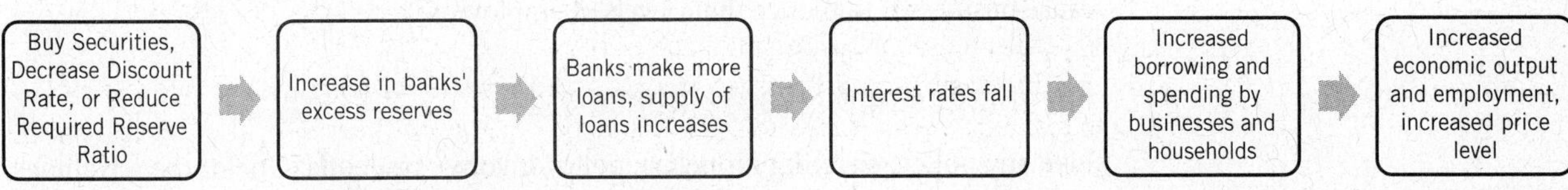

Expansionary monetary policy starts with Fed actions to expand the money supply by increasing banks' excess reserves. The excess reserves cause an increase in the supply of loans and a decrease in interest rates. Lower interest rates spur household and business borrowing and spending and result in increased employment.

When the Fed wants to promote employment, it will buy securities, decrease the discount rate, or decrease the required reserve ratio. These actions will generate increases in excess reserves for banks. Banks will make loans from these excess reserves, which will increase the supply of loans available. The increase in the supply of loans causes a decrease in interest rates and an increase in the quantity of loans demanded. With more loans available at lower interest rates, businesses and households increase their borrowing and spending. As a result, employment increases.

Contractionary monetary policy involves Fed actions to decrease the money supply,

When the Fed needs to encourage price stability in the face of rising prices, it undertakes contractionary monetary policy. **Contractionary monetary policy** includes actions designed to reduce the money supply, including selling securities, raising the discount rate, and raising the required reserve ratio. Figure 22.3 illustrates the impact of contractionary monetary policy.

Figure 22.3 **Impacts of Contractionary Monetary Policy**

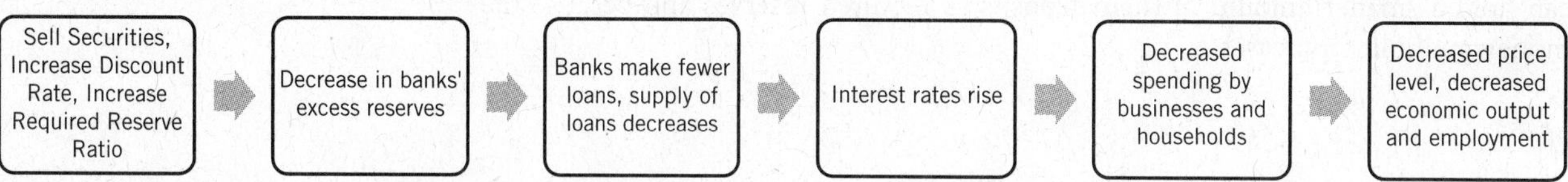

Contractionary monetary policy starts with Fed actions to decrease the money supply by decreasing banks' excess reserves. The reduction in excess reserves results in a decrease in the supply of loans and an increase in interest rates. Higher interest rates cause reductions in household and business borrowing and spending and results in reduced employment and lower prices.

The Fed can reduce the money supply by selling securities, increasing the discount rate, or increasing the required reserve ratio. This in turn will decrease banks' excess reserves and reduce the supply of loans. The reduction in the supply of loans will cause interest rates to rise. Higher interest rates will cause reductions in consumer and business borrowing and spending on goods and services. Reduced demand for goods and services will lower the price level in the economy.

The primary two missions of the Fed, promoting employment and promoting price stability, are often at odds with one another. If the Fed uses its monetary policy tools to promote employment and economic growth, it will seek to increase the money supply. Increases in the money supply cause reductions in interest rates. Falling interest rates spur increased spending as consumers take advantage of lower interest rates by increasing borrowing for new homes, for cars, or for other items. Businesses take advantage of lower interest rates by increasing borrowing for investment in new equipment or new buildings. These changes will increase demand for goods and services, and may result in increases in the prices of goods and services, which is at odds with the Fed's mission of promoting price stability. Alternatively, when the Fed reduces the money supply to combat inflation, it generates increases in interest rates and reductions in borrowing and spending. The reductions in spending cause businesses to reduce their levels of employment.

Advantages and Disadvantages of Monetary Policy

Like any policy, enacting monetary policy involves tradeoffs. One of the advantages of monetary policy is its flexibility. The FOMC meets often and can enact monetary policy immediately. Actions by congress to stimulate or dampen economic activity tend to take relatively longer as the process of debate and legislation moves forward. Another advantage of monetary policy is that it tends to be nonpolitical. The Federal Reserve is an appointed rather than elected body. This makes the Fed relatively insulated from the political forces faced by congress. Finally, Fed actions tend to generate relatively little interference with the market. The Fed influences interest rates and the money supply but does not restrict who can borrow or how loans are spent.

A disadvantage of monetary policy is the tradeoffs it involves. Fighting inflation involves reducing the money supply. This in turn causes a contraction in economic activity. Alternatively, engaging in expansionary monetary policy runs the risk of causing inflation. A second disadvantage of monetary policy comes as markets form expectations about Fed actions. If the Fed behaves as if they might raise interest rates, markets react quickly to anticipate higher interest rates. Fed policymakers must be extremely careful in their speeches and actions to ensure that they do not cause unwanted changes in expectations in financial markets.

SUMMARY

In this chapter, we examined the role of money in the economy. Money serves as a medium of exchange to facilitate transactions among buyers and sellers, as a unit of account to measure how much goods and services cost, and as a store of value for the future. The money supply is the money in circulation in the economy and is heavily influenced by the lending behavior of banks in the market for loans. Because banks are a primary source for loans, they exert substantial influence over the money supply in the economy. The Federal Reserve acts as a regulator of banks but also influences the money supply and economic activity through its control over monetary policy. Expansionary monetary policy generates an increase in the supply of money in the economy and stimulates economic activity. Contractionary monetary policy reduces the supply of money in the economy, lowering economic activity and inflation. Like all policies, monetary policy involves tradeoffs.

KEY CONCEPTS

- Barter exchange
- Medium of exchange
- Primary functions of money
- Unit of account
- Store of value
- M1 money supply
- Balance sheet
- Total reserves
- Required reserve ratio
- Required reserves
- Fractional reserve banking
- Excess reserves
- Money multiplier
- Bank run
- Monetary policy
- Open market operations
- Discount rate
- Federal funds rate
- Expansionary monetary policy
- Contractionary monetary policy

DISCUSSION QUESTIONS AND PROBLEMS

1. Describe the actions the Federal Reserve could take to increase the money supply.
2. Describe the functions of money. How well does cash fit these functions? How well does a checking account that earns zero interest fit these functions? How well does an interest-earning savings account fit these functions?
3. How is fractional reserve banking related to banks' ability to create money?
4. Describe the money multiplier. How does it influence the money supply?
5. How would the money multiplier change if businesses and consumers only used cash in transactions rather than depositing some of their money in banks?
6. Are credit cards part of the money supply? Why, or why not?

Assets		Liabilities	
Reserves	$30,000,000	Checking deposits	$150,000,000
Loans	$200,000,000	Savings deposits	$50,000,000
Total	$240,000,000	Total	$200,000,000

7. Consider the above balance sheet of a bank.
   a. If the required reserve ratio on checking deposits is 0.10, how much must the bank maintain in required reserves?
   b. How much money in excess reserves does the bank have?
   c. What is the total amount of money this bank could currently loan out?
   d. What is the value of the money multiplier?
   e. What is the maximum amount by which the money supply could increase if this bank lends out all its excess reserves?

MULTIPLE CHOICE QUESTIONS

1. If the Fed wants to combat inflation, it could
   a. decrease the required reserve ratio.
   b. increase the discount rate.
   c. buy securities on the open market.
   d. all of the above
2. The Fed could combat unemployment by
   a. increasing the required reserve ratio.
   b. increasing the discount rate.
   c. buying securities on the open market.
   d. all of the above
3. If the Federal Reserve sets a required reserve ratio of 0.2 and a bank has $100 million in loans and $80 million in deposits, what is the level of required reserves for the bank?
   a. $100 million
   b. $16 million
   c. $80 million
   d. $20 million
   e. $36 million
4. What interest rate does the Fed charge when it makes loans to banks?
   a. the prime rate
   b. the U.S. Treasury Bond rate
   c. the discount rate
   d. the federal funds rate
   e. the U.S. Treasury Bill rate
5. The Fed sometimes acts as a *lender of last resort*. This means that
   a. individuals can borrow from the Fed when the president declares a national disaster.
   b. individuals can try to borrow money from the Fed if they are unable to borrow from a bank.
   c. banks can go to the Fed to borrow money in order to purchase more government bonds.
   d. banks can go to the Fed to borrow reserves to meet their obligations to depositors.
   e. business firms can try to borrow money from the Fed if they are unable to borrow from a bank.
6. A bank wants to get rid of its excess reserves by making loans because
   a. it will be penalized if it does not get rid of the reserves.
   b. the reserves do not earn interest.
   c. it is afraid it will lose the excess reserves.
   d. firms will not borrow from a bank with excess reserves.
   e. the bank has too many liabilities.
7. If the reserve requirement is. 0.2 and demand deposits are $800, the banks must keep ______ as required reserves and can lend out ______.
   a. $800; $800
   b. $200; $6,000
   c. $160; $640

d. $640; $160
e. $0; $460

8. If the Federal Reserve buys $1,000 in bonds and the reserve requirement ratio is 0.5, what eventually happens to the money supply?
   a. The money supply decreases by $2,000.
   b. The money supply increases by $500.
   c. The money supply increases by $2,000.
   d. The money supply increases by $500.
   e. The money supply increases by $1,000.

9. If the Federal Reserve wishes to increase the money supply by $30,000 and the reserve requirement ratio is 0.4, how big of a purchase of bonds will the Fed need to make?
   a. $75,000
   b. $12,000
   c. $1,000
   d. $30,000
   e. $3,000

10. How would an increase in the required reserve ratio affect banks' ability to create money?
   a. Banks will be able to create more money because of the decrease in excess reserves.
   b. Banks will be able to create more money because of the increase in the demand deposit multiplier.
   c. It will have no effect on banks' ability to create money.
   d. It will reduce banks' ability to create money by forcing them to hold more reserves.
   e. It will reduce the banks' ability to create money by increasing excess reserves.

ADDITIONAL READINGS AND WEB RESOURCES

Friedman, Milton, and Friedman, Rose D. (1980) *Free to Choose: A Personal Statement*, Mariner Books. International bestselling book describing the negative relationship between personal freedom and many government policies.

Sowell, Thomas (2009) *The Housing Boom & Bust*, New York: Best Books. Provides a non-technical description of the sources of the financial and housing crisis that began in 2007.

The Federal Reserve website: www.federalreserve.gov includes extensive information about the different measures of the money supply, required reserves, and the money multiplier.

Federal Deposit Insurance Corporation website includes information on deposit insurance, bank regulations, and failed banks. www.fdic.gov

The PBS website "Inside the Meltdown" provides an overview of the 2007–2010 financial crisis. http://www.pbs.org/wgbh/pages/frontline/meltdown/

The Public Radio International broadcast, "This American Life: Giant Pool of Money," presents a Peabody Award–winning look at the financial crisis. http://www.pri.org/business/giant-pool-of-money.html

© Dieter Spears/iStockphoto

Fiscal Policy and the Federal Budget

After studying this chapter, you should be able to:

- Summarize how the federal budget is allocated
- Describe how the government raises money through taxes and borrowing
- Explain the difference between government deficits and debts
- Illustrate how fiscal policy impacts the economy using an aggregate demand and aggregate supply model
- Assess the tradeoffs associated with fiscal policy

In 2007–2010, the United States and many other nations experienced a severe economic downturn. Many financial institutions collapsed, housing prices plummeted, unemployment rose to over 10 percent, and the output of the U.S. economy fell rapidly. In response to the crisis, the U.S. Congress and President George W. Bush passed a $700 billion financial bailout package to help banks that were at risk of failing. Later, Congress and President Barak Obama passed an $800 billion stimulus plan that included tax rebates and various government spending plans aimed at saving or creating jobs. The combination of increases in government spending and reductions in government revenue meant that the federal government spent roughly $1.5 trillion more than it earned in revenue in 2010. Proponents of the high spending levels argued that the spending was necessary to stave off an even worse economic downturn. Opponents worried that the high spending would hurt the ability of the economy to grow in the long term. This chapter focuses on federal government spending, taxation, and borrowing. We'll learn how the government raises and spends money and assess the tradeoffs associated with these decisions.

THE FEDERAL BUDGET

Each year, the president is required to propose a federal budget to the U.S. Congress. The budget sets recommended spending and revenue generation for the federal government for the year. Congress then debates and adjusts the budget, eventually approving allocations of money to various programs through appropriations bills. Appropriations bills are laws that specify spending areas and authorize the government to spend money.

Spending

How is government spending determined? Some government spending is **nondiscretionary government spending**, which means that current laws, policies, and demographics, rather than presidential or congressional discretion, determine these spending levels. Social Security, Medicare, and the food stamp program are examples of nondiscretionary government spending because they provide benefits based on eligibility requirements rather than on year-to-year policy changes. Interest payments on federal borrowing are also nondiscretionary in the federal budget. Nondiscretionary spending accounts for about 60 percent of the federal budget.

Nondiscretionary government spending is determined by current obligations, policies, and demographics, rather than by policymaker discretion.

The other 40 percent of spending in the federal budget is **discretionary government spending**. Policymakers can make choices about the amount to fund discretionary programs. Discretionary spending items include spending on national defense, transportation, and education. Lengthening or shortening the length of time that the government pays unemployment insurance benefits is another example of a discretionary spending decision.

Discretionary government spending is determined by policymaker choices.

Figure 23.1 shows the mix of federal spending for 2012. Total federal spending in 2012 was $3.85 trillion. The largest categories of federal spending for 2012 include

Figure 23.1 **Federal Spending by Category, 2012 Percentages**

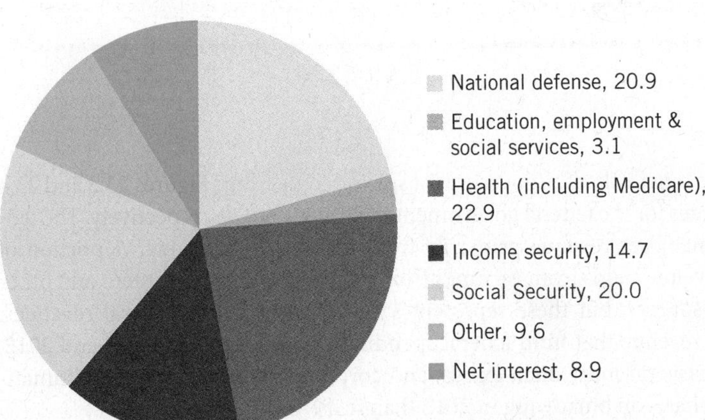

The largest categories of federal spending for 2012 include healthcare, national defense, and Social Security. Income security programs include federal employee retirement and disability, unemployment compensation, housing assistance, food and nutrition assistance, and other income security programs. The "other" category includes justice, general government functions, spending on science, space, and technology, natural resources and the environment, commerce and housing credits, community and regional development, research, transportation, energy, agriculture, and international affairs. *Source:* U.S. Office of Management and Budget Historical Tables.

Figure 23.2 **Federal Spending by Category, 1970 Percentages**

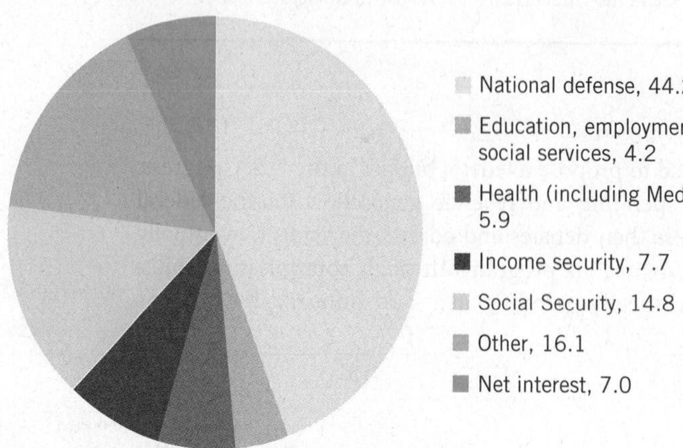

National defense made up a larger share of federal spending in 1970 than in 2012. Spending on health-care, income security, and Social Security has increased since 1970. *Source:* US Office of Management and Budget Histocical Tables.

health care, national defense, and social security. Figure 23.2 shows the mix of federal spending for 1970. Several changes in the federal budget have occurred since the 1970s. First, national defense accounted for roughly twice as much of the federal budget in 1970 than it did in 2012. Decreasing spending on national defense has been an ongoing trend in the U.S. since the 1960s. Second, spending on health care has increased dramatically, rising from 6 percent of federal spending in 1970 to 23 percent in 2012. Spending on income security and Social Security programs has risen dramatically as well.

What is the difference between discretionary and nondiscretionary government spending? Provide an example of each.

Revenue

Where does the money that the government spends come from? Figures 23.3 and 23.4 show the revenues for the federal government in 2012 and 1970, respectively. The federal government raises revenue primarily from taxes and borrowing. A portion of government revenue stems from earnings from the Federal Reserve System and other miscellaneous sources, but these represent a very small share of federal revenues. The sources of revenue that fund federal spending changed between 1970 and 2012, with less emphasis on individual, excise, and corporate income taxes and dramatically more emphasis on borrowing in 2012 than in 1970.

Taxes

*A **tax** is a financial obligation placed on taxpayers.*

Government revenue from taxes totaled about $2.9 trillion in 2012. A **tax** is a financial obligation imposed on individuals, corporations, or other legal entities.

Figure 23.3 **Federal Revenues by Category, 2012 Percentages**

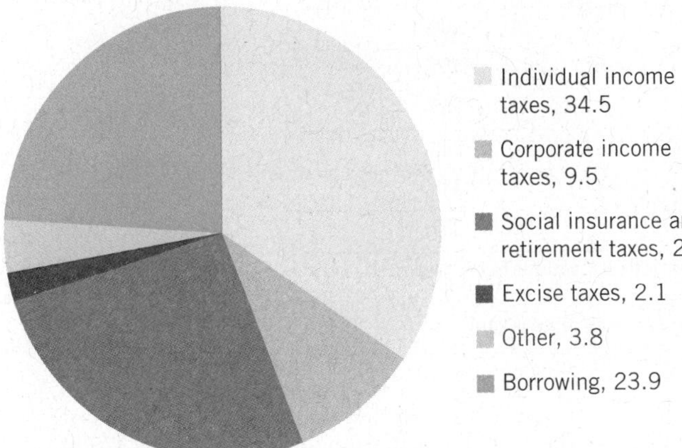

Borrowing made up the third largest source of federal revenues in 2012. The largest source of revenue was individual income taxes, followed by social insurance and retirement taxes. *Source:* U.S. Office of Management and Budget Historical Tables.

Figure 23.4 **Federal Revenues by Category, 1970 Percentages**

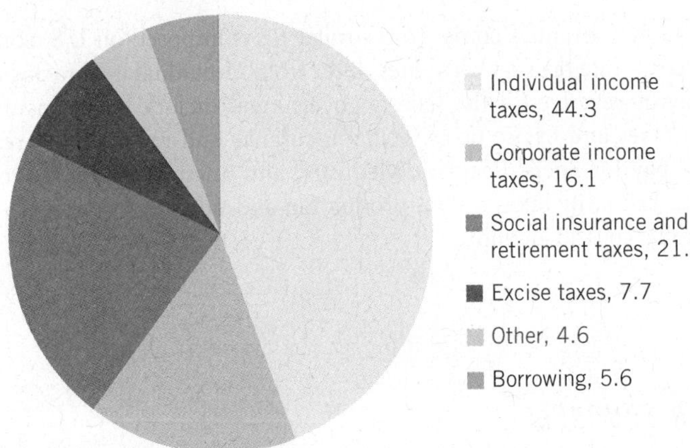

Individual income taxes made up a larger share of federal revenues in 1970 than in 2012. Borrowing accounted for 6 percent of federal revenues in 1970, but accounted for 24 percent of federal revenues in 2012. *Source:* U.S. Office of Management and Budget Historical Tables.

Most federal tax revenue comes from individual and corporate income taxes. **Income taxes** are taxes imposed as a percentage of income earned. The U.S. has a **progressive income tax system**, which means that as your income rises, you are required to pay a larger percentage of that income as taxes.

__Income taxes__ are taxes that are based on the amount of income a taxpayer earns. In a __progressive income tax system__, as taxpayers' incomes increase they are required to pay a larger percentage of that income as taxes.

There are currently six **income tax brackets** that are taxed at different rates. Each of these income tax brackets is charged a different **marginal tax rate**. The marginal tax rate is the tax rate on income within a tax bracket.

An __income tax bracket__ is a level of income that is taxed at a different marginal tax rate. The __marginal tax rate__ is the tax rate on income within a tax bracket.

Table 23.1 illustrates the federal income tax brackets and marginal tax rates for a single person in 2010. A simple example can illustrate how marginal tax rates are applied. Suppose your income is \$20,000. The first tax bracket applies to income below \$8,375, so your first \$8,375 of income will be taxed at the 10 percent marginal tax rate. The rest of your income will be taxed at the 15 percent marginal tax rate. In total,

$$\$20{,}000 - \$8{,}375 = \$11{,}635$$

Table 23.1 Income Tax Brackets and Tax Rates

Income Bracket ($)	Marginal Tax Rate
<8,375	10%
8,376–34,000	15%
34,001–82,400	25%
82,401–171,850	28%
171,851–373,650	33%
>373,651	35%

The progressive income tax system in the U.S. applies a higher marginal tax rate as income increases.
Source: www.irs.gov. Tax rates are for a single person in 2010.

of your income will be taxed at the 15 percent marginal tax rate and $8,375 of your income will be taxed at the 10 percent tax rate. Your total federal income tax bill would be

$$(\$8{,}375 * 0.10) + (\$11{,}625 * 0.15) = \$2{,}581$$

Corporate income tax revenues come from similar taxes imposed on U.S. corporations, although corporate tax bracket values differ from individual tax brackets. Other taxes that provide revenue for the federal government include social insurance and retirement taxes and excise taxes. Social insurance and retirement taxes include the taxes we pay for Social Security, Medicare, and unemployment insurance. Excise taxes are primarily taxes on the production and sale of certain goods, including gasoline, tobacco, and alcohol.

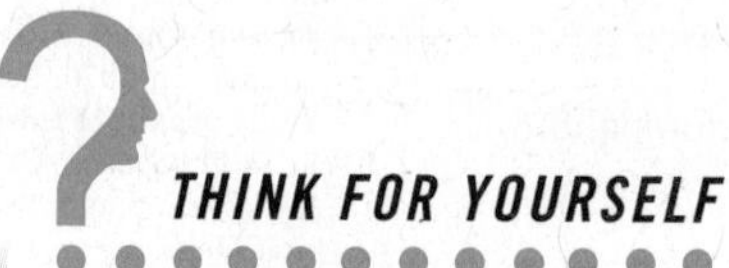

THINK FOR YOURSELF

Suppose your income is $100,000 per year. Using Table 23.1, compute your federal income tax bill.

Borrowing

To make up the difference between the amount that it spent and the amount it collected in revenue, the federal government borrowed $919 billion in 2012, making borrowing the third largest source of federal revenue. How does borrowing happen? The government borrows money from two primary sources: from the public and from itself. Borrowing from the public happens when the government issues U.S. Treasury securities including U.S. Savings Bonds, Treasury Bills, Treasury Bonds, or Treasury Notes that are available for purchase by households, business firms, other governments, or banks. The government borrows from itself when it exchanges Treasury securities for money from other government accounts, primarily from the Social Security Trust Fund. The Social Security Trust Fund is the fund where the government keeps money that has been paid as Social Security taxes but is not yet required to pay for Social Security benefits.

Figure 23.5 U.S. Federal Deficit ($ millions)

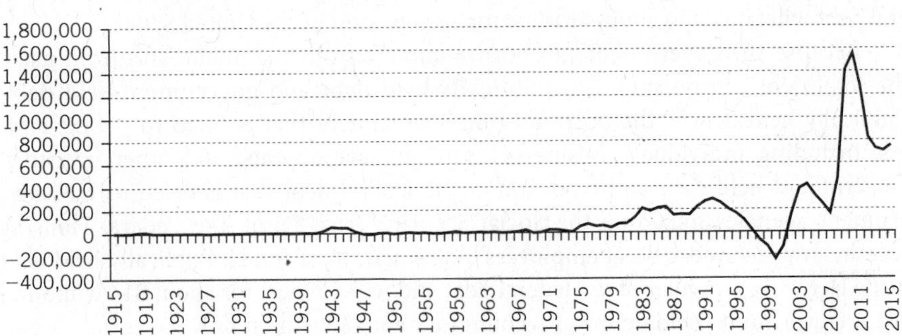

When the government spends more than it collects in tax revenue or other earnings, it runs a budget deficit. Budget deficits are financed by government borrowing. The U.S. federal deficit was near zero until the mid-1970s, but grew almost every year since then. *Source:* U.S. Office of Management and Budget. Values for 2010–2015 are estimates.

FEDERAL DEFICITS AND FEDERAL DEBT

When government spending is higher than the amount of tax revenue collected, the government runs a **budget deficit**. In order to make up the difference between spending and tax revenue, the government must borrow money.

A budget deficit occurs when the amount of government spending in a given period is larger than the amount of government revenue from taxes and earnings during that period.

Figure 23.5 illustrates the federal budget deficit since 1915. The federal government has run budget deficits many times in the past, including as far back as 1917. These deficits were generally small and were often followed by years with budget surpluses. The U.S. had relatively large budget deficits during the Great Depression and World War II in the 1930s and 1940s, but had either surpluses or small deficits during the 1950s and early 1960s. Beginning in the 1970s, federal budget deficits became the norm. Since 1975, the only years that the government ran a **budget surplus** were 1998–2001.

A budget surplus occurs when the amount of government spending in a given period is less than the amount of government revenue from taxes and earnings during that period.

Each period that the government borrows money to finance the deficit, it adds to its overall debt. The **federal debt** is the accumulation of deficit borrowing that has not been paid off.

The federal debt is the accumulated federal deficit borrowing that has not been paid off.

To illustrate the deficit and debt concepts, suppose you earn $1,000 per month and spend $1,200 each month on your credit card. You run a budget *deficit* of $200 each month because you spend more than you earn. The debt balance on your credit card will continue to increase if you spend this way. If we ignore interest charges your *debt* will be $2,400 after one year.

The U.S. federal debt over time is shown in Figure 23.6. The federal debt was close to $0 until the mid-1970s because prior budget deficits were very small and were followed by budget surpluses. The debt began to grow in the late 1970s and has

Figure 23.6 U.S. Federal Debt ($ millions)

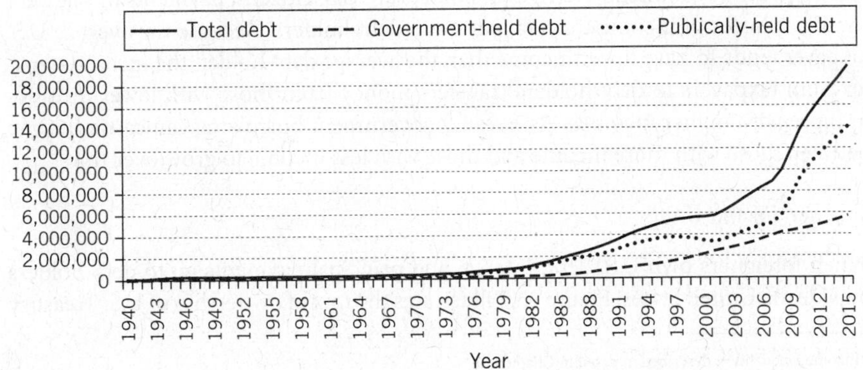

The U.S. federal debt is the accumulated federal budget deficit borrowing that has not yet been paid off. Publically held debt is the portion of the federal debt that is owed to public lenders including individuals, businesses, and other investors. Government held debt is the portion of the federal debt that is owed to government agencies including the Social Security Trust fund. *Source:* U.S. Office of Management and Budget. Values for 2010–2015 are estimates.

continued to grow since then. By 2015, the federal debt is projected to be almost $20 trillion. Since the U.S. population will be approximately 326 million in 2015, the federal debt will equate to about $61,000 for each person in the United States.

Publically-held debt is the portion of the federal debt that is owed to public lenders.

Government-held debt is the portion of the federal debt that is owed to government agencies.

Because the government can borrow money from the public and from itself, the total debt can be split into **publically-held debt** and **government-held debt**. Publically held debt is the portion of the federal debt that is owed to public lenders, including individuals, businesses, foreign governments, and other investors. Government held debt is the portion of the federal debt that is owed to U.S. government agencies including the Social Security Trust Fund, the Federal Housing Administration, and federal employees' retirement trust funds. Publically held debt is the largest component of the federal debt and will account for about $14 trillion in 2015. Government held debt will account for about $6 trillion in 2015.

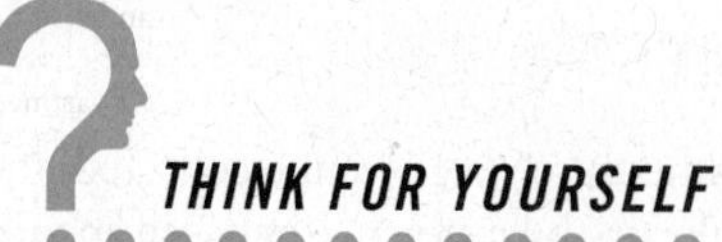

THINK FOR YOURSELF

What is the difference between a federal budget deficit and federal debt?

Controversies Surrounding Federal Deficits and Debts

Like any other choice, the choice to allow government deficits and debts involves tradeoffs. On the one hand, federal government borrowing can be used to smooth federal spending and increase economic stability during economic downturns or during periods of high demand on government spending (wartime, for example). Just like students might borrow money to pay for college or people might borrow money to pay for a home, some government borrowing might be desirable, particularly if it is used to invest in things that will generate income or output in the future. On the other hand, we have to pay interest payments on our debt, and those interest payments have opportunity costs. Apart from these general concerns, economists and policymakers have highlighted several other areas of controversy regarding federal debt.

Income Inequality

When the government borrows money from its own citizens, it generates a liability and an asset. The liability comes because taxpayers must make interest payments and repay the principal to the debt holders. The debt is an asset to the debt holders because lenders earn interest in exchange for their willingness and ability to loan money to the government. When debt holders are U.S. citizens, payments on the debt cause a transfer of income from taxpayers to debt holders. Because the average U.S. taxpayer tends to have lower income than the average debt holder, the income transfer from taxpayers to debt holders transfers money from those with lower incomes to those with higher incomes. As a result, government borrowing can cause the gap between those with more income and those with less income to grow over time.[1]

Foreign-Owned Debt

When foreigners own U.S. debt, interest and principal payments go to debt holders outside the United States. Figure 23.7 illustrates the mix of ownership of U.S. Treasury

1 Income inequality is described in detail in Chapter 20.

Figure 23.7 **Estimated Ownership of U.S. Treasury Securities (December 2010)**

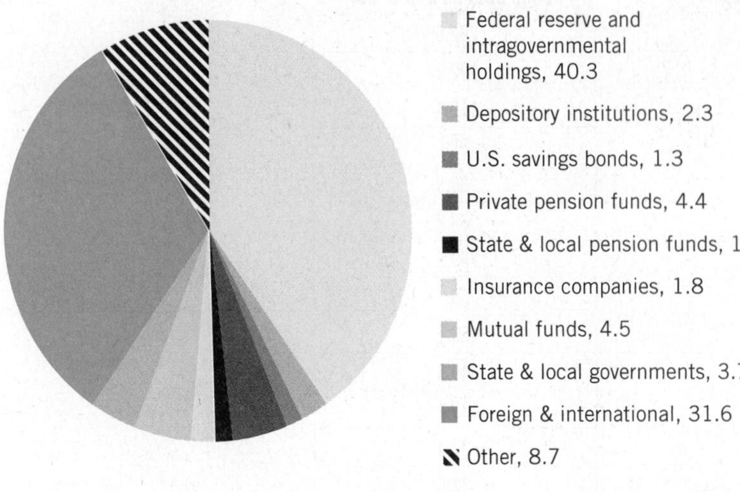

The largest holder of U.S. debt is the Federal Reserve and other intragovernmental agencies. Foreign and international debt holders own 32 percent of U.S. debt. *Source:* U.S. Department of the Treasury, Office of Debt Management, Office of the Under Secretary for Domestic Finance.

securities in December 2010. The largest share of federal debt is held by the Federal Reserve and other government agencies. The second largest share of the debt (31.6 percent) is held by foreign investors. Some economists worry that as a larger share of investment in U.S. debt comes from foreigners, policymakers may face increasing scrutiny from abroad when they enact economic policies.

Dangerous Levels of Debt?

If you need to borrow money to buy a car or a house, your first step is to find a lender willing to give you a loan. All else being equal, if you have a stable income and a good credit history you will probably be able to find a bank to lend you money at a reasonable interest rate. If your income is unstable or if you have a poor credit history, the bank faces more risk by lending you money, so it will be harder to obtain a loan, and you might be charged a higher interest rate.

The federal government faces the same situation, but on a larger scale. When the government wants to borrow money, it must find investors willing to lend it money. When governments have good credit histories and stable economies, they are low-risk borrowers and investors are willing to lend them money at relatively low interest rates. However, if a government's borrowing gets too large or its economy is unstable, it may have difficulty obtaining loans and it may face higher interest rates, both of which make borrowing more expensive.

One signal of a country's ability to repay its debt is its **debt-to-GDP ratio**. The debt-to-GDP ratio measures the size of a country's debt as a percentage of the country's gross domestic product.

*The **debt-to-GDP ratio** measures the size of a country's national debt as a percentage of its GDP.*

A low debt-to-GDP ratio is an indicator that a country is producing enough to pay back its debts relatively quickly if necessary, or that its productivity is enough to sustain its debt level into the future. A high debt-to-GDP ratio indicates that a country would have a more difficult time paying back its debt. Table 23.2 shows debt-to-GDP ratios for selected countries in 2009. Ceteris paribus, we would expect countries like China and Russia to have easier access to credit and borrowing than Japan and Greece because Chinese and Russian debt-to-GDP ratios are much lower than those of Japan and Greece.

Table 23.2 Debt-to-Gross Domestic Product (GDP) Ratios

Country	Public Debt as a % of GDP
Zimbabwe	282.6
Japan	192.9
Greece	113.4
Canada	82.5
Egypt	80.9
UK	68.2
Brazil	59.5
World	56
USA	53.5
Pakistan	49.3
Mexico	39.1
Hong Kong	37.4
Saudi Arabia	22.6
Venezuela	18
China	16.9
Russia	8.3
Libya	3.9

The debt-to-GDP ratio measures the size of a country's national debt as a percentage of its GDP. Lending to countries with low debt-to-GDP ratios is less risky for investors than lending to countries with high debt-to-GDP ratios.
Source: Author's table based on CIA World Factbook data 2009.

The 2011 U.S. Debt Crisis and U.S. Credit Downgrade

Mark Wilson/Getty Images, Inc.

During the summer of 2011, U.S. borrowing reached the level of the U.S. **debt ceiling,** which is the Congressionally mandated maximum amount of debt that the U.S. can have. Although the debt ceiling has been raised many times in the past, concern about the U.S. budget deficit prompted many lawmakers to refuse to raise the debt ceiling unless measures to reduce the deficit were also passed. Because a large fraction of federal spending is financed by borrowing, failure to raise the debt ceiling would have meant either a drastic cut in federal spending or a default on some U.S. debts. Although the debt ceiling was eventually raised after a series of negotiations between President Obama and House Speaker Boehner (pictured here), the situation affected consumer and investor expectations about the long-term health of the U.S. economy. The Standard & Poor's credit rating agency downgraded the U.S. credit rating from AAA (the best rating possible) to AA+, reflecting that lending to the U.S. had become riskier for investors. The U.S. had held the AAA rating since 1917.

*The **debt ceiling** is the Congressionally mandated maximum amount of debt that the U.S. government can have.*

Burden on Current and Future Generations

Another controversy surrounding government debt stems from the impact of debt payments on future generations. In order to make interest payments on its debt, the government can choose to borrow more money, increase taxes, or spend less. More borrowing involves a higher interest burden in the future. Reducing government spending is difficult politically, particularly for nondiscretionary government spending. Higher taxes make people's take-home pay smaller, reducing their ability to spend on goods and services, invest in businesses, or save for the future. If investment in business and infrastructure is lowered today, future generations will have less capital and technology available than they would have had otherwise.

Crowding Out

Another concern about government debt is that government borrowing has an impact on interest rates in the market for loans. Figure 23.8 illustrates the market for loans. The price of loans, measured on the vertical axis, is the interest rate that borrowers must pay in order to take out a loan. The quantity of loans, measured on the horizontal axis, reflects the amount of money borrowed and lent per period. The supply of loans (S) comes from savers and investors who are willing to lend their money to borrowers. The demand for loans (D) comes from individuals and businesses who want to borrow money. The demand for loans also comes from federal government borrowing.

Figure 23.8 **The Market for Loans**

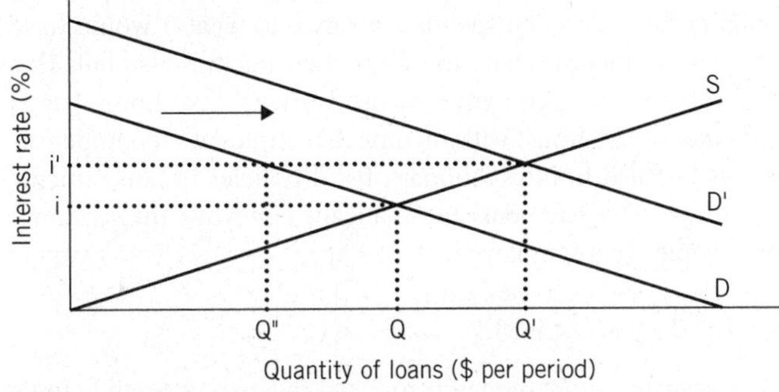

The supply of loans (S) comes from savers. The demand for loans (D) comes from borrowers. The initial equilibrium interest rate is i and the equilibrium quantity of loans is Q per period. If the government increases its borrowing, the demand for loans shifts outward to D' and the interest rate to rises to i'. The higher interest rate will make it more expensive for other borrowers to take out loans.

The intersection of the supply (S) and demand (D) for loans determines the equilibrium interest rate (i) and quantity of loans made in the market (Q). Suppose that an increase in government borrowing causes an increase in the demand for loans from D to D'. The increase in demand causes the interest rate to rise from i to i'. The higher interest rate reduces the ability of businesses and individuals to borrow and invest in new technologies and machinery or borrow to spend on consumption. Faced with higher interest rates, businesses and individuals will borrow less than they would have otherwise, as shown by the movement from Q to Q" on the original demand curve (D). This reduction in private borrowing is called **crowding out** because government borrowing causes a reduction in private sector borrowing and investment.

Crowding out occurs when government borrowing pushes up interest rates, which causes a reduction in private consumption and investment.

THINK FOR YOURSELF

Will crowding out be larger or smaller when the supply of loans is more elastic? Will crowding out be larger or smaller when the supply of loans is more inelastic?

FISCAL POLICY

Fiscal policy is the use of government spending and taxation to influence the economy.

Discretionary fiscal policy: When policymakers actively change government spending or taxation in response to changes in the economy.

Nondiscretionary fiscal policy: Automatic fiscal policy that stabilizes economic activity without active policy changes.

The use of government spending and taxation to influence the economy is called **fiscal policy**. Fiscal policy can be used to help stabilize economic downturns or to cool the economy when policymakers are worried that high demand for goods and services is putting too much upward pressure on prices.

Some fiscal policy results from government actively engaging to change taxes or spending to influence the economy. Policymakers use **discretionary fiscal policy** to change government spending or taxation in response to changes in the economy. When policymakers respond to economic downturns or expansions by cutting taxes or increasing government spending on various projects, they are engaging in discretionary fiscal policy.

Other fiscal policy impacts the economy automatically, without direct changes in policy. **Nondiscretionary fiscal policies** are sometimes called automatic stabilizers in the economy because they do not require policy action. Nondiscretionary fiscal policy is built into our progressive tax structure and our income-based welfare system. The U.S. progressive income tax structure is nondiscretionary fiscal policy because when people's incomes increase, a percentage of those higher incomes are collected as taxes. Higher tax payments have a stabilizing effect on an expanding economy because the higher taxes dampen spending relative to what it would have been. During recessions people's incomes tend to fall, so their tax bills also fall. This serves to help stabilize a recessionary economy because workers' take-home pay is more than it would be if taxes didn't adjust with income. Unemployment compensation and welfare payments are also nondiscretionary fiscal policies because unemployment compensation and welfare payments automatically rise when the economy is in recession and more people are unemployed.

Aggregate Demand/Aggregate Supply

The aggregate demand–aggregate supply model introduced in Chapter 6 can help us understand how fiscal policy impacts the economy. Aggregate demand (AD) represents the whole of the demand for all goods and services of the economy at different prices. Aggregate supply (AS) represents the whole of the supply of all the goods and services in the economy at different prices. Figure 23.9 illustrates a simple aggregate demand and aggregate supply (AD/AS) model. In the AD/AS model, the vertical axis measures the price level and the horizontal axis measures GDP per period. The intersection of AD and AS determines the equilibrium price level (P^*) and level of output in the economy (Q^*).

Expansionary fiscal policy is used to increase aggregate demand.

Contractionary fiscal policy is used to decrease aggregate demand.

Fiscal policy can include expansions or contractions in government spending or taxes. Both of these activities primarily impact aggregate demand. Fiscal policy that is used to help boost the economy during economic downturns is called **expansionary fiscal policy**. Fiscal policy used to dampen economic activity is called **contractionary fiscal policy**.

Figure 23.9 **Aggregate Demand/Aggregate Supply Model**

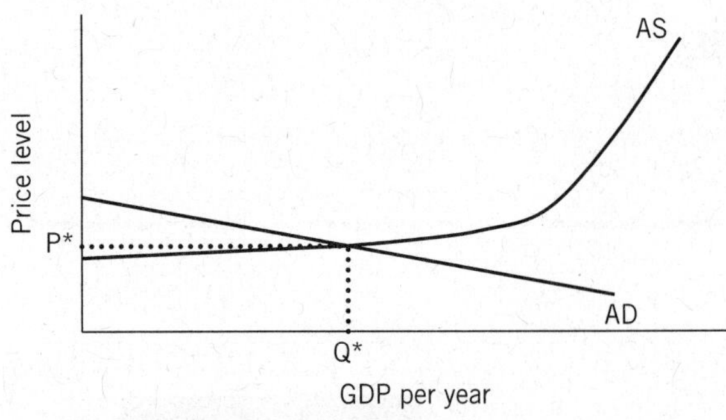

In the AD/AS model, the horizontal axis represents total output per period (GDP) and the vertical axis represents the price level in the economy. AD is the demand for all goods and services in the economy and AS represents the supply of goods and services in the economy. The intersection of AD and AS tells the equilibrium level of GDP and the equilibrium price level in the economy.

Expansionary Fiscal Policy

Expansionary fiscal policy can include tax cuts or rebates, increased government spending on military equipment or services, increased spending on education, or increased spending on infrastructure like roads and bridges. Increases in government spending cause increases in aggregate demand as the government hires workers or buys equipment. Lower taxes cause increases in aggregate demand because when businesses and households pay less in taxes they have more after-tax income to spend on investments or consumption.

Figure 23.10 illustrates the impact of expansionary fiscal policy on the economy. When the government expands its spending, AD shifts outward. The shift in AD causes the economy to move along the AS curve to a higher level of GDP and a higher price level. The size of the impact of expansionary fiscal policy depends on where the economy is on the AS curve.

Figure 23.10 **Expansionary Fiscal Policy**

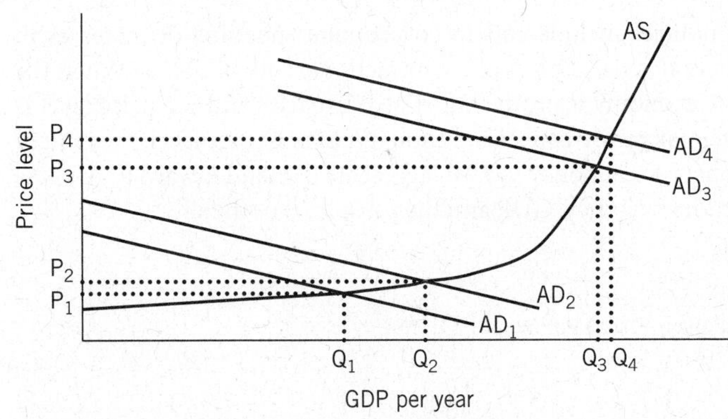

Expansionary fiscal policy causes outward shifts in aggregate demand. Expansionary fiscal policy that shifts AD from AD_1 to AD_2 causes a large increase in output but only a small increase in the price level. Fiscal policy that shifts AD from AD_3 to AD_4 does not cause a large increase in output, but does cause a large increase in the price level.

Suppose the economy is initially at equilibrium between AS and AD_1, so the level of output is Q_1 and the price level is P_1. If expansionary fiscal policy shifts aggregate demand outward to AD_2, output rises to Q_2 and the price level rises to P_2. If instead the economy were initially at equilibrium between AS and AD_3, the same expansionary fiscal policy will shift aggregate demand to AD_4. GDP will only increase from Q_3 to Q_4, but prices will rise from P_3 to P_4. In other words, fiscal policy can cause increases in output and employment when the economy is at a relatively low level of GDP, but fiscal policy will cause inflation when the economy is at a relatively high level of GDP.

Why doesn't expansionary fiscal policy have as large an impact on GDP between AD_3 and AD_4 as it does between AD_1 and AD_2 in Figure 23.10?

John Maynard Keynes and Expansionary Fiscal Policy

Walter Stoneman/Samuel Bourne/Getty Images

John Maynard Keynes (1883–1946) was a British economist whose influence on macroeconomics and governmental policy cannot be understated. During 1930s, Keynes argued that free markets would not move the economy out of the Great Depression but that active government policy to increase aggregate demand would. In his 1936 book, the *General Theory of Employment, Interest and Money*, Keynes demonstrated that it was possible for economies to stabilize at low levels of output and high levels of unemployment. To push economies out of these negative equilibriums, governments needed to increase aggregate demand by increasing government spending. His arguments supporting active government involvement in the economy form the foundation of Keynesian Economics, which is practiced to varying degrees in almost every developed nation in the world. Many of the government programs enacted during the Great Depression stemmed from Keynes' theory. In 1999, *Time* magazine named Keynes one of the 100 most influential people of the 20th century.

Contractionary fiscal policy is used to decrease aggregate demand.

Contractionary Fiscal Policy

Contractionary fiscal policies include cuts in government spending or increases in taxes. Figure 23.11 illustrates the impact of a contractionary fiscal policy. When the economy is at AD_1, the economy is producing at near capacity and the price level is relatively high. If policymakers are concerned about the rising price level, they might engage in a contractionary fiscal policy to push aggregate demand inward to AD_2. As a result of the contractionary policy, GDP and the price level both fall.

Figure 23.11 **Contractionary Fiscal Policy**

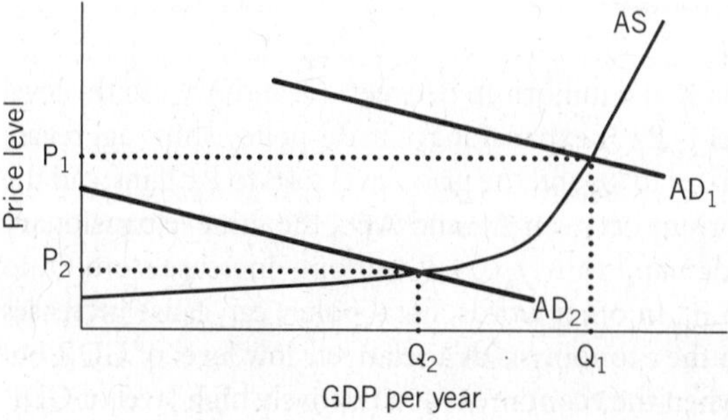

Contractionary fiscal policy causes inward shifts in aggregate demand. Contractionary fiscal policy that shifts AD from AD_1 to AD_2 causes a decrease in GDP and a decrease in the price level.

Controversies Surrounding Fiscal Policy

As with any policy choice, fiscal policy involves both costs and benefits. Expansionary fiscal policy can help policymakers to stabilize the economy during an economic downturn, which generates job and income stability for current citizens. If expansionary fiscal policy is financed by budget deficits, however, the costs of the policy include interest payments, changes in income inequality, and risks associated with foreign ownership of U.S. debt. Economists have also raised concerns about the ability of policymakers to time fiscal policy actions effectively and about the potentially destabilizing effects of fiscal policy if politicians use it for political gain.

Album/Oronoz/NewsCom

Friedrich Hayek and *The Road to Serfdom*

Friedrich Hayek (1899–1992) was an Austrian economist and philosopher best known for his support of free-market capitalism and minimal government. Along with his mentor Ludwig von Mises, Hayek is one of the most famous leaders of the Austrian School of economics, which supports free-market capitalism. Hayek's 1944 book, *The Road to Serfdom*, warned of the dangers associated with central planning and the potential tyranny associated with extensive government involvement in the economy. Extensive government involvement in the economy, Hayek asserted, would progressively lead to the will of a small minority being imposed on the majority of people in the pursuit of ambiguous centralized goals, including "social welfare" and "the good of the community," both of which run counter to the individual freedoms of democracy. Based on these arguments, Hayek warned that fascism and socialism both had roots in central economic planning and its associated power of the government over individual freedom. Hayek won the Nobel Prize in Economics in 1974 and the U.S. Presidential Medal of Freedom in 1991.

Fiscal Policy Timing Lags

Discretionary fiscal policy involves decisions by policymakers to actively change government spending or taxes. Actively changing policy involves many timing issues. Suppose, for example, that the economy has moved into a recession. It takes time for data on economic activity to be gathered, analyzed, and communicated to policymakers and the public. The time delay between an actual change in economic activity and the ability for policymakers and others to discern the change is called the **recognition lag**. The economy may be well into a downturn before we have the data to recognize that fiscal policy may be warranted. Once policymakers recognize the downturn, they must decide what to do about it. Some policymakers may want to enact tax cuts, others may want to increase government spending, and others may want both. The time it takes for Congress and the president to agree on what fiscal policy to use is called the **administration lag**. Finally, once the policy is enacted, it takes time for the policy to have an impact. For example, once increased government spending on infrastructure is authorized, it will take time for government agencies to advertise for contractors to bid on projects, for projects to be awarded, and for contractors to hire employees and start work. This is the **response lag** of fiscal policy. Each of these lags can vary in length depending on the complexity of the fiscal policy and the degree to which

The ***recognition lag*** *is the time between an actual change in economic activity and the ability for policymakers and others to recognize the change.*

The ***administration lag*** *is the time it takes for congress and the president to agree on what fiscal policy to use.*

The ***response lag*** *is the time it takes for government agencies to put fiscal policy into place.*

politicians can reach agreement and compromise. If expansionary fiscal policy comes after the economy has stabilized from a recession and started growing, it can exacerbate that growth and cause unnecessary inflation. Alternatively, if contractionary fiscal policy arrives as the economy has moved from a period of expansion into stability or into recession, fiscal policy can make the recession worse.

Fiscal Policy and Politics

Another concern with fiscal policy comes from worry that politicians have an incentive to use government spending and taxation to manipulate the economy in order to help them win elections. Politicians who are concerned about generating additional votes during an election have an incentive to engage in expansionary fiscal policy to help boost the economy, generate jobs in their districts, or increase voter incomes. Politicians also have incentives to direct government spending programs to their own districts, even if those districts might not be best suited for the projects.

SUMMARY

Government spending and taxation are an important part of the economy. Government expenditures include spending on interest payments, health care, national defense, Social Security, and other services. Government revenue comes from taxes and borrowing. When the government spends more than it brings in in revenue, it runs a budget deficit and must borrow money to make up the difference. Federal budget deficits have grown in recent years, raising concern among policymakers and others about the eventual impacts of the large federal debt.

Fiscal policy is the use of government spending and taxation to influence the economy. Expansionary fiscal policy is designed to increase aggregate demand and output in the economy. Contractionary policy reduces aggregate demand. Fiscal policy is controversial because it involves several timing lags and because of its potential to be abused for political gain.

KEY CONCEPTS

- Nondiscretionary government spending
- Discretionary government spending
- Tax
- Income taxes
- Progressive income tax system
- Income tax brackets
- Marginal tax rate
- Budget deficit
- Budget surplus
- Federal debt
- Publically-held debt
- Government-held debt
- Debt-to-GDP ratio
- Debt ceiling
- Crowding out
- Fiscal policy
- Discretionary fiscal policy
- Nondiscretionary fiscal policies
- Expansionary fiscal policy
- Contractionary fiscal policy
- Recognition lag
- Administration lag
- Response lag

DISCUSSION QUESTIONS AND PROBLEMS

1. What are some examples of expansionary fiscal policy? What are some examples of contractionary fiscal policy?
2. Why might the government want to enact contractionary fiscal policy? Why might the government want to enact expansionary fiscal policy?
3. When you accumulate debt on your credit card, does it add to the federal debt? Why or why not?
4. What are some of the tradeoffs associated with accumulating federal debt?
5. During the debt crisis of 2011, many people called for a balanced budget amendment to the federal constitution. What is a balanced budget amendment? What would be the costs and benefits of having a balanced budget amendment?
6. The chapter asserts that spending on Social Security is nondiscretionary government spending. During the 2011 debt crisis, several policymakers suggested altering the eligibility rules for Social Security. If the eligibility rules are altered, is Social Security spending still nondiscretionary? Explain.

MULTIPLE CHOICE QUESTIONS

1. If the government simultaneously raises taxes and cuts government spending, it is engaging in
   a. expansionary fiscal policy.
   b. contractionary fiscal policy.
   c. stable fiscal policy.
   d. expansionary monetary policy.

2. Some of the costs of government borrowing include
   a. impacts on income inequality.
   b. negative impacts on the ability of the economy to grow in the future.
   c. interest rate costs.
   d. crowding out.
   e. all of the above

3. When the economy is operating at a relatively low level of GDP, expansionary fiscal policy will cause
   a. large increases in output but small increases in the price level.
   b. large increases in output and large increases in the price level.
   c. small increases in output and small increases in the price level.
   d. small increases in output and large increases in the price level.

4. If the government increases borrowing at the same time that savers and lenders decrease the supply of loans,
   a. the interest rate will increase and the quantity of loans made will decrease.
   b. the interest rate will increase but the impact on the quantity of loans made is unknown.
   c. the interest rate will decrease and the quantity of loans made will decrease.
   d. the interest rate will decrease and the quantity of loans made will increase.

5. When government spending is more than government revenues, there is a(n)
   a. international trade deficit.
   b. interest rate deficit.
   c. federal budget deficit.
   d. federal budget surplus.
   e. interest rate surplus.

6. Examples of nondiscretionary fiscal policy include
   a. increases in government spending on roads and bridges during a recession.
   b. increased government borrowing to finance a budget deficit.
   c. interest payments on the federal debt.
   d. unemployment compensation.

7. The time that elapses between a change in economic activity and the time that policymakers see the need to respond is the
   a. administrative lag.
   b. recognition lag.
   c. implementation lag.
   d. operational lag.
   e. response lag.

8. The progressive income tax system is an example of
   a. inflationary fiscal policy.
   b. discretionary fiscal policy.

c. expansionary fiscal policy
d. nondiscretionary fiscal policy

9. If the economy is in a recession, discretionary fiscal policy to expand the economy could include
   a. raising taxes.
   b. lowering government spending.
   c. lowering taxes.
   d. increasing government spending.
   e. both a and b
   f. both c and d

10. Crowding out stems from
    a. the decrease in the demand for loans associated with federal deficits.
    b. the increase in GDP associated with federal deficits.
    c. the increase in interest rates associated with federal deficits.
    d. the increase in the supply of loans associated with federal deficits.

ADDITIONAL READINGS AND WEB RESOURCES

Hayek, Friedrich (1944) *The Road to Serfdom,* University of Chicago Press. Presents Hayek's arguments against central planning and in favor of free-market capitalism.

Keynes, John Maynard (1936) *The General Theory of Employment, Interest, and Money,* Kessinger Publishing. Presents Keynes' arguments for active governmental involvement in the economy.

The U.S. Congressional Budget Office provides congress with analyses related to the federal budget. www.cbo.gov

Congressional Budget Office (2010) "Federal Debt and the Risk of a Fiscal Crisis" http://www.cbo.gov/doc.cfm?index=11659. Presents a nonpartisan summary of the risks associated with the federal debt.

Congressional Budget Office (2010) "Federal Debt and Interest Costs" http://www.cbo.gov/doc.cfm?index=11999. Presents a nonpartisan summary of the interest costs associated with the federal debt.

The U.S. Office of Management and Budget website includes extensive data on government deficits and debt. www.omb.gov

The U.S. National Debt Clock website provides a real time update of the U.S. national debt, personal debt, and spending on various budget items. www.usdebtclock.org

The website http://econstories.tv/ includes several fun videos highlighting the differences between Keynes and Hayek and their differing views on fiscal policy.

Appendix A Answers to "Think for Yourself" Questions

CHAPTER 1

1. (1) The opportunity cost of taking a class involves the tuition, fees, and books associated with the class. It also involves giving up time that could be spent in other classes, at work, or enjoying leisure activities. (2) The opportunity cost of putting money in a savings account is the value of the items you could have purchased if you had spent the money instead of saving it. (3) The opportunity cost of having a mutually exclusive relationship is the opportunity to have a relationship with someone else.
2. The law of diminishing marginal utility implies that the utility we would get from watching each additional hour of TV would decline as more and more TV is watched, so TV watching would be less and less enjoyable as time passed. For most people, the marginal utility would eventually be low enough to entice them to do something else besides watch TV nonstop.
3. $18.00; 2

CHAPTER 2

1. Four points per day; 9 points per day; each point earned in economics per day has an opportunity cost of 1 point earned in finance per day; each point earned in finance per day has an opportunity cost of 1 point earned in economics per day.
2. The table shows the amount of housing gained and food given up as we move from E to D to C, and so on. The move from E to D generates a gain in housing of 8 units per year. The opportunity cost of this gain is the loss of 1 food unit per year. On average, this means that each unit of housing gained between point E and point D costs ⅛ unit of food. The move from D to C generates a gain in housing of 6 units per year at a cost of 1 unit of food per year. On average, each unit of housing gained between point D and point C costs ⅙ unit of food per year. The move from point C to point B generates a gain of 4 housing units per year at a cost of 1 food unit per year, or an average of 1 housing unit per ¼ food units. Finally, between point B and point A, 2 housing units are gained per year and 1 food unit is given up, so the cost per housing unit between point B and point A is ½ food unit. Because the amount of food given up to obtain each housing unit rose as we moved from point E to point D, C, and so on, the opportunity cost of housing increases as more housing is produced.

Opportunity Cost of Housing			
Move (in Figure 2.4)	Gain (housing units per year)	Cost (food units per year)	Cost (food units per housing unit)
E→D	8	1	1/8
D→C	6	1	1/6
C→B	4	1	1/4
B→A	2	1	1/2

3. The consumption possibilities frontiers are:

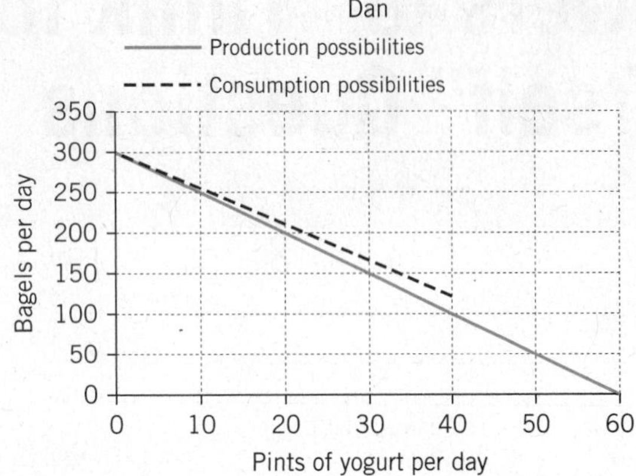

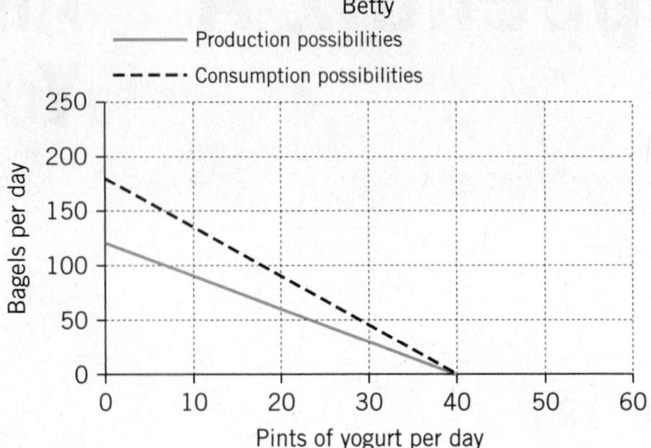

CHAPTER 3

1.

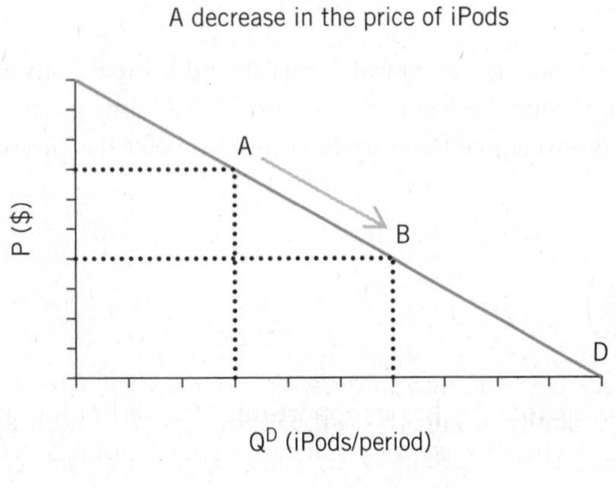

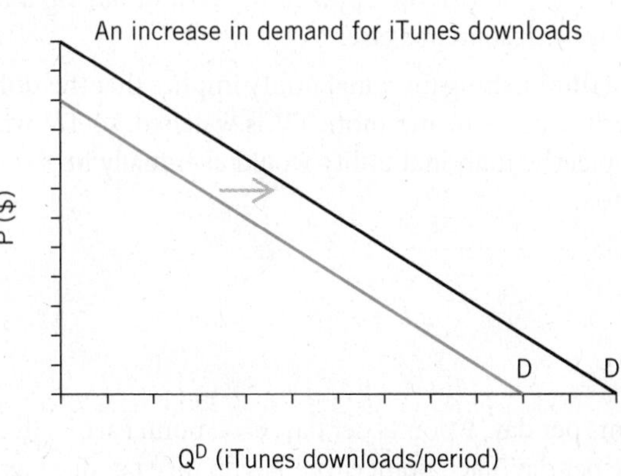

2.

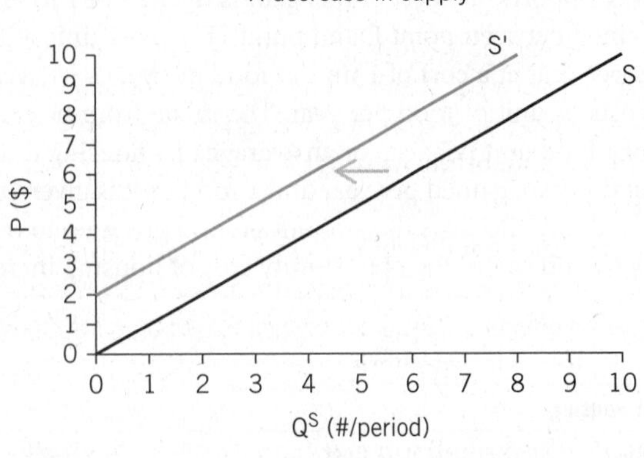

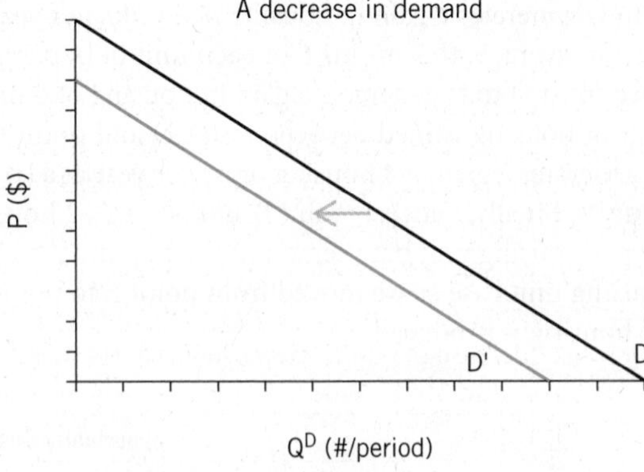

3.

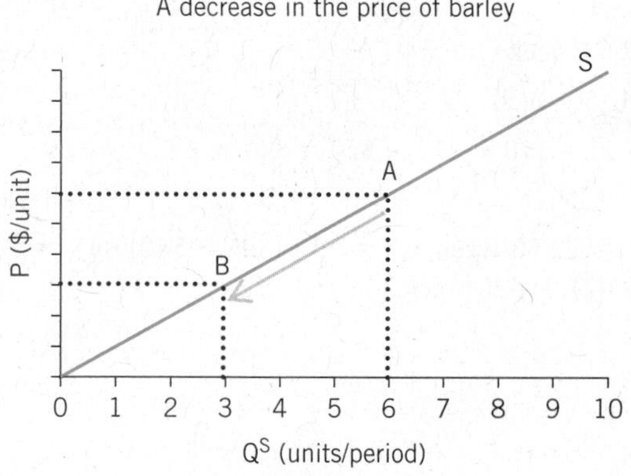

An increase in the supply of wheat
S
S'
P ($/unit)
Q^S (units/period)

4.

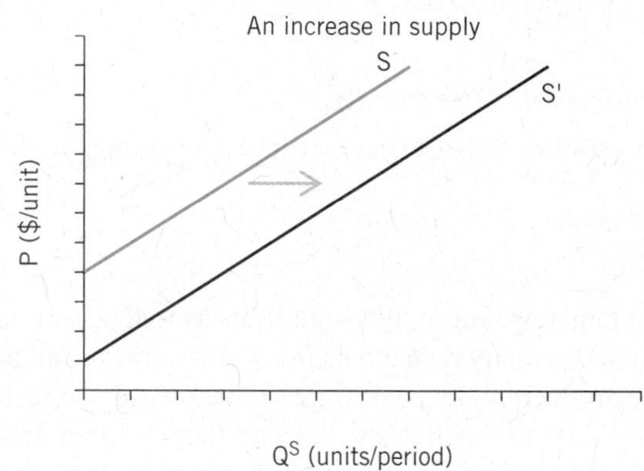

5. (1) The increase in supply would cause equilibrium price to fall and equilibrium quantity to rise. The decrease in demand would cause equilibrium price to fall and equilibrium quantity to fall. The demand and supply changes both contribute to a fall in equilibrium price but cause equilibrium quantity to move in opposite directions. On net, the equilibrium quantity will rise since the shift in supply is larger than the shift in demand. Thus, equilibrium price falls and equilibrium quantity rises.

(2) The decrease in supply would cause equilibrium price to rise and equilibrium quantity to fall. The increase in demand would cause equilibrium price and quantity to both rise. The demand and supply changes both contribute to an increase in the equilibrium price but have opposing effects on equilibrium quantity. Because the change in demand is larger than the change in supply, the net effect will be to increase equilibrium quantity. Thus, equilibrium price rises and equilibrium quantity rises.

(3) The decrease in supply would cause equilibrium price to rise and equilibrium quantity to fall. The decrease in demand would cause equilibrium price to fall and equilibrium quantity to fall. The demand and supply changes both contribute to a decrease in equilibrium quantity but have opposing effects on equilibrium price. Because the change in demand is larger than the change in supply, the net effect will be to reduce equilibrium price. Thus, equilibrium price falls and equilibrium quantity falls.

(4) The decrease in supply would cause equilibrium price to rise and equilibrium quantity to fall. The increase in demand would cause equilibrium price and quantity to both rise. The demand and supply changes both contribute to an increase in the equilibrium price but have opposing effects on equilibrium quantity. Because we do not know whether the shift in supply is larger or smaller than the shift in demand, we cannot make a prediction about what will happen to equilibrium quantity. Thus, equilibrium price rises, but the effect on equilibrium quantity is unknown.

CHAPTER 4

1. (.5 * ($45 – $25) * 4) = $40/week; (.5 * ($45 –$10) * 7) = $122.50/week
2. (.5 * ($20 – $15) * 1) = $2.50/week; (.5 * ($40 – $15) * 5) = $62.50/week
3. (.5 * ($45 – $35) * 2) + [(.5 * ($25 – $15) * 2) + ($35 – $25) * 2] = $10 + $10 + $20 = $40/week
4. (.5* ($40 – $20) * 2) = $20/week
5. PS = [(.5 * ($20 – $15) * 1) + ($40 – $20) * 1] = $2.50 + $20 = $22.50/week; CS = (.5 * ($45 – $40) * 1) = $2.50/week; Economic surplus = $25/week; DWL = (.5 * ($40 – $20) * 2) = $20/week.

CHAPTER 5

1. Q^D would fall by 13.2 percent; Q^D would rise by 26.4 percent
2. $E = -10/25 = -0.4$. If P rises by 1 percent, Q^D would fall by 0.4 percent; inelastic
3. Elastic; inelastic; total revenue would not change
4. When demand is unit elastic total revenue does not change in response to price changes.
5. Those in rural communities will have more inelastic demand for gasoline because there are fewer substitutes available.

CHAPTER 6

1. All final goods and services are traded in output markets, including new houses, bikes, and cars as well as entertainment services like movies and Broadway shows. Households are the primary demanders in output markets, and businesses are the primary suppliers in output markets. Factors of production are sold in input markets. These include the land used for production of food, the labor used in the production of medical services, and the machines used in the production of clothing. Households are the primary suppliers in input markets, and businesses are the primary demanders in input markets.
2. Answers to this question can vary. If consumers expect that economic activity will slow in the future, they may cut their spending today in order to save money to weather the economic downturn. Increased consumer saving will result in reduced consumption and reduced GDP.
3. A decrease in AD will cause a fall in GDP and the price level. Depending on where the AD curve intersects AS, the fall in GDP can be large, as when AD intersects the flatter portion of the AS curve, or small, as when AD intersects the steeper portion of the AS curve. A decrease in AS will cause a reduction in GDP and an increase in the average price level in the economy.

CHAPTER 7

1. The NASDAQ and the S&P 500 are other indexes of stock prices.
2. With three gallons of milk, the basket prices are 1980: $6.10; 1990: $7.75; 2000: $9.50; 2010: $10.50. If eggs cost $2.00 in 2010, the basket price in 2010 is $8.00 when two gallons of milk are in the basket and $11.00 when three gallons of milk are in the basket. The price index values given that eggs cost $2.00 in 2010 and three gallons of milk are in the basket are 1980: (6.10/7.75) * 100 = 79; 1990: 100; 2000: (9.50/7.75) * 100 = 123; 2010: (11.00/7.75) * 100 = 142.
3. Savers would win from deflation because their savings could purchase more in the future than when they put their money in the bank. Borrowers would lose from deflation because they would have purchased items at higher prices and would face interest charges on their loans.
4. If your earnings are $47,500, they are 7.3 times higher than your grandmother's earnings, but since prices are 7.4 times higher in 2009 than in 1960, your real income is lower than your grandmother's real income. If your earnings are $50,000, they are 7.7 times higher than her earnings. This means your real income would be greater than your grandmother's real income.
5. ($47, 500/220.2) * 100 = $21,571; ($50, 000/ 220.2) * 100 = $22,707

CHAPTER 8

1. Examples of command systems in the U.S. include the military, the public school system, and the rules regarding the use of national forests and parks. Examples of market systems include the local pizza parlor, clothing stores, and car dealerships. Command systems are characterized by public decisions about how resources are used. These decisions often take the form of government regulations. Market systems are characterized by private decisions about how resources are used, such as the private decision about how much pizza to buy, how much to work, which shirt to wear, and which car to drive.
2. Examples of socialist ownership systems include public buildings and spaces. Examples of capitalist ownership systems include private land ownership, private ownership of a business, and private ownership of stock in a business. Socialist systems are characterized by public or communal ownership of resources. Capitalist systems are characterized by private property ownership.
3. Societies trade efficiency for equity when they encourage unrestrained market capitalism. Allowing firms and employees to freely choose the wages they will pay and accept rather than setting limits on wages is one example of trading efficiency for equity. Having economic safety nets like the minimum wage, unemployment insurance, or federally funded financial aid for college students is an example of trading equity for efficiency.
4. Examples of ways that societies trade liberty for security include imposing income taxes in order to redistribute income to those with lower incomes and regulating product and worker safety. Examples of ways that societies trade liberty for security include allowing entrepreneurs the freedom to start their own businesses, which often entails substantial risk.

CHAPTER 9

1. An increase in the demand for movies would increase the equilibrium price of movies and thus increase Depp's VMP_L. A decrease in the demand for football would decrease the price of football-related items (tickets, TV advertising revenue, and merchandise) and would decrease the VMP_L of Manning.
2. Six workers per hour; 2 workers per hour; 5 workers per hour.
3. Workers in the U.S. have more access to capital and equipment than do workers in less developed countries. The access to capital increases U.S. workers' productivity and thus their VMP_L. Higher VMP_L for workers in the U.S. translates into higher wages for U.S. workers.
4. As workers age, their productivity in certain industries falls. For example, fashion and other magazines tend to favor photos of young models, and younger players tend to be more competitive than older players in some sports. As Armstrong has gotten older, his cycling times have slowed and he wins less often, which translated into a lower VMP_L in cycling.
5. Comparing the compensation of the CEO to that of other workers in a company does not compare the value of the CEO to the value of the company's workers because the salaries reflect the value of the marginal unit of labor hired, not the value of labor in total. A CEO like Ralph Lauren attracts millions of customers to the company, while a typical worker at Ralph Lauren is unlikely to generate as much additional revenue. The VMP_L of the CEO is thus higher than that of the typical worker, which is reflected in the higher CEO wage.

CHAPTER 10

1. The U.S. Bureau of Labor Statistics website (www.bls.gov) has extensive information on federal and state minimum wages, as well as information on average wages by state. In 2011, the federal minimum wage was $7.25. Some of the benefits of a minimum wage that automatically adjusts for inflation are that the minimum wage would move upward when inflation increases so that the real value of the minimum wage would not deteriorate over time and that the movements in the minimum wage would be less subject to political debate. One cost of an automatically adjusting minimum wage is that it can move down when inflation falls, reducing worker incomes.
2. When the minimum wage is $8 per hour instead of $7.25 per hour, the unemployment generated by the minimum wage would be larger because quantity demanded would be lower and quantity supplied would be higher at the higher

minimum wage. The unemployment generated by the minimum wage would be smaller if the minimum wage were $6 per hour instead of $7.25 per hour.

3. If the equilibrium wage is $7.50 per hour, a minimum wage of $10 per hour would generate unemployment in the local labor market. If the equilibrium wage is $7.50 per hour and the minimum wage is set at $6 per hour, the minimum wage would have no impact because it lies below the equilibrium wage.
4. For a given wage increase, firms change their quantity of labor demanded by a larger amount when demand is more elastic than when demand is more inelastic. An increase in the minimum wage will generate a larger decline in quantity demanded, and thus a larger increase in unemployment, when demand is more elastic.

CHAPTER 11

1. Absolute advantage occurs when a person, firm, or country can produce more of a good or service than another person, firm, or country. Comparative advantage occurs when a person, firm, or country can produce a good or service at a lower opportunity cost than another person, firm, or country. Comparative advantage is more important when determining whether it is beneficial to engage in international trade, because even a country with absolute advantage relative to another country can gain by trading if the other country has comparative advantage in production.
2. See the accompanying graphs. The solid lines represent the PPFs for Landia and Seavia. If Landia produces only computers and Seavia produces only shoes and the two countries trade with one another at the rate of 1S = 4.5C, the consumption possibilities curves are the dotted lines in the graphs.

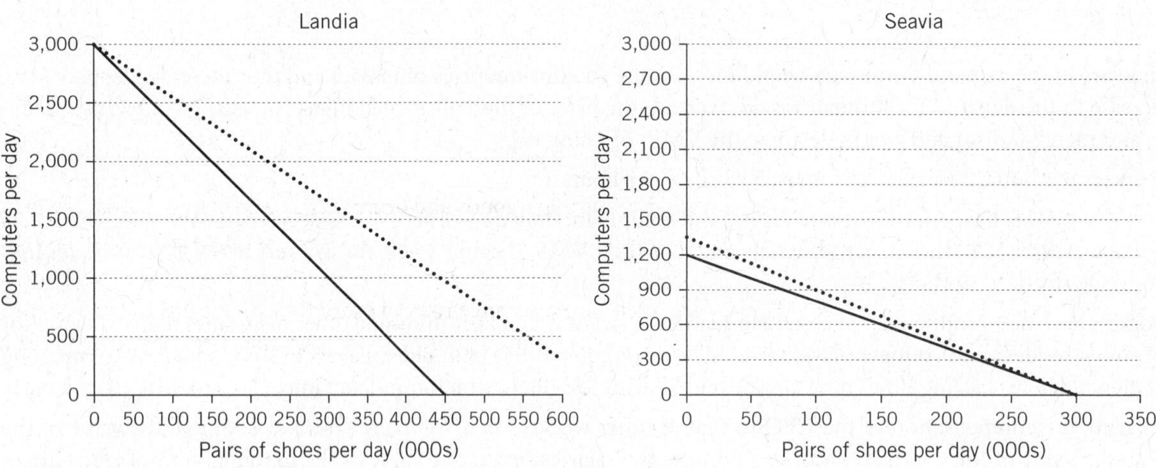

3. The more elastic the demand for the imported good, the smaller the price change in the good will be. The more inelastic the demand for the imported good, the larger the price change in the good will be.
4. Before the tariff, PS = ½ * 50 * $500 = $12,500 per day and CS = ½ * $(1000 − 500) * 50 = $12, 500 per day. After the tariff is in place, CS = ½ * ($1,000 − $600) * 40 = $8,000 per day and PS = ½ * $400 * 40 = $8,000 per day. The tax revenue is equal to ($200 * 40) = $8,000 per day. The deadweight loss is ½ * $(600 − 400) * 10 = $1,000 per day.

CHAPTER 12

1. Younger individuals are more likely to migrate than older individuals because younger individuals have more time to earn the higher earnings in the host country and to recoup the costs of immigrating. Immigrating involves transportation and moving costs, and those who immigrate are more likely than their non-migrating counterparts to have enough

income to cover these costs. A decrease in transportation costs lowers the cost of immigration and makes it more likely for someone to immigrate. A decline in the potential earnings in the host country lowers the benefits of immigrating and decreases the likelihood of immigration.

2. When immigrants and native workers are substitutes, native workers lose from immigration because their wages and employment levels will fall. Consumers and businesses win because lower costs of production generate lower prices for goods and services and higher profits for firms.
3. When immigrants and native workers are compliments, native workers win from immigration because the demand for their labor increases. Consumers and businesses also win because lower costs of production generate lower prices for goods and services and higher profits for firms.
4. In the original equilibrium, the supply curve $S_{(\text{native labor})}$ represents the supply of natives who do not emigrate and those who do emigrate, while the supply curve $S_{(\text{native - emigrant labor})}$ represents the supply of natives who do not emigrate. Since we are interested in the producer surplus of natives who do not emigrate, the supply curve $S(_{\text{native - emigrant labor}})$ should be used to compute producer surplus. This is the area above the native worker supply curve and below the original equilibrium price, so PS = .5 * $(15−12) * 300 = $450 per hour in the original equilibrium. In the post-emigration equilibrium, PS = .5 * $(16 − 12) * 400 = $800 per hour. Thus, the native workers are better off after the emigration.
5. Much debate arises over what to do about immigration and outsourcing, particularly for those who bear the cost of increased global competition in the labor market. Some groups advocate restrictions on immigration to protect domestic jobs. Although this may help those workers in the short term, it is likely to be detrimental to firms and domestic economies in the longer term because it hampers their global competitiveness. Alternative reactions to protectionist policies on immigration and outsourcing would include job training and educational opportunities for workers displaced by international trade in labor.

CHAPTER 13

1. $50; $200
2. 1 EUR = 0.5 USD; 1 EUR = 2 USD
3. A decrease in U.S. income would reduce the demand for European goods and decrease the demand for Euros. The price of Euros would fall, so it would take fewer USD to purchase each Euro. The Euro would depreciate against the USD and the USD would appreciate against the Euro.
4. The price of 700 CFA francs per Euro is above the equilibrium exchange rate. In order to keep the price above equilibrium, the Malian government would need to increase the demand for Euros or decrease the supply of CFA francs in Mali, so the government could either buy Euros or sell CFA francs.

CHAPTER 14

1. a. Price and quantity will both rise

   b. Price will rise and quantity will fall

   c. Price and quantity will both fall
2. A decrease in supply will cause the equilibrium price to rise and quantity to fall. The price increase will be larger when demand is relatively inelastic. The decrease in quantity will be smaller when demand is relatively inelastic. The price increase will be smaller when demand is relatively elastic. The decrease in quantity will be larger when demand is relatively elastic.
3. A price floor that is set below the equilibrium price will have no effect on the market because the market will be free to adjust to the equilibrium.
4. Because the demand for milk is relatively more inelastic than the demand for pork, the policy will cause a larger increase in price in the milk industry than it would cause in the pork industry.

CHAPTER 15

1. Benefits might include relaxation and relief from some health problems. Costs include the risk of fines or imprisonment as well as health risks. The costs of imprisonment would be larger for older people, those with more education, and the employed because older individuals and those with higher levels of education tend to have higher paying jobs, ceteris paribus.
2. The factors that shift the demand for Huxsoma include people's incomes, tastes and preferences, the prices of substitutes and complements to Huxsoma, people's expectations, and the number of consumers in the Huxsoma market. The factors that shift the supply of Huxsoma include the costs of production for Huxsoma, the prices of alternative goods that could be produced, producer expectations, and the number of sellers in the Huxsoma market.
3. Research on the negative externalities associated with drug use is relatively scarce. Advocates of marijuana legalization argue that the negative externalities associated with marijuana are smaller than the negative externalities associated with tobacco, alcohol, or methamphetamine, while those against marijuana legalization view the negative externalities associated with marijuana to be as large as or larger than those for other substances. The larger the negative externality associated with a drug, the greater the difference between the unregulated market and socially optimum levels of drug use will be.
4. If drugs are addictive at first use, learning by doing will not be a good method of assessing the costs and benefits of drug use. Once someone tries the drug, they could be addicted, and it would then be too late for those who decide that the costs of drug use are higher than the benefits of drug use to quit.
5. If drugs and alcohol are substitutes, policymakers could reduce the use of drugs through policies that reduce the price of alcohol. Obviously such policies would be unpopular among those who seek to reduce alcohol consumption.
6. Costs of marijuana legalization include an increase in the negative externalities associated with marijuana use plus costs of regulation of the marijuana market. Benefits of marijuana legalization could include decreased spending on law enforcement to keep marijuana off the market as well as potential tax revenues (assuming that legalized marijuana would be taxed). Whether the benefits outweigh the costs is a matter of debate.

CHAPTER 16

1. Laws prohibiting driving while on a cell phone or texting while driving are one way that cities have attempted to mitigate the negative externalities associated with cell phones. Cell phones are associated with a wide array of negative externalities, including increased traffic accidents and general "noise pollution" in public places.
2. Electric cars produce fewer pollutants from the cars themselves, but the generation of electricity to fuel electric cars produces air pollution and greenhouse gas emissions. Electric cars are also more expensive than traditionally fueled cars. In the U.S., approximately 45 percent of electricity is produced by burning coal, which contributes to global warming. To produce the same amount of energy, coal emits more carbon dioxide than gasoline. Evidence on the net pollution impact of electric versus traditional cars is mixed, with some researchers finding lower net carbon dioxide emissions from electric cars but others finding no difference in net pollution.
3. Banning elephant hunting involves tradeoffs. On the one hand, hunting elephants obviously reduces the elephant population. On the other hand, increasing the economic value of elephants by allowing nearby residents to sell safari hunts for elephants provides an incentive for nearby residents to preserve elephant habitat and elephants themselves. After Kenya banned all elephant hunting in 1977, the population of elephants in Kenya declined dramatically. In Zimbabwe, the World Wildlife Fund helped implement the Communal Areas Management Programme for Indigenous Resources (CAMPFIRE) in 1989. This CAMPFIRE program gave local residents the rights manage natural resources at the local level, including the right to allow safari hunting of elephants. By 2003, elephant numbers in Zimbabwe had doubled from 4,000 to 8,000.
4. Tax breaks to producers of ethanol provide an incentive for corn growers to divert their corn from food use to fuel use. In addition, growers of other crops have an incentive to switch their land to corn ethanol production. The result is a decrease in the supply of other crops as well as a decrease in the supply of corn on the food market. The decrease in supply causes the prices of food to rise.

CHAPTER 17

1. There are many ways to increase one's human capital including on-the-job training, self-study, and learning through experience.
2. Answers will vary here depending on the individual, the discipline, and the economy. Potential marginal benefits include increased job opportunities, potential earnings, and knowledge. Potential marginal costs include direct costs of tuition, books, and so on, and opportunity costs, which will be higher on average for a college graduate than for a high school graduate considering obtaining a bachelor's degree.
3. Economists argue that good neighbors tend to generate positive externalities for those nearby. Their yards may be pleasant to look at, they may be helpful in watching pets and plants while you are away, and they tend to raise the value of your property when it comes time to sell. Vaccinations also generate positive externalities because people around you benefit when you get a vaccination because your vaccination reduces their likelihood of getting sick.
4. The positive externalities associated with having a population with a basic literacy and skills are likely larger than those for having a population with more advanced knowledge. Since the positive externalities of K-12 education are larger than those of a university education, the university education system does not receive as much taxpayer funding per student as K-12 education.
5. If school choice results in more high-performing students attending schools with other high-performing students, low-performing students will not benefit from the positive peer effects associated with attending school with high-performing students. The concentration of high-performing students into some schools and low-performing students into others could potentially exacerbate differences in educational outcomes across these groups.

CHAPTER 17 APPENDIX

1. Answers here will vary depending on the individual, but individuals who carry balances on their credit cards likely have stronger preferences for present over future consumption. Ceteris paribus, the fact that you are in college indicates that you have a willingness to give up current consumption in exchange for future consumption.

CHAPTER 18

1. Marginal costs would not change if total costs were $5 higher at each output level. Marginal costs associated with the total costs listed are $35, $33, $30, $33, $35, $43, $50, $57, $65, $73.
2. If Econoweb charged $40 per report, Econoweb's marginal revenue would be $40 for each report.
3. The normal profits are TR − TC = $60,000 – ($30,000 + $30,000) = $0 per year. Your friend is earning zero normal profit. If total revenue were $100,000, normal profits would be $100,000 − $60,000 = $40,000. Because your friend would be earning normal profits above zero, she would be earning economic profits.
4. If pharmaceutical companies were not allowed to patent their new drugs, it would be more difficult for them to cover the large up-front investment required for the research and development needed bring the new drugs to market. As a result, fewer new drugs would be developed.
5. A price taker is a small firm in a large industry that cannot influence the market price of its good or service and instead must simply make its decisions based on the market price. A price setter is a firm that can influence the market price of its product.

CHAPTER 19

1. The black female/white male earnings ratio is 0.65, so white male/black female earnings ratio is 1/0.65 = 1.54. The pay gap between black females and white males is 0.54, meaning that white males earn 54 percent more than black females. The black male/white male earnings ratio is 0.75, so the white male/black male earnings ratio is 1/0.75 = 1.33.

The pay gap between black males and white males is 0.33, which implies that white males earn 33 percent more than black males.

2. Since earnings differences can arise for a wide array of reasons, including discrimination, it would be helpful to know about differences in the fields of specialization for male and female professors, since some fields pay more than others. If would also be useful to know about the professors' relative experience levels. If possible, it would be useful to compare the professors' relative productivity in terms of classes taught, research publication output, and success in obtaining research grants.
3. Answers will vary depending on the individual.
4. Yes. Insurance companies charge certain groups higher rates because most automobile insurance companies do not have adequate resources to verify that any particular driver is a safe driver. Instead, their rates are based in part on the driving records of those in the same demographic group. Because the rate of accidents is higher for younger drivers than for older drivers and for single drivers relative to married drivers, teenagers and single drivers face higher insurance premiums.
5. For teaching and clerical positions, the laws would result in a decrease in the supply of labor because women would no longer be able to work in those occupations. The decrease in supply from S to S', illustrated in the accompanying figure, would raise the wages for men in teaching and clerical positions. The laws increase the supply of labor in waitress, domestic servant, and manufacturing jobs from S to S' because women will move to these jobs and out of teaching and clerical jobs. The increased supply of labor in those jobs will cause wages to fall.

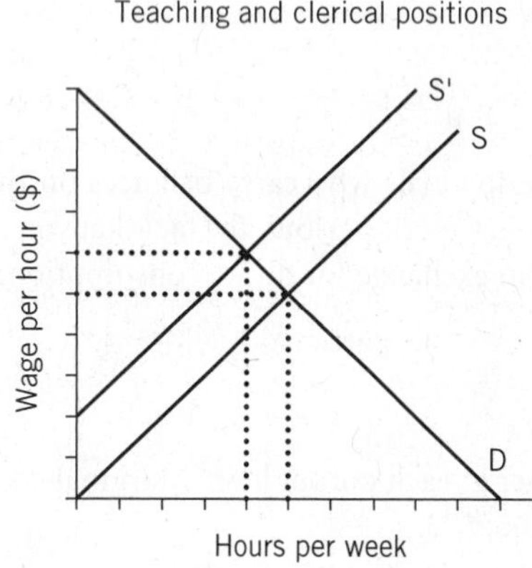

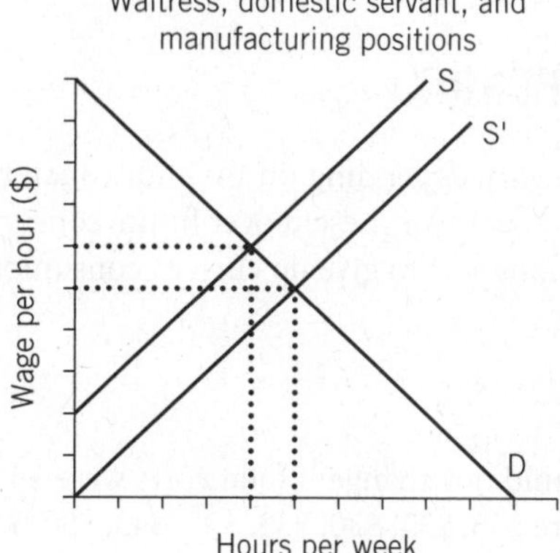

CHAPTER 20

1. Answers to this question can vary. One cost of having an unequal income distribution is that some people in the economy will be poor. If a society wants to ensure a minimum standard of living for its citizens, having an unequal income distribution may necessitate a redistribution of income from richer to poorer citizens. One benefit of having an unequal income distribution is that it provides strong work incentives for individuals because their income is not redistributed to others.
2. If the 90:10 ratio is 8, people at the 90th percentile of the income distribution earn 8 times higher incomes than people at the 10th percentile of the income distribution. A falling 80:20 ratio would indicate that the income distribution is becoming more equal.
3. Answers to this question will vary based on individual preferences and opinions.
4. If you use a relative measure of poverty, there will always be people in the U.S. who are poor based on that measure. For example, suppose your poverty threshold is set at half of the median income earned in the U.S. Unless the income in the U.S. is divided equally, there will always be people with less than half the median income in the U.S. For this reason, most poverty policies are evaluated based on an absolute measure of poverty.

5. The primary reason for our mix of poverty policies is that policymakers and taxpayers don't tend to want the poor to have unlimited choices on how their poverty assistance is spent. Instead, we want to ensure that spending is focused on food, housing, and health, particularly for children.

CHAPTER 21

1. Moral hazard implies that people with insurance will consume more health care than is optimal since they may engage in more risky activities and unnecessary surgery because they have insurance. Since cosmetic surgery is usually an optional procedure, insurance companies tend to make people pay the costs themselves to avoid the moral hazard problem.
2. It is likely that physician-induced demand would fall if physicians were paid based on the health outcomes for their patients rather than on a fee-for-service basis, since unnecessary lab testing or other procedures would be less common.
3. The marginal benefits of using an exercise program include things like increased stamina and energy, lower blood pressure, and lower weight. The marginal costs of using an exercise program include time, risk of injury, and any direct costs associated with joining a gym or obtaining exercise equipment. The MB curve for exercise is likely to be downward-sloping like the MB curve in Figure 21.6 because the law of diminishing marginal returns would lead to smaller and smaller incremental health improvements as exercise increases. The MC curve is likely upward sloping because the risk of injury increases as exercise increases.
4. The positive externality associated with health improvements falls because health improvements like vaccinations and hand washing can have large impacts on the probability that other people get sick, while health improvements like running six instead of five miles per day probably have only small impacts on public health. The government subsidizes vaccinations but not running shoes because the positive externalities associated with childhood vaccinations are large, but the positive externalities associated with people running more are smaller.
5. The benefit of not having health insurance is the money saved by not paying health insurance premiums, which could be in the tens of thousands of dollars per year. The cost of going without health insurance is the risk of having health care costs that are more than you can afford to pay. For some people, particularly those with low health risk and large savings, it may be optimal to go without health insurance.

CHAPTER 22

1. $20 million; $5 million
2. The interest rate and quantity of loans both increase; the interest rate decreases and the quantity of loans increases
3. $8.1 – (.1 * $8.1) = $7.29 million; $7.29 – (.1 * 7.29) = $6.56 million
4. $5 million * 10 = $50 million; $10 million * 5 = $50 million; $10 million * 20 = $200 million
5. Answers will vary depending on the individual.
6. Buy securities; sell securities
7. Lower the discount rate; increase the discount rate
8. 10; 33.33; $50 million; $1.67 billion

CHAPTER 23

1. Discretionary spending is subject to policymaker choice. Nondiscretionary spending is not determined by policymaker choices. Spending on national defense is an example of discretionary spending since policymakers can decide on the level of national defense spending each year. Spending on Social Security is an example of nondiscretionary spending because Social Security is paid based on eligibility rather than on policymaker choices from year to year.

2. Your tax bill would be (8,375 * 0.10) + ((34,000 − 8,375) * 0.15) + ((82,400 − 34,000) * 0.25) + ((100,000 − 82,400) * 0.28) = $21,710.
3. A federal budget deficit occurs when the government spends more than it collects in tax revenue in a given year. The federal debt is the sum of all of the budget deficits from the past, plus their associated interest charges.
4. Crowding out will be larger when the supply of loans is more elastic because the decline in the quantity of loans made will be larger. Crowding out will be smaller when the supply of loans is more inelastic because the quantity of loans made will not change by much when supply is relatively inelastic.
5. Between AD_3 and AD_4, the aggregate supply curve is relatively inelastic so changes in AD do not have very large impacts on GDP. Between AD_1 and AD_2, the aggregate supply curve is relatively elastic, so changes in AD cause larger changes in GDP.

Appendix B Glossary

Absolute advantage Absolute advantage is the ability to produce something with fewer resources than another producer, or to produce more with the same resources as another producer.

Absolute measure of poverty An absolute measure of poverty uses a fixed income or consumption level rather than an underlying income distribution to set the poverty line.

Administration lag In fiscal policy, the administration lag is the time it takes for Congress and the president to agree on what fiscal policy to use.

Affirmative action Affirmative action is a set of policies that mandate taking action to ensure the equal treatment of people regardless of their race, creed, color, or national origin. Affirmative action requires some organizations to take action to increase the representation of women and minorities.

Aggregate demand Aggregate demand (AD) is the demand for all goods and services in an economy, ceteris paribus.

Aggregate supply Aggregate supply (AS) is the supply of all goods and services in an economy, ceteris paribus.

Antitrust laws Antitrust laws are laws that promote competition between businesses and prohibit anti-competitive behavior by firms with large control over markets.

Appreciated In currency exchange markets, when the price of currency A rises relative to currency B, currency A has appreciated.

Attainable choices In the production possibilities model, points on or inside the production possibilities frontier represent attainable choices, ceteris paribus.

Balance sheet A balance sheet is a statement of assets (things owned) and liabilities (things owed).

Bank run A bank run occurs when a large number of customers withdraw their deposits from the bank because they worry that their bank might fail.

Barriers to entry Barriers to entry are obstructions that make it difficult for new firms to enter a market.

Barter exchange Barter exchange is the trading of goods and services directly for other goods or services, without using money.

Basic economic questions The three basic economic questions regarding resource allocation are: What to produce? How to produce it? For whom to produce?

Basic economic resources The basic resources of an economy include land, labor, and capital.

Benefit The benefit of a choice is what you gain when you make the choice.

Budget deficit A budget deficit occurs when the amount of government spending in a given period is larger than the amount of government revenue from taxes and earnings during that period.

Budget surplus A budget surplus occurs when the amount of government spending in a given period is less than the amount of government revenue from taxes and earnings during that period.

Business cycle Business cycles are recurring expansions and contractions in the level of aggregate economic activity.

Business cycle contraction Business cycle contractions or recessions are periods of decreasing economic activity, falling production, and falling employment.

Business cycle expansion Business cycle expansions are periods of increasing economic activity, rising production, and increasing employment.

Cap and trade In a cap and trade system of pollution reduction, polluters can buy tradable pollution rights that give the right to emit a specific amount of pollutant. The amount of tradable pollution rights issued is capped at the desired pollution level.

Capitalist systems Capitalist systems are characterized by private property ownership. See also "socialist systems."

Carbon offsets Carbon offsets are reductions in emissions of carbon dioxide in one place that offset emissions of carbon dioxide made elsewhere.

Ceteris paribus A Latin term meaning, "all else constant" or "all else equal."

Change in quantity demanded In the demand and supply model, a change in quantity demanded results from a change in the price of the good, ceteris paribus. It is represented by a movement along the demand curve.

Change in quantity supplied In the demand and supply model, a change in quantity supplied results from a change in the price of the good, ceteris paribus. It is represented by a movement along the supply curve.

Civil Rights Act The 1964 Civil Rights Act was the first federal legislation to prohibit employment discrimination.

Command capitalism Command capitalism is an economic system that uses private property ownership and public resource allocation decisions.

Command socialism Command socialism is an economic system that uses public property ownership and public resource allocation decisions.

Command systems Command systems are characterized by governmental regulation or central planning to allocate resources. See also "market systems."

Command-and-control Command-and-control methods of pollution reduction involve direct government regulation of pollution through taxes or emissions limits.

Commodity money Commodity money has value for its own sake, in addition to its value as money. Gold and silver are examples of commodity money.

Common property resources Common property resources are resources that are collectively owned.

Comparative advantage Comparative advantage is the ability to produce a good or service at a lower opportunity cost than another producer.

Complement Complements are goods that tend to be used together.

Consumer substitution effect In the demand and supply model, the consumer substitution effect describes the situation where consumers respond to a higher price of a good by decreasing their quantity demanded of that good and substituting instead into goods whose prices have not changed, ceteris paribus.

Consumer surplus Consumer surplus is the difference between what someone is willing to pay for a good or service and the price of the good or service. It is the net benefit buyers get from buying a good or service.

Contractionary fiscal policy Contractionary fiscal policy is used to decrease aggregate demand and aggregate economic activity.

Contractionary monetary policy Contractionary monetary policy involves Federal Reserve actions to decrease the money supply.

Cost The cost of a choice is what you give up when you make the choice.

Cost-push inflation Cost-push inflation arises from decreases in aggregate supply.

Crowding out Crowding out occurs when government borrowing pushes up interest rates, which causes a reduction in private consumption and investment.

Customer discrimination Customer discrimination occurs when customers base their purchasing decisions on the race, sex, or other demographic characteristics of the workers with whom they interact.

Deadweight loss Deadweight loss is the loss in economic surplus that results from disequilibrium market outcomes.

Debt ceiling The debt ceiling is the Congressionally mandated maximum amount of debt that the U.S. government can have.

Debt-to-GDP ratio The debt-to-GDP ratio measures the size of a country's national debt as a percentage of its GDP.

Decrease in demand A decrease in demand means that quantity demanded decreases at each price. As a result, the demand curve shifts inward to the left.

Decrease in supply A decrease in supply means that quantity supplied decreases at each price. As a result, the supply curve shifts inward to the left.

Deflation Deflation is negative inflation. Deflation indicates a period of declining prices of goods and services.

Demand Demand is the relationship between the price of a good and the quantity of the good that buyers are willing and able to buy at that price, ceteris paribus.

Demand-pull inflation Demand-pull inflation arises from increases in aggregate demand.

Depreciated In foreign currency exchange markets, when the price of currency A falls relative to currency B, currency A has depreciated.

Discount rate The discount rate is the interest rate that the Federal Reserve charges banks for loans.

Discretionary fiscal policy Discretionary fiscal policy occurs when policymakers actively change government spending or taxation in response to changes in the economy.

Discretionary government spending Discretionary government spending is determined by policymaker choices.

Discrimination Discrimination in the labor market occurs when workers who are equally productive are treated differently based on characteristics that are not related productivity, or when workers who are not equally productive are treated the same because of some arbitrary characteristic.

Disinflation Disinflation is a period of positive but falling inflation. Disinflation indicates a slowing of the rate of price increase in the economy.

Earnings ratio An earnings ratio measures the earnings of one group as a percentage of the earnings of another group.

Economic profit Economic profit occurs when a firm earns more than $0 in normal profits. A firm owner earning economic profit earns more than she would if she chose her next best alternative.

Economic surplus Economic surplus is the sum of consumer surplus plus producer surplus.

Economics Economics is the study of choices.

Efficient choices In the production possibilities model, combinations of output that lie on the production possibilities frontier represent efficient choices.

Elastic demand Elastic demand occurs when a given percent change in the price of a good causes a larger percent change in the quantity demanded of the good.

Elasticity Elasticity is a measure of responsiveness between any two variables.

Elasticity coefficient The elasticity coefficient is a numerical measure of elasticity. The price elasticity of demand coefficient is computed as the percent change in quantity demanded divided by percent change in price.

Emigrant An emigrant is someone who migrates out of their home country.

Emissions limits Emissions limits place controls or restrictions on specific sources of pollutant.

Employer discrimination Employer discrimination occurs when employers base their employment decisions on prejudice against certain workers.

Excess reserves Excess reserves are the difference between a bank's total reserves and its required reserves.

Exchange rate The exchange rate is the rate at which one currency can be exchanged for another. It is usually stated in terms of how many units of one currency can be bought with one unit of a different currency.

Expenditures approach to GDP The expenditures approach to measuring gross domestic product uses total expenditures on final goods and services.

Expansionary fiscal policy Expansionary fiscal policy is used to increase aggregate demand and aggregate economic activity.

Expansionary monetary policy Expansionary monetary policy involves Fed actions to increase the money supply.

Exports Exports are goods or services produced domestically but sold abroad. Exports involve the sale of goods and services to foreign buyers.

Federal debt The federal debt is the accumulated federal deficit borrowing that has not been paid off.

Federal funds rate The federal funds rate is the interest rate that banks charge one another for loans to cover required reserve shortfalls.

Fiat money Fiat money is money that has value because of government law or regulation.

Fiscal policy Fiscal policy is the use of government spending and taxation to influence the economy.

Fixed exchange rate system Under a fixed or pegged exchange rate system, exchange rates are kept constant through government action in foreign exchange markets.

Flexible or Floating exchange rate system In a flexible or floating exchange rate system, exchange rates are determined by demand and supply.

Fractional reserve banking Under a fractional reserve banking system, banks are required to hold only a fraction of their deposits as reserves.

Future value The future value is the value of a payment at a time in the future. See also "present value."

Gini coefficient The Gini coefficient measures income inequality on a scale from 0 to 1, with higher values indicating more income inequality.

Government held debt Government held debt is the portion of the federal debt that is owed to government agencies.

Gross domestic product Gross domestic product (GDP) measures the dollar value of all final goods and services produced in an economy in a given time period.

Home country An emigrant is someone who migrates out of their home country.

Host country An immigrant is someone who migrates into a host country.

Human capital Human capital is the acquired skills and knowledge that make workers more productive.

Immigrant An immigrant is someone who migrates into a host country.

Imperfect information Imperfect information occurs when demanders or suppliers do not know the true costs and benefits associated with a good or service.

Imports Imports are goods or services produced abroad but sold domestically. Importers purchase goods and services from foreign producers.

Income approach to GDP The income approach to measuring gross domestic product uses incomes earned by producers.

Income distribution An income distribution shows the levels of income in an economy and the percentage of individuals or households earning those income levels.

Income effect In the demand and supply model, the income effect of a price change implies that changes in the price of a good affect the amount of the good that you can afford, which results in a change in quantity demanded, ceteris paribus.

Income ratios Income ratios are measures of income inequality that compare the earnings of those at one point in the income distribution to the earnings of those at another point in the income distribution.

Income tax bracket An income tax bracket is a level of income that is taxed at a different marginal tax rate.

Income taxes Income taxes are taxes that are based on the amount of income a taxpayer earns.

Increase in demand An increase in demand means that quantity demanded increases at each price. As a result, the demand curve shifts outward to the right.

Increase in supply An increase in supply means that quantity supplied increases at each price. As a result, the supply curve shifts outward to the right.

Inefficient choices In the production possibilities model, combinations of output that lie inside the production possibilities frontier represent inefficient choices.

Inelastic demand Inelastic demand occurs when a given percent change in the price of a good causes a smaller percent change in the quantity demanded of the good.

Inferior good Goods for which an increase in income generates a decrease in demand.

Inflation Inflation is the rise in the general level of prices in an economy.

Inflation rate The inflation rate is the percentage change in the price level over time. It is measured as the percent change in the price index between two periods.

Investment Investments involve costs borne today in exchange for benefits received in the future.

Invisible hand The invisible hand is the self-regulating mechanism of market systems that generates allocation of resources based on self-interest, competition, and comparative advantage.

Law of demand The law of demand implies that there is an inverse relationship between price and quantity demanded.

Law of diminishing marginal benefit All else equal, as more and more of an activity is done, the marginal benefit derived from the activity tends to diminish.

Law of diminishing marginal product The law of diminishing marginal product implies that holding other inputs constant, as additional units of an input are added to a production process, at some point increases in total production come at a decreasing rate.

Law of diminishing marginal utility The law of diminishing marginal utility implies that the extra utility you get from consuming a good gets smaller as more of the good is consumed. As a result, your willingness to pay for another unit of a good decreases as more of the good is consumed.

Law of increasing marginal cost All else equal, as more and more of an activity is done, the marginal cost associated with the activity tends to increase.

Law of supply The law of supply implies that there is a positive relationship between price and quantity supplied.

M1 money supply The M1 money supply includes money in circulation: cash, demand deposits, traveler's checks, and other checkable deposits.

Macroeconomics The branch of economics that focuses on society-level choices such as taxes, government spending, and factors that influence overall economic performance.

Marginal benefit The additional or incremental benefit associated with a choice.

Marginal cost The additional or incremental cost associated with a choice.

Marginal cost of production The marginal cost of production is the change in total cost incurred when an additional unit of output is produced.

Marginal decision rule The marginal decision rule implies that decision makers can maximize the net benefit received from an activity by engaging in that activity until the marginal benefits are equal to the marginal costs.

Marginal product of labor The marginal product of labor is the additional output gained from hiring an additional worker, ceteris paribus.

Marginal revenue Marginal revenue is the change in total revenue earned when an additional unit of output is produced and sold.

Marginal tax rate The marginal tax rate is the tax rate on income within an income tax bracket.

Market basket Used for computing inflation, a market basket is a fixed set of goods or services whose prices are tracked across time.

Market capitalism Market capitalism is an economic system that uses private property ownership and private resource allocation decisions.

Market equilibrium In the demand and supply model, market equilibrium occurs at the price where quantity demanded is equal to quantity supplied.

Market failure Market failure occurs when the market generates an inefficient allocation of goods or services.

Market shortage A market shortage occurs when the price of a good is below its equilibrium price and quantity demanded is more than quantity supplied at that price.

Market socialism Market socialism is an economic system that uses public property ownership and private resource allocation decisions.

Market surplus A market surplus occurs when the price of a good is above its equilibrium price and quantity supplied is greater than quantity demanded at that price.

Market systems Market systems use decentralized interactions between buyers and sellers to allocate resources. See also "command systems."

Medium of exchange A medium of exchange is an item that is widely accepted as payment for goods and services. Money's role as a medium of exchange means that it can be used as a means of payment for goods and services or repayment of debt.

Microeconomics The branch of economics that focuses on individual-level choices by households, people, and businesses.

Minimum wage The minimum wage is the lowest wage that employers can legally pay workers.

Monetary policy Monetary Policy is the use of regulations or actions by the central bank to influence the money supply.

Money multiplier The money multiplier tells the maximum amount that the money supply can increase for a given increase in deposits. It is equal to the reciprocal of the required reserve ratio.

Monopoly A monopoly is a market with only one seller of a good or service.

Moral hazard Moral hazard occurs when people change their behavior to undertake more risk because they have insurance against that risk.

Negative externalities Negative externalities are costs that are imposed on third parties.

Net benefit The net benefit of an activity is the total benefit of the activity minus the total cost of the activity.

Nominal value of minimum wage The nominal value of the minimum wage is expressed in current dollar values and is not adjusted for inflation.

Nominal values Nominal values are values that have not been adjusted for inflation.

Nondiscretionary fiscal policy Nondiscretionary fiscal policy describes fiscal policy that stabilizes economic activity without active policy changes.

Nondiscretionary government spending Nondiscretionary government spending is determined by current obligations, policies, and demographics, rather than by policymaker discretion.

Normal goods Goods for which an increase in income generates an increase in demand.

Normal profit Normal profit is the profit that business owners could earn if they applied their resources and skills in their next best business alternative. Normal profit is equal to total revenue minus total cost, including opportunity cost.

Normative economics Normative economics deals with value judgments and decisions regarding how things should be. See also "positive economics."

Offshoring Offshoring is the movement of a firm's production from one country to another.

Open market operations Open market operations are the purchases and sales of federal government securities by the Federal Reserve.

Opportunity cost The value of the best alternative foregone when a choice is made.

Outsourcing Outsourcing occurs when someone hires another person or firm to produce a good or service.

Pay gap The pay gap is the percent difference in earnings between two groups.

Pegged exchange rate system Under a fixed or pegged exchange rate system, exchange rates are kept constant through government action in foreign exchange markets.

Perfect competition Perfect competition is a market characterized by many firms producing identical products for a large number of buyers. Buyers and sellers have complete information about prices, and firms can easily enter or exit the market.

Perfectly elastic demand Perfectly elastic demand describes the extreme subcategory of elastic demand that describes the situation where quantity demanded changes by an infinite amount in response to a price change.

Perfectly inelastic demand Perfectly inelastic demand describes the extreme subcategory of inelastic demand that describes the situation where quantity demanded does not change at all in response to a price change.

Physician-induced demand Physician-induced demand occurs when doctors prescribe more treatment than is necessary in order to increase their own incomes.

Pollution Pollution is contamination of the environment that causes instability, harm, or disruption to ecosystems. Pollution can be naturally occurring or human-induced.

Positive economics Positive economics provides descriptions of how things are. See also "normative economics."

Positive externalities Positive externalities are benefits that are bestowed on third parties.

Poverty line The poverty line is the income or consumption level below which a person is considered to be in poverty.

Poverty rate The poverty rate is the percentage of people with incomes below the poverty line.

Present value Present value tells us what a payment in the future is worth today.

Price ceiling A price ceiling is an upper limit on the price of a good or service. A price ceiling sets the maximum amount that can be charged for a good or service.

Price elasticity of demand The price elasticity of demand measures the responsiveness of the quantity demanded of a good to changes in the good's price.

Price floor A price floor is a lower limit on the price of a good or service. It sets the minimum amount that can be charged for a good or service.

Price index A price index is a measure of the average prices of a given set of goods or services across time.

Price level The price level is a measure of the average level of prices in an economy.

Price setters Price setters are firms that are able to set the prices for their products.

Price support A price support is a policy aimed at preventing the price of a given good or service from falling below a target level.

Price takers Price takers are firms that cannot set the price of their good, but instead must take the market price as given.

Primary functions of money The three primary functions of money are a medium of exchange, a unit of account, and a store of value.

Private marginal benefits Private marginal benefits are marginal benefits that accrue only to individual decision makers.

Private marginal costs Private marginal costs are marginal costs that accrue only to the producers of a good or service.

Producer substitution effect In the demand and supply model, the producer substitution effect of a price increase changes the relative price of a good and causes producers to move their production into the now relatively higher priced goods.

Producer surplus Producer surplus is the difference between the price at which a seller is willing and able to sell a given good and the actual price received for the good. It is the net benefit sellers get from selling a good or service.

Production function A production function shows the amount of output that can be produced with different amounts of inputs.

Production possibilities frontier A production possibilities frontier (PPF) illustrates the maximum amount of output that can be produced with a given set of resources and technology, ceteris paribus.

Production possibilities model A production possibilities model tells us combinations of goods or services that can be produced by an individual, a group, or an entire economy given the resources available and the state of technology.

Profit The difference between total revenue and total cost.

Profit-maximizing level of output The profit-maximizing output level for a firm occurs where marginal revenue equals marginal cost. If marginal revenue is greater than marginal cost, increasing output will increase profits. If marginal revenue is less than marginal cost, decreasing output will increase profits.

Progressive income tax system In a progressive income tax system, as taxpayers' incomes increase they are required to pay a larger percentage of that income as taxes.

Protectionism Protectionism is the limiting of free trade between countries by using tariffs, quotas, or other regulations.

Public good A public good is one for which the seller cannot exclude non-buyers from using it.

Publically-held debt Publically-held debt is the portion of the federal debt that is owed to public lenders.

Purchasing power of money The purchasing power of money reflects the amount of goods and services that a given unit of money could be used to acquire.

Quantity demanded In the demand and supply model, quantity demanded describes the amount of a good that buyers are willing and able to buy at a given price, ceteris paribus.

Quantity supplied In the demand and supply model, quantity supplied describes the amount of a good that sellers are willing and able to sell at a given price and time, ceteris paribus.

Quota A quota is a limit on the quantity of a good that can be sold. An import quota is a restriction on the quantity of a good than can be imported into a country.

Real value of minimum wage The real value of the minimum wage is expressed in constant dollar or inflation-adjusted values.

Real values Real values are values that have been adjusted for inflation.

Recession Business cycle contractions or recessions are periods of decreasing economic activity, falling production, and falling employment.

Recognition lag In fiscal policy, the recognition lag is the time between an actual change in economic activity and the ability for policymakers and others to recognize the change.

Regional trade agreements Regional trade agreements are agreements by countries in a region to reduce trade restrictions among themselves.

Relative measure of poverty A relative measure of poverty uses position in the income distribution to determine the poverty line.

Required reserve ratio The required reserve ratio is the percentage of deposits that a bank must hold as reserves by law.

Required reserves The dollar amount that a bank is required to hold as reserves.

Resource allocation The resource allocation decisions of a society determine how the resources are shared or allocated among society's citizens.

Resource ownership The resource ownership decisions of a society determine the property rights over the resources in a society.

Response lag In fiscal policy, the response lag is the time it takes for government agencies to put fiscal policy into place.

Scale effect In the demand and supply model, the scale effect of a price increase generates increased incentives for producers to expand their scale of production, thus increasing the quantity supplied.

Scarcity Scarcity occurs when we have fewer resources than we have uses for those resources.

Slope of the PPF In the production possibilities model, the slope of the PPF equals the opportunity cost of producing one more unit of the good measured on the x-axis.

Social marginal benefits Social marginal benefits are marginal benefits that accrue to society as a whole.

Social marginal costs Social marginal costs are marginal costs that accrue to society as a whole.

Socialist systems Socialist systems use public property ownership. See also "capitalist systems."

Statistical discrimination Statistical discrimination occurs when people use information about the average characteristics of a group when making decisions about an individual member of that group.

Store of value A store of value is something that can be saved and used at a later time. Money's role as a store of value means that it can be saved and used to purchase goods and services at a future time.

Subsidy A subsidy is a program of financial or other assistance given to a business or industrial sector.

Substitute Substitutes are goods that tend to be used in place of one another.

Sunk cost A cost that, once incurred, cannot be recovered.

Supply Supply is the relationship between the price of a good and its quantity supplied, ceteris paribus.

Tariff A tariff is a tax on imported goods or services.

Taste-based models of discrimination In taste-based models of discrimination, people are assumed to have preferences not to work with, hire, or buy from the discriminated group.

Tax A tax is a financial obligation placed on taxpayers.

Terms of trade The terms of trade describe the price or rate of exchange of one good for another. In order for two countries to be better off by trading, the terms of trade need to be between the two countries' opportunity costs of production.

Third-party payment A third-party payment occurs when the provider or seller of a good or service is paid by someone other than the buyer of the good.

Time preference Time preference describes the idea that people prefer money in the present more than money in the future.

Total costs of production Total costs of production include the direct costs and opportunity costs associated with producing a given level of output.

Total product Total product is the total output produced at a given level of input use.

Total reserves A bank's total reserves are deposits that it has received but has not lent out.

Total revenue Total revenue is the amount of money earned when a supplier sells a given quantity of a good. It is equal to the price of the good multiplied by the quantity of the good sold.

Tradable pollution rights In a cap and trade system of pollution reduction, polluters can buy tradable pollution rights that give the right to emit a specific amount of pollutant. The amount of tradable pollution rights issued is capped at the desired pollution level.

Trade deficit A trade deficit occurs when a country's level of imports exceeds its level of exports.

Trade surplus A trade surplus occurs when a country's level of exports exceeds its level of imports.

Tragedy of the commons The tragedy of the commons describes how collective ownership of a resource can lead to overuse and destruction of the resource.

Unattainable choices In the production possibilities model, points outside the production possibilities frontier are unattainable choices, ceteris paribus.

Unemployment Unemployment occurs when there is a surplus of labor in the market.

Unit elastic demand Unit elastic demand describes the situation where a given percent change in the price of a good causes an equal size percent change in the quantity of the good demanded.

Unit of account A unit of account is a standard measure of the value of goods and services. Money's role as a unit of account means that it provides a common measure of the worth of goods or services.

Utility A synonym for satisfaction or happiness. Economists assume that utility is the benefit that individuals get from their choices.

Value of the marginal product of labor The value of the marginal product of labor is the increase in total revenue earned when the firm hires an additional worker. The value of the marginal product of labor is equal to the marginal product of labor multiplied by the price of the output being produced.

Value-added approach to GDP The value-added approach to measuring gross domestic product uses total sales minus the value of inputs.

World Trade Organization The World Trade Organization (WTO) is an international organization of 153 member states with the goal of reducing trade barriers throughout the world.

Index

Pages numbers in **bold** refer to marginal definitions

Q

R

S

T

U